The Early Christian World

The Early Christian World presents an exhaustive, erudite and lavishly illustrated treatment of how the small movement which formed around Jesus in Galilee became the preeminent religion of the ancient world.

The work begins by firmly situating early Christianity within its Mediterranean social, political and religious contexts, before charting the history of the First Christian centuries. The creation and perpetuation of Christian communities through various means, including mission and monasticism, is explored, as is the everyday experience of early Christians, through discussion of gender and sexuality, religious practice, communication and social structures. The intellectual (particularly theological) and artistic heritage of the period is fully considered, and a vivid picture painted of the internal and external challenges faced by early Christianity. The book concludes with profiles of the most notable figures of the age.

Comprehensive and accessible, this work provides up-to-date coverage of the most important topics in the study of early Christianity, together with an invaluable collection of visual material. It will be an indispensable resource for anyone studying this period.

Philip F. Esler is Vice-Principal and Provost, and Professor of Biblical Criticism at the University of St. Andrews. He is the author of *Community and Gospel in Luke-Acts, The First Christians in their Social Worlds* and *Galatians*, and editor of *Modelling Early Christianity* and *Christianity for the Twenty-First Century*.

D1290084

THE EARLY CHRISTIAN WORLD

Volume II

Edited by

Philip F. Esler

Routledge
Taylor & Francis Group

LONDON AND NEW YORK

Every attempt has been made to obtain permission to reproduce copyright material. If any proper acknowledgement has not been made, we would invite copyright holders to inform us of the oversight.

First published 2000
by Routledge
2 Park Square, Milton Park, Oxon, OX14 4RN

Simultaneously published in the USA and Canada
by Routledge
270 Madison Ave, New York, NY 10016

Routledge is an imprint of the Taylor & Francis Group

First published in paperback 2004

© 2000 Philip F. Esler selection and editorial material; individual chapters, the contributors

Typeset in Garamond by RefineCatch Limited, Bungay, Suffolk
Printed and bound in Great Britain by Bell & Bain Ltd, Glasgow

British Library Cataloguing in Publication Data
A catalogue record for this book is available from the British Library

Library of Congress Cataloging in Publication Data
The early Christian world/edited by Philip F. Esler
p. cm.
Includes bibliographical references and indexes.
1. Church history—Primitive and early church, ca. 30–600.   I. Esler, Philip Francis.

BR165.E17 2000
270.1—dc21
99-056667

ISBN 0–415–33312–1 (2 vol set)
ISBN 0–415–35093–X (Vol II)

CONTENTS

———— •◆• ————

— Contents —

ILLUSTRATIONS

————— •◆• —————

PART VI

THE ARTISTIC HERITAGE

CHAPTER TWENTY-SEVEN

ARCHITECTURE: THE FIRST FIVE CENTURIES

—— •✦• ——

L. Michael White

By the time the early Christians began to build monumental church buildings, during the reign of Constantine the Great (313–37 CE), there had been a recognizable, public religious architecture in the Graeco-Roman world for over a millennium. Yet, the Christians did not adopt a traditional Greek or Roman style of temple architecture for their churches. Instead, they adapted the basilica. Modelled after a standard type of audience hall used by municipal courts and imperial administrators, the basilica effectively became the norm and hence the rootstock for the evolution of all later types of Christian architecture down to modern times. To understand the forces of tradition and change at work in this religious arena is critical to understanding the development of early Christianity itself. There are important implications in terms of Christianity's social location, its liturgical evolution, and its self-understanding.

Because of this distinctive role in Christian history, it has been suggested that the basilica was a radical departure from the religious architecture of the pagan world, a symbol of the triumph of Christianity over its environment (MacDonald 1977: 12). Christianity's religious architecture, it is thus argued, avoided the sacralization of objects and places typical of pagan temples and shrines.[1] In reality, however, the story is more complex; the cultural disjunctures less clear. The evolution of a typically Christian architecture was a long process that reflected the appropriation of traditional Jewish as well as pagan forms and practices. Local traditions and influences abound, especially in the earlier stages. Prior to the time of Constantine, there was no normative Christian architecture in any strict sense. One could not walk down the streets of Rome, Corinth, or Carthage and pick out a Christian church by its distinctive plan or façade. There was not yet an iconography of architectural planning that had become identifiably Christian. Features that seem familiar today, such as steeples and stained–glass windows, were still a millennium away as symbolic markers of Christian religious architecture.

In the age of Constantine, then, Christianity developed its first normative public expression of religious architecture after nearly three centuries of social evolution. For this reason, the study of the origins and development of early Christian architecture is usually broken into two main chronological phases: that before the time of

Constantine and that after. In examining this process, then, we shall take up the material as follows:

1. The architectural environment: public and private
   (a) 'Public' religion: temples in classical Greece and Rome
   (b) Domestic space and 'private' religion
   (c) Foreign religions and architectural adaptation
2. From houses to church buildings: Paul to Constantine
   (a) The synagogue and Diaspora Judaism
   (b) The house–church
   (c) The *domus ecclesiae* and architectural adaptation
   (d) The *aula ecclesiae*
3. The birth of the basilica: the fourth and fifth centuries
   (a) Constantine's building programme
   (b) Local and regional variations
   (c) Other types of Christian architecture: martyria and baptisteries
   (d) The Christian landscape of late Roman cities

THE ARCHITECTURAL ENVIRONMENT: PUBLIC AND PRIVATE

For people living in the Hellenistic-Roman world the norms of religious architecture would have been well known and readily recognizable both in the public and private spheres. None the less, there are some key differences between the religious environments of classical Greece and imperial Rome that must be noted.[2]

'Public' Religion: temples in classical Greece and Rome

From the late archaic to the Hellenistic period (seventh to third centuries BCE) the centre of religious life in a Greek city became the monumental podium temples associated with particular deities or mythic foundations. The interior *cella*, surrounded by one or more colonnades, housed the statue of the deity; it was tended by a coterie of professional priests often assisted by city magistrates, leading citizens, and other individuals. A cycle of festivals, processions, and sacrifices were managed by the priests and the city as part of its ritual calendar. As at Athens, the most important temples were often set up on the citadel of the city, called the *acropolis* (or 'upper city'). In some cases, however, the principal sanctuary might be otherwise set apart from the main city, as in the case of the temple of Ephesian Artemis, especially after the city was relocated in Hellenistic times. Other temples, smaller sanctuaries and shrines, and altars were spread about the areas of the *agora* (or 'marketplace') and other important or sacred localities, such as springs, civic boundaries, and the like. Religious architecture from great to small emulated the iconography of temples and was a part of the civic landscape.

In classical Greek religion, however, there were numerous other sanctuaries that were not exclusively associated with a single city. Often they were associated with places of awe and majesty or with important mythic events, as in the case of the oracular sanctuary of Apollo at Delphi, the temple of Zeus at Olympia, the sacred precincts of Apollo at Delos, the sanctuary of Apphaia on Aegina, the temple complex of Poseidon and Athena at Cape Sounion, or the Telesterion or sanctuary of the mysteries at Eleusis. Some of these came to be closely linked at times with Athenian political control, yet they retained their mystique even after Athens' decline. Centuries later a host of travelling Romans – emperors and senators, Herod and Paul – still knew them as sacred places and favourite tourist destinations. From Hellenistic times other important sanctuaries also developed, such as those associated with the hero and healing god Asclepius that grew up at Epidaurus, Kos, and Pergamum. Then there were lesser shrines that dotted the landscape, such as Herms used to mark key locations, sacred groves, or the tomb of a local hero (called a Heröon). Finally, there were the shrines and religious appurtenances of the household itself. Thus, Greek religion had a continuity of expressions across the public and private spheres that integrated the cultural ideals of Greek society.

The monumental temples of ancient Rome were influenced by both Etruscan and Greek architectural traditions (cf. Edlund-Berry 1988). By the second century BCE Rome had developed its own norms of city planning and sacred architecture. A Roman temple complex (literally a sacred precinct) centred on a podium temple, but traditionally without peripteral colonnades. Elevated several steps, the *cella* enclosed the sides of the podium with a colonnade along the façade only. Round temples with colonnades were also used, and gradually Greek temple styles with peripteral colonnade became more prominent in Rome.

While temples and sanctuaries might be inside or outside the walls of a Roman city, the *pomerium* (or boundary) of the city also marked a sacred enclosure; burials, for example, were usually prohibited within the *pomerium*. Roman city planning was oriented around the forum. By the second century BCE it was typically dominated by a temple of the Capitoline gods (Jupiter, Juno, Minerva), also called the *Capitolium*. The foundation and siting of a temple required the assent of religious officials (the *collegium pontificum*) and the Senate (Stambaugh 1978, 1988). Temples for other deities were then located according to traditional functions and events. New temples, sanctuaries, and altars were introduced with regularity in the republican period and even more frequently during the empire.

In the Hellenistic and Roman world temples functioned as banks, social welfare agencies, places of political sanctuary, and the centres of public festivals and processions. The sacred precincts accommodated crowds of people on special holy days or when particular rituals and sacrifices – 'liturgies' (*leitourgiai*) in Greek, 'offices' (*officia*) in Latin – were performed. Often major festivals functioned as civic banquets, and sacrifices were publically distributed as part of the festivities. Yet, a temple in the strict sense, as the house of a god (the *cella* in architectural terms), was not normally a place for public assembly or religious 'worship' in any modern sense. The order of procedures for acts of worship and devotion, whether for major festivals or for individual devotion, at most temples was carefully prescribed. In Greek religion there were few exceptions where a gathering of people was convened in a large hall as part of a religious ceremony. One such was the Greater Mysteries, the annual ritual of initiation celebrated at the Telesterion of Eleusis. Otherwise, most corporate religious activity of a public nature was conducted out of doors in processions and festival activities. A number of ancient Greek and Roman temples (such as the sanctuary of Demeter at Corinth or the sanctuaries of Asclepius) made provision for smaller groups to gather in dining rooms in the temple complex, but not in the temple-*cella* proper. On the other hand, both Greeks and Romans viewed the civic assembly (*ekklêsia* and *curia*, respectively)[3] as sacred gatherings, and their architecture reflected this sacralization.

Domestic space and 'private' religion

While the elements of such public and official religious activities, and their architectural forms, were monumental and distinctive in style, the continuum between public and private forms of religiosity was not clearly differentiated in the Hellenistic-Roman world. In contrast to modern cultural distinctions between public/civic and private/domestic, a number of recent archaeological and cultural studies have shown that many elements of domestic life were considered part of the public sphere (Wallace-Hadrill 1994, 1995; Laurence 1994, 1995, 1997). *Compita* (or 'crossroads' shrines) marked key sections of the city, including voting districts (the *vici*) or neighbourhoods (Bakker 1994). Domestic religion and the household shrine (or *lararium*) stood at the intersection between these spheres of activity, especially where key social rituals (patronage, hospitality, and dining) were concerned (Orr 1978; Clark 1991; Wallace-Hadrill 1997; Foss 1997; Osiek and Balch 1997: 5–47; White 1998: 177–81).

Apart from the family, the most important social groupings in Roman cities were the guilds and clubs (Latin: *collegia* or *sodalicia*; Greek: *thiasoi*). Comprised of people in a common trade, veterans, ethnic enclaves, or funerary societies for the freeborn poor, they afforded social cohesion and networks of support for members of the group. Guilds and *collegia* participated in regular public festivals, often in some special capacity. Yet the majority of their religious activities were conducted in a non-public arena, usually in dinner gatherings for their members. Most had a patron deity or deities, frequently with a special shrine or a private temple set aside within the society's headquarters (sometimes called a *schola*). Dining halls were another common feature. Their banquets were frequently accompanied by sacrifices and other acts of piety by the group or its individual members. Such communal gatherings could at times find their way into the precincts of the public temples, but most often kept to the more private confines of their own buildings.

In the Hellenistic world these collegial halls typically resembled domestic architecture, as in the case of the 'Association of Merchants and Shippers from Berytus' who in the second century BCE established a headquarters in the important trade centre of Delos. Based on the grandiose inscription from the peristyle of their building, their hall was known as the 'House of the Poseidoniasts from Berytus'. Their patron deity, Greek Poseidon, was an amalgamation with their local form of Ba'al from Syria. Architecturally the building resembles a house with a typical peristyle court and a large room for assembly. Instead of regular domestic quarters, however, it featured a separate room with altars and statues of the gods (Picard 1921; Bruneau 1970: 623–4).

From the Roman period we find analogous groups, such as the Tyrian merchants at Puteoli who maintained a collegial hall and sanctuary dedicated to their ancestral god (Ba'al of Serapta), whom they called by the Hellenized name Helios Seraptenos (Nock 1939: 66; White 1996–7: I, 32). At Ostia we find the *collegium* of the *Fabri Navales* (the Ship-builders Guild), whose headquarters (III.2.2) was located along the main street, the *Decumanus maximus*, a few blocks west of the forum. The edifice (Figure 27.1, locus A) was installed in a lot previously occupied by a typical private house: the peristyle was turned into a small *temenos* (sacred enclosure), with the *cella* proper set on a podium in the area previously occupied by the *tablinum* (or main living room) of the house. The rear areas of the complex were used for other activities and gatherings of the group (Meiggs 1973: 327; Hermansen 1981: 63).

Immediately across the street hall (see Figure 27.1, locus B) stood another collegial hall (IV.5.15). Usually known as the 'School of Trajan' (*Schola Traiani*) it probably belonged to the 'Shipowners Association' (*Naviculariei*).[4] Their building similarly took over and renovated a large peristyle house dating from the early first century CE; the reconstruction dates to the late second century CE. In addition to offices, an imperial shrine, a large peristyle court with central fountain (a nymphaeum), and porticoes, the rear of the complex contained a large and richly decorated dining hall with an apsidal niche for a statue of Fortuna. For such groups social interaction, especially banquets, were closely aligned with their religious activities.

Like the headquarters of the *Fabri Navales*, a number of these guild halls at Ostia clearly included small temples within their confines, even though the buildings themselves came from the realm of domestic architecture.[5] Some groups adopted explicitly religious designations such as the obscure group known only from inscriptions as 'The Order of the Guildbrothers who contributed funds for enlargement of the temple' (Meiggs 1973: 335; Hermansen 1981: 59, 241). Two further cases known from epigraphic remains reflect this continuum between public and private arenas of religious activity. One is the household of Pompeia Agripinilla which in *c.* 127 CE was organized as a cult of Dionysus; the nearly 500 members of her household were called 'initiates' (Greek: *mystai*) and were assigned hierarchically to ranks and offices within the 'cult.' Agripinilla, the *mater familias*, held the highest rank as priest and patron of the cult (White 1996–7: I, 45, with references). From Rome another inscription refers to 'the Association which is in the house of Sergia Paullina' (*Collegium quod est in domu Sergiae Paullinae*, CIL 6.9148). In the former case the household is identical to the cult; in the latter, it appears that the *collegium* meets in the house of the patron, likely overlapping somewhat with the household but not entirely.[6]

Foreign religions and architectural adaptation

Beginning in Hellenistic times there was a growing trend for new religious groups to move into the urban environment alongside the traditional cults. These new groups came from the Eastern Mediterranean and Middle East in the wake of Alexander's conquests and the subsequent centuries of Hellenistic rule. By the first century BCE these regions came under Roman rule, but by then the pathways of migration and cultural interaction had been well worn. As with the shippers and

Figure 27.1   Ostia: regions III and IV along the Decumanus Maximus. From White (1996–7: II. fig. 41).

merchants on Delos in the Hellenistic period and those at Puteoli and Ostia in the imperial age, many people were drawn by trade and migration to the large cities. With them they carried their cultural heritage and their religious traditions. Their collegial halls thus served both as commercial agencies and as religious and social centres.

Once out of the realm of the official cults associated with the state or the city, there was much more variety in religious activity and in its architectural forms. Dining and social functions were closely linked to religious activities. Houses might be turned into cult centres or collegial halls. A wealthy homeowner might also install his/her own private 'chapel' in honour of a favourite deity or as part of a small religious confraternity. For example at Ephesus, a wealthy city official (*alytarch*) of the early second century CE, named C. Flavius Furius Aptus, owned a palatial house (*Hanghaus* 2) along the *Embolos* (or Processional Way). Off a peristyle court reached from a mosaic portico along the street, he installed a small apsidal shrine to Dionysus next to an opulent dining hall. It seems that these rooms were meant for formal entertaining of small elite groups (Wiplinger and Wlach 1995: 103–4).

Similarly, at Rome a group using the collegial title 'Association of the Treebearers' (*Collegium Dendrophororum*) met in an apsidal hall in the house of its patron, Manius Publicius Hilarus, who lived on the Caelian. Though located in a domestic setting, the hall was marked off by a formal inscription of dedication and invocation (*CIL* 6.641, 30973). It would appear that this was a private cultic association loosely tied to the cult of Magna Mater, but it maintained its own distinct social and religious functions apart from the public cult (White 1996–7: I, 46). Architectural adaptation and renovation was the order of the day, and such groups relied on the patronage of leading individuals.

It seems that many of the so-called 'mystery cults' made their way into the Hellenistic and Roman world by means of architectural adaptation and private patronage, either before or alongside of establishing formal public temples of classical design. A common phenomenon, this practice was especially noteworthy in the case of the cults of the Egyptian gods, where communal dining was a prominent feature (White 1996–7: I, 32–9, 43–6). The cult of Mithras, which became popular in the Roman world in the second century CE, developed a distinctive type of religious architecture for its sanctuaries, called mithraea (Figure 27.2).

There was a typical plan for most mithraea in the Roman world. In imitation of a cave, the mithraeum was usually a long narrow hall with elevated benches along the two side walls and a central aisle leading to an altar platform at one end. On the side benches the members of the cult assembled, socialized, and ate communal dinners. The halls might be decorated with religious art and symbols, but the altar platform, usually decorated with mythic scenes of Mithras slaying the bull (or *tauroctony*) served as the focus of attention and cultic actions.

Despite these common features, the actual design and architecture of each mithraeum might be vastly different owing to the fact that most of them were quite small and usually constructed from or within some existing building (White 1996–7: I, 47–50). Very few ancient mithraea were *de novo* or purpose-built edifices for religious purposes; the vast majority (nearly 90%) of excavated mithraic buildings were created by renovation and architectural adaptation of houses, baths, cryptoportici, warehouses, vaulted storerooms, courtyards, and even nymphaea (White 1996–7: I, 48; II, no. 87). All of the known mithraea from Rome and Ostia were renovated from existing buildings. In some cases the renovations were minimal (White 1996–7: II, no. 79). In other cases they could be quite extensive, with lavish decorations

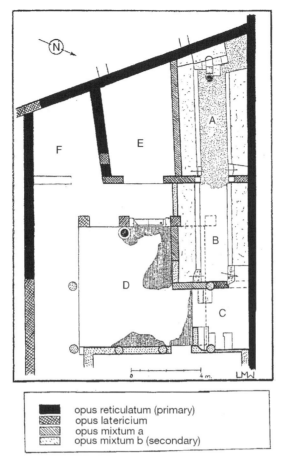

■	opus reticulatum (primary)
▨	opus latericium
▨	opus mixtum a
▨	opus mixtum b (secondary)

Figure 27.2 Plan of the Mithraeum of the Painted Walls in Ostia – 'Mitreo delle pareti dipinte'. From White (1996–7: II, fig. 42; adapted from Becatti, *Mitrei Ostia*).

and muiltiple stages of enlargement (White 1996–7: I, 49–52; II, nos. 59, 79, 81, 89). For example, the 'Mithraeum of the Painted Walls' (Figure 27.2; and Figure 27.1, locus C) at Ostia (III.1.6) was constructed in two stages in the courtyard and a side room of a house (White 1996–7: II, no. 81). Similarly, at Rome, the mithraeum found beneath the apse of San Clemente (Figures 27.3, 27.14) had been installed in the second or third century in the cortile of a private house; before renovation the same space had been used as a nymphaeum (White 1996–7: II, no. 87).

What sets the mithraic cult apart architecturally from other traditional religions of the Hellenistic-Roman world is the lack of a formal temple architecture apart from these small sanctuaries. Still, they participated in public temple activities as part of daily life, even though their own cultic dining and social activities took place within the sanctuary. In this sense it was more 'private', both in setting and in operations, despite the fact that a limited iconography of architecture had evolved.

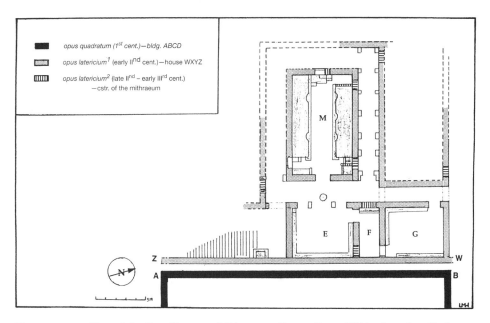

Figure 27.3   Plan of the San Clemente Mithraeum, Rome. From White (1996–7: II, fig. 44; after Guidobaldi).

In some ways it was closer to a *collegium*, even though it was publicly recognized as a religion by Roman standards. As with most other forms of religious architecture, public or private, the bulk of construction, renovation, and decoration fell to the private acts of devotion of individual members, and especially to the wealthy. They usually functioned as patrons and leaders within the cultic community (White 1996–7: I, 53–7).

FROM HOUSES TO CHURCH BUILDINGS: PAUL TO CONSTANTINE

In its earliest stages the Christian movement was not a separate religion but a sect within first-century Judaism. As such it observed the rhythms of religious life in the same way as other Jews; therefore, in terms of architecture the centre of religious identity was the temple at Jerusalem. The temple was rebuilt and enlarged extensively under the Hasmoneans and even more under Herod the Great; Herodian construction continued from *c.* 20 BCE down to 62 CE, not long before the outbreak of the war that would see it finally destroyed in 70 CE. It was a centre of sacrifical activity and national identity; it was an architectural showpiece set in an elevated position within the 'sacred' city, Zion. The area surrounding the Jewish temple (the outer courts, or 'Court of the Gentiles') was a gathering place for religious festivals and other public and commercial activities. Jewish men alone could approach the entrance to the building through the inner courts, but the temple proper, and especially its inner sanctum, was restricted to the priests alone. In this sense, it functioned much like other ancient temples. Despite the fact that no Jew would say that their God actually lived there, it was still conceived as the place where God's presence dwelt as a symbol of national election.

According to the New Testament, the first followers of the Christian movement continued in traditional forms of Jewish piety, attending the temple, observing annual feasts and purity rules.[7] As such they initially had no need of other forms of religious architecture, especially since the movement was limited to a Jewish following in the Homeland (White 1996–7: I, 102–3). Like other Jewish sects, these earliest Christians also met in homes for private meals, fellowship, and prayer (Acts 2–5). The Pharisees were another Jewish group that used homebased fellowships as a locus for study and prayer alongside the normal religious functions of the temple.[8] Only after the temple was destroyed in 70 CE would the synagogue emerge as the new centre of Jewish worship and identity.[9] A normative synagogue architecture and liturgy did not evolve until the fourth century CE as part of the consolidation of rabbinic Judaism. Consequently, it did not serve as the architectural model for the development of Christian architecture, the basilica in particular, as has sometimes been supposed.[10]

The synagogue and Diaspora Judaism

Early on synagogues were usually just called 'prayerhalls' (Greek: *proseuchai*). In the Homeland prior to 70 CE they are known from scant references of Josephus (*JW* 2.285–9; *JA* 19.300–305; *Life* 277–80) and early Christian writings (the Gospels and Acts); however, it is significant that all were authored well after the war. Only in Philo (*De vita Mosis* 2.215–16; *De legibus specialibus* 2.62) do we find securely dated pre-70 references, but these come from the Alexandrian Jewish community, not the Homeland (Grabbe 1995: 20–1).

Archaeological evidence for pre-70 synagogues is even more perplexing, since it now appears that the vast majority date to the centuries after the First Revolt; they occur either from the Galilee or from provisions for Diaspora Jews. Moreover, these cases arise only in the post-Hasmonean period, i.e., late first century BCE, or later (Grabbe 1995: 21–3; Flesher 1995: 30–4). By contrast, archaeological and epigraphic evidence points to the origins of Jewish prayerhalls in the second and first centuries BCE in Ptolemaic Egypt and the Eastern Mediterranean Diaspora (Grabbe 1995: 18–19; Griffiths 1995; White 1987). In other words, the synagogue originated in regions away from Judaea, where access to the temple was limited. In the Diaspora it functioned as a social as well as religious centre, and there was neither a fixed liturgy nor architecture in the pre-70 period (Kasher 1995; White 1987).

When we look at the archaeological remains of Diaspora synagogues (Figure 27.4) we discover that all were adapted from previously existing buildings, usually over several phases of renovation and development (Figure 27.5).

There are six such edifices known of that date (Figure 27.5), at least in part, from the pre-Constantinian period. Listed in more or less chronological order for their earliest phases, they are: Delos (second-first century BCE), Ostia, Dura-Europos,

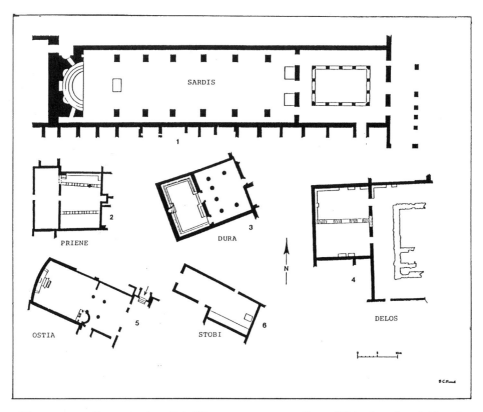

Figure 27.4 Synoptic plan of six Diaspora synagogues. From White (1996–7: I, Fig. 9).

Priene (second century CE), Stobi (third century CE), and Sardis (third-fourth centuries CE). Of these six, four were clearly renovated from existing private houses, and one (Ostia) was likely some sort of insula complex. The Sardis synagogue, the largest known from antiquity (see also Figure 27.22), was renovated in at least three distinct phases from a municipal bath-gymnasium complex (Kraabel 1979; White 1996–7: I, 60–77, II, nos. 60, 66, 69, 70, 72, 83).

Both the archaeological and epigraphic record from these edifices attest to the significant role played by patrons, both men and women, in their growth and architectural development (White 1996–7: I, 77–93; Brooten 1982). The fundamental role of patronage in the Mediterranean world of this time is discussed in Chapter 1 of this volume. In many ways the use of space, and the social organization of these communities, most resembles that of other religious clubs or *collegia*, especially during the Roman period (White 1987, 1997; Richardson 1996). Three further points are worth noting in the architectural development of these edifices. First, as A.T. Kraabel (1981: 89) has noted, the form of these buildings and their adaptation was determined by local social and economic conditions more than by any architectural norms (cf. White 1996–7: I, 93–101). The Dura-Europos synagogue is a good example since we can see its evolution from an ordinary house in the

Site	No. of phases	Building type	Dates*	First Synagogue phase date
SYRIA Dura-Europos	3	[1] house [2] renov.synag.i [3] renov.synag.cmplx. [3a] paintings	Late I *c.* 150–200 244/5	2/*c.* 150–200
LYDIA Sardis	4	[1] apodyterion [2] hall [3] synag./court [4a] refurb.	*c.* 166 late-II beg.-III IV	3/III
Priene	3	[1–2] house [3] renov.synag.	I BCE	3/II
INSULAE AEGEAE Delos	2	[1] house [2] synag. [2a] refurb.?	II BCE I BCE I	2/I BCE
MACEDONIA Stobi	5	[1–2] house [3] synag.i [4] synag.ii [5] Xn.basilica	I–II III III–IV IV–V	3/III
ITALY Ostia	4	[1] insula? [2] synag.i [3] synag.ii [3b] aedicula [4] synag.iib	I II–III III–IV IV IV–V	2/III

* All dates are CE unless otherwise indicated.

Figure 27.5 An archaeological survey of the building history of Diaspora synagogues. From White 1996–7: II, 30.

midst of a block of houses (Figure 27.6) into a formal synagogue edifice in three distinct phases (Figure 27.7) (White 1996–7: II, no. 60).

Second, over time, each building achieved more monumental scale and formal liturgical articulation. In particular, four of the six were outfitted with Torah shrines that stood as the focus of the assembly and worship arena (Figure 27.4). As an

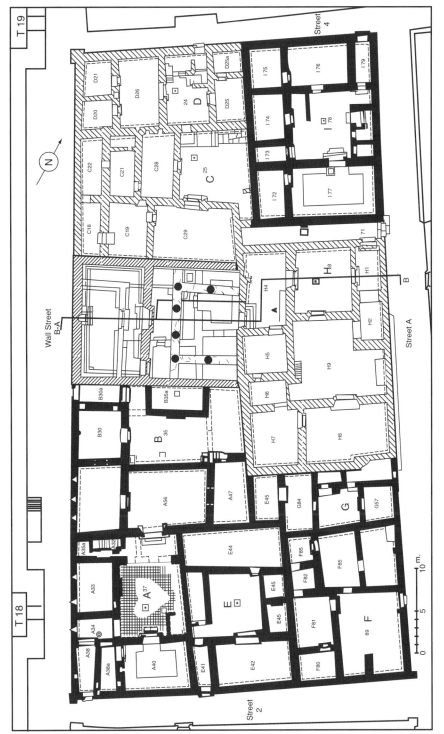

Figure 27.6 Plan of the block containing the synagogue in Dura-Europos. From White (1996–7: II, fig. 28).

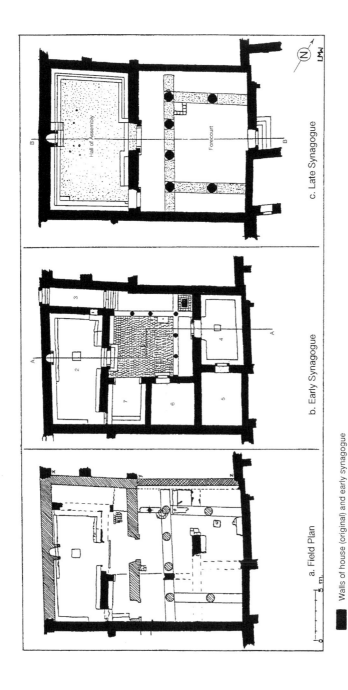

a. Field Plan

b. Early Synagogue

c. Late Synagogue

■ Walls of house (original) and early synagogue

▨ Renovation work (late synagogue cstr.)

▨ Renovation work B (late synagogue, secondary)

Figure 27·7 Plan of earlier and later phases of the synagogue in Dura-Europos. From White (1996–7: II, fig. 29).

architectural edifice, the Torah shrine does not appear before the late second century CE, and becomes more prominent in the third and fourth centuries. It marks an articulation of sacred space in the synagogue and is closely associated with the evolution and formalization of liturgy. Its development resulted from new religious functions and symbolism of the synagogue as sacred architecture that emerged after the destruction of the temple, correlated with the consolidation of the synagogue as a religious institution in the rabbinic tradition (White 1996–7: I, 93–101; Rutgers 1995; Fine 1996). Despite the absence of a fixed architectural form for the external building, by the end of this process one finds broad or elongated halls with the Torah shrine as focal point becoming the norm for internal plan. In their final stages, the synagogues at Ostia and Sardis, both of which lasted beyond the fifth century CE, reflect the influence of basilical architecture, probably from contemporaneous Christian usage. So the emergence of the Christian basilica from the fourth century onward influenced later synagogue architecture in the Homeland as well as the Diaspora (Foerster 1995: 92–4).

Third, most of the Diaspora synagogues made provision for social functions, especially dining, during some or all of their renovations. In earlier stages, it appears that dining might be more closely associated with the areas of assembly, while in later stages more segregation occurred. For example, in the Ostia synagogue (Figure 27.8) benches seem to be operative in two distinct areas from its first phases of renovation as a synagogue, while in its later phase, a separate dining hall seems to be annexed to the building (White 1996–7: II, no. 83; 1997). But this pattern varies significantly from building to building and group to group (Kraabel 1981; White 1998). Thus it may be argued that the process of growth and adaptation was an organic social function and only gradually took on more discrete liturgical planning.

Since the earliest Christian communities arose out of this Jewish matrix, it is not surprising to discover that they began with household meetings. Only gradually over time did they begin to adapt existing structures for their religious usage. Thus, two steps, the house-church and the *domus ecclesiae*, mark the beginnings of Christian architectural development.

The house-church

Writing near the end of the first century CE, the author of Luke-Acts noted that the earliest Christians, in addition to attending the temple, assembled to break bread 'from house to house' or 'at home' (*kat' oikon*) (Acts 2:46; 5:42; White 1996–7: I, 188, n.7). Acts also characterizes the ministry of Paul as typically holding meetings in domestic quarters (Acts 20:7), and it was common for whole households to be baptized following the conversion of the *pater* or *mater familias* (Acts 16:15, 34; 18:8). These household heads were also Paul's sponsors and hosts in the cities of the Roman East (Acts 18:3, 7, 24). While the account of Acts is likely idealized and intended for a theological and apologetic purpose (White 1995a: 256–61; 1995b: 36–8; Balch 1995: 232–3; cf. Esler 1987: 207–19), the basic picture of the house-church is substantiated by Paul's own letters, the earliest writings in the New Testament.

Paul's letters regularly relayed greetings both to and from 'so-and-so and the church in his/her/your/their house' (so 1 Cor. 16:19: Aquila and Prisca *syn tê kat'*

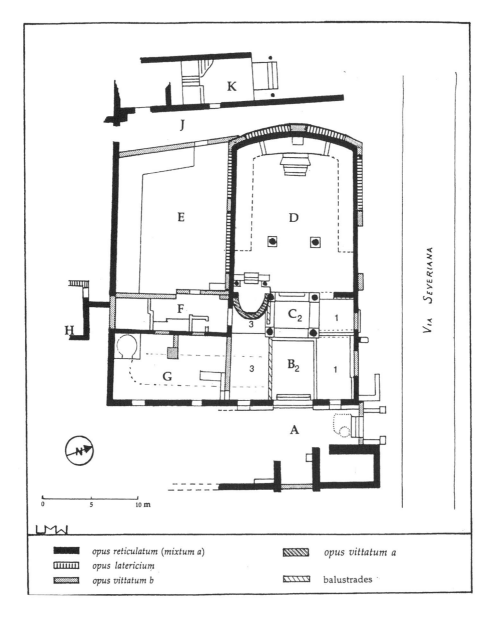

Figure 27.8 Composite plan of the synagogue at Ostia. From White (1997: fig. 3).

oikon autôn ekklêsia; cf. Rom. 16:5; Philem. 2; Col. 4:15). Other references confirm the fact that key households served as the nucleus of congregations (1 Cor. 1:11, 16; 16:15). From these descriptions has come the terminology of the 'house-church' as the designation for this early stage of development and organization at the time of the Pauline mission.[11] Some of the larger cities were made up of several house-churches. In Paul's day Corinth had six or more house-church groups (Acts 18:3, 7;

1 Cor. 1:11, 16; 16:15; Rom. 16:2, 23) while Rome had at least eight (Rom. 16:5–16).

The owner of the house served as patron of the community as well as host to Paul and his co-workers (Rom. 16: 2, 23; Philem 22). As a result of this social and economic dependency conventions of patronage, hospitality and friendship – the social interstices of public and private – were important virtues in the social organization of these congregations and explain much about the character of Paul's relationship with them (Marshall 1987: 133–50; Osiek and Balch 1997: 193–212; Malherbe 1983: 92–103; White 1990b: 210–15; Fitzgerald 1996b; Mitchell 1997). Women such as Phoebe (Rom. 16:2), Chloe (1 Cor. 1:11), Prisca (1 Cor. 16:19; Rom. 16:3), Mary and Junia (Rom. 16: 6–7), and Nympha (Col. 4:15) are named as house-church patrons or leaders of household groups. It seems, therefore, that the house-church context afforded social standing and religious leadership roles to prominent women, much as it did in pagan cults and Jewish synagogues (Schüssler Fiorenza 1983: 162–8; Torjesen 1995: 53–110; Osiek and Balch 1997: 103–55).

Several characteristic features of Pauline worship and assembly can also be gleaned from these texts. First, the typical setting for worship was in the context of the communal meal, presumably in the dining room of the host's house. This is the setting presupposed for both the Lord's Supper in 1 Cor. 11: 17–34 and for the worship in 1 Cor. 14. At this stage, there was no formal distinction between the communal meal and the Eucharistic observance (White 1998: 178–80). Second, there seems to be no direct basis for seeing 'privacy' or cost as constraining factors for choosing the house setting, since dining and collegial activities were commonly held in domestic settings (contra Blue 1994: 121; cf. Krautheimer 1979: 24–5). Instead, already in Paul's day the house-church setting presupposed that at least some members of the community were of higher social and economic standing and used these means to host the church and its assembly (Meeks 1983: 51–73; Osiek and Balch 1997: 96–102; White 1996–7: II, 142–8).

Third, there was no peculiar synagogue organization that had become normative by this stage or that was taken by Paul when he was 'kicked out'. This notion is based on the polemic of Acts and imposes later Jewish norms than were actually operative in the mid-first century. The synagogues of the Diaspora were still in an early stage of development; hence, they were very diverse, and, as already noted, often used domestic contexts where the social organization closely resembled that of the surrounding Graeco-Roman culture (contra Burtchaell 1992: 228–63 and others; cf. Ascough 1998: 22–3). Hence unidirectional models of influence do not tell the whole story. While similarities certainly exist, they likely stem from the common social context and the reliance on patronage rather than on strict organizational or architectural norms. As long as the temple was standing, local Jewish congregations of all types, including Jewish-Christian groups at Antioch and Paul's predominantly gentile house-churches in the Aegean, followed local patterns of household and collegial assembly and organization.

Finally, and most importantly, the house-church, by definition, implies no special architectural articulation beyond that typical of houses, apartments, and other unrenovated spaces. This leaves us with an archaeological problem, however, since the lack of adaptation and spatial articulation means that the Christian places of meeting are physically impossible to distinguish from other architecture. We are left only with literary remains that must be handled with caution.

According to the literary sources, houses were not the only places of meeting for the earliest Christians. Others include collegial or school halls, such as the 'hall' (*scholê*) of Tyrannus at Ephesus (Acts 19:9) and warehouses (*horrea*) at Rome (*Passio Pauli* 1; cf. White 1996–7: II, no. 9b). Even so, houses are by far the most prominent throughout the early literature. Even in the middle of the second century it appears that Justin Martyr was still meeting with other Christians in some sort of domestic complex or an apartment building, 'above the baths of so-and-so' (*Passio Sancti Justini et socii* 3; White 1996–7: II, 7b). Even the worship and organization presupposed in early to mid-second century sources (e.g., *Didache* 12–14 and Justin's *Apology* I, 61–7, do not reflect more formal places of assembly; apparently there was no special place for baptism (White 1996–7: I, 110).

In later centuries it became common to associate formal church buildings with putative claims that there had originally been a house-church in the same location. This tendency shows the influence of the earlier house-church and *domus ecclesiae* in the evolving tradition, even though many of these later legends were spurious (cf. White 1996–7: II, nos. 42 and 50). In the case of the so-called *tituli* or house-churches of Rome, such as San Clemente, Christian usage of a house or private property in the early stages has proved difficult to maintain on archaeological grounds (White 1996–7: II, 1–10, no. 58, and appendix A; Snyder 1985: 67–81).

Because the house-church was not archaeologically distinguishable, our first glimpses of the architectural development must come from the first attempts at spatial adaptation. There is, thus, a kind of transitional phase when houses and other buildings began to be partially altered by Christians for specific religious purposes based most likely on continued patterns of usage.[12] Over time certain areas might be given over to virtually exclusive Christian usage or decorated with Christian symbols. Once physical adaptation of the space and the edifice commenced, then the architecture was moving beyond the house-church both in physical terms and in the minds of the users.

By the early second century we begin to see some shifts in the way that some Christians thought about their assembly space in terms of its religious and communal significance. For example, in the Johannine epistles (2–3 John), which likely come from Asia Minor, the setting still clearly presupposed a localized house-church under a patron (Malherbe 1983: 103–9). The local patron, Diotrophes, had refused to welcome some travelling Christians with letters of recommendation into his assembly and even expelled some of his own congregation who wished to admit them (3 John 9–10). Thus, tensions erupted between several different house-church cells, and the role of local patrons was significant.

Perhaps even more telling is the other letter (2 John) by the same Christian 'elder' who opposed Diotrophes, since his directives for dealing with travelling Christians closely parallel the actions taken by Diotrophes. It says, 'if anyone comes to you and does not bring this doctrine (*didachên*) do not receive him into the house or give him any greeting (*mê lambanete auton eis oikian kai chairein autô mê legete*); for the one who gives him greeting shares (*koinônei*) in his evil works' (2 John 10). The formal greeting was a sign of hospitality and fellowship; it was not offered lightly.

The visitor, therefore, was stopped at the door of the house and either welcomed or refused admission, in this case based on an anti-docetic creedal affirmation (2 John 7). The procedure makes it clear that admission to the house, and hence to the church's assembly space, had become an important symbol of fellowship. The door of the house and the ritualized greeting enacted there had begun to function both spatially and symbolically as boundary markers of the church. In effect, they had moved one step closer to identifying the space where the church met with the 'church' as some idealized entity.

This shift in conceptualization is very important to the later development of both ecclesiology and church architecture. It must be remembered that the term 'church' (*ekklêsia*) originally just meant the assembled group or congregation. In the Septuagint it was used to translate the symbolically loaded phrase 'congregation of Israel' (Deut. 23:1–3, 8; 31:30; 1 Kgs 8:14, 22, 55, 65; Neh. 8:2, 14; Sir. 15:5; 1 Macc. 4:59; 5:16; 14:19) and was synonymous with synagogue (*sunagôgê*; Exod. 16:9–10; 35:1; Deut. 5: 22; 1 Kgs 12: 20–21; Sir. 1:30; 1 Macc. 14: 28). The two terms could also be used in combination as subject and verb (so 1 Kgs 12:21: *exekklêsiasen tên sunagôgên*) not unlike the phrasing typically found in Paul's letters (so 1 Cor. 11:18: *sunerchomenôn humôn en ekklêsia*, cf. 11:20; 14:23; and 1 Cor. 5:4 which explicitly uses the verb *sunagôgein*).

Only in the period well after the destruction of the temple do these terms become clearly differentiated along sectarian lines. Within the Jewish-Christian matrix of Matthew's gospel, the terms were used to distinguish two distinct congregations in social conflict – '[our] church' (Matt. 18:15–20) and 'their/your synagogue' (Matt. 4:23; 9:35; 10:17; 12:9; 13:54; 23:34). Symbolization of the assembled congregation reinforced boundary definition of the group. It was analogous to that in the Johannine epistles, albeit on quite different grounds (cf. White 1991: 215–16 and n. 17). Growing tensions and boundary definition would result in the separation of the Christian movement from Judaism, at least in most regions, and thereupon the stage was set for a new kind of ideology of religious assembly to develop for both Jews and Christians (White 1998: 195–7). None the less, local influences would still be determinative for each.

The *domus ecclesiae* and architectural adaptation

As Christianity became more firmly rooted in the urban social context of the Roman world, it followed patterns of architectural adaptation and rebuilding. The cities themselves were constantly under construction, especially from Trajan to the Severans. Churches, like all sorts of other edifices, were built and rebuilt, remodelled and transformed with the urban growth of cities (see Figure 27.9). The progression towardss a distinctive Christian architecture moved gradually to renovation of existing buildings in order to transform them into places set aside for assembly and other liturgical and social functions. To distinguish this phase from the house-church we use the term *domus ecclesiae* ('house of the church') based on terminology found in Eusebius (*Historia Ecclesiastica* 7.30.19) and others (Rordorf 1964: 117; Krautheimer 1979: 27; White 1996–7: I, 111, II, 25–6; Finney 1988: 325, 331–5).

The clearest example of this shift can be seen in the Christian building discovered

Site	No. of phases	Building type	Dates (CE)	First Xn. phase date
SYRIA (including Arabia)				
Dura-Europos	2	[1-2] house/church	231–56	2/*c.* 240
Qirqbize	5	[1-2] house/hall [3-5] basilica	330–VI	1/*c.* 330
Umm el-Jimal	3	[1-2] house, [3] basilica	IV–VI	2?–3/IV
PALESTINE				
Capernaum	3	[1] house, [2] hall [3] octagonal church	IV–VI	2/IV
MACEDONIA				
Philippi	3	[1] Heröon, [2] hall church, [3] octagon	IV–VI	2/*c.* 334
ISTRIA				
Parentium	5	[1-2] Roman edifice, [3] hall, [4] bas., [5] cathedr.	III–V	3/IV
Aquieleia	4	[1] house, [2] commerc. bldg. [3] hall cmplx., [4-5] basilica	III–VI	3/IV
ITALY Rome Ss Giovanni e				
Paolo	6	[1-3] insula, [4] hall, [5-6] basilica	II–V	3/III
S. Clemente	5	[1-2] Mag./domus [3] hall?, [4-5] basilica	I/III–V	3/III
S. Martino al Monti	4	[1-2] commerc.bldg. [3-4] hall/bas.	III–VI	4/IV
S. Crisogono	4	[1-2] hall [3-4] basilica	IV–VI	1/*c.* 310
BRITAIN				
Lullingstone	5	[1-4] villa/chapel	IV–V	4/*c.* 350

Figure 27.9 Prebasilical church buildings: an archaeological survey of adaptation and renovation. From White (1996–7: II, 27).

at Dura-Europos in 1931 (Figure 27.10). It was a typical Durene house that had been adapted through a single phase of internal renovations to serve as a place of Christian assembly. In other words, through the process of renovation and adaptation it had become a building set aside for Christian religious functions. The nature of the renovations indicate that ordinary domestic functions ceased after the renovations; it had become a 'church building'. The house had been built about 231 CE

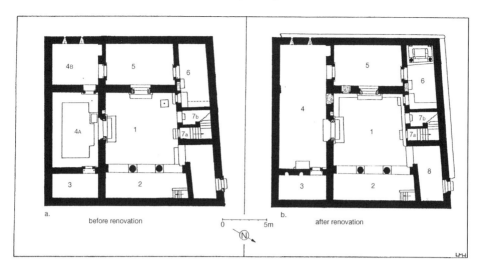

Figure 27.10 The Christian building at Dura-Europos, before and after renovation. From White (1996–7: II. Fig. 2).

and renovated as a *domus ecclesiae* in *c.* 240/1 (White 1996–7: I, 120–2; II, 18–24 and no. 36; Kraeling 1967). Because the city was destroyed in 256 CE during Sassanian incursions, it provides a rare case in early Christian architecture where there is clear evidence of an early stage of adaptation without later phases of rebuilding. It is also significant that along the same street were found two other houses that had been remodelled by religious groups – one a mithraeum that went through three phases of adaptation; the other, a synagogue that went through two. In both cases donor inscriptions commemorated the renovation work (White 1996–7: II, 10–18; II, nos. 58–61). The last phases of renovation in the mithraeum and the synagogue were contemporaneous with the single phase of renovation in the *domus ecclesiae*.

Among private dwellings at Dura, the house was fairly large but otherwise typical with several rooms grouped around a central courtyard. On the exterior the house was almost untouched and retained its domestic appearance. On the interior, the main structural modifications occurred in three areas: (a) the courtyard, (b) the south suite (rooms 3, 4A, and 4B), and (c) the west suite (rooms 5 and 6). Renovation of the courtyard was minimal; it included raising and paving the floor and installing two banks of L-shaped benches, and various finishing touches.

In the south suite a formal door led from the court into room 4A, originally the dining room of the house. With plaster benches and a brazier box, the dining room was typical of the Durene domestic *diwan*. Room 3 was most likely a pantry, while room 4B was connected to other living areas of the house. In the remodelling of the edifice, the partition wall between rooms 4A and 4B was removed. The floor was then filled in to the height of the benches to create one large room for assembly, with a dais installed at its east end. Room 3 continued to serve as a storage or preparation area. Other than plastering of the walls and memorial graffiti there was little or no decoration in this area; a low shuttered window was cut through to the courtyard.

On the west side of the courtyard another formal doorway led to room 5.

Originally, rooms 5 and/or 6 might have served as the women's quarters. Only minimal changes were made in room 5; another shuttered window to the courtyard was introduced, and the door from room 5 to room 6 was fitted with more elaborate trim. Such formal trimwork is unusual for an interior doorway and suggests that this door had become part of a new pattern of movement through the edifice.

Room 6 had originally been only a modest chamber, but in the Christian renovations received the most extensive makeover of all. It was converted into a formal baptistery. A font basin nearly 1 metre in depth was set into the floor on the west end of the room. Above it was a decorated canopy carried by pilasters and two plaster columns painted to look like marble. Above the canopy a new ceiling/floor structure divided the space vertically to create an upstairs apartment. On the south wall a small niche between the two doors was enlarged and arcuated, and low steps or benches were set along the east and west ends of the room. Then the entire room was decorated with an extensive pictorial programme containing some of the earliest datable examples of Christian biblical illustrations.

Along the east and north walls of room 6 there were two registers that appear to wrap around the corner. The lower contained a scene of five women approaching the tomb (a sarcophagus) of Jesus. The composition suggests a processional towards the font, so that movement of initiates paralleled the scene from the gospels. All that is preserved of the upper register are two scenes depicting Jesus' miracles, both of which were associated with water. The lunette above the font contained a good shepherd scene and a small vignette of Adam and Eve. Immediately to its south side was a scene of the Samaritan woman at the well (more water symbolism from John 4), and between the windows was a scene of David slaying Goliath. In the borders of this scene two Christian graffiti were incised, and a similar text appeared in room 4 (White 1996–7: II, no. 37). The individuals commemorated by these graffiti might have been martyrs or, more likely, Christian leaders or those who assisted in the renovation of the building.

Taken together, the renovations indicate a conscious plan to adapt the building for particular patterns of religious usage. One area was for assembly and worship, presumably including a Eucharistic liturgy and teaching. The courtyard might also have been used for assembly and fellowship functions, but there is no direct evidence of communal dining. Rooms 5 and 6 seem to have been set aside for other specialized functions, especially baptism. It affords the earliest surviving evidence of a formally designed baptistery set within an actual Christian building. Nothing can be ascertained regarding the usage of the upper floor rooms.

The Dura-Europos Christian building thus marks a full transition to a specialized church edifice, a *domus ecclesiae*. While it is possible that this house was already in use by Christians before the renovation there is no direct evidence. It is likely, however, that most local Christian congregations made a more gradual transition by partial adaptation. It is also likely that these stages of adaptation varied significantly from place to place. One might guess that the Dura-Europos building, located in a relatively remote garrison town on the Eastern frontier, was not the first to devise such modes of spatial usage or artistic decoration, even though their appropriation was local and idiosyncratic.

The only other direct evidence of partial adaption of a house for Christian assembly comes from the Lullingstone Roman villa (Figure 27.11) near London (White 1996–7: I, 125; II, no. 57). In one wing of the house, away from the formal dining area and an adjacent bath complex, a moderately sized room (locus C) and antechamber were decorated with Christian symbols. It appears that this wing also had a separate entrance allowing for Christian gatherings that did not interfere with continuing domestic functions in the remainder of the house. Like Dura, this case is remarkable for its date, since the installation of the Christian chapel occurred in the second half of the fourth century, well after basilical church buildings were being built at Rome and elsewhere. Hence, the phases suggested here are not meant to suggest strict chronological limits but rather developmental stages. The progression might vary widely from place to place. Nor is it the case that every church building will have gone through all these stages.

Other instances of partial renovation are indicated in two of the titular churches of Rome, San Clemente and San Giovanni e Paolo. (See White 1996–7: I, 114–5; II, nos. 52–3; see also this volume pp. 720–2, 730.) In both cases there is archaeological evidence of Christian usage by the third century; both were renovated to create large assembly halls before being thoroughly rebuilt in basilical form in the early fifth century. In the case of San Clemente, there is no clear evidence of a *domus ecclesiae* phase in between the earlier Roman warehouse building and the Christian hall of the third–fourth centuries. Since tradition holds that there were congregations associated with both at earlier times, it has been assumed that some sort of spatial provisions had already been made; however, direct archaeological evidence is lacking (Krautheimer 1979: 29–30; White 1996–7: II, 1–6; Snyder 1985: 76).[13]

At least some literary texts suggest that such changes were already at work by the beginning of the third century in some of the more populous regions. Clement of Alexandria, writing near the turn of the third century, preferred to call 'not the place, but the assembly of the elect, the church' (*Stromateis* 7.5; White 1996–7: II, no. 12a). Indeed, his emphatic tone suggests that the terminology had already begun to blur. Even Clement himself on another occasion refers to 'going to church' in such a way as to suggest both a regular time and *place* of assembly; in regard to dress and deportment he further draws distinctions between *inside* and *outside* the church assembly (*Paedagogus* 3.11; White 1996–7: II, no. 12b).

Moreover, Clement seems to reflect a worship context where the Eucharist and the *agape* or fellowship meal had already become fully separated (*Paedagogus* 2.1). Writing at the same time in North Africa, Tertullian shows no clear distinction (*Apology* 39; White 1996–7: II, no.13a); however, within two decades at Rome the liturgical tradition of Hippolytus makes the separation explicit and further regulates the convening of private Christian dinners (*Apostolic Tradition* 21–6; White 1996–7: II, no. 14; White 1998: 181–5; cf. Bobertz 1993). It is likely that such localized patterns of liturgical development were reflected in the physical arrangements and adaptations. The spatial articulation of the Dura *domus ecclesiae* presupposed a separate and more formal Eucharistic assembly with no social dining. One must guess that this change marked a broader shift in the spatial articulation and layout for Christian assembly.

The Dura *domus ecclesiae* is also important because it suggests that the edifice had become the property of the church and was publicly identifiable even though it

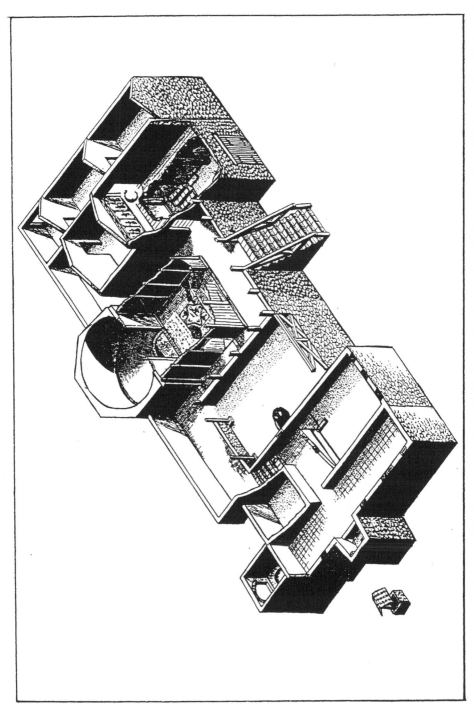

Figure 27.11   Isometric drawing of the late Roman villa, with Christian chapel (*c.* 390), at Lullingstone. From White (1996–7: II, fig. 23).

had not yet become a distinctive church architecture. Other literary and documentary sources provide important historical indicators to support this shift. The *Edessene Chronicle*, a fifth-century Syriac court record, reports 'a temple (or sanctuary) of the church of the Christians' that was destroyed along with other buildings by a flood in the year 201 CE (§ 8; White 1996–7: II, no. 26). Later the *Chronicle* (§ 12) mentions a new church foundation in the year 313 by the bishop Kûnê. Given the nature of these references, it does not suggest a more formal type of architecture in the year 201, but rather the wording of a door plaque from an earlier type of *domus ecclesiae* (White 1996–7: I, 118).

The *aula ecclesiae*

By the end of the third century church buildings were clearly recognized by local civic officials in many cities. Such can be seen from villages in Egypt, where census and court records openly mention Christian 'church buildings' (*P. Oxy.* I, 43; VI.903; *P. Gen. Inv.* 108) as well as property transfers and ownership by the church (*P. Oxy.* XII.1492; *P. Gen. Inv.* 108; White 1996–7: II, nos. 43–5, 47). In two other cases there are court records of the search and seizure of church property during the Diocletianic persecution. From Egypt the reader of a village church near Oxyrhynchus filed a property declaration after their church building was seized in 304 (*P. Oxy.* XXXIII.2673; White 1996–7: II, no. 46). From the previous year a court record from Cirta in Numidia records the search of the local church building and describes its dining hall (*triclinium*), a library, and a large cache of clothing, apparently for charitable distribution; however, no description is given of the assembly room proper (*Acta Munati Felicis* from the *Gestae apud Zenophilum*; White 1996–7: II, no. 31). One might well guess that the edifice was still in the form of a *domus ecclesiae*, but certainty is impossible. Clearly the church edifice at Nicomedia, whose destruction Diocletian is reported to have witnessed from his palace, was a publically recognized edifice even though it was not a monumental church building (Lactantius, *De mortibus persecutorum* 12; White 1996–7: II, no. 24).

These records suggest that in between the renovation of existing structures to form a *domus ecclesiae* and the building of monumental basilicas after the peace of Constantine there was an intermediate stage of development in which further enlargement and specialized adaptations were introduced. Although local variations must be allowed, this stage occurred generally in the second half of the third century CE. It continued in some localities, including Rome itself, through the fourth century. This type of development is what Eusebius describes regarding the rebuilding of older church buildings in the period of growth before the Great Persecution. He says:

> With what favour one may observe the rulers in every church being honoured by all procurators and governors. Or how could anyone describe those assemblies with numberless crowds and the great throngs gathered together in every city as well as the remarkable concourses in the houses of prayer? On account of these things, no longer being satisfied with their old buildings (*tois palai oikodomêmasin*), they erected from the foundations churches of spacious

dimensions in every city (*eis platos ana pasas tas poleis ek themeliôn anistôn ekklêsias*).

(*Historia Ecclesiastica* 8.1.5; White 1996–7: II, no. 23b)

Eusebius' comments ring with some realistic elements, including rebuilding and enlarging the old structures 'from the foundations'.[14] Because many of these new buildings include larger hall-shaped structures in their building plans, we may designate this phase the *aula ecclesiae* (or 'hall of the church'); still, it does not imply the architectural elements or the scale that would be introduced with the basilica.

Eusebius' comments were doubtless hyperbole, since he interpreted this period of popular growth as a cause of the ensuing persecutions (*H.E.* 8.1.9–2.5). None the less, there is considerable evidence that it was a period of new growth and adaptation in church building. Unfortunately the literary sources rarely give physical and architectural descriptions of these buildings; however, a few passing references may provide some clues. For example Cyprian's letters from the middle of the third century occasionally mention accoutrements of assembly. In referring to the ordination of a reader, he spoke of placing him 'upon the pulpit (*pulpitum*), that is upon the tribunal of church', which was 'propped up in the place of highest elevation and conspicuous to the entire congregation' (*Epistle* 39.4.1; White 1996–7: II, no. 16.a). In other places it appears that the phrase 'to ascend the platform' (*ad pulpitum venire*) had become a technical term for ordination (cf. *Epp.* 38.2; 40).

So it seems that by the middle of the third century, in Carthage at least, the church building had been outfitted with a raised dais or platform (called *pulpitum* or *tribunal*) for some clerical and liturgical functions. While the general plan of Cyprian's church building cannot be ascertained, it suggests something of a larger rectangular hall with a dais on one end. In a letter to the bishop of Rome Cyprian referred to this space as 'the sacred and venerated *congestum* of the clergy' (*Ep.* 59.18.1; White 1996–7: II, no. 16.d). Such a construction may have been the forerunner of the chancel as a segregated area for clergy.

This picture is supported in other large urban centres of the empire during the latter half of the second century. At Antioch the ecclesiastical crisis precipitated by the episcopate of Paul of Samosata (261–70 CE) similarly provokes passing references to activities inside their church buildings. Among the charges levelled against Paul prior to his expulsion as a heretic was that he had installed a throne and a *secretum* on the *bema* in his church at Antioch (Eusebius, *H.E.* 7.30.9; White 1996–7: II, no. 20). The terminology used here explicitly comes from the arena of Roman civic architecture since the Greek text mentions the Latin *secretum* (*sêkrêton*), the private chamber of a Roman magistrate, while *bema* (*bêma*) is the usual Greek equivalent for the Latin *pulpitum*, the raised platform on which the magistrate sat. To Paul's outraged opponents, these elements of public architecture were less a threat in themselves than they were symptomatic of Paul's inordinate self-aggrandizement and his other faulty theological ideas. There is no indication that these installations were removed from the building when Paul was expelled. Thus, it appears that by the year 270 the church at Antioch had become a large hall of some sort with several accoutrements of public architecture. It had become an *aula ecclesiae*.

It is also noteworthy that other buildings from the same period lagged far behind in size and architectural articulation. The simpler *domus ecclesiae* at Dura-Europos was roughly contemporaneous with the more elaborate buildings suggested for Carthage and Antioch. On the other hand, household meetings were still common during the Diocletianic persecution, and other church buildings still presupposed some elements of domestic architecture (White 1996–7: I.126; II, nos. 21, 36). Sources from this period indicate further elaborations in the ordering of assembly, at least in some areas. The Syriac *Didascalia*, for example, is the earliest church order text to prescribe a seating arrangement for various members of the congregation in a pattern that fits a rectangular hall plan, whether of larger or smaller dimensions (§ 12; White 1996–7: II, no. 18).

The archaeological evidence supports this picture of a gradual progression towards rectangular assembly halls. The clearest case of a pre-Constantinian church building, apparently planned *de novo* for Christian use, is that of San Crisogono in Rome's Trastevere region (Figures 27.12, 27.13b). It was apparently designed as a large rectangular hall of irregular proportions (length: 35.35 metres; width: 17.25–19.25 metres) with an exterior portico on one side but no interior divisions (White 1996–7: II, 55; Krautheimer 1979: 37–8; Snyder 1985: 81–2). It was built by about the year 310 and continued in this rudimentary form for over a century before it was remodelled. In the early sixth century its western wall was levelled, the hall was extended, and an apse added on to the new west end. On the east end, a crossing wall was introduced to divide the assembly hall (or nave) from a vestibule (or narthex), thereby giving it some features of basilical architecture. Even so, the edifice lacked the colonnaded aisles typical of true basilical architecture; only in the twelfth century was the church thoroughly rebuilt as a basilica on top of the original buildings (Figure 27.13a).

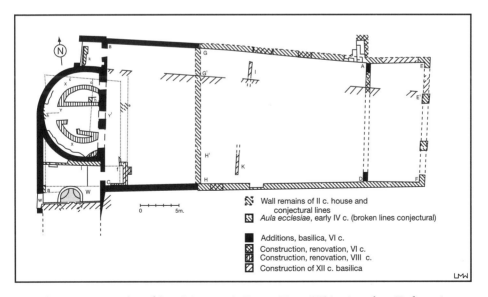

Figure 27.12 Plan of San Crisogono in Rome. From White (1996–7: II, fig. 19).

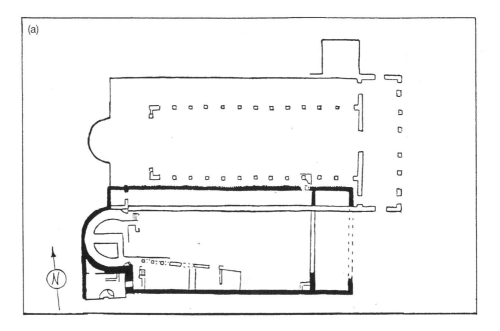

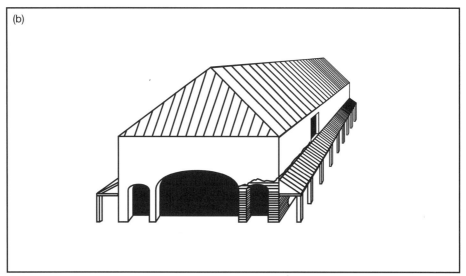

Figure 27.13 Siting plan (a) and restoration drawing (b), of early *aula ecclesiae*, San Crisogono, Rome From White (1996–7: II, fig. 20a-b).

Two of the Roman *tituli* (the traditional 'parish' churches) seem to reflect a stage of adaptation from existing buildings directly to the *aula ecclesiae*. One is San Clemente (Figure 27.14), where a plain hall edifice was constructed on the upper floor level of the late third century and survived to the beginning of the fifth century before the first basilica was built on this basic plan (White 1996–7: II, no. 53).

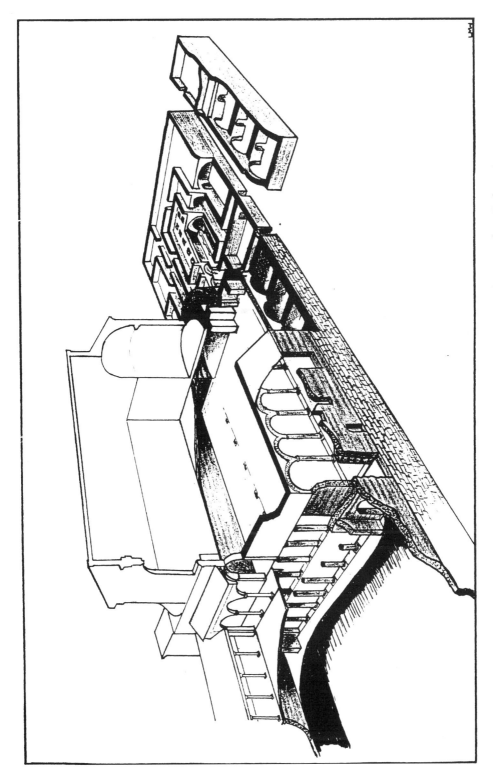

Figure 27.14   Isometric drawing of San Clemente, Rome. From White (1996–7: II, fig. 17).

The basilica of SS Giovanni e Paolo was built *c.* 410 CE over an earlier apartment building with ground-floor shops. The nave of the basilica was set at the level of the second storey of this apartment complex, where it appears that the rooms had already been renovated to form a large hall before the beginning of the fourth century (Figures 27.15, 27.16). The walls of this hall were later preserved in the construction of the basilica. It has been suggested that Christians might have earlier used one or more of the ground-floor shops before and after this initial renovation; however, the first indication of Christian usage appears to be the construction of the large hall of the upper storey (White 1996–7: II, no. 52; Krautheimer 1939–56: I, 4: 267–303; Snyder 1985: 78–80).

The prevalence of the *aula ecclesiae* is shown by the fact that throughout the fourth century new church construction continued in this form alongside the introduction of basilical architecture. Three cases are worth noting. First is the so-called 'basilica of Paul', a small hall edifice found beneath the fifth-century octagonal church D at Philippi (Figure 27.17, 27.18). The name comes from an inscription in its mosaic floor, which also identifies its bishop, Porphyrios; on this basis it can be dated roughly between 330–40 CE (White 1996–7: I, 134–6; II, no. 49). Despite the terminology of the inscription it was not a true basilica architecturally; however, this usage suggests that the term 'basilica' had already been applied to 'church buildings', apart from its more precise architectural signification (White 1996–7 I, 196 and n. 92 and Voelkl 1954).

Second is the simple hall from Qirqbize (near Aleppo in Roman Coelesyria), built in the first third of the fourth century. The nature of the construction shows that it was modelled in part after a domestic plan, with a porticoed courtyard flanking the

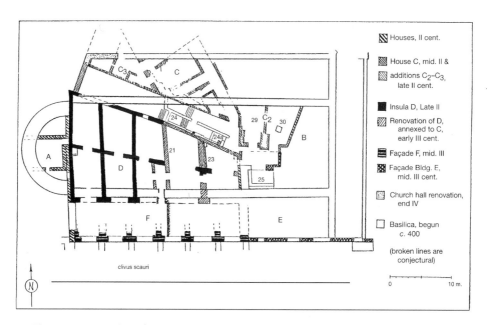

Figure 27.15   Plan of SS Giovanni e Paolo, Rome. From White (1996–7: II, fig. 14).

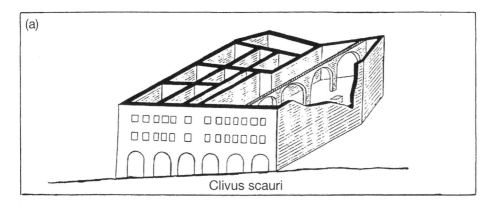

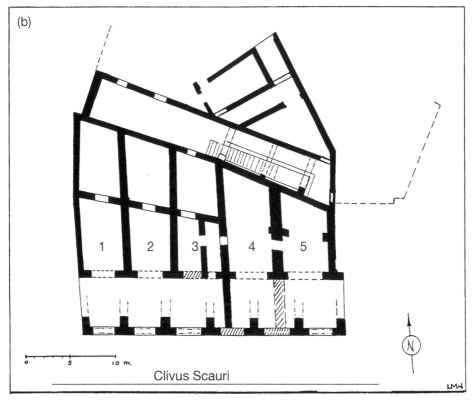

Figure 27.16. Isometric reconstruction (a) and plan (b) of SS. Giovanni e Paolo, Rome. From White (1996–7: II, fig.15).

hall proper; however, it was designed for Christian usage from the beginning. In its later stages, the hall was adapted to a basilical style on the interior, in keeping with typical Syrian church architecture of the fifth and sixth centuries. It likely served as a village church, and might have been built by the owner of the estate next door (White 1996–7: II, 38 with plans).

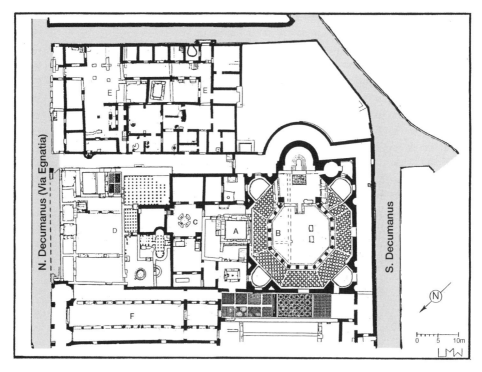

Figure 27.17   Plan of the octogonal church at Philippi. From White (1996–7: II, fig. 9).

Third is the early church edifice found beneath two later layers of basilical construction at Parentium, Istria (modern Parenzo or Poreč). The sixth-century complex is known as the basilica of Eufrasius. It stood over a fifth-century basilica with
elaborate mosaic floors, which in turn stood over a fourth-century *aula ecclesiae* that
also contained Christian mosaic floors. Legends associated with the fifth-century
construction held that the earlier building had been the house of a martyr, bishop
Maurus, and the earlier edifice was thought to be a *domus ecclesiae*. While some earlier
domestic structures may be present, it appears that the first Christian construction
belongs to the fourth-century building, a *de novo* Christian edifice with two small
parallel halls and other associated rooms (White 1996–7: 122; 194 n. 73; II, no. 50,
with plans).

THE BIRTH OF THE BASILICA: THE FOURTH AND FIFTH CENTURIES

The period immediately after the Edict of Milan (313 CE) saw a new burst of church
building, which Eusebius contrasts to the 'destruction of the churches' during the
persecutions (*H.E.* 10.3.1). His programmatic interests are none the less visible:

a divine joy blossomed in all as we beheld every place which, a short time

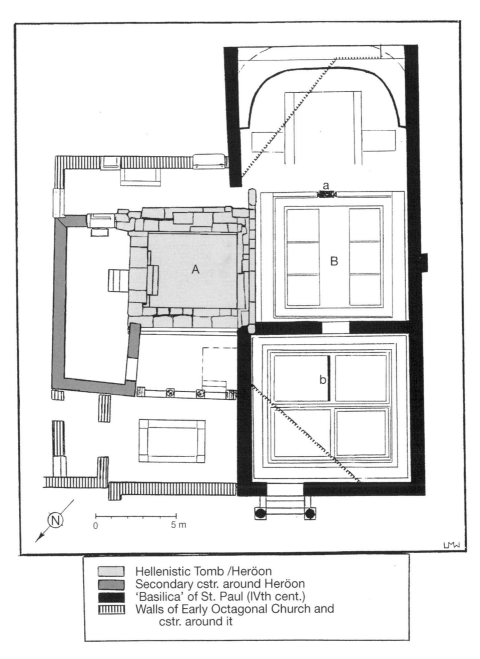

Figure 27.18 Plan of the 'basilica' of Paul at Philippi (White 1996–97: II, fig. 10).

before, had been torn down by the impious deeds of the tyrants. Reviving as from long and deadly mistreatment, the *temples* were raised once again from the foundation to a lofty height and received in far greater measure the magnificence of those that had formerly been destroyed.

(*H.E.* 10.2.1; emphasis added)

While some churches were doubtless destroyed, it was not uniform. Lactantius describes the demolition of the church building at Nicomedia in 303 (*De mortibus persecutorum* 12); however, *aula ecclesiae* already built at Rome (San Clemente, SS Giovanni e Paolo) show no signs of destruction and rebuilding from the early decades of the fourth century. In fact, new and larger churches, such as San Crisogono, were being built during the period when the edicts of persecution were still in effect (303–13). It is likely that the majority of church buildings, if they were touched at all, were merely 'seized' by state or local officials. Implementation of the imperial orders varied from region to region. The edicts of toleration and largesse under Constantine and his co-regents consistently called for restoration of these church properties to the Christians. None the less, it appears that the period of peace and growth beginning in 313 stimulated new building programmes both on the local and the imperial level.

Eusebius' principal example is the church at Tyre rebuilt by the young, aristocratic bishop Paulinus. At its dedication in 317 CE Eusebius himself delivered the sermon, in which he likened it to Zerubbabel's rebuilding of Solomon's temple (*H.E.* 10.4.36–45; White 1996–7: II, no. 23d). He went on to develop an extended allegory on the church as God's new, triumphant temple of God on earth (*H.E.* 10.4.46–68). Despite Eusebius' elaborate description of its embellishments, the newly rebuilt church at Tyre does not appear to be a basilica in architectural form, but rather a monumental *aula ecclesiae* (White 1996–7: I, 136; cf. Krautheimer 1979: 45–6). It is also noteworthy that the project seems to be a local initiative undertaken, at least in large measure, by the young bishop of Tyre as an act of public benefaction.[15] Even so, it is clear that Eusebius was applying notions of sacred space and architecture to the church buildings both before and after the persecutions (Finney 1984: 217–25). The entry of Constantine into this process would add yet another dimension, but the architectural revolution did not occur overnight (Voelkl 1953).

Constantine's building programme

A number of earlier theories regarding the origins of the Christian basilica attempted to find a genetic progression from houses (and the house-church) or other non-public type of architecture (White 1996–7: I, 11–17). Some relatively recent studies continue to argue that the basilica had already been introduced into Christian usage during the third century (Rordorf 1964: 127–8). Typically, these theories have carried two underlying assumptions: (a) that the basilica as monumental church architecture consciously avoided traditional Roman religious forms, and (b) that Christian liturgy was the determining factor in shaping its distinctive architectural plan.

A new consensus has emerged since the work of Richard Krautheimer (1939, 1979) and J. B. Ward-Perkins (1954). They argued instead that the basilica was a conscious feature of Constantine's policy towards the Christians in the years following 313. The plan was taken from standard forms of monumental civic architecture at Rome. Constantine and Maxentius had only a little earlier (306–10) built a new public audience hall in the *Forum Romanum*. Christian basilicas derived their basic plan and construction from such civil and imperial halls; they were then adapted self-consciously under imperial patronage to fit the new social and legal status of Christianity. This monumental type of architecture was intended to make a statement about the public acceptance and imperial favour of Christianity and to give it a formal style within the urban landscape. None the less, it shows continuities with earlier patterns of architecture, where a 'hall' of assembly had already emerged. Thus, the basilica as an accepted form of public 'assembly' architecture was a natural choice. Given its traditional civic and military functions, not to mention specific rituals employed in imperial usage, the basilica may properly be considered a type of religious architecture for corporate activity long before its Christian adaptation (Krautheimer 1979: 42). It thereby offered more grandiose elements of style as well as notions of sacred space. Liturgy was also anticipated in the choice of the architecture, but at the same time it was transformed by this choice.

Constantinian patronage set the tone for the transformation of Christian architecture, but prior to *c.* 350 there still was no set form of basilical church planning (Krautheimer 1979: 43). Regional variations would also evolve, and local builders experimented with designs, as in the cross-arcaded basilica of Santa Croce in Gerusalemme at Rome (completed in *c.* 329 CE; Krautheimer 1979: 51). Initially at least, adaptation both of basilical form and of existing buildings was still the norm. The first Christian basilica in this strict sense was the church of St John Lateran in Rome (Figure 27.19). Originally an imperial palace and barracks complex donated by Constantine himself, the church was begun in 314, the same year that the emperor called for the church council at Arles to consider the Donatist question. The construction was completed by 319/20 (Ward-Perkins 1954: 85–7; Krautheimer 1979:42–9). A five-aisle hall measuring 75 metres by 55 metres with an apsidal sanctuary and synthronon extending 20 metres more, it soon became the seat of the bishop of Rome. The exterior was finished in a plain plaster while the interior was lavishly decorated, no doubt from imperial gifts.

The plan of the Lateran basilica would eventually become typical of western church architecture, albeit with modifications. The classical Christian basilica comprised a central, rectangular *nave* oriented on its long axis and flanked by either two or four side aisles separated by columns. This style of construction allowed for a wide hall while still providing a high central clerestory for windows. The entry to the Lateran basilica, as with earlier *aula ecclesiae*, was not mediated through a portico or propylaion; later it became typical to front the nave proper with a lateral entry hall (or *narthex*), usually with either three or five doors. Eventually, church buildings were turned to face east, towards the rising sun, as a symbol of resurrection; however, the Lateran basilica, like San Clemente and a number of others, had its apse on the west end. Initially orientation of basilicas was not fixed and depended on the existing buildings and other factors in the sighting of the plan.

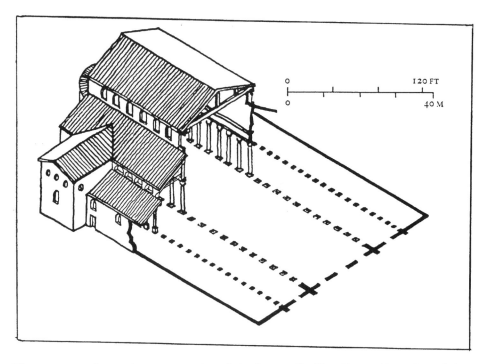

Figure 27.19 Isometric reconstruction of the Lateran Basilica, Rome. From Krautheimer (1979: 47, fig. 11).

Finally, it became common for basilicas to include an atrium or forecourt before the entrance and narthex. Rather than the traditional atrium of Roman domestic architecture, however, it was more properly a tetrastoa or peristyle court. The first Constantinian building to incorporate the atrium was St Peter's at Rome, begun in *c.* 317–19 but as a funerary basilica rather than a regular church building (Figure 27.20). Even so, it is possible that the atrium was added subsequent to the initial construction (Krautheimer 1979: 57–9). According to Eusebius, the rebuilt church at Tyre (dedicated in 317) already contained an open-air court with four *stoai*, probably a peristyle, but his description implies that it was a viewed as a novel design (*H.E.* 10.4.40).

St Peter's also introduced another architectural innovation over the plan of the Lateran basilica in the form of a transverse hall (or *transept*) crossing between the nave and the apse. In other basilicas the end of the nave just before the apse served for the altar and clergy, with the bishop and others seated in the synthronon of the apse. At St Peter's, the transept formally and spatially divided the nave from the apse; immediately before the apse stood a *baldachino* over the altar and the venerated tombs that lay beneath the floor (Krautheimer 1979: 57). The transept did double duty, serving as a place for the clergy during regular services but also serving for commemorations of the shrine of St Peter, legendarily identified with one particular tomb structure in the earlier necropolis adjacent to the hippodrome of Nero. The church complex was intentionally placed above this necropolis by an elaborate

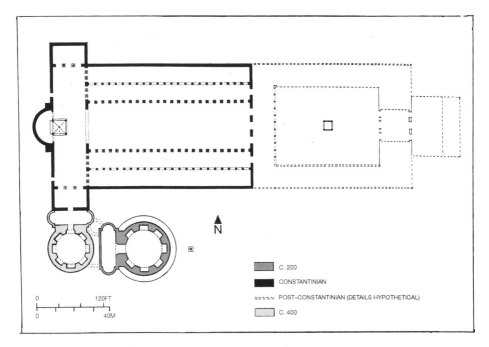

C. 200
CONSTANTINIAN
POST–CONSTANTINIAN (DETAILS HYPOTHETICAL)
C. 400

Figure 27.20 Plan of the Constantinian Basilica of St Peter's, Rome. From Krautheimer 1979: 56, fig. 22).

architectural design to adapt the foundations to the slope of the hill along which the necropolis was set (Snyder 1985: 105–15, with further bibliography). The result was a monumental edifice measuring 119 by 64 metres on the interior, not counting the atrium forecourt (Krautheimer 1979: 57).

While Constantine supported the building of basilical churches at Rome and elsewhere, the construction of St Peter's reflects another conscious element in his building programme through the architectural commemoration of Christian sacred sites. Near the end of Constantine's life Eusebius dedicated a biography to the emperor in which he recited the list of his major building projects (*Vita Constantini* 3.25–43; 51–3); his interests turned especially to the Holy Land, as it was coming to be called (Wilken 1992: 82–97). His agent in identifying key sites was his mother, Helena Augusta (*c.* 250–330 CE), who visited Jerusalem in 326. According to tradition she found the site of the cross and burial of Jesus, on which Constantine would build the Church of the Holy Sepulchre (Drijvers 1992). Constantine also supported the building of the Church of the Ascension on the Mount of Olives and the Church of the Nativity at Bethlehem; he also gave permission to others to build churches at sites associated with events in the life of Jesus, such as the site called the house of St Peter at Capernaum where a memoria was built by Joseph of Tiberias (White 1996–7: II, 155).

The Constantinian foundations at both Golgotha (completed *c.* 330 CE) and Bethlehem (333) followed the basilical architecture already pioneered at Rome for the memoria of Peter. They were five-aisle basilicas with atrium forecourt

(Krautheimer 1979: 60–5). In both cases, however, the actual sacred locus was commemorated by a building of central plan extended from the apse end of the basilica proper. In the Church of the Nativity, an octagonal room memorializing the birthplace of Jesus replaced the apse proper; in the Church of the Holy Sepulchre, a rotunda was connected to the basilica's apse by a porticoed court (MacDonald 1977: 20–1). Thus, Constantine's building programme anticipated the blending of central-plan buildings with the longitudinal plan of the basilica; however, central plan architecture (polygonal or rotunda type) was generally reserved for special memorial edifices, either for the dead or for gods (Krautheimer 1979: 66). At least in the beginning, the longitudinal plan of the basilica was primarily the one reserved for traditional Christian assembly and worship.

Local and regional variations

It is likely that over the next few centuries pilgrimage traffic to key sites in Rome and the Holy Land was a powerful force in disseminating the 'Constantininan' type of basilica (Krautheimer 1979: 66). By the end of the fourth century it had become pervasive, especially in the West. Even so, it must be remembered that many of the older *domus ecclesiae* and *aula ecclesiae* structures continued in uninterrupted use alongside these new constructions. At Rome itself, both San Clemente and SS Giovanni e Paolo remained unchanged until *c.* 400–10 at which time they were both rebuilt in basilical form (Figures 27.14, 27.15; White 1996–7: II, nos. 52–3).

In many other cases new churches were founded in the post-Constantinian era by loosely adapting existing buildings to a rudimentary basilical plan. It sometimes meant little more than spatially marking off a hall and constructing an apse in an otherwise substantial building or complex, as in the case of Santa Croce in Gerusalemme and a number of the fourth century *titular* churches of Rome (Vaes 1984–6: 316; White 1996–7: II, 437–8). This practice continued through the fourth century and into the fifth, especially in the larger cities of the Eastern empire. They were able to appropriate and convert various other types of buildings, including libraries, market halls, an odeion, and other public edifices (Vaes 1984–6: 318–21). At Ostia (Figure 27.1, locus D), for example, a bath complex and an adjacent building were adapted to form an unusual basilica (Meiggs 1973: 397–9), while the Constantinian basilica, a monumental *de novo* construction, has only recently been discovered (1996) outside the city walls on the Via Laurentiana (cf. Meiggs 1973: 395). It was also at Ostia that the wealthy Christian senator Anicius Auchenius Bassus dedicated a shrine to Monica, mother of St Augustine, after she died there in 388 CE (Meiggs 1973: 213, 399; Augustine, *Confessions* 9.10–3). Gradually, such cities were being 'Christianized' at the level of public architecture.

Even more noteworthy was the fact that Christians began to take over traditional pagan temples and convert them loosely to basilical form. This process can be seen most clearly in fifth-century Athens, where the Parthenon of the Acropolis and the Hephasteion of the agora were converted to churches; a similar fate awaited the Pantheon at Rome, the temple of Apollo at Daphne (Julian, *Misopogon* 361A-363A), and many others (Vaes 1984–6: 326–33; Hanson 1978). Despite the appeals of Firmicus Maternus (*De errore profanarum religionum* 28.6), it is not likely that many cases of destruction or conversion of pagan religious architecture took place before the end of the fourth-century. The process was facilitated by edicts of Theodosius banning pagan *cultus* and ordering destruction of rural temples (*Codex Theodotianus* 16.10.10, 16). At the local level, however, tensions and outbreaks of violence arose on both sides. At Alexandria, Christian mobs sacked and burned the Sarapeion and murdered the philosopher Hypatia (Theodoret, *Historia Ecclesiastica* 5.22.3–6; Socrates, *Historia Ecclesiastica* 7.15). Elsewhere, pagans rioted to preserve their local temples (Libanius, *Pro templis* 8.9; Sozomen, *Historia Ecclesiastica* 7.15.11–15).

A special case in this regard is the Church of Mary, also known as the Church of the Councils, at Ephesus, which has long been thought where the Council of Ephesus of 431 was held (Krautheimer 1979: 113–15). The edifice is unique among Christian churches, a double basilica measuring some 275 metres in length with an apse on either end. It has now been found that the church structure was built in the south hall of the outer ambulatory of the Temple of Zeus Olympus (or Hadrianeion), originally built by Hadrian. The south hall was further elaborated in the early third century with an imperial cult sanctuary for Macrinus (Karwiese 1995: 314–15). The entire temple complex was destroyed by Christians in *c.* 400; however, the magnificent double church was not constructed until near the end of the fifth century using spoils from the temple complex (Karwiese 1995: 316). This means that the council of 431 must have been convened elsewhere in another church building so far not discovered. Ephesus' associations with the cult of Mary apparently also faced a difficult time in this period (Limberis 1995). All the same, new church constructions continued in the ruins of monumental imperial architecture. At Rome in *c.* 400 CE a mithraeum installed some 200 years earlier in an imperial palace was destroyed and the church of Santa Prisca built on top of it (White 1996–7: II, no. 89). Church construction put a new, 'Christian' face on the urban landscape, but often by renovating or replacing traditional forms of public religious architecture with its own.

Christians took over Jewish synagogues as well. Despite an imperial edict protecting Jews and pagans who 'live quietly and attempt to do nothing disorderly or contrary to law' (*Codex Theodotianus* 16.10.24) Christian triumphalism turned violent. The case of the destruction of the synagogue at Callinicum in 388 CE by a mob of local Christians is well known from the exchange between Ambrose and Theodosius (Ambrose, *Epistles* 40.6–7; 41.25–8). At Gerasa in the Transjordan, the local synagogue was taken over to build a church. Also near the end of the fourth century, in northern Macedonia at Stobi, another synagogue that had been in use for nearly two centuries and in two distinct phases of rebuilding was systematically destroyed and the remains incorporated into a Christian basilica (Figures 27.4, 27.21). It is thus noteworthy that some of its earlier architectural elements and dedicatory inscriptions were reused, apparently without alteration, in the new Christian edifice (White 1996–7: II, nos. 72–3).

Jews in other cities fared far better. For example at Sardis, the Jewish community was apparently given possession of one wing of the municipal bath/gymnasium complex sometime in the third century. By the late fourth century, after several stages of renovation, it had become an elaborately decorated basilica in keeping with, and perhaps influenced by, contemporaneous architectural developments

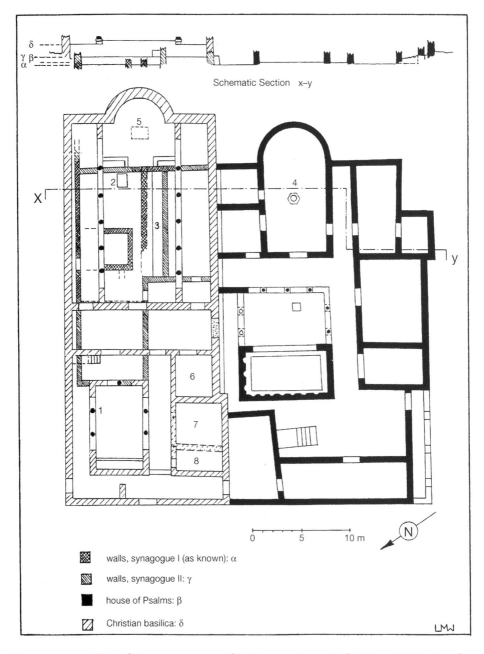

Schematic Section x–y

Figure 27.21 Plan of the synagogue and basilica complex at Stobi. From White (1996–7: II, fig. 38).

Legend:

- walls, synagogue I (as known): α
- walls, synagogue II: γ
- house of Psalms: β
- Christian basilica: δ

among Christians (Figures 27.4, 27.22). With interior dimensions of 82.5 by 18 metres, it was by far the largest synagogue now known from antiquity (White 1996–97: II, nos. 66–7). It continued in uninterrupted operation until the city was destroyed in 616 CE.

While basilical planning became predominant in the course of the fourth century, there were local and regional variations. By the early fifth century there emerged in the Aegean coastlands (Greece and Turkey) a distinctive adaptation of the basic basilical plan, typically with a much squarer nave and often with cruciform transept (Krautheimer 1979: 126–32). When later combined with central planning this style would result in some of the great domed church buildings of the Byzantine tradition, including the monumental Hagia Sophia at Constantinople as rebuilt by Justinian in 561 CE. At Philippi during the fifth century the earlier *aula ecclesiae* dedicated in the name of Paul was finally renovated as a hybrid basilica. From the exterior, the edifice appeared to be a squarish basilica with an apse on its east side (see Figure 27.17). On the interior, the nave was an octagonal colonnade with clerestory cupola; four apsidal *exedrae* were tucked into the corners. The apse extended from one of the sides of the octagon. The buildings surrounding the church were remodelled and incorporated into an ecclesiastical complex. They included a baptistery, converted from an earlier bath building, and a large complex that likely served as *Episkopeion* or bishop's residence (White 1996–7: II, no. 49, with further bibliography). A similar suggestion has been made regarding the complex around the church of St Augustine at Hippo Regius, since it was a typical western basilica but surrounded by what appear to be contiguous domestic structures (Marrou 1960).

Syrian churches were influenced by this Aegean tradition (Krautheimer 1979: 145), but also developed peculiar traits. Rather than entering on the end opposite the apse, Syrian churches often had their main doors (usually two or three) on the side of the nave (see Figure 27.23). The doors might have been designated clergy and laity, or men and women, respectively. These Syrian churches sometimes had external apses, but many had only internal apsidal constructions flanked by *exedrae*. The *ambo* – a semi-circular enclosure with interior benches and steps to a rostrum – was a peculiar adaptation to the Syrian liturgical tradition. This structure was situated in the middle of the nave and probably housed the bishop and attendants during some portion of the service (Lassus and Tchalenko 1951). Finally, many Syrian churches seem to comprise large complexes of buildings with differentiated functions, perhaps reflecting a monumental version of the different rooms of an earlier style of *domus ecclesiae* (White 1996–7: I. 122–3; Krautheimer 1979: 149–51; Lassus 1947: 22–3; Lassus and Tchalenko 1951). A good example is the church of St Paul and Moses at Dar Qita (Figure 27.23).

Other types of Christian architecture: martyria and baptisteries

As already noted, buildings with a central plan (square, polygonal, or round) had originally been associated more with memorial architecture, mausolea, and sanctuaries rather than assembly. Thus, in the pre-Constantinian period the architecture of assembly developed in a different realm and different architectural medium from the

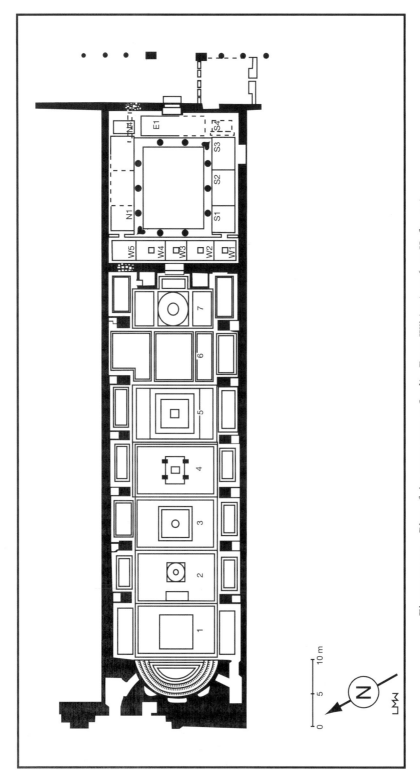

Figure 27.22 Plan of the synagogue at Sardis. From White (1996–7: II. fig. 33).

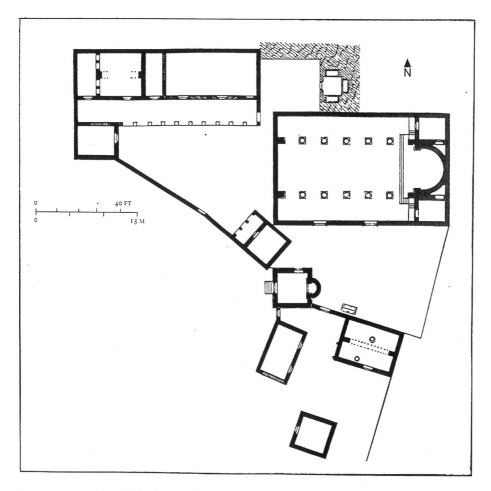

Figure 27.23 Plan of the church of St Paul and Moses at Dar Qita. From Krautheimer 1979: 150, fig. 97).

cult of the dead (Krautheimer 1979: 30). The adaptation of central plan to temple architecture began in the second-century when Hadrian had the Pantheon rebuilt after it had long been favoured for imperial mausolea. Such memorial associations probably account for appropriation of central plan edifices in conjunction with the basilicas at Golgotha and Bethlehem. Gradually, the central plan was integrated with the basilical plan especially in the Aegean regions, later the centre of Byzantine Christianity. It was especially popular for martyria or churches built to memorialize key events in the biblical tradition and in the life of Christ, or to commemorate martyrs who had died for the faith (Grabar 1946; Ward-Perkins 1966). Octagonal churches became common in the fourth to sixth centuries. When blended with the rectangular plan of the basilica it resulted in monumental domed churches, such as Hagia Sophia at Constantinople, San Vitale at Ravenna, and the church of St John at Ephesus. While central planning was thus integrated with basilical style two other

specialized appropriations continued in Christian architecture apart from the ordinary assembly and worship setting.

Martyria, catacombs and cemetery basilicas

The architecture of the martyrium continued beyond the time of Constantine. It was
usually a square or central plan focusing on either a sacred locus (e.g. the monastery
of St Catherines at Mount Sinai) or the relics of a martyr and saint (church of St
Philip at Hierapolis: Figure 27.24). Andre Grabar (1946) has identified several other

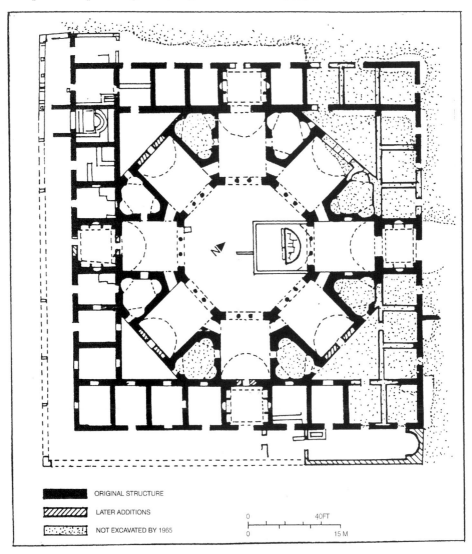

ORIGINAL STRUCTURE

LATER ADDITIONS

NOT EXCAVATED BY 1965

0   40FT

0   15 M

Figure 27.24 Plan of the Martyrium of St Philip, at Hierapolis (Pamukkale). From
Krautheimer (1979: 171, fig. 124).

variations on this architectural scheme, including the triconch (a square building with apses on three sides) and cruciform buildings. One of the most elaborate was the church built to commemorate the life of St Simeon the Stylite at Qal'at Siman (Figure 27.25).

Cemeterial basilicas also became popular, especially around Rome. As in the case of St Peters, they may have originated to memorialize a burial site identified with a saint or apostle, but they also needed to enclose larger burial areas while accommodating crowds during festivals of religious commemoration. St Paul's Outside the Walls marks one of the sites associated with the apostle Paul. Several of the large cemetery basilicas grew up in association with the Christian catacombs, especially San Sebastiano, also known as the Church (or *memoria*) of the Apostles. Originally a pagan necropolis, it was already being commemorated by Christians as the burial place of both Peter and Paul as early as the third-century. These legendary associations gradually transformed it into a regular place of pilgrimage, and many Christians wanted to be buried there, near the apostles. The basilica was built early in the fourth-century to sacralize both traditions (Snyder 1985: 98–104).

It was this same site that actually gave its local place name (*ad catacumbas*, 'at the hollows') to the growing practice, especially around Rome, of digging out long underground tunnels for burial (Stephenson 1978: 7, 24–5). The first tombs at San Sebastiano were typically Roman 'housetombs' dug into the tufa escarpment of the hill face. Gradually tunnels were extended far into and under the ground.

Most of the other catacombs began as small family tombs or *columbaria* with an entrance at ground level and a vault or room for multiple burials dug into the

Figure 27.25 Isometric reconstruction of the Martyrium of St Simeon, at Qal'at Siman, Syria. From Krautheimer (1979: 156, fig. 102).

ground. Beginning in the second century CE, the older Roman practice of cremation gave way to inhumation as the preferred mode of burial. All burials at Rome had to be outside the *pomerium* (or sacred boundary) of the city; in practical terms, this meant outside the city walls. A result of the growing popularity of inhumation among pagans as well as Jews and Christians was that land for burial came at a premium (Stephenson 1978: 25–44). Tunnelling into the layers of soft igneous rock (*tufa*) indigenous to Rome offered a cheap solution and also fostered a new profession: the *fossores* (or 'grave diggers'). Although not alone, Christians figured prominently in this new enterprise. In some cases (such as the Domitilla catacomb), several independent family tombs were interconnected by tunnels, which then grew into an ant-like network of catacombs. By the early fourth century this site had been memorialized by construction of a cemeterial basilica of unusual plan above the cemetery complex.

Baptisteries

In the earliest days it seems that Christians performed baptism in natural streams or pools or wherever they could find water (*Didache* 7; Tertullian, *De baptismo* 4). By the middle of the second-century they also used Roman *balinea* or baths (White 1996–7: 110). At some point, however, Christians began to build special areas for baptism. In part it came as a result of the increasingly complex ritual process that grew around baptismal liturgy. Privacy and decorum were concerns since baptism was undertaken nude. These factors in the liturgical development likely paralleled the process of architectural adaption from house-church to *domus ecclesiae*, where specialized areas might be set aside. Gradually they were adapted and further articulated to meet the ritual and symbolic needs of baptismal liturgy.

The earliest known example of such a specially constructed baptistery comes from the *domus ecclesiae* at Dura-Europos (Figure 27.10). One modest chamber (room 6) was particularly adapted to suit their liturgical and symbolic needs. A small basin or *font* (2.57 metres long by 1.83 wide by 0.95 deep) was set partially into the floor on one end of the room. The shape of the font and its arched canopy is similar to a small shrine or tomb. It may well be that this funerary symbolism was self-consciously appropriated in conjunction with the practical considerations of a washing ritual. The decorative programme also seems to have been tailored to the baptismal liturgy as it juxtaposed scenes of death (the tomb and Goliath) with scenes of salvation from or through water (White 1996–7: II, no. 36). The font itself was barely large enough to allow for immersion, but the precise practice is uncertain. A large amphora was also found and could have been used in some way either for pouring (as recommended by the *Didache* when running water was not available), or for filling the basin.

Perhaps because of the symbolism of death and resurrection, the architecture of later Christian baptisteries seems to have a strong affinity for memorial style architecture, especially central planned buildings and/or fonts. Over four hundred early Christian baptisteries have been catalogued dating from the third to the seventh centuries. They exhibit considerable architectural diversity, especially in the external building forms. Most are artistically unexceptional and clearly designed for utilitarian purposes. There are, however, some general features of font design and siting that suggest patterns of spatial articulation at least by the fourth to sixth centuries.

Most baptisteries were attached as rooms or as auxiliary buildings to the main church building. Eventually, it became the norm that only the bishop's church in each locality should have a baptistery; however, many cities had more than one. Other baptisteries were built as freestanding structures or complexes of rooms. The freestanding baptistery buildings were of various shapes, but central plan buildings (square, round, or octagonal) became the most popular, especially in northern Italy. The octagonal baptistery of St John at the church of Santa Thecla in Milan (built by Ambrose in *c.* 350) perhaps set the pattern for others (Krautheimer 1979: 187). The octagonal font was set in the centre of the octagonal building and the decorative programme consolidated its imagery of death and rebirth. The shape of various fonts have been correlated with this symbolism: cruciform and hexagonal fonts more with the 'tomb' imagery; round or octagonal fonts with the 'womb' of rebirth (Bedard 1951; Davies 1962; Khatchatrian 1962, 1982). Other rooms in the building served for dressing and waiting areas; at Salona the large complex seems to have included an auditorium and room for catechumens as well.

The most elaborate architectural and decorative programme in baptismal buildings was that of the Orthodox Baptistery at Ravenna (completed between 450–70 CE). The octagonal building was over 11 metres in diameter; in its centre stood a font nearly 3.5 metres in diameter, with a depth of 0.85 metres. The central mosaic of the cupola depicted the baptism of Jesus by John. Surrounding it were two concentric bands of decoration. The upper band, still in the circular dome, showed a procession of the apostles in two groups of six each led by Peter and Paul. Each carries a crown, and they meet below the axis of the cupola scene. The lower band of mosaic drew the scene down to the octagonal walls. It depicted four thrones alternating with four altars. The thrones bear a cross; the altars, one of the gospels (Kostoff 1965; Krautheimer 1979: 187–9). The iconography seems to reflect orthodox Trinitarian doctrine, over against the nearby Arian baptistery. The combined effect of the spatial and decorative programmes was designed to pilot the initiate around and through the font in a particular way so as to maximize the aesthetic, psychological, and theological significance of the experience. Art and architecture were played in harmony and thus facilitated the consolidation of Christian culture.

The Christian landscape of late Roman cities

By the end of the fifth century the cities of the later Roman empire had become predominantly Christian. Urban planning and architecture reflected continuities as well as change. Traditional temple architecture had largely been abandoned or converted to give it a Christian façade. In its place stood monumental Christian basilicas as the visual and symbolic marker of Christian identity and ritual activity. Festivals and processions at sacred centres and on holy days ordered civic life, while every neighbourhood could boast its local shrine. Some became pilgrimage centres to mark the great events and archetypal stories of the founder's life or the exemplary accomplishments of heroes past. Architecture and ritual were media of cultural integration and construction of a new symbolic universe. But now the architectural norm was drawn from the basilica and its varied Christian adaptations and associations. They were attended by a coterie of professional clergy who figured prominently in daily social life. State and civic leaders held important seats in religious festivals. An identifiable religious architecture, great and small, now emulating the basilical style, dotting the rebuilt urban landscape. On some levels, at least, not so much had changed after all (MacMullen 1981: 131–7; 1984: 1–9).

NOTES

1 This is the view traditionally taken in more theologically oriented discussions of the origins of Christian architecture as reflected in Deichmann (1964); Süssenbach (1977); and Turner (1979). On the Calvinist theological orientation towards ritual and 'sacred space' implicit within these studies, see Finney (1988: 320–328). Compare also Harnack (1908: II, 86).

2 The extensive bibliography on Greek and Roman architecture, city planning, and archaeology will not be recapitulated here. The reader is referred to the following for further references: Connolly and Dodge (1998); Wycherly (1978); Boethius (1978); Ward-Perkins (1974, 1981); and Jones (1940).

3 For the Latin *curia*, which means either the assembly or the place of assembly (the 'Senate' or the 'Senate house'), used of the Christian gatherings see Tertullian, *Apology* 39.21.

4 It has often been assumed that both buildings belonged to the Shipbuilders Association; however, Hermansen (1981: 71–4) makes a strong case for the Shipowners Association instead.

5 For collegial halls with small temples at Ostia, in addition to the Shipbuilders Association discussed above, note the House of the Triclinia (I.12.1), seat of the Housebuilders Association (*Fabri tignuari*), even though they may be associated with another temple at V.11.1 (Hermansen 1981: 62, 64); The Guild of the Grain Measurers (*Mensores frumentarii*) located next to their warehouse (I, 19.1–3; Hermansen 1981: 65); and the *schola* of the *hastiferi* located in the precincts of the Magna Mater (IV.1.4; Hermansen 1981: 69–70).

6 Based on the patron's name in relation to Sergius Paulus, proconsul of Cyprus mentioned in Acts 13.7 as a 'convert' of Paul, it has been suggested that this *collegium* represents an early Christian house-church at Rome; however, there can be no certainty (White 1996–7: I, 46 with references).

7 So see Acts 2–5, although this might well be an idealized portrayal of the earliest days of the movement.

8 *m.Shabbath* 1.4; *b.Menahoth* 41b; Neusner (1979: 81–96); White (1996–7: 103).

9 On the vexed questions surrounding the origins of the synagogue see White (1987: 133–134); Gutmann (1975b: 72–6); Urman and Flesher (1995: xx-xxiv); Griffiths (1995); Grabbe (1995); and Flesher (1995).

10 White (1996–7: I, 12) and bibliography cited there; see also Groh (1995); Tsafrir (1995); and Hachlili (1996: 101–2). While architectural studies have long since abandoned synagogue models as an explanatory category in basilical origins, such suppositions continue to find a voice, especially in studies of liturgy and church organization, and should be treated with caution.

11 The house-church in the New Testament period has become a fixture in recent discus-

sions and the bibliography is now quite lengthy. *Inter alia* see Meeks (1983: 29–30; 74–84); Malherbe (1983: 60–91); White (1996–7: I, 102–9); Theissen (1982: 73–96; 147–55); Schüssler Fiorenza (1983: 175–83); Klauck (1981); Banks (1994). Two recent works deserve special notice: Osiek and Balch (1997) (which gives the most thorough treatment of archaeological and cultural issues in housing and family life relative to the social organization of house-churches), and Ascough (1998) (with an excellent review of the scholarship).

12 I am grateful to Corby Finney (1988: 334–5) for recognizing the significance of these intermediate moments or transitional stages in my earlier discussions of this 'dynamic model'.

13 Two other archaeological sites deserve special mention in this connection. First, at Umm el-Jimal in the Hauran (Roman Syria/Arabia), the so-called 'Julianos church' appears to be a later basilical hall protruding from one side of a house in a domestic insula complex. The addition of the basilical hall and apse dates to the late fourth century; however, there are indications that a portion of the edifice preserved in this construction may have already been in use at an earlier stage, but not likely for domestic functions. An earlier stage of partial adaptation for Christian usage, i.e. a possible *domus ecclesiae*, may be indicated but is awaiting further excavations (White 1996–7: II, 40).

Second, at Capernaum excavations since the mid-1960s have revealed an area of houses dating to the first century over which was built an octagonal church complex in the fifth and sixth centuries CE. In an intermediate phase, datable to the early to mid-fourth century, a simple quadrangular complex had been built, and it appears that it was meant to sacralize a particular room in the domestic complex, which then later stood at the centre point of the octagonal structure. It is clear that in the fourth century the first building was a Christian shrine built to commemorate what they thought was the house of St Peter. Although the evidence is sketchy and archaeologically problematic, it is possible that the site had already been identified with the legend of Peter at a slightly earlier stage (late third–century; so Corbo 1969: 71). However, initial claims that the edifice had already begun to function as a *domus ecclesiae* prior to the building of the fourth century memorial edifice are archaeologically unwarranted. There is no evidence that it was ever used as a regular place of Christian assembly and worship or was adapted for specifically Christian purposes prior to the fourth century project (White 1996–7: II, no. 42). Even so, the site is of considerable interest for some of the later tendencies in the development of Christian holy sites.

14 This phrase (*ek themeliôn*) is commonly found in building inscriptions from synagogues, mithraea, and the like, and suggests a full-scale rebuilding on an existing structure. It does not necessarily imply a prior catastrophic 'destruction'. See White (1996–7: I, 128; II, 93, 119, 175, 177, 357).

15 Compare the epitaph of Marcus Julius Eugenius at Laodicea Combusta for another case of a local bishop who undertakes a special rebuilding programme 'from the foundations' in this period; inscription in *MAMA* I, 170 and White (1996–7: II, no.48).

BIBLIOGRAPHY

Ascough, Richard S. (1998) *What are They Saying about The Formation of Pauline Churches?* New York: Paulist Press.

Bakker, Jan Theo (1994) *Living and Working with the Gods: Studies of Evidence for Private Religion and its Material Environment in the City of Ostia (100–500 AD).* Dutch Monographs on Ancient History and Archaeology XII. Amsterdam: J. C. Gieben.

Balch, David L. (1991) *Social History of the Matthean Community: Cross-Disciplinary Approaches.* Minneapolis, Minn.: Fortress Press.

—— (1995) 'Rich and Poor, Proud and Humble in Luke-Acts', in White and Yarbrough 1995: 214–33.

Balch, David L., Ferguson, Everett, and Meeks, Wayne A. (1990) *Greeks, Romans and Christians: Essays in Honor of Abraham J. Malherbe.* Minneapolis, Minn.: Fortress Press.

Banks, Robert (1994) *Paul's Idea of Community: The Early House churches in their Cultural Setting.* 2nd edn. Peabody, Mass.: Hendrickson.

Bedard, Walter M. (1951) *The Symbolism of the Baptismal Font in Early Christian Thought.* Washington, DC: Catholic University of America Press.

Blue, Bradley (1994) 'Acts and the house-church', in Gill and Gempf 1994: 119–89.

Bobertz, Charles (1993) 'The Role of the Patron in the *Cena dominica* of Hippolytus' *Apostolic Tradition*', *Journal of Theological Studies* 44: 170–84.

Boethius, Axel (1978) *Etruscan and Early Roman Architecture.* London: Harmondsworth.

Brooten, Bernadette (1982) *Women Leaders in the Ancient Synagogue: Inscriptional Evidence and Background Issues.* Brown Judaic Studies 36. Chico: Scholars Press.

Bruneau, Philippe (1970) *Recherches sur les cultes de Délos.* Paris: Bocard.

Burtchaell, James T. (1992) *From Synagogue to Church: Public Services and Offices in the Earliest Christian Communities.* Cambridge: Cambridge University Press.

Clark, John (1991) *Houses of Roman Italy, 100 BC–AD 250: Ritual, Space and Decoration.* Berkeley: University of California Press.

Connolly, Peter and Dodge, Hazel (1998) *The Ancient City: Life in Classical Athens and Rome.* New York: Oxford University Press.

Corbo, Virgilio C. (1969) *The House of St. Peter at Capharnaum, a preliminary report of the first two campaigns of Excavations, 1968.* Studium Biblicum Franciscanum, Collectio minor 5. Jerusalem: Studium Biblicum Franciscum.

Cornell, Timothy J. and Lomas, Kathryn (1995) *Urban Society in Roman Italy.* London: University College of London Press.

Davies, J. G. (1962) *The Architectural Setting of Baptism.* London: Barrie & Rockliff.

Deichmann, Friedrich Wilhelm (1964) 'Vom Tempel zur Kirche', *Mullus: Festschrift Theodor Klauser.* JAC Ergänzungsband 1. Münster: Aschendorff.

Drijvers, Jan Willem (1992) *Helena Augusta.* Leiden: E. J. Brill.

Edlund-Berry, Ingrid E. M. (1988) *The Gods and the Place: Location and Function of Sanctuaries in the Countryside of Etruria and Magna Graecia (700–400 BC).* Acta Instituti Romani Regni Sueciae, IV.43. Stockholm: Svenska Institutet i Rom.

Esler, Philip F. (1987) *Community and Gospel in Luke-Acts: The Social and Political Motivations of Lucan Theology.* SNTS Monograph Series 57. Cambridge: Cambridge University Press.

Fine, Steven (1996) *Sacred Realm: The Emergence of the Synagogue in the Ancient World.* New York: Oxford University Press and Yeshiva University Museum.

Finney, Paul Corby (1984) 'TOPOS HIEROS und christlicher Sakralbau in vorkonstantinischer Überlieferung', *Boreas: Münstersche Beiträge zür Archäologie* 7: 193–225.

—— (1987/8) 'Early Christian Art and Archaelogy I/II (AD 200–500): A Selected Bibliography 1945–1985', *The Second Century: A Journal of Early Christian Studies* 6: 21–42, 203–38.

—— (1988) 'Early Christian Architecture: The Beginnings (A Review Article)', *Harvard Theological Review* 81: 319–39.

Fitzgerald, John T. (1996a) *Friendship, Flattery, and Frankness of Speech: Studies on Friendship in the New Testament World.* Supplements to Novum Testamentum 82. Leiden: E. J. Brill.

—— (1996b) 'Philippians in the Light of Some Ancient Discussions of Friendship', in Fitzgerald 1996a: 141–61.

—— (1997) *Graeco-Roman Perspectives on Friendship*. SBL Resources for biblical Study 34. Atlanta, Ga.: Scholars Press.

Flesher, Paul V. M. (1995) 'Palestinian Synagogues before 70: A Review of the Evidence', in Urman and Flesher 1995: 27–39.

Foerster, Gideon (1995) 'Dating Synagogues with a 'Basilical' Plan and Apse', Urman and Flesher 1995: 87–94.

Foss, Pedar (1997) 'Watchful *lares*: Roman Household Organization and the Rituals of Cooking and Dining', in Laurence and Wallace-Hadrill 1997: 196–218.

Gill, David W. J. and Gempf, Conrad (1994) *The Book of Acts in its First Century Setting*, vol. 2: *Graeco-Roman Setting*. Grand Rapids, Mich.: Eerdmans.

Grabar, André (1946) *Martyrium: recherches sur le culte des reliques et l'art chrétien antique*, 2 vols. Paris: College de France.

Grabbe, Lester L. (1995) 'Synagogues in pre–70 Palestine: A Re-assessment', in Urman and Flesher 1995: 17–26.

Griffith, J. Gwyn (1995) 'Egypt and the Rise of the Synagogue', in Urman and Flesher 1995: 3–16.

Groh, Dennis E. (1995) 'The Stratigraphic Chronology of the Galilean Synagogue from the early Roman Period through the Early Byzantine Period', in Urman and Flesher 1995: 51–69.

Gutmann, Joseph (1975a) *The Synagogue: Studies in Origins, Archaeology, and Architecture*. New York: KTAV.

—— (1975b) 'The Origins of the Synagogue: The Current State of Research', in Gutmann 1975a: 72–6.

—— (1981) *Ancient Synagogues: The State of Research*. Brown Judaic Studies 23. Chico: Scholars Press.

Hachlili, Rachel (1996) 'Synagogues in the Land of Israel: The Art and Architecture of Late Antique Synagogues', in Fine 1996: 96–129.

Hanson, R. P. C. (1978) 'The Transformation of Pagan Temples into church Buildings in the Early Christian Centuries', *Journal of Semitic Studies* 23: 257–67.

Harnack, A. von (1908) *The Mission and Expansion of Christianity in the First Three Centuries*, 2 vols., 2nd edn., trans. and ed. J. Moffatt. London: Williams & Norgate.

Hermansen, Gustav (1981) *Ostia: Aspects of Roman City Life*. Edmonton: University of Alberta Press.

Jones, Arnold Hugh Martin (1940) *The Greek City from Alexander to Justinian*. Oxford: Clarendon.

Karwiese, Stefan (1995) 'The Church of Mary and the Temple of Hadrian Olympos', in Koester 1995: 311–20.

Kasher, Aryeh (1995) 'Synagogues as 'Houses of Prayer' and 'Holy Places' in the Jewish Communities of Hellenistic and Roman Egypt', in Urman and Flesher 1995: 205–20.

Khatchatrian, Andreas (1962) *Les baptistères paléochrétiens*. Paris: Imprimerie Nationale.

(1982) *Origine et typolofie des baptistères paléochrétiens*. Mulhouse: Centre de Culture Chrétienne.

Klauck, Hans-Josef (1981) *Hausgemeinde und Hauskirche im frühen Christentum*. Stuttgarter Bibelstudien 103. Stuttgart: Verlag Katholisches Bibelwerk.

Kloppenborg, John S. and Wilson, Stephen G. (1996) *Voluntary Associations in the Graeco-Roman World*. London: Routledge.

Koester, Helmut (1995) *Ephesus Metropolis of Asia: An Interdisciplinary Approach to its Archaeology, Religion, and Culture*. Harvard Theological Studies 41. Valley Forge: Trinity Press International.

Kostoff, Spiro (1965) *The Orthodox Baptistery of Ravenna*. (New Haven, Conn.: Yale University Press.

Kraabel, Alf Thomas (1979) 'The Diaspora Synagogue: Archaeological and Epigraphic Evidence since Sukenic', in Wolfgang Haase and Hildegard Temporini (eds.) *Aufstieg und Niedergang der Römischen Welt*, II, 19.1: 477–510; (reprinted in Urman and Flesher 1995: 95–126).

—— (1981) 'The Social Systems of Six Diaspora Synagogues', in Gutmann 1981: 79–92.

Kraeling, Carl H. (1967) *The Christian Building*. Excavations at Dura-Europos, Final Report 8.2; New Haven, Conn.: Yale University Press.

Krautheimer, Richard (1939) 'The Beginnings of Early Christian Architecture', *Review of Religion* 3: 144–59.

—— (1939–1956) *Corpus Basilicarum Christianarum Romae*. 5 vols. Vatican City: Pontifical Gregorian Institute.

—— (1967) 'The Constantinian Basilica', *Dumbarton Oaks Papers* 21: 117–40.

—— (1979) *Early Christian and Byzantine Architecture*. 3rd edn. New York: Penguin.

Lassus, Jean (1947) *Sanctuaires chrétiennes de Syrie*. Paris: P. Geuthner.

—— (1965) 'Les édifices du culte autour de la basilique', in *Actes de VI° Congresso Internazionale di Archeologia Cristiana. Studia di Antichità Cristiana* 26: 581–610.

Lassus, Jean and Tchalenko, Georges (1951) 'Ambons Syriens', *Cahiers archeologique* 5: 75–122.

Laurence, Ray (1994) *Roman Pompeii: Space and Society*. London: Routledge.

—— (1995) 'The Organization of Space in Pompeii', in Cornell and Lomas 1995: 63–78.

—— (1997) 'Space and Text', in Laurence and Wallace-Hadrill 1997: 7–14.

Laurence, Ray and Wallace-Hadrill, Andrew (1997) *Domestic Space in the Roman World: Pompeii and Beyond*. Journal of Roman Archaeology Supplements 22. Portsmouth: JRA.

Limberis, Vasiliki (1995) 'The Council of Ephesus: The Demise of the See of Ephesus and ·the Rise of the Cult of the Theotokos', in Koester 1995: 321–40.

MacDonald, William (1977) *Early Christian and Byzantine Architecture*. New York: George Braziller.

MacMullen, Ramsay (1981) *Paganism in the Roman Empire*. New Haven, Conn.: Yale University Press.

—— (1984) *Christianizing the Roman Empire*. New Haven, Conn.: Yale University Press.

Malherbe, Abraham J. (1983) *Social Aspects of Early Christianity*. 2nd edn. Philadelphia, Pa.: Fortress Press.

Marrou, Henri Irenee (1960) 'La basilique chrétienne d'Hippo d'après le résultat des derniers fouilles', *Revue des Études Augustiniennes* 6: 109–54.

Marshall, Peter (1987) *Enmity at Corinth: Social Conventions in Paul's Relations with the Corinthians*, Wissenschaftliche Untersuchungen zum Neuen Testament, II. 23. Tübingen: J. C. B. Mohr (Paul Siebeck).

Meeks, Wayne A. (1983) *The First Urban Christians: The Social World of the Apostle Paul*. New Haven, Conn.: Yale University Press.

Meiggs, Russel (1973) *Roman Ostia*. 2nd edn. Oxford: Clarendon.

Mitchell, Alan C. (1997) ' 'Greet the Friends by Name': New Testament Evidence for the Greco-Roman *Topos* on Friendship', in Fitzgerald 1997: 225–60.

Neusner, Jacob (1979) *From Politics to Piety: The Emergence of Pharisaic Judaism*. 2nd edn. New York: KTAV.

Nielsen, Inge and Nielsen, Hanne Sigismund (1998) *Meals in a Social Context*. Aarhus Studies in Mediterranean Antiquity 1. Aarhus: Aarhus University Press.

Orr, David G. (1978) 'Roman Domestic Religion: The Evidence of Household Shrines', in Wolfgang Haase and Hildegarde Temporini, *Aufstieg und Niedergang der Römischen Welt*. Berlin/New York: DeGruyter. II, 16.2: 1557–91.

Osiek, Carolyn and Balch, David L. (1997) *Families in the New Testament World: Households and House churches*. Louisville: Westminster/John Knox Press.

Picard, Charles (1921) *L'établissement des Poseidoniastes de Berytos*. Exploration archeologiques de Délos 6. Paris: Bocard.

Richardson, Peter (1996) 'Early Synagogues as Collegia in the Diaspora and Palestine', in Kloppenborg and Wilson 1996: 90–109.

Rordorf, Willy (1964) 'Was wissen wir über die christlichen Gottesdiensträume der vorkonstantinischen Zeit?', *Zeitschrift für die Neutestamentliche Wissenschaft* 55: 110–28.

—— (1971) 'Die Hausgemeinde der vorkonstantinischen Zeit', *Kirche: Tendenzen und Ausblicke* 190–6; 235–7.

Rutgers, Leonard V. (1995) *The Jews in Late Ancient Rome: Evidence of Cultural Interaction in the Roman Diaspora*. Religions in the Graeco-Roman World 126. Leiden: E. J. Brill.

Schüssler Fiorenza, Elisabeth (1983) *In Memory of Her: A Feminist Theological Reconstruction of Christian Origins*. New York: Crossroad Press.

Snyder, Graydon F. (1985) *Ante Pacem: Archaeological Evidence of Church Life before Constantine*. Macon: Mercer University Press.

Stambaugh, John E. (1978) 'The Functions of Roman Temples', in Wolfgang Haase and Hildegarde Temporini (eds). *Aufstieg und Niedergang der Römischen Welt*. Berlin and New York: De Gruyter II, 16.1: 540–607.

—— (1988) *The Ancient Roman City*. Baltimore, Md.: The Johns Hopkins University Press.

Stephenson, James (1978) *The Catacombs: Life and Death in Early Christianity*. London: Thames & Hudson.

Süssenbach, Uwe (1977) *Christuskult und kaiserliche Baupolitik bei Konstantin*. Bonn: Hanstein.

Theissen, Gerd (1982) *The Social Setting of Pauline Christianity: Essays on Corinth*, trans. by John H. Schütz; Philadelphia, Pa.: Fortress Press.

Torjesen, Karen Jo (1995) *When Women Were Priests: Women's Leadership in the Early Church and the Scandal of their Subordination in the Rise of Christianity*. San Francisco: Harper Collins.

Turner, Harold W. (1979) *From Temple to Meeting House: The Phenomenology and Theology of Places of Worship*. Religion and Society 16. The Hague/Paris/New York: Mouton.

Tsafrir, Yoram (1995) 'On the Source of the Architectural Design of the Ancient Synagogues of the Galilee: A New Appraisal', in Urman and Flesher 1995: 70–86.

Urman, Dan and Flesher, Paul V. M. (1995) *Ancient Synagogues: Historical Analysis and Archaeologial Discovery: Volume I*. Studia Post-Biblica 47.1; Leiden: E. J. Brill.

Vaes, Jan (1984–6) 'Christlichen Wiederverwendung Antiker Bauten: Ein Forschungsbericht', *Ancient Society* 15–7: 305–443.

Voelkl, Ludwig (1953) 'Die konstantinischen Kirchenbauten nach Eusebius', *Rivista di archeologia cristiana* 29: 60–94.

—— (1954) 'Die konstantinischen Kirchenbauten nach dem literarischen Quellen des Okzidents', *Rivista di archeologia cristiana* 30: 99–136.

Wallace-Hadrill, Andrew (1994) *Houses and Society in Pompeii and Herculaneum*. Princeton: Princeton University Press.

—— (1995) 'Public Honor and Private Shame: The Urban Texture of Pompeii', in Cornell and Lomas 1995: 39–62.

(1997) 'Rethinking the Roman Atrium House', in Laurence and Wallace-Hadrill 1997: 219–40.

Ward-Perkins, J. B. (1954) 'Constantine and the Origins of the Christian Basilica', *Papers of the British School at Rome* 22: 69–90.

—— (1966) 'Memoria, Martyrs Tomb, and Martyrs Church', *Journal of Theological Studies* 17: 20–38.

—— (1974) *Cities of Ancient Greece and Italy: Planning in Classical Antiquity*. New York: George Braziller.

—— (1981) *Roman Imperial Architecture*. London: Harmondsworth.

White, L. Michael (1987) 'The Delos Synagogue Revisited: Recent Fieldwork in the Graeco-Roman Diaspora', *Harvard Theological Studies* 80: 133–60.

—— (1990a) *Building God's House in the Roman World: Architectural Adaptation among Pagans, Jews, and Christians*. Baltimore: The Johns Hopkins University Press [reprinted as White 1996–7, vol. I].

—— (1990b) 'Morality between Two Worlds: A Paradigm of Friendship in Philippians', in Balch, Ferguson, and Meeks 1990: 201–15.

—— (1991) 'Crisis Management and Boundary Maintenance: The Social Location of the Matthean Community', in Balch 1991: 210–47.

—— (1995a) 'Visualizing the "Real" World of Acts 16: Toward Construction of a Social Index', in White and Yarbrough 1995: 234–63.

—— (1995b) 'Urban Development and Social Change in Imperial Ephesos', in Koester 1995: 27–80.

—— (1996–97) *The Social Origins of Christian Architecture*, Vol. I: *Building God's House in the Roman World: Architectural Adaptation among Pagans, Jews, and Christians*; Vol. II: *Texts and Monuments of the Christian Domus Ecclesiae in its Environment*. Harvard Theological Studies 42. Valley Forge, Pa.: Trinity Press International.

—— (1997) 'Synagogue and Society in Imperial Ostia: Archaeological and Epigraphic Evidence', *Harvard Theological Review* 90: 23–58.

—— (1998) 'Regulating Fellowship in the Communal Meal: Early Jewish and Christian Evidence', in Nielsen and Nielsen 1998: 177–205.

White, L. Michael and Yarbrough, O. Larry (1995) *The Social World of the First Christians: Studies in Honor of Wayne A. Meeks*. Minneapolis, Minn.: Fortress Press.

Wilken, Robert (1992) *The Land Called Holy: Palestine in Christian History and Thought*. New Haven, Conn.: Yale University Press.

Wiplinger, Gilbert and Wlach, Gudrun (1995) *Ephesus: 100 Years of Austrian Research*. Vienna: Böhlau Verlag.

Wycherly, Rachel (1978) *How the Greeks Built Cities*. 3rd edn. Princeton: Princeton University Press.

CHAPTER TWENTY-EIGHT

ART

—— •✦• ——

Robin M. Jensen

ORIGINS AND DEVELOPMENT

Since the earliest examples of Christian visual art usually are dated to the end of the second century, many scholars have concluded that first- and second-century Christians generally observed the Jewish prohibition against the production or use of figurative images for religious purposes – a prohibition established by the second commandment (Exod. 20:4–5). Sometimes scholars also have attributed this supposed reticence by Christians about the making of art objects to the distinction early Christians wished to draw between themselves and their idol-worshipping neighbours, whose cult statues or religious images were understood to be the work of the demons.[1] For instance, Justin Martyr cites the honouring of pagan cult images with sacrifices and floral garlands, and says that by contrast Christians know the images are lifeless, and deem it an insult to the true God to be confused with material objects that are formed or shaped by human hands (*1 Apology* 9.1–9). Likewise, both Clement of Alexandria and Tertullian assert the folly of idol worship and superstition – attributing to objects of wood or stone (some of them even slightly obscene), the qualities of infinite divinity. Tertullian deemed it more than bizarre to purchase one's gods at auction – buying and selling images of Minerva – or melting down Saturn to make a cooking pot (Clement, *Exhortation to the Greeks* 4; Tertullian, *Apologeticum* 1 and *On Idolatry* 3 and 4). And although Tertullian explicitly cites the second commandment against the making or consecration of images, he also reminded his readers that idolatry was yet still practised, as much as in ancient times, and is associated particularly with the surrounding polytheistic culture.[2]

Nevertheless, at the same time as ancient authors condemned the production or worship of cultic art objects, either as prohibited by the divine command or because they entrapped Christians in the idolatrous practices of contemporary culture, many of these same writers provide testimony that Christians both used and perhaps produced small, everyday objects that carried specific Christian symbols. These items – many of them still surviving in museum collections, including lamps, gems and glassware – were most likely made by ordinary artisans selling to a mixed clientele, although especially designed for Christian customers. Tertullian describes goblets with images of the Good Shepherd, and Clement discusses which images Christians might have engraved on their signet rings (doves, fish, ships and anchors were acceptable).[3] Consequently, neither early Christian theologians nor simple everyday believers seem to have rejected material signs or symbols of their faith altogether. Perhaps the lack of extant larger or more expensive art objects from the first two centuries is the result of a general lack of material wealth of first- and second-generation Christians, or (more likely) by their fairly gradual adaptation of familiar objects and the relative modesty of their early worship spaces.[4]

So while textual evidence shows that certain early Christian theologians inveighed against both the production and use of cultic art objects (a sign that such practice must have been going on therefore necessitating the admonitions), they perhaps understood functional distinctions between art that was decorative, symbolic, or didactic and cult objects that were worshipped in themselves. Ordinary Christians may have understood their smaller objects as belonging to a mundane, domestic world. When larger art objects eventually appeared, they were not understood as subjects for worship and therefore presented no danger of idolatry. Moreover, Christian converts from polytheism came from a rich material culture and were as inclined to adapt certain habits and objects to their new faith as to reject other former customs as altogether incompatible. As clear illustration of this trend to incorporate a pagan past into the artistic or material production of the emerging church, many of the earliest 'Christian' artistic motifs appear to have been modelled on Graeco-Roman prototypes, albeit reinterpreted to have particular Christian significance.

Probably the foremost example of this translation from polytheist to Christian artistic type is the Good Shepherd, displayed as a youth dressed in short tunic and boots, carrying a ram or lamb over his shoulders (see Figure 28.1). This extremely popular figure had a direct antecedent in the figure of Hermes as psychopomp (a guide to the underworld – often found in funerary contexts), and in the allegorical personification of philanthropy. Given the biblical use of the Good Shepherd as a metaphorical type for both Christ and God (e.g., John 10), Christians easily and understandably adapted this image as a symbol belonging to their particular set of beliefs (Shumacher 1977; Finney 1990).

In a similar way, a female figure shown as veiled and praying with outstretched hands (*orans*), and who in classical art personified the virtue *pietas*, comes directly into Christian iconography with little change in meaning. A third figure, a seated reader who often appears in conjunction with the shepherd and praying figure, possibly represents the classical value of philosophy. Neither the praying figure nor the philosopher portray a particular biblical figure or historical character, but rather to suggest certain values (piety or wisdom) that belong as much to Graeco-Roman religion as to the Christian faith. Other directly transferred motifs include a range of birds, animals, or floral motifs (peacocks, dolphins, lambs, grape vines, etc.), some clearly popular for their decorative functions while others may have been more symbolically significant. Sometimes the only way to distinguish certain objects or compositions as 'Christian' is their inclusion of (or close proximity to) recognizable biblical themes. For instance, a shepherd becomes definitely identified as a Christian Good Shepherd (rather than as Hermes) when it occurs next to an image of Jonah or of John the Baptist.

Figure 28.1   The Good Shepherd from the Catacomb of Callixtus. Photo Estelle Brettman, with the permission of the International Catacomb Society.

In conclusion, what scholars might recognize as a distinctly 'Christian' body of iconographic themes only began to appear around the year 200 CE. Prior to that time, Christians may have produced works of art, but historians may not be able to distinguish them from examples belonging to the wider cultural context (Finney 1994: 109). Thus in its earliest stage, the basis for characterizing certain materials as 'early Christian art' is primarily iconographic (noting certain themes or motifs) rather than stylistic or functional. In other words, certain new or uniquely Christian figures began to appear, often on objects or in places common to both pagans and Christians (e.g., lamps and tomb walls). Neither the setting, medium, nor style of the art was necessarily Christian. In almost every case, only the content or subject matter reveals the object's particular Christian character and significance. For instance, archaeologists have found decorative terracotta wall tiles bearing representations of the Good Shepherd, Noah, Abraham offering Isaac, or Jesus raising Lazarus – images that conveyed aspects of the Christian faith, illustrated key Bible stories, and identified their owner's religious affiliation.

CHRONOLOGICAL PERIODS

Early Christian art may be roughly divided into two general periods, distinguished partly by iconographic motifs but also partly by certain key transitions in style after the initial stages. Beginning during the era of the Severan emperors (180–240 CE), the earliest phase generally coincides with the last century of pagan rule, and covers the period of the Decian and Diocletianic persecutions, lasting through to the elevation and conversion of the emperor Constantine. During this early stage, Christian art shows the most influence of classical or pagan Roman prototypes in its conventions, decorative motifs and style, as well as much of its subject matter. For instance Christ may be represented as (or shown in the guise of) the Good Shepherd, Orpheus, or Sol Invictus. Popular decorative motifs, including grape vines or dolphins, were transferred to Christian settings and probably were understood to have particular Christian symbolic significance. Other themes of more clearly Christian character were extremely popular during this period and include a cycle of scenes from the Jonah story (by far the most frequent), presentations of Noah in the ark, and Moses striking the rock in the wilderness.

The second period of Christian art covers the era of the Constantinian dynasty through the early sixth century, the time when the church passed from being persecuted to being the officially recognized state religion. The art of this era was largely supported by the wealth of the imperial family or new Christian aristocracy, and certain motifs that characterize it have come to be commonly identified as exemplary of a so-called 'imperial style'.

The conversion of the Roman imperial family was a watershed moment for the church and, by extension, for Christian art. Almost as soon as the emperor Constantine gave his patronage to the Christian cause, he in turn financed the building and rich artistic embellishment of the first great public Christian buildings in Rome, the Holy Land, and especially in his new capital in Constantinople – the 'New Rome'. Consequently, Christian art in this period moved from being largely private or funereal to being public and monumental in character. As part of this transition, certain motifs from the earlier phase dropped out (e.g., the Good Shepherd and Jonah) and new iconographic themes emerged (e.g., Christ enthroned or giving the law to his apostles – the *traditio legis*).

This second phase actually bridges the late Roman and the early Byzantine eras, ending with the reign of the emperor Justinian (527–65), whose artistic patronage helped to make his western capital, Ravenna, into a city best known today for its glorious mosaics. However, Ravenna, which replaced Milan as the western capital in the early fifth century, had already been a centre of art and architecture well before Justinian's general Belisarius regained it for the Byzantine empire from the Ostrogoths. Ravenna's buildings therefore are a combination of artistic work that was begun during the reigns of Honorius (395–423), continued under the Ostrogothic ruler Theodoric (493–526), and finally completed after the re-establishment of the exarchate in Ravenna in 535.

In brief, while the definitive characteristic of 'Christian' art in the earlier period was its iconography (i.e. subject matter and themes), the criteria for such identification expanded to include both context and function during the post-Constantinian era when the material, economic, and social status of Christianity changed radically. While in the third century distinguishable Christian and pagan art works are just beginning to emerge, and are only identifiable by their content, by the first decades of the fifth century, and through the early Byzantine era, the culture was so permeated by Christian interests that the categories 'secular' and 'sacred' were less sharply defined, and the appellation 'Christian art' came to be as much defined by context or patron as by iconographic programme.

PROVENANCE AND CONTEXT

Aside from the lack of first- or second-century evidence, the extant corpus of pre-Constantinian Christian art is limited in two additional respects. First, much of the evidence is of limited geographical provenance. Although significant exceptions exist, most extant examples of earliest Christian art derive from the environs of Rome. In fact, among the earliest and most significant examples of Christian art are frescoes on the walls of the third-century Christian catacombs found just outside Rome itself. The oldest known example of these underground burial sites, the Catacomb of Callistus, was named for an early bishop of Rome (*c.* 217–22) who, while still a deacon of the church, was put in charge of this first subterranean Christian cemetery (Hippolytus, *Refutation of All Heresies {the Philosophumena}* 9.12.14).

Roman-Italian dominance of extant pre-Constantinian Christian imagery is not absolute, however. Scholars have assumed that the Cleveland marble sculptures, generally dated to the third century, came from a Christian family tomb in Asia Minor. Asia Minor may also have been the source of partially finished marble sarcophagi that were sent to workshops in Rome for completion. Additionally, ateliers in Gaul produced many surviving examples of early Christian relief sculpture on sarcophagi, although the influence of Roman workshops is apparent in their technique and style.[5] Archaeologists have also discovered what may be some third-century frescoes in catacombs in North Africa and Thessalonica. The single most important pre-Christian monument, moreover, may be the mid-third-century house church in Dura-Europos, which was located on the Roman/Parthian border (modern-day western Syria). When archaeologists excavated the site in the 1940s, they found the baptistery of this converted domestic structure with its ceiling and wall frescoes intact, thus discovering a unique example of early Christian architecture and interior decoration (see Figure 28. 2).

To a great degree, the limited geographical provenance of early Christian art is an accident of history and, unlike the lack of pre-third century data, not a factor that can be explained by the nature of the data itself. Much of the other non-Roman material, which must have existed, has been lost – presumably to wars, outbreaks of iconoclasm, or the continuous urban renewal of cities and towns. Accordingly, the fact that existing artistic data derive from Rome is neither positive proof of Roman superiority in the crafts nor of the particular authority of the church at Rome at this early date. Although Rome was the political centre of the empire, the Roman church (and presumably Roman Christian art) was distinctly regional and, although

Figure 28.2   The baptistery from the Christian building at Dura-Europos. With the permission of the Yale University Art Gallery.

influential, not necessarily dominant in matters of theology or artistic style.[6] Early Christian theology and practice in other regions of the Roman empire, including Spain, Egypt, Syria, Greece, the British Isles and North Africa, show much regional character and variation – variations that are paralleled by stylistic and thematic distinctions in the surviving examples of non-Roman Christian art from a slightly later period.

The second, and perhaps more important, limiting characteristic of earliest Christian art is the fact that it derives largely from funereal contexts. The major portion of extant pre-Constantinian artwork appears to have served primarily as decoration for tomb chambers or stone coffins – the two largest bodies of Christian art before the mid-fourth century are catacomb frescoes and relief sculpture on marble sarcophagi. Even certain rare small sculptures in the round, or everyday or domestic items bearing recognizably Christian symbols (e.g., pottery lamps), mostly derive from sepulchral environments.

The significance of this fact is difficult to determine given the lack of comparative material from non-funereal contexts. Apart from the unique example of the house-church at Dura-Europos, and a few rare examples from other parts of the world, including Aquileia in north-eastern Italy (whose double basilica may date from both before and after the Constantinian era), scholars may only speculate whether church walls or pavements were regularly decorated with religious imagery (and destroyed in the rebuilding process) and, if so, whether that religious imagery would have been similar to the art work found in the catacombs. The Spanish Council of Elvira in the early fourth century condemned the decoration of church walls with religious paintings (Canon 36); a prohibition that suggests that such decorations existed. The acts of the council, however, omit any description of the offending paintings (Grigg 1976). Later in the fourth century, Paulinus, the aristocratic monk and later bishop of Nola, described the paintings he had commissioned for the church he had built and dedicated to the saint, Felix, as primarily of saints and biblical figures. Paulinus, obviously uncomfortable with the use of art in churches, defends his use of art by giving it a didactic purpose – to counter the popularity of pagan idols and to elevate and inspire his Christian flock (*Poems* 27 and 32).

Nevertheless, based on the single example of the Dura-Europos baptistery and some of the stylistic parallels to Roman wall painting in domestic structures, it seems likely that church-wall frescoes or floor mosaics shared common themes and similar painting techniques with the catacomb frescoes. The Dura frescoes included representations of the Good Shepherd, Adam and Eve, the healing of the paralytic, and the woman at the well – all scenes also found in the catacombs. Even so, the sample is too small for any clear assertions about either the existence or the specific appearance of religious images in other Christian buildings.

During the fourth century, both the provenance and the context of Christian art were radically changed. Churches were built as public buildings, paid for from the imperial treasury, decorated by the best artisans, and patronized by wealthy families. At the same time as art began to appear on the walls and in apses of basilicas in Rome, Constantinople, Greece, and the Holy Land, Christians apparently ceased to use the catacombs for their burial places. By the end of the fourth century the primary venue of Christian art was entirely changed. Whereas in the earliest period the distinction between Christian and pagan art was almost entirely in their different themes or iconographical motifs, by the mid-fourth century the setting of the art was determinative. A peacock on the wall of a Roman tomb might have been painted either for a pagan or for a Christian client, while a peacock in mosaic above the arch of an apse in a Christian basilica clearly had a Christian symbolic significance. In time, Christian art made for church buildings or public Christian worship completely dominated the scene, while the more private funerary art faded into the background.

WALL PAINTING

Apart from the house-church at Dura-Europos (and possibly other early examples such as the fourth-century Christian buildings in Lullingstone, Kent), extant frescoes that belong to the earliest period of Christian art mostly appeared in a funerary context, on the walls and ceilings of tomb chambers in the Roman catacombs (Wilpert 1903). Among the best known of these are the paintings in the catacombs of Callistus, Domitilla, and Priscilla. Although such cemeterial art mainly had died out by the fifth century, it continued into the Constantinian era, and some of the most significant examples of fourth-century wall painting come from the catacombs of Saints Peter and Marcellinus and the new catacomb under the Via Latina, both also in Rome.

Fresco painting on tomb walls had been a Roman custom prior to the Christian adaptation of that tradition. The continuity with this pagan Roman practice may clearly be seen in the composition and style of the paintings themselves, along with many of the decorative elements (borders, urns, birds, garlands, etc.) – features that also may be seen on the walls of Roman villas of the same period. In fact, many of the earliest paintings contained subjects that were as likely to have been pagan as Christian in meaning, including the ubiquitous praying figure (*orans*), the shepherd with sheep, or a funeral banquet (see Figure 28.3).

Although still within the broad tradition of Roman wall painting, the particular technique or style of the Christian catacomb frescoes was often more sketchy and expressionistic than the more finely crafted pagan examples, and these images are sometimes disparagingly described by historians as being crude, of poor quality, or carelessly executed. These features, however, may be less due to a lack of skill, time, or money expended, and more the result of an attempt to achieve a symbolic short-hand designed to communicate certain aspects of the faith. Figures were often awkwardly rendered with a limited colour palette, sometimes difficult to identify, flat and two-dimensional, and supported by a minimum of narrative details. Noah, for example, is shown standing with his arms up in prayer in a mail-box-like ark, while a dove often flies into the scene carrying an olive branch in its beak. This simple or abbreviated image may be all that is necessary to remind the viewer of the entire story and its significance, making other details (Noah's wife, sons, elaborate boat stocked with lots of animals), or even careful rendering of the figures, superfluous.

Figure 28.3   Funeral banquet from the Catacomb of Callistus. Photo Estelle Brettman, with the permission of the International Catacomb Society.

Furthermore, the paintings in the Roman catacombs were not intended for a large public audience, but were private and personal in their character. They were in small spaces, neither well-lit nor much frequented. Unlike the ancient Egyptians, Christians did not believe that tomb paintings had particular value to the deceased in transition to the afterlife. The function of these paintings was most likely entirely devotional and decorative – meant to comfort, inspire, or instruct relatives or friends during their regular visits to the graves of loved ones on festival or anniversary days.

The subject matter of these paintings was primarily based on biblical stories or characters as well as adapted from such classical Roman prototypes as the shepherd or praying figure. Iconographic references to biblical stories are the primary basis for identifying these paintings as Christian in character. The most common of these biblical themes are Jonah (usually shown in a unique three or even four-part narrative sequence); Moses striking the rock to get water in the wilderness; Abraham about to offer his son Isaac; Noah in his ark; and Daniel flanked by lions. Representations of New Testament stories also appear, but are outnumbered by the Hebrew Bible images almost five to one. Those New Testament scenes that occur mostly show Jesus in the role of teacher, healer, or wonder-worker. The most frequent images include Jesus healing the paralytic or the woman with the haemorrhage, multiplying loaves and fishes, or raising Lazarus from the dead.[7] Also depicted is the meeting of Jesus and the Samaritan woman from John 4 (see Figure 17.1). Scenes portraying the incarnation, birth, passion or resurrection of Jesus are almost unknown in this early period.

The preference for art images based on Old Testament narratives has led scholars to theorize that Roman artists were particularly influenced by Jewish iconography, or had access to certain illustrated bibles of the Jews – bibles that provided the basic models of many of the compositions in the Christian catacomb paintings.[8] However, no such illuminated Bibles have been discovered, and the unique example of Jewish art from this early period, the wall frescoes from the synagogue at Dura-Europos, show quite different biblical scenes and, in the few examples of parallel scenes, have very different compositions. Furthermore, the Hebrew scripture-based images that appear in the catacombs are usually abbreviated rather than detailed, and not always what to modern eyes would be obvious choices. For instance, Moses striking the rock is far more common in Christian catacomb art than Moses and the burning bush or even Moses receiving the Law.

The predominance of Old Testament motifs may in part lie in the tradition of scriptural interpretation of the early church. Whether in homilies, catechetical lectures, or in liturgy (prayers and hymns, in particular), preachers and theologians constantly held up episodes or characters from the Old Testament as figures or 'types' referring to the life of Jesus Christ and the salvation offered by the church. The Hebrew Bible was, in fact, the basic scripture of the early Christian church, and understood to foretell the coming of Christ and his message of deliverance from sin and death. The paintings in the catacombs can be understood as interpreting the texts in the same way, although in visual rather than in written form. Thus, representations of Jonah point to the death and resurrection of Christ as well as to the death and rebirth of Christian baptism. Abraham offering Isaac was a way to both prefigure and suggest the sacrifice of the beloved Son on the cross. This form of visual exegesis also may account for the lack of certain narrative details in the scene, or (to our eyes) the preference for more obscure stories over the obvious. All that was needed was the visual cue as reminder – a symbol that carried far more meaning than its simplicity would suggest (Jensen 1993).

One particular image, that of John the Baptist baptizing a youthful (or even childlike) Jesus in the waters of the Jordan, is almost the exception to the otherwise general presentation of Jesus as wonder-worker or healer. Along with certain other figures or motifs that have no particular scriptural referents (e.g., a banquet scene, images of a fish and loaves, or grapevines ripe with fruit), these images may be understood as representing actual liturgical events of the early church, or perhaps symbolizing certain important events in the life and worship of the early Christian community. Baptism and participation in the Eucharistic meal not only were critical points in the communal life of early Christians; they were the liturgical signs that incorporated the deceased's hope of both the general resurrection and Messianic banquet at the end of time. Thus, early Christian painting must be understood not as literal illustration, but rather as a shorthand method to remind the viewer of the deeper or hidden meanings those stories or symbols held for both their religious life and self-identity.

During and after the Constantinian era, the range of subjects increased for all of Christian art, at the same time as the art began to appear in large public buildings instead of in more private, funereal contexts. New biblical stories appeared in paintings, including the crossing of the Red Sea and the finding of Moses by the Pharaoh's daughter. Meanwhile, certain previously popular figures began to disappear, including the Shepherd, Jonah, and Noah. In general, however, wall paintings were replaced, first by the monumental mosaics of the fifth and sixth centuries, as well as by manuscript illuminations, carved ivories, and images on liturgical implements of silver and gold, with the most characteristic motifs of the new era appearing on these monuments or on the carved sarcophagi of the fourth and fifth centuries.

RELIEF SCULPTURE ON SARCOPHAGI

Many of the same iconographic motifs that appeared in paintings from the early period also appeared on the relief carvings of stone sarcophagi created for Christian patrons. Most Roman sarcophagi (literally 'flesh-eaters' – a term applied by later historians) were lidded stone coffins designed to be placed against a wall. Usually box-shaped, but sometimes rounded like bathtubs, backs were left unfinished while the other three sides (front and the two ends), as well as the lids, were decorated with relief sculpture. Only the most wealthy classes could afford to bury their dead in this way, and because of their great expense sarcophagus reliefs often were of a different type or quality of craftsmanship from the wall paintings. Sarcophagi were carved with drills and chisels in white marble, but occasionally also in limestone. They were sometimes painted lightly to make them polychrome but the use of colour was normally restrained. In the earlier era, most sarcophagus images were portrayed on the same level or register, and by the end of the third century designs began to become more detailed, even crowded with smaller figures and multiple scenes. In the early fourth century, double-registered sarcophagi gave more structure or order to the multiple images. The quality ranges from high relief with beautifully polished details to flatter and less finely carved work, often in a lower grade of marble or softer limestone. Like the tomb frescoes, stone sarcophagi were produced by workshops of artisans who also served a pagan clientele and adapted common Roman motifs for their Christian customers, although it seems most likely that the designs were more or less customized for each client. These common motifs included shepherds milking or carrying animals over their shoulders, praying figures (*orans*), seated readers, and scenes of small children (putti) harvesting wheat or grapes. One or two extant sarcophagi from this period show that faces of the seated reader or praying figure may have been left unfinished in the expectation that portraits of the deceased could have been added to these particular figures. Later, such portraits would have been added to medallions (often of scallop shell design) in the centre of the front frieze.

The earliest Christian sarcophagi can be dated to the late third century. Among the best known and most beautiful is the so-called Jonah sarcophagus, now in the Museo Pio Cristiano in the Vatican and dated to approximately 270 CE (Figure 28. 4). The main image on this sarcophagus portrays Jonah being tossed overboard and into the mouth of the waiting sea creature, and then being spat up on dry land again. Jonah reclines nude on the dry ground in a posture similar to depictions of the sleeping Endymion of Greek legend (another familiar Roman art motif). The water in which Jonah's boat floats also supports Noah's ark and a number of fish and sea creatures being caught by anglers on a bank. The boat's mast breaks into the upper portion of the sarcophagus' frieze, which contains images of Jesus raising Lazarus and Moses striking the rock to give water to the Israelites in the wilderness.

Sarcophagi produced for Christian clients in the fourth century showed fewer of the pagan influences in their iconographic programmes and motifs became exclusively Christian in character. The Shepherd, praying figure, or seated reader disappeared and their places were taken by familiar biblical images. Most of the same biblical themes that had appeared in catacomb painting found their way onto

Figure 28.4   Jonah cycle from the late third-century 'Jonah sarcophagus' in the Museo Pio Cristiano, Vatican. Photo Graydon Snyder.

the often crowded fronts of sarcophagi, including the most popular of the Old Testament images – Adam and Eve, Moses (or Peter) striking the rock, Abraham about to slay his son, or Daniel with his lions. Comparatively more New Testament images appeared on the sarcophagi, but the standard portrayals of Jesus as healer and wonder-worker remained consistent. Alternating with images from the Hebrew scriptures are representations of Jesus healing (the paralytic, the man born blind, the woman with the issue of blood, etc.) and working wonders (e.g., changing water to wine at Cana, multiplying the loaves and fishes, and raising Lazarus: Figure 28.5).[9]

However, many new iconographic themes appeared on these expensive funerary monuments in the mid-fourth century. Among these new themes is Christ handing a scroll (the 'new law', the *traditio legis*) to his apostles (Figure 28.6). In these images Christ either sits on a throne-like chair (sometimes with his feet on the head of the God, Caelus), or stands on the rock of Golgotha out of which spring the four rivers of paradise symbolizing the beginning of the new creation. The gesture of passing a scroll is based upon the traditional gesture of the transfer of imperial authority or power from the Roman political scene. Christ here is delegating his authority to his apostles – his earthly magistrates – from his position in heaven.

To this dignified and hieratic scene come other new themes to the programmes of fourth-century sarcophagi. The magi are portrayed bringing their gifts to the Christ-child, and Christ is depicted entering Jerusalem riding on a donkey, for example. However, perhaps, the most striking additions are the presentations of

Figure 28.5 Double-registered mid-fourth-century sarcophagus from the Museo Pio Cristiano in the Vatican, with various Old and New Testament scenes. Photo Robin Jensen.

Figure 28.6   Late fourth-century sarcophagus showing the *traditio legis*, now in Arles. Photo
Robin Jensen.

scenes from Christ's passion, a theme that is particularly noteworthy at this time
because of its earlier absence from Christian art (and its later great popularity).

The actual crucifixion – Jesus hanging on the cross – is omitted from these
compositions (as it is generally before the fifth century), but other episodes in the
story are shown, including Christ's arrest, Simon of Cyrene carrying the cross, Jesus'
crowning with a wreath (laurel instead of thorns), and appearance before Pilate.
These separate scenes, sometimes combined with figures from the Old or New
Testaments (e.g., Adam and Eve, Abraham offering Isaac, Daniel, the raising of
Lazarus, or arrest of Peter) are often each separated into architectural niches, set off
by columns or gabled roofs. In the centre niche of two of these sarcophagi, now in
the Vatican Museo Pio Cristiano, stands an empty cross surmounted by a laurel
wreath enclosing the chi-rho monogram. Below, two sleeping soldiers appear, while
above their heads, perched on the arms of the cross, are two doves. The whole
composition suggests triumph and victory rather than suffering and sacrifice. In
fact, the empty cross with the wreath looks very much like the Constantinian
imperial insignia, or military standard, and the parallelism may have been
intentional.

The omission of the image of Christ's actual suffering on the cross and replacement by images of a hero standing nobly before the Roman governor, or with
symbols of victory, may arise from a desire to emphasize the triumph of resurrection
rather than the pathos of painful death. Since theological writings from the same
period are in no way reserved about the crucifixion itself, it cannot be that the
crucifixion was of minor importance. Rather it may have been that an artistic
presentation of Christ's passion on the cross itself was deemed too graphically disturbing or the subject too holy to be appropriate for viewing. The figure of Abraham
offering Isaac may have been substituted as a 'type' of the crucifixion and intended to
convey the meaning of the event (Jensen 1993: 85–100). When crucifixion portrayals began to appear in art, they may have been modelled upon an image found in
the Church of the Holy Sepulchre in Jerusalem (no longer extant). Some of the
earliest such images were imprinted on small pilgrimage tokens (ampullae of
pottery or lead) that pilgrims carried back to the West from the Holy Land.

The implications of this iconographic shift during the fourth century, shown so clearly on the sarcophagi of the period, are several. First the new presentations of Jesus as calm and heroic, resurrected and enthroned and giver of the new law, show a definite shift from an earlier artistic stress on Jesus as healer, teacher, or wonder-worker. Moreover, these new images are more dogmatic in nature and less consistently narrative-based. The emphasis of the imagery is on Jesus' divine person who is judge, heavenly lord, and redeemer, rather than on Jesus' earthly ministry.

Changing social or political circumstances may explain this shift away from the earlier scripturally oriented images towards those with more dogmatic emphases. Often the shift in Christianity's status and patronage has been cited to explain representations of Christ as an enthroned heavenly king, sometimes with his feet placed upon the mantle of the god of the heavens, Caelus. Such an image has long been assumed to have political associations – Christ as ruler of the cosmos is icono-graphically paralleled with the emperor as ruler of the world below. These motifs are identified as imperial, and supportive not only of the Christian faith but also of the emperor cult.[10] This would suppose that Christian visual art of this era was used to advance the programme of the Christian emperors, a programme aimed at unifying the empire both under one faith and under one ruler who was granted authority from the Christian god.

Recently this hypothesis has been re-examined and refined (Mathews 1993). Scholars have challenged the idea that fourth-century art in some sense 'sold out' to imperial interests and have pointed out the similarities of Christ in this iconography with the ruling pagan gods, Jupiter and Dionysus in particular. As Christianity went from being the personal faith of the ruling family to the official religion of the state, images of the pagan gods were replaced with images of Christ, sometimes shown in remarkably similar guise.[11] Thus many of the new dogmatic themes of fourth-century painting and sculpture may be attributed to the triumph and power of the Christian god and Christian teachings over the traditional (but dying) Roman pantheon.

A related, but somewhat different, explanation for the changing in iconographic motifs in the fourth century may be the shift from the private, funerary context of art to a public and monumental venue. Enormous sums of money were used to erect grand buildings and decorate them. They were intended to impress the masses of both locals and pilgrims who daily crowded into them. The art in these spaces was not commissioned to console the bereaved or to make a statement about particular beliefs of individual Christians, but to express the glory, as well as the faith, of the church triumphant. Many favourite scriptural themes and sacramental motifs remained, but through the fourth and fifth centuries new pictures appeared: representations of a majestic Christ, ruling and judging; the heroes of the church (apostles, martyrs, prophets, and patriarchs); the nativity with Mary and the magi; and scenes from Jesus' arrest, trial, and crucifixion. The apse mosaic of Hosios David in Thessalonica (*c.* 425) shows Christ as the enthroned One as described in Revelation 4, sitting on a rainbow, surrounded by the four living creatures (ox, lion, eagle and man). This theme of apocalyptic majesty is paralleled in the slightly earlier apse mosaic of Sta Pudenziana in Rome (*c.* 400), which adds the apostles and female personifications of the churches of the Jews and the gentiles offering them wreathes of victory (see Figure 28.7).

Figure 28.7   The apse in St Pudenziana, Rome. Photo Robin Jensen.

SCULPTURE IN THE ROUND

Few examples of early Christian sculpture in the round exist, which suggests that Christians were less inclined to this medium of art than either painting or relief carving. This form of art may have been most closely associated with pagan idolatry and the imperial cult and thus shunned as a form of decorative or funerary art by Christian clients. Nevertheless, a few significant examples of sculpture assumed to have Christian associations are dated between the third and seventh centuries; in particular a number of third- and fourth-century Good Shepherd statuettes.

A series of small sculptures whose provenance is unknown and therefore usually referred to as the 'Cleveland marbles' (because they are now housed in the Cleveland Museum of Art), includes figures of the Good Shepherd as well as four statues of Jonah (Jonah swallowed, cast up again, reclining under the vine, and praying in the *orans* position). Dated to the late third century on stylistic grounds, these pieces are thought to have come from a family tomb in Asia Minor (Kitzinger 1978).

Other rare examples of early Christian sculpture have been found to depict Christ seated, St Peter holding a cross, and a nearly life-sized figure of the theologian and bishop (or anti-bishop), Hippolytus. Although this material evidence might be enough to support the conclusion that Christians tolerated a certain amount of sculpture in the round, additional textual evidence also exists as back up. Eusebius of Caesarea referred to a bronze statue representing Jesus and the woman with the issue of blood that had been set up near the gates of her alleged home in Caesarea

Philippi as well as bronze images of Daniel and the Good Shepherd which decorated fountains in Constantinople (*Ecclesiastical History* 7:18; *Life of Constantine* 3:49). The *Liber Pontificalis* similarly describes statuary, in this case given by Constantine to adorn the baptistery of the Lateran Basilica: seven silver stags, a golden lamb, and nearly life-sized figures of Christ and John the Baptist (*Book of the Popes* 34:9 and 13 {Sylvester}). Although none of these figures have been found, these texts give testimony to the inclination to identify particular pilgrimage sites or to beautify church settings with statues – an inclination consistent with Roman tradition and decor.

MOSAICS AND IVORY CARVING

Even as the iconographic themes evolved and the settings of Christian art changed, many traditional motifs and popular themes were retained. Thus the end of catacomb painting in the fourth century did not put an end to narrative iconography in general, but only to certain themes that seem to have belonged to an earlier era. Christian art still continued to employ scripture-based imagery, even as both new and old biblical images appeared on the walls of church buildings, on small ivory diptychs or gospel covers, or in early illuminated manuscripts. For example, the early fifth-century mosaic panels along the nave of the basilica of Sta Maria Maggiore (*c.* 432–40), and those from a century later in the upper nave of S. Apollinare Nuovo in Ravenna (*c.* 493–525), continue to present certain familiar and now 'ancient' biblical motifs along with new and heretofore unknown ones. The basilica at Sta Maria Maggiore was adorned with an impressive cycle of Old Testament images in mosaic, especially with scenes from the books of Exodus and Joshua. Among the 27 (of an original 42) surviving images are scenes from Moses' life, including Moses with the Pharaoh's daughter, Moses' marriage to Zipporah, and the battle with the Amelekites. The basilica of S. Apollinare Nuovo, on the other hand, shows new images from the New Testament such as Christ separating the sheep from the goats or Jesus calling Peter and Andrew to be 'fishers of men'.

Ivory plaques, book covers, boxes designed to hold consecrated bread and reliquary caskets also contain small narrative images, many of which were common in catacomb or sarcophagus iconography. Although most Christian ivory carving is dated from the fifth century, the craft was well established in Rome from the second century and used for luxurious items of every kind from beds to combs. Small hinged ivory tablets known as diptychs were used in the Christian liturgy to hold lists of names of saints, bishops, or important church dignitaries. The ivory plaques of these diptychs, as well as other ivory objects, including gospel covers and even a bishop's chair, were decorated with carved images of Christ, the Virgin Mary, and the saints, and with episodes from the lives, or with narrative scenes from biblical stories (Figure 28.8).

Ivory carving was used for small pieces and had a kind of intimacy not intended for public view. By contrast, from the fourth to the sixth centuries, mosaic decoration of churches became one of the most important and beautiful modes of Christian artistic expression on a large scale. As with ivory carving, mosaic decoration did

Figure 28.8 Mid-fifth-century ivory diptych (the Andrew diptych) with miracles of Christ. Photo by Art Resource, New York, with the permission of the Victoria and Albert Museum, London.

not originate with Christian art. The use of decorative mosaics for both walls and floors was widespread in the ancient Mediterranean world and workshops of skilled artisans merely needed to adapt well-practised techniques to a new programme of images. A few wall and floor mosaics with Christian themes or from Christian contexts are known to date from the pre-Constantinian or very early Constantinian era, and have been discovered in church buildings as well as in funerary contexts.

One of the best known of the latter is the mosaic found in the so-called 'tomb of the Julii' (or mausoleum M), under St Peter's basilica in Rome, which has been roughly dated to the end of the third or beginning of the fourth century. The most famous image (and only truly extant mosaic) from this tomb was placed on the ceiling and presents Christ in the guise of the sun-god (Sol Invictus), complete with radiate halo and riding in a chariot drawn by four white horses. Such an image, clearly a conflation of a pagan image with the Christian saviour, certainly was intended to illustrate an aspect of Christ's divinity (the light of the world or the 'sun of righteousness' of Malachi 4) or to signal Christ's superseding the pagan gods.[12] All around him in this image are grapevines, which were a common decorative motif in Roman art and found their way into Christian iconography, perhaps to pictorially represent the text of John, 'I am the true vine' (John 15:1).[13]

Another example of early mosaic decoration exists in the double church in Aquileia, Italy. The newer church should be dated to the early fourth century and may barely pre-date Constantine. The older (north) church building may be dated some decades earlier, and either incorporated the mosaic pavements of an earlier structure, or was built and originally decorated to serve a Christian community. Both floors are covered with mosaic decoration, and while the mosaic motifs in the older building are ambiguous and show various images of birds and animals, the floor of the newer edifice is clearly Christian in its symbolism, judging by its several scenes from the Jonah story as well as a representation of the Good Shepherd (Menis 1965).

Mosaics were used to decorate both ceilings and floors of Christian churches in the fourth century, all across the Roman empire, from Britain to North Africa and from Spain to Syria. Archaeologists discovered an unusual Christ portrait on a floor mosaic in a late fourth-century Christian building in Dorset at Hinton St Mary and subsequently removed to the British Museum. The portrait, a bust in the centre of a medallion decorated with patterned bands, shows Christ as a beardless Roman youth, dressed in a toga. A chi-rho monogram is placed behind his head and on either side are pomegranates, the significance of which are somewhat mysterious. The placement of a portrait of Christ on the floor of a Christian building is both surprising and unique. In Roman Africa and Numidia (modern Libya, Tunisia, and Algeria), mosaics carpeted the floors of basilicas, covering the tombs of the 'special dead' (martyrs, clergy, or wealthy patrons).

Mosaics began decorating the vaulted ceilings and apses of Christian churches in the mid-fourth century, in conjunction with the Constantinian building programme. One of the earliest examples, the mosaics decorating the round mausoleum of Constantine's daughter, Constantina (now known as the church of Sta Constanza), clearly shows an adaptation of traditional Roman motifs – twining grapevines and harvesting cupids, bird, flowers, and portrait busts of Constantina and her husband. In contrast with these religiously neutral images, however, are the two apse mosaics in the ambulatory that show images of Christ with his apostles, Peter and Paul. These two mosaic portraits present two strikingly different presentations of Christ. In one, Jesus is represented as youthful and fair (beardless and with light hair and eyes), with a mild expression. In the other apse mosaic, an older, bearded and darker-skinned Christ is seated on the orb of the world as if on a throne and his expression is solemn and regal. These latter two mosaics may post-date the floral and harvesting motifs by twenty years or more, and show the transition from a generic Roman decor to a more specific Christian iconographic programme (Stern 1958). The different images may have been an intentional modelling after portraits of Dionysus (or Apollo) and Jupiter, expressing the triumph of the Christian god over those pagan deities by subsuming the characteristics of both.

Although the churches of Sta Maria Maggiore and S. Apollinare Nuovo continue to show biblical narrative images in their nave mosaic panels, the medium of mosaic was applied most effectively to the apse and dome mosaics that generally emphasized the theological or dogmatic images of Christ transfigured, resurrected, or giving the Law. Typical of these are the early fifth-century apse of Sta Pudenziana, which shows Christ ruling from the Heavenly Jerusalem (Figure 28.7), or SS Cosmas and Damian, which presents Christ standing in a darkened sky, wearing a golden tunic, surrounded by apostles and saints holding out their martyrs' crowns to their Lord.

The presentation of crowns is repeated in several places in Ravenna (the western capital of the Byzantine empire in the fifth and sixth centuries), in the church of S. Apollonare Nuovo, and in the famous mosaic-covered domes of the two baptisteries in that city – the baptistery of the Orthodox and the baptistery of the Arians. Apostles or martyrs marching in a row and carrying jewelled wreaths as an offering either to the child Jesus seated on his mother's lap or to the adult being baptized in the waters of the Jordan present a solemn, hieratic, and suggestively liturgical procession (Figure 28.9). These scenes seem to have connections to particular courtly rituals in which the lesser nobility pay homage to their newly crowned king. Some decades later, the designers of the mosaic decoration for Ravenna's jewel-like church of S. Vitale chose to present two actual courtly processions – one of the emperor Justinian and his courtiers with the bishop, and the other of the empress, Theodora, with her ladies in waiting. Instead of crowns of martyrdom, however, Justinian carries the loaf of Eucharistic bread in an offertory procession while his wife carries the chalice.

The focal point of the chancel (or presbyterium) in S. Vitale is the altar where the bishop would have presided over the Eucharistic sacrifice. Above the altar the viewer sees a dominating image of Christ enthroned on the orb of the world, and below and on the side walls of the apse are the offertory processions of Justinian and Theodora. Directly above the altar itself, on either side, is a different kind of liturgical commentary in mosaic – representations of ancient prototypes of the Eucharistic offering or sacrifice. On one side Melchizedek (drawing on the text in Hebrews 7) and Abel present their offerings, standing on either side of a cloth-draped table that must have looked strikingly similar to the draped altar below. Directly across the chancel and at the same level of vision are two scenes of Abraham combined into one composition, the first showing Abraham serving his three visitors (probably intended to represent the Trinity), and the second showing Abraham about to slay his son Isaac as sacrifice. The imagery and the liturgy here are in perfect harmony – the first non-verbally reflecting and interpreting the language, actions and symbols of the second.

Figure 28.9 Medallion from the mid fifth-century dome mosaic, Orthodox baptistery, Ravenna. Photo Robin Jensen.

MANUSCRIPT ILLUMINATION

In contrast to the monumental character of the mosaics installed in the great churches of the empire, manuscript illuminations were small images preserved and cherished in the codices of the scriptures or gospel books, which were kept on the *ambo* or altar, or in church treasuries when they weren't in use. Beginning in the second century, the parchment codex (a bound book with separate leaves) replaced the scroll as the primary form of the book, particularly for Christians (Jews continued to use scrolls), and very gradually these codices began to be illuminated with miniature paintings. Some of these manuscripts are illustrated with full-page images, while others combine text with illuminations. The paint used for this work was egg tempera, often accented by silver or gold inks, sometimes on purple-stained parchment, underscoring the great value of the book itself.

The oldest known Christian manuscript was discovered at the monastery of Quedlingburg. The *Quedlingburg Itala* (so named for its place of discovery and because it contained a portion of the Old Latin Bible), dates to the early fifth century and consists of five leaves from the books of Samuel and Kings. Historians have assumed this work was produced in a Roman scriptorium that also served pagan clients because of its compositional similarities to a contemporary illuminated manuscript of the *Aeneid* (the *Vergilius Vaticanus*). Such cooperation and adaptation demonstrate the continued adaptation of Christian themes by artisans who were the inheritors of an already established tradition and well-honed craft.

The direct proximity of text and image, however, encouraged the continuing development of narrative art, particularly in sequenced cycles that represent the details of the text fairly literally. The abbreviated, sketchy, and symbolic images of the earlier catacomb frescoes are supplanted here by intent to illustrate the story directly. The four illustrated leaves of the *Quedlinburg Itala* show four scenes on three of its pages and two on another, each representing a relatively small detail of a story in the accompanying columns of text. Calculating that some of these manuscripts had fifty or sixty pages, the volume of artistic work must have been substantial and quite impressive in its richness and detail (Levin 1985; Weitzmann 1977).

Surviving illuminated manuscripts from the sixth century include codices with fragments of the Pentateuch, particularly the book of Genesis (the *Cotton Genesis* and the *Vienna Genesis*) as well as portions of the gospels (the *Gospel of Augustine*, the *Rossano Gospels*, and the *Rabbula Codex*). These manuscripts originated in all parts of the empire, including Egypt and Syria, and Constantinople. The *Vienna Genesis*, perhaps the most beautiful and most complete of these early manuscripts (having 48 existing leaves), was executed in the early sixth century on purple parchment, suggesting that it was made for a member of the imperial family. One of the most impressive of the miniatures in this codex is the presentation of the flood, which differs in almost every possible way from the image of Noah in his ark found in catacomb painting or sarcophagus carving. Here the ark, shown as a boat with a double-decker cabin, barely floats in a dark blue swirling sea in which people and animals are struggling but drowning. Another remarkable miniature from the Vienna Genesis is that of Rebecca and Eliezer at the well, from Genesis 24 (see Figure 28.10).

The *Rossano Gospels* (named for the Italian city which still houses the book) is made up of excerpts from the gospels of Matthew and Mark. It illustrates a series of episodes in the life of Christ, including several healings, the raising of Lazarus and Christ's arrest and trial before Pilate. The image of Christ raising Lazarus is filled with narrative detail, even showing the onlookers holding their noses for fear of the stench coming from the tomb. The trial scene of Jesus before Pilate is shown in two parts – Christ first appearing before Pilate, and Pilate asking the people to choose between Barabbas and Jesus. The background of these scenes presents what was probably a typical sixth-century court interior, populated with officials, scribes and Roman guards.

The *Rabbula Codex* is extremely important in the history of Christian art, if for no other reason than that it contains one of the earliest extant images of the crucifixion. Originating in Mesopotamia, but probably based on iconographic models in Palestine, the cycle of images suggests a visit of pilgrims to the sacred shrines of the Holy Land, and certain topographical details – particularly in the representation of the crucifixion itself – not only lend a concrete literalism to the image but suggest that the creators of the prototype had a familiarity with that particular landscape. Like the mosaic processions and offerings in the churches of Ravenna, which represented or commented upon actual liturgical events, here art works draw upon what was known about actual spaces and geography to conflate image with reality and history with sacred narrative.

Christians also produced an entire range of smaller objects, both personal and

Figure 28.10   Rebecca and Eliezer at the well, from the Vienna Genesis. Photo by Giraudon/ Art Resource, New York, with the permission of Oesterreichische Nationalbibliothek, Vienna.

private in character or communal and liturgical. Jewellery (cameos and signet rings), furniture, domestic ware (silver spoons or caskets, pottery lamps, bowls, or glass bowls and cups), as well as liturgical implements, including reliquaries, incense burners, lamps, chalices, flagons, and patens, constitute a large corpus of important objects for historians of Christian art. Pilgrimage tokens and reliquaries made of pottery, lead, enamelled metal or wood were painted or stamped with images of events corresponding to particular sites in the Holy Land. Even coins, bearing Christian legends or details of reverse imagery are a record of the way faith was made visual in daily life. Whether part of a church's treasury or primarily designed for personal and private use, these goods often are hardly distinguishable from common, everyday items, and their function or Christian character may be identified only by their physical context or small design details. What might be an ordinary drinking cup may be used for a chalice, a serving plate for a paten.

Depending on their base material, some of these items have survived better than others. Metal and glass remains endure better than textiles or wooden objects. Most of the textiles were garments, altar cloths, or curtains and made of linen or wool which bore Christian symbols or occasionally more elaborate Christian imagery, including images of the Virgin and the saints. The best of these textiles come from Egypt, where the arid climate helped to preserve them.

CONCLUSION

Although Christian theologians at various times worried about the problem of idolatry and may have tried to enforce restrictions on Christian use of artistic imagery, in practical application Christians were making and using art, probably even from the first generations, although those images have not survived or been identified as definitively Christian. But, taking care not to fall into idolatry, Christians used visual images as identity with community, to enhance their worship, to inspire or educate, to aid devotion, or even to give honour to God and the saints. Not to be confused with those who actually worshipped cult statues or mistook them for living (and circumscribed) realities, Christians might respect, or even give homage to, a symbol or image without mistaking the mundane elements of wood, paint, or stone for the divine presence itself. Thus what might at first appear as a difference between 'official' theological stance and popular practice, may be more properly a careful definition of form and function.

Several characteristics of Christian art emerge and appear to be foundational. The first is its narrative source. Most early Christian art was related (either directly or indirectly) to sacred narrative – either the Old Testament or the Christian gospels. In the earliest days, these texts were, however, more illuminated than illustrated. The art works were shorthand references to familiar stories already interpreted and given secondary significance in the life of the community, its liturgy, its faith, and its present circumstances. Certain stories were more popular for representation, were particular favourites, and were represented in a kind of modified shorthand form in order to attract the viewer's attention. The rest existed in memory. Only later, when the illuminations were absolutely juxtaposed with text did the images become more faithfully narrative, but even these were interpretations of the key points and meanings contained in the accompanying texts.

The second key point about Christian art is its transmitting tradition, whether through instruction, or through the creation of sacred image and space and the formation of a kind of visual spirituality. Christian art was the work of the community, perhaps patronized by the wealthy, the aristocracy, or even the imperial family, but even so, open to all eyes and on display. To this end, Christian art had to be revolutionary with respect to its surrounding culture – to forge new identity and to draw community around a group of core images or symbols that were its own, even if drawn from earlier traditions or prototypes. As the community grew and changed, so did the art that reflected the church and its people. As the content of theology changed, so did the art advance the concerns of the church, reflected in liturgy and life. When the imagery didn't directly reflect the written sacred texts, it was likely associated with the liturgy or sacraments of the church.

The last characteristic of Christian art is that it functioned symbolically and socially. No matter how fundamentally textual in origins, art did more than merely illustrate or reinforce community, it encompassed and reflected the content and meaning of the faith, in ways beyond mere words. The art interpreted and reinforced the meaning and key symbols of the Christian faith and the hopes of those who were members of the community. Like any set of communal symbols, the images from art were most clear to the insiders, but they communicated as well to outsiders, identifying members and providing a visual summary of their core ideology. Whether simple and sketchy, or majestic and monumental, the art of the early church perhaps expressed the hopes and expectations of those who belonged to the community better than words alone could do. For them, the materials and contents of art needed no corresponding interpretation. Over time, those symbols evolved, primarily because the community changed, grew, or understood itself in new terms. Different aspects of the faith would come to the fore and find their expression in visual form. Each of these developments was keyed to changing theological emphases as well as shifts in the social, cultural, and political circumstances of the church, and each shift would be mirrored in other aspects of Christian life, such as liturgy, theological writings, and institutional structures.

NOTES

1 For example, see the standard argument in Chadwick (1967: 277–8), and by such prominent art historians as Kitzinger (1977: 3). For a very helpful summary of the modern scholarship Finney (1994: 7–12). See also Finney (1994: 99–145) for his critique of other arguments for early Christian aniconism, including a presumption that the earliest Christians were more 'spiritual' or 'otherwordly' than their pagan neighbours and later Christian art-users.

2 Murray (1977) summarizes the early patristic sources on this subject, as well as their use in the later iconoclastic controversy. Most of these ancient texts have appeared in collections, including that of Koch (1917).

3 Both Tertullian (*On Modesty* 7.1–4; 10.12) and Clement of Alexandria (*The Tutor* 3.11.59) give second-century testimonia to Christian use of etched Eucharistic cups and engraved signet rings.

4 The lack of material wealth as a reason for the lateness of Christian artwork was suggested by Finney (1994: 108).

5 These sarcophagi are well-presented and discussed by Benoit (1954).

6 Finney summarizes the ideological aspects of scholarly assertions that Rome was the source and centre for Christian artistic output (1994: 151 and 264, nn. 8, 9). For an example of how scholars take Roman dominance for granted see Snyder (1985: 3).

7 For a chart of these images and a short discussion of each, see Snyder (1985).

8 For discussion and elaboration of these arguments see Goodenough (1962), Weitzmann (1971) and Weitzmann and Kessler (1990).

9 Abraham offering Isaac, Moses striking the rock, Daniel and the lions, Jesus before Pilate, Jesus raising Lazarus, and Jesus healing the man born blind.

10 See Grabar (1968: 39–50), for a clear statement of what he calls the 'imperial invention'.

11 The strongest case (and probably the first significant argument) for this is in Mathews (1993). For a short summary of some of the arguments see Jensen (1997).

12 To see how this is paralleled in text see Clement of Alexandria, *The Instructor* 9, in which the author directly refers to Christ as 'the Sun of Righteousness, who drives his chariot over all,' thereby conflating the prophecy of Malachi with the figure of the sun god.

13 For a general survey see Volbach (1946).

BIBLIOGRAPHY

Beckwith, J. (1970) *Early Christian Art*. Harmondsworth: Penguin.

Brenk, B. (1977) *Spätantike und frühes Christentum*. Frankfurt: Propyläen.

Benoit, F. (1954) *Sarcophages paléochrétiens d'Arles et de Marseille*. Paris: Centre Nationale de la Recherche Scientifique.

Chadwick, Henry (1967) *The Early Church*. London: Penguin Books.

Deichmann, F. W., Bovini, G. and Brandenburg, H. (eds) (1967) *Repertorium der christliche-antiken Sarkophage*. Wiesbaden: Steiner.

Du Bourguet, P. (1971) *Early Christian Art*. New York: Reynal.

Finney P. C. (1990) 'Good Shepherd', *Encyclopedia of Early Christianity*. New York: Garland, 845–6.

—— (1994) *The Invisible God: The Earliest Christians on Art*. Oxford: Oxford University Press.

Goodenough, E. (1962) 'Catacomb Art', *Journal of Biblical Literature* 81: 113–42.

Gough, M. (1973) *The Origins of Christian Art*. London: Thames & Hudson.

Grabar, A. (1967) *The Beginnings of Christian Art 200–395*. London: Thames & Hudson.

—— (1968) *Christian Iconography: A Study of Its Origins*. Princeton, N.J.: Princeton University Press

Grigg, R. (1976) 'Aniconic Worship and Apologetic Tradition: A Note on Canon 36 of the Council of Elvira', *Church History* 45: 428–9.

Jensen, R. (1993) 'Isaac's Sacrifice in Jewish and Christian Tradition: Image and Text', *Biblical Interpretation* 2,1: 85–110.

—— (1997) 'The Femininity of Jesus in Early Christian Art', *Studia Patristica* 29: 269–82.

—— (2000) *Understanding Early Christian Art*. London and New York: Routledge.

Kitzinger, Ernst (1977) *Byzantine Art in the Making*. Cambridge, Mass.: Harvard University Press.

—— (1978) 'The Cleveland Marbles', *Congresso Internazionale di Archeologia Cristiana* I: 653–75.

Koch, G. (1996) *Early Christian Art and Architecture*. London: SCM Press.

Koch, Hugo (1917) *Die altchristliche Bilderfrage nach den literarischen Quellen*. Göttingen: Vandenhoeck & Ruprecht.

Levin, Ira (1985) *The Quedlingburg Itala: The Oldest Illustrated Biblical Manuscript*. Leiden: Brill.

Lowden, John (1997) *Early Christian and Byzantine Art*. London: Phaidon.

Mathews, T. F. (1993) *The Clash of Gods: A Reinterpretation of Early Christian Art*. Princeton, N.J.: Princeton University Press.

Menis, Gian Carlo (1965) *I mosaici cristiani di Aquileia*. Udine: del Bianco.

Milburn, R. L. (1988) *Early Christian Art and Architecture*. Berkeley: University of California Press.

Murray, Mary Charles (1977) 'Art and the Early church', *Journal of Theological Studies* n.s. 28,2: 304–45.

Shumacher, W. N. (1977) 'Hirt und Guter Hirt', *RQS Supplementheft* 34. Freiberg: Herder.

Snyder, Graydon (1985) *Ante Pacem: Archaeological Evidence of church Life before Constantine*. Macon, Ga.: Mercer University Press.

Stern, H. (1958) 'Les mosaïques de l'Église de Sainte Constance', *Dumbarton Oaks Papers* 12: 157–218.

Volbach, W. F. (1946) *Early Christian Mosaics*. New York: Oxford University Press.

Volbach, W. F. and Hirmer, M. (1962) *Early Christian Art*. New York: Abrams.

Weitzmann, Kurt (1971) 'The Illustration of the Septuagint', in H. Kessler (ed.) *Studies in Classical and Byzantine Manuscript Illumination*. Chicago: University of Chicago Press.

—— (1977) *Late Antique and Early Christian Book Illumination*. New York: George Braziller.

Weitzmann, Kurt and Kessler, H. (1990) *The Frescoes of the Dura Synagogue and Christian Art*. Washington, DC (Dumbarton Oaks Papers 28).

Wilpert, Giuseppe (1903) *Roma Sotterranea: Le Pitture delle Catacombe Romane*. 2 vols: Volume I (text) and II (plates). Rome: Desclèe Lefebure &Co.

CHAPTER TWENTY-NINE

MUSIC

———— .◆. ————

James W. McKinnon

INTRODUCTION

The earliest preserved monuments of Christian music date from the Middle Ages. There are a handful of ninth-century manuscripts from Carolingian centres such as Corbie and Compiègne that provide the texts (but not the music) of the Mass Proper chants for the entire liturgical year.[1] These are followed around CE 900 by books from locations such as St Gall, Laon and Chartres that have the same texts with a primitive type of musical notation.[2]

Figure 29.1 shows the beginning of the Mass chants for the second Sunday of Advent from St Gall 359, perhaps the earliest of all extant notated chant manuscripts. It is an example of a *cantatorium*; that is, a book reserved to the solo cantors – hence the introit *Populus sion*, a choral chant, is given only with its incipit, whereas the gradual *Ex sion*, a solo chant, is provided in its entirety.

Nothing of the sort exists from the early Christian period; we have, instead, only literary references to music. It is true that one third-century musical fragment has come down to us by a freak of preservation, the so-called 'Oxyrhynchus Hymn', the much-mutilated closing portion of a Trinitarian hymn from Egypt (Figure 29.2).

The Greek text is surmounted by letters that appear to be a kind of musical notation, purportedly decipherable with the aid of Greek theoretical treatises. Precious as this fragment is, it may have served to distort the historiography of early Christian music. We have no indications that the hymn is particularly representative of early Christian song, and by attracting so much attention to itself it may have retarded the task of exploring the vast repository of evidence about early Christian musical practice and attitudes that is available in the writings of the church Fathers.

If this fund of material is studied systematically (that is, by collecting virtually all of it and arranging it regionally and chronologically, rather than citing it selectively as has been the custom in music histories since the eighteenth century), four major themes or subject matter areas emerge.[3] Most obvious, perhaps, is the harsh denunciation of pagan musical display, typically focusing on musical instruments. Then there is musical imagery, again, generally involving instruments, especially those mentioned in the Psalms. A category of reference less frequently encountered, but not without considerable significance, is that which treats of the liberal art

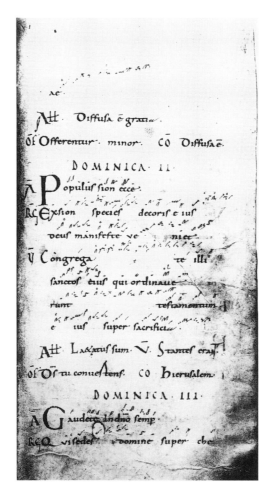

Figure 29.1   The beginning of the Mass chants from the second Sunday of Advent, from the ninth-century manuscript St Gall 359. Copyright Stiftsbibliothek St Gallen, Switzerland.

musica, a subject towards which the church Fathers display an attitude of acceptance seemingly at variance with their condemnation of everyday music in pagan society. Finally there are passages that speak of Christian music itself; that is, the singing of hymns and psalms at Christian gatherings, practices from which the great wealth of medieval ecclesiastical chant will develop. It is this last type of material, surely the most important from a historical point of view, that has proved to be particularly difficult for scholars to control.

THE PATRISTIC POLEMIC AGAINST PAGAN MUSIC

Even the most casual observer will not fail to be struck by the harshness of the patristic utterance against pagan musical practice. John Chrysostom (died 407) calls

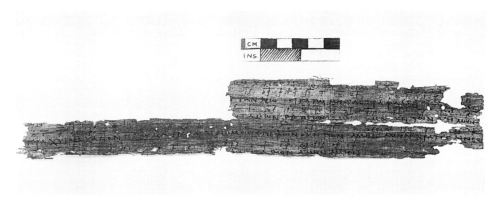

Figure 29.2   Oxyrhnychus Papyrus 1786, showing a fragmentary closing portion of a Trinitarian hymn from Egypt. Copyright the Committee of the Egypt Exploration Society.

cymbals and *auloi* (pipes or flutes) 'rubbish of the devil' (Chrysostom, *In 1 Corinthios*, Hom. 12.5; *MECL* 183), while Arnobius of Sicca (died *c.* 330) asks: 'Was it for this that he sent souls, that as members of a holy and dignified race they practise here the arts of music and piping . . . that in men they become male prostitutes, and in women harlots, sambucists[4] and harpists?' (Arnobius, *Adversus nationes* 2.42; *MECL*).

The kind of musical puritanism involved here is not without its precedents in antiquity. Plato, already, calls for a ban on the *aulos* and on 'many-stringed instruments' in his ideal state (*Republic* 399d), while Livy includes 'women harpists and sambucists' among the undesirable Eastern luxuries introduced into republican Rome by the Asiatic army of Scipio Africanus (39.6.7). Similarly the prophet Isaiah said of the new urban rich of ancient Judah: 'They have lyre and harp, tympanum and flute, and wine at their feasts; but they do not regard the deeds of the Lord' (Isa. 5:12), and centuries later rabbi Johanan commented on the passage: 'Whoever drinks to the accompaniment of the four musical instruments brings five punishments to the world' (*Sotah* 48a).

But the patristic reaction against musical abuse is far more intense than anything of the sort encountered in pagan or Jewish antiquity. It is intense and at the same time virtually universal; there is hardly a major early Christian author who did not take part in it. In seeking to explain this, scholars have pointed to the association of various ancient musical practices with pagan religion – for example – the presence of musical instruments at animal sacrifice (see Figure 29.3) or the music of the theatre with its cultic origins.[5]

Tertullian (died *c.* 225) demonstrates his awareness of the latter when he says of the theatre: 'Whatever transpires in voice, melody, instruments and writing is in the domain of Apollo, the Muses, Minerva and Mercury. O Christians, you will detest those things whose authors you cannot but detest' (Tertullian, *De spectaculis* 10.8–9; *MECL* 76). But surely just as powerful as such theological motivation is that of moralism. This is clear from the words of Arnobius, quoted above, and from numerous other passages. To quote just one, Pseudo-Basil has this to say of a young prostitute:

Figure 29.3   Sarcophagus relief from Mantua of a Roman general sacrificing a bull, accompanied by music. Copyright Archivi Alinari Florence.

> You place a lyre ornamented with gold and ivory upon a high pedestal . . . and some miserable woman, rather than being taught to place her hands upon the spindle, is taught by you . . . to stretch them out upon the lyre . . . So she stands at the lyre and lays her hands upon the strings, her arms bare and her expression impudent . . . All in the house are silent, charmed by the lascivious song.
>
> (Pseudo-Basil, *Commentary on Isaiah* 5.158; *MECL* 143)

The attitude of the church Fathers is better understood when the various contexts of their condemnations are considered.[6] Chiefly three social institutions are involved: the wedding, the theatre and the banquet; the three, apparently, were frequently the occasion of musical ribaldry in antiquity. John Chrysostom's reference to musical instruments as the 'rubbish of the devil' came in the course of a diatribe against pagan nuptial celebrations, while the quotation from Tertullian involved the theatre. Isidore of Pelusium (died *c.* 435) speaks of the banquet when he tells us that 'a carousal . . . is the intoxicating *aulos*, together with prolonged drinking, which arouses one to sensuality, and makes of the symposium a shameful theatre, as it bewitches the guest with cymbals and other instruments of deception' (*Epistle* 1.456; *MECL* 122).

Some historians have misread this polemic against musical immorality, with its typical singling out of instruments, as evidence for the employment of musical instruments in Christian church services. Why constantly rail against instruments, they asked, if their intrusion into liturgical chant was not a frequently encountered abuse? The answer, obviously enough, is that the patristic denunciation of instruments involves the sort of circumstances just cited, such as the theatre, banquets, etc., but not church services. We have no patristic passage that can in any way be construed as a condemnation of instruments in church. The issue is an anachronistic reading of nineteenth-century attitudes (when 'worldly' instruments were in fact pitted against the purity of *a cappella* church music) into entirely different early Christian circumstances. It is true that Christian ecclesiastical music has been, throughout much of its earlier history, an exclusively vocal art, but this was a matter of historical circumstances not the result of ecclesiastical edict; it is only in comparatively recent times that we see religious authorities striving to keep liturgical song free from the intrusion of worldly instruments. In the later fourth century, as liturgical services took on the basic shape that they would maintain for centuries, and the singing of psalms was established in set places in these services, the question of instrumental accompaniment simply did not arise. The declamation of psalms was in its origin a form of biblical reading. As it took on a more consciously musical form in the later fourth century (a development treated on p. 778), its essential nature as scriptural cantilation was not forgotten, and we have not a hint from the voluminous fourth-and fifth-century Christian literature that there was any felt need to bring musical instruments into the process.

At the same time we cannot say that musical instruments were absolutely never used in early Christian song. One can well imagine, for instance, particularly in the earlier centuries when evening meals figured more prominently in Christian religious gatherings, that the discreet accompaniment of a lyre might have been fairly common in the hymnody that was heard in the homes of well-to-do Christians.

A final question about instruments: why is it that they are evoked so consistently in the patristic denunciation of pagan music? Lascivious texts, for example, are occasionally mentioned in connection with wedding music, but musical instruments are by far the more consistent target of criticism, whether in the context of weddings, banquet or theatre. The answer lies, I think, in the very special physical properties of musical instruments, both aural and visual. They have a unique capacity, as much by their striking appearance as by their highly individual sonic qualities, to attract attention to themselves. They tend to stand out, then, as the concrete sign of music in all its dimensions. Take, for example, the visual arts, where it is all but impossible to portray music except by the depiction of instruments.

MUSICAL IMAGERY

It comes as no surprise, then, that instruments have a pre-eminent role in early Christian musical imagery. Paul of Tarsus already tells us that the eloquent person without charity has 'become sounding brass or a clanging cymbal' (1 Cor. 13:1), and more positively Ignatius of Antioch (died *c.* 107), in writing to the Christians of Ephesus, compliments them on their collegiality: 'For your most renowned presbytery, worthy of God, is attuned to the bishop as strings to a cithara' (*Ephesians* 4.1–2; *MECL* 21).

The principal source of early Christian musical imagery is the rich fund of instrumental allusion in the Book of Psalms, as treated by the allegorical manner of exegesis employed in the typical patristic psalm commentary.[7] The practice of psalmic instrumental allegorization has its origins with the third-century Alexandrians Clement (died *c.* 215) and Origen (died *c.* 265), and becomes all but universally employed by patristic commentators of the fourth century. Clement cites the instruments of Psalm 150 in order, applying to each of them an appropriate allegorical interpretation:

> The Spirit . . . sings: 'Praise him with the sound of the trumpet', and indeed he will raise the dead with the sound of the trumpet. 'Praise him on the cithara', let the cithara be taken to mean the mouth, played by the Spirit as if by a plectrum. 'Praise him with tympanum and chorus' refers to the Church meditating on the resurrection of the flesh in the resounding membrane . . . 'Praise him on the clangorous cymbals' speaks of the tongue as the cymbal of the mouth which sounds as the lips are moved.
>
> (Clement of Alexandria, *Paedagogus* 2.4; *MECL* 52)

As the practice of allegorical exegesis becomes customary in the later fourth-century psalm commentaries, the figures employed for the individual instruments become standardized; indeed, trite and repetitious. Some of them have a measure of poetic aptness such as the 'evangelical trumpet'; that is, the trumpet as a symbol for proclaiming the good news of the gospel. But others seem contrived – for example, the tympanum (a small hand drum) as a sign of mortified desire. We might have expected some imaginative evocation of a percussion instrument's elemental thumping, but instead the figure has to do with the stretching of an animal's skin on the circular frame of the drum, and hence the death of the flesh.

The allegorical mode of Psalter exegesis, with its consistent employment of instrumental imagery, has created a measure of confusion among certain historians. These individuals, insufficiently mindful that the authors of the psalm commentaries are engaged in the exegesis of an Old Testament book rather than discoursing on contemporary musical life, allow themselves to see in the equanimity of the patristic instrumental reference an implicit approval of instruments and a contradiction of the polemic described above. A corrective to this confusion is provided by the fourth-and fifth-century exegetes of the Antioch school, figures such as John Chrysostom and Theodoret of Cyrus (died *c.* 466). These authors eschew the typical Alexandrian allegorical method in favour of a more literal or historical approach. Hence in speaking of the instruments of the Psalter, they seek to explain them in their historical context. Thus Theodoret has the following to say about the instruments of Psalm 150, in a passage not altogether lacking in the anti-Semitism for which the Antiochenes have been frequently reproached:

> 'Praise him on psaltery and cithara. Praise him with tympanum and dance. Praise him on strings and instrument. Praise him on well-sounding cymbals, praise him on loud-clashing cymbals' (Ps. 150:4–5). The Levites employed

these instruments long ago as they hymned God in his holy Temple, not because God enjoyed their sound but because he accepted the intention of those involved. That the Deity does not take pleasure in singing and playing we hear him saying to the Jews: 'Take away from me the sound of your songs; to the voice of your instruments I will not listen' (Amos 5:23). He allowed these things to happen because he wished to free them from the error of idols. For since they were fond of play and laughter, and all these things took place in the temples of the idols, he permitted them and thereby enticed them, thus avoiding the greater evil by allowing the lesser.

Interpretatio in Psalmos 150; *MECL* 229)

But it is the allegorical approach which is dominant in early Christian literature and which remains a staple of medieval psalm commentaries. There is a fascinating parallel to patristic musical imagery encountered in the manuscript illumination of the Middle Ages, even if it is more characteristic of psalters themselves than of psalm commentaries. Artists, for reasons already suggested, love to draw and paint musical instruments. They take full advantage, then, of the instruments mentioned in the Psalms as well as those mentioned in a frequently encountered psalter preface that is attributed to Venerable Bede, but is clearly derived from the introduction to the psalm commentary of Eusebius of Caesarea (died *c.* 340).[8] In the later Middle Ages these psalmic instrumental depictions spread by a kind of contagion from the psalters themselves to all manner of illuminated manuscripts, where they decorate the margins in riotous profusion. There they form a visual analogue to the musical imagery of the early Christian psalm commentary.

THE LIBERAL ART OF MUSIC

Musica is one of the seven liberal arts; it finds place amid the four mathematical arts of the quadrivium (*arithmetica, geometrica, musica* and *astronomia*), which follow the three propaedeutical language arts of the trivium (*grammatica, rhetorica* and *dialectica*). It took about a millennium, from the time of Plato to that of Martianus Cappella (fifth century), for the system to become fixed in the form just described, but *musica* was an established subject virtually from the beginning. It had little to do with the modern notion of what constitutes music, and it would be a mistake even to identify it with the contemporary subject of music theory. Our music theory strives honestly, if not always successfully, to explain the workings of actual music, but the *musica* of antiquity focused upon itself; it had nothing to do with the everyday music of its time and concentrated instead on the construction of abstract tonal systems (scales), which utilized the full repertory of ancient mathematical learning. It was at the same time a subject of some grandeur, because these tonal systems were thought not only to reside on the pages of treatises but to echo throughout the cosmos. The 'music of the spheres' was just that – the seven planets, each revolving at a precisely determined rate so as to create its own pitch, with the seven together created an all encompassing scale, a phenomenon that had achieved its classic exposition already in the *Timaeus* of Plato. It is no accident that the greatest of the ancient music theorists was the renowned astronomer Ptolemy, who, for all we know, could have been tone deaf.

Music, as an abstract science, posed none of the problems for early Christians that the pagan music of everyday existence did. To the extent, then, that Christians accepted the educational system of antiquity as a whole, they would accept *musica* as a matter of course. Origen, for example, cites 'music' as one of the subjects propaedeutic to Greek philosophy, which, in turn, can be propaedeutic to Christianity:

> I would wish that you take from Greek philosophy that which has the capacity, as it were, to become encyclical and propaedeutic studies for Christianity, and whatever of geometry and astronomy might be useful in the interpretation of the Holy Scriptures, so that just as the children of the philosophers speak of geometry and music, grammar, rhetoric and astronomy as being ancillary to philosophy, we too may say this of philosophy itself in relation to Christianity.
>
> (*Letter to Gregory* 1; MECL 63)

Origen mentions here that Greek learning can be useful in the interpretation of Scripture, and this is the more particular role that early Christian savants assign to *musica* and the other sciences. Still more particularly, a Christian scholar might look upon his allegorical exposition of the instruments of the Psalter as an application of the discipline *musica*. Augustine demonstrates this in his *De doctrina christiana*:

> Indeed, an ignorance of certain musical questions shuts off and conceals much. For on the basis of a distinction between psaltery and cithara a certain writer has aptly explained some figures of things, and among the learned it is fittingly queried whether the psaltery of ten strings obeys some law of music which required that number of strings, or whether . . . that number should be considered to result from . . . the Ten Commandments.
>
> (*De doctrina christiana* 2.16.26; MECL 381)

Augustine closed his disquisition on the application of *musica* to scriptural exegesis with a clear distinction between this use of music and the 'theatrical frivolities' of actual instruments:

> We must nevertheless not shun music because of the superstition of the heathen, if we are able to snatch from it anything useful for the understanding of the Holy Scriptures. Nor should we be involved with their theatrical frivolities, if we consider some point concerning citharas and other instruments which might be of aid in comprehending spiritual things.
>
> (*De doctrina christiana* 2.18.28; MECL 383)

Augustine, it should be noted, contemplated at one time the authorship of a series of works on the seven liberal arts. It was never completed, and not all that he did manage to write has come down to us. Surviving are the six books of *De musica*, a treatise on the rhythmic and metric aspects of music, while a planned treatise on the tonal material of music, the subject favoured by Ptolemy and most other ancient theorists, was never begun. The sixth book of Augustine's *De musica* was written just after his conversion, and in it he soars to unprecedented heights to create a Christianized, albeit neo-Platonic, philosophy of rhythm, which has influenced aesthetic thinking down to modern times.

Augustine's *De musica* aside, the early Christian adaptation of classical music theory may strike us as trivial and perfunctory, but it had enormous unintended consequences for the history of western music. Christian authors of succeeding centuries, figures such as Boethius, Cassiodorus, and Isidore of Seville, maintained the early Christian stance towards the liberal art of music and compiled their own digests of classical music theory. These works maintained the classical abstract manner of extreme isolation from contemporary musical reality, although this was to change in the Middle Ages. Carolingian scholars took the basic concepts and terminology of these transitional authors, especially Boethius, and made direct application of them to the Gregorian chant of their own time (we noted on p. 773 the ninth-century 'invention' of music notation). The result was a powerful theoretical thrust in western music, a horizontal rationalization, so to speak, creating rhythmic systems, and a vertical rationalization creating harmonic systems. This sent western music on its course of constructing monumental architectonic forms, distinguishing it from the music of other high cultures, which maintained more fluid, improvisational approaches to musical creation.

EARLY CHRISTIAN HYMNODY AND PSALMODY

If the early Christian acceptance of classical music theory eventually influenced the direction taken by European art music, then early Christian ecclesiastical song itself played an even more central role in that development. The hymnody and psalmody of the ancient church developed into the Gregorian chant of the early Middle Ages which, in turn, developed into the great polyphonic art of the High Middle Ages and Renaissance.

Christian song in the earliest centuries

Christianity was warmly receptive to religious song from the beginning. There are several New Testament references to the singing of hymns and psalms, the most significant of which, perhaps, has Jesus and his disciples singing a 'hymn' at the close of the Last Supper (Matt. 26:30 and Mark 14:26). If the Last Supper took place on the evening of the Passover, as the synoptic gospels indicate, then this hymn was the Hallel (Pss. 113–18),[9] which was traditionally sung by Jewish families on this occasion.[10] That the singing, moreover, took place at an evening meal has a significance of its own. The majority of references to Christian song from the first three centuries are to singing at common meals, whether the meal be part of an *agape* service (love feast), or some less formal occasion. The latter seems to be the case in the following affecting passage from Cyprian, bishop of Carthage (martyred in 258), where he asks a musical friend to sing a 'psalm' (the term is used interchangeably with 'hymn' in the first Christian centuries) at his table:

And since this is a restful holiday and a time of leisure, now as the sun is sinking towardss evening, let us spend what remains of the day in gladness and not allow the hour of repast to go untouched by heavenly grace. Let a psalm be heard at the sober banquet, and since your memory is sure and your voice pleasant, undertake this task as is your custom. You will better nurture your friends, if you provide a spiritual recital for us and beguile our ears with sweet religious strains.

(Cyprian, *Ad Donatum* 16; MECL 94)

The conventional wisdom has it that in these earliest centuries newly composed hymns were more commonly sung than psalms from the Psalter. Indeed one school of thought sees the New Testament text shot through with fragments of early Christian hymns. This view has met with considerable scepticism in the most recent years,[11] and many of the passages in question are now taken to be simply instances of rhetorical prose rather than hymn texts, but the more basic notion that hymns predominate over psalms in very early Christian song remains in favour.[12] A corollary to this view is that the singing of biblical psalms became common only in the fourth century, and that at the same time, as the concept of a scriptural canon was more firmly established, the singing of individually composed hymns (*psalmi diotici*) came to be frowned upon. There is no doubt a good deal of truth in all this, but one must take care not to oversimplify. I find it hard to imagine that favourite biblical psalms, or portions thereof, were not sung with some frequency in early Christian gatherings from the beginning. It may be true, as advocates of the position in question maintain, that the Old Testament Psalter was at first looked upon primarily as a book of readings rather than a hymnary. But the lyric character of the Psalms is undeniable; many of them were singled out for musical performance in the Temple of Jerusalem, and it seems inevitable that something of the sort must have taken place in primitive Christianity as well.

The venue, however, where psalmody appears *not* to have been a regular practice in the earliest centuries is the Eucharist, that is, the Eucharist once it had been divorced from the evening meal and moved to a morning celebration.[13] Justin Martyr (died *c.* 165) provides us with our most detailed description of this service, and he makes no mention of psalmody during the pre-Eucharistic service of readings and instruction (hereafter 'synaxis'), the place where we might expect it to be included:

And on the day named for the sun there is an assembly in one place for all who live in the towns and in the country; and the memoirs of the Apostles and the writings of the Prophets are read as long as time permits. Then, when the reader has finished, he who presides speaks, giving admonishment and exhortation to imitate those noble deeds. Then we all stand together and offer prayers.

(*1 Apology* 1.67; MECL 25)

Justin mentions three distinct elements – reading, exhortation (homily), and prayer – whereas it was maintained until recently by historians of liturgy and music alike that there were four essential elements: reading, psalmody, exhortation and prayer. Essential to this view is the proposition that the pre-Eucharistic synaxis was taken over *en bloc* from the synagogue service, which itself consisted in the four essential elements of reading, psalmody, exhortation, and prayer. During the past decade or so, however, scholars (liturgical and musical, Christian and Jewish) have substantially revised the earlier view of ancient synagogue liturgy.[14] Certainly the reading and exposition of scripture were common practices in the synagogues of Jesus' time, and no doubt prayer of some sort was also involved. But it is unlikely that anything like a formal liturgical order was established until some time after the destruction of the Temple by the Romans in 70 CE. As for psalmody, the evidence is overwhelming that it did not become a regular part of the synagogue service until centuries after the Temple's destruction; indeed, the close connection of Temple psalmody with the act of sacrifice, and the stated intention to restore the Temple some day, functioned as an inhibiting factor in the development of synagogue psalmody.

To say that the early Christian pre-Eucharistic synaxis is not a direct borrowing of an ancient synagogue liturgy is not to deny the obvious debt of early Christian liturgy to Judaism in general and to the synagogue in particular. The concept of a weekly day of rest and celebration is part of that debt, along with the provision of an annual cycle of feasts. Even more essential perhaps is the part played in the new religion by a collection of sacred books, read and commented upon at meetings – at meetings, moreover, which are held in the confines of a home or communal hall

Figure 29.4   Relief from the Arch of Titus in Rome, showing musical instruments from the Jerusalem Temple at his triumph in 71 CE. Copyright Archivi Alinari Florence.

rather than an open square before a temple. It is only the notion of a fixed liturgical placement for psalmody in the pre-Eucharistic synaxis, borrowed from an identical synagogue service that must be rejected.

In fact, the early Christian evidence viewed only with reference to itself speaks against the existence of pre-Eucharistic psalmody in the second and third centuries. We know that such psalmody was an essential feature of the service in the later fourth century; how, then, did this come about? The answer to this question must await a description of broader musical and liturgical developments of the fourth century.

Desert monasticism and the fourth-century psalmodic movement

There was a virtual explosion of psalm singing in the later decades of the fourth century, and the chief impetus for this came from an unlikely source – desert monasticism.[15] Led by figures such as the hermit Anthony (died 356) in the north and the coenobite Pachomius (died 346) in the south, thousands of stalwart souls flooded the deserts of Egypt seeking to recover the purity of apostolic Christianity. They sought to put into practice, literally, Paul's admonition 'to pray without ceasing' (1 Thess. 5:17), and the means they employed towards this end was the recitation of the Psalter. This was not a matter of selecting particular psalms for appropriate occasions, but the declamation of the Psalms in continuous order for extended periods of time. Indeed some monks would recite the entire Psalter in a single night.

We must not imagine here anything like the psalmody of, say, eleventh-century Cluny; rather than a splendid choral sacrifice of praise this was the murmured chanting of unschooled individuals, utilizing the Psalms as an aid to meditation. Yet it no doubt had a beauty of its own, inspiring Palladius (died *c.* 431), for example, to describe what he heard when visiting the great monastery of Nitria:

> They all make linen with their hands so that they are all without need. Indeed one who stands there at about the ninth hour can hear the psalmody issuing forth from each cell, so that he imagines himself to be high above in paradise.
> (Palladius, *Lausiac History* 7; *MECL* 117)

Palladius was not the only prominent ecclesiastical figure to visit the Egyptian monasteries. Basil, Jerome, Cassian, Rufinus, Paula, and many others made the same pilgrimage, some staying for extended periods of time. Monastic spirituality became the ideal form of Christianity in the later fourth century, and virtually no important ecclesiastical figure failed to spend several years of spiritual apprenticeship as a monk. Ambrose of Milan is perhaps the one significant exception to this, and he, too, fostered monasticism in his diocese. The monastic movement, in any event, spread from the deserts to the cities, and there greatly influenced the Christian way of life.

And the hallmark of monasticism remained psalmody. The two seemed always to be mentioned in the same breath, whether it be Basil the Great (died 379) recommending his monastic retreat to Gregory of Nazianzus: 'What is more blessed than to imitate the chorus of angels here on earth; to arise for prayer at the very break of day and honour the Creator with hymns and songs' (*Epistle* 2.2; *MECL* 138); or the Pseudo-Chrysostom in that oft-quoted paean to Davidic psalmody:

> In the monasteries there is a holy chorus of angelic hosts, and David is first, middle, and last. In the convents there are bands of virgins who imitate Mary, and David is first, middle, and last. In the deserts men crucified to this world hold converse with God, and David is first, middle, and last. And at night all men are dominated by physical sleep and drawn into the depths, and David alone stands by, arousing all the servants of God to angelic vigils, turning earth into heaven and making angels of men.
>
> (De poenitentia, PG 64.12–13; MECL 195)

Monastic psalmody had two demonstrable influences on Christian life in the second half of the fourth century: it virtually inundated the newly developing Office with continuous psalmody, and it inspired the creation of the popular psalmodic vigil. As for the first of these developments, two daily public offices had developed in the course of the fourth century after the emancipation of Christianity with the Edict of Milan in 313. The two services, one in the morning and another in the evening, constituted the so-called 'cathedral office'. They made carefully selective use of psalms: in the morning, for example, Psalm 62:1 (LXX), 'Oh God my God, I rise before thee at the break of day' was sung, and in the evening Psalm 140 (LXX) with its verse two, 'Let my prayer be directed to thee as incense, and the lifting up of my hands as an evening sacrifice.' These psalms formed part of elegantly designed sequences of song and prayer, presided over by the bishop, which varied somewhat from city to city, but which maintained none the less a recognizably homogeneous shape and a common core of material (Taft 1986: 36–56).

In the second half of the century the urban monastic office radically transformed the cathedral office; it did so mostly by addition, leaving the cathedral nucleus more or less intact. The morning cathedral service, the predecessor of early medieval lauds, was preceded by a lengthy vigil of monastic psalmody, the forerunner of matins. During the day three shorter services of monastic psalmody were added, at the third, sixth and ninth hours. Finally, the evening cathedral service, our vespers, was preceded by a prelude of monastic psalmody. The monastic components of the hybrid office were clearly distinct from the cathedral components; they consisted essentially of continuous psalmody, and they were in fact performed by monks and nuns, in the absence, moreover, of the local bishop, who presided only over the original cathedral portions of the Office. Robert Taft (1986: 75–91) has made an impressive effort to reconstruct the offices of the various ecclesiastical centres, making good use of the not always adequate sources; for Jerusalem, however, one can read a complete and detailed description of the late fourth-century office in the diary of the pilgrim nun Egeria.[16]

It is Egeria, too, that provides the most telling evidence for the monastic influence on the people's pre-Eucharistic vigil. She describes the early morning vigil that monks and nuns (*monazontes* and *parthenae* in the Jerusalem idiom) perform on six days of the week in the great Constantinian basilica of the Anastasis; it consists of continuous psalmody with interspersed prayers, the prayers being said by local clergy, thus providing a sort of ecclesiastical sanction for the monastic service. Lay people are in attendance at these weekday gatherings, and then on Sunday morning the monks and nuns are absent, and the laity, assisted by the local clergy, participate in a vigil that is more or less identical to that held during the week by the monks and nuns. Such vigils became common throughout the East and eventually the West in the closing decades of the fourth century. It is such a practice that Augustine refers to when he says of Milan in the year 386: 'At that time the custom began that hymns and psalms be sung after the manner of the Eastern regions lest the people be worn out with the tedium of sorrow. The practice has been retained from that time until today and imitated . . . by almost all your congregations throughout the rest of the world' (*Confessions* 9.6.14–7.15; *MECL* 351).

Related, no doubt, to the phenomenon of the popular psalmic vigil are the extended encomiums of psalmody penned by several outstanding ecclesiastical figures including Athanasius, Basil, John Chrysostom, Ambrose and Niceta of Remesiana. These passages suggest that psalmody had become central to the Christian piety of the time. Ambrose, for example, tells us:

> Old men ignore the stiffness of age to sing a psalm . . . young men sing one without the bane of lust . . . young women sing psalms with no loss of wifely decency . . . and the child who refuses to learn other things takes pleasure in contemplating it . . . A psalm is sung by emperors and rejoiced in by the people . . . a psalm is sung at home and repeated outdoors; it is learned without effort and retained with delight.
>
> (*Explanatio psalmi* 1.9; *MECL* 276)

The 'delight' that Ambrose refers to here speaks to the aesthetic dimension of what has taken place in the later fourth-century upwelling of enthusiasm for singing the Psalms. One has the distinct impression that the urban psalmody of the period is generally a much more musical affair than the psalmody of desert monasticism, which had had so much to do with the origins of the fourth-century psalmodic movement. There are numerous references from the time to the way that the pleasurable melody of psalmody aids human nature in its spiritual quest. Niceta of Remesiana (died after 414), for example, argues:

> Through David the Lord prepares for men this potion which is sweet by reason of its melody and effective in the cure of disease by reason of its strength. For a psalm is sweet to the ear when sung, it penetrates the soul when it gives pleasure, it is easily remembered when sung often, and what the harshness of the Law cannot force from the minds of man it excludes by the suavity of song.
>
> (*De utilitate hymnorum* 5; *MECL* 306)

Niceta expresses the majority view of the time. There are some, it is true, who are less hospitable to the idea of musical delight; Jerome, for example, on more than one occasion argued that the Christian should sing psalms in such a way 'that not the voice of the singer but the words that are read give pleasure' (*Commentary on Ephesians* 3.5.19; *MECL* 333). Augustine, with characteristic psychological perception, gives us the most nuanced view of this conflict when he tells of his scruples over experiencing pleasure in hearing the psalmody of the church of Milan. He speaks first of his pleasure: 'How much I wept at your hymns and canticles, deeply moved by the voices of your sweetly singing church', then expresses his guilt over his reaction: 'I sin thus in these things'. But ultimately he accepts melodious psalmody: 'I err by excessive severity . . . When I recall the tears which I shed at the song of the Church in the first days of my recovered faith . . . I acknowledge again the great benefit of this practice' (*Confessions* 10.33.49–50; *MECL* 352).

The psalmody of the later fourth-century Eucharist

The question of how psalmody came to be a regular feature of the morning Eucharist was left open above. Certainly the phenomenon of the later fourth-century psalmodic movement provides at least part of the answer: the near universal enthusiasm for the singing of psalms must have furnished the context for the establishment of Eucharistic psalmody as a formal liturgical event. Psalmody, in any case, came to be employed regularly at two places in the later fourth-century Eucharist: in connection with the readings of the pre-Eucharistic synaxis and during the distribution of communion.

The second of these is less complex from a historiographic point of view. There are several references from the time to the singing during communion of Psalm 33 with its highly appropriate verse eight, 'Taste and see that the Lord is good.' The communion psalm would generally be sung in the responsorial manner; that is, a solo lector or cantor would declaim each verse, and at certain intervals, perhaps after every verse, the congregation would respond by singing the refrain verse, 'Taste and see'. Most of the evidence for singing this particular psalm comes from the East, while the more scanty western evidence suggests a less selective approach to communion psalmody. This state of affairs is corroborated by the situation in the Middle Ages, when the most common Byzantine communion chant is the original *Geusasthe kai idete* ('Taste and see'), whereas the Roman *Gustate et videte* is simply one in a series of undifferentiated post-Pentecost communions.

The psalmody of the later fourth-century pre-Eucharistic service is attested to in numerous patristic passages, well over a hundred of them in the works of Augustine alone.[17] Generally the reference appears in a sermon (or homily) preached by a church Father at Saturday or Sunday morning Eucharist, in which he makes reference to the psalm that had been sung earlier in the service. The fourth-century pre-Eucharistic service was simpler than it would come to be in the Middle Ages. It began with a brief greeting by the celebrant such as 'Peace be to you', and moved immediately to the readings, which were followed by homily and prayers, and then the dismissal of the catechumens. The psalmody was part of the readings; the psalm, in fact, was one of the readings, as is clear from numerous passages such as this from Augustine: 'We heard the Apostle [epistle], we heard the Psalm, we heard the Gospel; all the divine readings sound together so that we place hope not in ourselves but in the Lord' (*Sermo* 165, *de verbis Apostoli, Ephesians* 3.13–18, 1; *MECL* 371).

It might surprise some to learn that this psalm was spoken of as a reading in Augustine's time, and it might lead them to think that it was simply recited rather than sung. But that this particular 'reading' is at the same time a musical event (an instance of the kind of responsorial psalmody described above in connection with the communion) is clear from numerous other passages; for example, this, in which Augustine reminds his congregation in speaking of Psalm 99 (LXX): 'The psalm which we have just now heard sung and responded to in singing, is short and highly beneficial' (*In psalmum* 119.1; *MECL* 364). At least some of these response verses must have been sung to particularly attractive tunes. In speaking of the first verse of Psalm 132 (LXX), 'Behold how good and sweet it is when brothers dwell in unity', Augustine seems to chide his congregation for their undue focus on its singular charm: 'That sound is so sweet that even those who do not know the Psalter quote this verse . . . this sweet sound, this lovely melody' (*In psalmum* 132.1–2; *MECL* 365).

In this seeming contradiction between the psalm being spoken of at the same time as a biblical reading and as a melodious song, I believe, lies a clue to reconstructing the history of the pre-Eucharistic responsorial psalm. At an earlier stage (the second and third centuries) psalms must have figured occasionally among the Old Testament readings of the pre-Eucharistic service. It is possible that as psalms, their inherent lyric qualities might have been exploited by at least some lectors, and that they might have been declaimed in somewhat more musical fashion than the other readings. Still they were essentially readings, not set musical pieces. But in the late fourth-century wave of enthusiasm for the singing of psalms, it is possible that the pre-Eucharistic psalm moved from an occasional to a regular liturgical event, and while still referred to as a reading, was performed in the responsorial manner that had come into vogue during the psalmodic movement.

Bringing further plausibility to this reconstruction is a consideration of the broader historical background. With the emancipation of the church in 313 came a transformation of Christianity into a more public religion. Domestic gatherings, whether to celebrate the Eucharist or to attend morning and evening prayer, developed into elaborate services in great stone basilicas, calling for a style of declamation and song matching the new acoustical environment.

Still, the Eucharistic psalmody of the later fourth and earlier fifth centuries, and the Office psalmody as well, was just that: psalmody; that is, the solo declamation of psalms (with accompanying congregational responses) by lectors, cantors, monks and nuns, all of whom were essentially amateurs. The ecclesiastical song of the time was not yet the medieval Byzantine or Roman chant, which consisted of elaborate set pieces recorded in liturgical books, sung as part of a complex annual cycle by quasi-professional clerical and monastic choirs. Yet the psalmody of the early Christian period lay in a direct line of development with that splendid musical outcome which is one of the glories of Christian civilization.

NOTES

1 The texts are edited in Hesbert (1935).
2 Several of the earliest notated manuscripts have been published in facsimile by the monks of St-Pierre de Solesmes in the series *Paléographie musicale*, which commenced in 1889 with the manuscript pictured in Figure 29.1.
3 I attempted such a survey in McKinnon (1987a). All patristic quotations in the present chapter will be quoted from that work; after each quotation the abbreviation *MECL* will

follow in parentheses with the *MECL* number (not page) of the item quoted. The complete citation for each quotation, including the place in the patristic author's work and in modern editions, is available in *MECL*.

4 A sambuca was a triangular instrument with four strings, of Eastern origin.

5 See especially Quasten (1930: 81–3). This classic volume of the eminent patristics scholar serves as the starting point for much of my own work.

6 Much of the following two paragraphs is summarized from McKinnon (1965).

7 Much of this section on 'musical imagery' is summarized from McKinnon (1968a).

8 See *MECL* 205.

9 The numbering of the Psalms given here is that of the Hebrew Bible; subsequent numbering in this chapter will be from the Greek-Latin tradition.

10 See McKinnon (1987b: 93–5).

11 See especially Foley (1992: 58).

12 For a finely nuanced summary of the issues involved, see Bradshaw (1982: 43–6).

13 See McKinnon (1987b: 95–8).

14 See, for example, Smith (1981), McKinnon (1968b), Bradshaw (1992: 21–3) and Smith (1994).

15 This entire section is summarized from McKinnon (1994).

16 See *MECL* 242–53, selections from the *Itinerarium Egeriae*.

17 On the subject of patrisitic references to the psalmody of the pre-Eucharistic synaxis, see Martimort (1982) and McKinnon (1996b).

BIBLIOGRAPHY

Bradshaw, Paul F. (1982) *Daily Prayer in the Early Church*. Oxford: Oxford University Press.

—— (1992) *The Search for the Origins of Christian Worship*. Oxford: Oxford University Press.

Foley, Edward (1992) *Foundations of Christian Music: The Music of Pre-Constantinian Christianity*. Brancote, Nottingham: Grove Books Limited.

Hesbert, René-Jean (1935) *Antiphonale Missarum Sextuplex*. Brussels: Vromant.

Martimort, Aimé Georges (1984) 'A propos du nombre des lectures à la messe', *Revue des sciences religieuses* 58: 42–51.

McKinnon, James (1965) 'The Meaning of the Patristic Polemic against Musical Instruments', *Current Musicology* 1: 69–82.

—— (1968a) 'Musical Instruments in Medieval Psalm Commentaries and Psalters', *Journal of the American Musicological Society* 21: 3–20.

—— (1968b) 'On the Question of Psalmody in the Ancient Synagogue', *Early Music History* 6: 159–91.

—— (1987a) *Music in Early Christian Literature*. Cambridge: Cambridge University Press.

—— (1987b) 'The Fourth-Century Origin of the Gradual', *Early Music History* 7: 91–106.

—— (1994) 'Desert Monasticism and the Later Fourth-Century Psalmodic Movement', *Music & Letters* 75: 505–21.

—— (1996a) 'Preface to the Study of the Alleluia', *Early Music History* 15: 213–49.

—— (1996b) Review of Aimé Georges Martimort, *Les Lectures liturgiques et leurs livres*. Typologie des sources du moyen âge occidental, Fasc. 64. Turnhout: Brepols, in *Plainsong and Medieval Music* 5: 211–26.

Quasten, Johannes (1930) *Musik und Gesang in den Kulten der heidnischen Antike und christlichen Frühzeit*. Liturgiewissenschaftliche Quellen und Forschungen 25. Münster in Westphalia: Aschendorf.

Smith, John (1981) 'The Ancient Synagogue, The Early Church and Singing', *Music & Letters* 65: 1–16.

—— (1994) 'First-Century Christian Singing and it Relationship to Contemporary Jewish Religious Song', *Music & Letters* 75: 1–15.

Taft, Robert (1986) *The Liturgy of the Hours in the East and West*. Collegeville, Minn.: Liturgical Press.

IMAGINATIVE LITERATURE

—— •✦• ——

Richard Bauckham

INTRODUCTION

Most early Christian literature was didactic, devotional or theological. But there is also imaginative literature, some examples of which we shall consider in this chapter. Such works, of course, had religious aims, but aims which were fulfilled by the telling of imaginative stories. Works of the narrative imagination are found especially among some of the so-called apocryphal works produced from the second century onwards. In this connection the term 'apocryphal' should not be given much weight. These were not necessarily works which might have been included in the canon of the New Testament but in fact were excluded. Most were never candidates for canonicity. They were not necessarily works condemned as heretical by the emerging orthodoxy of the Catholic church, though some of them were. Many were widely read in thoroughly orthodox circles as edifying and entertaining literature, and some, even when roundly condemned by councils and theologians, were thought too good to lose by scholars and monks who preserved them, and much too interesting to abandon by ordinary readers with whom they remained popular. English translations of the Christian apocryphal works discussed in this chapter can be found in Elliott (1993) and Schneemelcher (1991–2).

We might expect apocryphal gospels to be prominent among works of the Christian narrative imagination, but in fact no non-canonical gospel of the type that narrates the story of Jesus, as the canonical gospels do, survives in more than fragments. Surviving apocryphal gospels (mostly gnostic) are collections of sayings of Jesus or dialogues between the risen Jesus and his disciples, not narratives. For stories of Jesus we must turn to more specialized off-shoots of the Gospel genre: 'proto-gospels' and gospels of the Passion and Resurrection. The latter type (including especially the cycle of narratives known either as the *Gospel of Nicodemus* or as the *Acts of Pilate*), though important for its medieval influence, developed only in the later patristic period and will not be studied here. But 'proto-gospels' (often called birth and infancy gospels) which narrate Jesus' background (from before the birth of his mother), birth and childhood began to be written in the second century. We shall comment on the two second-century works of this type from which all later such works developed: the *Protevangelium of James* and the *Infancy Gospel of Thomas*.

These works illustrate how the Christian narrative imagination blossomed, especially in the gaps left by the Christian story as the New Testament itself told it. This also happened in the case of stories about the apostles. The canonical Acts of the Apostles, the only canonical narrative about the early church, leaves a great deal untold. Even Paul's story is cut off an indeterminate time before his death. The other most famous apostle, Peter, drops out of the narrative of Acts half way through the book, and not even his later presence in Rome, well known to all later Christians, is mentioned. About the ministries of most of the 12 apostles, all of whom the risen Jesus commissions, at the beginning of Acts, to take the gospel to the ends of the earth, Acts has practically nothing to say. For this reason – and other reasons which will become apparent – apocryphal narratives of the deeds and deaths of individual apostles flourished from the second century onwards. We shall study the five oldest of these apocryphal acts of apostles.

THE *PROTEVANGELIUM OF JAMES*

The *Protevangelium of James* is one of the most attractive of the early Christian apocryphal works, as well as one of the most influential (see Cothenet 1988; Vorster 1988). It tells a delightful story with considerable narrative skill. The title *Protevangelium* is not ancient, but is reasonably apt in that it describes the work as the beginning of the Gospel story. It begins in fact at a chronological starting-point prior even to that of Luke's Gospel, with a story about Mary's parents that leads to her birth, and ends shortly after the birth of Jesus. But the ascription of the work to James is probably original. He is James the brother of Jesus, here understood (as in other Christian literature of the second and third centuries) as one of Joseph's children by his first marriage. Already adult at the time of Jesus' birth, James was an eyewitness of the later parts of the narrative, though only in the conclusion does he reveal his authorship. Pseudonymity presumably supports one purpose of the work, which, as we shall see, is apologetic against derogatory stories of Jesus' birth and background. The *Protevangelium* was written in the second century.

The narrative

Like the first two chapters of Luke's Gospel, the narrative strongly evokes a Palestinian Jewish context, with an emphasis on the Temple in Jerusalem, though, unlike Luke's Gospel, much of the Jewish detail is fanciful rather than historically informed. At the outset of the work, Mary's parents, Joachim and Anna, a wealthy couple resident in Jerusalem, are childless. Their sorrow over this is poignantly described. Joachim retires to the wilderness, apparently with his flocks (*Protevangelium of James* 1.2 and 4.2; see Figure 30.1)

In response to their prayers, an angel informs them that they are to have a child who will become world famous. Like her Old Testament prototype and namesake Hannah, Anna vows to give the child to God, and so at three years old Mary leaves her parents to live in the Temple, where she is miraculously fed by an angel. This

Figure 30.1 Joachim retires to the sheepfold; drawing after Giotto's painting in the Arena chapel in Padua. From Quilter (1880).

part of the story, known as 'the presentation of Mary in the Temple', has inspired numerous artistic renditions (see Figure 30.2).

At 12, approaching puberty, Mary cannot stay in the Temple without defiling it, and so an angel instructs the high priest Zechariah (evidently the Zechariah of Luke 1, the father of John the Baptist) to assemble the widowers of Judaea, so that by a miraculous sign one may be selected to take Mary as his wife. Widowers are specified because it is intended that Mary remain a virgin and her husband be in reality a guardian. The choice goes to Joseph.

At the age of 16, Mary is addressed by an angel, as in Luke's annunciation story, and visits her kinswoman Elizabeth, as in Luke's Gospel. When she returns home, Joseph's reaction to her evident pregnancy and the angelic explanation to him in a dream are expansions of Matthew's account. When Mary's pregnancy becomes known to an outsider, Joseph is accused to the high priest of having defiled the virgin in his care. Both Mary and Joseph protest their innocence, and they are vindicated when the high priest puts them through the ordeal of drinking water that would harm them were they guilty.

Joseph and Mary appear to be living in Jerusalem, from where they set off for

Figure 30.2   The presentation of Mary, aged three, in the Temple; drawing after Giotto's painting in the Arena Chapel in Padua. From Quilter (1880).

Bethlehem when the census is decreed. In one of its permanent contributions to the Christian imagination, the *Protevangelium* depicts Joseph seating the heavily pregnant Mary on a donkey for the journey. Another such contribution is its location of the birth of Jesus in a cave (a detail also found in Justin Martyr, writing at about the same time). They are only halfway to Bethlehem when Mary is about to give birth. Joseph leaves her with his sons in the cave, the only shelter in this desert region, while he goes to seek a midwife. He soon meets one who, entering the cave, witnesses the miraculous birth of Jesus. A cloud overshadows the cave; then an unbearably bright light appears in the cave; the child appears as the light withdraws. The midwife, deeply impressed, meets Salome outside the cave, and tells her she has witnessed a virgin give birth. (Salome is probably Joseph's daughter, though in later versions of the story she becomes a second midwife.) The sceptical Salome refuses to believe unless she can put her finger on Mary's intact flesh. (There is clearly an echo of the Fourth Gospel's story of Thomas refusing to believe without himself touching the risen Christ.) Because she has tempted God with it, Salome's hand is consumed, but is healed when she prays and touches the new-born child.

The story of the visit of the magi is then told, following Matthew's account. When Herod decrees the slaughter of the children, Mary hides Jesus by wrapping him in swaddling clothes and laying him in a manger. Elizabeth flees from her home in fear with her son John, and a mountain opens to receive and to hide them. When Herod's officers can get no information from Zechariah as to the whereabouts of his son, Herod orders his death. He is murdered in the Temple, where the priests later find his blood petrified, though his body has vanished.

Literary character

The literary tradition to which the *Protevangelium* most obviously belongs is that of Jewish narrative works (sometimes called 'rewritten Bible' or, less accurately, 'midrash') which retell the biblical histories, expanding on the biblical versions in order to explain problems raised by the biblical texts, to fill in the gaps, to satisfy curiosity, to put a particular theological or ideological slant on the stories, and to enable readers imaginatively to enter the world of the biblical stories and characters more fully (see Cothenet 1988). Such works often create new stories inspired by – though deliberately also differing from – those told in the Bible about other characters. This is what happens in the *Protevangelium* when the story of Mary's conception and birth echoes those of Isaac, Samson and especially Samuel, or when the story of Salome's scepticism about the virgin birth parallels the Fourth Gospel's story of Thomas's scepticism about the resurrection. The imaginative account of Mary's birth and childhood satisfies the sense that someone of such significance as Mary in the history of salvation must have been marked out and prepared for this role from before her birth, just as Jewish literature told extra-biblical stories about the births of Noah (*1 Enoch* 106), Melchizedek (*2 Enoch* 71) and Moses (Pseudo-Philo, *Biblical Antiquities* 9). The later part of the *Protevangelium* is the first literary attempt to reconcile the two canonical narratives about Jesus' birth in the Gospels of Matthew and Luke. The freedom with which it sometimes treats these latter (especially in matters of geography) is surprising, but not entirely unparalleled in the Jewish 'rewritten Bible' texts. Typical of Jewish exegetical method is the way the *Protevangelium* creates stories which explain some feature of the scriptural text. For example, Luke's statement that Mary laid the child Jesus in a manger (Luke 2:7) is explained as a way of hiding the child from Herod's soldiers. The Gospels' reference to the murder of Zechariah in the temple (Matt. 23:35; Luke 11:51) seemed to imply that this was a recent event (rather than the event narrated in 2 Chr. 24:19–22) and so required a story to explain it. The *Protevangelium*, following the common exegetical technique of assuming characters with the same name to be identical, therefore tells a story of the murder of Zechariah the father of John the Baptist, in consequence of Herod's attempt to destroy the Messianic child.

Apologetic and polemic

Several features of the narrative suggest that it was at least partly designed to deflect charges made about Jesus' background and origins in Jewish polemic against Christians, which we know to have been current in the second century, principally from the citation of them in the work of the pagan anti-Christian writer Celsus. Since both Jews and pagans were contemptuous of Jesus' humble origins, the *Protevangelium* begins by pointing out that his grandfather Joachim was very wealthy, while

Joseph's trade is portrayed as that of a master builder. The fact that no mention is made of Nazareth is probably due to concern to deny that Jesus' origins were obscure. Mary was not a girl forced to earn her living by spinning, as the polemic asserted; she did spin, but what she made, according to the *Protevangelium*, was the curtain for the Temple. Against the slander that Jesus was conceived through extra-marital union, the *Protevangelium* is at great pains to relate how Mary's virginity was safeguarded and her innocence demonstrated in a way the Temple authorities them-selves accepted. It may not be accidental that the flight into Egypt goes unmentioned, since Jewish polemic portrayed Jesus as a magician who learned his magic in Egypt.

Along with these responses to Jewish polemic goes a Christian counter-polemic against the Jews. On the way to Bethlehem, Joseph is puzzled that Mary appears to be mourning and laughing at the same time. She explains: 'I see with my eyes two peoples, one weeping and lamenting and one rejoicing and exulting.' While the passage echoes Genesis 25:23, it evidently means that Mary's son is to be the occasion for the sorrow of the Jews as well as for the rejoicing of Christians. From this perspec-tive the way the *Protevangelium* ends, with the story of the murder of Zechariah, often thought to be a later addition, is appropriate and effective. When Zechariah's blood is found in the Temple, a voice declares that it will not be wiped away until his avenger comes, referring no doubt to the destruction of the Temple in 70 CE.

Mariology

The way the *Protevangelium* develops the theme of Mary's virginity is a major step on the way to the mariological doctrines of a later period. To the canonical Gospels' claim that Mary was a virgin when she conceived Jesus, the *Protevangelium* adds the claim that Jesus' birth was miraculous, such that Mary's virginity was preserved through it (the *virginitas in partu*), while it also implies that Mary remained a virgin thereafter, in that it depicts Joseph's children as those of his first wife, not Mary. These ideas are found in other second-century texts and so were not original to the *Protevangelium*, but it undoubtedly promoted them. It is not clear that they consti-tute an idealization of virginity as such. The idea of the miraculous birth probably has a scriptural origin (Isa. 66:7), while the emphasis on Mary's virginity seems related to her consecration for a unique role. That she remained a lifelong virgin may reflect a sense that the womb which had borne the Son of God should not be subsequently used for other and ordinary births (cf. 1 Sam. 6:7). Mary's special consecration for her extraordinary role in God's purposes is the focus of the work, rather than her lifelong virginity as an example to be imitated. On the other hand, sexual asceticism was certainly already current as an ideal in some Christian circles in the later second century, as the apocryphal Acts testify (see pp. 808–9), and so the *Protevangelium* may owe something to that context.

It is noteworthy that the *Protevangelium*'s interest in Mary is not properly bio-graphical (by contrast with medieval lives of the Virgin). It does not continue her story beyond her role in salvation history, which it does not extend beyond the birth of Jesus. Its interest is solely in the way Mary was prepared for and fulfilled her unique vocation to be the virgin mother of the Saviour.

THE INFANCY GOSPEL OF THOMAS

Both curiosity and convention required appropriate stories, not only about the background and birth of a great man, but also about his childhood. Such stories, like the only one the canonical Gospels tell about the boy Jesus (Luke 2:41–51) or one which Jewish tradition told about the young Abraham (*Jubilees* 11.18–24), should prefigure the role which the adult is going to play in history. The *Infancy Gospel of Thomas*, also from the second century, complements the *Protevangelium of James* by telling stories of the miracles done by Jesus between the ages of five and twelve, concluding by reproducing Luke's story of the 12-year-old Jesus in the Temple, thereby attaching itself to the canonical Gospel story (see Gero 1971).

The fact that a non-biblical character, Annas the scribe, appears in both the *Protevangelium* and the *Infancy Gospel of Thomas* suggests that the author of the latter knew the former and deliberately filled the chronological gap left between the *Protevangelium* and the canonical Gospel story. The title *Infancy Gospel* is modern, but the attribution to the apostle Thomas is ancient, and probably indicates that the work derives from the Christian tradition of the east Syrian area, which connected itself especially with Thomas (cf. the *Acts of Thomas*, discussed on pp. 798, 807–9). However, it displays none of the special theological characteristics of that tradition.

This work has none of the literary sophistication of the *Protevangelium of James*. What literary skill it displays consists in the telling of stories concisely and vividly. The miracles the boy Jesus performs anticipate, within the world of Jesus' childhood in Nazareth, the kinds of miracles he would perform in his adult ministry. Miracles of cursing and destruction occur disproportionately often, but there are also, for example, a miracle of raising the dead and a miracle of multiplication of wheat. The effect these miracles have in the stories corresponds to the way the gospel miracles were commonly understood in the patristic period: they demonstrate to people that Jesus is no mere human. One of the more sophisticated and attractive is the first story, in which the 5-year-old Jesus, playing at the ford of a brook, 'gathered together into pools the water that flowed by, and made it at once clean, and commanded it by his word alone'. Then 'he made soft clay and fashioned from it twelve sparrows', who later, at his word, flew away. Jesus thus imitates his Father's work in creation, gathering the waters and creating living things. The fact that these miracles occur on a Sabbath indicates that he claims his Father's prerogative to give life on the Sabbath, as the adult Jesus does in John 5.

Later writings in the tradition of the *Protevangelium of James* and the *Infancy Gospel of Thomas*, especially the Latin apocryphal *Gospel of Matthew* (usually known as Pseudo-Matthew) which was very influential in the medieval West, drew on both works, taking over most of their contents and supplementing them in order to tell a continuous story from the birth of Mary through the childhood of Jesus. Thus, even where the two second-century works themselves were not known, the stories they told continued to be told, as well as illustrated in art, throughout the medieval period and later.

APOCRYPHAL ACTS OF THE APOSTLES

The literary genre in which the narrative imagination of early Christianity was most extensively expressed was that of apostolic acts (see Findlay 1923; Bovon 1981). The earliest of the apocryphal acts of apostles date from the mid-second century or even a little earlier, and such works continued to be written for centuries in a tradition continued also to some extent in the lives of post-apostolic saints. Here we shall focus on the five oldest of these acts, written between the early second and early third centuries: the *Acts of John* (Bremmer 1995), *Andrew* (Prieur 1989; Pao 1995; Bremmer 1998b), *Peter* (Perkins 1994; Bremmer 1998a), *Paul* (Brock 1994; Bremmer 1996), and *Thomas* (Germond 1996; Tissot 1998). (This may be the chronological order, but, although there are undoubtedly literary connections between some of these works and influences of some on others, the directions of dependence and influence are not agreed, and the chronological sequence therefore quite debatable.) Only in the case of the *Acts of Thomas* has the complete text survived (probably best in the Greek version, although the work was probably composed in Syriac). In the other four cases, the text has to be reconstructed – with more or less confidence and with larger or smaller lacunae – from fragments and later adaptations of parts of the text, so that in no case do we have a complete text, though in most cases a large proportion is reasonably secure. These five texts were put together as a corpus only in the fourth century by the Manichaeans, but they have evident affinities.

These various acts are similar in that each narrates the final part of the apostolic ministry of the apostle in question, ending with his death (martyrdom except in the case of John, who dies peacefully). The *Acts of Thomas* begins with a scene in Jerusalem, in which the nations of the world are divided among the apostles and India is allotted to Thomas. Thomas, despite his initial unwillingness to accept this allocation, travels by sea to India, where the rest of the work is set. The *Acts of Andrew* probably began with the same scene in Jerusalem, with Andrew receiving Achaea as his allotted mission field, and went on to describe Andrew's travels in northern Asia Minor and Greece, especially Philippi, Corinth and Patras, where he suffers martyrdom. The original form of the *Acts of Peter* evidently also began in Jerusalem, where Peter is said to have stayed for 12 years after the resurrection; in the surviving text we are told only of his voyage to Rome and his ministry there. The *Acts of Paul* relates the apostle's travels in much the same areas as those which feature in the account of Paul in the canonical Acts, ending with a journey from Corinth to Italy and Paul's martyrdom in Rome. This has usually been understood as an alternative account of Paul's missionary career, paralleling that of the canonical Acts, but it can also plausibly be seen as a sequel to Acts, narrating travels Paul was believed to have undertaken between the end of Luke's narrative and his later return to Rome (see Bauckham 1993). Finally, the *Acts of John* tells of the apostle's ministry in Ephesus and other cities of the province of Asia, concluding with his death in Ephesus. The beginning of the narrative is lost, but the fact that John is depicted as an older man implies that only the final period of his life was covered.

The apocryphal Acts and the canonical Acts of the Apostles

These five works are each distinctive in structure, style, content and ideology, but they also have much in common and clearly constitute a genre of literature not quite like anything else, although they have been and can be profitably compared with several other types of ancient literature. They are certainly modelled to varying degrees on the canonical Acts of the Apostles. It was Luke's work, especially when read as a work distinct from Luke's Gospel, that structured salvation history in such a way as to make the missionary activity of an apostle, beginning at some point after the resurrection, readily conceivable as a narrative unity. None of the apocryphal Acts narrate – except in flashbacks in speeches – either the early lives of the apostles or their time with the earthly Jesus. For this reason, they cannot be classified simply as biographies. They are biographical only in a special sense determined by the Christian concept of the role of an apostle in salvation history. On the other hand, they are more biographical than the canonical Acts is. Even though Luke's narrative focuses almost exclusively on Paul in the second half of Acts, the fact that it ends at the point it does shows that the interest in Paul is subordinated to a non-biographical conception of the work as a whole. The fact that each of the apocryphal Acts tells one apostle's story and ends it with his death demonstrates a more biographical interest, which is in line with the growing popularity of biographical works in the period when the apocryphal Acts were written. To second-century Christians the canonical Acts seemed unfinished in that it did not continue its story as far as Paul's death, while Peter and John both disappear from its narrative at early stages without explanation. It is easy to see how, to a more biographical interest than Luke's, his Acts seemed in need of completion and supplementation.

A striking feature which distinguishes the *Acts of Paul* in particular from Luke's narrative of Paul, and aligns the former with Graeco-Roman biography in a way that is not true of Acts, is the inclusion of a physical description of Paul. Such descriptions were a standard feature of Greek and Roman biography. They are often conventional to some degree, reflecting the theories of physiognomics, which were popular in the second century and understood physical features as revelatory of character and aptitudes (see Malherbe 1986; Malina and Neyrey 1996: 100–52). The Roman historian Suetonius' physical descriptions of the emperors, for example, are determined as much by physiognomical theory as by the actual appearances of the emperors, even when these were readily available in the form of statues and images on coins. The description of Paul in the *Acts of Paul* – short, bald, bowlegged, with meeting eyebrows and a somewhat hooked nose – is to a large extent conventional, and was certainly not unflattering, as it appears to modern readers. Bowleggedness and meeting eyebrows were admired, the hooked nose was a sign of magnanimity, and a moderately small stature indicated quickness of intelligence (since the blood flowed more quickly around a small area and more quickly reached the heart, the seat of intelligence). The only feature which is surprising is the bald head, which might therefore reflect a historical reminiscence.

Despite the more biographical character of the apocryphal acts, it was the Lucan Acts that provided for them the model of an episodic travel narrative, including the deeds, especially miracles, and the words of an apostle, which all the apocryphal Acts follow to some extent, those of Paul and Andrew most fully. It is not surprising that the *Acts of Paul* resembles the canonical Acts more than any other of the apocryphal acts, but in one respect the *Acts of John* is more similar. While its narrative is for the most part told in the third person, there are passages in the first person plural, which begin and end unaccountably in the midst of third-person narrative. This phenomenon is not easily explicable except as a deliberate imitation of the 'we-passages' of Acts. Unlike Acts, the *Acts of John* also uses the first-person singular, though only on two or three occasions (61; 73; 86?). The implied author is evidently one of John's close companions who travel with him, much like Luke's role in the canonical Acts according to the traditional understanding of the 'we-passages'. The beginning of the *Acts of John*, which might have identified the pseudonym to whom the first-person accounts were attributed, is not extant, but this supposed disciple of John may well have been Leucius, to whom all five of the apocryphal Acts were later attributed, but who is also attested as particularly related to John. (It has been suggested that the name was chosen for its similarity to the name Luke, suggesting a role parallel to that of Luke in his Acts.) The *Acts of Peter* also contains very brief occurrences of the first-person plural in the midst of third-person narrative, which are probably remnants of a wider usage in the original text. While the *Acts of Peter* differs both from the canonical Acts and from the other apocryphal Acts in that it seems to have contained only one journey by the apostle – from Jerusalem to Rome – it is related to the canonical Acts in a different way: Peter's conflict with Simon Magus (Acts 8) is continued and brought to a dramatic climax in Rome. The work ends with the crucifixion of Peter – but upside down at his request, a scene commemorated in many European paintings (see Figure 30.3).

Alongside these forms of dependence on the Lucan Acts, the apocryphal Acts also share significant differences from the canonical Acts. Their more biographical character has already been noticed. The miracles the apostles perform are, in general, more dramatic and impressive than those of the canonical Acts. Miracles of resurrection are especially common, and seem to be related to an understanding of conversion as rising to new life, which is not to be found in the canonical Acts. The predominance of upper-class characters, among both converts and opponents of the apostles, is not paralleled in Luke's Acts, nor are the stories, recurrent in the apocryphal Acts, of betrothed or married people, especially women, who practise sexual abstinence as part of their new Christian lifestyle (see pp. 808–9). While the canonical Acts contains episodes of excitement and adventure, such as Peter's escape from prison or Paul's sea voyage and shipwreck, intended to entertain while also instructing readers, the stories in the apocryphal Acts have far more sensational and fantastic elements: murder, parricide, self-castration, necrophilia, suicide, murderous demons, talking animals (even converted ones), a flying magician, a visit to hell, close encounters with wild animals in the amphitheatre, miraculous escape from execution by fire. Readerly pleasure is served by both melodramatic and humorous episodes, sometimes deliberately alternated. Among the light-hearted stories are the tale of the bed-bugs in the *Acts of John*, in which the apostle procures an uninterrupted night's sleep at an inn by banishing the bed-bugs temporarily from the bed, and the story which the *Acts of Andrew*, employing a stock motif, tells of a wife who

Figure 30.3   The martyrdom of Peter; drawing after a painting by Filippino Lippi in the
Brancacci Chapel, Santa Maria del Carmine, Florence. From Phillimore (1881).

abstained from sexual relations with her husband by substituting her maid for
herself in the marital bed.

The apocryphal Acts and the Greek novel

The elements of travel, upper-class setting, prominent female characters, adventure
and excitement have prompted comparison with the Greek novel (or romance). The
novel proper, i.e. the erotic novel (such as Chariton's *Chaereas and Callirhoe* or
Xenophon's *Ephesiaca*), whose popularity seems to have been at its height in the
period when the apocryphal Acts were written, tells a story of two lovers who remain
faithful to each other through separations, trials and dangerous adventures, before
arriving at a happy and final reunion. To some degree these novels carry a moral
message as well as being designed for maximum entertainment. In that sense, the
combination of entertainment and edification at which the apocryphal Acts seem to
aim brings them close to the erotic novel. Moreover, the stories – to be found in all
the apocryphal Acts – of upper-class women who forsake their husbands or deny
conjugal rights to their husbands in order to follow the apostle's teaching, employ
an erotic motif which could be seen as paralleling and subverting the themes of
faithful love and sexual consummation around which the plots of the novels revolve.
But these similarities are not sufficient to place the apocryphal Acts in the genre of

the novel. Travel, for example, which in the plots of the novels functions to separate the lovers, serves a quite different purpose in the apocryphal Acts, where the travels are those of a Christian apostle charged with a mission of evangelism and care of the churches. More generally, the novels concern individuals in their private capacities, and their plots are limited to the personal lives and emotions of these individuals, whereas the apocryphal Acts portray the apostles as public figures, whose mission belongs to the purpose of God for the world and affects whole populations and regions. However much the emotions and aspirations of individuals are stressed in the stories these Acts tell, especially of conversions, such private affairs take their place in an overall story of public significance.

What we can conclude, from the features they share with the Greek novels, is that the apocryphal Acts may well have appealed – and have been designed to appeal – to a readership similar to that of the novels. Unfortunately, the nature of that readership is debatable. The view that the novels were a relatively popular literature, circulating more widely than other literary works, and attracting especially a female audience, has been challenged by the evidence of surviving papyrus fragments, whose relative numbers do not support the hypothesis of wide circulation, and by the observation that the literary sophistication of the novels presupposes not only a literate audience, but an educated one. On the other hand, it is likely that the novels which have survived are those of higher literary quality and sophistication, while the relatively unsophisticated apocryphal Acts (with the exception of the *Acts of Thomas*) resemble, in this respect, a somewhat more popular level of novelistic writing. The prominence of upper-class characters, including women who exercise considerable initiative and independence, cannot prove that either the novels or the apocryphal Acts were intended to appeal only to readers of the same class and gender. Popular literature often features characters from the social elite. (Marcellus, the Christian senator who appears prominently in the *Acts of Peter*, is unlikely to correspond to any historical Christians who were members of the Roman Senate at the time of writing.) But it is reasonable to assume that the target audience included women, who would find a variety of strong female characters to identify with, and who, in households wealthy enough to have educated slaves, would have slaves to read to them for entertainment.

If we envisage the apocryphal Acts as intended primarily to attract outsiders to the faith, and only secondarily to edify believers, we can easily understand the literary resemblances to the novels. If the targeted audience were primarily the literate elite, this does not mean that the apocryphal Acts pander to aristocratic prejudice. On the contrary, such frequent themes as the disobedience of upper-class Christian wives to their husbands and the apostle's conflict with civil and religious authorities, usually ending in martyrdom, are aimed against established order, while some of the Acts, especially those of Peter, encourage a kind of solidarity with the poor and marginal that was both alien to the elite of the Graeco-Roman world and also early Christianity's most distinctive socio-economic concern. Unlike the *Protevangelium of James* (see pp. 792–6), the *Acts of Peter* provides no refutation of the dismissive description of Jesus it puts on the lips of Simon Magus: 'Jesus the Nazarene, the son of a carpenter and a carpenter himself.'

Before leaving the subject of the resemblances between the apocryphal Acts and the Greek novel, we should observe that one section of one of these Acts bears a much closer resemblance. The story of Thecla in the *Acts of Paul* (which later circulated as an independent narrative work, the *Acts of Paul and Thecla*, no doubt in the interests of the cult of Thecla) must be seen as a deliberate small-scale equivalent to one of the erotic novels. Thecla, like the heroines of the novels, is a beautiful young woman of aristocratic birth who preserves her chastity and remains faithful to her beloved through trials and dangers in which she comes close to death but experiences divine deliverance. She escapes two unwanted and malevolent suitors, Thamyris and Alexander, as do the heroines of the novels. Unlike these heroines, her chastity is not, of course, temporary but permanent, and represents her total devotion to God. But her devotion to God is also devotion to his apostle Paul, who preaches sexual abstinence as essential to the Christian way. This devotion to Paul is depicted in terms which are certainly not to be read as sexual, but nevertheless parallel erotic passion. As in the case of the heroes and heroines of the novels, the plot partly turns on the separation of Paul and Thecla, her search for and reunion with him. When she offers to cut her hair short in order to follow him everywhere and when she adopts male dress to travel in search of Paul, these may be not primarily signs of her liberation from patriarchal structures, though there is no doubt that she is so liberated, but echoes of the novelistic theme of a woman travelling in male disguise in order to escape detection. It seems clear that Thecla's story has been directly modelled on the Greek novel, both in order to entertain a readership similar to that enjoyed by the novels, but also in order to express the message of sexual continence for the sake of devotion to God in an attractively symbolic way.

The apocryphal Acts and novelistic biography

The Greek novels were pure fiction, even if they originated as imitations of historiography and were apt to use some of the conventions of historiography (Morgan and Stoneman 1994; Holzberg 1995). While it is hard to believe that the frequently tall stories of the apocryphal acts were taken entirely literally by, at least, their more sophisticated readers, nevertheless it seems unlikely that their authors would have been happy for them to be regarded as wholly fictional. At least the apostles themselves were real historical figures. This suggests that, in search of the literary affinities of the apocryphal Acts, we should return to the category of biography, which we introduced when observing that these Acts are more biographical in form than the canonical Acts.

Momigliano makes this important comment on ancient biography:

The borderline between fiction and reality was thinner in biography than in ordinary historiography. What readers expected in biography was probably different from what they expected in political history. They wanted information about the education, the love affairs, and the character of their heroes. But these things are less easily documented than wars and political reforms. If biographers wanted to keep their public, they had to resort to fiction.

(Momigliano 1971: 56–7)

This comment needs qualification in the sense that some biographies were as scrupulously historical as the best ancient historiography. Indeed, one can perhaps speak of the emergence, by the time of writing of the apocryphal Acts, of two genres of biography: the historical, which remained close to good historical method, and the (for want of a better word) novelistic, which, while using sources, allowed more or less freedom to creative imagination. It is instructive to compare the works of a contemporary of some of the authors of the apocryphal Acts: Flavius Philostratus. His *Lives of the Sophists*, dependent on oral sources, no doubt share the limitations of the sources, but in these Philostratus does not indulge in free invention. Quite different is his *Life of Apollonius of Tyana*. Here the point where novelistic creativity takes over from history is impossible to determine, and scholars differ over whether even Philostratus' supposed source, Damis, is a novelistic invention. A quite different example of the same kind of contrast is between the histories of Alexander the Great and the freely imaginative Alexander romance.

There is no doubt that, if we are to associate the apocryphal Acts with ancient biography, then it is with the semi-fictional, novelistic biography that we should associate them. This is a category which made some claim to be historiography, but which allowed very wide scope for various kinds of historical imagination. Readers who put the apocryphal Acts in this category would expect them to be biographies of real historical persons, but would also expect a considerable and indeterminate admixture of fiction. Given only sparse historical details for their imagination to work on, authors of such works would be expected to make the most of these but not to be constrained by them. Entertainment and edification required an approach much more flexible than the methods of more scrupulous kinds of historiography.

Scholars have found it difficult to classify Philostratus' *Life of Apollonius* generically. It seems to be a combination of biography with the novel. But, rather than confusing its genre with that of the novel proper, it would be more appropriate to say that this example of novelistic biography borrows themes from the novel proper, just as the *Acts of Paul* does. The way in which erotic subplots are included in the story of the ascetic philosopher Apollonius, presumably to appeal to the same kind of readership as enjoyed the novels, is parallel to, though not the same as, the way erotic themes are introduced into the apocryphal Acts. The semi-fictional or novelistic biography can be influenced by the novel proper, but it is not this influence that makes it semi-fictional. It is in any case a semi-fictional genre, novelistic in its own way. What the influence of the novel in this case illustrates is the way the novelistic biography was a genre particularly hospitable to influence from other genres. Such hospitality helps us to understand the variety of literary elements that go to make up the various apocryphal Acts (e.g. the *Acts of Paul* contains letters passed between Paul and the Corinthian church; the *Acts of John* contains virtually a short Gospel; the *Acts of Thomas* contains poems and hymns; the *Acts of Andrew* shows particular affinities with the biographies of philosophers; folktale motifs are evident in some of the stories in the various Acts).

The *Life of Apollonius*, written in the early third century, tells the story of a first-century philosopher in a way which is based in history but is also freely imaginative. Another example is the *Life of Secundus the Philosopher* (Perry 1964). Secundus, put to death by Hadrian for keeping to his vow of silence in defiance of the emperor's command to speak, also lived at roughly the same chronological remove from his biography as the apostles did from the time of composition of their apocryphal Acts. The plainly novelistic story which his *Life* tells to explain his vow of silence is plausibly understood as a sensational story woven around the historical fact of the philosopher's silence, which would no doubt have been actually connected with Pythagorean asceticism. That Secundus is portrayed, like the apostles, as a martyr also illustrates how at this period stories of heroic deaths for philosophical or religious principle appealed to both pagans and Christians. The martyrdoms of the apostles at the conclusions of the apocryphal Acts could serve the propagandist aims of these Acts, just as historical martyrdoms in the amphitheatres and elsewhere did.

The apocryphal Acts are best described, then, as works of novelistic biographical character (not strictly biographies) suited to the telling of the story of a Christian apostle and defined as the semi-fictional narrative of the missionary activity of an apostle subsequent to the resurrection of Jesus and ending with the apostle's death. While modelled in part on the canonical Acts, they are at once more biographical and more fictional than the canonical Acts. They partake in several ways in the literary currents of the period in which they originated, a period in which biography in general and the novelistic biography in particular were popular, as was the erotic novel and the martyrology (whether as an element in biography or as a distinct genre).

Apocryphal Acts and Jewish 'rewritten' Bible texts

One further category of literature belongs to the literary context which accounts for the particular features of the apocryphal Acts. In discussion of the *Protevangelium of James* we have already encountered the tradition of Jewish narrative works which retell the biblical histories, explaining and expanding the biblical text with the imaginative development of stories about the biblical characters. Such works include both those which retell the biblical story with creative expansions (e.g. *Jubilees*, Pseudo-Philo's *Biblical Antiquities*, Artapanus) and those which tell largely extra-biblical stories about biblical characters (e.g. *Joseph and Aseneth, Jannes and Jambres*). This Jewish literature was widely read by Christians in the early centuries of Christianity. (In fact, most of it has been preserved only through Christian channels of transmission.) Most Christians who read, enjoyed and were instructed by it did not regard it as canonical scripture, as they regarded the Old Testament. Such Jewish works could well have suggested how the writings of the emerging New Testament canon could be extended (as by the *Acts of Paul* and the *Acts of Peter*) or supplemented (as by the *Acts of John* and the *Acts of Andrew*) by extra-canonical stories about the apostles. Some of these Jewish works use various forms of exegesis of the biblical text as the starting-point and stimulus for exercises in historical imagination, while others are more straightforwardly fictional creations.

We can observe both types among the apocryphal Acts. When its relationship to the canonical Acts of the Apostles and the Pauline letter corpus (including the Pastorals) is carefully studied, it becomes evident that the *Acts of Paul* uses many of the usual Jewish exegetical practices to explain and to expand the available information about the period of Paul's missionary activity the author believed to have intervened between the end of Acts and the apostle's martyrdom (see Bauckham 1993). (It should also be noted that some of these techniques were also used by Hellenistic biographers of writers, faced with the need to eke out the minimal historical data available to them and to develop entertaining stories about their subjects: see Lefkowitz 1981.) The same kinds of methods as we observed in the case of the *Protevangelium of James* can also be identified in the *Acts of Paul*. References to persons and events in the Pastoral epistles, for example, are the basis for the creation of stories which explain them. Persons with the same names are identified. Metaphorical references, such as Paul's references to fighting with wild animals in Ephesus (1 Cor. 15:32) and being delivered from the lion's mouth (2 Tim. 4:17), are taken literally and an appropriate story created to explain them (Paul is thrown to the wild animals in the amphitheatre of Ephesus and escapes death when the lion turns out to be one he had befriended on an earlier occasion). New stories are formed on the model of existing ones, similar but also deliberately different: for example, Luke's story about Eutychus (Acts 20:7–12) inspires another story about the emperor's cup-bearer Patroclus in the *Acts of Paul*. The latter is not, as some have argued, a variant of the same oral tradition as Luke knew, but an example of a well-evidenced literary practice of modelling new stories on old, especially new stories about biblical characters on biblical stories about the same or other characters. While this practice is rare in the other apocryphal Acts, the comparable practice of modelling a new story about one apostle on a story about another apostle in his apocryphal Acts is common, and accounts for the various narrative motifs which, unknown elsewhere, recur in these texts. (Of course, the repetition of narrative motifs was common in all forms of ancient narrative literature, and, when used in historiography, did not impair historical credibility as it would for modern readers.) In comparison with the *Acts of Paul*, the other apocryphal Acts clearly had far less biographical data about their respective apostles already available to base their creative storytelling on, but there are a few other examples of exegetical imagination. The famous 'Quo Vadis?' story in the *Acts of Peter* is probably inspired by John 13:36–7. In the main the non-Pauline apocryphal Acts resorted to narrative invention unrelated to New Testament texts.

Evangelism or edification

We have already raised the question whether the apocryphal acts are evangelistic works envisaging pagan readers and seeking their conversion, or whether they are edificatory works for established believers. There are several indications of the former. The entertaining nature of these works as narrative literature may well be calculated to appeal to outsiders who enjoyed similarly entertaining narrative literature of other types, though there is no reason to think that Christian readers would not also appreciate this feature of the Acts. Many of the stories in the Acts are stories of the conversion of individuals or a group of related individuals to faith. There are more than thirty such stories in the five apocryphal Acts (including the restoration of apostate believers in the *Acts of Peter*), as well as general references to the conversions of large numbers of people through the miracles and preaching of the apostles.

In many cases, the miracle stories, which are so plentiful in the apocryphal Acts, function as demonstrations of the Christian God's power to deliver, to heal, to raise the dead, to outdo his demonic or human opponents, in such a way as to lead to the conversion of people who experience or witness these miracles.

This is probably the main reason why miracles of resurrection are so common in the apocryphal Acts (at least twelve such miracles in conversion stories). It is not simply that they are a particularly impressive form of miracle, but that they demonstrate the Christian God's power over life and death, and point to the eternal life that he gives to those who believe in Jesus. Like the raising of Lazarus in John 11, the miracles of resurrection point beyond the mere resuscitation to mortal life which is their physical effect, and function as signs of resurrection to eternal life, effected by God for the convert. As in John 11 (which has probably influenced the *Acts of John*), this coheres with the emphasis, in the *Acts of John* and the *Acts of Thomas*, on eternal life as Christian experience in the present. The *Acts of John* in particular interprets its resurrection stories with a theological understanding of conversion as resurrection from the state of death in which the sinful and unconverted person is. They are parables of the need to die in order to live. As the characters in the story recognize this, we should expect that the implied reader should also understand and experience conversion.

However, while many of the conversion stories seem designed for outsiders to the faith, it is not clear that we can generalize about the aims of the apocryphal Acts. Conversion stories are less prominent in the *Acts of Paul*, which often portrays Paul ministering to established churches. The *Acts of Thomas* is a work of considerable literary sophistication and theological depth, whose seemingly simple narratives are packed with symbolic and typological significance. It may well be a work designed to be read at more than one level or in a process of increasing penetration through the entertaining surface to the profounder message. Lalleman (1998) argues that, while the miracles stories and missionary preaching in the *Acts of John* aim at the conversion of outsiders, the gnostic section, which is not original to the work (chs 97–102), aims to initiate readers, who may well be non-gnostic Christians, into a gnostic understanding of Christ and salvation.

This gnostic section of the *Acts of John* is polemical in the sense that it expresses contempt for the non-gnostic Christians who do not – and, indeed, cannot – understand the true mystery. Only one other section of the apocryphal Acts seems to be written as propaganda for one form of Christianity against another. This is the correspondence between Paul and the Corinthian church in the *Acts of Paul*, whose polemic runs in the exact opposite direction from that of the *Acts of John*. The Corinthians are troubled by teachers of gnostic heresy which Paul rejects and refutes. But this polemic against gnosticism is confined to this section of the *Acts of Paul*, and cannot be understood as the overall aim of the work. The *Acts of Peter* gives much attention to Peter's restoration of Christians who have been led into apostasy by Simon Magus, but since there is virtually no account of Simon's teaching the work can scarcely be understood as polemic against heresy. In general the apocryphal Acts do not seem to aim at winning Christians of a different persuasion to their own brand of Christianity. Their polemic is confined to paganism, and their aims seem to be the conversion of pagans to the faith and the (non-polemical) edification of believers in the faith. The balance of these two elements evidently varies from one work to another.

Asceticism and dualism

The Christian way entails the renunciation of the things of this world. This theme is common to all the apocryphal Acts, as to most Christianity of the period in which they were written. Such renunciation includes contempt for wealth and luxury and worldly honour, and may also include frugality in diet (it is a peculiarity of Eucharistic celebrations in the apocryphal Acts that wine is not used), but its most prominent feature in the apocryphal Acts is sexual abstinence. Most of the apostles in them preach the ideal of complete celibacy, and many stories illustrate this preaching and its socially disruptive effects.

A story which survives only as a fragment but probably belonged to the lost first part of the original *Acts of Peter* tells of the apostle's daughter. To save her from an unwanted suitor who abducted her, she was miraculously paralysed on one side of her body from head to toe. She remains so until someone asks Peter, who heals all others brought to him for healing, why he does not heal his own daughter. Peter does then heal her in order to show that God is able to do so, but at once restores the paralysis. The reason is that the girl is too beautiful for her own good, and needs the paralysis to protect her. Extreme as this story is, it should be remembered as counter-evidence to the claim that sexual abstinence functions in the apocryphal Acts as a form of female autonomy and liberation from male dominance.

More typical are stories of women who, under the influence of the apostle's preaching, abandon sexual relations with their husbands. In some cases the husband is won over to the same practice, but in three cases (Andrew, Peter, Thomas) it is a story of this kind that leads to the apostle's martyrdom. Thecla is the most prominent example of an unmarried woman who, against all the pressures of family and society, succeeds in remaining unmarried, as the apostle's teaching requires of her. The extent to which the Acts regard such sexual abstinence as necessary is debatable, and probably varies to some extent from one work to another. The *Acts of Thomas* seems the most emphatic in considering sexual activity wholly incompatible with Christian faith and salvation, and in this it reflects the encratite (from *enkrateia*, continence) Christianity of its context of origin, the second-century Christian tradition of the east Syrian area. In other Acts there are married couples who do not seem to be required to abstain from normal marital relations, but there is no doubt that celibacy is an ideal expressing the Christian's absolute devotion to God.

It is important to notice, however, that the theological context in which this sexual asceticism is understood is different in each case. The stories of sexual abstinence are a prime example of the way narrative motifs pass from one to another of these works but serve subtly or even obviously different theological agendas in each case. In the *Acts of Paul* the theological context is a kind of eschatological radicalism based especially on 1 Corinthians 7 ('Blessed are those who have wives as if they had them not . . . '). The dualism involved is the eschatological dualism of this world and the next, not at all a matter–spirit dualism. Sexual abstinence implies no depreciation of the body. On the contrary, it keeps the body pure ('Blessed are they who have kept the flesh pure, for they shall become a temple of God'). Not the body but passions that defile the body are evil. So there is no contradiction involved when the Paul of the *Acts of Paul* also, in correspondence with the Corinthians, decisively condemns the gnostic dualism which denies that God created the human body, that Christ has come in the flesh and that there will be a resurrection of the flesh.

The much more developed theology of the *Acts of Thomas* is not dissimilar. Sexuality is bound up not with the body as such, but with death (since it is death that makes procreation necessary), sickness and other evils of the flesh which became part of human life at the fall. Sexual continence is restoration of the condition of Adam and Eve in paradise, and is associated with immortality. Enormous importance is attached to *enkrateia* because it is the key point in human life at which the forces of evil, which plague human life, can be resisted and overcome. The dualism here is between the transitory and the eternal, but not between the material and spiritual. In the *Acts of Andrew*, on the other hand, there is clear influence from the matter–spirit dualism with which the transitory–eternal dualism was associated in Greek philosophical traditions: Platonism and neo-Pythagoreanism. Salvation is the liberation of the soul, which is of divine origin, from the captivity of the body, and its reunion with God. Only through common affinities with Platonism does the *Acts of Andrew* resemble Gnosticism, but its Greek philosophical flavour, distinctive among the apocryphal Acts, differs markedly from the mythological idiom of Gnosticism.

Gnosticism itself is found only in that section of the *Acts of John* which is probably to be regarded as an addition to the original text: chapters 97–102. Here the cosmos is not the creation of the high and good God, but of an evil demiurge, who is identified with the God of the Old Testament, while the human spirit of the gnostic is alien to the body and the material world, discovering in gnosis its true home in the world above. This radical cosmic dualism, which characterizes Gnosticism in the useful sense of that term, is confined, among the apocryphal Acts, to this section of the *Acts of John*. While the rest of the *Acts of John* displays a spiritualizing tendency, stressing the new life of the spirit rather than the flesh, and so would have been congenial to a gnostic editor, it does not espouse the radical cosmic dualism of the gnostic section. On the other hand, there are no allusions to the Old Testament in the whole of the *Acts of John*, and thoroughgoing rejection of the Old Testament was distinctive of Gnosticism. The gnostic character of the form of the *Acts of John* that we have may not be entirely confined to the clearly gnostic section.

With these various forms of dualism are associated a variety of Christologies in the various Acts. In the *Acts of Andrew*, in so far as the text can be reconstructed, there is no reference at all to the life, death and resurrection of Jesus. Christ is indistinguishable from God, and it is the apostle Andrew who is both the revealer and the embodiment of salvation. In the *Acts of John* and (probably derivatively) in the *Acts of Peter*, with some traces also in the *Acts of Thomas*, is found a distinctive polymorphous Christology, which attributes to Christ no fixed form of earthly appearance, but one that changes at will, so that he is seen, even in his earthly life and even at the same time, in different forms by different people. The function of this in the *Acts of John* is clearly to remove the divine Christ from any real incarnation. This is a fully docetic Christology, whose Christ is explicitly not human at all. However, the same motif is differently interpreted in the much more 'orthodox' but rather eclectic *Acts of Peter*. Here the milder docetism that is found also in the Alexandrian Fathers – a Jesus who did not need to eat or drink but did so for our sakes – understands the polymorphy as Christ's accommodation of himself to the capacities of the people he met. Once again we see a literary motif passed from one of the apocryphal Acts to another, but its significance shifting according to the theological outlook of the work in question.

Women in the apocryphal Acts

We have already noted the prominence of women, especially aristocratic women, among the converts to Christian faith in all of the apocryphal Acts, and the adoption of sexual continence by many of them. Some recent scholarship (see Davies 1980; MacDonald 1983; Burrus 1987) has given this feature of the Acts a strongly feminist interpretation, understanding celibacy as a form of liberation for women from the patriarchal structures of marriage and the family. It was the one way in which women could exercise autonomy and independence. The Acts are then thought to reflect circles of female ascetics in second-century Christianity, whose form of Christian life ran deliberately counter both to the patriarchal structures of society in general and to male-dominated forms of Christianity. Female authorship of some of the Acts, notably the *Acts of Paul*, or oral storytelling in circles of Christian women as the source of the stories about women in the apocryphal Acts, have been postulated (Kaestli 1990). These latter hypotheses are particularly fragile, since there is no good reason to doubt Tertullian's evidence (see below) that the author of the *Acts of Paul* was male, while our observations above about the literary modelling of stories on other stories in the apocryphal Acts themselves and the difficulty of detecting oral forms behind literary versions of stories make guesses about traditions behind them perilous.

The general approach of the apocryphal Acts to marriage does not, in fact, seem to be opposed to the patriarchal structure of marriage as such but to the sexual relationship within marriage. Certainly Christian wives intent on sexual continence are defying their husbands' authority in a way that the narratives approve. We should not forget that being a Christian wife to a non-Christian husband was itself a quite serious defiance of the patriarchal structure of marriage, a defiance to which all forms of Christianity were committed. In the stories in the apocryphal Acts, this assertion of the right to be a Christian by the wife of an unconverted husband is intensified and dramatized (in a way that makes for engaging narratives) by giving it the form of refusing sexual relations. That women among the social elite converted more readily than their husbands (for whom social impediments were a greater obstacle) is true to the social realities of Christianity at the time, and the narratives of the apocryphal Acts no doubt encourage such women to persevere bravely and to hope for their husbands' conversion. But it must also be noticed that in the apocryphal Acts marriage is no longer a problem when both partners are Christian and both agree to live together without sexual relations. This shows that the authority structure of marriage is seen as problematic only when profession and faithful practice of the Christian way by the wife are opposed by the husband.

However, in the case of Thecla we can find some truth in the feminist interpretation. This story instantiates the preference for the unmarried state for the sake of the gospel and the equal rights of women and men to remain unmarried that Paul, at his most socially radical, expresses in 1 Corinthians 7. (The influence of this text on the Thecla story has not been sufficiently appreciated.) As an independent, unmarried woman she is no more subordinated to Paul's authority than his male disciples are, and she soon moves on to her own mission field and a lifetime of 'enlightening many with the word of God'. It was to this feature of the *Acts of Paul* that Tertullian objected, complaining of women who appealed to Thecla's example in order to defend the right of women to teach and to baptize (*De baptismo* 17). Whether this was the reason why, as he relates, the presbyter who wrote the work was condemned and deposed, is not clear. It certainly did not prevent the *Acts of Paul* remaining a popular work among Christians in general for quite some time after Tertullian wrote.

BIBLIOGRAPHY

Baars, W. and Helderman, J. (1993–4) 'Neue Materialien zum Text und zur Interpretation des Kindheitevangeliums des Pseudo-Thomas', *Oriens Christianus* 77: 191–226; 78: 1–32.

Bauckham, Richard (1993) 'The Acts of Paul as a Sequel to Acts', in B. C. Winter and A. D. Clarke (eds) *The Book of Acts in Its Ancient Literary Setting*. Grand Rapids, Mich.: Eerdmans and Carlisle: Paternoster Press, 105–52.

Beyers, Rita and Gijsel, Jan (1997) *Libri de natiuitate Mariae*, 2 vols. Corpus Christianorum Series Apocryphorum 9–10. Turnhout: Brepols.

Bovon, François (ed.) (1981) *Les Actes apocryphes des Apôtres*. Geneva: Labor et Fides.

—— (1991) 'The Suspension of Time in Chapter 18 of *Protevangelium Jacobi*', in B. A. Pearson (ed.) *The Future of Early Christianity: Essays in Honor of Helmut Koester*. Minneapolis, Minn.: Fortress, 393–405.

Bremmer, Jan N. (ed.) (1995) *The Apocryphal Acts of John*. Studies on the Apocryphal Acts of the Apostles 1. Kampen: Kok Pharos.

—— (ed.) (1996) *The Apocryphal Acts of Paul and Thecla*. Studies on the Apocryphal Acts of the Apostles 2. Kampen: Kok Pharos.

—— (ed.) (1998a) *The Apocryphal Acts of Peter*. Studies on the Apocryphal Acts of the Apostles 3. Leuven: Peeters.

—— (ed.) (1998b) *The Apocryphal Acts of Andrew*. Studies on the Apocryphal Acts of the Apostles 5. Leuven: Peeters.

Brock, Ann G. (1994) 'Genre of the *Acts of Paul*: One Tradition Enhancing Another', *Apocrypha* 5: 119–36.

Burrus, Virginia (1987) *Chastity as Autonomy: Women in the Stories of the Apocryphal Acts*. New York/Queenston: Mellen.

Cothenet, Edouard (1988) 'Le Protévangile de Jacques: origine, genre et signification d'un premier midrash chrétien sur la Nativité de Marie', in W. Haase (ed.) *Aufstieg und Niedergang der Römischen Welt*, Vol. 2.25.6. Berlin and New York: de Gruyter, 4252–69.

Davies, Stevan L. (1980) *The Revolt of the Widows: The Social World of the Apocryphal Acts*. New York: Seabury.

Dunn, Peter W. (1993) 'Women's Liberation, the *Acts of Paul*, and Other Apocryphal Acts of the Apostles', *Apocrypha* 4: 245–61.

Elliott, J. Keith (1993) *The Apocryphal New Testament*. Oxford: Clarendon Press.

Findlay, Adam Fyfe (1923) *Byways in Early Christian Literature: Studies in the Uncanonical Gospels and Acts*. Edinburgh: T&T Clark.

Gallagher, Eugene V. (1991) 'Conversion and Salvation in the Apocryphal Acts of the Apostles', *Second Century* 8: 13–29.

Germond, Paul (1996) 'A Rhetoric of Gender in Early Christianity: Sex and Salvation in the *Acts of Thomas*', in S. E. Porter and T. H. Olbricht (eds) *Rhetoric, Scripture and Theology: Essays from the 1994 Pretoria Conference*. Journal for the Study of the New Testament Supplement Series 131. Sheffield: Sheffield Academic Press, 350–68.

Gero, Stephen (1971) 'The Infancy Gospel of Thomas: A Study of the Textual and Literary Problems', *Novum Testamentum* 13: 46–84.

Holzberg, Niklas (1995) *The Ancient Novel*. London and New York: Routledge.

Junod, Eric and Kaestli, Jean-Daniel (1982) *L'Histoire des Actes apocryphes des apôtres du IIIe au IXe siècles*. Cahiers de la Revue de théologie et de philosophie 7. Lausanne: Labor et Fides.

—— (1984) *Acta Johannis*, 2 vols. Corpus Christianorum Series Apocryphorum 1–2. Turnhout: Brepols.

Kaestli, Jean-Daniel (1990) 'Fiction littérarire et réalité sociale: que peut-on savoir de la place des femmes dans le milieu de production des Actes apocryphes des Apôtres?', *Apocrypha* 1: 279–302.

Lallemann, Pieter J. (1998) *The Acts of John: A Two-stage Initiation into Johannine Gnosticism*. Studies on the Apocryphal Acts of the Apostles 4. Leuven: Peeters.

Lefkowitz, M. R. (1981) *The Lives of the Greek Poets*. London: Duckworth.

MacDonald, Dennis Ronald (1983) *The Legend and the Apostle: The Battle for Paul in Story and Canon*. Philadelphia, Pa.: Westminster Press.

Malherbe, Abraham J. (1986) 'A Physical Description of Paul', *Harvard Theological Journal* 79: 170–5.

Malina, Bruce J. and Neyrey, Jerome H. (1996) *Portraits of Paul: An Archaeology of Ancient Personality*. Louisville, Ky.: Westminster/John Knox.

Momigliano, Arnaldo (1971) *The Development of Greek Biography*. Cambridge, Mass.: Harvard University Press.

Morgan, J. R. and Stoneman, Richard (eds) (1994) *Greek Fiction: The Greek Novel in Context*. London and New York: Routledge.

Pao, David W. (1995) 'The Genre of the *Acts of Andrew*', *Apocrypha* 6: 179–202.

Perkins, Judith (1994) 'The Social World of the *Acts of Peter*', in J. Tatum (ed.) *The Search for the Ancient Novel*. Baltimore, Md.: Johns Hopkins University Press, 296–307.

Perry, Ben Edwin (1964) *Secundus the Silent Philosopher*. Philological Monographs 23. Ithaca, N.Y.: Cornell University Press for the American Philological Association.

Phillimore, Catherine M. (1881) *Fra Angelico*. London: Sampson Low, Marston, Searle & Rivington.

Prieur, Jean-Marc (1989) *Acta Andreae*, 2 vols. Corpus Christianorum Series Apocryphorum 5–6. Turnhout: Brepols.

Quilter, Harry (1880) *Giotto*. London: Sampson Low, Marston, Searle & Rivington.

Schneemelcher, Wilhelm (ed.) (1991–2) *New Testament Apocrypha*. 2 vols. trans. and ed. R. McL. Wilson. Louisville, Ky.: Westminster/John Knox Press and Cambridge: James Clarke.

Tissot, Yves (1988) 'L'encratisme des Actes de Thomas', in W. Haase (ed.) *Aufstieg und Niedergang der Römischen Welt*, Vol. 2.25.6. Berlin and New York: de Gruyter, 4415–30.

Vorster, Willem S. (1988) 'The Protevangelium of James and Intertextuality', in T. Baarda, A. Hilhorst, G. P. Luttikhuizen and A. S. van der Woude (eds) *Text and Testimony: Essays in Honour of A. F. J. Klijn*. Kampen: K. H. Kok, 262–75.

PART VII

EXTERNAL CHALLENGES

CHAPTER THIRTY-ONE

MARTYRDOM AND POLITICAL OPPRESSION

——— •✦• ———

W. H. C. Frend

MARTYRDOM AND ITS JEWISH LEGACY

Why were the early Christians so unpopular with their contemporaries and subjected to political oppression and martyrdom? The question has been asked by scholars ever since the Enlightenment. Ludwig Mosheim writing his *Ecclesiastical History Ancient and Modern* at Göttingen in the 1750s asks, 'how it was that the excellent nature of the Christian religion, its admirable tendency to promote both the welfare of the state and the private felicity of individuals' (1767: 48) should have brought persecution on itself rather than the protection of the state. Gibbon asked the same question in slightly different words 20 years later. The Christian religion's 'Sanctity of its moral precepts and the innocent and obscure lives' of the first Christians 'should have been received with due reverence, even by the unbelieving world' (1802: ch. xvi, opening sentence). Yet even though persecutions were comparatively rare – Polycarp, bishop of Smyrna, for instance, could assert (as reported by Eusebius) that he had served Christ 'eighty and six years' before he was brought to trial before the Proconsul of Asia as a Christian (*Historia Ecclesiastica* 4.15.20)[1] – there was always an underlying hostility towards the Christians. Tacitus in *c.* 115 CE describes them as a 'race of people hated for their abominations' and Christianity as a 'deadly superstition' (*superstitio*) at the time of the Neronian persecution in 64 (*Annals* 15.44.3), while even the heroism of the martyrs of Lyons, martyred in the amphitheatre of Lyons in August 177, evoked only uncomprehending pity among the Gallic provincials as their ashes were swept into the Rhone (*HE* 5.1.60, 62).

As we trace the saga of political oppression suffered by the Christians, we must also ask ourselves how far Christian attitudes and, in particular, a desire for martyrdom contributed to their fate. In the first generations of the church's existence the clue lies in the close association between Christianity and Judaism, that lasted through the first two centuries. Down to around 100 CE members of the Christ-movement regarded themselves as 'the new Israel'. Two of the later books of the New Testament, namely 1 Peter and the Letter of James, are addressed to the (Jewish) tribes of the Dispersion, and in particular, the Jews of the Roman provinces in Asia Minor (James 1.1; 1 Pet. 1.1). Reading *1 Clement (the First Epistle of Clement of Rome to the Corinthians*, written in Rome *c.* 95–100, it is clear also that the author regarded Christianity as a lineal progression from Judaism, quoting the Septuagint more than a hundred times and treating the Jewish hierarchy as foreshadowing the Christian ministry (*1 Clement* 42.5). During the second century, while the Christians were never able to make good their claim to be the legitimate successors of Judaism and Jesus Christ as the expected Messiah they remained in the eyes of the authorities a Judaistic sect, or as the Platonist and anti-Christian writer, Celsus, expressed it, apostates from Judaism (cited in Origen, *Contra Celsum* 2.1, 4).[2] It is interesting that at Smyrna in the mid-third century, the martyr, Pionius, not only quotes loud and long in his speeches from stories in the Old Testament, such as the destruction of Sodom and Gomorrah as the fate awaiting pagans, but recounts how he had heard since his childhood Jews discussing the story of the witch of Endor and the return of the prophet Samuel to life through her necromancy (*Martyrium Pionii* 13 and 14).[3] In western Asia Minor Jews and Christians had retained close if unneighbourly relations throughout this period.

The continued cultural affinity with Judaism and use of the Septuagint provided the Christians with models for attitudes towards the pagan world. Christ, as the martyrs of Lyons proclaimed in 177, was the 'faithful and true martyr' (*HE* 5.2.3; cf. Rev. 1:5), but running through Jewish scripture was the theme of the persecuted remnant. This was the faithful remnant of Israel oppressed but ultimately victorious over foreign overlords and idolators, looking forward to the establishment of a kingdom where God alone would be sovereign. Throughout the books of the Old Testament the loyal minority finds its champion in the prophets of Israel. The prophet was represented as a heroic figure destined to die rather than condone practices contrary to the Law. He is the prototype of the Christian martyr. In legend Isaiah and even Moses were added to Daniel and 'the Three Holy Children' as examples of those who were prepared to suffer rather than obey idolatrous rulers or the backsliders of their own race.[4] The Hasmonean period (167–63 BCE) unloosed a whole series of heroic accounts of victorious suffering for the sake of upholding the purity of God's Law. The Teacher of Righteousness himself is recorded in the Dead Sea Scrolls as being persecuted and hounded by the Wicked Priest (*Commentary on Habbakuk* 1.10–15). In the literature of the time the tradition of the noble deaths of the 'Maccabean' youths and their mother rather than bow to the idolatrous demands of the Seleucid king, Antiochus IV Epiphanes (179–165 BCE) became part and parcel of the martyr-literature of the church, even though the term 'martyr' was not used by the Jewish writers of the day. More than three centuries later in the account of the martyrs of Lyons, Blandina the confessor was compared to 'the noble mother who had encouraged her children and sent them forth triumphant to the king, having herself endured all the tortures of her children, hastened to them' (*HE* 5.1.55). The direct quotations from 2 Macc. 7:23–9, 41 show the author steeped in the Jewish Maccabean tradition. Sixty years later, in 236, Origen wrote his *Exhortation to Martyrdom* to his friend Ambrosius who appeared to be in danger from the persecution initiated by the emperor Maximin (235–38). Origen recounts in detail the story of the youths and their mother, paraphrasing 2 Macc. 6 and 7, and characterizing their deaths as 'an example of courageous martyrdom' (*Exhortation to Martyrdom* 22–3; Oulton and Chadwick 1954: 408–9). He then recalls the refusal of

Ananias, Azarias and Misael to sacrifice at the order of Nebuchadnezzar (*Exhortation to Martyrdom* 33). Jewish literature certainly, but 'even now', he claimed, Nebuchadnezzar is saying the very same thing to us, the true Hebrews 'whose home', Origen adds, 'is in the next world'. In the West, Cyprian recalls the seven Maccabean martyrs as examples for Christian martyrs to follow (Cyprian, *Epistle* 58.6 and *Ad Fortunatum* 11). During the Great Persecution of 303–13, Secundus of Tigisis, primate of Numidia compared (falsely!) his conduct with that of Eleazer the heroic priest in 2 Macc. 6:21–8 (Augustine, *Breviculus Collationis cum Donatistis* 3.13.25), while the confessors of Abitina (in western Tunisia) modelled their conduct on these heroes of Judaism (*Acta Saturnini* 16 [= PL 8, col. 700] 'Machabaeo more').

Apart from the glory and indeed the duty of dying rather than commit an act of idolatry another aspect of remnant theology absorbed by the Christians is revealed in the story of the 'Maccabean' mother. In a final speech put into her mouth by the writer of a tract, known as 4 Maccabees and probably composed in Antioch in *c.* 40 CE, the mother recounts how the boys' father read to them of Abel who was slain by Cain, and of Isaac who was offered as a burnt offering, and of Joseph in the prison. He spoke to them of Phineas the zealous priest, and he taught them about Ananias, Azarias and Misael in the fire. He sang the praises of Daniel in the den of lions and blest him, and he recalled the saying of Isaiah: 'Even though you pass through the fire, the flame shall not harm you.' He sang to them the psalm of David which says 'Many are the afflictions of the just' (4 Macc. 18.11–18).[5] The allusive style of the passage suggests that the writer expected his audience to be fully acquainted with the stories. Persecution and suffering were the lot of the righteous from the beginning of time and would endure until the end of the present age. This aspect of remnant theology found a ready reception by Christians in the early centuries. Appreciation that they were enacting a process decreed by God since creation steeled their resolve in the face of political oppression and persecution. In the Donatist church in fourth-century North Africa it survived the conversion of Constantine and the triumph of Christianity.[6]

The inspiration of Jewish tradition for Christian martyrdom and its continuing influence at least in the first half of the fourth century should be evident enough. The heroes of Judaism, not least the Maccabees, remained heroes of the Christians in East and West alike down to the early fifth century. This view has, however, been challenged by the eminent classical historian G. W. Bowersock in his Wiles Lectures given at Queen's University, Belfast in May 1993. Bowersock believed that the Christian idea of martyrdom originated among the Christian communities in the cities of western Asia Minor, and that rather than having 'anything to do with Judaism or with Palestine, it had everything to do with the Greco-Roman world, its traditions, its language and its cultural tastes'. 'Martyrdom', he adds 'was thus solidly anchored in the civil life of the Greco-Roman world of the Roman empire', running its course in 'the great urban spaces of the agora and amphitheatre, the principal settings for public discourse and for public spectacle' (Bowersock 1995: 28, 54).

It is true, of course, that to die for truth or for a noble cause were acts remembered and praised in Graeco-Roman provincial society. Regulus, Socrates and Empedocles passed into its folk-memory as examples of heroic deaths. There is also an interesting passage in Celsus' *True Word*, quoted by Origen, suggesting that valorous death extended to religion. 'If you happen to be a worshipper of God and someone commands you to act blasphemously or say some other disgraceful thing, you ought not to put any confidence in him at all. Rather than this, you must remain firm in the face of all tortures and endure any death rather than think anything profane about God.' Origen was surprised at Celsus' 'apparent recovery from demonic possession', though he rejects Celsus' subsequent naming of Helios or Athena as deities through whom 'the great God' was worshipped (Origen, *Contra Celsum* 8.66–7). It is clear that so far as concerns Origen, dying if necessary for the honour of a pagan 'great God' had not inspired the conduct of Christians. In his *Exhortation to Martyrdom* Origen makes no reference to Stoic or pagan martyrdom, but only to biblical and Maccabean examples of heroism. In the West, Tertullian cites the example of the death of Socrates with approval 'because he was destroying the gods' (*Apol.* 11.15 and 14.7–8), but elsewhere he criticizes him severely for his immorality. He was 'a pander' and his death was therefore no model for Christian martyrdom (*Apol.* 39.13, where 'the philosopher a pander' refers to Socrates).

If one looks closely at examples of pagan self-sacrifice in the first two centuries CE, one can see that much of it was inspired on behalf of avowedly political causes. 'Come up Romans', shouts the Alexandrian Appian on his condemnation to death in Rome for denouncing the emperor (Commodus?) as a tyrant, 'see a unique spectacle, an Alexandrian gymnasiarch and ambassador being led to execution' (*Acts of the Pagan Martyrs [Acta Alexandrinorum]*; Musurillo 1972: 69). Here one can see the latent pride of the Macedonian-descended citizen of Alexandria outraged at the 'crudity' of his imperial adversary (and no doubt, the Roman authorities), but there is no transcending religious motive, no call on the Name of God as we find in the Maccabean Acta. All one can say is that in the first two centuries CE there was a living pagan tradition of self-sacrifice for a cause, a preparedness if necessary to defy an unjust ruler, that existed alongside the developing Christian concept of martyrdom inherited from Judaism. The two ideals ran parallel, but the Christians were almost exclusively indebted to their Jewish past.

The distance separating them is emphasized by another aspect of Christian conduct that alienated pagan opinion both official and popular – namely, voluntary martyrdom. Martyrdom as stated by Tertullian was the mark of election,[7] the supreme honour to which a Christian might aspire. Little wonder then that it was eagerly sought. To quote Celsus again, Christians 'deliberately rush forward to arouse the wrath of an emperor which brings upon us blows and tortures and even death' (*Contra Celsum* 8.65). A well-known example of this attitude is quoted by Tertullian. In his address to the proconsul Scapula he tells how in *c.* 185 a mob confronted the proconsul of Asia, Arrius Antoninus, while he was on a judicial tour. They declared themselves to be Christians and clamoured to be put to death. The exasperated official, after ordering a few to be executed, replied, 'You wretches, if you want to die, you have cliffs to leap from and ropes to hang by' (*Ad Scapulam [To Scapula]* 5.1). Mass suicidal tendencies, *pace* Bowersock, belong to the Semitic rather than the Graeco-Roman tradition. It can be illustrated by the action of the Carthaginian survivors from their defeat at the battle of Himera in 480 BCE, or by the citizens of Carthage in 146 BCE, when they realized the hopelessness of resistance against the besieging Roman armies. Among the Jews, Philo records in *c.* 40 CE how his people were used to accepting death willingly as if it were immortality in order not to allow any of their ancestral customs, even the smallest, to be abrogated (*Legatio ad Gaium* 16.117; cf. the edition of Smallwood 1961). When the danger intensified of Caligula placing his statue within the Temple precincts in Jerusalem in 40–1 CE, scores of Jews went out to appeal to the governor of Syria, Petronius, to do his utmost to prevent this. They were organized in orderly units, unarmed, but, 'offering our own bodies as targets for the unerring missiles of those who wish to kill us' and threatening to 'bring our own wives to the Temple to slay them with our own hands' (Philo, *Legatio ad Gaium* 32.229–30, 234), if Caligula's plan went ahead. Not surprisingly, Petronius temporized, and by the time his messenger had reached Rome, Caligula was dead (24 January 41).

The Christians of Arrius Antoninus' time were continuing this Jewish tradition to the unfeeling amazement of their contemporaries. All in all, Roman authorities were tolerant of dissent if it was kept within the bounds of philosophical argument and was not considered dangerous to the state and its institutions (see Francis 1995). What was feared was malevolence towards these by magical practices and sub-versive attitudes and actions (Francis 1995: 93–4). The Christians were perceived as deviants. Christ, in Celsus' view, was a magician like his followers, preying on the gullible. These were the 'actions of one hated by God, and a wicked sorcerer' (*Contra Celsum* 1.71; Francis 1995: 139–40). The Jews were tolerated as worshippers of an ancient (if repulsive) religion (*Contra Celsum* 5.25), and they were prepared to pray for the emperor's welfare.[8] The Christians tried to subvert family life and traditional institutions (*Contra Celsum* 3.55), and were not prepared to give any recognition whatsoever to pagan rites or respect for the *genius* of the emperor.[9] They put them-selves beyond the pale of Graeco-Roman society. During the first two centuries CE, popular hatred previously reserved for the Jews was directed against them. Persecu-tions, sporadic but violent, were to be their lot. For their part, these provided Christians with the chance to bear witness to the truth of their faith. By the time the Book of Revelation was written (*c.* 90) witness had become witness to the death or 'martyrdom'. Antipas, it was stated (Rev. 2:13) was not deterred from his witness by fear of death. During the first three centuries CE two systems of religion and life confronted each other. In the end there could only be one victor, and Constantine decided that this must be Christianity.

POLITICAL OPPRESSION

It was against an already existing background in which persecution and readiness to die for the truth were accepted in Jewish tradition[10] that the Crucifixion took place. The death of Jesus followed in the wake of the priestly persecution of the Teacher of Righteousness, and the execution of John the Baptist at the orders of Herod Antipas. Jesus himself is represented in Luke's Gospel as the prophet-martyr going to his death in Jerusalem as the prophets of Israel had done so before him (Downing 1963: 284–93; Frend 1965: 79–83). His followers, as mentioned, looked back on his death as that of the 'faithful and true martyr', whose fate it was an honour to imitate.

Not surprisingly then, the story of the early church in Jerusalem was one characterized by oppression by Jesus' enemies, especially the Pharisees. According to the Acts of the Apostles, Stephen was stoned to death (7:54–8:1), and *c.* 41 the Christians suffered their first state-organized persecution through the execution of James, the brother of John, and the imprisonment of Peter at the orders of the conservative-minded King Herod Agrippa (Acts 12:1–5). The effect, however, was to disperse the Christians throughout Palestine and to spread their message accordingly. Barnabas became leader of this first Dispersion, while in Jerusalem, James, Jesus' brother, emerges as head of the church with Peter as his chief missioner.[11]

The period 40–62 sees the expansion of the church, first into Judaea and Samaria, then under Barnabas and Paul into Asia Minor, and finally through the Pauline missions and their influence to the Greek mainland and south Italy. The decisions of the Council of Jerusalem, which possibly occurred in 48 (Acts 15), enabled gentiles to become full members of the Christ-movement without first submitting to the Law of Moses. This decision imaginatively made by James opened the way for Paul's missions through Asia Minor, first with Barnabas, and then with his own personal followers. By 52, Paul had crossed from Troas into Macedonia and set up communities in Philippi, Thessalonica and Corinth, before settling for three years in Ephesus (54–7). He planned to travel to Rome and from Rome to the edge of the Mediterranean and Jewish world in the towns of south-Eastern Spain. However, he arrived in Rome *c.* 60 CE under conditions he may not have anticipated.

Everywhere Paul had preached had resulted in bitter divisions among the Jewish community. While members of Paul's new communities in Thessalonica and Beroea may not have been actually oppressed, there is little doubt that their lives were not secure. 'The men who have made trouble all the world over have now come here', was the cry of the local Jews (Acts 17:6). Paul himself was subjected to beatings in the synagogues and seems to have been forced out of Ephesus and mainland Asia Minor through mob action (Acts 19:23ff.). When he arrived in Jerusalem in 58 he was in danger from a conspiracy to murder him. Eventually, in Rome, the Jewish delegation which met him told him that while they had heard nothing from Judaea to his discredit, 'all we know about this sect [of Christians] is that no one has a good word to say for it' (Acts 28:22).

The scene was now set for the first great clash between the Christians and the Roman authorities and the former's first experience of political oppression at the latter's hands. On 19 July 64 Rome was the victim of a conflagration that gutted three entire quarters of the city. It lasted for six days and seven nights. Thousands were made homeless. There is no eyewitness record of the disaster, but from Tacitus' account, well documented though written 60 years later, suspicion soon fell on the emperor Nero himself (*Annals* 15.44). His grandiose schemes for town planning were well known, and an unexpected high wind may have turned intended controlled destruction of buildings that lay in its path into a catastrophe. What was to happen now is matter for speculation. The likelihood, however, is that Nero tried to make the Jews scapegoats and the latter diverted the odium on to the upstart synagogue of the Christians. The latter were already being tarred with the same brush as the Jews as 'haters of the human race'.[12]

A 'huge number' (perhaps including Peter and Paul) were rounded up and done to death, possibly in the Circus of Gaius and Nero near Vatican Hill. The macabre character of their deaths was designed to appease the gods whom the Christians were presumed to have outraged and to strike terror among the sectaries (Tacitus, *Annals* 15.44; cf. *1 Clement* 6.2). Suetonius, writing in *c.* 120, a few years after Tacitus, adds that the Christians were guilty of introducing a new and dangerous cult associated with magic.[13] For the senatorial writers of the day Nero's action, though cruel, had crushed a dangerous conspiracy fomented by a new type of malevolent Jewish sectary.

Christianity was now an illegal religion, though the persecution does not seem to have been extended outside Rome. Christians could be arrested and tried as Christians, with associated crimes (*flagitia*) forming a secondary charge. This situation was to persist until the end of the Great Persecution in 312.[14]

Although the evidence for relations between Christians and the Roman authorities during the next half century is relatively scanty, it indicates harassment and persecution by the authorities. 1 Peter, written probably in western Asia Minor *c.* 80, speaks of Christians being maligned by pagans 'as criminals' (1 Pet. 2:12), being called to account (3:15), and encountering shame 'as a Christian' (4:16). Not long after, when Revelation was written (*c.* 90) there were martyrs, such as Antipas killed in Pergamum (Rev. 2:13), while in Smyrna the Jews are blamed for oppressing the faithful (2:9). Whether the execution of Flavius Clemens and the exile of his wife Flavia Domitilla to the island of Pandetaria (Pantellaria) by Domitian in 95 on the charge of 'atheism' was an act of political oppression aimed at upper-class Christians is uncertain (Dio Cassius 67.14; Frend 1965: 212–13). Christians, however, were being arrested, as shown by the letters of bishop Ignatius of Antioch written to churches in Asia Minor during his slow progress under guard to Rome *c.* 107. Among the Christians themselves attitudes to the empire were ambivalent, extending all the way from outspoken loyalty by Paul (Rom. 13) and the writer of 1 Peter (2:17) to equally intense hostility demonstrated by the writer of Revelation, sustained by hopes of vengeance on the pagans at the Last Day (Rev. 6:9–10)

The curtain is finally raised by the correspondence between the emperor Trajan and Pliny the Younger, his governor of the Black Sea province of Bithynia in 111–13. Pliny had been sent out with special powers to check the widespread corruption and abuses to which the province had fallen victim. Christianity was one of these. A slow progress had taken him to Amastris at the Eastern end of the province where he was confronted by a number of denunciations against individual Christians.[15]

Though Pliny tells the emperor that he had never participated in investigations of Christians and did not know therefore the precise nature of 'the crime usually punished' (whether the name itself or the secret crimes [*flagitia*] connected with it), he knew that Christianity was illegal for he had no hesitation in ordering that those who confessed be executed. Roman citizens were despatched to Rome for judgement. What he terms the 'obstinacy and unbending perversity' of the Christians deserved in any case to be punished. Christianity was an illegal cult with the aggravating circumstance of the disloyal attitude of its members.

So far, so good. What prompted Pliny to consult Trajan however, was that he had been presented with an anonymous pamphlet denouncing a large number of people as Christians. Many of these protested that they had renounced Christianity, three, five and even 20 years ago.[16] There was also the practical problem, which must have been obvious, of feeding the large number of those incarcerated. They should be either executed or freed as soon as possible.

Before writing, Pliny had made his own investigations. He had weeded out some who had obviously recanted, having them recite a prayer to the gods at his dictation, making supplication with incense and wine to the emperor's statue, and finally, cursing Christ – as a malevolent demon – 'none of which acts, it is said those who are really Christians can be forced into performing' (10.96.5). Other former Christians explained in some detail the liturgy of the cult and the suspension even of the common meal, which they claimed consisted of ordinary food, on Pliny's order banning associations (*hetaerias*). Further inquiry, assisted by the torture of two female slaves who were styled 'deaconesses' convinced the governor that though the cult might be extravagant (*immodicam*) and depraved (*pravam*) it should not be regarded as a conspiracy (10.96.7). The situation had appeared serious, with Christian adherents in both town and country, but Pliny believed that his firm measures were already having their effect. Temples were being frequented once more, and animals brought forward for sacrifice. 'From this it may easily be supposed what a multitude of men can be reclaimed if there is place for repentance' (10.96.10).

The final sentence seems to have influenced Trajan's reply. While 'nothing can be laid down as a general ruling involving something like a set form of procedure', he said Christians were not to be sought out (i.e. treated as sacrilegious, *ipso facto* malefactors), but 'if they are accused and convicted they must be punished'; that is, Christianity remained illegal. However, anyone who recanted and 'worshipped our gods' should be pardoned. Anonymous accusations were not to be accepted. 'They were a very bad example and unworthy of our time' (10.97).

The emperor had attempted to square the circle and in the upshot had succeeded better than most similar compromises. He had praised Pliny's handling of the situation, and so long as they behaved with discretion Christians were unlikely to be denounced. None the less, their cult remained a 'superstition' – to other contemporaries such as Tacitus, a 'deadly' one – and hence anyone fairly convicted would be punished.

Trajan's ruling remained in force at least until the end of the century, when it was a subject of Tertullian's sarcastic wit (*Apologeticum* 2.6–9). It was reinforced in *c.* 125 when Hadrian sent a rescript to Minucius Fundanus, the proconsul of Asia, laying down that Christians had to be proved to be doing something 'contrary to the laws' before being punished. The courts were still open to genuine accusations, but libellous charges would be punishable 'by heavier penalties in accordance with their heinous guilt'.[17]

Justin Martyr attached a copy of the rescript to his First Apology (*1 Apol.* 68) written *c.* 155, suggesting that it secured the Christians from persecution, and 20 years later Melito of Sardes thought the same. They were wrong. We do not know the contents of the original petition to Fundanus' predecessor Serenius Granianus, but James Stevenson's suggestion that it may have contained charges of cannibalism, incest and sacrilege (1967: 22), such as Justin mentions, may not be far off the mark. They could have been included among the 'abominations' of which Christians were accused by the populace, according to Tacitus writing in *c.* 115. If that were so, Hadrian said, and if the petitioners could prove their case in the courts, the Christians would be punished. In effect, however, it needed an exceptionally determined individual to await the arrival of the provincial governor on judicial circuit to bring an accusation involving the death penalty against a Christian, especially because if he failed the charge could rebound on his shoulders (Sherwin-White 1952). The other contingency was that some natural disaster, such as as earthquake, would prompt the provincials to blame the Christians, and set off a persecution against them. The remainder of the second century provides examples of both situations.

The middle years of the second century provide instances both of martyrdom and political oppression. The second Jewish revolt saw the Christians persecuted by Bar Kochba's men. Bar Kochba, Justin claimed, gave orders that Christians alone should be led to cruel punishments, unless they would deny Jesus Christ and utter blasphemy (*1 Apol.* 1.31). Thirty years later, in the 160s, the Jews of Smyrna made common cause with the pagan provincials against bishop Polycarp.

The main conflict was, of course, between the Christians and the Roman authorities and the populace. The church was beginning to develop into a powerful organization. By 150, the great majority of, if not all, mainstream churches were organized hierarchically under a bishop or presbyter. Justin shows that a distinctive liturgy centred on the Eucharist was in place and that the canon of the New Testament was taking shape, to be read alongside traditional Jewish scripture. Under the pressure of gnostic and Marcionite deviations, the church was beginning to establish a distinctive canon of scripture and a theology based on its understanding of the nature of the Trinity. Credal statements were designed to exclude heretics, especially gnostics, by emphasizing the true humanity of Christ. Finally, throughout the Greek-speaking world bishops and other representatives of communities were keeping in contact with each other and setting out their views by correspondence over considerable distances. In 177/8 an account of the martyrdoms of the Christians at Lyons was on its way to their 'brethren in Asia and Phrygia who have the same faith and hope of redemption as you' (Eusebius, *HE* 5.1.3). A little later, (*c.* 190) the tombstone of Avircius Marcellus, bishop of Hieropolis in Phrygia, shows a merchant who was also an orthodox bishop travelling from Nisibis on Rome's Euphrates frontier all the way to Rome, finding the same Eucharistic and baptismal liturgy in force throughout all the communities he had visited.[18] Near the end of the century, Irenaeus' five books *Against the Heresies* shows a self-confident and well-organized church firmly based on senior communities that could claim Apostolic foundation, of which Rome was the pre-eminent example. The challenge to the primacy of the pagan cults and the immortal gods of Rome was increasing.

But it was not yet regarded as formidable. One may agree with Gibbon's assessment of the second century CE of a Graeco-Roman world, prosperous, tolerant of local religious differences and ruled by a succession of rulers of exceptional ability (1802: opening sentences of ch. 1). Their success is shown by the growth of towns and cities all over the Roman empire, by an expansion of agriculture into areas previously semi-desert, by the fine pottery (Samian ware) found even on insignificant sites in distant Roman Britain. The urban classical civilization was sure of itself, and its representatives could afford to be tolerant within the framework of the law of mavericks and religious fanatics. Authentic accounts of the trials of Christians that have survived show that even in the Great Persecution senior administrators, including proconsuls, often did their best to save Christians from what they considered dangerous folly. 'Respect your age . . . Swear by the genius of Caesar and say "Away with the atheists"', urged the proconsul of Asia on Polycarp (Eusebius, *HE* 4.15.15). 'We too are a religious people and our religion is a simple one: we swear by the genius of our lord, the emperor and we offer prayers for his health – as you also ought to do.' Thus, Vigellius Saturninus strove to persuade the Scillitan martyrs at Carthage in July 180, and he offered them a time for reflection before he passed sentence (*Acta Scillitanorum*; Musurillo 1972: 86–9). The offer was spurned, but that it was made indicates that oppression as such was far from the minds of second-century senior provincial administrators. All they wanted was conformity as proof of loyalty.

Oppression when it took place came from the people, stirred by irrational fears that by 150 were beginning to find expression also in deep-felt prejudices among some members of the senatorial class. Thus, Marcus Cornelius Fronto, tutor to the emperor Marcus Aurelius (161–80) was already painting a picture of Christian depravity which provincials would be accepting as true.[19] Incest, lust and black magic were to be the popular charges against the Christians for the next half century and act as a spur to their harassment, torture and death. In contemporary accounts of the martyrdom of Polycarp and the martyrs of Lyons, the initiative for persecution came from the people. 'All the multitude of heathen and Jews living in Smyrna cried out with uncontrollable wrath and loud shouts, "This is the teacher of Asia [Polycarp], the father of the Christians, the destroyer of our gods, who teaches many neither to offer sacrifice nor to worship"'. They begged Philip the Asiarch to let loose a lion on Polycarp.[20] In the end Polycarp was burnt alive, Jews and gentiles making common cause against him.

At Lyons, it is doubtful whether the governor would have acted on his own against the Christians. He and his predecessors had let bishop Pothinus reach the age of 90 as leader of the community, which suggests a long period of official tolerance. The authorities' hands were forced by popular clamour in 177 CE. There was a mob uprising of increasing intensity against the Christian community (Eusebius, *HE* 5.1.7–8). The city authorities reacted, and had the Christians arrested and imprisoned until the governor arrived. Judgement could only be pronounced by him. Confronted by a semi-riotous situation the latter first allowed matters to take their course, letting the Christians be tortured. He went further, and condemned to death as murderers and perpetrators of other horrific crimes (the *flagitia*, about which Pliny had written to Trajan) those who had first denied that they were Christians. He was, however, a stickler for legality, and when he heard that one of the confessors was a Roman citizen, halted the proceedings to write to the emperor for advice (Eusebius, *HE* 5.1.44). Marcus Aurelius replied, on the lines of Trajan's answer to Pliny, that those who confessed should be 'tortured to death', but those who recanted should be freed (Eusebius, *HE* 5.1.47). Few seem to have benefited from the emperor's decision, and Blandina and the 47 Christians who perished in the amphitheatre of Lyons with her became heroines and martyrs for posterity.

By *c.* 200 however, the Christians in the Greek-speaking world were beginning to earn respect from some of their contemporaries. One of these was the physician Galen. Christians were known, he said, to be self-controlled in their food and drink

Figure 31.1 The amphitheatre at Lyons, scene of the mass martyrdom of Christians in 177 CE. Photo J. C. N. Coulston.

and 'in their pursuit of justice have attained a pitch not inferior to that of genuine philosophers'.[21] This was a different view from that of Celsus, but the emergence of Christianity in Latin-speaking North Africa *c.* 180 was once again to sharpen the impact of religious conflict and emphasize the irreconcilable difference between the Roman gods and Christianity. The confessor Speratus' words to the proconsul of Africa in 180 illustrate the depth of alienation some North African Christians felt towards the empire. He refused to recognize 'the empire of this age'. His lord was the 'king of kings and emperor of all nations'. And he and his companions went cheerfully to their deaths. 'Today we are martyrs in the heavens. Thanks be to God'.[22]

There was also a theological basis for this defiance; namely the primary role of the Holy Spirit in North African Christian thought. In the East, discussions on doctrine had ranged round the relations between God the Father and the Divine Word Incarnate. The Holy Spirit's existence was accepted, but no particular role had been assigned to Him. For Origen, he was still less 'than the Father and Son and dwelt within the saints alone' (*De Principiis* 1.3.5). He was the highest of the angels with correspondingly slight influence on human affairs. In the West, however, and in particular among the North African Christians, the role of the Spirit was crucial. The Spirit that inspired the Hebrew prophets was deemed to inspire the confessors. The church in North Africa was the Church of the Martyrs, and it deserved the title thoroughly. Christians in Carthage were as unpopular as their counterparts were in

825

Lyons and for the same reasons – namely, suspicion of incest, adultery and black magic practised in their rites,[23] and as the cause of natural disasters.[24] But they were also 'ever ready for death' (Tertullian, *De Spectaculis* 1). Already in *c.* 197 we hear of Christians being imprisoned, and as Tertullian (*c.* 160–240) declared, 'the Holy Spirit entered the prison with them' (*Ad Martyras* 1.3.) The Spirit was to be the force that sustained their faith, and their willingness to die cheerfully for their cause.

At the end of his Apology, written in *c.* 197, Tertullian claims that 'we multiply whenever we are mown down by you. The blood of Christians is seed' (*Apol.* 50.13). He was exaggerating. For some individuals, perhaps former Stoics like himself, the courage of the Christians in the face of death provided the impulse to 'enquire further', as he says, 'into what lay within their religion and having inquired to join it' (*Apol.* 50.15). But for countless others, the Christians were simply fanatics, 'faggot-fellows' and 'half-axle men, because we are tied to a half-axle post', who wished to die (*Apol.* 50.3).

One important test of opinion came in 202–3 with the execution of Perpetua, Felicitas and their companions in the amphitheatre at Carthage (see Figures 40.4, 40.5) on 7 March 203 (Musurillo 1972: 106–31). We cannot be sure whether these Christians converts, Perpetua coming from a well-known Carthaginian family, were the victims of a rescript directed by the emperor Septimius Severus against conversion either to Judaism or Christianity.[25] All that can be said is that between 202 and 206 Christians were arrested in Carthage, Rome, Corinth and Alexandria, four cities that are mentioned in contemporary literature (Frend 1965: 322–3), and that while senior clergy do not seem to have been troubled, converts faced the death penalty. While in prison Perpetua and her companions exercised considerable influence on their gaolers,[26] but once committed to the amphitheatre the spectators saw them as fanatics, traitors to the established order, threatening doom and destruction against the authorities who had condemned them. They alternated between horror at witnessing women being sent to their deaths naked, and pleasure at seeing the presbyter Saturus struck down by a leopard's single bite. 'Well washed, well washed' (*Salvum lotum, salvum lotum*), they cried in crude satire at Christian baptism (*Passiones sanctarum Perpetuae et Felicitatis* 21.2). Martyrdom was not to be a seed for Christians generally, until the Great Persecution (303–12) produced a gradual but permanent revision of attitudes towardss them. At the time, 'Christianos ad leonem' was the popular cry (Tertullian, *Apologeticum* 40.2).

The persecutions of the first decade of the third century may have been partly official-inspired as well as expressions of popular antipathy. They were followed by a period of calm until the murder of Alexander Severus in 235. That emperor (222–35) was remembered later as having 'allowed the Christians to be' ('Christianos esse passus est'; Lampridius, *Alexander Severus* 22.8.4[27]) and it was in this period that the earliest Christian catacombs came into existence.[28] But mob attacks against Christians did not cease.[29] There was still pride in Rome for the worship of Jupiter, and one of the reasons for their hostility towardss Elagabalus was that he had preferred Syrian gods to him.[30] Christians also suffered at the same time and it is now believed Pope Callistus was thrown down a well by the mob in the year 222.[31]

The tolerance of Alexander Severus towards the Christians was roughly reversed by his successor, the Thracian soldier Maximin. This time one may speak of 'political

Figure 31.2 The Colosseum in Rome. Photo J. C. N. Coulston.

oppression'. Around 236 CE a short, sharp persecution was directed against the church's leaders – lay as well as clerical (Eusebius, *HE* 6.28). It inspired Origen to write his *Exhortation to Martyrdom* to his friend Ambrosius. On Maximin's removal in 238, the church enjoyed another spell of toleration under his successors, Gordian III (238–44) and Philip the Arab (244–9). The Christians' sudden reversal of fortunes under Decius (249–51) was as much due to the ever-increasing threats to the frontiers of the empire as to Decius' hostility towards the religious policies of his predecessor. Christianity had now emerged as one of the main internal problems in the empire.

With the advent of Decius a new situation arose. For the first time, perhaps with the exception of Severus' rescript, we enter a period of state-sponsored persecution. Popular perception of the Christians seems to have been no more favourable than in the past. In 248 Alexandria had witnessed a veritable pogrom when mobs turned on the Christians; some were seized and lynched, while others were dragged into temples and forced to sacrifice (Eusebius, *HE* 6.41). Origen, writing at the same period in Caesarea, foresaw the likelihood of a universal persecution.[32] The event itself, however, was to some extent accidental. In 249 Gothic tribes crossed the Danube and invaded the Balkan provinces of the empire. The emperor Philip failed to drive them out and in the autumn of 249 was removed in favour of his general and prefect of Rome C. Quintus Messius Decius. On 3 January 250 Decius, it would appear, ordered that the usual annual sacrifice to Jupiter and the Roman gods on the Capitol should be repeated throughout the empire.[33] The edict was not specifically aimed against the Christians, but they were caught in a dilemma. Either they obeyed the emperor's orders or they stood by their obligation not to sacrifice, and risked death.

The vast majority chose the former course. At Carthage, Cyprian, who had only recently become bishop, laments the mass apostasies that were taking place and records how crowds besieged the temples so much so that priests asked them to return the next day.[34] The sacrifice had become a token of loyalty to the empire, of solidarity 'with the Romans'. An inscription from Aphrodisias, the provincial capital of Caria, shows the emperor thanking the citizens for their support 'of our empire' and for 'their just sacrifices and prayers' (*Monumenta Asiae Minoris Antiqua* 8.424, of Oct.–Nov. 250). Decius' aim was the restoration of the values of the past, and he himself adopted the name Trajanus to emphasize his kinship with the ideals of that 'Optimus princeps'.

Resisters were few. In Smyrna every effort was made to persuade the presbyter Pionius and his small band of followers to sacrifice, and follow the example of bishop Euctemon 'and everyone else' who had performed pagan rites in the temple of Nemesis.[35] Pagan officials openly ridiculed the Christian religion. There were loud guffaws when Pionius proclaimed his faith in the 'crucified one' (*Martyrdom of Pionius* [*Martyrium Pionii*] 16). To the very last moment, efforts were made to save him from the results of what the townspeople of Smyrna regarded as a useless act of folly (*Martyrdom* 21).

In Egypt a series of 43 certificates (*libelli*) have been discovered on papyri which show how the act of sacrifice was regarded as a solemn, formal act taking place before a supervisory commission. One example may be quoted:

> First hand. To the commission chosen to superintend the sacrifices at the villae of Alexander's Isle. From Aurelius Diogenes, son of Satabous of the village of Alexander's Isle, aged 72 years with a scar over the right eyebrow. I have always sacrificed to the gods and now in your presence and in accordance with the edict I have made sacrifice and poured a libation and partaken of the sacred victims. I request you to certify this below. Farewell. I, Aurelius Diogenes have presented this petition.

It was a civic act formally witnessed and exactly dated, undertaken by an individual often on behalf of his family.[36]

Meantime, Decius had swept the Goths out of Illyricum, and commemorated his success on his coinage, notably the 'Pannonia' type on Decius' *antoniniani* and *sestertii*. The church faced the severest test in its history. It was still an overwhelmingly urban organization, which meant that its leaders were usually well-known though not well-liked by their fellow-citizens. They could be denounced, and their congregations marked out for repression. By the end of 250, Rome had lost its bishop. Fabian had been one of the first to be executed (20 January 250), the emperor allegedly saying that he would rather face a usurper than another bishop (Cyprian, *Ep.* 55.9 (Hartel, *CSEL* iii.2, p. 630). Babylas of Antioch had suffered similarly (Eusebius, *HE* 6.39.4). Presumably Antioch was too tempting a target for Persian attack to risk disloyalty among its prominent citizens. In Carthage and Alexandria only a core of dedicated believers survived. Rescue came, however, first from the fact that no follow-up had been planned which was designed to extirpate Christianity. A day set aside for sacrifices was proclaimed, and when it passed no further measures were apparently taken. Christians who lay low escaped. Second, in June 251 Decius was killed in battle against the Goths at Abrittus, among the marshes of the Danube delta whither he had advanced too hastily. The persecution ended with his death. Though there was a brief return under Gallus and Aemilian, this time apparently directed against the Christian leaders specifically, the crisis was over. Cyprian and Dionysius of Alexandria returned to their respective sees and were free to begin the work of salvage and reconstruction.

This is not the place to discuss Cyprian's policy towards the lapsed or its consequences for the North African theology of the church, a matter dealt with by James Alexander in Chapter 37. Suffice it to say that within a few years the church had recovered its numbers and on 1 September 256 Cyprian was able to assemble 87 bishops to support his view that heretics and schismatics coming into the church should be rebaptized, against the opposite view held by Pope Stephen.

The renewal of persecution by the emperor Valerian (253–60) in the summer of 257 may have had an economic as well as a religious motive. The 40 years between the death of Gordian III in 244 and the accession of Diocletian in 284 witnessed a decline in the standard of living throughout the cities of the empire. In North Africa, for example, few new public buildings were built in this period and dedications, whether private or public, are scarce. There was increasing insecurity in Numidia and Mauretania.[37] There was a catastrophic decline in the value of the currency, the silver content of the *antoninianus*, the coin most frequently used, dropping in *c.* 260 from 15% to a bare 2% by 265, represented by a thin silver wash on base metal (Mattingly and Sydenham 1927: 5–8). Local bronze coinage, the pride of the cities of the East, ceased. Aqueducts and other public buildings were neglected, and dedications to the gods declined correspondingly. The church, however, seems to have weathered the storm. In Carthage, the clergy were paid a stable monthly stipend.[38] In Rome the church had resources enough to maintain '1500 widows and poor persons' on its payroll (Eusebius, *HE*, 6.43.11). When Kabyle tribes struck in North Africa in 253, the church in Carthage was able to subscribe 100,000 sesterces for the ransom of prisoners (Cyprian, *Ep.* 62.4; *CSEL* 3.2, p. 700). Amid increasing signs of economic decline the relative wealth of the Christian church was a tempting target.

This time persecution was directed specifically against the church, as an institution, and its leaders. Eusebius puts the blame for the events that took place in the summer of 257 on Macrianus, Valerian's finance minister (*curator summarum rationum*), rather than on the emperor himself, whom he describes as having previously been well disposed towards the Christians (Eusebius, *HE* 7.10.3; Frend 1965: 422–3). The actual texts of Valerian's edicts have perished, but we can get a very fair idea of their tenor from Cyprian's letters and from Dionysius of Alexandria's account of his encounter with the deputy prefect of Egypt. The empire was in peril. Dura-Europos, the main fortress on the Euphrates frontier, had fallen to the Persians after a heroic defence (autumn 256). The favour of 'the gods' must be regained. Hence, Christians were required to 'recognize' the Roman gods, the 'saving gods' as the deputy prefect of Egypt, Aemilian told Dionysius.[39] The counterpart was that no

Christian services were to be held and the cemeteries where these would take place would be confiscated.[40] The authorities struck at the Christian leadership and institutional worship. Both Cyprian and Dionysius were summoned before high officials, and both refused to compromise. Cyprian asserted 'I am a Christian and a bishop. I know no other gods except the one true God', but he added that prayer was offered for the safety of the emperors (*Acta Proconsularia* 1). Dionysius answered the deputy prefect similarly but more courteously. For the latter the gods preserved the empire, and the Christian God was 'contrary to nature'. The Christians, however, were at liberty to worship their God so long as they worshipped 'the gods whom we all know' (Eusebius, *HE* 7.11.7). Like Cyprian, Dionysius refused and both bishops were sent into exile. Some of Cyprian's fellow-bishops fared less well, being committed to hard labour in the mines (Cyprian, *Ep*. 79).

The second edict a year later was more severe. Cyprian is our chief authority.[41] Bishops, presbyters and deacons were to be arrested and punished. For the first time laymen were included. Senators, *viri egregii* and knights (*equestres*) would lose their dignities and property; likewise the *matronae* would be banished. In addition, the *Caesariani*, imperial civil servants, would be reduced to slavery and sent in chains to work on the imperial estates (*Ep*. 80.2). This was an attempt to deprive the church of its leaders, any social standing it possessed, and its property, in effect to root it out; and one notices that upper-class Roman women (*matronae*) were significant enough to require special measures.

In North Africa, Cyprian was summoned before the new proconsul, Galerius Maximus. The ensuing dialogue showed clearly the political character of the conflict that had now developed between the two religious systems. Within a few years the church had become a state within a state. Cyprian was condemned as the ringleader of 'an unlawful association'. He had lived an 'irreligious life'. He was 'an open enemy of the religion of Rome'.[42] Despite being given a chance to conform to the religious observances of the emperors, he had refused to do so. He would therefore be executed. He died a martyr on 14 September 258. In Rome, Pope Xystus II and four deacons were discovered in the catacomb of Callistus and executed on the spot on 6 August 258.[43]

This time the persecution continued. During 259 Theogenes, bishop of Hippo, and two other bishops were executed, and Cirta, the capital of Numidia, could boast the martyrs Marianus (a reader) and Jacobus (a deacon) and their companions. The populace was still strongly hostile. Political oppression had not yet outrun popular opinion.[44] The hand of the authorities was only stayed when news of the capture of Valerian by the Persians, near Edessa, filtered through. By 20 July 260 a new bishop of Rome, Dionysius (260–9) had been elected.[45] A rescript of Gallienus to the bishops in Egypt restoring their 'places of worship' (261) formally ended three years of repression (Eusebius, *HE* 7.13).

In the 'little peace' that lasted for the next 43 years, the church gained the advantage. Apart from Paul of Samosata, bishop of Antioch from 261 until deposed by a council in 268 for heresy, the church produced no outstanding leader that has left his mark on history. The emperors for their part were engaged in repelling attacks by Germanic barbarian invaders or dealing with usurpers, and had little time for the Christians. Only Aurelian (270–5), first acting as an arbitrator between Paul of Samosata and his opponents over the ownership of the bishop's house in Antioch in 271 (Eusebius, *HE* 7.30.19–21), and then threatening to renew persecution in 275,[46] concerned himself with the affairs of the church. Christianity, however, remained illegal, especially in the army,[47] and a scattering of martyrs are recorded from these times. Yet all the while the church was prospering. In Rome, the catacombs underwent a huge expansion. By *c.* 300, that of Peter and Marcellinus contained about 11,000 burials in galleries that extended over two kilometres (Guyon 1987: 96–102). Sixty years later, Optatus of Milevis records that there were 40 churches in Rome at this time (*De Schismate Donatistarum* 2.4.5; *CSEL* 26, p. 39). Dated burial inscriptions begin to appear in Rome and Thessalonica, testifying perhaps to the dedicants' belief in the freedom and stability of their church. More significant was the decline of the pagan cults in some of the major provinces of the empire. In Numidia the last dated dedications to Saturn, hitherto the supreme deity in North Africa, end in 272.[48] In Cyrenaica the last dedications to Apollo date to 287–8 (Roques 1988: 318). Ancient expressions of language, such as inscriptions in hieroglyphics, fade out after the 250s, and in rural Egypt as well as in rural North Africa and parts of Asia Minor the pagan cults were being replaced by the Christian church. The beginnings of Coptic monasticism through Anthony in *c.* 270 typified the change that was coming over the Mediterranean world.

Diocletian (284–305) had been emperor for 18 years before he and his colleague Maximian (286–305) seriously considered a trial of strength with the Christians. They had found the empire in dire straits, threatened the length of its frontiers by enemies, the army mutinous, the economy at a low ebb even after Aurelian's reform of the coinage. In turn, the central and provincial administration, army, coinage, the economy represented by the Edict of Prices (in 301) had been reformed; also the cults, and in particular the imperial cults, had been restored in the cities along with public buildings that had decayed or collapsed in the previous half century.[49] The most pressing enemy, Persia, had been defeated in 297. Moral discipline was the subject of edicts, and in 298 (or 302) what Diocletian regarded as a noxious import from Persia, Manichaeism, proscribed. Manichaean literature was to be handed over to be burnt and members of the sect were made liable to execution. Old religious beliefs must be protected, said the emperors.[50] It would be the turn of the Christians next.

Pressure against them gradually built up. During the 290s a bitter propaganda campaign had been launched against them by Porphyry of Tyre (*c.* 232–304) and his Neoplatonist allies. They sought to discredit the New Testament, in particular Christ's disciples, and to downgrade Christ himself to the level of a wonderworking prophet.[51] After 298, however, the emperors became involved. In that year, Christians were believed to have disrupted a sacrifice at Antioch at which Diocletian and his Caesar, Galerius, were present. Galerius was strongly anti-Christian, and after his defeat of the Persians in 297 his star was in the ascendant. Measures were undertaken to expel Christians from the Roman army. In North Africa there were martyrdoms among soldiers who refused to perform customary sacrifices.[52] As Eusebius records, 'little by little persecution against us began',[53] until in the winter of 302–3 after a visit to the oracle of Apollo at Miletus the emperors' minds were made up. On 23 February 303 the first edict in a ten-year battle with the Christians was promulgated in the imperial capital, Nicomedia. The feast of Terminalia would mark the beginning of the end of the Christian church (Lactantius, *De mortibus persecutorum* [*On the Death of the Persecutors*] 12.1).

The first edict recalled those of Valerian, without the sanction of the death penalty – Diocletian, according to the Christian writer and teacher Lactantius who was at Nicomedia at the time, had forbidden bloodshed (*De mortibus persecutorum*, 11.8). There were to be no martyrs. Churches were to be destroyed and scriptures handed over to the authorities for burning. Church property, including chattels, would be confiscated, and Christian officials removed from their offices. In civil life, Christians were subjected to a variety of annoyances. The *honestiores* were to lose privileges of birth and status, and Christians were banned the courts, where litigants were expected to cast incense on an altar before pleading their case.[54]

In the provinces the edict was enforced to the letter, though not always with enthusiasm. Courtesies were observed up to a point, if events at Cirta, the capital of Numidia, are typical. There was a good deal of prevarication there by the clergy before bibles and church property were handed over to the municipal authorities.[55] Elsewhere, however, as at Caesarea in Palestine, there was more harshness.[56] During the summer of 303 further instructions were despatched to the provinces aimed against the episcopate. Bishops were to be arrested and forced to sacrifice, and meantime, the impossibility of a bloodless persecution was being demonstrated. In Phrygia, the seizure of a church in a nameless town resulted in the killing of the entire Christian congregation within it (Eusebius, *HE* 8.11.1).

In the autumn, Diocletian left Nicomedia for Rome where he intended to celebrate his Vicennalia. In the course of the customary amnesty for criminals bishops and others who had been arrested were compelled to make some gesture that implied 'sacrifice' and then freed. On his return from Rome, however, Diocletian became ill and unable to govern. Power fell to his Caesar, Galerius. In the spring of 304 the latter ordered a general sacrifice by the Christians. The edict was also enforced in the dominions of Diocletian's western colleague, Maximian.[57]

This was the turning point in the persecution, and also in the fortunes of the Christians. Up to that moment, obdurate congregations, such as that of Abitina (Henchir Souar) in western Tunisia, had been arrested and imprisoned,[58] but, as Eusebius points out, in the East measures had been confined to the clergy.[59] Now, all Christians were involved. Would they rebel against 'our gods' or comply? The names of 34 North African martyrs were preserved on an inscription inscribed on a balustrade found in the church of Candidus at Ammaedara (Haidra, in south-west Tunisia) to be repeated on a celebratory mosaic in Byzantine times.[60] At Milevis in Numidia other martyrs suffered at the hands of the governor, Valerius Florus, on the 'day of incense burning' (*dies thurificationis*).[61] In Palestine Eusebius chronicles scrupulously the names and sufferings of Christians there. A large number were sent to the mines (*Mart. Pal.* 8.1).

As in previous persecutions there were some purely voluntary martyrs. At Catania in Sicily the deacon Euplus shouted from outside the governor's (*consularis*) office, 'I wish to die for the name of Christ, for I am a Christian.' Carrying the Gospels he was brought before the startled governor, and after some argument reinforced by torture he was granted his wish (12 August 304, Musurillo 1972: 310–19).

Throughout the short but very sharp persecution in North Africa, the same irreconcilables remained. The last dated trial that has survived, that of Crispina of Thagora at Theveste, shows confessor and judge enunciating the same sentiments as had their predecessors a century or more before.[62] The proconsul Annius Anullinus is shown to be as reasonable as his predecessors, far from the raging tyrant of later legend. 'Do you know of what is commanded by the sacred decree?' he asks Crispina. 'No, but I have never sacrificed and shall not do so save to the one true God and to our Lord, Jesus Christ, his Son who was born and died.' 'Break with this superstition', said Anullinus 'and bow your head to the sacred rites of the gods of Rome.' That was all that was asked. Crispina's refusal echoed that of the Scillitan martyrs in 180. Anullinus tried persuasion and argument, but, even without some gruesome details added possibly by a Donatist editor, the end was inevitable. Crispina, accompanied by five companions, was executed. A *martyrium* was raised on the site of her execution, to be succeeded by a vast (Donatist?) pilgrimage centre designed as a permanent memorial to her defiance and fortitude.[63]

By now, the martyrdoms and steadfast conduct of many of the Christians were having their effect on pagan morale. Lactantius again; he claims that the numbers of Christians were increasing continuously and that persecution was one means permitted by God.[64] Elsewhere, he describes how 'great numbers were driven from the worship of the gods by their hatred of cruelty'. People, but in far greater numbers than in Tertullian's day, were questioning 'whether it was without reason that worship of the gods was so hated that men and women would rather suffer torture and death than participate'. These things, he added, had great effect.[65] The initiative for the first time, but decisively, now lay with the Christians. They were at last winning the argument.

Diocletian and Maximian abdicated amid great military displays on 1 May 305. Their successors were Constantius in the West and Galerius in the East. The persecution was not renewed in the West, but was continued in the East after a respite of about eleven months. The new Caesar, Maximin, was as strong a pagan as Galerius, but more prudent. There was a fifth edict in 306 which again required all to sacrifice, military officers checking the names of those who approached the temples (Eusebius, *Mart. Pal.* 4.8). Maximin, however, was not content with repression. He reorganized the pagan priesthood in his domains, which included Egypt, Palestine and Syria, on hierarchical lines in imitation of the Christian hierarchy (*HE* 8.14.9; 9.4.2), and unleashed a propaganda attack on the Christians. A supposed account by Pontius Pilate of Christ's trial was circulated in schools (*HE* 9.5; 7.1). It had enough effect to influence Eusebius of Caesarea to write his *Ecclesiastical History* relating the church's struggles and political oppression and heresy down to and including the present persecution.

Decisive help for the Christians was now at hand. In the spring of 311 Galerius became seriously ill. Realizing his end was near, and that he could not defeat the Christians, he drafted an edict recognizing his failure, allowing the Christians to 'exist again' and beseeching their prayers for his recovery. In vain, the edict was promulgated on 30 April and he died on 5 May (Lactantius, *De mortibus* 34–5; Stevenson 1967 [Document 246]).

There was now one final, dreadful flicker of state oppression. Maximin seized the opportunity to take over Galerius' dominions in Asia Minor with the imperial capital, Nicomedia. Galerius' edict was either sidestepped or ignored. In Asia Minor a 'plebiscite' was organized through the provincial councils to vote the expulsion of the 'atheists' from beyond the provincial boundaries.[66] Egypt, however, witnessed the worst horrors, which would leave an indelible mark on the memory of the Copts. On 25 November 311 bishop Peter of Alexandria was executed, and the persecution extended to the now Christianized Coptic villages. Eusebius of Caesarea was in Egypt at the time and wrote down what he saw, 'And we ourselves beheld, when we were at these places many all at once in a single day, some of whom suffered decapitation others punishment of fire; so that the murderous axe was dulled and worn out ... As soon as sentence was given against the first, some from one quarter and others from another would leap up before the tribunal and declare themselves Christians' (*HE* 8.9; 4–5). The martyrs had at last triumphed. Not surprisingly, the Coptic church commemorates its martyrs by beginning its era as 'the era of the Martyrs' with the accession of Diocletian in 284.

The end of the persecutions was decided, however, by events in the West. In the Gallic and Danubian provinces of the empire, Christians were not numerous and persecution had amounted to little. Constantius had died in 306, and after a series of political manoeuvres his son Constantine became ruler of the Gallic provinces and Spain in 310. Two years later he challenged Maxentius, son of the former emperor Maximian who had seized Italy and Africa, for control of the whole of the West. He succeeded. Maxentius was defeated and killed at the battle of the Milvian Bridge, five miles north of Rome, on 28 October 312. Constantine had previously been a convinced worshipper of the Sun-god to whom he had attributed his successes.[67] Now, as the result of a vision on the eve of his decisive battle with Maxentius, he came to believe that Christ, represented by a cross of light in his vision, was indeed God (Lactantius, *De Mortibus* 44.3–6), and persecution of his ministers and adherents must cease forthwith. During the winter of 312–13 confiscated lands were restored to the church, and in Africa the emperor had taken the side of bishop Caecilian of Carthage against those who claimed that he had been consecrated by a bishop who had handed over the Scriptures to the authorities (a *traditor*) and hence, that his consecration was invalid (*HE* 10.6 and Optatus of Milevis, *Against the Donatists* 1.20).[68]

In February 313 Constantine met Licinius who ruled the Balkan provinces of the empire at Milan. They agreed not only that the persecution should end, and all lands and properties belonging to the church should be restored, but that there should be complete toleration for all to worship as they thought best. However, in the statement, which came to be known as the Edict of Milan, the Christians were represented positively as against 'the others', i.e. the pagans.[69] Licinius made a marriage alliance with Constantine, and two months later defeated Maximin. In the summer of 313 Maximin committed suicide. Twelve years later, the Council of Nicaea confirmed Christianity as the preferred religion of the empire as well as Constantine's personal conviction.

The story of official oppression and martyrdom was continued in Persia through the fourth and fifth centuries. Christians in the Persian empire were considered disloyal and pro-Roman, and were subjected to periods of repression.[70] They never attained official status nor did they become a majority. In North Africa, on the other hand, the opponents of Caecilian had prevailed under their leader, Donatus. Throughout the fourth century this majority church among the North African Christians rejected the effects of Constantine's conversion. They regarded themselves still as aliens in the contemporary world and looked forward to a martyr's death. The church in the rest of the empire, however, had survived and triumphed. As Origen had said, it had spread its teaching despite the opposition of kings, governors, the Roman Senate, rulers everywhere and the common people' (*Contra Celsum* 2.79). Soon, alas, it would itself begin to persecute and make martyrs of those who disagreed with its teaching.

It is not easy therefore to speak of political oppression, except in the sense that all authority may be deemed oppressive by those who refuse obedience and deny its validity. The Roman empire, like the Seleucid rulers of Syria before it, was never able to come to terms with a monotheistic religion. It solved the problem with the Jews by marginalizing them and restricting them to narrow identifiable national limits. But with the Christians spread through all classes and throughout the Mediterranean world, and carrying no distinctive marks or emblems, this was impossible. Moreover, the fanaticism shown by some aroused a fanaticism among the pagan provincials, fuelled by rumours of vile and harmful magical practices by the Christians. The authorities were far from being the diabolical characters portrayed a century later by Prudentius in *Peristephanôn Liber* and in later martyr-legends. They had no choice but to act against adherents of a religion deemed since the Neronian persecution to be illegal, and which had become regarded increasingly as disloyal to the empire and its gods. That generally the authorities acted as reasonable men confronting a distasteful situation is clear from the *Acta Martyrum*. Only when Christianity revealed itself as the major threat to the empire's internal security in the 250s did administration of justice become political oppression.

NOTES

1 Eusebius is cited in this chapter in the edition of Kirsopp Lake (1926, 1932).
2 *Contra Celsum* is cited here in the edition of Chadwick (1953).
3 For the *Martyrium Pionii*, see Musurillo (1972).
4 For this association in the minds of some early Christians, see Heb. 11.32–40.
5 See Frend (1965: 57–8).
6 Petilian, cited by Augustine, 2.89.196 (martyrdom as the goal of Christian life), and compare 2.92.202 (standing persecution of the Just of Israel and Christianity by unjust rulers).
7 Tertullian, *De Baptismo* 16 (*CSEL* 20.214): 'Nos faceret aqua vocatos, sanguine electos.'
8 See Philo, *Legatio ad Gaium* 24.157 for Augustus' favour to the Jews, and also 45.356 for sacrifices in honour of Caligula.
9 Thus, Polycarp among very many others – Eusebius, *HE* 4.15.21.
10 Thus, Philo, *Legatio ad Gaium* 29.192: 'A glorious death in defence of the Law is a new kind of life.'
11 On this period see Eisenman (1997), which is over-detailed but useful.
12 Tacitus, *Histories* 5.5.3, largely on the grounds of their religious exclusiveness leading to alleged contempt of their pagan contemporaries.

13 Suetonius, *Nero*, 16.2: 'Punishment was inflicted on the Christians, a class of men given to a new and wicked [*maleficus*, having the overtones of magic] superstition.'

14 See the excellent study by de Ste. Croix (1963).

15 Pliny, *Epp.* 10.96 and 97. See de Ste. Croix (1963: 18–21) and Sherwin-White (1966: 691–712).

16 Pliny, *Ep.* 10.96.6. This is an interesting commentary on the character and effect of the Christian mission in the post-Pauline era. Perhaps, when the Last Days failed to occur, converts returned to their former pagan allegiance.

17 The original Latin is given by Rufinus in his translation of Eusebius, *HE* 4.9. Translated by Stevenson (1967: 21–2).

18 Text translated in Stevenson (1967: 110–11 [Document No. 92] and Frend (1996: 94–8).

19 Cited in Minucius Felix, *Octavius* 9 (*c.* 230); Rendall (1931).

20 Eusebius *HE* 4.15.26. Compare *HE* 4.15.6: 'Kill the atheists. Let Polycarp be sent for.'

21 Galen, (lost) *Commentary on Plato, Republic Bk. 10*. Cited from Walzer (1949: 15).

22 *Acta Scillitanorum*; Musurillo (1972: 86–9): 'Hodie martyres in coelis sumus . . . Deo gratias.'

23 Tertullian, *Apologeticum* 8.6–9 (Glover 1931) and compare *Passio Perpetuae* 16.2.

24 Tertullian, *Apol.* 40.2.

25 Spartian, *Vita Severi*, 17.1; discussed by Frend (1974: 333–51) and Barnes (1968b: 40–1).

26 *Passio Perpetuae* 16.4: 'By this time the adjutant (*optio*) who was head of the gaol was already a Christian'; and compare 17.2: 'many of them [sightseers at the prison] began to believe'.

27 Also see dal Covolo (1989: 77).

28 Hippolytus, *Refutation of All Heresies* 9.12.14.; Pope Zephyrinus recalled Callistus from Antium and 'appointed him over the cemetery', *c.* 200 CE.

29 Tertullian, *Apol.* 49.6

30 For Elagabalus' unpopularity in Rome, because of his downgrading of Jupiter, see Dio Cassius, *Epitome* (LCL edn) 80.11.

31 His tomb with an inscription alluding to his martyrdom was found in the catacomb of Calepodius (see Frend 1996: 369, and n. 68).

32 Origen, *In Matth.* 24.9. *Sermo 39* (ed. Lommatzsch 1831–48: 4.270) 'Ut tunc fiant persecutiones iam non ex parte sicut ante, sed generaliter ubique.'

33 For the dating, see Saumagne (1975: 29).

34 Cyprian, *De Lapsis* 8 (Hartel 1868: 242). Christians 'running to the forum to sacrifice'. Cf. *Ep.* 11.1 (Hartel: 495).

35 *Martyrdom of Pionius and his companions*, paras 4 and 15 (Musurillo 1972: 136–67). See Fox (1986: 462–92).

36 Cited from Stevenson (1967: 218); see Knipfing, (1923: 345ff.) and Alföldi (1938), who are still the best authorities on the Decian persecution.

37 See Décret and Fanjar (1981: 331–2).

38 Cyprian, *Ep.* 34.4 (*CSEL* 3.2, p. 571) 'divisione mensurna'.

39 Eusebius, *HE*, 7.11.7, 'the gods that preserve the empire'.

40 Cyprian, *Ep.* 77.2–3 (*CSEL* 3.2, pp. 834–5); the statement by the proconsul of Africa, Paternus, 30 August 257, after ordering Cyprian into exile, adds, 'They [the emperors] further ordain that no meetings be held in any place and that Christians shall not enter their cemeteries. If any transgress this wholesome ordinance, he shall suffer death' (*Acta Proconsularia* 1 [*CSEL* 3.3. p. cxi]. Also, Eusebius, *HE*, 7.11.4 (Egypt).

41 *Ep.* 80, which throws light on the exact sources of information at Cyprian's disposal in Rome.

42 *Acta Proconsularia* 4 (pp. cxii–cxiii): 'Diu sacrilega mente vixisti et plurimos nefariae tibi conspirationis homines adgregasti et inimicum te diis Romanis et religionibus sacris constituisti . . . sanguine tuo sancietur disciplina.'

43 Cyprian, *Ep.* 80.1 (p. 840). The prefect of the City had ordered the execution of any Christian (clergy?) who was caught and the confiscation of his goods.

44 *Passio Sanctorum Mariani et Iacobi* 2.2: 'blind madness of the pagans and the action of military officials' (Musurillo 1972).

45 Dating discussed in Marichal (1953).

46 Eusebius, *HE* 7.30.21, and Lactantius, *De mortibus persecutorum* 6; Moreau (1954).

47 Eusebius, *HE* 7.15 (the case of the soldier, Marinus in Palestine). Trophimus in Asia Minor (from the museum at Brusa) is an example of a martyr in these years. See Frend (1996: 135–6).

48 See Frend (1952: 83–5). The evidence has not been superseded.

49 A good overview of these reforms remains that of Ensslin (1939).

50 The text of Diocletian's edict is reproduced in Stevenson (1967: 267–8 [Document 236]).

51 See Frend (1987), Beatrice (1988) and Stevenson (1967 [Document 237 – extracts from Porphyry]).

52 Thus, the centurion Marcellus, executed at Tingis (Tangier) 31 July 298. See *Acta Marcelli* in Musurillo (1972: 250–9). Marcellus, though a Christian, was executed specifically, however, for throwing down his arms.

53 Eusebius-Jerome, *Chronicle*, ad. ann. 301; Lactantius, *De mortibus persecutorum* 11–13.

54 Eusebius, *HE* 8.2, 4–5 (text of edicts 1 and 2); Lactantius, *De mortibus persecutorum* 13.1.

55 See the account in *Gesta apud Zenophilum* (appendix to Optatus of Milevis, *De Schismate*, *CSEL* 26, pp. 186–8) and Stevenson (1967 [Document 240]).

56 Eusebius, *On the Martyrs of Palestine* 1.1 (Lawlor and Oulton 1954: 331–3), the martyrdom of Procopius.

57 For arguments, I believe mistaken, against its enforcement, see Ste. Croix (1954).

58 See *Acta Saturnini* PL. 8, 689–703 (particularly paras 2 and 3).

59 *Mart. Pal.* 3.1, but in North Africa disobedient congregations were liable to arrest.

60 See Duval (1982: I, 105–15).

61 *CIL.* Viii. 6700 = 19353.

62 *Passio sanctae Crispinae* (Musurillo 1972: 310–9). Discussed by Monceaux (1905: 158–61) and Rosen (1997).

63 Christern (1976: 297–303). For the suggestion of a Donatist connection see Frend (1996: 364).

64 Lactantius, *Divine Institutes* 5.22 (ed. S. Brandt, *CSEL* xix) .

65 Ibid. 23; cf. ibid. 13.1: The gods 'were decaying' (ibid. 12).

66 For instance, the inscription from Arycanda in Lycia, *CIL* 3.12132 (Stevenson 1967 [Document 247]). Maximin's answer to these petitions is given in Eusebius, *HE* 9.7.

67 Constantine's vision of the Sun-god, Anon. *Panegyrici Latini* 6 (7) 21.3–6; Stevenson (1967 [Document 248]).

68 Ed. Zinsa, *CSEL* 20, 21; Frend 1952: 20.

69 Lactantius, *De mortibus* 48.2–12; Stevenson (1967 [Document 250]).

70 Sozomen, *HE* 2.9.1–5.

BIBLIOGRAPHY

Alföldi, A. (1938) 'Zu den Christenverfolgungen in der Mitte des 3 Jahrhunderts', *Klio* 31: 323–48.

Andresen, C. (1975) 'Der erlass des Gallienus an die bischöfe Aegyptens', *Studia Patristic* xvii: 358–90.

Barnes, T. D. (1968a) 'Pre-Decian *Acta Martyrum*', *Journal of Theological Studies*, n.s. 19: 509–31.

—— (1968b) 'Legislation against the Christians', *Journal of Roman Studies*. 58: 32–50.

Beatrice, P. F. (1988) 'Oracle antichrétien chez Arnobe', *Studia Ephemeridis Augustiniani'* (Rome) 27: 107–29.

Bowersock, G. W. (1995) *Martyrdom and Rome*. Cambridge: Cambridge University Press.

Bickerman, E. B. (1968) 'Trajan, Hadrian and the Christians', *Revista di Filolocia e di Istruzione Classica (Torino)* 96: 290–315.

Chadwick, Henry (ed.) (1953) *Origen*, Contra Celsum. Cambridge: Cambridge University Press.

Christern, J. (1976) *Das frühchristliche Pilgerheiligtum von Tébessa*. Wiesbaden

Covolo, Enrico dal (1989) *Severi e il cristianesimo*. Las-Roma.

Décret, F. and Fanjar, Mhamed (1981) *L'Afrique du Nord dans l'Antiquité*. Paris: Payot.

Downing, J. (1963) 'Jesus and Martyrdom', *Journal of Theological Studies* n.s. 14, 2: 279–93.

Duval, Yvette (1982) *Loca sanctorum Africae* I. (Haïdra) Collection de l'Ecole de Rome 58. Rome, 105–15.

Eisenman, Robert (1997) *James the Brother of Jesus*. London: Faber.

Ensslin, W. (1939) 'The Reforms of Diocletian', *CAH*, Vol. 12, Ch. 9.

Fox, R. Lane (1986) *Pagans and Christians*. London: Viking Press.

Francis, James A. (1995) *Subversive Virtue: Asceticism and Authority in the Second-Century Pagan World*. University Park, Pa.: Pennsylvania State University.

Frend, W. H. C. (1952) *The Donatist Church*. Oxford: Oxford University Press.

—— (1959) 'The Failure of the Great Persecution', *Past and Present* 16: 10–30.

—— (1965) *Martyrdom and Persecution in the Early Church*. Oxford: B. H. Blackwell.

—— (1974) 'Open Questions Concerning the Christians and the Roman Empire in the Time of the Severi', *Journal of Theological Studies* 25: 333–51.

—— (1987) 'Prelude to the Great Persecution: The Propaganda War', *JEH* 38: 1–18.

—— (1996) *The Archaeology of Early Christianity: A History*. London: Geoffrey Chapman.

Gibbon, E. (1802 edn) *The Decline and Fall of the Roman Empire*. London.

Glover, T. R. (ed.) (1931) Tertullian, *Apology, De Spectaculis with an English Translation*. Loeb Classical Library. London: Heinemann.

Guyon, J. (1987) *La cimitière aux Deux Lauriers*. Rome: Bibliothèque des Ecoles françaises d'Athènes et de Rome.

Hartel, W. (ed.) (1868) Cyprian, *De Lapsis. CSEL* III. 1, 235–64 and Epistulae 3.2, 463–842.

Keresztes, P. (1968) 'Marcus Aurelius a Persecutor?', *Harvard Theological Review* 61, 3: 321–41.

Knipfing, J. R. (1923) 'The Libelli of the Decian Persecution', *Harvard Theological Review* 16: 345–90.

Lake, Kirsopp (1926, 1932) *Eusebius: The Ecclesiastical History*. Loeb Classical Library. London: Heinemann.

Lawlor, H. J. and Oulton, J. E. L. (eds) (1954) *Eusebius, The Ecclesiastical History and the Martyrs of Palestine*. London: SPCK.

Lommatzsch, C. H. E. (ed.) (1831–48) Edition of Origen's works. 25 vols. Berlin. (In large part superseded by successive *Griechische Christlichen Schriften* edns of Origen's works.)

Marichal, R. (1953) 'La date des graffiti de la basilique de Saint-Sebastien à Rome', *Nouvelle Clio* 5: 119.

Markus, R. A. (1974) *Christianity in the Roman World*. London: Thames & Hudson.

Mattingly, H. and Sydenham, E. A. (1927–36) *Roman Imperial Coinage*, especially Vol. V (by P. A. Webb), Part i (Valerian to Florian) and Part ii (Probus to Diocletian).

Molthagen, Joachim (1970) *Der römische Staat und die Christen im zweiten und dritten Jahrhundert*. Göttingen: Vandenhoeck & Ruprecht.

Monceaux, P. (1905) *Histoire littéraire de l'Afrique chrétienne*, Vol. 3. Paris: Ernest Leroux.

Moreau, Joseph (ed.) (1954) *Lactantius, De Mortibus Persecutorum*. Sources Chrétiennes 39. Paris: Éditions du Cerf.

Mosheim, L. A. (1767) *Ecclesiastical History*, trans. A. Maclaine. Dublin.

Musurillo, H. (ed.) (1972) *Acts of the Christian Martyrs*. Oxford: Clarendon Press.

Olmstead, A. T. (1942) 'The mid-3rd century of the Christian Era', *Classical Philology* 37: 241ff., 398ff.

Oulton, J. E. L. and Chadwick, Henry (eds) (1954) *Origen*. Exhortation to Martyrdom. SCM Press, 393–428.

Rendall, G. H. (ed.) (1931) *Minucius Felix with an English Translation, Based on the Unfinished Version by W. C. A. Kerr*. Loeb Classical Library. London: Heinemann.

Roques, D. (1988) *Synésios de Cyrène et la Cyrénaique du Bas Empire*. Paris: Editions de CNRS.

Rosen, Klaus (1997) 'Passio Sanctae Crispinae', *Jb AC* 40: 106–25.

Rouselle, Alain (1974) 'La Persécution des Chrétiens à Alexandrie au iiie Siècle', *Revue Historique de droit français et étranger*, 2: 222–51.

Saumagne, Charles (1975) *Saint Cyprien: Evêque de Carthage, 'Pape' d'Afrique*. Paris: CNRS.

Sherwin-White, A. N. (1952), 'The Early Persecutions and Roman Law again', *Journal of Theological Studies* n.s. 3: 199–213.

—— (1966) *The Letters of Pliny: A Historical and Social Commentary*. Oxford: Clarendon Press (especially 691–712).

Ste. Croix, G. E. M. de (1954) 'Aspects of the "Great" Persecution', *Harvard Theological Review* 47: 75–113.

—— (1963) 'Why were the early Christians persecuted?', *Past and Present* 26, 2: 6–38.

Smallwood, E. M. (ed.) (1961) *Legatio ad Gaium: Philonis Alexandri*. Leiden: E. J. Brill.

Sordi, Marta (1965) *Il cristianesimo e Roma*. Bologna: Licinio Cappelli.

Stevenson, J. (1967) *A New Eusebius*. London: SPCK (rev. 1987).

Vittinghoff, F. (1984) 'Christianus sum', Das 'Verbrechen von Aussenseiten der römischen Gesellschaft, *Historia* 33, 5: 331–57.

Vogt, J. (1962) *Zur Religiosität der Christenverfolger im römischen reich*. Heidelberg: Akademie der Wissenschaften, 28.

Walzer, R. (1949) *Galen on Jews and Christians*. Oxford: Oxford University Press.

Wilken, R. L. (1984) *The Christians as the Romans Saw Them*. Yale: Yale University Press.

CHAPTER THIRTY-TWO

GRAECO-ROMAN PHILOSOPHICAL OPPOSITION

—— •✢• ——

Michael Bland Simmons

THE HOSTILE ENVIRONMENT

Christianity was born and developed in a hostile environment. Though pregnant with a great deal of theological and spiritual meaning for many throughout the ages, the cross nonetheless symbolized the insoluble conflict between Christianity and paganism already present in the life and teachings of Jesus (Meyer 1992). Hostilities described in the Acts of the Apostles between Jews and Christ-followers preceded the greater conflict between the early church and gentiles in the Graeco-Roman world during the first-century missionary expansions (Frend 1984: 11–109; Chadwick 1992). The delineation of correct (orthodox) doctrines in the face of heretical teachings, and the definition of a canon of scripture, were two of the major challenges of the church beginning (but not ending) in the second century (González 1970; Pelikan 1971; Chadwick 1993: 32–83; Kelly 1978: 52–82; McDonald 1995). As these issues of identity were being clarified, both the pagan intelligentsia and the political administration of the Roman empire were able, beginning with Nero (54–68), to distinguish between Judaism and the Christ-movement as separate religious entities (Suetonius, *Caesar* 16.25; Tacitus, *Annals* 15.44; Griffin 1984; Harnack 1972). Owing to such factors as the church's continued growth in the provinces, the belief in the deity of Christ, and the exclusiveness of the Christians (which appeared strange and unacceptable to the tolerant polytheists of the empire), an increasingly inimical attitude towards Christianity became inevitable (Chadwick 1993: 66–131; Daniélou 1973). Christian leaders were now thrown on the defensive, and began to write *apologies* which had the twofold objective of offering reasonable explanations of doctrines and practices, and evangelistically attempting to convince the pagans that Christianity is the only true religion (see Chapter 21 of this volume and Frend 1984: 229–70). Thus by the second century there emerged such erudite apologists as Justin Martyr, Tertullian, Athenagoras, Theophilus, and the Alexandrian theologians Clement and Origen (Kelly 1978: 83–108; Chadwick 1993: 54–115). As we shall see, the latter wrote a refutation of the first work published against Christianity, *The True Discourse* by Celsus.

Though official state persecutions of Christians had occurred as early as Nero (54–68) and Domitian (81–96), by the 250s under the emperors Decius (249–51) and

Valerian (253–60), the first universal persecutions took place, clearly indicating the perceived threat now posed by the church to the imperial *pax deorum* (Frend 1981). The latter formed the conceptual basis of the empire's religious propaganda, and because it possessed theological and political implications, it was often used as a test of the individual citizen's loyalty to the Roman government. Often given the name of *imperial cult*, it had been continuously developed and variously interpreted by Roman leaders since the time of Livy. Its central thesis posited that the right order and success of the empire would be maintained as long as the worship of the Roman gods was perpetuated. From Tertullian to Eusebius, the misfortunes which befell the empire, whether natural, economic, or military, were regularly blamed on the Christians for their refusal to worship the very gods held responsible for Rome's greatness (Tertullian, *Apologeticum* 40; *Ad Scapulam* 3; Arnobius, *Adversus nationes* 1.1; Eusebius, *Historia ecclesiastica* 9.7.3–14). The church took maximum advantage of the cessation of state persecutions between Gallienus (260) and Diocletian (284). But storm clouds soon gathered. Already by the 290s, beginning with the executions of Christians in the Roman legions (see Simmons 1995: 38–40), a very destructive two-edged sword was being prepared by the pagans for their upcoming unprecedented attack upon the church. This double threat came in the form of, first, the most damaging obloquys ever written (to date) against the Christians; and, second, the most formidable state persecution ever launched against the church in its 300-year history (Simmons 1995: 22–46; Woods 1992; Davies 1989; Barnes 1973; de Ste. Croix 1954).

Moreover, the Great Persecution which began in February 303 would not end until Constantine's victory in 311 at the Milvian Bridge in Rome and the subsequent 'Edict of Milan'.

THE CASE OF PHILOSOPHICAL OPPOSITION

Yet we must keep in mind that within this environment hostile to Christianity another kind of opposition developed. It was led by learned philosophers and communicated both in the formal debates and lectures of their schools in places like Rome, Athens, and Alexandria and in their published works which vituperated Christian beliefs and practices. Appearing for the first time in the late second century and continuing throughout the fourth, these writings served a twofold purpose. First, they contained well-reasoned arguments against such Christian doctrines as monotheism, the incarnation, Christ's deity and passion, and the resurrection of the flesh. Second, they attempted to prove the superiority of traditional polytheism and the Hellenic *paideia* upon which Graeco-Roman culture was founded.

During the period from 150–363 CE, the three philosophers whose anti-Christian works are examined in this chapter (Celsus, Sossianus Hierocles and Porphyry of Tyre), and a fourth, Julian the Apostate, an emperor with philosophical interests whom I profile in Chapter 50, contributed to this philosophical opposition to Jesus and his followers. In this chapter I shall outline the individual and collective contributions of Celsus, Sossianus Hierocles and Porphyry, consider the major

Figure 32.1 *The Crucifixion*, 1515–16, by Grünewald. Pagan philosophers rejected the Christian doctrine of the passion of Christ. Photo by permission of Oxford University Press, from McManners (1992: 2).

themes of one of the works they produced (*The True Discourse* of Celsus) and finally assess their significance for the conflict between Christianity and paganism in the Roman empire.

CELSUS

A recent study estimates that during the period in which Celsus wrote *The True Discourse* (= *Discourse*) against Christianity (*c.* 178 CE: see pp. 851–60), there were *c.* 100,000 Christians dispersed among two hundred or more communities in the empire (Hopkins 1998). A concern about the growth of the church may have been a corollary factor which motivated Celsus to write his book (Frend 1984: 310–11, 443), but the immediate cause appears to have been the need to write an erudite rejoinder to the apologies of Justin Martyr written *c.* 150.[1] We know nothing of Celsus beyond the pages of the *Discourse*, of which about 70% has been accurately preserved in Origen's *Contra Celsum* (Rougier 1977: 19; Hoffmann 1987: 45; Origen, *Contra Celsum* 5.53). Its significance as the oldest literary attack upon Christianity by a member of the pagan intelligentsia of which details have survived reveals invaluable insight into the hostile conflict that was occurring between Christianity and paganism during our period. The central thesis of my argument in this chapter

Figure 32.2 Christ raises Lazarus, from a third-century sarcophagus. The doctrine of the resurrection of the body contradicted Platonic soteriology and eschatology and was often a focus of anti-Christian writers. Photo by permission of Oxford University Press, from McManners (1992: 21).

will stress the truculent nature of the conflict between the two religious traditions, a good illustration of the conflict-ridden character of Mediterranean culture discusssed in Chapter 1 of this volume, rather than to follow the often superficial trend in modern scholarship which has explained the relationship between Christianity and paganism on the basis of intentionally worn-out, ambiguous, and anachronistic words like *pluralism* or *syncretism*. It is extremely doubtful that either side would have explained the conflict in this manner. A fresh appraisal is necessary to get a better understanding, even though it will be tantamount to swimming against the currents. The fashionable argument (pluralism/syncretism) leaves too many unanswered questions and should be no longer accepted as a viable interpretation of the problem.

Although Origen informs us that Celsus was a professed adversary of Christianity

(*Contra Celsum* 8.62; 4.47), and his erudition in pagan and Christian literature was conspicuous (*Contra Celsum* 4.11; 4.36; 2.32; 2.76), the school of philosophy which he espoused has been the focus of scholarly debate. Origen calls Celsus an Epicurean in *Contra Celsum* 1.8, but elsewhere he expresses doubt (4.54; 4.75). It has been suggested that Celsus was the Epicurean who lived in the second century to whom Lucian of Samosata dedicated his *Alexander the False Prophet*,[2] but passages in the *Contra Celsum* which betray either Stoic (*Contra Celsum* 4.67; Chadwick 1947) or Platonic (*Contra Celsum* 1.32; Chadwick 1947: 47; Quasten 1953: 52; Baumeister 1978) doctrines eliminate him as the anti-Christian author of the *Discourse*. It would therefore be prudent to conclude that Celsus was an unknown eclectic philosopher with strong Platonic leanings whose major focus was practical ethics rather than abstract metaphysical concepts (Chadwick 1947: 46).

Turning to the date of the *True Discourse*, Celsus (*Contra Celsum* 8.69) refers to contemporary Christians who were sought out and punished with death. This appears to be an allusion to the rescript of Marcus Aurelius which initiated the persecution of Christians at Lyons and Vienne in 177 CE (Chadwick 1953: xiv). Also, in the preface to *Contra Celsum*, Origen remarks that Celsus had been dead a long time, and this makes sense in light of Eusebius' statement (*HE* 6.36.2) that Origen wrote his refutation during Philip the Arab's reign (244–9 CE; Chadwick 1953: xxv–xxvi; Borret 1967: 15–21). Finally, a reference to joint emperors in the *Discourse* (*Contra Celsum* 8.71) again strongly suggests the period of Marcus Aurelius. It appears likely that Celsus wrote the *True Discourse against the Christians c.* 178 CE.

More difficult to answer is the question of Celsus' provenance. Suggestions have ranged from Rome to Alexandria as the place of origin for the *Discourse* (Chadwick 1953: xxviii–xxix), and it is quite possible that Celsus may have acquired knowledge of Christian heretical doctrines by attending lectures given in the schools of people like Marcion and Valentinus in Rome (Amphoux 1992: 250). However, *Contra Celsum* 7.3–11 undoubtedly reveals personal knowledge of contemporary Near Eastern prophetic practices, and this would appear to provide unambiguous evidence that Celsus most probably came from Syria (Frend 1984: 177; Burke 1984: 3).

With respect to the structure, method, and style of the *Discourse*, we first note that Books 1–3 of the *Contra Celsum* respond to the attacks of a Jew (Fox 1987: 482) – presumably a literary device used to express Celsus' views – found in the early part of the work; Books 4–5 give Celsus' criticism of the Jewish religion from which Christianity originated; Books 6–7 inform us that Celsus argued that the Christians borrowed from Greek culture, and that their religion encouraged sedition in the empire:

> For Celsus has quoted several passages especially from Plato, comparing them with extracts from the holy scriptures such as could impress an intelligent person, saying that those ideas have been better expressed among the Greeks, who refrained from making exalted claims and from asserting that they had been announced by a god or the son of a god.
>
> (*Contra Celsum* 6.1)

Some of the basic components of classical anti-Christian polemics make their appearance here: the superiority of Graeco-Roman culture, a criticism of scripture,

Figure 32.3 The beginning of John's Gospel from the Codex Sinaiticus, written in uncial script on vellum and discovered in the Monastery of St Catherine on Mount Sinai in 1844. The Christian scriptures were often ridiculed by Graeco-Roman philosophers for their inelegant style and mythological contents. Photo by permission of Oxford University Press, from McManners (1992: 21).

and a dependence upon Plato to prove the weaknesses of Christian doctrine. In Book 7 Origen responds to Celsus' concepts of demonology, divine providence, and his poignant accusation that Christianity has caused sedition against the Roman government. Noteworthy here is Celsus' silence on such topics as cannibalism, incest, infanticide, and orgies which were popular criticisms of Christianity in the second century (Fox 1987: 427). As a learned philosopher he evidently felt himself to be above the clamour of the ignorant masses. His overall method of argumentation seems to have been inspired by anti-Jewish writers like Lysimachus, Chaeremon, and Apion (Feldman 1990: 106). Moreover, if we keep in mind the important fact that it was an enemy of Celsus (Origen) who edited the *Discourse*, it is obvious that we cannot always get a clear picture of the details of his argument (Hoffmann 1987:

44). Suffice it to say that the method and style of the *Discourse* can be generally characterized by (1) the use of historical and 'scientific' facts; (2) the use of irony (often humorous); (3) deliberate distortion of his enemies' beliefs; (4) literary retortion; (5) the allegorization of (e.g.) Homer, but at the same time refusing to allow the Christians to allegorize scripture; (6) the use of Stoic and Platonic doctrines to support his argument; and (7) criticism of scripture to show the superiority of pagan culture.[3] These salient features of Celsus' argument contributed to his major goal to convert the Christians 'by shaming them out of their religion' (Quasten 1953: 52).

Though Celsus emphasized the superiority of Greek culture, he nevertheless employed his knowledge of the Bible in his attack upon Christianity. It is true that Origen says that Celsus was not acquainted with the words of scripture (6.12), but this probably means that he was ignorant of the different levels of biblical interpretation (literal, moral, spiritual) used in the Alexandrian exegetical schools. Many passages in the *Discourse* quoted in the *Contra Celsum* confirm Celsus' knowledge of scripture. The question is how much of the Bible did he know? In beginning to answer this, we must remember that by 180 CE the New Testament canon had not been closed (Rougier 1977: 115–18), and we often find Celsus citing non-canonical books like the Epistle of Barnabas and the Book of Enoch (1.63; 5.54) along with canonical books. Origen is explicit that he knew Matthew (1.34) and the other gospels (6.16) very well, and many passages in the *Contra Celsum* attest to this (e.g. 1.34–8). Origen also admits that Celsus had read Genesis (4.42), and one study has demonstrated that the text he used was the Septuagint, based on the verbal agreements between it and passages of Celsus quoted in the *Contra Celsum* (Burke 1986: 242). Of the rest of the Pentateuch, the books of the Prophets, the historical and wisdom literature, the Pauline corpus, Acts, and Revelation, Celsus knew either little or nothing (Benko 1984: 148–9; Wilken 1984: 101; Burke 1986: 245; Pichler 1980: 43–50; contra Rougier 1977: 113–14).

In order to give examples of Celsus' criticism of scripture, we begin by noting his great aversion for the allegorical method of interpretation. He denounces the Christian allegorical interpretation of the Mosaic histories (1.17) because the language of Moses, particularly the Genesis account of creation, will allow no such meaning for the text (1.20). In any event, he argues, Christians give an allegorical meaning to the creation story of Gen. 2:21–2 because they are ashamed of it (4.38). Finally, this hermeneutical method produces an interpretation of scriptural passages more absurd than the fables themselves (4.51; 4.87). Often Celsus attacks the Bible by attempting to show the superiority of a philosophical doctrine, as he does in 1.19–20, where he rejects the Christian doctrine of creation (in Genesis) by saying that the world is uncreated, and here he bases his argument on the Platonic concept of the eternity of the world (*Timaeus* 22f.) combined with the Stoic doctrine of cyclical conflagrations. Another contention is that the stories of the Bible are simply invented by its writers. Thus the 'twelve legions of angels' (Matt. 26:52–4) is a fiction of the evangelists (2.10). Jesus' genealogy was made up by Matthew to make it appear that he descended from royalty (2.32). Moses and the prophets have written pure nonsense (6.50). Celsus also accentuates the inconsistencies of the Bible. For example, Jesus' injunction to turn the other cheek is an infraction of the Old Testament *lex talionis* (6.50). One Gospel says that one angel came to the tomb, another says two (5.52).

Jesus forbade his disciples to be ambitious (Mark 10:44; Matt. 20:25; Luke 22:25), which contradicts his prophecy that they would rule over the nations (7.23). Celsus also attacks the style of scripture: its language lacks the elegance of Greek literature (6.2); it is very simple and commonplace (4.87), and even vulgar (3.68). Finally, even though the writers of the Bible borrowed from the wise men of antiquity, they often misunderstood and misconstrued what they wrote (1.21; 6.7). This critique may have been provoked by Justin Martyr who wrote that God's divine Logos had been revealed to the wise men of old like Socrates. They were in a true sense 'Christians before Christ'. Origen, moreover, following one of the basic arguments of Christian apologetics (e.g., 6.43), is determined to prove that Moses' writings are much older than Homer. The borrowing went in the opposite direction.

Although Celsus overwhelmingly reviled orthodox Christianity, his knowledge extended also to heretical groups or movements of the second century (Burke 1984: 5–6). In the *Discourse* reference is made to gnostic sects, apocryphal works (e.g., the Preaching of Peter), Marcionite doctrines (especially 6.74; Fox 1987: 515; Jackson 1992), and sects founded by the women apostles Helen of Samaria, the consort of Simon Magus, Marcellina, Salome, Mariamne and Martha. Even heresies that were unknown to the learned Origen are mentioned (8.16). It appears from this that Celsus had a broad knowledge of the religion that he was assailing, and his purpose for alluding to the diverse doctrines that were disseminated in the name of Christianity is clear. By opposing the teachings of the heretics to those of the orthodox, he was able to prove the disunity, and therefore falsity, of Jesus and his followers to his readers (Martinez 1990–1: 203).

Although I will cover the themes of the *Discourse* as a case study in philosophical opposition to early Christianity later in this chapter, it is worth while at this point to make a few observations about Celsus' legacy. In the history of ancient thought, particularly as it relates to the conflict between Christianity and paganism in the Roman empire, the *True Discourse* and the *Contra Celsum* reveal the respective positions of the educated representatives of the old polytheism and the new monotheism. Celsus is important for our understanding of this conflict because he is the first learned pagan to write against Christianity, and the *Discourse* is significant for setting a precedent for later anti-Christian polemicists regarding scripture, the superiority of Graeco-Roman culture, and the use of pagan philosophy, especially Platonism, to disprove the credibility of Christian doctrine. Even though some scholars question the influence of Celsus upon later periods (Quasten 1953: 52; González 1970: 216; Hauck 1985–6), others have equally argued that many Christian writers before Origen wrote in response to the *True Discourse* (Chadwick 1953: xiii; Baumeister 1978: 175; Benko 1984: 140; Burke 1984: 1–7). While it may be true that a direct influence cannot be established in many cases, it would certainly be rash to suggest that later writers like Hierocles and Porphyry, and even a philosophically inclined emperor like Julian, had not become familiar with many of the anti-Christian themes of the *Discourse*.

SOSSIANUS HIEROCLES

Sossianus Hierocles was successively governor of the province in which Palmyra was located (*c.* 297), *vicarius* probably of the diocese of Oriens, *praeses* of Bithynia (303), and prefect of Egypt (310–11).[4] By 23 February 303 when Diocletian promulgated his first edict against the Christians, Hierocles had already exerted considerable influence upon imperial officials in Nicomedia to launch the 'Great Persecution'. Lactantius informs us that he was the author and instigator of the persecution (*De mortibus persecutorum* 16). Christians who crossed themselves at Antioch during sacrifices ordered by Diocletian before the persecution interfered with the *hauruspices'* ascertaining the proper omens (*De mor. pers.* 10.1–5; Eusebius, *HE* 8.4.3f.), and this precipitated the imperial *concilium* (late 302/early 303) at Nicomedia where Diocletian, Galerius, and representatives from the government and the military met to decide what to do with the Christians. Hierocles was there persuading Diocletian to begin the persecution (Lactantius, *De mor. pers.* 11). After Diocletian consulted the oracle of Apollo at Didyma he was convinced that it was the will of the gods to initiate the persecution (Eusebius, *Vita Constantini* 2.50; Lactantius, *De mor. pers.* 2.7f.; Arnobius, *Adversus nationes* 1.26; Zosimus, *Historia nova* 2.12 and 2.36f.).

It may have been just before the outbreak of the persecution that Hierocles wrote the *Philalethes (Lover of Truth)*, although this is debatable, and some scholars date it to *c.* 311–13 (Barnes 1976: 240–3 and 1981: 22; Forrat and Des Places 1986: 18, 23; Des Places 1989). However, an attempt to explain the contradictory descriptions of the *Philalethes* found in Lactantius and Eusebius, who were contemporaries of Hierocles and were familiar with his work, may help to solve the problem. Lactantius is explicit that Hierocles wrote the Philalethes not *against*, but *to* the Christians (Lactantius, *Div. inst.* 5.2). Eusebius offers a different interpretation, referring to the work written 'against us' (*Contra Hieroclem* 1: *kath' hêmôn*). Hierocles may have published two editions, one which possessed a more conciliatory tone (*c.* 303) to which Lactantius refers; and a later edition with an overt hostile message, perhaps when Hierocles was prefect of Egypt (310–11). Eusebius' description 'against us' may refer to this later edition. Whether there were indeed two editions, it is clear that from *c.* 303 the *Philalethes* was circulating in the Eastern provinces. Hierocles draws his materials from *The Life of Apollonius of Tyana* which was written by Philostratus (*c.* 217) at the demand of Septimius Severus' wife, Julia Domna.[5] Apollonius appears to have been an ascetic who lived during the first century, but by Philostratus' period a rich hagiographic tradition had already developed, and it is for this reason that the latter makes him not only a Greek hero but a wonder-working holy-man possessed with divine qualities (Forrat and Des Places 1986: 53f.). Hierocles' *Philalethes* undoubtedly depended on earlier anti-Christian sources, and Celsus is a good possibility. Eusebius himself admits that Origen in the *Contra Celsum* had so sufficiently answered Hierocles' criticisms that he only needed to focus on Hierocles' comparison of Jesus and Apollonius (*Contra Hieroclem* 1; Junod 1988: 41). Even though it was written hastily in the midst of controversy and is therefore lacking in style and orderly argumentation, the *Contra Hieroclem* is a book-by-book criticism of the work of Philostratus[6] as it was used by Hierocles (Eusebius, *C. Hier.* 1). It would appear that the *Philalethes* was not published for the public, which may explain why it had apparently little influence upon later writers.

Nor can we describe Hierocles as a philosopher occupied with speculative thought. None the less, it would be rash to discount the importance of the *Phila-lethes*. First, this work reveals significant information about the intellectual background to the pagan–Christian conflict during the period immediately before the outbreak of the Great Persecution. Second, it reveals the close association between pagan intellectuals and the anti-Christian policies of the Tetrarchy (Simmons 1995: 24–46). Third, it is significant for the historical development of pagan and Christian apologetics and polemics as literary genres in the late Roman empire. Fourth, it gives us some understanding about the development in the history of comparative religions. Next, it helps us to understand the evolving concept of the 'Holy Man' in ancient Mediterranean society. Finally, it demonstrates the importance that both sides of the conflict placed upon such religious concerns as miracles and prophecy (Kertsch 1980; Gallagher 1982: 165–6). Note that after mentioning Apollonius, Hierocles informs us of his purpose for writing:

> What then is my reason for mentioning these facts? It was in order that you may be able to contrast our own accurate and well-established judgment on each point, with the easy credulity of the Christians. For whereas we reckon him who wrought such feats not a god, but only a man pleasing to the gods, they on the strength of a few miracles proclaim their Jesus a god.
>
> (Eusebius, *C. Hier.* 2)

In these lines we have the heart of Hierocles' message: (1) Jesus is not God, and (2) the basis of Christian faith cannot be proven. By constructing an argument that employs the same method of literary retortion which Porphyry used in his *Contra Christianos*, it is noteworthy that Eusebius says very little about Jesus and Christianity in general, and rather attacks Hierocles by using his weapons against him. Its main themes are Apollonius, Jesus and his disciples, miracles (including healings and exorcisms), fideism, prophecy, and Fate and Free Will.

PORPHYRY OF TYRE

Originally given the Semitic name Malchos ('King') after his father,[7] Porphyry was born in the Phoenician city of Tyre in *c.* 232 CE.[8] By *c.* 250 he came to Caesarea in Palestine where for a period he probably studied biblical exegesis and hermeneutics, particularly the Alexandrian allegorical method of interpretation, under Origen.[9] Porphyry may have been a Christian during this time, and it may have been while he was in Caesarea that he was assaulted by a group of Christian youths (Socrates, *Historia Ecclesiastica* 3.23.37), which may have initiated the development of a great hatred for Christianity and eventually gained for him a reputation as a 'defensor simulacrorum' (F. Maternus, *De err. prof. relig.* 13.4). Sometime later Porphyry went to Athens where he studied philology and philosophy under Longinus. Here the critical linguistic, literary, rhetorical, and historical skills were developed that he would later successfully use against the Christians (Eunapius, *Vitae philosophorum*

456). Such works as the *Philosophia ex oraculis*, the *Epistle to Anebo*, and the *De antro nympharum* belong to this period.[10] In 263 Porphyry left Athens for Rome, where he became the disciple of Plotinus and studied in his Neoplatonic school there. After a period of time in the city Porphyry became suicidal, and his master advised him to go on holiday (268). He went to Sicily (Eusebius, *HE* 6.19; *Vit. Plot.* 4, 11) and while there took at least one trip to North Africa to do zoological research for the *De abstinentia*, and may have begun a Neoplatonic school in Africa Proconsularis (Simmons 1995: 29, n. 310). Plotinus died in 270, and Porphyry returned to Rome to assume leadership in the Neoplatonic school. Late in life he married a widow with seven children named Marcella, and informs us that at around sixty-eight years of age he had a mystical experience similar to those of his master (*Vit. Plot.* 23; Simmons 1995: 219, nn. 24–5). He completed the edition of the *Enneads* before his death, which occurred sometime around 305.

Porphyry appears to have had a significant influence upon the events at Diocletian's court which led to the outbreak of the Great Persecution in February 303. In his *Epistle to Marcella* (Ch. 4) he alludes to an important trip to the East because, he says, of 'a need of the Greeks', which took place around the time that Diocletian and Galerius were devising a programme for the persecution. Lactantius informs us that a 'priest of philosophy' who taught abstinence and wrote three books against the Christians dined regularly at Diocletian's palace in Nicomedia (*Div. inst.* 5.2). This is undoubtedly a reference to Porphyry, who in the *De abstinentia* calls the philosopher 'a priest of the Supreme God' (*Abst.* 2.49.1), and the three books allude to the anti-Christian *Philosophia ex oraculis*. Porphyry was probably in attendance at the same imperial consilium that Hierocles and other magistrates attended in late 302. Porphyry was the ideal person to attend the meeting, and Diocletian will have listened intently to his advice about the impending persecution. He was the leading scholar of his day, concerned both about the decline of pagan culture and the increasing number of intellectuals going over to the church. He was the most famous anti-Christian activist who had already published several works against Christianity. As we noted above, the *Philosophia ex oraculis* contained a number of oracles against the Christians, and in the *Ad Marcellam* he stated that the greatest expression of piety was to honour the gods according to ancestral customs. Porphyry also believed in the superiority of Graeco-Roman culture to the man-made ludicrous fables of the Christians. All of these will have admirably suited Diocletian's policies against the Christians (*Ad Marc.* 18). Arnobius of Sicca, the first Christian author to write in response to Porphyry, provides evidence that the anti-Christian works of Porphyry were circulating in the western Roman empire by the late third century, as I have argued elsewhere (1995), which probably resulted from Porphyry's trip to Africa Proconsularis, and this may indeed indicate that Diocletian supported the dissemination of Porphyrian anti-Christian propaganda in association with the official imperial legislation of the Great Persecution (Beatrice 1988).

Porphyry was a polymath whose scholarly interests led him to study history, philosophy, religion, the natural and medical sciences, philology, and rhetoric.[11] He wrote perhaps between 66–81 works, and three of these are particularly important: the *Contra Christianos*, *Philosophia ex oraculis*, and *De regressu animae*. The *Contra Christianos* was a systematic attack in 15 books against Christian scripture, which provoked responses from Arnobius, Methodius, Eusebius, Apollinaris, Philostorgius, Firmicus Maternus, Diodore of Tarsus, Theodore of Mopsuestia, Didymus the Blind, John Chrysostom, Severian, Cyril, Jerome and, of course, Augustine. The latter admired Porphyry for his scholarly qualities, and he was highly respected in North Africa in his time (Augustine, *Civ. Dei* 7.25; 8.12; 10.10; 10.28; 10.29; 10.31). The *Contra Christianos* posed such a threat to the church that Constantine's edict of 333 refers to the Arians as 'Porphyrians' (Socrates, *HE* 1.9.30; *Codex Theodosianus* 15.5.66), and an edict issued in February 448 by Theodosius II and Valentinian III ordered all copies of it to be put to the flames (*Codex Justinianus* 1.1.3).[12] Surviving fragments are found only in Christian writings. The *Philosophia ex oraculis* was a collection of oracles which offered a Chaldaean-Neoplatonic soteriology, and the *De regressu animae* was a philosophical work about the ascent of the soul to God.

THE THEMES OF THE *TRUE DISCOURSE* OF CELSUS

The final section of this chapter consists of a discussion of the themes of the *True Discourse* of Celsus, both because of the importance of this text in founding the tradition of philosophical opposition to Christianity and for its approach and contents, which were regularly utilized by later pagan critics.

Jesus

The brunt of Celsus' attack focused upon the person and works of Jesus Christ principally to disprove his deity. Philosophically the incarnation is impossible because this compromises the (Platonic) doctrine of divine immutability (Chadwick 1966: 101; Pelikan 1971: 14; Wallis 1972: 101). Rejecting the virgin birth as a fable invented by Jesus himself (*Contra Celsum* 1.28), the Jew of Book 1 explains his birth as the result of Mary's adultery with a Roman soldier named Panthera (1.39). Anyway, if Jesus was really God, why was he forced to escape to Egypt (1.66)? True divinity, moreover, does not possess physical characteristics: God cannot have been enclosed in Jesus' body, eaten food, or spoken with a voice (1.69–70). Besides, why did God have to *descend* in the first place? To learn what goes on in the world? Does he not know all things (4.3)? The incarnation is not only illogical, it is also unnecessary. God did not have to breathe his spirit into a womb, full of pollution, because he could have simply created a body for Jesus. More people would have believed in him because of his immediate existence from above (6.73). Underlying Celsus' attack upon the incarnation here is Platonic soteriology which affirmed the affinity of the soul with God, disparaged corporeal and material existence, and placed first priority on purifying one's inner being with philosophy. Life in a physical body was depreciated and hence shameful. Even so, the Christian doctrine was rejected for its particularity: why did God send his son to an obscure corner of earth to live as a Jew (6.78)? Finally, by relocating God the incarnation would disrupt the natural order of things foreordained by providence (4.5).

To disprove the deity of Christ required an explanation of his miracles which were recorded in scripture. Celsus does not deny the fact of Jesus' miracles, but rather concentrates on the means by which they were performed. Perhaps influenced by rabbinical sources, Celsus attributes Jesus' miracles to his great skills as a magician (8.9).[13] By associating magic with ignorance and immorality (Gallagher 1982: 43–6), Celsus could prove to the educated classes of the empire that Jesus, who had learned sorcery in Egypt, and his followers, were deceived persons from the lowest classes of society (2.52–3; Kee 1986: 121–3). Magic cannot deceive true philosophers, who are educated and moral (6.41). But Jesus' magic was not just a result of innocence or naivety. His intentions were quite malicious and hypocritical because, although he performed miracles by sorcery, he excluded others from his kingdom who did (1.6). The miracles have nothing to do with God, therefore, nor do they benefit mankind (1.6; 1.46; 2.8; 2.9; 2.14; 2.48–9; 2.51). Origen's response is that magicians do not call their audience to a reformation of character (1.38; 1.68).

As the first writer of antiquity who criticized the central figure of Christianity, Celsus moved beyond the incarnation and miracles to discredit the belief in the deity of Christ. Origen informs us that many times in the *Discourse* Celsus assailed the life of Jesus as being the most infamous (7.56). Again, the central point was to prove that Jesus was a mere man (3.41). He asks how could Jesus really be God when he tried to escape from the Jews disgracefully, was betrayed by his own disciples, and could not even save himself on the cross (2.9)? Why did Jesus, though challenged, not manifest any visible sign in the temple that he was God's son? Relying upon the belief in the superiority of the Graeco-Roman religious *mos mariorum* which affirmed that 'older is better', Celsus criticized the recent appearance of this 'God' in history (1.26). The moral turpitude of Jesus' character was a salient feature of Celsus' obloquy: Christ obtained his living, he says, in a shameful and importunate manner (1.62); God hated him for his sorcery (1.71; on John 13:8 and Luke 22:37); he deluded a few Jews into following him (2.4), and they were men of worthless character (2.4; 2.6; 2.22; 2.39; 2.45–6). The crux of Celsus' argument here was important in the intellectual debates about the nature of the God-man in antiquity who was conceived as a person with an upright moral character whose miracles bestowed good things upon humanity. Because Jesus deceived people by sorcery, possessed a base character, and could only win over to his deceptive cause the lowest classes of society, in Celsus' mind he could not be given the title *God, Son of God*, or even *great man* (1.57; 2.33; 2.41–2; 2.76). And in order to strike at the foundation of Christian beliefs about Jesus (scripture), Celsus says that either the gospels were corrupted from their original meaning and rewritten to answer refutations (2.26–7); or that Jesus himself borrowed from, and perverted, the wisdom of Greek philosophy (6.16; 7.58). Celsus does not, however, leave his criticism at the historical level. Inquiring about the relevance of Christianity to contemporary society, he asks why does Jesus not prove his deity now? Why is he not recognized by those (the Jews) who have been looking for their Messiah? Why do many people not believe in Jesus if indeed he came to earth as God (7.35; 2.74–5; 2.78)? Finally, to the amazement of Origen, Celsus argued that not only was Jesus bad, he was also an evil demon:

> *Do you see, my excellent man, that anyone who stands by your daemon not only blasphemes him, but proclaims his banishment from every land and sea, and after*

binding you who have been dedicated to him like an image takes you away and crucifies you; but the demon or, as you say, the Son of God, takes no vengeance on him? This reply might have been effective if we used such words as he has put into our mouth; and yet not even on his own premises did he speak correctly, since he said that the Son of God is a daemon.

(Discourse 8.39)

Divine impassibility was a basic theological tenet of the kind of Middle Platonism espoused by Celsus (Pelikan 1971: 189; Gallagher 1982: 150; Borret 1984: 177–9), and thus the doctrine of the crucifixion which posited that Christ's death was efficacious for the salvation of all humanity was attacked vehemently by Celsus. We may give five major criticisms. First, since Jesus died the ignominious death of a criminal on a cross, he certainly was not God (2.5). Many robbers have died on crosses, he says, so why should we not call them 'God' (2.44, 47)? By stripping Christ's death of its theological interpretation, Celsus concluded that Jesus was sentenced by the Jews as one deserving of death (2.10). Second, the disciples betrayed Jesus at his death (2.11–12). Next, Jesus neither received help from God, nor was he able to save himself from the cross (1.54; 2.34; 2.72). To prove his deity Jesus should have disappeared from the cross (2.68). Fourth, a true God feels no pain, and in any event, what father would allow his son's torture (8.41; 2.37; 2.23)? Opposing gnostic with orthodox views of Christ's passion, Celsus will venture to say that Jesus only appeared to suffer on the cross (2.25). Finally, Celsus finds it strange, even if the crucifixion story is accepted, that those who were responsible for Jesus' execution received no punishment from God (8.39, 41). The notion of the 'suffering of God' contradicted the Platonic doctrine of divine impassibility. Moreover, by basing the premises of his argument on the view that the Passion narratives in the gospels were inventions (2.10; 2.24; 2.43; 2.59), Celsus can conclude that the story of the cross concerns the death of a man who was a criminal (2.16).

Celsus had a special disdain for the resurrection of Christ. Owing to the Platonic doctrine of the dichotomy between soul and body, Celsus finds bodily resurrection philosophically impossible. It would have been impossible for God to receive back Jesus' spirit after being contaminated by contact with a body (6.72). As we have seen, Jesus only appeared to die, but he later reappeared, and by the use of sorcery deceived an insane woman and others with good imaginations to believe that he had been raised from the dead (2.55; 2.56; 2.60). Anyway, if the story had been true, Jesus as God should have appeared to all men universally (2.63; 2.67; 2.70). In reality Jesus could not open his own tomb (5.52; 5.58).

His conclusion strikes at the heart of Christian faith: no one has been raised from the dead with a body (2.56–7), the resurrection story is a myth (2.58), and the Christians therefore worship a dead man (7.36). People become Christians because of a false hope in Jesus' resurrection (2.54–5).

Another criticism of Celsus is associated with his belief that the exploits of the Greek heroes are superior to the miracles of Jesus (1.67). During this period both pagans and Christians believed in miracles (Dodds 1965: 84). Although Jesus performed miracles by magic for evil purposes (1.68), Celsus insists that many who lived before the founder of Christianity performed wonders and foretold the future for the benefit of humanity. Asclepius, Cleomedes, the Dioscuri, Hercules, and Dionysus are a few examples (3.3; 3.22). Besides, Aristeas of Proconnesus, Abaris the Hyperborean, and the Clazomenian are much better candidates for divinity than Jesus (3.26–9; 3.31; 3.32). The glorious deaths of such great ones as Hercules, Asclepius, Orpheus, Anaxarchus, and the Sibyl are superior to the ignoble demise of Jesus (7.53, 55). If Asclepius heals, gives predictions, and does good to humanity (3.24), there is no room in Graeco-Roman religion for a deceiving magician who deluded the ignorant masses.

God

One of the greatest weaknesses of Christianity for Celsus was the concept of a God who constantly changed his mode of being, since this idea contradicted the classical Platonic doctrine of divine immutability:

> I have nothing new to say, but only ancient doctrines. God is good and beautiful and happy, and exists in the most beautiful state. If then He comes down to men, He must undergo change, a change from good to bad, from beautiful to shameful, from happiness to misfortune, and from what is best to what is most wicked. Who would choose a change like this? It is the nature only of a mortal being to undergo change and remoulding, whereas it is the nature of an immortal being to remain the same without alteration. Accordingly, God could not be capable of undergoing this change.
>
> (*Discourse* 4.14)

We have already seen how this concept relates to Celsus' argument about the crucifixion, but now it is necessary to observe how it relates to creation. Celsus relied on Marcionite teaching which distinguished between a Superior God and an inferior God in several passages where he calls the creator God of the Old Testament an 'accursed divinity' (6.28; 6.29; 6.51; 6.53; 6.59; Chadwick 1966: 26).

According to Plato in the *Timaeus*, the creation of mortal beings who descend into the World of Becoming is the work of the Demiurge. Following this Academic doctrine, Celsus punctiliously disparages the stories of creation in Genesis (4.38; 4.39; 4.52–3; 4.54–6). Christian teaching about a heavenly creator thus is a perversion of the *Timaeus* account which resulted from the biblical writers' borrowing from Plato (6.19; Baumeister 1978: 163–4; Borret 1984: 185–7). To the Christian views Celsus opposes the Platonic doctrines of the eternity of the world, and the Stoic concept of cyclical periods in time characterized by intermittent conflagrations (4.11; 4.65; 4.67–9).

Teleology was an important aspect of the pagan–Christian debate about the nature of God and his relationship to the natural world (de Andrés Hernansanz 1976; Lanata 1987: 36). Celsus ridicules the Judaeo-Christian belief that God created the world for man (4.74). He asks how can anyone believe that man is superior to animals? They are intelligent (4.78–81; 4.81–5: ants and bees), they converse and possess reason (4.84), and are more beloved by God (4.97). Divine providence has allocated a proper place for humans and animals, but man cannot claim superiority over any other species in the world (4.99). Nor can man even boast of a better knowledge of God. Celsus bases his argument on Roman augury and divination and asseverates that serpents and eagles have the power of sorcery (4.86), birds can predict future events (4.88), and elephants are observant of oaths (4.88).

With respect to God's nature, again Celsus adopts the standard teaching of the Academy: 'Ultimate being, colourless, formless, and impalpable, visible only to the mind that is guide of the soul, round which is the species of true knowledge' (6.19). This quotation from Plato demonstrates that Celsus' understanding of God is permeated with a distinct apophatic meaning, and may be one reason for his abhorrence of Christian doctrines like the incarnation, divine intervention in human affairs, and the ridiculous concept of God's chosen people. Hence God is unspeakable (7.43). He has neither mouth nor voice (6.62), He has no form, colour, nor does he partake of motion or substance (6.64). God cannot be reached by word, nor expressed by nature (6.65). He is incorporeal and impassible (6.64–5; 8.49). It is impossible to say, as Genesis 2 maintains, that God created man in his image because God is dissimilar to any other species of visible things (6.63). Yet the soul needed salvation. Following Platonic soteriology which emphasized the need to purify the soul and flee the passions of corporeal existence, Celsus affirms that man 'ought never to forsake God at all, neither by day nor by night, neither in public nor in private. In every word and deed . . . let the soul be continually directed towards God' (8.63). There was already by the second century a development in philosophy towards a rational monotheism which attempted to accommodate the old polytheism (Chadwick 1953: xvi–xxii). While rejecting the new monotheism of Christianity, Celsus insists that it makes no difference if we call the One God Zeus, Zen, Adonai, or Sabaoth (5.41–5; Baumeister 1978: 163–4; Hovland 1984: 202; Bregman 1984). This concept of the One true God, who is transcendent, conceived apophatically, and approachable only through rational thought, forms an essential part of Celsus' central thesis: there has been handed down a True Doctrine from ancient times which is the foundation of Graeco-Roman civilization, and it has given to mankind a true understanding of God's nature.

Prophecy

By 150 CE the Christian apologetic tradition had already developed a cogent argument based on the belief that Christianity must be true because Jesus Christ fulfilled all the Old Testament prophecies about the Messiah (Hauck 1989: 137). Prophetic revelation, whether oral or written, was thought to reveal a divine, secret, and beneficial knowledge accessible only to a few qualified recipients (MacMullen 1984: 25; Hauck 1989: 137). The *argument from prophecy* was central to the pagan–Christian conflict during our period (150–363), and we know of a few pagan philosophers, such as Justin Martyr (*Dialogue* 8) and Theophilus of Antioch (*Ad Autolychum* 1.14), who were so convinced by it that they converted to Christianity. Both Christians and pagans believed in their respective prophetic traditions, and each in turn attempted to prove the falsity of their opponents positions.

Origen's argument, which followed second-century apologetics, maintained that the Old Testament prophets were inspired by the One true God, they spoke the truth, preceded the wise men of Greece, were men of honourable characters, and their prophecies have come true in the life and death of Jesus Christ (7.4–42). Celsus ridicules the idea of a particular revelation, bases his argument on Stoic premises, and vehemently attacks the Christian 'fulfilled prophecy' argument (2.30; 3.1; 4.28; 7.36). His primary objective was to disprove the deity of Christ based on Old Testament prophecies. We may give five points of his argument.

First, Celsus maintains that the Old Testament prophecies are illogical and contradictory. This became an important theme in classical anti-Christian polemics, influencing later writers like Porphyry and Julian. Celsus says that the prophecies depict God as favouring evil (7.13). The prediction that the Jews will fill the earth and slay their enemies is ridiculous (7.19). Concerning the contradictions of the prophets, he asks if they really foretold that the son of the same Hebrew God would come into the world, how could he command one law through Moses and a different one through Jesus? Either he forgot what he had told Moses, or changed his mind with Jesus (7.18; 7.20; 7.25).

Second, Celsus rejects the claim that Jesus fulfilled Old Testament Messianic prophecies primarily because they can easily be applied to many other men more credible than Jesus (1.57; 2.28), they are inconsistent with the character of God (7.15–7), and they are more suitable to events other than those of Jesus' life (1.50). In any event, if the prophecies were so clearly fulfilled in Jesus, why have the Jews not received him as their Messiah (1.52)? Philosophically the heart of Celsus' argument here is based on Stoic epistemology, which held that reality is material and knowledge is derived from sense-perception. Inasmuch as Christian *prophetic revelation* was produced by sense-perception, it was carnal, unreliable, and certainly not divine (7.33–40; Hauck 1988: 242–9 and 1989: 121–9).

Celsus' third point is that Jesus himself was not a prophet. Miracles and prophecy were signs of genuine divine power in Graeco-Roman religions, and consequently Celsus attempts to discredit Jesus as a wonder-working prophet (Kolenkow 1987). Christ did not foreknow all that happened to him (2.13). The prophecies about Judas and Peter at the Last Supper are ludicrous (2.19): a man who banquets with a god will not plot against him (2.21)! And even if the fictions about Jesus' foreknowledge are accepted as true (2.15), one must keep in mind that Jesus deceived people by sorcery to believe that he was the one predicted by the Old Testament prophets (3.1).

Not only does Celsus attempt to destroy the credibility of Christian prophetic revelation, he also demonstrates the superiority of pagan oracles. Civilization, he asserts, has benefited greatly from oracles given at Delphi, Dodonna, Clarus, and other sites throughout the empire's history (7.3). As a result of obeying the commands of these oracles, many have been miraculously healed, magnificent cities have been built, colonies were established, rulers have prospered, and barren women have given birth (*Contra Celsum* 8.45). Furthermore, the oracular responses were given by priests and priestesses who were under divine influence (8.45). To some of these the gods appeared in visible form (8.45). Conversely, it is historical fact that those who disregarded the oracles have brought divine disfavour on themselves, causing entire cities to perish and individuals to suffer (8.45).

Celsus' fifth point is very significant for our study here and in relation to Porphyry and Julian as well. In *Contra Celsum* 7.9, Celsus derides *contemporary* prophetic experiences in Syria:

> As Celsus professes to describe the style of prophecy in Phoenicia and Palestine as though he had heard it and had a thorough first-hand knowledge of it, let us also consider this . . . There are many, he says, who are nameless, who prophesy at the slightest excuse for some trivial cause both inside and outside temples; and there are some who wander about begging and roaming around cities and military camps; and they pretend to be moved as if giving some oracular utterance. It is an ordinary and common custom for each to say: 'I am God (or a son of God, or a divine Spirit). And I have come. Already the world is being destroyed. And you, O men, are to perish because of your iniquities. But I wish to save you. And you shall see me returning again with heavenly power. Blessed is he who has worshipped me now! But I will cast everlasting fire upon all the rest, both on cities and on country places. And men who fail to realize the penalties in store for them will in vain repent and groan. But I will preserve for ever those who have been convinced by me.' Then after that he says: Having brandished these threats they then go on to add incomprehensible, incoherent, and utterly obscure utterances, the meaning of which no intelligent person could discover; for they are meaningless and nonsensical, and give a chance for any fool or sorcerer to take the words in whatever sense he likes.

Note Origen's remark about first-hand knowledge, the reference to many of these Syrian prophets during the period (late second century), and the apparent continuation of the (Christian) charismata mentioned in 1 Corinthians 12 and 14, especially prophecy and glossolalia (Aune 1983: 359, n. 221). And even though Origen attests to a few in the third-century church who possessed prophetic gifts, he nonetheless rejects the claim that prophets similar to those of the Old Testament lived in Celsus' day (7.8–9). Celsus' principal purpose in mocking these fanatical practices was to show how contemporary Christian prophets deceived weak people just as their leader had done in Palestine many years before (Chadwick 1953: 406, n. 6 and 1966; Gillespie 1978).

Eschatology

The Christian belief that the future life of blessedness is reserved only for those who live according to Christ's teaching was greatly ridiculed by Celsus (3.81). Doctrines concerning the blessed life and communion with God are vain hopes (3.80), and the biblical writers borrowed the idea of heaven as the soul's eternal resting place from Homer and Plato (7.28). Origen retorts that these borrowed the idea from Moses and the prophets. Celsus did believe in life after death, for as a Platonist his eschatological soteriology affirmed the belief in the immortality of the soul, the ability of philosophy to purify the soul, the need to escape from corporeal contamination, a release from the cycles of reincarnation, and being with God in the afterlife (Simmons 1995: 264–303). Where Celsus parts company with the Christians is the doctrine of the resurrection of the flesh. Platonism could teach a final salvation *in* and *from* the body, but never, as Christians professed, *of* the body. The resurrection of the body is philosophically impossible. God indeed may give immortality to the soul, but he will not raise to life flesh which is, as Heraclitus taught, more worthless than dung (5.14). Finally, calling the Christian God a 'cook', Celsus mocks the belief in an eternal hell where all except the Christians will burn with fire (5.15–17). The Christians again borrowed this from Homer, he says, and besides, more noble doctrines about eternal punishments are found in the Mystery Religions (8.39–40; 8.48). Furthermore, the idea of hell is used by Christians to scare people into becoming believers in Jesus. Christian eschatology is untenable because it is philosophically deficient in the 'true doctrine' of cyclical time – the same things happen and God does not amend his work anew – and the correct theodicy which posits that the same number of evils remain constant in the world at all times.

Jesus' followers: the church

Celsus has much to criticize about the church. To cast aspersions on the origins of Christianity, and its doctrines and practices, he uses a Jew (1.28). And although he finds the Jews contemptible for having forsaken polytheism and for other reasons (1.2; 1.14; 1.16; 1.22; 2.4; 3.6; 4.31; 4.33–5; 4.36; 5.6–9; 5.50; 5.59),[14] at least they worship according to their ancestral customs (5.25–6; 5.34–5). On the other hand, Christians revolted from Hebrew traditions and became apostates (5.33). Celsus' objective in assailing the Jews was to show that Christianity must not be true because it derived from the false religion of the Hebrews (1.22). Connected with the charge of apostasy is the allegation that Christians hold secret associations which violate Roman law (1.1; 1.3; 1.7; 8.17; 8.39).[15] Christianity therefore is an illegal religion.

Throughout the *Contra Celsum* Origen informs us that his opponent consistently attacked the doctrines of the church. Celsus primarily argues that Christianity is based on a corruption of the True Doctrine passed down from ancient times by ignorant and superstitious men who misunderstood what they had received (5.65; cf. 3.79). Comparing Christian teaching with the silly theriomorphic religion of Egypt (3.17, 19, 21), Celsus concludes that it is vulgar, unreasonable, and it easily persuades the illiterate masses (1.27). He will also rather frequently stress the variety of heretical doctrines circulating in the church to prove the disunity of the Christians. If they really possessed the truth, should they not all profess the same beliefs (5.62; 5.63–5; 6.30; 6.33–5; 6.38; 7.53)? Many Christian doctrines resulted from the corruption of ancient Greek authors, especially Plato (6.17–18; 7.14; 7.61). It is therefore not surprising for Celsus to find inconsistencies in such teachings as cosmology (6.49), soteriology (6.68–9), pneumatology (7.45; 6.70; 6.71; 6.72), and universalism.

As a Platonic philosopher who emphasized the importance of living in accordance with reason, Celsus regularly attacks Christian faith, and this eventually developed into a major criticism in pagan polemics by the time of Porphyry. Hence he says that men should follow reason to acquire wisdom which comes from the World of Being after the soul is purified by philosophy. Otherwise opinions from the World of Becoming will impede his attainment of the truth. Because Christians follow opinions, they are ignorant and easily deceived (1.9). Wisdom is thus foolishness to those who say 'only believe', and 'don't ask any questions' (6.12). Christians believe erroneous and make-believe doctrines about Jesus because they cannot offer any sound reason for their 'faith' (1.13; 3.39; 4.11; 6.10; 6.12). Inasmuch as faith is inferior to reason, it is no wonder to Celsus that ignorant people are easily converted (6.12).

The new religion begun by a Jewish carpenter's son has borrowed many things from the Greeks and lacks the authority of antiquity. 'For Celsus it is axiomatic that nothing can be both new and true' (Chadwick 1966: 23). The novelty of Christianity was a major criticism of Christianity found frequently in the *Discourse* (7.53; 8.12; 8.41; 8.43). Celsus' central thesis is the belief in an ancient doctrine passed down by wise men of old which contains the True Doctrine for humanity and has had a great civilizing influence upon the Mediterranean world. Without a foundation in truth, Christian worship and ritual are demonic in origin, and worse than the practices of barbarian nations (1.5; 1.6; 1.8; 6.40; 7.62; 7.68; 8.13; 8.48).

The character and social status of Christians is the final criticism of the church made by Celsus. He maintains that Jesus' disciples were notorious and wicked (1.62), and contemporary believers are ignorant, unintelligent, carnal, and win over no one to their cause who is wise or prudent (3.44–9; 7.39). Only low-class persons of the markets who are easily deceived by sorcery, and who would never associate with cultured people, are converted to Christianity (3.50–4). The church welcomes 'sinners' because it cannot appeal to the righteous (3.65).

Christians and the Roman empire

A disregard for the True Doctrine passed down from antiquity which has preserved polytheistic culture can only lead to rebellion against the empire. Traditional polytheism is justified according to the divine providence which governs all things through the mediation of angels, demons, and heroes. To these are assigned various geographical areas, so whoever worships God should also worship his subordinate powers (7.68–70; cf. 5.25). Christians cause sedition against the Roman government in the same way that the Hebrews originated in rebellion against Egypt (3.8; cf. 3.5, 7, 14). The Christians' rebellion against the empire stems from refusing to honour the daemons in the lower atmosphere who belong to God (8.2), assist him in governing the world in their assigned territories (8.33–5), receive sacrifices and prayers (8.24–7), and bless those under their care in conjunction with providence (8.7, 9, 34, 36, 38). History informs us that many have become sick, mad, or committed suicide for disregarding polytheistic worship (8.45).

If Christians honoured these polytheistic customs, they would be tolerated (8.12), but since they worship a dead man who only recently lived, and who was the leader of a seditious movement (8.14), they revolt without reason from the common belief (8.49; cf. 8.2). Christianity divides the 'Kingdom of God', raises factions, and worships one who is God's enemy (8.11). If on the other hand the Romans abandoned their ancestral religious customs, their world would disintegrate because it is the worship of the gods that made the empire great (8.69). All people should swear by the emperor, for the material and spiritual fortunes from the gods come through him (8.63, 66, 67, 68, 71). Christians should support the emperor to maintain justice (8.73); serve in the army to defend their country (8.74); and hold public offices in the government for the maintenance of the laws and the support of religion (8.74–5). But since they stand aloof from the government, the military, and society generally, they provoke the gods' wrath and anarchy, and should therefore be executed and driven to extinction (8.56).[16]

The superiority of Greek culture

As we have already observed, Celsus believed that Jesus and his followers borrowed many of their doctrines from the wise men of the Greeks who passed down the True Doctrine to posterity. This cultural *mos maiorum* contained the truth in such areas as philosophy, religion, and literature, its claim to authority was found in its antiquity, and it has formed the basis for the high culture (*paideia*) of the Greeks. It has preserved Roman civilization. Celsus goes further, however, by explaining the affinities between Christianity and Graeco-Roman culture on the basis not only of the new borrowing from the old, but also of corrupting the *Discourse* by the use of sorcery. Hence there may be found a few admirable things about Christianity, but on the whole, because of its ludicrous practices and doctrines, this new and strange religion is greatly inferior to the traditional polytheism of the empire.

Celsus initially develops his argument by saying that Greek culture is superior to the customs of barbarian nations (1.2). Since Christianity has much in common with barbarous customs, it too is inferior to Greek culture. Owing to its style and accuracy, Greek literature is superior to Christian scripture (6.1). And many of the writings of the Greeks are more ancient than those of Moses and the prophets (7.31). Celsus consistently relies upon Plato to prove his thesis (6.6–8). For example, he says that Plato taught many great theological truths, yet he never espoused a belief in a particular God who descended to earth to talk with him (6.8). Plato is a more effective teacher of the problems of theology. Quoting *Timaeus* 28C, Celsus says, 'Now to find the Maker and Father of this universe is difficult, and after finding him it is impossible to declare him to all men' (6.42). Greek philosophers have demonstrated that God is knowable by synthesis, analysis, and analogy, but the Christians cannot comprehend him because their theological epistemology is based on sense-perception (7.36). And their Logos concept is wedded to the flesh (7.42).

Celsus here follows the Platonic doctrine which affirmed that things are either intelligible, originating in the realm of Being; or sensible–visible, deriving from the realm of Becoming. Truth comes from Being which is apprehended by pure thought. Error, which is based on opinion, derives from Becoming. Intelligible objects are known by the soul trained by philosophy. If the Christians believe that a divine spirit came to earth in order to reveal truths to men, it was the same spirit that announced these Platonic truths long ago. But in fact the Christians are really lamed in mind, follow errors newly created by the magician Jesus, and live a sensual-carnal life far removed from the True Doctrine passed down from antiquity.

CONCLUSIONS

Whether we speak about the True Doctrine of Celsus or the other ideas enunciated by the philosophers I have considered, it should be clear to the reader that the anti-Christian literature published by philosophers during the period 150–363 CE was characterized by an increasingly *hostile* attack upon Christianity by some of the best representatives of the cultured classes of the Roman empire. This description ('increasingly hostile attack') of the relationship between paganism and Christianity takes issue with current trends in modern scholarship which has often reinterpreted the *conflict* along the lines of *pluralism* and *syncretism*, rather than accepting the argument which we have presented in this chapter. There is no doubt that there were areas during our period where the pagans and Christians cooperated and collaborated with each other, and because of this more conciliatory ambience, relatively speaking, we may in a limited sense use words like pluralism and syncretism to attempt to define the pagan–Christian relationship. But on the whole, and especially as it relates to the continuing debate between educated Christians and pagan philosophers, 'increasingly hostile attack' would appear to be quite appropriate words to describe the pagan–Christian conflict during our period. We started with a rather dispassionate and concerned critic of Christianity (Celsus), and then moved to a magistrate in the Roman government who claimed to be benevolently correcting the errors of a man-made myth (Hierocles), and who at the same time 'behind closed doors' energetically persuaded Diocletian to launch the Great Persecution in February 303. The double threat posed by Porphyry to the Christians was his widely circulated anti-Christian works, one of which (the *Contra Christianos*) appears to have exclusively used the scriptures against his enemies; and his apparently close collaboration with Diocletianic officials to initiate the persecution. Neoplatonic philosophers like Porphyry particularly opposed the Christian doctrines of revelation, eschatology, creation, God, soteriology, and Christology. The latter's tenets of the incarnation, the passion, and the resurrection of the body grossly contradicted such cardinal Platonic teachings as divine immutability and impassibility, and simply seemed absurd to many philosophers who conceived reality as hierarchical and the cosmos as being divided into distinct ontological levels with the highly transcendent supreme principle at the top, and the material world at the bottom. As we will see in Chapter 50, with the advent of an apostate emperor (Julian), we witness an anti-Christian programme which began with a number of non-aggressive policies, predominantly in favour of the pagans, but which over a short period of time continued to develop into an increasingly hostile move against the Christians. One can only imagine what Julian would have done if his Persian campaign had been successful. What we do know is that during its most critical period when the pagan intelligentsia excoriated the doctrines of the church and caricatured the Christians as ignorant, gullible, and demonized, the church was consistently growing throughout the empire, and this may indeed be the principal reason why the pagan attack became increasingly hostile.

Of the three pagan philosophers whom we have discussed in this chapter, Porphyry represents the most formidable, and indeed we have identified him as the greatest opponent of Christianity in antiquity. His threat was in his subtle and deceptive treatment of the founder of Christianity, acknowledging him as pious and dwelling with the gods in heaven, while at the same time totally rejecting his deity; and attempting to prove that his disciples misconstrued his teachings which were in conformity with traditional Graeco-Roman polytheism. Unlike other pagan polemicists, Porphyry apparently never described Jesus as a demonized magician whose primary objective was to deceive the masses, nor did he attribute his miracles to the operation of malignant spirits. This does not, however, mean that he was genuinely complimentary of Jesus, nor that he desired to incorporate him into the religions of the empire, at least from the perspective of the Christians who believed that he was God incarnate and the saviour of the world exclusive of all other gods.

The theme of this chapter is significant for a number of reasons. First, it reveals something of the truculent nature of the *intellectual conflict* between pagans and Christians in the Roman empire. Second, it demonstrates the struggle with the meaning of a truly universal religion, and whether this would be defined as a tolerant and inclusive polytheism supported by ancient religious customs, or as an intolerant and exclusive monotheism characterized by its particularity and a strong conviction that a recent and new divine revelation had been given to humanity. Third, the importance of the belief in *divine revelation*, espoused and defended by both pagan and Christian writers and focusing upon *prophetic revelation*, was one of the most important aspects of the pagan–Christian debate in antiquity, as has emerged in the discussion of the *True Discourse* of Celsus. This is a fact that has not been given the recognition that it deserves, and further research will undoubtedly produce admirable dividends. Fourth, we have shown that there was a continual debate between both groups concerning the true nature of the 'God-man' as he was perceived in the classical Mediterranean world. Finally, the close collaboration between pagan Neoplatonic philosophers and the Roman government, represented in the writings of Hierocles, Porphyry and Julian, but hinted at in the *True Discourse* of Celsus, accentuates the hostile nature of the opposition to Christianity during the period. Considering both the intensity of the criticism and the superb literary skills of the critics of Christianity that we have surveryed in this chapter, the most fascinating fact of all is not that the church eventually survived among so many cults in the Graeco-Roman world, but that it emerged triumphant.

NOTES

1 The thesis of Andressen (1955) is that Celsus develops a philosophy of history to oppose that of Justin. Some scholars concur: Chadwick (1966: 22), Hovland (1984), Wilken (1984: 101), Hauck (1985–6: 211–25, 220 and Amphoux (1992: 251). On the other hand, Burke (1985: 107–16) seeks to refute Andressen's thesis.

2 Although most scholars reject this idea: Chadwick (1953: xxiv–xxv; his translation is used here), Gallagher (1982: 115), Benko (1984: 108), Wilken (1984: 95), Hoffmann (1987: 31) and Lanata (1987: 12–13).

3 On allegory see Pelikan (1971: 31) and Chadwick (1947: 43). Chadwick (1953: x) points out that when Celsus uses Platonic arguments, Origen relies on Stoic refutations and vice versa. See also Hovland (1984: 210).

4 For the context, see Lactantius, *Divinae institutiones* 5.2; Eusebius, *Contra Hieroclem* 4, 19;

On the Martyrs of Palestine 5.3. Also Barnes (1976 and 1981: 21–3 and 165), Forrat and Des Places (1986: 1–14 and 17), Junod 1988, Speyer (1989) and Simmons (1995: 32–46). These secondary authors are also relied on extensively in my discussion.

5 For the Greek text and English translation, see Conybeare (1912).

6 The structure is: Chapters 1–6 (introduction); 7–12 (Philostratus Book 1); 13–15 (Book 2); 16–22 (Book 3); 23–6 (Book 4); 27–9 (Book 5); 30–2 (Book 6); 33–40 (Books 7–8); 41–2 (on Fate and Necessity). See Campanini (1991: 20).

7 Porphyry, *Vita Plotini* 17: 'Basileus' in Greek. Cf. Rinaldi (1982) and *Vit. Plot.* 23.12–14.

8 For his life and works see: Kroll (1894), Bidez (1913), Courcelle (1953), O'Meara (1959), Wolff (1962), Hagedorn and Merkelbach (1966), Hadot (1968), Demarolle (1972), Grant (1973), Smith (1974), Bouffartigue and Patillon (1977), Geffcken (1978), Meredith (1980), Des Places (1982), Croke (1983, 1984), Goulet (1984), Frend (1987), Evangliou (1989), Edwards (1990, 1991), Simmons (1995: 1–46, 216–27), Beatrice (1996) and Simmons (1997).

9 Eusebius, *HE* 6.19; Porphyry, *Vit. Plot.* 3, 14, 20; Hoffmann (1994: 16, 155); De Labriolle (1929); Hadot (1960); Pezella (1962).

10 For analysis of his works, see Smith (1993). For the *Philosophia ex oraculis*, see Augustine, *Civ. Dei.* 10.32; also Bidez (1913: 20–36), Hadot (1960: 240), Dodds (1961), Pezella (1962: 303), Rist (1964), O'Meara (1969), Des Places (1971) and Majercik (1989).

11 There is a huge literature on his scholarly achievements. (As a selection see Bidez 1913; O'Meara 1969; Hadot 1968; De Labriolle 1929: 386; Frassinetti 1953; Pezella 1962: 302–5; Dodds 1965: 126; Brown 1967: 316; Hadot 1960: 244; Demarolle 1972: 120; Meredith 1980: 1123–5; Beatrice 1989: 267; Simmons 1995: 18–32, and 218–22.)

12 For some of the literature on the *Contra Christianos*, including its biblical criticism, see Harnack (1916), Hulen (1933), Frassinetti (1953), Schröder (1957), Anastos (1966), den Boer (1974), Casey (1976, 1990), Ferch (1982), Evangeliou (1989: 55), Sellew (1989) and Beatrice (1993).

13 Also see Feldman (1990: 122), Benko (1984: 150), Borret 1984: 175–6), Mossetto (1986) and Puiggali (1987).

14 For Celsus' criticism of the Jews see Chadwick (1953: xx), Frend (1984: 163), Wilken (1984: 112–17), Hoffmann (1987: 36) and Martinez (1990–1: 201–2).

15 On illegal associations see Chadwick (1953: xvi) and Hoffmann (1987: 35).

16 On the charge of sedition against Christians, see Chadwick (1953: xix), Dal Covolo (1979), Benko (1984: 46–7, 56), Frend (1984: 177–8) and Hovland (1984: 194–6, and 202), Wilken (1984: 117–25), Hoffmann (1987: 34), Feldman (1990: 124–5) and Markus (1990: 100).

BIBLIOGRAPHY

Amphoux, Christian-Bernard (1992) 'Un Echo de la Devise de l'Académie de Platon chez Celse?', *Revue des Études Greques* 105: 247–52.

Anastos, M. V. (1966) 'Porphyry's Attack on the Bible', in L. Wallach (ed.) *The Classical Tradition*. Ithaca, N.Y.: Cornell, 42–50.

Andressen, Carl (1955) *Logos und Nomos. Die Polemik des Kelsos Wider das Christentum*. Berlin: de Gruyter.

Aune, David E. (1983) *Prophecy in Early Christianity and the Ancient Mediterranean World*. Grand Rapids, Mich.: Eerdmans.

Barnes, T. D. (1973) 'Porphyry Against the Christians: Date and Attribution of Fragments', *Journal of Theological Studies* n.s. 24: 424–42.

—— (1976) 'Sossianus Hierocles and the Antecedents of the Great Persecution', *Harvard Studies in Classical Philology* 80: 239–52.

—— (1981) *Constantine and Eusebius*, Cambridge, Mass.: Harvard University Press.

Baumeister, Theofried (1978) 'Gottesglaube und Staatsauffassung – ihre Interdependenz bei Celsus und Origenes', *Theologie und Philosophie* 53: 161–78.

Beatrice, Pier F. (1988) 'Un oracle antichrétien chez Arnobe', in Y. de Andia *et al.* (eds) *Memorial Dom Jean Gribomont*. Rome: Institutum Patristicum Augustinianum, 248–81.

—— (1989) 'Quosdam Platonicorum Libros', *Vigiliae Christianae* 43: 248–81.

—— (1993) 'Pagans and Christians on the Book of Daniel', *Studia Patristica* 25: 27–45.

—— (1996) 'Porphyrius', *Theologische Realenzyklopädie* 27. Berlin: de Gruyter, 54–9.

Benko, Steven (1984) *Pagan Rome and the Early Christians*. London: Batsford.

Bidez, J. (1913) *Vie de Porphyr*. Gand /Leipzig (= Hildesheim 1964).

Bolton, Charles A. (1968) 'The Emperor Julian Against "Hissing Christians"', *Harvard Theological Review* 61: 496–7.

Borret, Marcel (1967) *Origène Contre Celse Tome I (Livres I et II)*. Sources Chrétiennes 132. Paris: Editions du Cerf.

—— (1984) 'L'Ecriture d'après le païen Celse', in Claude Mondésert (ed.) *Le monde grec ancien et la Bible*. Paris: Beauchesne.

Bouffartigue, J. and Patillon, M. (1977) *Porphyre De L'Abstinence Tome I Livre I*. Paris: Belles Lettres. *Bulletin de l'Association Guillaume Budé*.

Bregman, Jay (1984) 'Logismos and Pistis', in Robert C. Smith and John Lounibos (eds) *Pagan and Christian Anxiety*. Lanham, Md.: University Press of America, 217–31.

Brown, Peter (1967) *Augustine of Hippo*. Los Angeles: University of California Press.

Burke, Gary T. (1984) 'Walter Bauer and Celsus', *Sources Chrétiennes* 4: 1–7.

—— (1985) 'Celsus and Justin: Carl Andrensen Revisited', *Zeitschrift für die Neustestamentliche Wissenschaft und die Kunde des Urchristentums* 76: 107–16.

—— (1986) 'Celsus and the Old Testament', *Vetus Testamentum* 36: 241–5.

Campanini, Saverio (1991) 'Un Cristiano e l'irrazionale: Il Contra Hieroclem di Eusebo di Cesarea', *Giornale Ferrarese di Retorica e Filologia* 1: 17–25.

Casey, P. M. (1976) 'Porphyry and the Origin of the Book of Daniel', *Journal of Theological Studies* 27: 15–33.

—— (1990) 'Porphyry and Syrian Exegesis of the Book of Daniel', *Zeitschrift für die Neutestamentliche Wissenschaft und die Kunde des Urchristentums* 81: 139–42.

Chadwick, Henry (1947) 'Origen, Celsus, and the Stoa', *Journal of Theological Studies* 48: 43–9.

—— (1953) *Origen: Contra Celsum*. Cambridge: Cambridge University Press.

—— (1966) *Early Christian Thought and the Classical Tradition*. Oxford: Oxford University Press.

—— (1992) 'The Early Christian Community', in John McManners (ed.) *The Oxford Illustrated History of Christianity*. Oxford: Oxford University Press, 21–61.

—— (1993) *The Early Church*. rev. edn. London: Penguin.

Conybeare, F. C. (1912) *Philostratus. The Life of Apollonius of Tyana*, 2 vols. Loeb Classical Library. Cambridge, Mass.: Harvard University Press.

Courcelle, Pierre (1953) 'Les Sages de Porphyre et les "uiri noui" d'Arnobe', *Religion* 31: 257–71.

Croke, Brian (1983) 'Porphyry's Anti-Christian Chronology', *Journal of Theological Studies* 34: 168–85.

—— (1984) 'The Era of Porphyry's Anti-Christian Polemic', *Journal of Religious History* 13, 1: 14.

Dal Covolo, Enrico (1979) 'Il Regno di Dio in Alcune Testimonianze del Secondo Secolo', *Rivista Biblica* 27: 313–24.

Daniélou, Jean (1973) *A History of Early Christian Doctrine Before the Council of Nicaea*. Vol. II: *Gospel Message and Hellenistic Culture*, Philadelphia, Pa.: Westminster.

Davies, P. S. (1989) 'The Origin and Purpose of the Persecution of 303', *Journal of Theological Studies* 40: 66–94.

de Andrés Hernansanz, Teodoro (1976) 'La Sintesis filosofica del Intelectual Pagano del Siglo II D.C., A travers del "Alethes Logos" de Celso', *Miscellanea Comillas* 34: 145–95.

De Labriolle, Pierre (1929) 'Porphyre et le Christianisme', *Revue d'Histoire de la Philosophie* 3: 385–440.

Demarolle, Jeanne-Marie (1972) 'Un aspect de la polémique païenne à la fin du IIIe siècle: Le vocabulaire chrétien de Porphyre', *Vigiliae Christianae* 26: 117–29.

den Boer, W. (1974) 'A Pagan Historian and his Enemies', *Classical Philology* 69: 198–208.

Des Places, Edouard (1971) *Oracles Chaldaïques*. Paris: Belles Lettres.

—— (1982) *Vie de Pythagore. Lettre à Marcella*. Paris: Belles Lettres.

—— (1989) 'Le Contre Hiéroclès d'Eusèbe de Césarée à la lumiere d'une édition récente', *Studia Patristica* 19: 37–42.

Dodds, E. R. (1961) 'New Light on the Chalcedon Oracles', *Harvard Theological Review* 54: 263–73.

—— (1965) *Pagan and Christian in an Age of Anxiety*. New York: Norton.

Edwards, M. J. (1990) 'Porphyry and the Intelligible Triad', *Journal of Hellenic Studies* 110: 14–25.

—— (1991) 'Two Episodes in Porphyry's Life of Plotinus', *Historia* 40: 456–64.

Ehrhardt, C. T. H. R. (1979) 'Eusebius and Celsus', *Jahrbuch für Antike und Christentum* 22: 40–9.

Evangeliou, C. (1989) 'Porphyry's Criticism of Christianity and the Problem of Augustine's Platonism', *Dionysius* 13: 51–70.

Feldman, Louis H. (1990) 'Origen's Contra Celsum and Josephus' Contra Apionem: The Issue of Jewish Origins', *Vigiliae Christianae* 44: 105–35.

Ferch, A. J. (1982) 'Porphyry: An Heir to Christian Exegesis?' *Zeitschrift für die Neutestamentliche Wissenschaft und die' Kunde des Urchristentums* 73: 141–7.

Forrat, M. and Des Places, E. (1986) *Eusèbe de Césarée. Contre Hiéroclès*. Sources Chrétiennes 33. Paris: Editions du Cerf.

Fox, Robin Lane (1987) *Pagans and Christians*. New York: Knopf.

Frassinetti, P. (1953) 'Porfirio Esegeta del Profeta Daniele', *Rendiconti Classe di Lettere e Scienze Morali e Storiche* 86: 194–210.

Frend, W. H. C. (1981) *Martyrdom and Persecution in the Early Church*. Grand Rapids, Mich.: Eerdmans.

—— (1984) *The Rise of Christianity*. Philadelphia, Pa.: Fortress.

—— (1987) 'Prelude to the Great Persecution: The Propaganda War', *Journal of Ecclesiastical History* 38: 1–18.

Gallagher, Eugene V. (1982) *Divine Man or Magician? Celsus and Origen on Jesus*. Society of Biblical Literature. Dissertation Series No. 64 (William Baird, ed.). Chico: California.

Geffcken, J. (1978) *The Last Days of Greco-Roman Paganism*. trans. S MacCormack. Amsterdam: North-Holland.

Gillespie, T. W. (1978) 'A Pattern of Prophetic Speech in First Corinthians', *Journal of Biblical Literature* 97: 74–95.

González, Justo L. (1970) *A History of Christian Thought*, 3 vols. Nashville, Tenn.: Abingdon.

Goulet, R. (1984) 'Porphyre et Micaire de Magnésie', *Studia Patristica*, Part I, *Texte and Untersuchungen* 128: 448–52.

Grant, Robert M. (1973) 'Porphyry Among the Early Christians', in den Boer *et al.* (eds) *Romanitas et Christianitas*. Amsterdam: North-Holland, 181–7.

Griffin, Miriam T. (1984) *Nero. The End of a Dynasty*. New Haven, Conn.: Yale University Press.

Hadot, Pierre (1960) 'Citations de Porphyre chez Augustin', *Revue des Études Augustiniennes* 6: 205–44.

—— (1968) *Porphyre et Victorinus*. Paris: Études Augustiniennes.

Hagedorn, D. and Merkelbach, R. (1966) 'Ein neues Fragment aus Porphyrios "Gegen die Christen"', *Vigiliae Christianae* 20: 86–90.

Harnack, Adolph (1916) *Porphyrius 'Gegen die Christen', 15 Bücher: Zeugnisse, Fragmente und Referate*. Akademie der Wissenschaften, Philosophisch-historische Klasse Nr. 1. Berlin.

—— (1972) *The Mission and Expansion of Christianity in the First Three Centuries*, trans. and ed. James Moffat. Gloucester, Mass.: Peter Smith.

Hauck, Robert J. (1985–6) 'Omnes Contra Celsum?', *The Second Century* 5: 211–25.

—— (1988) '"They Saw What They Said They Saw": Sense Knowledge in Early Christian Polemic', *Harvard Theological Review* 81: 239–49.

—— (1989) *The More Divine Proof. Prophecy and Inspiration in Celsus and Origen*. American Academy of Religion. Academy Series. Atlanta, Ga.: Scholars Press.

Hoffmann, R. Joseph (1987) *Celsus On the True Doctrine, A Discourse Against the Christians*. Oxford: Oxford University Press.

—— (1994) *Porphyry's Against the Christians. The Literary Remains*. Amherst, N.Y.: Prometheus.

Hopkins, Keith (1998) 'Christian Number and its Implications', *Journal of Early Christian Studies* 6, 2: 185–226.

Hovland, C. Warren (1984) 'The Dialogue Between Origen and Celsus', in Robert C. Smith and John Lounibos (eds) *Pagan and Christian Anxiety*. Lanham, Md.: University Press of America, 191–216.

Hulen. A. B. (1933) *Porphyry's Work Against the Christians: An Interpretation*. Scottdale, Pa.: Mennonite Press.

Jackson, Howard M. (1992) 'The Setting and Sectarian Provenance of the Fragment of the "Celestial Dialogue" Preserved by Origen from Celsus', *Harvard Theological Review* 85: 273–305.

Junod, Eri (1988) 'Polémique Chrétienne Contre Apollonius de Tyana', *Revue de Théologie et de Philosophie* 120: 475–82.

Kee, Howard Clark (1986) *Medicine, Miracle and Magic in New Testament Times*. Cambridge: Cambridge University Press.

Kelly, J. N. D. (1978) *Early Christian Doctrine*, rev. edn. San Francisco: Harper & Row.

Kertsch, Manfred (1980) 'Traditionaelle Rhetorik und Philosophie in Eusebius' Antir-rhetikos gegen Hierocles', *Vigiliae Christianae* 34: 145–71.

Kolenkow, A. Bingham (1987) 'Relationships between Miracle and Prophecy in the Greco-Roman World and Early Christianity', in Wolgang Haase (ed.) *Aufstieg und Niedergang der Römischen Welt*. Berlin: Gruyter, II: 36.2.

Kroll, W. (1894) *De Oraculis Chaldaicis*. Breslau: Vratislaviae (*apud* G. Koebner).

Lanata, Giuliana (1987) *Celso II Discorso Vero*. Milan: Adelphi.

McDonald, Lee M. (1995) *The Formation of the Christian Biblical Canon*, rev. and expanded edn. Peabody, Mass.: Hendrickson.

McManners, J. (ed.) (1992) *The Oxford History of Christianity*. Oxford: Oxford University Press.

MacMullen, Ramsay (1984) *Christianizing the Roman Empire (A.D. 100–400).* New Haven, Conn.: Yale University Press.

Majercik, Ruth (1989) *The Chaldean Oracles.* Leiden: Brill.

Markus, Robert A. (1990) *The End of Ancient Christianity.* Cambridge: Cambridge University Press.

Martinez, M. G. (1990–1) 'En torno a la Polemica entre christianos y paganos a traves de la obra de Celso', *Memorias de Historia Antigua* 9–10: 199–212.

Meredith, Anthony (1980) 'Porphyry and Julian Against the Christians', *Aufstieg und Niedergang der Römischen Welt.* Berlin: Gruyter, II. 23.2: 1119–49.

Meyer, Ben F. (1992) 'Jesus Christ', in David N Freedman, *The Anchor Bible,* 6 vols. New York: Doubleday, 3: 773–96.

Mosetto, Francesco (1986) *I Miracoli Evangelici nel Dibattito tra Celso e Origene.* Biblioteca di Scienze Religiose 76. Rome: Libreria Ateneo Salesiano.

O'Meara, John J. (1959) *Porphyry's Philosophy from Oracles in Augustine.* Paris: Études Augustiniennes.

—— (1969) 'Porphyry's Philosophy from Oracles in Eusebius's Praeparatio Evangelica and Augustine's Dialogues of Cassiacum', *Études Augustiniennes* 6: 103–39.

Pelikan, Jaroslav (1971) *The Christian Tradition. A History of the Development of Doctrine,* 5 vols. Vol. 1: *The Emergence of the Catholic Tradition (100–600).* Chicago: University of Chicago Press.

Pezella, S. (1962) 'Note sul pensiero filosofico e sociale di Porfirio', *Eos* 52: 299–307.

Pichler, Karl (1980) *Streit um das Christentum.* Regensburger Studien zur Theologie Band 23. Frankfurt: Peter Lang.

Puiggali, J. (1987) 'La Démonologie de Celse Penseur Médio-Platonicien', *Les Études Classiques* 55: 17–40.

Quasten, Johannes (1953) *Patrology,* 4 vols. Vol. 2: *The Ante-Nicene Literature After Irenaeus.* Utrecht and Antwerp: Spectrum.

Rinaldi, G. (1982) 'L'Antico Testamento nella polemica antichristiana di Porfirio di Tirio', *Augustinianum* 22: 97–111.

Rist, J. M. (1964) 'Mysticism and Transcendence in Later Neoplatonism', *Hermes* 92: 213–25.

Rougier, Louis (1977) *Celse Contre les Chrétiens.* Paris: Éditions Copernic.

Ste. Croix, G. E. M. de (1954) 'Aspects of the "Great Persecution"', *Harvard Theological Review* 47: 75–113.

Schröder, H. (1957) 'Celsus und Porphyrios als Christengegner', *Die welt als Geschichte* 17: 190–202.

Sellew, P. (1989) 'Achilles or Christ? Porphyry and Didymus in Debate over Allegmal Interpretation', *Harvard Theological Review* 82: 79–100.

Simmons, Michael Bland (1995) *Arnobius of Sicca. Religious Conflict and Competition in the Age of Diocletian.* Oxford: Oxford University Press.

—— (1997) 'The Function of Oracles in the Pagan–Christian Conflict during the Age of Diocletian: The Case of Arnobius and Porphyry', *Studia Patristica* 31: 49–56.

Smith, Andrew (1974) *Porphyry's Place in the Neoplatonic Tradition.* The Hague: Martinns Nijhoff.

—— (1993) *Porphyrii Philosophi Fragmenta.* Leipzig: Teubner.

Smith, Rowland (1995) *Julian's Gods. Religion and Philosophy in the Thought and Action of Julian the Apostate.* London: Routledge.

Speyer, Wolfgang (1989) 'Hierocles I', *Reallexikon für Antike und Christentum* 15: 103–9.

Wallis, R. T. (1972) *Neoplatonis.* London: Duckworth.

Wilken, Robert L. (1984) *The Christians as the Romans Saw Them.* New Haven, Conn.: Yale University Press.

Wolff, G. (1962) *Porphyrii de Philosophia ex oraculis haurienda librorum reliquaiae*. Hildesheim: Georg Olms.

Woods, D. (1992) 'Two Notes on the Great Persecution', *Journal of Theological Studies* n.s. 43, pt 1: 128–43.

POPULAR GRAECO-ROMAN RESPONSES TO CHRISTIANITY

———— •✦• ————

Craig de Vos

Modern historians have noted that there was no official persecution of Christians before the mid-third century. That is to say, there was no empire-wide ban on Christianity enforced from the top down. Rather, prior to that time, any actions that were taken against Christians were local and sporadic. As such, they would have been largely due to public opinion.[1]

After all, the Roman legal system was accusatorial. It relied upon an accuser who laid the charge and presented the case, rather than on official investigation.[2] Consequently, for a Christian to be charged before a provincial governor meant that he or she would have been denounced and prosecuted by neighbours, family or friends (e.g. Pliny, *Epistulae* 10.96.2; 10.97.2; Eusebius, *Historia Ecclesiastica* 4.9; Justin Martyr, *Apology* 2.2). That such a major step would be taken suggests that Christians would have been disliked, resented, and/or feared. Indeed, for neighbours, family or friends to bring them to trial suggests that animosity and resentment would have built up over a considerable period.

This is consistent with social-scientific analysis of conflict. 'Conflict' is understood as a process that involves 'an escalating sequence of responses between two disputants'. It begins with the recognition of differences in attitudes, norms, values and beliefs between those concerned, which may be accompanied by feelings of resentment. Conflict-proper only occurs when these differences become intolerable. For this second step to occur, some sort of 'trigger' (that is, some significant incident or event) is normally required (de Vos 1999a: 11–12). However, whether or not overt conflict occurs also depends on other social factors, especially the nature of social ties in that society. For example, if a Christian community was itself socially diverse and its members had significant ties to the different social strata of its local society (especially if there were strong and positive ties to the ruling elite) the incidence of conflict with non-Christians would have been much less than a Christian community that had a much more restricted pattern of social ties (de Vos 1999a).

Consequently, the incidence of recorded conflict does not necessarily have any bearing on the general perception of Christians. In other words, the fact that actual cases of harassment of Christians are recorded only infrequently does not weaken the assertion that the Christians were the subject of popular resentment. Such accusations are quite literally the 'tip of the iceberg'. Apart from feelings of resentment that were not acted upon, there also would have been a spate of (unofficial) social and economic sanctions and verbal and physical abuse that simply would not have been recorded. Presumably this would have occurred before Christians were ever brought before magistrates .[3] After all, history tends to preserve the unusual and the extreme, not the ordinary, average and everyday.

Therefore, the question we face is, what did the average person in the Graeco-Roman world dislike about Christians? Or, to put it another way, what did Christians do, or not do, that elicited such resentment and hostility? We will begin our exploration of this issue by looking for traces of popular opinion in the later New Testament, followed by Christian and non-Christian sources from the second and subsequent centuries. Following that we will seek to answer the question of why they perceived Christians in this light.

EVIDENCE FROM THE LATER NEW TESTAMENT

The author of 1 Peter suggests that his readers are experiencing conflict and oppression because of their severance of social ties and their generally separatist way of life (Elliott 1986: 67–8; Goppelt 1993: 39–40; Achtemeier 1996: 177; Kraybill 1996: 44). Indeed, he specifically asserts that 'they are surprised that you do not now join them in the same wild profligacy, and they abuse you' (1 Pet. 4:4; see also 1:14–19; 2:11–12; 4:2–4). Given John's emphasis on a similar withdrawal and separatism in the Letters to the Seven Churches (Revelation 2–3), it is likely this also lay behind the sufferings his readers were experiencing (Kraybill 1996: 42). In other words, Christians were being harassed by their neighbours because they were seen as anti-social. They had stopped taking part in normal social activities (which were now considered immoral from the perspective of Christian morality) and they had thereby strained their relations with family, friends and neighbours.

Intimately linked to this separatism and social withdrawal was the Christians' withdrawal from the traditional cults of their cities. After all, religion was completely integrated in Graeco-Roman society. Temples and shrines were ubiquitous, and they performed a range of religious, political, economic and social functions. For example, the major religious festivals (which included public feasts and often gladiatorial or athletic games) were the high-points of the city's social calendar. It is quite clear that 'everyone' ordinarily participated in these festivals (see, for example, Pausanias, 10.32.8ff.; Xenophon, *Ephesiaca* 1.2.2–3; Augustine, *De civitate Dei* 2.26; Macmullen and Lane 1992: 45–9. Apart from joining the processions, it was customary for small altars to be set up outside houses and households would offer sacrifices as the processions passed by (Price 1984: 111–12; Kraybill 1996:53, n.97). Although participation was not 'compulsory', as such, there generally was no good reason not to take part. Therefore, when Christians stopped doing so their changed behaviour must have been immediately noticeable to their family, friends and neighbours (Oakes 1995: 116; see also de Ste. Croix 1963: 25; Price 1984: 123).

In addition, travelling markets and fairs were often held in temple precincts and in conjunction with religious festivals. A Christian would not take part in these if she or he took seriously the requirement to avoid idolatry. Similarly, Christians could no longer belong to a social club or a trade guild (*thiasos/collegium*) since this would mean participating in religious rites in honour of its patron deity. Consequently, withdrawal from these activities because of their cultic association would have meant an almost complete non-participation in society. In other words, not to take part in processions, sacrifices, feasts, fairs, clubs and guilds would have meant shunning their neighbours.[4]

This Christian attitude of separatism and socio-religious exclusivity is quite explicit in 1 Peter:

> As obedient children, do not be conformed to the passions of your former ignorance, but as he who called you is holy, be holy yourselves in all your conduct . . . You know that you were ransomed from the futile ways inherited from your fathers, not with perishable things such as silver or gold, but with the precious blood of Christ.
>
> (1:14–15, 18–19a)

> Let the time that is past suffice for doing what the Gentiles like to do, living in licentiousness, passions, drunkenness, revels, carousing, and lawless idolatry. They are surprised that you do not now join them in the same wild profligacy, and they abuse you.
>
> (4:13–14)

Indeed, the New Testament is full of exhortations to avoid 'idolatry' (for example, Acts 15:20, 29; 21:25; 1 Cor. 6:9–11; 10:7–14; 2 Cor. 6:16; Gal. 5:20–1; Eph. 5:5; 1 Thess. 1:9–10; 1 John 5:21; Rev. 2:14–16, 20–5; 21:8; 22:15). If involvement in 'idolatrous' practices were avoided, this would have meant social withdrawal and offence to ordinary Greeks and Romans. Obviously some early Christians, such as the elite Christians at Corinth (1 Cor. 8:1–11:1) and some among the seven churches in Revelation (Rev. 3:1–4), did not. Where Christians did not withdraw from 'idolatrous practices', conflict with non-Christians does not appear to have been a significant issue (Kraybill 1996: 44; de Vos 1999a: 205–31, 271–5). This, in itself, attests to the connection between the early Christian tendency towards socio-religious exclusivity (as reflected in the majority of the New Testament authors), and the reprisals that were exacted against Christians.

Added to this, of course, would be the Christians' offence to Graeco-Roman religious sensibilities. Rejection of the gods and their cults was greatly resented by the common people (de Vos 1999a: 46–8; see also Stoops 1989: 83). It would have been a personal affront to their values and beliefs, indeed their whole world-view. The traditional gods and their cults were still held in high esteem, and were the subject of strong personal devotion among the common people (de Vos 1999a: 43–5, 48–50). Furthermore, the people's relationship with the gods was understood in a contractual sense. This relationship was described by the Romans as *pax deorum* – the belief that they had peace with the gods provided they kept up their end of the contract. In reality this meant that their personal safety and well-being, along with that of their town, depended upon them maintaining the good favour of the gods by correctly performing the appropriate rites (Garnsey and Saller 1987: 163, 175; de Vos 1999a: 43–56).

Consequently, since the gods were understood to protect the town and its inhabitants, the behaviour of the Christians was seen as a direct threat to their welfare and safety (Janssen 1979: 141; Sordi [1988] 1994: 203; de Vos 1999a: 51–3). This alone would have been sufficient to provoke considerable hostility against Christians.

Such resentment would have been even greater due to the increase in popularity and importance of the imperial cult. Although Thompson has rightly pointed out that the imperial cult predated Domitian (81–96 CE), and that Domitian may not have demanded the use of divine addresses (1990: 96–116, 159; see also Collins 1984: 71–2; Friesen 1993: 165–6; contra Cuss 1974: 57–8), there is no doubt that there was a change or growth in the cult during his reign (Friesen 1995: 249; Slater 1998: 233–8). Many remains exist of temples built for the cult (see Figure 33.2, for Pisidian Antioch). We also know that under Domitian a new provincial imperial cult was established at Ephesus and the Ephesian Olympics were instituted in his honour (Kraybill 1996: 27–8; see also Friesen 1993: 147–9, 160–4). Furthermore, imperial cult images were quite frequent on coins from the latter half of the first century (see Figures 33.1a, b and c).

As it happens, the seven churches of Revelation 2–3 were all located in major imperial cult centres. Revelation 13 strongly suggests that the imperial cult, described as the worship of a haughty and blasphemous beast (Rev. 13:1–10), was both prevalent and popular in the late first century.[5] Therefore, when John attacked the cult (as he did, for example, in Rev. 14:9–12) he attacked something that was a major socio-religious institution, a significant vehicle for the expression of loyalty to Rome by provincials (Friesen 1995: 249), and the product of local, popular enthusiasm (Price 1984: 78–9; Garnsey and Saller 1987: 165). Furthermore, even as early as Tiberius' reign (14–37 CE), Tacitus claims that 'the town of Cyzicus was charged with neglecting the cult of the deified Augustus' (*Annals* 4.36). So criticism of and opposition to this institution would also have been perceived as a threat to the city's welfare. If John's attitude was at all common among Christians in this period an apparent increase in anti-Christian sentiment should not be surprising.[6]

At the same time, rejection of the traditional gods and cults, as well as the imperial cult, could have had a significant impact on the local economy. Cult festivals, with their processions, sacrifices, feasts, fairs and games, were a major source of revenue.[7] Resentment of Christian practices due to loss of income is quite apparent in Acts 16:19–21 (see de Vos 1999b) and especially in Acts 19:23–41. In the latter, the Ephesian silversmiths feared the impact of the preaching of Paul and his companions on their livelihoods, which were intimately associated with the cult of Ephesian Artemis. Therefore, they incited the mob to gather in the theatre (see Figure 33.3), dragging two companions of Paul and Barnabas along with them. After much confusion, the town clerk managed to quiet them down and the crowd left the theatre (Acts 19:23–41; see also Stoops 1989: 73, 83–4; Sordi [1988] 1994: 203). It is likely that such a scenario would have been repeated in many other cities.

In summary, then, it would seem that the Christians were resented because they refused to take a full part in society, snubbed their neighbours, spurned the gods and thereby threatened their neighbours' livelihoods and the safety of their towns, and

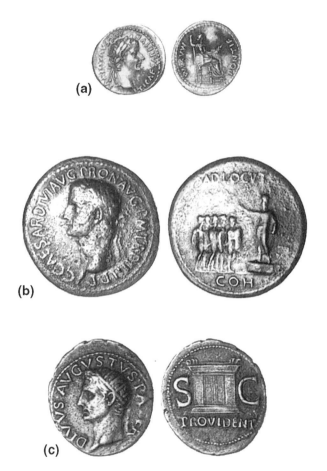

Figure 33.1a, b   Coins of Tiberius and Gaius (Caligula) in which each is described as the son of the divine Augustus.

Figure 33.1c   A coin issued by Tiberius commemorating Augustus after his death and describing him as 'Divine Father Augustus'.

offended their neighbours' social, political and religious values and beliefs. Consequently, it is not surprising that Christians were abused and harassed. Nor is it surprising that they were denounced to the authorities, even if this is recorded somewhat infrequently.

At the same time, it is clear that the Christians were denounced for what they thought to be trumped-up charges. For example, the author of 1 Peter suggests that his readers were the subject of abuse and slanderous accusations. Unfortunately, he does not explicitly indicate what these accusations might have been, except that he repeatedly uses the terms 'to do wrong' and 'wrongdoers' (2:12; 3:16–17; 4:14). The fact that both his readers and some among the readers of Revelation are denounced and suffer for the 'name' of 'Christ' or 'as a Christian' (1 Pet. 4:14–16; Rev. 2:17;

Figure 33.2 Remains of the Temple of Augustus and Roma at Pisidian Antioch. Photo J. C. N. Coulston.

3:5, 10, 12) would suggest that there was some overwhelming stigma or crime associated with belonging to the Christian community.[8] But the nature of these charges is not explicit. Given the circumstances that Luke describes in Acts 16:19–21, the most likely accusation against the historical Paul and Silas at Philippi would have been one of practising magic or witchcraft (de Vos 1999b). However, due to Luke's apologetic agenda this charge is down-played. Instead, the charge that Luke records (or constructs), 'they advocate customs which it is not lawful for us Romans to accept or practice' (Acts 16:21), is quite ambiguous. Therefore, while it is clear that Christians were denounced simply for being Christians, and this was due to an association with some crime or stigma, the nature of this is nowhere explicit in the New Testament. It only becomes explicit when we turn to subsequent writers.

EVIDENCE FROM OTHER SOURCES

Tacitus claims that Nero blamed the Christians for the Great Fire of Rome in 64 CE because they were 'hated for their atrocities' by the mob (*Annals* 15.44).[9] Suetonius also describes the Christians as a group 'given to a new and vile superstition', and records Nero's harassment of them. But he does not specifically link this to the fire (*Nero* 16.2; see also Cuss 1974: 150). Therefore, although a connection between actions against Christians and the fire may be somewhat tenuous, there is little

Figure 33.3   The theatre in Ephesus. Photo Philip F. Esler.

doubt that in the later half of the first century and the first half of the second century the Roman mob disliked Christians because they believed them to be guilty of a range of anti-social vices.

This is most apparent in the 'lynching' at Lyons in 177 CE (see Figure 33.4). On this occasion, Eusebius tells us:

> the local Christians endured with dignity the assaults that the entire company of the people inflicted upon them: mockery and insults yelled at them, blows and beatings, dragging, lootings, stonings and imprisonments, and everything that an enraged mob is able to unleash against its foes and enemies. Then they were taken to the public square by the authorities and questioned before the entire populace before being imprisoned ... After that they endured unimaginable tortures. ... Maturus, Sanctus, Blandina and Attalus were thrown into the amphitheatre to struggle with wild animals to be a public spectacle for pagan cruelty, ... they ran the gauntlet of lashings, as is customarily done there; they were dragged by wild animals; they suffered everything that the frenzied mob demanded, first from one side of the arena, then from the other; finally, they were strapped to an iron chair above a fire, which burned their bodies and smothered them with smoke. Even then the pagans did not stop ... Blandina, trussed to a stake, was exposed to the wild animals which

Figure 33.4   Amphitheatre at Lyons, scene of the martyrdom of Christians in 177 CE. Photo
Everett Ferguson.

were released against her . . . And after the floggings, after the wild animals,
after the iron-chair, she was finally thrown into a basket as a play-thing for a
bull. For a while it tossed her about . . . Then she too was slaughtered.

(Eusebius, *HE* 5.1.7–8, 16, 38, 41, 56; my trans)

What is significant, however, is that Christians at Lyons who denied their faith were
not spared. Eusebius notes that 'those who had denied when the Christians were first
arrested were also imprisoned with them and shared the same fate; for on this
occasion their denial had profited them nothing' (Eusebius, *HE* 5.1.33). This
strongly suggests that they were specifically executed because they were thought to
be guilty of various anti-social crimes. Indeed, Eusebius himself suggests the fury of
the crowd was a result of rumours of 'Thyestean feasts and Oedipean intercourse, and
things which it is not possible to say aloud or to think' (*HE* 5.1.14).

Similarly, when the magistrate reads out the charge of 'being a Christian' against
Polycarp the crowd immediately demands his execution (*Martyrdom of Polycarp*
12.2). Even at the end of the second century, Tertullian still can exclaim that in
trials of Christians 'only one thing is looked for, and only one, what is needful for
popular hatred is the confession of the name' (*Apol.* 2.3).

From this it seems likely that to be a Christian in the second century meant that
one was perceived to be some sort of criminal or engaged in illicit, antisocial,
immoral activity. This is no different from what we saw in relation to the later New

Testament. However, in the second century the nature of such accusations do become explicit. Indeed, it is clear that, for the common people at least, Christianity was strongly associated with crimes such as ritual murder and the sacrifice of infants, cannibalism, incest and other illicit sexual activity, conspiracy to commit arson, 'hatred of humanity', and the practice of magic (Justin Martyr, *Apol.* 1.26; Minucius Felix, *Octavius* 8.4–5; 9.2–5; Tertullian, *Apol.* 7.1; Athenagoras, *Leg. pro Christ.* 3; *Acts of Paul and Thecla* 15, 20; Pliny, *Ep.* 10.96).[10] For example, Tertullian sarcastically exclaims that Christians ought to be tortured to find out 'how many butchered babies each of us had eaten, how many acts of incest each had performed in the dark' (*Apol.* 2.5). Minucius Felix has an imaginary 'pagan' critic describe Christians as a 'band of questionable and illegal outlaws' who 'unite themselves against the gods'. Furthermore, he claims they are

> people who assemble illiterates from the dregs of society . . . and so organise a rabble of impious conspirators, banded together by nocturnal meetings, ritual fasts and abnormal feasts, not for any religious devotion but for superstitious rites . . . everywhere they introduce a 'so-called' religion of lust, a promiscuous fraternity by which promiscuous behaviour becomes incest, under the guise of a sacred title.
>
> (*Octavius* 8.4–9.3)

Apuleius says of one woman, whom most scholars consider a Christian, that:

> She was like a filthy toilet into which virtually every vice had flowed. She was cruel and debauched, addicted to sex and wine, recalcitrant and stubborn, greedy in her petty thievery and extravagant in her loathsome excesses, an enemy of fidelity and a foe to chastity . . . She despised and mocked all of the gods, and, instead of following true piety, she hid behind a false and wicked god, whom she called 'the one and only god', to create hollow rites in order to deceive everyone, including her wretched husband. She gave herself over to liquor from day-break and to licentiousness until sunset.
>
> (*Metamorphoses* 9.14)

In this regard, Christians were also thought to worship the head of an ass (Tertullian, *Apol.* 16; Damocritus, *Fr. Hist. Gr.* 4.377; see also McGowan 1994: 417). For example, the imaginary pagan critic of Christianity in Minucius Felix's *Octavius* claims that:

> their empty and idiotic superstition actually boasts of criminal activity . . . unless there was some foundation to it, perceptive rumour would not associate it with blatant and shameful forms of depravity. I am led to believe that by some stupid impulse they consecrate and worship the head of an ass, the basest of all beasts, a religion worthy of the morals that sired it.
>
> (*Octavius* 9.3)

This accusation, which is also reflected in a famous graffito from the Palatine area of Rome (see Figure 9.6 in this volume), would appear to be linked to a similar accusation made against the Jews by several Hellenistic writers. In particular, Apion specifically linked worship of an ass's head to ritual murder and cannibalism

(Josephus, *Against Apion* 2.79–80, 91–102), and this link may be implied in the passage just cited from Minucius Felix (McGowan 1994: 417). It is possible that this derogatory scrawling was also intended to convey this same accusation.

Not surprisingly, given the nature of these accusations, Christians were seen as a threat or danger to society. In particular, they were thought to be corrupt teachers who deceived women and young people. They were also accused of undermining family life; that is, of seeking to split households (*Acts of Paul and Thecla* 8–15, 20).[11] In this regard, it is possible that heads of households may have become suspicious of adulterous affairs if their wives were entertaining strange men in their homes during the day, or were getting up early to go to secretive pre-dawn rituals (MacDonald 1997: 71; see also Benko 1984: 126).

Although we cannot be certain how much the average Greek or Roman knew of Christian rituals, certain practices, such as exorcism, speaking in tongues, praying 'in the name of Jesus', and the sign of the cross, could have been seen as magical rites.[12] Accusations of practising magic would have been particularly important if, as Wypustek claims, there was a growing fear of harmful magic over the course of the second and third centuries (1997: 283, 287). Such a fear may indeed be implied by Suetonius' reference to Christianity as a 'wicked' or 'criminal' superstition (*malefica superstitio*; Suetonius, *Nero* 16.2; see also Janssen 1979: 157).

In the second and subsequent centuries the refusal of Christians to worship the traditional gods is also very prominent. They are frequently accused of 'atheism' (Justin Martyr, *Apol.* 1.5–6; Tertullian, *Apol.* 10.1; *Martyrdom of Polycarp* 12.2; Lucian, *Alexander the False Prophet* 38; Apuleius, *Met.* 9.14).[13] For example, Minucius Felix's imaginary pagan critic claims that 'they disdain shrines as if tombs; they mock the gods; they ridicule at our most sacred rituals; deserving sympathy themselves, they pity our priests (if you can believe it)' (*Oct.* 8.4). Indeed, such a complaint was probably the primary problem, as everything else stemmed from it (Benko 1984: 4; Sordi [1988] 1994: 160; MacDonald 1997: 59). This would also explain why Pliny only dismissed charges against people who denied they were Christians 'once they had recited after me a prayer of invocation to the gods and had made wine and incense offerings to your statue' (*Ep.* 10.96). Correspondingly, they became the scapegoats for the natural disasters experienced by local communities.[14] Although somewhat sarcastic, Tertullian's famous jibe is not an outrageous exaggeration:

> If the Tiber rises to the city walls, if the Nile does not cover the flood-plains, if the heavens don't move or if the earth does, if there is a famine or a plague, the roar is at once: 'The Christians to the lion!' Really! All of them to one lion?
>
> (*Apol.* 40.2)

Indeed, there was mob violence against Christians in Asia Minor during the reign of Antoninus Pius (138–61) as a result of natural disasters (Williams 1997: 897; see also Justin Martyr, *Apol.* 1.68; Eusebius, *HE* 4.26.10). For example, they were blamed for earthquakes in about 152, and plagues and a Parthian attack in about 165. Christians were also blamed for earthquakes in the 230s.[15] Frend even suggests that the Decian persecutions (250–1) can largely be attributed to this popular reaction against Christians in the face of natural disasters (1987: 6).

Popular resentment of Christians in this period can also be linked to the increasing importance of the imperial cult (McGowan 1994: 440). Thompson, however, contends that the role of the cult should not be overemphasized, because the issue of adherence to traditional cults was the main issue (1990: 164).[16] Yet, in a sense, the cult *was* traditional – at least in the Hellenistic East. As we have seen, even in the first century it was both widespread and popular. Furthermore, there is evidence to suggest that mob violence towards Christians was more pronounced during the major imperial festivals.[17] This is not surprising if observance of the cult was seen as a direct expression of loyalty to Rome and the emperor, upon whose goodwill cities in the Hellenistic East relied for their stability and prosperity.

Finally, ordinary people may also have denounced Christians to the authorities for economic reasons. Some, conceivably, may have denounced relatives, friends or neighbours in the hope of gaining their goods. After all, Roman law rewarded in that way those who could successfully prosecute another (Lane Fox 1986: 425; see, for example, Suetonius, *Nero* 10.1). It is more likely, however, that economic motivation was linked to the impact of Christian attitudes and practices on people's livelihoods, as we saw earlier in the case at Ephesus (Acts 19:23–41). For example, Pliny notes that following his actions against Christians 'meat from sacrifices is again being sold everywhere, although until recently hardly anyone seemed to be buying it' (*Ep.* 10.96). In other words, there had been a decline in the sale of meat left over from sacrifices that he directly attributed to the Christians. In the context of the numerous denunciations he mentions, it would not be surprising if many of the informers had been those most affected by this (Thompson 1990: 131; Kraybill 1996: 52–3). Anyone whose occupation was associated with temple practice would have been disadvantaged by Christian withdrawal.

As we saw in relation to the New Testament writings, it seems quite clear from later Christian and non-Christian sources that Christians were disliked, or even feared, because of the threat they posed to society. They rejected the gods, which was believed to harm people's very livelihoods and welfare. Christians destroyed families and households, thus also weakening the very fabric of society. They were thought to engage in magic, and they were suspected and accused of engaging in a range of illicit, immoral and criminal acts. Indeed, by the end of the second century such anti-social attitudes and activities had become synonymous with the very name of 'Christian'.

WHY WERE THE CHRISTIANS RESENTED?

It seems quite clear that Christians were the objects of popular resentment. On the surface this appears to derive from their separatist and anti-social tendencies, and their failure to worship the traditional gods. However, scholars generally argue that the popular belief that Christians were involved in immoral or illicit activity arose from misunderstandings of the Christians' practices, liturgies and language. For example, it is suggested that the accusations of cannibalism arose from outsiders misinterpreting the words of the Eucharist. Expressions such as 'this is my body . . .

this is my blood' would have naturally lead to the assumption that Christians practised cannibalism. Similarly, the Christian ban on abortion and the exposure of infants was linked to this accusation of cannibalism; that is, the ban was introduced so that there would be excess infants for their cannibalistic practices.[18]

Accusations of incest are said to have arisen from a misunderstanding of the Christians' use of terms such as 'brother' and 'sister' or 'love' (Wagner 1994: 133; see also Sordi [1988] 1994: 32–3), and the practice of kissing one another.[19] Similarly, accusations of adultery are attributed to women entertaining strange men in their homes during the day (MacDonald 1997: 71).

Accusations of magic are said to have arisen from the way that Christians sang hymns, spoke in tongues, prayed 'in the name of Jesus', made the sign of the cross and engaged in exorcism. All such activities would have been seen as 'magical' by outsiders. Indeed, the use of gesture, speaking in gibberish, and invoking the name of a powerful god were all common in magical incantations.[20] Furthermore, accusations of practising magic would have been linked to the Christian practice of holding secretive nocturnal rituals.[21] Some have even suggested that these accusations arose because outsiders confused Christians with gnostics or Montanists, who probably did engage in such activities (Benko 1984: 67; Wypustek 1997: 277–9).

Nevertheless, can this popular perception of illicit and immoral activity be attributed simply to misunderstanding? In the first place, if accusations of immoral and illicit activity were simply based on misunderstanding how do we account for the fact that the same accusations were made repeatedly over a very long span of time? As we saw, such accusations may have been made in the time of the later New Testament. Even if they were not, they certainly were by the time of Pliny (early second century), and they continued until at least the early third century (de Ste. Croix 1963: 20–1; Krodel 1971: 261). Surely it is unreasonable to attribute a belief that is sustained over a period of more than a century (if not two centuries) to a misunderstanding.

Furthermore, the claim of misunderstanding assumes that ordinary outsiders had little substantial knowledge of Christian beliefs and practices. Given the nature of life in ancient cities, however, this is highly questionable. The common people in Graeco-Roman cities spent much of their time in communal spaces and in public activities, because their places of residence were very small. An average flat or apartment was really used only for sleeping and storing possessions – people relied upon baths, public latrines, temples, shops, cafés and inns for everything else. At the same time, streets were generally very narrow (seldom more than a few metres wide) and there was an extremely high population density. Consequently, Graeco-Roman cities were face-to-face communities; that is, they lived very public lives. Gossip was rampant. There was little privacy and few secrets, especially as town-planning, social structures and social institutions specifically sought to minimize them (de Vos 1999a: 28–37).

In light of this, it is hard to imagine that outsiders did not know a considerable amount about Christian practices and beliefs. Since early churches generally met in houses, workshops and apartments (de Vos 1999a: 147–50, 258–61), streets were very narrow (see Figures 33.5 and 33.6 as an indication of how narrow the streets

Figure 33.5   First-century street in Jerusalem. Photo Merrill Kitchen.

were and how closely people lived together), and housing was very dense, many outsiders would have heard quite a lot of Christian preaching and teaching.

For example, in the *Acts of Paul and Thecla*, Thecla sat at her window across the street listening as Paul preached to the church that met in the house of Onesiphorus. She became a Christian as a direct result of what she heard. On the other hand, Thecla's mother (who no doubt also heard Paul's preaching) announced to Thecla's husband-to-be that 'she is obsessed with a foreigner teaching deceptive and crafty teachings . . . He claims we must fear only one God and live in abstinence' (*Acts of Paul and Thecla* 7–9). This is hardly a gross misunderstanding or misrepresentation of early Christian beliefs. Given the communal nature of city life, Christian beliefs and practices no doubt became a topic of conversation when people met at the local wells, the baths, the latrines, the shops, the cafés and so on.

Therefore, the argument that the popular accusations arose from misunderstanding due to ignorance or limited knowledge is hard to sustain, even if the Christians continually protested that their teachings and practices were being misunderstood (for example, Justin Martyr, *Apol.*; Minucius Felix *Oct.*; Tertullian, *Apol.*; Origen, *Contra Celsum*). After all, people could have made inquiries about the Christians, as Pliny did of those brought before him (*Ep.* 10.96), if they were concerned and wanted to get all of the facts. Consequently, if there was any 'misunderstanding' it must have been because outsiders were quite satisfied that they already knew the truth. They did not feel any need to investigate. Rather, as a number of scholars have suggested, because the Christians were seen as anti-social (both withdrawing from normal socio-religious activities and engaging in secret nocturnal gatherings) and they refused to worship the gods it was simply *assumed* that they must have been

Figure 33.6   Part of the Via Dolorosa in Jerusalem. Photo Merrill Kitchen.

involved in immoral and illicit activity.[22] People who did such things were surely capable of doing anything!

This popular assumption that the Christians must have been involved in a range of immoral and illicit activity is consistent with social-scientific analyses of Graeco-Roman society. As a number of scholars have noted (for example Malina and Neyrey 1996), the ancient Mediterranean world appears to have been a group-oriented or 'collectivist' society. In other words, Greeks and Romans gave priority to group rather than personal goals and their sense of identity was largely dependent upon the groups to which they belonged. Within such cultures people tended to think 'sociologically' rather than psychologically. As such, they were not really concerned with understanding each other in terms of the 'introspective, psychological ways' characteristic of modern western cultures (Malina and Neyrey 1996: xiii). Rather, they assessed themselves and others in terms of group-determined stereotypes. People were classified according to their family, race, place of origin and class. Indeed, if you knew these, you knew the person (Malina and Neyrey 1996: 7–17).

This 'stereotypic' approach is also very evident in the body of ancient work known as the 'physiognomic' literature. Such literature assumed that one could tell another person's character from the way that he or she looked (Malina and Neyrey 1996: 100–8). In other words, it assumed that 'all internal qualities may be known rather easily from external traits and behaviors', which were held to be fixed and unchanging (Malina and Neyrey 1996: 149–50). Consequently, from their observation of Christian beliefs, values and practices it could be concluded that Christians *were* anti-social. And if they were anti-social then it was to be expected that they would be capable of any manner of anti-social activity. Furthermore, if one Christian was an anti-social atheist, then they all were.

This use of stereotypic accusations is also consistent with a sociological understanding of deviance: specifically, the labelling theory of deviance. According to this theory, 'deviance' is behaviour that is perceived to violate a group's norms and values. As such, deviance is not so much an inherent characteristic as a reaction. A person becomes a deviant via a 'labelling process' such that the person's behaviour is perceived to violate the group's norms and values, this perception is disseminated within the group, and the person is subjected to a status degradation ritual and receives the appropriate punishment.[23] Deviance labelling is particularly common in collectivist societies (de Vos 1999b), where it serves to establish and maintain social boundaries (Esler 1994: 141; with some modification also Barclay 1995: 117). This particular theory is helpful because it shows that people can be labelled as deviants, and treated as such, simply based on the way their actions are perceived. Provided their actions are seen to violate the norms and values of the dominant group, so that they constitute a threat to that group, it does not matter whether they have actually done what they are said to have done.

In light of this, it would appear that the popular perception of Christians as engaged in immoral and illicit activity involves stereotypic thinking. The specific accusations (such as cannibalism, incest and magic) should be seen as examples of deviance labels. As such, they do not require any basis in 'reality'. Rather, they simply function to label those so accused as anti-social, in order to strengthen the boundaries within society and exert social control. That these accusations against the Christians are deviance labels becomes quite apparent when we look at the similar accusations that were made against other individuals and groups. These same accusations were extremely common, and in many cases it is quite apparent that they were levelled in the absence of any teachings or practices that could have been misunderstood (see McGowan 1994: 413–14).

For example, Lucius Catilinus and his co-conspirators were accused of incest, human sacrifice and cannibalism. Sallust claims they drank blood to seal their conspiracy, whereas Dio Cassius accuses them of sacrificing a child and eating his intestines (Sallust, *Catiline* 22; Dio, 37.30; see also Benko 1984: 61; McGowan 1994: 431). Plutarch goes even further. He claims that Catilinus had 'once been accused of raping his own daughter and of murdering his own brother' and 'had corrupted a large number of the city's youth', but together with his co-conspirators had taken oaths among themselves, one of which involved sacrificing a man and eating his flesh (*Cic.* 865–6).

Such accusations were common against those suspected of conspiracy (Corbett 1997: 849; MacDonald 1997: 60). Cicero makes an accusation of cannibalism against another political opponent (*In Vatinium interrogatio* 6.14; see McGowan 1994: 432). Such accusations were also levelled against Apollonius of Tyana who, with his associates, was said by Domitian to have 'sacrificed a boy in order to foresee the future' (Philostratus, *Vita Apollonii* 7.9; see also McGowan 1994: 432). Apuleius was brought to trial on charges of practising magic simply because he had married a wealthy widow in a town where he was an outsider (Apuleius, *Apologia* 25–8, 42–7; see also Kolenkow 1976: 108–9; Remus 1983: 70; de Vos 1999b). Agrippina was accused of adultery and using magic by someone who, Tacitus suggests, was simply trying to make a name for himself (Tacitus, *Annals* 4.52). It is doubtful that these accusations can be attributed to 'misunderstanding'.

Many foreign nations were also suspected of practices such as human sacrifice, cannibalism and incest, especially those on the fringes of the civilized (that is, the Graeco-Roman) world. For example, accusations of cannibalism and/or child sacrifice were levelled against most African tribes, some Egyptian tribes, some Gallic tribes (especially the Druids), Scythians, Carthaginians and the people of the Caucasus region.[24] Indeed, Aristotle claimed that 'there are many foreign races that tend toward murder and cannibalism' (*Politics* 8.3.4). Similarly, Pliny the Elder asserts that

> some Scythian tribes, indeed most of them, feed on human flesh – a claim that may seem unbelievable if we do not consider that races of this ominous character have lived in the central part of the world, named Cyclopes and Laestrygones, and that until relatively recently the tribes just beyond the Alps routinely practised human sacrifice.
>
> (*NH* 7.9–10.)

Accusations of incest were made against most devotees of Eastern religions (Benko 1984: 22, 62). Christians also made these same accusations against heterodox groups in the second century, particularly gnostics (Irenaeus, *Adversus Haereses* 1.25; 2.31; Hippolytus, *Refutation of All Heresies* 7.32; Clement, *Stromateis* 3.2.10; see also de Ste. Croix 1963: 20–1; Frend 1967: 188; Benko 1984: 65–6, 71; MacDonald 1997: 59–64).

There are also numerous examples of individuals or groups who were accused of practising magic.[25] Furthermore, ritual murder was also commonly associated with the practice of magic (Benko 1984: 60–1). In fact, accusations of magic and conspiracy were traditionally linked in Graeco-Roman thought with secret nocturnal rituals. Since the Christians practised the latter it would simply have been assumed that they practised the former.[26]

Rather than attributing many of the popular Graeco-Roman accusations against Christians (such as incest, illicit sexual behaviour, cannibalism, human sacrifice and the practice of magic) to misunderstanding, they should be seen as the stereotypic charges levelled against those who were perceived to threaten society. In other words, they were used to label those perceived to be deviants. Therefore, while those who claim that the accusations against the early Christians were based on misunderstanding assume that they were regarded as anti-social because they were thought to engage in such activity, it is more likely that because the Christians were regarded as anti-social it was assumed that they would engage in such activity.

The popular perception of and accusations against Christians simply reflect the stereotypic way that Graeco-Roman society described those who were perceived to be 'outsiders' and threats to their society.[27] Overall, it seems quite clear that Christians were resented by ordinary Greeks and Romans because they were dangerously deviant.

Therefore, on the whole, it would appear that ordinary Greeks and Romans disliked and resented Christians because of the threat they posed to society. Christians rejected the traditional gods and cults (including the imperial cult), an action that was believed to harm people's very livelihoods and welfare. They split families and households, thereby damaging the fundamental building-block of society. They were suspected (and accused) of engaging in magic and a range of illicit, immoral and criminal acts. Indeed, such anti-social attitudes and activities became synonymous with the very name of 'Christian'.

While scholars have attributed many of these accusations to misunderstanding, it is more likely that these were stereotypic accusations applied to those who were considered dangerous deviants. After all, these accusations were made over a long period of time – too long to be explained away as misunderstandings. Furthermore, similar accusations were also made against other individuals and groups who were perceived to be threats to Graeco-Roman society. When understood in terms of deviance labels, it is also clear that there need not have been any specific basis to these accusations, apart from the perception of the ordinary Greeks and Romans who made them.

NOTES

1 de Ste. Croix (1963: 6–7), Krodel (1971: 261), Lane Fox (1986: 423, 450), Garnsey and Saller (1987: 174), Barnes (1991: 236–7), Sordi (1988] 1994: 194–5), Williams (1997: 896) and Wypustek (1997: 276).

2 Benko (1984: 7–8), Lane Fox (1986: 425), Johnson (1988: 417), Phillips (1991: 263–4) and de Vos (1999b).

3 See Frend (1967: 156–7), Collins (1984: 98), Downing (1988: 115), Slater (1998: 245), see also Eusebius, *H. E.* 5.1.7; Athenagoras, *Legatio pro Christ.* 1.

4 See de Vos (1999a: 35–8), see also Wilken (1984: 63–5), Goppelt (1993: 39–40), Oakes (1995: 118–22), Achtemeier (1996: 282–5), Kraybill (1996: 52) and Slater (1998: 244, 250–1).

5 See Cuss (1974: 96–101), Price (1984: 252–65), Esler (1994: 132), Slater (1998: 253), even Thompson (1990: 160).

6 See Cuss (1974: 77, 84), Collins (1984: 101), Price (1984: 78–9), Achtemeier (1996: 285), Friesen (1995: 249–50), Kraybill (1996: 29–34) and Slater (1998: 238).

7 Thompson (1990: 161–2), Kraybill (1996: 29, 53) and de Vos (1999a: 35–6).

8 Downing (1988: 115), Goppelt (1993: 39–41, 327), Achtemeier (1996: 28–9;) and Slater (1998: 243).

9 See de Ste. Croix (1963: 8), MacMullen ([1966] 1992: 142), Frend (1967: 124, 155), Krodel (1971: 259) Cuss (1974: 149), Sordi ([1988] 1994: 31), Barnes (1991: 231), Goppelt (1993: 43) and Slater (1998: 247–8).

10 See also de Ste. Croix (1964: 31), Frend (1967: 195), Krodel (1971: 259), Janssen (1979: 151–4), Cunningham (1982: 8), Benko (1980: 1090–1 and 1984: 24, 60–70, 98), Lane

Fox (1986: 427), Wagner (1994: 133), MacDonald (1997: 64–72), Reasoner (1997: 911) and Wypustek (1997: 277).

11 See also Frend (1979: 35), Benko (1984: 46) and MacDonald (1997: 64).

12 See Aune (1980: 1545), Remus (1983: 60), Benko (1984: 113–19), Wypustek (1997: 282), de Vos (1999b), see also Tertullian, *Ad uxorem* 2.5.

13 See also Frend (1967: 200), Janssen (1979: 151–4) Cunningham (1982: 8), Wagner (1994: 132) and Wypustek (1997: 277).

14 See de Ste. Croix (1963: 24–6) Frend (1967: 177), Janssen (1979: 132–3), Wilken (1984: 63), Lane Fox (1986: 425–6), and Sordi ([1988] 1994: 56–7, 70, 160).

15 So Frend (1967: 177, 198) Reasoner (1997: 912) and Williams (1997: 897).

16 See also de Ste. Croix (1963: 10), Lane Fox (1986: 426), even Price (1984: 221).

17 Cuss (1974: 158), Bowersock (1995: 48), Friesen (1993: 154, 166), see also Price (1984: 73–83, 111–12, 123–4).

18 See Wagner (1994: 133), see also Benko (1984: 60), Sordi ([1988] 1994: 32–3, 197), and Goppelt (1993: 41).

19 Benko (1984: 79, 98), see also Rom. 16:16; 1 Cor. 16:20; 2 Cor. 13:12; 1 Thess. 5:26; 1 Pet. 5:14.

20 Aune (1980: 1545), Remus (1983: 60), Benko (1984: 12, 24, 113–19) and Wypustek (1997: 282).

21 Minucius Felix, *Oct.* 8.4–5; 9.4; see also Benko (1984: 10–12, 125–6) and Remus (1983: 60).

22 See Krodel (1971: 261), Frend (1979: 35), Sordi ([1988] 1994: 31, 202), Phillips (1991: 262) and McGowan (1994: 437).

23 See, for example, Malina and Neyrey (1991: 97–122) Barclay (1995: 114–27) Still (1996: 75–86), and de Vos (1999b).

24 See Minucus Felix, *Oct.* 30.3–4; Philostratus. *Vit. Apoll.* 6.25; Herodotus, *Histories* 1.216; 3.38, 99; 4.26, 64, 106; Strabo, *Geog.* 15.1.56; and also Benko (1984: 17, 61–6), Collins (1984: 87) and McGowan (1994: 425–6, 431).

25 For example, Tertullian, *De virginibus velandis* 15.1; *De spectaculis* 2.8; *De pudicitia* 5.11; Tacitus, *Annals* 2.69; Plutarch, *Conjug. praec.* 141B; *Dion.* 3.3; see also Aune (1980: 1523), Remus (1983: 52).

26 Minucius Felix, *Oct.* 8.4–5; 9.4; Pliny, *Ep.* 10.96; Apuleius, *Met.* 9.14; see also Benko (1984: 10–12, 125–6), Remus (1983: 60).

27 See Wilken (1984: 31–2), McGowan (1994: 433–4), MacDonald (1997: 60) and Slater (1998: 246).

BIBLIOGRAPHY

Primary sources

Ehrman, Bart D. (1998) *The New Testament and Other Early Christian Writings: A Reader*. New York: Oxford University Press.

MacMullen, Ramsay and Lane, Eugene N. (eds) (1992) *Paganism and Christianity 100–425 C.E: A Sourcebook*. Minneapolis, Minn.: Fortress.

Shelton, Jo-Ann (ed.) (1988) *As the Romans Did: A Sourcebook in Roman Social History*. New York: Oxford University Press.

Stevenson, J. (ed.) (1957) *A New Eusebius: Documents Illustrative of the History of the Church to A.D. 337*. London: SPCK.

Secondary Sources

Achtemeier, Paul J. (1996) *1 Peter*. Minneapolis, Minn.: Fortress.

Aune, David E. (1980) 'Magic in Early Christianity', *Aufstieg und Niedergang der römischen Welt* 2.23.2: 1507–57.

Baker, Derek (ed.) (1979) *The Church in Town and Countryside*. Oxford: Blackwell.

Barclay, John M. G. (1995) 'Deviance and Apostasy: Some Applications of Deviance Theory to First-Century Judaism and Christianity', in Esler 1995:114–27.

Barnes, Timothy D. (1991) 'Pagan Perceptions of Christianity', in Hazlett 1991:231–43.

Benko, Stephen (1980) 'Pagan Criticism of Christianity during the First Two Centuries A.D., *Aufstieg und Niedergang der römischen Welt* 2.23.2: 1055–118.

—— (1984) *Pagan Rome and the Early Christians*. Bloomington: Indiana University Press.

Benko, Stephen and O'Rourke, John J. (eds) (1971) *The Catacombs and the Colosseum*. Valley Forge, Pa.: Judson.

Bowersock, Glen W. (1995) *Martyrdom and Rome*. Cambridge: Cambridge University Press.

Collins, Adela Yarbro (1984) *Crisis and Catharsis: The Power of the Apocalypse*. Philadelphia Pa.: Westminster.

Corbett, John H. (1997) 'Paganism and Christianity', in Ferguson *et al.* 1997:848–51.

Cunningham, Agnes (1982) *The Early Church and State*. Philadelphia Pa.: Fortress.

Cuss, Dominique (1974) *Imperial Cult and Honorary Terms in the New Testament*. Fribourg: Fribourg University Press.

de Ste. Croix G.E.M. (1963) 'Why Were the Early Christians Persecuted?', *Past and Present* 26: 6–31.

—— (1964) 'Why Were the Early Christians Persecuted – A Rejoinder', *Past and Present* 27:28–33.

de Vos, Craig S. (1999a) *Church and Community Conflicts: The Relationships of the Thessalonian, Corinthian and Philippian Churches with their Wider Civic Communities*. Atlanta, Ga.: Scholars Press.

—— (1999b) 'Finding a Charge that Fits: The Accusation against Paul and Silas at Philippi (Acts 16.19–21)', *Journal for the Study of the New Testament* 74:51–63.

Downing, F. Gerald (1988) 'Pliny's Prosecutions of Christians: Revelation and 1 Peter', *Journal for the Study of the New Testament* 34: 105–23.

Elliott, John H. (1986) '1 Peter, Its Situation and Strategy: A Discussion with David Balch', in Talbert 1986: 61–78.

Esler, Philip F. (1994) *The First Christians in their Social Worlds: Social-Scientific Approaches to New Testament Interpretation*. London: Routledge.

—— (ed.) (1995) *Modelling Early Christianity: Social-Scientific Studies of the New Testament in Its Context*. London: Routledge.

Faraone, Christopher A. and Obbink, Dirk (eds) (1991) *Magika Hiera: Ancient Greek Magic and Religion*. New York: Oxford University Press.

Ferguson, Everett *et al.* (eds) (1997) *Encyclopaedia of Early Christianity*.Vol 2, 2nd edn. New York: Garland.

Frend, W. H. C. (1967) *Martyrdom and Persecution in the Early Church*. New York: New York University Press.

—— (1979) 'Town and Countryside in Early Christianity', in Baker 1979: 25–42.

—— (1987) 'Prelude to the Great Persecution', *Journal of Ecclesiastical History* 38:1–18.

Friesen, Steven J. (1993) *Twice Neokoros: Ephesus, Asia and the Cult of the Flavian Imperial Family*. Leiden: E. J. Brill.

—— (1995) 'The Cult of the Roman Emperors in Ephesos: Temple Wardens, City Titles, and the Interpretation of the Revelation of John', in Koester 1995:229–50.

Garnsey, Peter and Saller, Richard P. (1987) *The Roman Empire: Economy, Society and Culture.* Berkeley: University of California Press.

Goppelt, Leonhard (1993) *A Commentary on 1 Peter.* Trans. by John E. Alsup. Grand Rapids Mich.: Eerdmans.

Hazlett, Ian (ed.) (1991) *Early Christianity: Origins and Evolution to AD 600.* London: SPCK.

Janssen, L. F. (1979) ' "Superstitio" and the Persecutions of the Christians', *Vigiliae Christianae* 33: 131–59.

Johnson, Gary J. (1988) '*De conspiratione delatorum*: Pliny and the Christians Revisited', *Latomus* 47: 417–22.

Koester, Helmut (ed.) (1995) *Ephesos: Metropolis of Asia. An Interdisciplinary Approach to its Archaeology, Religion, and Culture.* Valley Forge, Pa.: TPI.

Kolenkow, Anitra B. (1976) 'A Problem of Power: How Miracle-Doers Counter Charges of Magic in the Hellenistic World', *Society of Biblical Literature Seminar Papers 1976*: 105–10.

Kraybill, J. Nelson (1996) *Imperial Cult and Commerce in John's Apocalypse.* Sheffield: Sheffield Academic Press.

Krodel, Gerhard (1971) 'Persecution and Toleration of Christianity until Hadrian', in Benko and O'Rourke 1971: 255–67.

Lane Fox, Robin (1986) *Pagans and Christians.* New York: Viking.

McDonald, Margaret Y. (1997) *Early Christian Women and Pagan Opinion: The Power of the Hysterical Woman.* Cambridge: Cambridge University Press.

McGowan, Andrew (1994) 'Eating People: Accusations of Cannibalism against Christians in the Second Century', *Journal of Early Christian Studies* 2: 413–42.

MacMullen, Ramsay ([1966] 1992) *Enemies of the Roman Order: Treason, Unrest and Alienation in the Empire.* London: Routledge.

Malina, Bruce J. and Neyrey, Jerome H. (1991) 'Conflict in Luke-Acts: Labelling and Deviance Theory', in Neyrey 1991: 97–122.

—— (1996) *Portraits of Paul: An Archaeology of Ancient Personality.* Louisville, Ky.: Westminster/John Knox Press.

Martin, Ralph P. and Davids, Peter H. (eds) (1997) *Dictionary of the Later New Testament and Its Development.* Downer's Grove, Ill.: IVP.

Neyrey, Jerome H. (ed.) (1991) *The Social World of Luke-Acts: Models for Interpretation.* Peabody, MA: Hendrickson.

Oakes, Peter (1995) 'Philippians: From People to Letter', Unpublished D.Phil. thesis, University of Oxford.

Phillips, Charles R. (1991) '*Nullum Crimen sine Lege*: Socioreligious Sanctions on Magic', in Faraone and Obbink 1991: 260–76.

Price, Stephen R. F. (1984) *Rituals and Power: The Roman Imperial Cult in Asia Minor.* Cambridge: Cambridge University Press.

Reasoner, Mark (1997) 'Persecution', in Martin and Davids 1997: 907–14.

Remus, Harold (1983) *Pagan–Christian Conflict over Miracle in the Second Century.* Cambridge, MA: Philadelphia Patristics Foundation.

Slater, Thomas B. (1998) 'On the Social Setting of the Revelation to John', New Testament Studies 44: 232–56.

Sordi, Marta ([1988] 1994) *The Christians and the Roman Empire.* trans. Annabel Bedini. London: Routledge.

Still, Todd D. (1996) '*Thlipsis* in Thessalonica: A Study of the Conflict Relations of Paul and the Thessalonian Christians with Outsiders', Unpublished Ph.D. thesis, University of Glasgow.

Stoops, Robert F. Jr. (1989) 'Riot and Assembly: The Social Context of Acts 19:23–41', *Journal of Biblical Literature* 108: 73–91.

Talbert, Charles H. (ed.) (1986) *Perspectives on First Peter.* Macon, GA.: Mercer University Press.

Thompson, Leonard L. (1990) *The Book of Revelation: Apocalypse and Empire.* New York: Oxford University Press.

Wagner, Walter H. (1994) *After the Apostles: Christianity in the Second Century.* Minneapolis, Minn.: Fortress.

Wilken, Robert L. (1984) *The Christians as the Romans Saw Them.* New Haven, Conn.: Yale University Press.

Williams, Robert Lee (1997) 'Persecution', in Ferguson *et al.* 1997: 895–9.

Wypustek, Andrzej (1997) 'Magic, Montanism, Perpetua, and the Severan Persecution', *Vigiliae Christianae* 51: 276–97.

PART VIII

INTERNAL CHALLENGES

INTERNAL RENEWAL AND DISSENT IN THE EARLY CHRISTIAN WORLD

————— .✦. —————

Sheila E. McGinn

Perhaps one of the most significant debates of this century among scholars of early Christianity is the extent to which it is appropriate to speak of 'orthodoxy' and 'heresy' before the Council of Nicaea (325 CE). The rise of historical criticism and its application to the development of doctrine shattered scholars' former straight-forward assumption of the canon of Vincent of Lérins – that orthodoxy is what was believed by everyone, everywhere, at every time. Before many had come to terms with the evidence calling this assumption into question, a second and more significant challenge was raised by the German scholar Walter Bauer. In his *Rechtgläubigkeit und Ketzerei im ältesten Christentum* ('Orthodoxy and Heresy in Earliest Christianity'; 1934), Bauer called into question even the more modest assumption retained by late nineteenth- and early twentieth-century scholars – that orthodoxy was the common faith from which heretics then diverged. On the contrary, Bauer argued, heresy came first, and then orthodoxy.

The working assumption of the priority of orthodoxy, however, was not easily unseated. Its durability is illustrated by the fact that it took an entire generation before Bauer's challenge really gained much attention. Not until the mid-1960s did Bauer's work reach international recognition with its second German edition (1964), and then its English translation (1971). Prior to this, most scholars seem to have ignored it in the hope that its challenge would go away.

Such a substantial critique of the former scholarly approach could not be brushed aside forever. With the rise of 'engaged' scholarship in the 1970s (for example, in liberation theology and feminist hermeneutics) many began to press the question of what social, economic, and political factors may have influenced the doctrinal controversies of the first Christian centuries. Ecclesiastical decisions privileging certain doctrines over others were no longer viewed in a theological vacuum, but came to be seen in the context of wider social processes. All this transpired just as Bauer's work was finding a wider audience.

The title of this chapter illustrates how far the pendulum has swung. Even a few years ago, this section of a volume on the Early Christian World would have been entitled 'Heresy and Heresies'. Now the discussion is set in the framework of 'Internal Renewal and Dissent in the Early Christian World'. Individual movements still are given their traditional names – Gnosticism, Montanism, Donatism, and

Arianism – although without attempting to prejudge the question of their propriety, which currently itself is a matter of considerable debate, as the subsequent four chapters will show.

Some scholars of the early church period ('patristics') bemoan this interest in 'heresy' (see Henry 1982). The scholarly shift away from privileging conciliar decisions and statements of the 'Fathers of the church' is seen as bad enough, but at least it is understandable in light of the rise of historical critical methods. What has developed instead, they claim, is not an even-handed historical analysis, but rather the privileging of the heretics:

> I believe we are the heirs of a third stage of development, one which goes beyond even-handedness. In much current writing about Christian origins, the Fathers are no longer put on a par with the heretics; they are put on the defensive, and it is assumed that the heretics are the true religious geniuses, and even more, the bearers of the authentically radical spiritual breakthrough inaugurated by Jesus.
>
> (Henry 1982: 124)

Given the significance of the present debate and the breadth of evidence being adduced, attempting to summarize the sea of current thinking feels somewhat like walking on water. Nevertheless, a few broad strokes can be drawn, as long as one remembers that such generalizations will always have their exceptions in specific cases.

INSIDERS AND OUTSIDERS

'Heretics' according to the traditional definition, are 'outsiders', those who have gone beyond the boundaries of the true faith. The Vincentian canon stipulated that 'orthodoxy' is what has been believed in the church by everyone, in every place, throughout time. Thus, if one adheres to some other kind of belief, by definition that places the person 'outside' the church. According to this view, there can be no such thing as 'internal dissent' in doctrinal matters, since a belief contrary to the established or majority view defines a person as 'outside' the church. Even after the rise of modern historical methods and the advent of a critical approach to doctrinal developments, this canon remained unchallenged for quite some time. Throughout the nineteenth century, and even into our own, church historians often simply repeated the sentence of their uncritical forebears when it came to determining 'orthodoxy' of insiders and the 'heterodoxy' or 'heresy' of 'outsiders'.

One of the first signs that this uncritical dike was beginning to leak came in 1881 with G. Nathanael Bonwetsch's *Die Geschichte des Montanismus* ('The History of Montanism'), where he noted a shifting view of whether or not Tertullian had been a heretic and, therefore, the beginnings of a question of whether the Montanist movement itself was or was not heretical. This attested to an increasing awareness of the fact that ancient authors gave the name 'heresy' indiscriminately both to movements which were doctrinally at variance with 'the great church' and ones which evidenced no such doctrinal variations but rather showed variations in ecclesiastical

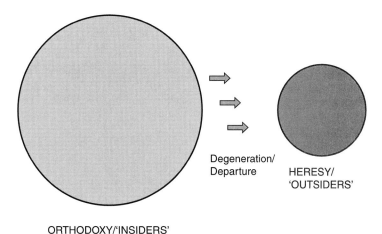

Figure 34.1   Orthodoxy and heresy in early Christianity as constituted by insiders and outsiders.

practice or discipline. Hence, scholars began to distinguish between 'heresy' as divergences from the belief system of 'the great church' and 'schism' as divergences in practice or discipline. Of course, at the same time, although they often were not cognizant of the significance of this language shift, they began to develop a new mapping of 'insiders' and 'outsiders' in the history of early Christianity. And with this boundary shift began a new paradigm shift in the historical approach to opposing views in early Christianity.

The recognition of 'schism' as a distinct category from 'heresy' blurred the once clear boundary between 'insiders' and 'outsiders'. In the past, it was assumed that all those who were 'insiders' must have believed the same doctrines, worshipped the same ways, followed the same disciplinary practices and accepted the same leadership models. Any recognizable variation on these points was taken as a sign of being an 'outsider' to the great church – a heretic. Now it was argued that doctrine alone provided the dividing line between the 'insiders' versus the 'outsiders'. One potentially could find a set of believers who engaged in different rituals, followed different disciplinary practices and also lived under a totally different ecclesiastical leadership structure than the great church, and yet evaluate them as 'insiders' – as long as there was no evidence of doctrinal disagreement. Thus was born the notion of internal 'dissent' or renewal as a historical reality for early Christianity.

It is perhaps not coincidental that this paradigm shift in evaluating early Christianity occurred towards the middle of this century, when there was a concomitant shift taking place in the relationships among major Christian denominations. The rise of the 'ecumenical' movement and of 'interfaith' dialogue among Catholics, Orthodox, Anglicans and Lutherans, among others, shows the fruits of the *resourcement* movement, where historians took a fresh look at Christian origins and what these sources might provide for the life of the contemporary church. The pastoral effect of the historians' paradigm shift was the eventual recognition among different Christian groups that this is precisely what they were – different groups within Christianity, rather than one Christian church assailed by many heretical groups.

At the same time, one notices a growing awareness of the social and political uses (and abuses) of religion. The manipulation of the German ecclesiastical structure by the Nazi powers was lamented as one of the more serious causes of the Holocaust. The devastating, immoral, social and political affects of the branding of one group as 'heretics' and 'outsiders' could no longer be ignored. This gave church historians an added impetus to seek out the origins of such labels, as well as their social and political uses.

EARLY CHRISTIAN TRAJECTORIES

A watershed of this new discussion was the 1971 work of James M. Robinson and Helmut Koester, *Trajectories through Early Christianity*, where they laid out the evidence for early Christianity being a multiform reality, with differing characteristics dependent upon the geographical, social and cultural location in which it was found. At almost the same time, Robert Wilken directly confronted the Vincentian canon in *The Myth of Christian Beginnings* (1971). These studies were followed almost immediately by a wave of discussions of diversity in the early church, and even in the New Testament itself, as in James Dunn's 1977 work, *Unity and Diversity in the New Testament*. Koester furthered the argument for the diversity of the early Christian movement in his two-volume New Testament introduction (1982), breaking one further barrier by including apocryphal writings contemporaneous to the NT materials. Within two decades, what was taken for granted in discussions of the NT texts was no longer their consistency, but rather their variety; the unity of their thought was what required an argument (see Reumann 1991; Achtemeier 1987).

Perhaps the most significant feature thereby raised in the 'orthodoxy vs. heresy' discussions in the last quarter of this century has been the oft-repeated question of 'by whom are they considered heretics?' None of the extant literature of early Christianity claims the title heretic for its author; on the contrary, each author views her/himself as teaching true doctrine. If a 'false doctrine' is in view, it is that taught by others who are stigmatized as 'outsiders' to the teacher's group. The dynamic of 'insiders' (those who know the truth) versus 'outsiders' (those who teach and believe falsely) had been previously noted. Unquestioned before the late nineteenth century, even then, the 'insider' vs. 'outsider' distinction was taken by most scholars as descriptive of the historical situation, rather than being viewed as prescriptive for the ancient audience. But now the sociological and political dimensions of this language were noticed, and scholars began to undertake a serious analysis of its significance.

The new 'theologies of liberation' both arose out of and expanded upon this social and political analysis. Sociologist George Zito summarizes the common view of liberation theologians, as well as of many contemporary historians of early

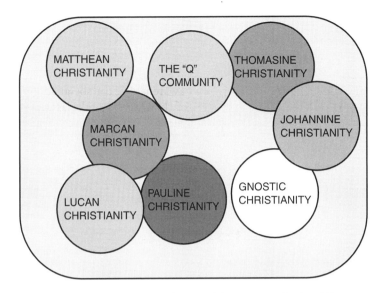

Figure 34.2   Christianities in the New Testament and related literature.

Christianity, when he explains that the heretical status of an articulated opinion is determined by the institutionalized legitimation of the discourse within which a heresy is voiced (1983). 'Heresy' is a thought-world which threatens established power relations, whether ecclesiastical or political. 'Heresy' is a semiotic phenomenon employing words that result in cognitive disorientation of those who accept the status quo, thereby categorizing themselves as true believers. In short, scholars must recognize that speech is contextual and perspectival; whether overtly or covertly, it both expresses and reinforces group boundaries. One can no longer speak simply of orthodoxy and heresy without defining *whose* orthodoxy or *whose* heresy. And the determination of which view will become orthodoxy is not only a theological process, but a social and political one as well.

Framing the discussion of theological trends or movements within early Christianity as a question of 'internal renewal and dissent' – rather than of 'orthodoxy versus heresy' – presumes this paradigm shift from the notion of a universal Christianity with uniformity of belief and practice to that of an ecumenical Christianity with some consistent patterns as well as distinctive features in every place where it was found. The boundaries between 'insider' and 'outsider' become very hazy indeed. If we suspect as prescriptive, rather than descriptive, the statements of ancient authors who charge another group with 'heresy', then the only boundary guidelines that remain are those which are self-selected by the groups themselves. This shift of the burden of proof is one of the developments that troubles scholars such as Henry, on p. 894. And unsettling it well may be, for it certainly has complicated the issues. It has broadened the scope of early Christianity so much that most scholars today would speak of 'early Christianities' rather than referring to a singular, univocal description of the movement.

In this context, the notion of 'internal renewal and dissent' comes to have two

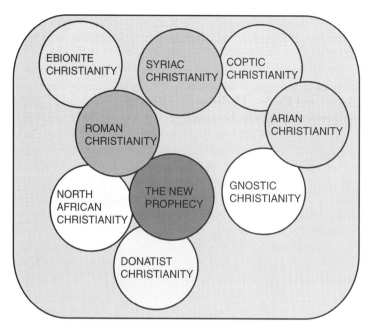

Figure 34.3 Christianities in the first four Christian centuries.

meanings. In the broadest sense, it simply refers to the pluralism which we find among these different trajectories of early Christianity due to their varied geographical, social and cultural contexts – whether or not there actually seems to have been any overt historical conflict over these different developments of the Christian movement. In the second place, it refers to the actual differences of opinion which did indeed arise among various sectors of Christianity in its formative period.

RE-VISIONING THE PAST

While the terms 'renewal' and 'dissent' may imply a prior standard to which one wants to return or from which one wishes to diverge, they need not be read that way. On the contrary, the scholarly consensus at this point seems to be that variety preceded the development of a universal standard among the early churches. Taking into account the gradual development of agreement on issues of doctrine and practice, what appears in retrospect as 'dissent' seems to have originated as one legitimate option among many. It is only after an alternative becomes the dominant view that we can see the former as dissenting. Similarly, what appears in retrospect to be an 'internal renewal' movement may well have begun as one viable option, maintained by one group within the churches, and then later spread to other sectors of the church. Each case must be decided on its own grounds.

The remainder of this chapter is devoted to three examples of how such alternative approaches might change the way we envision the earliest history of Christianity.

To attain a sense of how powerful this paradigm shift might be, I have taken examples from across the spectrum of the early Christian movement: a case of orthodoxy, a case of heresy, and a case of schism.

The first example is from an 'orthodox' movement and leader, to see how our picture of orthodoxy changes if we re-contextualize this particular trajectory within it. Paul of Tarsus and Pauline Christianity (considered in detail in Chapter 7 of this volume) are a perfect case study, because Paul's teaching is often seen as the hallmark of orthodoxy; indeed, Paul sometimes has been considered 'the founder of Christianity' itself. If Paulinism is viewed as one of the many choices in first-century Christianity, how does this change our understanding of Paul's teaching and practice? What if Paulinism is no longer the hallmark of the 'insider' but rather a version of Christianity which may have been 'outside' the mainstream?

The second example is Gnosticism (see Chapter 35 of this volume), a movement traditionally understood as a heresy. But what would we find if we tried to understand Gnosticism as simply one of the many alternatives available during the formative period of Christianity? What would the Christians labelled as gnostics tell us about Christian faith and life if we viewed them as Christians, rather than as 'gnostics?'

Finally, we will turn to Montanism (see Chapter 36 of this volume), a late second-century prophetic movement which its earliest opponents labelled a heresy, but which since has been understood as a schism. What difference does it make if we construe Montanism as a renewal movement *within* early Christianity, rather than a movement *breaking away from* early Christianity? Renewal means a revival of some lost practice and/or belief from the past. If Montanism really was a renewal movement, what was it that the Montanists saw being lost to early Christianity that needed to be recovered?

Paul of Tarsus, the first dissident

Antique historians and heresiologists (e.g., Irenaeus of Lyons, Eusebius of Caesarea) viewed Simon Magus as 'the first author of all heresy' (Eusebius, *Historia Ecclesiastica* 2.13.5; *cf.* Irenaeus, *Adversus Haereses* 1.23.1), but Gerd Lüdemann has recently challenged this view (1996). Following up on a comment of Walter Bauer (1971: 236, n. 83), Lüdemann names Paul of Tarsus as 'The Only Heretic of the Earliest Period' (1996: 61). What he means to emphasize, of course, is that the notion of 'heresy' is perspectival and contextual. However, the further point is that, given Paul's context in the first decades of the Christian movement, his views were divergent from the 'mainstream' understanding of what it meant to be a follower of the Messiah Jesus – assuming that one defines the 'mainstream' from the viewpoint of the mother church of Christianity, the Jerusalem church.

Although we may demur from his label for Paul, Lüdemann's basic point is well taken. If we take into account the New Testament materials that pertain to Paul and his teachings, including Paul's own letters, it becomes clear that Paul is arguing for an alternative understanding of Christianity than that which is dominant in the Jerusalem church of the 40s–50s, and probably also in Rome as well. According to both Acts 15 and Galatians 2: 1–10, the 'Council of Jerusalem' was convened at least

Figure 34.4   Mosaic of Saint Paul in the Museo Arcivescovile in Ravenna, Italy, dated 300–600 CE. Credit: Scala/Art Resource, NY.

in part to adjudicate between these two divergent presentations of the gospel. Acts 15:2 mentions that the reason for the meeting is 'dissension' between Paul and others. (Luke uses the term *stasis*, which can even mean 'revolt'.) Clearly Paul believes that some Christians from Jerusalem are behind the 'Judaizing' troubles in Galatia, and he goes to great lengths to refute their position. In Gal. 2:11–14, Paul even mentions a later public confrontation with Peter in Antioch about the proper behaviour in fellowship meetings, possibly indicating deep division between Paul on the one hand and Peter and James on the other (Esler 1998: 126–40). Whether or not Paul was successful among the Galatians, we do not know; but he seems never to have returned to Antioch after this incident with Peter, which suggests that Paul's view was not the winner in Syria. Nor does his apparent foreboding about his return to Jerusalem (in Rom. 15:30–2) bespeak a victory there.

We are left with a picture not of Paul as a spokesperson for the 'orthodox' or 'mainstream' view, but rather a marginalized Paul dissenting from the prevailing view, working from within – or perhaps along the fringes – for reform of an apparently well-established practice of having two ranks of converts, the first for men of Jewish origin, and the second for women and gentile men. This dissident Paul is castigated by many of his contemporaries for teaching an inadequate gospel, and is even rejected for engaging in practices which are called idolatrous (e.g., Rev. 2:14, 20; *cf.* 1 Cor. 8)!

One hundred years later, this picture is dramatically changed. No longer the minority voice, Paul's view on church practice has become the dominant one and the Jewish Christian view has become the one marginalized. To achieve membership in the Christian movement, one must accept the faith of Christ and receive baptism; circumcision is no longer an issue. The question of male–female relations in the church is not so easily resolved, but Paul's argument for equal treatment of Jews and gentile converts in the church has won the day. In fact, it is nearly a moot point given that the overwhelming majority of new Christians come from gentile origins. Eventually, the hard-liners who want to retain a more Jewish identity as Christians, rather than labelling Paul, are themselves the ones who are labelled, and these 'Ebionites' gradually fade out of our historical picture.

Which is it to be, Paul as 'apostle to the gentiles' or 'first among the heretics'? Was Paul of Tarsus an 'insider' or an 'outsider'? If we follow this new paradigm, then the answer must be 'both'. This is no mere equivocation, but rather a judgement imposed on us by the facts of the case. How we will use Paul's teachings in our time is a decision open to Christians of all stripes – laity, clerics and theologians – but how to evaluate Paul in his own time is a historical judgement which must be faithful to the historical data. And, as discomfiting as it may be to us, the data do not agree. To many of his contemporaries, Paul was a dissident and troublemaker. Later believers saw him rather as a great teacher and visionary. They can both be 'right'. John Barclay recently has argued for the need to take the perspective of the observer into account in assessing how Paul (and other ancient Jews of questionable status) were assessed by their contemporaries (1995).

For the most part, Paul's proponents were looking at the same features of Paul's theology as his detractors (e.g., the relationship between Torah and gospel; the circumcision question), but they evaluated these features differently because they came from different social and cultural contexts and, hence, were interested in fostering different social relations. Uncovering the context of their evaluations has provided greater depth and breadth to the historical understanding of early Christianity. This same kind of 'contextualizing' approach also is underway in the study of such movements as Gnosticism, Montanism, Donatism, and Arianism – movements that once were known as 'heresies'. If the first dissident, Paul, can become a valuable resource for later believers, perhaps we may yet glean at least some small insights from these other dissenting groups as well. And we certainly can discover why these groups, who viewed themselves as Christians, believed that their particular understanding of Christianity was preferable to the other options of the time.

What was it that the gnostics knew?

One of the earliest attempts to read dissenting voices from their own point of view was Elaine Pagels' study of the gnostics. Best known for her study of *The Gnostic Gospels* (1982), she already had published two earlier studies of gnostic exegesis of New Testament materials (1973, 1975). In *The Gnostic Gospels*, Pagels begins with the assertion that, in addition to its religious or theological content, 'the doctrine of bodily resurrection also serves an essential *political* function: it legitimizes the authority of certain men who claim to exercise exclusive leadership over the churches as the successors of the apostle Peter' (Pagels 1982: 38). The gnostic gospels, on the other hand, promote a spiritualized understanding of Christ's resurrection that involves a 'direct, personal contact with the "living One" ... [which] offers the ultimate criterion of truth, taking precedence over all second-hand testimony and all tradition' (1982: 53). This notion of the resurrection, in giving pride of place to direct experience, thereby undercuts any possibility of developing an institutional structure of authority. The 'orthodox' view, on the other hand, centring as it does on the validity of a past historical experience granted to certain of Jesus' earliest disciples, necessarily makes those disciples and their experience an external criterion of truth, and thereby provides a solid ground on which to establish an institutional authority structure.

This notion that there are socio-political dynamics involved in 'heresy-making' has by now become a commonplace in early Christian studies. Pagels may have overstated the case in attributing primarily political motives to the proponents of the 'bodily resurrection' view versus the gnostics; for example, Mark's Gospel (16:1–8) reports the empty tomb, which presumably indicates a belief in the bodily resurrection of Christ, yet it does not privilege certain witnesses since there are no resurrection appearances reported. Hence, it is possible to hold to the 'orthodox' view of bodily resurrection without the political motives she outlines. Still, if somewhat reductionistic, her point is well taken that more than theology was at stake in these debates. Religions are human social organizations and, as such, they include human structures of power which are legitimated by the religious ideology. Scholars now recognize that early Christianity is not an exception, but rather a clear example of this rule.

So, what does it seem that the gnostics knew? First of all, they certainly recognized that repeating stories of Jesus' post-resurrection appearances to certain individuals made those few individuals privileged witnesses to the event of the resurrection. Hence, telling such stories would be a way not only to proclaim the resurrection but also to proclaim the authority of those witnesses. Second, it seems reasonable to infer that the gnostics recognized that such a privileged status would generalize beyond authority concerning this one event to authority for interpreting the entire body of Jesus' teaching; no one else could experience the resurrected Lord the way these witnesses did, thus no one else could understand or teach the Lord's message as thoroughly as they did. Did they also envision that, third, this generalized authority would lead to a permanent, hierarchical rank for those witnesses – and, finally, for their 'successors' as well? This is less certain, although also possible – and they would have been right on all these points.

The gnostics provided the following alternative to this scenario. (1) Individuals become witnesses to the resurrection by means of a direct encounter with the Risen One, (2) thereby becoming reliable witnesses both to the resurrection and to the entire body of Jesus' teaching. (3) Although Pagels seems not to think so, it is possible that some individuals might even be granted a rank above others in the gnostic church, due to the depth of their spiritual experience, their teaching ability, or some other distinguishing feature (cf. the importance of demonstrating charismatic gifts in 1 Cor. 12–14). However, stage four in the preceding scenario could never take place; no one could 'succeed' someone in such an office, precisely because the office was based upon a direct experience of the foundational event of Christianity – the resurrection of the Lord. Each leader must begin with step one. And the leadership rank would not mean the same thing in the gnostic church, for any member could become a leader; they all could expect to experience the resurrection in a direct and immediate way, regardless of teacher or training.

As with Paul, there are lessons to be learned from the gnostics. The following are four which in fact have been taken up by different trajectories within Christianity, perhaps most noticeably since the Reformation period. First, the most powerful and compelling religious experience is 'unmediated'; it is an experience that believers have for themselves, rather than one that is reported to them. Second, for authenticity as a religious leader, it is necessary to have had this kind of compelling, first-hand experience. For example, to speak with authority as a leader of a Christian community, one must have had a personal experience of the Risen One. Third, hierarchical leadership is one model, but not the only model of leadership. Finally, leadership need not be limited on the basis of sex or other physical traits.

What did the New Prophecy reclaim?

The New Prophecy of Asia Minor (called 'Montanism' by its opponents – see Chapter 36 in this volume) was one example of a Christian movement which seems to have taken hold of these four lessons from Gnosticism, but without adopting the gnostic context for them. Montanism appears on the scene in Asia Minor during the third quarter of the second century. The movement originated in Phrygia, a region in the south-western portion of the Roman province of Asia. Three initial leaders are known by name: Maximilla, Montanus, and Priscilla. All three were prophets who seem to have had ecstatic experiences during worship, and who also gave prophetic speeches in discursive language. Several of their oracles survive, but none in their original context. A few are recorded by Tertullian of North Africa, but most appear only as fragments reported by anti-Montanist writers in order to refute them.

Montanism arose as a 'renewal movement' within the church to combat at least some of the teaching of Gnosticism. Over against a denial of the full humanity of Christ and of the historical reality of the resurrection, the surviving oracles proclaim the reality of Christ's incarnation and affirm a Trinitarian view of the Godhead (McGinn-Moorer 1989: 312–14). They insist on the salvation of 'the little ones' (not only the gnostic elect), the importance of moral discipline in the Christian life, and the value of martyrdom as a share in the power of Christ. Both of these latter were viewed by libertarian gnostics as pointless acts, since they had to do with the flesh rather than the spirit.

The New Prophecy was often linked by its opponents with Gnosticism, however, because of the leadership patterns noted above. The leaders of the New Prophecy clearly had the kind of 'unmediated' religious experience noted above, for their leadership roles were based upon their prophetic gifts. Most scholars of Montanism view their leadership structure as more egalitarian than hierarchical, particularly given that leaders were selected based upon a charismatic gift. Their leadership consisted in the ability to share that gift of prophecy with the Montanist community, not on any kind of inherited rank. Two of the three prophets were women, which illustrates that sex was not a criterion for selection of Montanist leaders. Nor do other inherent physical traits appear to have been used as selection criteria. We do find that Maximilla and Priscilla separated from their husbands, presumably to lead a celibate lifestyle, but this is a status choice rather than an inherent physical characteristic.

The New Prophecy looks like a 'renewal movement' in its lively worship, and especially in its focus on the continuing revelation of God through prophetic speech and visions, precisely because this is not an innovation but a return to (or continuation of) an earlier tradition. Many first- and second-century Christian texts speak of prophets, prophecy, preachers speaking under the influence of the Spirit of God, worship in the Spirit, and similar themes (see 1 Cor. 11–14; Acts 2, 4, 9, etc.; *Didache* 10.7; 11.7). Clement of Rome (fl. 92–101) insists that his letter to Corinth is 'prompted by the Holy Spirit' (*First Epistle to the Corinthians* 63.2); in the opening greeting of each of his letters, Ignatius of Antioch (?-107) claims the title 'Theophorus' – God-bearer – because of his prophetic gifts (cf. his *Epistle to the Philadelphians* 7.2), and he encourages Polycarp of Smyrna (70?-156) to seek spiritual revelations (*Epistle to Polycarp* 2.2); the martyrs were known to have visions and revelations of Christ in their last hours (*Martyrdom of Polycarp* 2.2; 9.1), and even crowds of onlookers were said to see miraculous visions (*Martyrdom of Polycarp* 15.1–2). *The Shepherd of Hermas* is even a full-blown second-century apocalypse, including visions and revelations. In such a context, the prophetic activity found in Montanism can certainly be no novelty. However, it can be a revival of prophecy and other manifestations of the Spirit in the face of a rising emphasis on an authoritative teaching tradition that is 'handed down' by word of mouth.

The New Prophecy may have been a threat to the 'orthodox' church not because of its novelty but precisely because it maintained or revived an older, prophetic tradition rather than giving way to the new hierarchical tradition of authoritative teachers. Montanist insistence on prophecy posed a similar threat as did Gnosticism because of its understanding of leadership as arising out of a specific and immediate religious experience – in this case, the experience of prophetic revelation. The charismatic nature of this experience did not lend itself to the kind of control which was sought by those who claimed the name 'orthodox'. Direct and new revelation could threaten the existing beliefs of the church, and certainly could not be controlled by human agents in the same way that a teaching tradition could be. In addition, the Montanists permitted women to lead prayer and worship, whereas the orthodox increasingly wanted to restrict these roles to influential men.

SOMETHING OLD, SOMETHING NEW, SOMETHING BORROWED – WHICH IS TRUE?

As can be seen from the three preceding examples, the paradigm shift represented by this discussion of 'internal renewal and dissent' will have a profound impact on how we understand the development of 'the early Christian world'. Particularly in regard to doctrinal and institutional developments, the most significant difference which results from this change in assumptions – i.e., that there were a variety of early Christian models from the very beginning, rather than one, static reality – is that early Christians become much less alien than we thought. The history of early Christianity is a history of choices amid pluralism, not of a *deus ex machina* and an unthinking mob response. Some of these choices were later evaluated as orthodoxy, some as heresy, and some as schism. But such evaluative hindsight does not mean that any Christian *chose* heresy or schism. As today, believers followed their best lights, disagreed on significant issues, argued about them, and sometimes castigated, stereotyped and marginalized those who disagreed with them. It remains important to learn what these early Christian groups borrowed from outsiders, revived from older traditions, or generated anew in light of their changing circumstances. Yet perhaps the most important thing we gain from this paradigm shift is that we now can learn how these diverse early Christian groups negotiated their differences, and what criteria they used to determine which of their old, new, and borrowed traditions would be retained for posterity. Whether we agree or disagree with their selections, whether we judge their decisions ultimately to be 'heresy' or 'orthodoxy', understanding the decision-making process is at least as important as recognizing its outcome.

Whether or not we know this history, contemporary Christians are not merely repeating but also continuing it. We can do so blindly, or we can do it intentionally, with openness to the lessons of these early Christian 'dissenters' and innovators. Perhaps we can arrive not at the divisive judgements of 'heresy' or 'orthodoxy,' but rather at a unity of purpose and understanding that might have been – and still might be.

BIBLIOGRAPHY

Achtemeier, Paul J. (1987) *The Quest for Unity in the New Testament Church*. Philadelphia, Pa.: Fortress.

Barclay, John (1995) 'Deviance and Apostasy: Some Applications of Deviance Theory to First-Century Judaism and Christianity', in Esler 1995: 114–27.

Bauer, Walter (1934) *Rechtgläubigkeit und Ketzerei im ältesten Christentum*. Tübingen. Second German edn. G. Strecker, [ed.] Tübingen: Mohr, 1964. English trans. *Orthodoxy and Heresy in Earliest Christianity*, R. A. Kraft and G. Krodel [eds] Philadelphia, 1971, and London, 1972.

Bonwetsch, G. Nathanael (1881) *Die Geschichte des Montanismus*. Erlangen: Andreas Deichert.

Dunn, James D. G. (1977) *Unity and Diversity in the New Testament*. London: SCM Press.

Esler, Philip F. (ed.) (1995) *Modelling Early Christianity: Social-Scientific Studies of the New Testament in Its Context*. London and New York: Routledge.

—— (1998) *Galatians*. New Testament Readings. London and New York: Routledge.

Henry, P. (1982) 'Why is Contemporary Scholarship so Enamored of Ancient Heretics?', *Studia Patristica* 17, 1: 123–6.

Koester, Helmut (1982) *Introduction to the New Testament*. 2 vols. New York: Walter de Gruyter.

Lüdemann, Gerd (1996) *Heretics: The Other Side of Early Christianity* Louisville, Ky.: Westminster/John Knox. (Trans. from the German *Ketzer. Die Andere Seite des frühens Christentums*. Stuttgart: Radius, 1995).

McGinn-Moorer, Sheila E. (1989) 'The New Prophecy of Asia Minor and the Rise of Ecclesiastical Patriarchy in Second Century Pauline Traditions'. Ph.D. dissertation. Evanston, Ill: Northwestern University.

Pagels, Elaine (1973) *The Johannine Gospel in Gnostic Exegesis: Heracleon's Commentary on John*. Nashville, Tenn.: Abingdon Press.

—— (1975) *The Gnostic Paul: Gnostic Exegesis of the Pauline Letters*. Philadelphia, Pa.: Fortress Press.

—— (1982) *The Gnostic Gospels*. Harmondsworth, New York, etc.: Penguin (repr. from Weidenfeld & Nicolson, 1980).

Reumann, John (1991) *Variety and Unity in New Testament Thought*. Oxford: Oxford University Press.

Robinson, James M. and Koester, Helmut (1971) *Trajectories through Early Christianity*. Philadelphia, Pa.: Fortress.

Wilken, Robert (1971) *The Myth of Christian Beginnings*. Garden City, N.Y.: Doubleday (repr. University of Notre Dame, 1980).

Zito, George V. (1983) 'Toward a Sociology of Heresy', *Sociological Analysis* 44: 123–30.

CHAPTER THIRTY-FIVE

GNOSTICISM

—— ·✦· ——

Alastair H. B. Logan

INTRODUCTION

The early meanings of 'Gnosticism'

'Gnosticism' is the modern designation, probably coined in the eighteenth century, for a religious movement or group of movements of Late antiquity which claimed to possess a specific and superior type of knowledge, *gnosis*. That knowledge was of their origin in a heavenly world and fall into this lower world of evil, error and illusion, the handiwork of subordinate beings, and their awakening and return to that transcendent world through a saving call issued by a heavenly revealer. Knowledge is thus essentially saving knowledge, salvation is through self-acquaintance, and this knowledge tends to be reserved for an elite. Proponents of such a view seem first to have been identified and attacked by Christian writers of the middle to late second century, such as Justin Martyr and Irenaeus of Lyons, as representing a form of Christian 'heresy' deriving from Simon Magus (Acts 8:9–24), although, as we shall see, there existed contemporary pagan forms of such *gnosis*, e.g. the *Poimandres* of the Corpus Hermeticum, and what has been argued to be evidence of pre-Christian, Jewish forms of it.

Justin Martyr seems to have been the first Christian author to write a treatise against all heresies (*1 Apology* 26.5), and the parallel he draws between heresies and the philosophical schools named after their founders, with their successions of teachers and pupils, developing novel lines of interpretation and thus increasingly disagreeing among themselves and departing further from the truth, seems to have profoundly influenced all later heresiology. Thus, echoing Justin, the major heresiologists, Irenaeus in his *Adversus haereses* of around 185, Pseudo-Hippolytus of Rome in his *Refutation of All Heresies* of the second decade of the third century, Hippolytus (d. 235), in his lost *Syntagma* against 32 heresies,[1] and Epiphanius of Salamis in his *Panarion* against 80 heresies of 375–7, reflect an increasingly stereotyped catalogue of Jewish and Christian heresies which includes groups called 'gnostics', seeing them as inspired by the Devil and Greek philosophy.

Now Justin himself does not mention a sect which called itself or was called 'gnostic', but simply refers to groups who claimed to be Christians but who were in fact heretics, followers of and named after Simon Magus, his pupil Menander and Marcion, or who were called Marcionites, Valentinians, Basilidians and Saturnilians, etc., like the philosophical schools of Platonists, Stoics, Peripatetics and Pythagoreans (*1 Apol.* 26; *Dialogue with Trypho* 35, 80). It is Irenaeus writing his five books of detection and refutation (*Adversus haereses*) of 'the falsely so-called *gnosis*' (cf. 1 Tim. 6:20) in the 180s who seems to identify groups who called themselves 'gnostics/ *gnostikoi*' in his additions to the heretical catalogue in Book 1 (chs 23–31), whose kernel ultimately derives from Justin. Thus he asserts of the libertine Carpocratian followers of a certain Marcellina who came to Rome in the time of Anicetus (154 CE on), 'they call themelves gnostics' (*Adv. haer.* 1.25.6). And at the end of Book 1, he deals at some length, apparently on the basis of written texts, with two mythological systems of a 'mass of gnostics' (*multitudo Gnosticorum*) whom he claims have arisen from the Simonians.

The first group are usually known as 'Barbelognostics', a secondary designation evidently derived from the name of the supreme female aeon of the myth, and the second as 'Ophites', again a later appellation derived from the prominence of the snake in their system; but Irenaeus plainly considers both to belong to the collective '*gnostikoi*', from whom he claims his chief targets, the Valentinians, derive (*Adv. haer.* 1.30.15; 2 Praef). Indeed his polemic against 'the falsely so-called *gnosis*' is directed against those who distinguish the supreme God and father of Christ from the Creator God of the Old Testament, the heavenly Christ from Jesus (or at least teach a docetic Christology), and claim only a part of us is saved (soul or spirit), denying the resurrection of the body, whom he repeatedly identifies as Valentinians, Basilidians, gnostics and Marcionites. His somewhat loose use of the term 'gnostic' has been the object of recent vigorous debate; does it apply to an actual group or is it just a general term for all the heretics of his catalogue as descendants of Simon Magus (Logan 1996: ch. 1)? I have argued that Irenaeus does have a particular group in mind, whose myth and initiation ritual profoundly influenced the Valentinians, and who are also represented by the Naassenes (from the Hebrew for snake) of Pseudo-Hippolytus, who called themselves '*gnostikoi*' (*Refutation of All Heresies* 5.6.4), and the Christian 'heretics' mentioned by Porphyry who attended Plotinus' philosophy classes in Rome in the 260s, and are the 'Gnostics' whom he attacks in *Ennead* 2.9.[2]

However, the problem is that such 'Gnostics' seem to disappear in later heresiologists such as Epiphanius, among whom the sects or groups who seem to correspond most closely to Irenaeus' 'Gnostics' are called by different names ('Sethians' and 'Archontics'), while the 'Gnostics' so-called represent a licentious branch of a predominantly ascetic movement (Porphyry, *Vita Plotini* 16). Furthermore although Clement of Alexandria in the early third century can appeal to the ideal of the true Christian gnostic,[3] and preserve valuable fragments of Basilides and his son Isidore, of Valentinus and of Carpocrates and his son Epiphanes, he makes only fleeting passing references to the false, heretical *gnosis*, which he attributes to a certain Prodicus.[4] Conversely it is Clement who is responsible for preserving in a collection of excerpts attributed to Theodotus, a disciple of Valentinus, a famous formula which many take as the key to Gnosticism and which would confirm Irenaeus' portrayal of Valentinians as representatives of the falsely so-called *gnosis*:

Until baptism, they say, Fate is effective, but after it the astrologers no longer speak the truth. It is not the bath alone that makes us free, but also the knowledge (*gnosis*): who were we? what have we become? where were we? into what place have we been cast? whither are we hastening? from what are we delivered? what is birth? what is rebirth?

(Excerpta ex Theodoto 78.1–2)

It is this kind of knowledge, of our ultimate origin, our fall into this world and its hostile powers and rescue from it, which seems to underlie the mythological schemes of Irenaeus' gnostics and Valentinians (as well as Basilidians and even perhaps Simonians), which we might take as characteristic of the falsely so-called *gnosis* attacked by Irenaeus and his successors. It is the lack of such a scheme that tends to rule out Marcion as a proper representative of *gnosis*, despite Irenaeus' inclusion of him.

The problem of the definition of *gnosis*, gnostics and Gnosticism

Such then is the evidence about the gnostics and *gnosis* among the heresiologists, which in the end still seems ambiguous about the existence and variety of groups of Christians who can be classed as 'gnostics' – do they really hark back to Simon? Do they include Marcion or the Carpocratians, or the amazing variety of groups and systems in Pseudo-Hippolytus' *Refutation*?[5] What happens to them after the third century? Until recently the patristic evidence tended to determine the way we saw such groups and defined Gnosticism, since the primary evidence to supplement that picture that emerged in the eighteenth century reflected an evidently late and degenerate form.[6]

But the discovery first of the Berlin Codex BG 8502 in 1896 (although not published till 1955), then of the Nag Hammadi library of Coptic texts in December 1945 (see Figure 35.1 showing the site), contained in 12 codices still in their original leather covers (see Figure 35.3) and leaves from a thirteenth, and including most sensationally the *Gospel of Thomas*, transformed the situation by its infusion of primary texts, the vast majority hitherto unknown, some possibly dating back in their original form to the second century or earlier. Here at last was a chance to put the patristic Fathers' claims and judgements to the test. The Nag Hammadi and Berlin texts are conveniently available in English translation (Robinson 1977).

For the striking thing about the Berlin Codex and the Nag Hammadi Library was the existence in them of no less than four versions of a post-resurrection revelation discourse of the Saviour to his disciples, the *Apocryphon of John* (see Figure 35.2, showing the end of this document, and the beginning of the *Gospel of Thomas*), whose first part bore a remarkable resemblance to Irenaeus' account of the 'Barbelognostics', while its second part was related, if more indirectly, to his account of the 'Ophites' in the following chapter. Further, the Nag Hammadi Library contained treatises of apparently Valentinian provenance which tended to confirm both the overall picture and certain divergent details of the Valentinian systems built up from study of Irenaeus, Pseudo-Hippolytus and Clement.[7]

Figure 35.1 The place of discovery of the Nag Hammadi library at the foot of the Djebel-el-Tarif. Photo by courtesy of The Institute for antiquity and Christianity, Claremont, California.

None of the texts, however, contained the self-designation 'gnostic', and both discoveries contained works which did not seem compatible either with the heretical classifications of the Fathers or with their categorization of *gnosis*. Thus we find in the collection some works which seem at first sight to bear no trace of Christian influence,[8] some clearly pagan works, philosophical, ascetic and Hermetic,[9] and the rest with varying degrees of Christian colouring, including one, the *Sophia of Jesus Christ*, which was an unmistakable Christianization of the apparently non-Christian *Eugnostos*. The first western scholar to examine and publicize the texts, Jean Doresse, tried to identify them as the library of Epiphanius' 'Sethians' (Doresse 1960), but his interpretation was not widely accepted.

Nevertheless, the publication of the most well-preserved and interesting texts

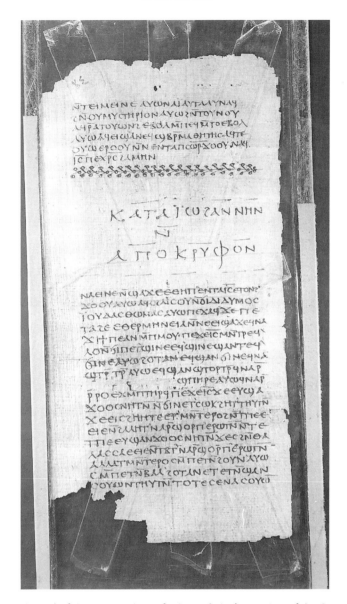

Figure 35.2 The end of the Apocryphon of John and the beginning of the Gospel of Thomas from the Nag Hammadi codices. Photo by courtesy of The Institute for antiquity and Christianity, Claremont, California.

such as the *Gospel of Truth*, evidently Valentinian and echoing Irenaeus' lapidary summary of that form of *gnosis*,[10] the *Apocryphon of John* and the *Sophia of Jesus Christ*, supplementing the information Doresse was able to provide from his cursory examination of the bulk of the Nag Hammadi texts (Figure 35.3), allowed a major colloquium on the origins of Gnosticism to take place in Messina in 1966. Building, if critically, on the scholarship of the German History of Religions school, which had sought to see Gnosticism (or *Gnosis* in German) as a relatively independent Hellenistic religion of salvation emanating from the Orient, with a developed Redeemed Redeemer myth which had influenced Christianity (Bousset 1907; Reitzenstein 1904, 1921; Bultmann 1962), the Colloquium explored all kinds of possible contexts for the origins of Gnosticism/gnosis, Jewish, pagan, even Buddhist. However, it also attempted to produce, via a small international committee, a definition of the phenomenon, differentiating between the more general term '*gnosis*', defined as 'knowledge of divine mysteries reserved for an elite', and 'Gnosticism' as applied more specifically to an assortment of religious systems beginning in the second century CE as attested by the heresiologists.

The Colloquium suggested as a working definition of the latter the following:

> a coherent series of characteristics that can be summarized in the idea of a divine spark in man, deriving from the divine realm, fallen into this world of fate, birth and death, and needing to be awakened by the divine counterpart of the self in order to be finally reintegrated. Compared with other conceptions of a 'devolution' of the divine, this idea is based ontologically on the conception of a downward movement of the divine whose periphery (often called Sophia [Wisdom] or Ennoia [Thought]) had to submit to the fate of entering into a crisis and producing – even if only indirectly – this world, upon which it cannot turn its back, since it is necessary for it to recover the *pneuma* – a

Figure 35.3 The Nag Hammadi codices, with their original leather covers, from a photo taken by Jean Doresse in Cairo in 1949. Photo by courtesy of The Institute for antiquity and Christianity, Claremont, California.

dualistic conception on a monistic background, expressed in a double movement of devolution and reintegration.

The type of *gnosis* involved in Gnosticism is conditioned by the ontological, theological and anthropological foundations indicated above. Not every *gnosis* is Gnosticism, but only that which involves in this perspective the idea of the divine consubstantiality of the spark that is in need of being awakened and reintegrated. This *gnosis* of Gnosticism involves the identity of the *knower* (the Gnostic), the *known* (the divine substance of one's transcendent self), and the *means by which one knows* (*gnosis* as an implicit divine faculty to be awakened and actualized. This *gnosis* is a revelation-tradition of a different type from the Biblical and Islamic revelation tradition.)

(Bianchi 1967: xxvi–xxvii)

The Colloquium also accepted the concepts of pre- and proto-gnosticism, to allow in the first case for elements which later became gnostic in the sense of the developed systems of the second century, and in the second for earlier, pre-Christian, embryonic forms of the latter.

Building on the evidence from the Nag Hammadi texts, coupled with Epiphanius' account of the Sethians, Hans-Martin Schenke claimed to detect the existence of a group of Sethian gnostics with their distinctive treatises, on the basis of shared characteristics (self-designation as 'seed of heavenly Seth', Seth as redeemer, the Mother Barbelo, the Autogenes and his four illuminator aeons, the Demiurge Ialdabaoth, the threefold advent of the redeemer, etc.), and certain shared features (including ritual practices and signs of later Christianization) (Schenke 1974, 1981). The category of 'Sethian' he expanded to include not only Christian groups (such as Irenaeus' Barbelognostics, Epiphanius' gnostics, Sethians and Archontics and the Christian 'heretics' of Plotinus), and Christian texts (such as the *Apocryphon of John*, the *Gospel of the Egyptians*, *Trimorphic Protennoia* and the Untitled Text from the Bruce Codex), but apparently non-Christian texts (such as the *Apocalypse of Adam*, the *Three Steles of Seth*, *Zostrianos* and *Marsanes*), even when such texts did not feature heavenly Seth. He suggested that such a group of pre-Christian gnostics could well have arisen in a Samaritan milieu, and then in the encounter with Christianity have given their texts a superficial Christianization, while still retaining their distinct and alien essence and not ultimately synthesizing with Christianity (Schenke 1981: 607–13).

The severest critic of Schenke's 'Sethian Gnostic' hypothesis has been Frederik Wisse (1971, 1981), who has also been the most sceptical about the classifications of the heresiologists and has seen the Nag Hammadi texts not as evidence for the teaching of a sect or sects, but rather as the inspired creations of individuals who did not feel bound by the opinions of a religious community (1981: 575). However, Wisse's sceptical essay was published in a two-volume treatment (Layton 1980–1) of what had come to be accepted by many as the two main schools of Gnosticism, the (Christian) Valentinians and the (pre-Christian) Sethians. Indeed, what the editor of the volumes, Bentley Layton, has identified as classic gnostic scripture with its 'classic Gnostic myth', is virtually identical with Schenke's 'Sethian' texts (Layton 1987: xii–xiii).

Yet it is not only the attempted definitions of Messina and the suggested classification of main gnostic schools that have recently been radically questioned, but the entire concept of Gnosticism (Williams 1996). Williams argues that since there is no true consensus even among experts on a definition of the category 'gnosticism', and since it evidently only succeeds in generating greater confusion, it should be abandoned for something better. Thus, although there is some agreement about certain features, such as that the material cosmos was created by one or more lower demiurges, other claimed defining features of 'gnosticism' are much more problematical. They have usually included the idea of a radically new attitude to the created order, one of 'protest' or 'revolt', an 'anti-cosmic attitude', as illustrated in the way gnostics treated Scripture (by reversing its sense in a kind of 'protest exegesis', particularly of Genesis), viewed the material cosmos (by allegedly reject-ing it), looked at society (supposedly despising it) and felt about their own bodies (hating them). Apparently lacking any ethical concern, their view of themselves as 'saved by nature' by their inner spiritual character is supposed to have led to two characteristic responses, either of fanatical ascetic renunciation of the world, sex and the body, or of unrestrained licence and lawlessness (Williams 1996: 4f.).

Williams then proceeds to test each of these defining characteristics after setting out four case studies of what has been classed as 'gnosticism'; namely the *Apocryphon of John*, the Valentinianism of Ptolemy, the *Baruch* of Justin in Pseudo-Hippolytus and Marcion. He concludes that none of the characteristics (hermeneutical, anticos-mic and antisomatic, parasitical, ascetic or libertine) adequately corresponds to the sheer diversity of the evidence, and that if we need a general category, 'gnosticism' or even 'gnosis' cannot provide it. He suggests as a better, more suitable and less restrictive category, 'biblical demiurgical', which does avoid the mistakes and mis-interpretations bound up with 'gnosticism', and does more justice as a typology to what are for him a series of related religious innovations and new religious movements.

Is 'gnosticism' as a category therefore simply to be abandoned as too vague and misleading? Williams' case that too wide and vague a definition has been offered in the past is convincing, as is his description of the movements involved. Indeed one of the strengths of his approach is the utilization of insights from sociologists of religion such as Rodney Stark to cast light on the way new religious movements arise and grow or decline. Thus he would argue we should not think of a single phenomenon, Gnosticism or the gnostic religion, and try to define a single essence or seek a single origin for it; the chief error has been to confuse the issue of definition with the question of historical origins. However, he does allow the validity of exploring individual traditions, such as the 'Sethian', and the way they tend to resemble the schismatic 'church movements' or 'sect movements' identified by Stark and other sociologists of religion.

Williams here refers primarily to the distinction between church and sect in terms of 'ideal types' pioneered by Ernst Troeltsch, a pupil of Max Weber (Troeltsch 1931: 331–43). But Troeltsch's 'ideal types' with their half a dozen characteristics have proved impossible to use for theorizing. Thus Stark, building on the narrower definition that churches accept their social environment while sects reject it, sug-gested that churches are nearer the low tension pole and sects to the high, with the latter becoming more church-like and sparking off new sects desiring greater tension with their social environment (Stark and Bainbridge 1985: 19–67). On this basis Williams would see the Valentinians and Basilidians as 'church movements' aiming to reduce tension, and the Marcionites as 'sect movements'.

More promisingly, perhaps, he also draws attention to Stark and Bainbridge's use of the term 'cult' as distinct from church and sect. They define cults as non-schismatic deviant groups which are innovatory, introducing an alien (external) religion or inventing a new indigenous one. They proceed to distinguish three types of contemporary cults: audience cults, client cults and cult movements. The first are literary, involving no formal organization or group commitment to a dogma (e.g. astrology); the second involve a therapist–client relationship (e.g. psychoanalysis), while only the third are genuinely religious, seeking to satisfy all the religious needs of believers (Stark and Bainbridge 1985: 24–30). Alan Scott has recently suggested that Schenke's 'Sethian' gnostic sect is more like an audience cult, based on texts as objects of individual meditation, than a cult movement or sect (Scott 1995). While Williams admits the validity of Scott's application to some of the relevant circles, he objects to Scott's characterization of Sethian and other groups as highly deviant and in high tension with their environment, appealing to 'church movements' like the Valentinians (Williams 1996: 113).

However, neither Williams nor Scott have sufficiently taken in the full import of the Stark–Bainbridge definitions. Williams still treats his biblical–demiurgical movements as basically sects, of which some are more church-like than others, rather than as cults, while Scott has overlooked the communal, exclusive and sacramental character of groups like the Sethians, whom I prefer, with Layton, to call gnostics. Indeed, one only has to ask the question in terms of the Stark–Bainbridge definitions of sect and cult to see that 'cult movement' seems most appropriate. To supporters of the majority opinion that Gnosticism emerged from Judaism (e.g. Rudolph 1984: 276ff.) and of the minority view which sees it as an offshoot of Christianity (e.g. Pétrement 1991), one has to pose the question: is it then a schismatic, revival movement or series of movements harking back to the past (a sect), or rather a new religious movement or movements offering new answers to old problems (a cult)? Are such movements exclusivist, cutting themselves off from the Catholics, establishing a rival church organization (like the Marcionites), or do they not rather seek to mingle with the Catholics while claiming to be the true, perfect Christians? Is it not instructive in this regard that while Marcion was excommunicated and expelled from the Roman church, Valentinus was not, and even almost became a bishop.[11] And the consistent complaint from Justin to Eusebius about groups such as the Simonians is that they claim to be Christians and are so hard to spot precisely because they disguise themselves as Catholics![12]

THE GNOSTICS, THEIR BELIEFS AND PRACTICES

So perhaps the most promising approach to the questions of defining Gnosticism, identifying its adherents and illuminating its origins, lies in seeing the phenomenon as involving a related series of cult rather than sect movements, which arose within the general religious milieu of Judaism and Christianity, and sought to answer pressing questions within that milieu in new ways. Stark has recently suggested the key role played by religious geniuses, unusually creative individuals with deep religious concerns who perceive shortcomings in conventional faiths, something which increases during periods of social crisis. During such periods the numbers of people who receive novel revelations and the number willing to receive them is maximized. The more reinforcement the recipient receives, the more likely they are to have more revelations. And the interaction between successful founders and their followers tends to amplify heresy. The result of these interactions is more radical revelations (Stark 1992: 19–34).

Such a scenario of visionary geniuses founding cults to offer new solutions to pressing problems, arising out of social, political and cultural pressures but expressed in predominantly religious terms, may go a long way to account for the movements labelled 'gnostic', and help distinguish them from other, more sectarian movements such as Marcionitism. Such cult movements may have arisen in Judaism and may be reflected in such phenomena as the *minim* of the rabbis and belief in two powers in heaven, or in paganism as with the Jewish-influenced hermetic *gnosis* of the *Poimandres* (Pearson 1990: 139–47), but we have insufficient evidence to work with in such cases, and are soon led into uncontrolled speculation. We are on much firmer ground if, mindful of Williams' strictures, we confine ourselves to those movements from the late first century which either call themselves 'gnostic' or appeal to a higher, saving knowledge, knowledge of the divine self, and which embrace a Platonic hierarchical world-view and myth and related ritual of fall and restoration of the divine, and seem to arise in a dialectic with a Judaism in crisis over its identity.

Thus it is surely no coincidence that the earliest movements which seem to meet our criteria of what is 'gnostic' seem to occur in areas where there is long-standing opposition to Judaism, such as Samaria in the first century (Simon and Menander), or in communities in which emergent Christianity is locked in conflict with a dominant Judaism, such as Antioch in the early second century (Ignatius, Saturninus, Irenaeus' gnostics), or where Jews are facing the threat of extinction, such as Egypt, and Alexandria in particular, in the wake of the great Jewish revolt under Trajan (Basilides and Valentinus). Even the Jewish-hermetic *gnosis* of the *Poimandres* could fit into this scenario (Pearson 1990: 135–47). For Stark and Bainbridge have drawn attention to the fact that increasingly secularized Jews, of whatever era, are strikingly more liable to join cult movements (Stark and Bainbridge 1985: 400–3). The other feature Stark and Bainbridge isolate as significant for the rise of cults is also characteristic of these places and this period; namely, the lack of a dominant religion, which is also true of Rome (Simonians, gnostics, Valentinus).

When, where and why did such gnostic cult movements originate? The picture of the phenomenon I have presented so far suggests that, if we are to continue to speak of 'gnosticism', it can only accurately be applied to cult movements within a general Jewish and Christian milieu which called themselves 'gnostic' or understood salvation in terms of self-knowledge, awareness of the essential kinship between the inner self, soul or spirit and the divine. Such movements only make sense in the light of an overall myth or system which consciously reflects a Platonic world-view with its hierarchical levels of reality and myth of the soul and its fall and reascent. Further, such cult movements, if we accept the Stark–Bainbridge thesis, tend to emerge as novel attempts to resolve pressing problems, social, political, religious, in a period of crisis.

This would seem to suggest that, although elements which later became 'gnostic' in the above sense were undoubtedly present in the first century when Christianity was emerging, they cannot be said to be 'gnostic' in the strict sense, and thus one is not really entitled to speak, for example, of a pre-Christian 'gnosticism' or of 'gnosticism' in Corinth. On the other hand, once we do enter the second century it may be possible to detect traces of what we have called 'gnostic' groups and ideas in Colossians and the Pastorals, as also in Ignatius of Antioch. R. M. Grant made a bold attempt to explain the rise of 'gnosticism' in terms of a reaction to the destruction of the Jerusalem Temple in 70 CE (Grant 1966: 27–38), but that seems on the one hand too limited a factor to explain the entire varied phenomenon, and too early to take into account the general assimilation of Platonism into Judaism and Christianity that appears to be a specific characteristic of gnostic cults.

Further, although Simonianism as a cult movement seems well-attested from the second century on, and must have some relation to Simon, it is extremely difficult to determine what Simon taught and what part, if any, he himself had in the development of the myth involving Helen which the later sources attest, and which might justify classifying Simonianism as 'gnostic'. Clearly Simon was a charismatic, prophetic figure, who from his portrayal emerges, not as a Samaritan heretic or schismatic founder of a Messianic sect, but, with his novel claim to be God himself, as an entrepreneurial cult founder. This role corresponds to the second of Stark and Bainbridge's three models of cult formation, the first being the psychopathological and the third the subcultural-evolutionary (Stark and Bainbridge 1985: 171–88). The first, preferred by many social scientists, but rejected by Stark as inadequate to explain the data (Stark 1992: 19–34), implies that cult founders are ill or mad. The second is self-explanatory and the third suggests that cults can emerge without authoritative leaders, achieving radical developments by group interaction via many small steps. All three, which Stark and Bainbridge insist are compatible, supplemented by Stark's concept of the creative religious genius operating in a period of crisis, can help illuminate the origins and development of the related cult movements which merit the classification 'gnostic'.

If we exclude pre-Christian and first-century phenomena, including Simon's original cult, as candidates for the title 'gnostic', we come to figures and movements at the beginning of the second century, such as Saturninus, Basilides and the shadowy opponents of Ignatius and also perhaps of the writers of Colossians and the Pastorals. Irenaeus' summary of Saturninus' views includes a single Father, unknown to all, seven angelic creators of the world and humanity, made after the image of the supreme power (cf. Gen. 1:26), but inferior until animated because of the likeness by that power with a divine spark which ascends to the supreme Father at death. To this hierarchical and dualistic picture are added a certain anti-Jewish animus and a docetic Christology: the unbegotten, incorporeal Saviour, Christ, appears like a human being to destroy the creator angels, including the God of the Jews, for their enmity to the Father, and to wipe out the evil class of humans and their assisting demons, while saving the other, good class, those with the divine spark. The final element is an ascetic rejection of marriage, procreation and animal food. All this is based on a distinctive critical interpretation of the Old Testament prophecies: some were spoken by the world-creating angels, some by Satan, an apostate angel resisting the seven, and the Jewish God in particular (Irenaeus, *Adv. haer.* 1.24.1–3).

In view of this, it is no wonder that Layton, who includes Saturninus in his section on classic gnostic scripture, has remarked that, despite its extreme compression and brevity, it refers to almost all parts of the gnostic myth and related topics, including anthropology, principles of biblical interpretation, Christology and ethics (Layton 1987: 159). Saturninus' system seems to reflect controversies between Jews and Christians in Antioch over vexed topics such as the proper interpretation of Scripture (in the Greek, or 'Septuagintal' version) on issues like the origin of evil and the goodness of the created order, the meaning of humanity being made in the image and likeness of God, the accuracy of Messianic prophecy, etc. And even if we cannot identify Saturninus and his followers as among the direct targets of Ignatius in his letters, the same range of issues seems to be involved, as he battles with Judaizers who reject his Christological interpretation of the Septuagint and docetists who deny the reality of Christ's humanity and suffering and reject the materiality of the Eucharist.

But Saturninus' system has inbuilt tensions and inconsistencies, especially between the idea of the spark in all and the idea of two races (Logan 1996: 168f.), no real explanation of how everything originated, no proper myth, or developed assimilation of Platonic philosophy, and he does not seem to have engendered a lasting movement. Basilides, associated with him by Irenaeus but based in Alexandria, goes some way to make up those deficiencies. Irenaeus' account, again based on Justin, begins with a cosmogonic myth: from the supreme unengendered Father is engendered Intellect (*nous*), from Intellect Word (*logos*), from Word Prudence, from Prudence Wisdom (*sophia*), and Power. Wisdom and Power produce powers, rulers and angels who create the first of 365 heavens by a series of emissions, corresponding to the number of days in the year. The last heaven, this visible one of ours, was created by the lowest group of angels, of whom the god of the Jews is the chief. Here Basilides' anti-Jewish animus becomes evident in what may be a veiled allusion to the Jewish revolt of 115–17 CE: because the Jews' god wished to subject all nations to them, the rest opposed him and the Jewish nation. This provoked the nameless Father to send his first-born, Intellect, called Christ, to save those who believed in him from the world-creating powers. Again the Christology is docetic: Christ appeared on earth as a man, but did not suffer; Simon of Cyrene was crucified in his stead, while Jesus, in his form, stood by laughing. As an incorporeal power he could transform himself as he liked. He ascended to his Father unimpeded and invisible. So those who have this knowledge(!) have been liberated from the world and its rulers (*archons*), and should not confess the man who was crucified, but the one who came in human form to destroy the works of the creator powers. Thus salvation involves only the soul; the body is by nature corruptible. Basilides too has a distinctive, anti-Jewish way of interpreting Scripture: the prophets were created by the world-creating powers while the Law was the special handiwork of the god of the Jews. Finally, his ethical stance was one of indifference both regarding meat offered to idols and other kinds of behaviour and pleasure (Irenaeus, *Adv. haer.* 1.24.4–6).

Irenaeus' sketch is complemented by Clement of Alexandria, writing at the turn of the second century CE. He is quite sympathetic at times and offers perhaps the most accurate, if limited, information. He implies that Basilides taught an original ogdoad, and was an eclectic Christian philosopher blending Stoic ethical concerns with a Platonic and Pythagorean belief in reincarnation (Layton 1987: 415–44). But our knowledge of Basilides remains fragmentary and we cannot reconstruct his myth in any detail, although we do have evidence of a continuing movement, and Basilidians are one of the very few groups named in the Nag Hammadi texts, criticized along with Simonians and Valentinians for their liberal attitudes towards marriage.[13] And Basilides is also clearly relevant for our definition of what constitutes 'gnostic' in that he seems among the first to have properly assimilated Platonic philosophy, its hierarchy and emanative system, its belief in the superiority of the soul and its reincarnation.

But it is with the gnostics of Irenaeus that we can confidently speak of a group that did call itself and fully deserves the title 'gnostic', that does represent a successful cult movement which developed a 'classic myth' and ritual of initiation which profoundly influenced the greatest and most Christian gnostic movement of all, that of the Valentinians. Indeed I would contend that it is this cult movement that embraces all the phenomena which Schenke classes as 'Sethian' and also takes in the Naassenes, the mysterious Aurelii with their hypogeum in Rome (Frend 1996: 209–11), the gnostics of Plotinus and Porphyry as well as the Borborites and other related licentious groups. Futhermore, it was this group I would claim which was responsible for collecting the Nag Hammadi texts as their library.

But can we determine where, when and why they began? As we have noted, Justin does not seem to be aware of them. But in attempting to reconstruct their beliefs and practices I have argued that behind the shadowy figures in Antioch whom Ignatius has in his sights, particularly in his letters to the Ephesians, Trallians and Smyrneans, may lie the pioneers of the gnostic cult. Ignatius implies that the breakaway group he is combating claims to be Christian, has shared with the community in the initiation rite of chrismation, but rejects the reality of the incarnation, cross and resurrection of Christ, as attested by law, prophets and gospel, and does not recognize or share in the Eucharist (*Ephesians* 7–9, 14, 17–20; *Trallians* 6–7, 9–11; *Smyrnaeans* 1–7). Now the key to understanding the identity of the gnostics and the factor which unites the varied phenomena which Schenke and Layton and others have identified, would seem to lie in the interaction of myth and initiation ritual which underlies such apparently disparate texts as the *Apocryphon of John*, the Naassene Preaching and the *Pistis Sophia*.

The creative genius behind the gnostic myth and ritual clearly shared the concerns of Saturninus and Basilides, the proper interpretation of Scripture as regards creation, humanity, the Messiah, law and ethics, etc., in opposition both to the Jews who had recently expelled Christians from their synagogues and to Judaizing Christians, but he/she seems to have started with the intoxicating experience of being born again as a Christian in the initiation rite of baptism and chrismation. What he or she adds to the systems of Saturninus and Basilides seems to have been developed out of that culminating saving experience in which the gnostic imitates the birth, naming and chrismation of the heavenly Son in the rite of baptism in the name of the gnostic triad followed by the five seals rite of chrismation (Logan 1997: 188–93). This frees him/her from the consequences of a primal fall, that of heavenly Wisdom/Sophia. The new elements are thus the heavenly triad and related ritual of Father, Mother (heavenly Sophia but renamed Barbelo to distinguish her from the Sophia who falls), and Son, and the myth of Sophia, but they are evidently based on the same Old Testament evidence used by mainstream Christians to construct their theologies (i.e. Prov. 3:19; 8:22ff.; Wisd. 7:25f.; Pss. 2, 8, 45, 110) and on existing initiation rites. The other key element, alluded to in Saturninus but given a fundamental role reflecting the greater assimilation of Platonic ideas, is that of heavenly archetype and earthly copy.

The myth, whose first, cosmogonic, part is summarized in Irenaeus *Adv. haer.* 1.29, occurs in full in the *Apocryphon of John* supplemented by other Nag Hammadi treatises such as the *Gospel of the Egyptians* and *Trimorphic Protennoia* (Logan 1996). It first relates the origin of the heavenly triad of Father, Mother and Son, and traces the development of the heavenly world by male–female pairs of aeons, culminating in the appearance of heavenly Adamas, the archetype of humanity. It then recounts the genesis of this visible world through the error of the lowest aeon, Sophia. She tries to produce without her partner and without the consent of the supreme Father, and the result is the ignorant and arrogant Demiurge, Ialdabaoth, creator and ruler of this world and God of the Old Testament. His hubristic claim to be the only God results in the appearance of heavenly Adamas, whom he then gets his seven archons to copy (Gen. 1:26f.).

Genesis 1–4, suitably reinterpreted, thus becomes the second act of the cosmic drama, not the first. Earthly man is made after the heavenly image, but his/her essence is the divine power of Sophia inbreathed by the Demiurge (Gen. 2:7) to enable him to stand upright. Alarmed by such autonomy, Ialdabaoth plots to recover the divine power, and the events of Genesis and the rest of human history till the coming of the Saviour are represented as a series of moves by Sophia and countermoves by Ialdabaoth and his seven archons, rulers of the planets. Thus, the human fleshly body, the division of the sexes, life in this world, law and ethics, sexual intercourse, fate itself, the efforts of the angels to mate with human women (Gen. 6:4) and in these last days the counterfeit spirit (i.e. the Antichrist), are all devices of Ialdabaoth to entrap the gnostics in this world and rob them of their divine power. The 'Ophites' of Irenaeus vividly illustrate the distinctive exegesis of the Old Testament of these gnostics: the prophets from Moses on are the mouthpieces of Ialdabaoth, but unwittingly transmit some true prophecies through the activity of Sophia (Irenaeus, *Adv. haer.* 1.30.11). Intriguingly, however, David and Solomon are omitted from the list of deluded prophets of Ialdabaoth, surely on the grounds that David's Psalms and Solomon's Proverbs and Wisdom, as primary source material for Christian (including gnostic) theology, had to be true, entirely inspired by Sophia!

Salvation, as with Basilides, only involves the soul, not the spiritual element as with the Valentinians, as we shall see. The present versions of the *Apocryphon*, particularly the long recension with its triple descent of a female Saviour figure, the last in the form of Christ, seem to have obscured the original pattern suggested by the 'Ophite' myth, of Sophia's interim interventions to ensure the survival of the divine power until the Saviour's final saving descent and revelation. The dialogue on the fates of different souls, however, better preserves the basic gnostic understanding of salvation in its intriguing and subtle solution to the classic dilemma faced by all Christians: how to balance divine initiative (the promise of universal salvation and the irresistibility of divine grace) and human response (the reality of human free will and human refusal). Thus they were able to avoid both the terrible predestinarian tangles of a salvation by nature approach (with which Valentinians were charged) or an appeal to the irresistibility of grace (to which Augustine was forced), on the one hand, and the unrealistic perfectionism of Pelagius, on the other.

The gnostic solution is to understand the light power of the Mother present in all humanity as the *capacity* for salvation, which yet needs the descent of the Father's Holy Spirit in the rite of sealing/chrismation for completion. Salvation depends on which spirit dominates; the Holy Spirit or its demonic counterpart, the counterfeit spirit. Those souls on whom the Holy Spirit descends will be saved; all they need is ascetic freedom from the passions, using the flesh as a mere vehicle until on death they ascend to heaven. But those souls on whom the counterfeit spirit descends will be led astray, although there is always the possibility, via transmigration, of gaining the saving knowledge and ascending. Nevertheless, not all souls will be saved; those who had the saving knowledge but rejected it and repudiated the descent of the Spirit in the five seals rite of chrismation (the blasphemy against the Holy Spirit) will suffer eternal punishment.[14]

Despite the awkward fact we noted at the outset that these gnostics tend to disappear as such in the later heresiological accounts, there is plenty of evidence of the spread and success of movements and groups inspired by them, their myth and their ritual, right on into the eighth century (Layton 1987: 6f.). It is in the very nature of such cult movements, after all, to change and transmute, a charge brought against them by Irenaeus himself. Indeed the very prominence of the figure of heavenly Seth in the Nag Hammadi documents, which contributed both to modern arguments for the pre-Christian Jewish character of 'gnosticism' and to Schenke's 'Sethian' sect hypothesis, I have argued, is in fact the result of a later Sethianizing reinterpretation at the end of the second and beginning of the third centuries, in response both to Catholic criticism of the novelty of the gnostic claims, and to the general rise of interest in the figure of Seth (Logan 1996: 47f.). But what is striking about the evidence from Nag Hammadi and elsewhere is the way that, despite such reinterpretation, basic features and figures of the myth recur, even in such distant and degenerate forms of the myth as the Untitled Text from the Bruce Codex and the gnostic (or Borborite), Sethian and Archontic systems described by Epiphanius.

What then of Valentinus and the Valentinians, whom I have described as the most Christian of the gnostic movements? Irenaeus, again probably echoing Justin, speaks of Valentinus as the first to adapt the fundamental principles of the so-called gnostic sect (*hairesis*) to his own brand of teaching (*Adv. haer.* 1.11.1), while at the end of his sections on the gnostics he remarks that from these teachings, like the Lernaean hydra, was born the many-headed wild beast of the school of Valentinus.[15] This is not just another piece of heresiological rhetoric, for we do indeed find remarkable similarities between the two systems, particularly as regards the heavenly world of the aeons, the Sophia myth, and the ritual of initiation, but Valentinus was a great poetic genius in his own right, a visionary who attracted creative pupils, more of whose names have been preserved than those of any other such cult founder. Thus the heresiologists tell of the Italian school of Ptolemy (whose system is summarized by Irenaeus at length) and Heracleon, the first to write a commentary (on John, first accepted by gnostics as authoritative), of Secundus, Marcus the magus (whose followers were active in the Rhône valley in Irenaeus' time), of Theotimus and Theodotus (from whom Clement collected valuable excerpts), and of the Eastern school of Axionicus of Antioch and Ardesianes, who saw the Saviour's body as spiritual (like Valentinus, but unlike the Italian school which considered it psychic).[16]

Valentinians crop up all over the ancient world, from Lyons to the valley of the Tigris, from the second to the eighth centuries (Layton 1987: 10f.; see Figure 35.4), and the Nag Hammadi Library has contributed several texts which appear to be Valentinian,[17] adding priceless original material to the few fragments in the Fathers, and thereby helping us to assess with much greater confidence the accuracy and objectivity of their accounts. Unfortunately, besides the Justin/Irenaeus material, we only have fragments of Valentinus himself, largely preserved by Clement of Alexandria and more concerned with his ethics than his theology. Christoph Markschies, basing his thoughts on the fragments, has recently denied that Valentinus was responsible for the Valentinian myth; he was a Christian Platonist whose followers developed the characteristic myth Irenaeus describes (Markschies 1992).

But over against such a judgement based on such limited evidence we have to set, on the one hand, the picture we get from other sources of a visionary, founder of a cult with one of the most evocative myths of all time, and, on the other, the fact that even the fragments seem to hint at that myth (Logan 1994: 310–13). Thus Pseudo-Hippolytus records how Valentinus saw a small child, newly born, and asked him who he was, and he answered that he was the Logos. Then he added to this an imposing myth and on this, says Pseudo-Hippolytus, wants to base the sect (*hairesis*) founded by him (*Refutatio Haer.* 6.42.2). The 'imposing myth' is evidently that of the gnostics, particularly as it involves Sophia. The Valentinus of the fragments comes over as a very winning personality, author of letters, homilies and books, not so much the cult founder as dominating entrepreneur à la Simon Magus (Stark and Bainbridge model two), as the cult founder involved in creative interaction with his pupils (Stark and Bainbridge model three). For what is again striking about Valentinianism, which must be due in large part to the character and contribution of its founder, is the way that his pupils, despite all their variations and innovations gleefully charted by the heresiologists and present in original texts, retain certain key features and do not break away to form spin-off cults.

So what was Valentinus' contribution? What was the crisis to which he creatively responded? We have noted Basilides' likely response to the Jewish Revolt and his assimilation of contemporary philosophy, Stoic and Platonic. Valentinus, a younger fellow Alexandrian, seems to have followed a similar path. Colin Roberts has drawn attention to the vacuum in Egypt caused by the virtual extinction of Judaism and the Jewish Christianity associated with it (Roberts 1979). The failure of yet another Jewish Messianic uprising, and by implication of their understanding of God, may have represented that crisis. Valentinus seems to have sought to fill that vacuum by

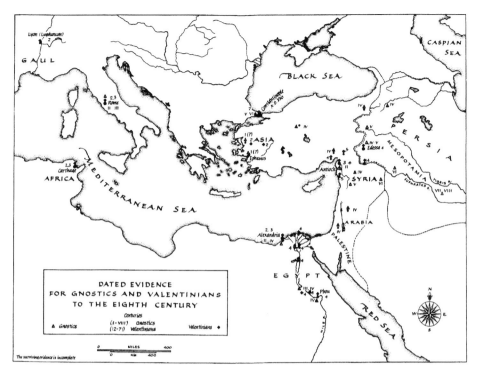

Figure 35.4 A map of dated evidence for the Gnostics and Valentinians to the eighth century; from *The Gnostic Scriptures*, by Bentley Layton. Copyright 1987 by Bentley Layton; used by permission of Doubleday, a division of Random House, Inc.

the introduction, perhaps for the first time in Egypt, as an alternative to the discredited Jewish understanding, of a Pauline theology of divine grace and election, of spiritual versus psychic, and by further assimilation with pagan thought, particularly Platonism. His theogony and cosmogony involve a sophisticated reworking of the gnostic scheme, borrowing Pythagorean categories (dyad, tetrad, ogdoad) to produce a heavenly world or Pleroma of 30 aeons as mental aspects of God, and developing the gnostic pairing of male and female aeons into the fundamental ontological and soteriological principle of syzygy.

Irenaeus' account, again from the Justin material, has Valentinus start from an original dyad of Father and Silence who emanate the remaining 28 aeons, which Tertullian notes were entirely in the mind of God (Irenaeus, *Adv. haer.* 1.11.1; Tertullian, *Adv. Val.* 4). One of the final 12 falls away (i.e. Sophia) and produces Christ outside the Pleroma. He immediately returns within, while she, bereft of spiritual substance, produces the Demiurge and a left-hand ruler (i.e. Satan), as with the gnostics, comments Irenaeus. He notes Valentinus' distinction between Christ and Jesus (as with the 'Ophites'), and the role of the Holy Spirit fructifying the aeons of the Pleroma. The rest of Valentinus' system has to be conjectured from the fragments and the systems of his pupils, but what does emerge seems to be a systematic expansion of the Platonic theme of archetype and image, a rather hostile view of the Demiurge and his creator angels (like Saturninus, Basilides and the gnostics), a development of the idea of the divine as a spiritual seed rather than a power (as with the gnostics), an emphasis on the Pauline themes of the grace of God and the law written on the heart, and an understanding of Christ as entirely spiritual, body and all.[18]

The remaining accounts of Valentinian theology and original texts seem to represent variations on these themes, often in an attempt to soften the monstrous claim of a divine error or fall by positing two Sophias (Ptolemy), or in a very sophisticated exculpation of God for allowing the whole process (the *Tripartite Tractate*), or in a mystical meditation demythologizing the all-too-ugly details which has been attributed to Valentinus (the *Gospel of Truth*). Finally the Valentinian treatise from Codex XI, while presenting certain idiosyncratic features, does roughly correspond to the main lines of the picture presented by the heresiologists, being often close to what we have attributed to Valentinus himself.

What is new in all this is the sophisticated treatment of the themes of fullness and deficiency, of spirit and matter, of male angel and female elect, of the derivation of the cosmos from the emotions of fallen Sophia and the consequent division of reality into three categories and three types of humanity: the spiritual (the seed from Sophia sown in the world through the Demiurge, which is sometimes referred to as 'being saved by nature'[19]), the psychic, the handiwork of the Demiurge and consubstantial (*homoousios*) with him, and the hylic or material, the work of Satan. Thus the heart of the developed myth, as found for example in Ptolemy, is the repeated pattern of fall and restoration at successively lower levels, first of Sophia, then of her offsping Achamoth, then of the spiritual seed, the gnostic elect, sown in this world, and the salvation or rescue of what is fallen by a series of Christ figures, the last being Jesus, supplying form and knowledge to remove the deficiency. Salvation into the Pleroma is only for the spiritual seed who are depicted as female, united in marriage with their male angelic counterparts in the Valentinian sacrament of the bridal chamber, their equivalent of the Catholic Eucharist. A vivid allusion to this is found on the tombstone of the Roman Valentinian, Flavia Sophe (Quispel 1974). The psychics, to whom the ordinary Christians belong, are the creatures of the Demiurge and may attain a middle level of salvation by good works, while the hylics are doomed to destruction.

But despite the deterministic sounding language, grace seems to be the keynote and 'become what you are' the motto (on Valentinian theology, see especially Pagels 1972). And the Valentinians seem increasingly keen to be accepted both by Catholic Christians and by pagan society, to form a kind of bridge, modifying the fierce extremes of Christian asceticism and denial of the world, by seeing the world, fallen as it is, as nevertheless the theatre for the formation and salvation of the elect seed, with a Demiurge who is ignorant, not evil, and who attains a degree of salvation. Their cultic rather than sectarian character, and their ability to assimilate to Catholic Christianity, enabled them to survive for centuries as a kind of fifth column, and this perhaps helps to explain both the apparent lack of evidence for distinctive Valentinian hierarchies and forms of organization, on the one hand, but also the continuing obsession in church and state with trying to flush them out, on the other. The similarities with modern 'New Age' movements are evident here as elsewhere.

But what of the other texts found at Nag Hammadi, neither gnostic nor Valentinian? What of the most sensational find there which has generated more debate and literature than the rest put together, and which has barely been mentioned, the *Gospel of Thomas*? How does it fit in? The best solution seems to be to see the whole collection as the library – or better libraries – of a gnostic cult movement, with their classic myth and scripture, supplemented, as we see is attested for the Naassenes and Archontics,[20] with holy books and authoritative works and fragments of whatever provenance on the soul, its nature, vicissitudes and salvation, reflecting a basically ascetic standpoint. Hence the inclusion both of gnosticized Christian ascetic works of the Syrian Thomas tradition such as the *Gospel* and *Book of Thomas*, of pagan ascetic literature like the *Sentences of Sextus* and pagan *gnosis* such as the hermetic works, as well as appropriate Valentinian material. However, the absence both of any sign of sexual exclusiveness (e.g. in the salvation of souls) as of any scriptural commentaries, and the relative sophistication of the texts might suggest a mixed, well-educated community like Epiphanius' 'Gnostics' or 'Archontics' (or the Roman Aurelii) as the owners, weakening the popular hypothesis that the texts were preserved and copied by Pachomian monks in their monasteries in the areas of Achmim and Chenoboskia.

CONCLUSION

'Gnosticism' and 'gnostic' as designations of a clearly defined religious phenomenon of Late antiquity have rightly been criticized for being too vague and misleading, unable to contain the great variety of phenomena usually so described. But if understood of and restricted to a related family of cult movements springing up within the religious milieu of Judaism and Christianity of the late first century on, which either used the self-designation 'gnostic' or understood themselves within a Platonically influenced mythological scheme of 'fall' and restoration through a heavenly revealer-redeemer, then both can still be valid and useful. If such an understanding focuses primarily on the gnostic and Valentinian movements described above, it can also embrace, as the gnostics and their library did, the Jewish-influenced pagan *gnosis* of the Corpus Hermeticum. As cult movements seeking new answers to old problems and perhaps in the end alien to the spirit of Christianity, they yet were able to operate within it and exert a powerful influence on the emergence of what came to be 'orthodoxy'. They forced opponents like Irenaeus to develop an even better, more adequate, biblical and incarnational theology, and in turn, as so often in the history of Christian doctrine, were plundered by mainstream figures like Clement and Origen for good ideas.[21]

NOTES

1 Cf. Photius, *Bibliotheca* 121. The work is perhaps reconstructable from Ps. Tertullian, *Adversus omnes haereses* and Epiphanius, *Panarion*, etc. On the distinction between the two authors, see Brent (1995).

2 Porphyry, *Vita Plotini* 16.

3 Cf. *Stromateis* 2.11; 4.4.8f., 21ff.; 6–7 *passim* on the true gnostic.

4 Cf. *Strom.* 2.11; 3.4.30, 1; 7.7.41, 1. On Prodicus see Tertullian, *Scorpiace.*

5 Cf. Foerster (1972), who includes alongside the Barbelognostics, Naassenes and Valentinians, Simon, Saturninus, Basilides, the Carpocratians and the systems of Pseudo-Hippolytus as well as the pagan hermetic *Poimandres* and the Christian encratite *Acts of Thomas.*

6 It consisted of three Coptic works of the fourth–fifth centuries CE: the treatise *Pistis Sophia* of the Codex Askewianus in the British Library, a third-century revelation discourse of Jesus to his disciples about the fate of Pistis Sophia (Faith–Wisdom), and the 2 *Books of Jeu* and Untitled Text of the Bruce Codex – the former another revelation discourse of Jesus about the heavenly world, the latter an account of the topography of the heavenly world involving aeons mentioned in Irenaeus' account of the Barbelognostic system.

7 For the latter, see Sagnard (1947).

8 E.g. *The Apocalypse of Adam, The Paraphrase of Shem, Thunder: Perfect Mind, Eugnostos, The Three Steles of Seth, Marsanes*, etc.

9 E.g. Plato, *Republic* 588A–589B, *The Sentences of Sextus*, and the hermetic works *On the Eighth and Ninth*, a *Prayer of Thanksgiving* and part of the *Asclepius.*

10 Cf. *Gospel of Truth* (Nag Hammadi Codex I) 18.7–11; 24.28–25.19; *Adv. haer.* 1.21.4. See Jonas (1992: 309ff.).

11 Cf. Tertullian, *Adversus Valentinianos* 4. His lumping of Valentinus with Marcion as '*semel iterum ejecti*' in *The Prescription of Heretics* 30 is never attested elsewhere, and seems typical exaggeration.

12 Cf. Justin, *1 Apol.* 26; *Dial.* 35; 80; Eusebius of Caesarea, *Historia ecclesiastica* 2.1.11f., 2.13.1.6f.

13 Cf. *Testament of Truth* [Nag Hammadi Codex IX] 56.1–58.6.

14 Nag Hammadi Codex II 25.16–27.31; Berlin Codex BG 64.14–71.2.

15 *Adv. haer.* 1.30.15. Pétrement (1991) tries to derive the gnostics from the Valentinians. See Logan (1996: Ch. 1).

16 Cf. Pseudo-Hippolytus, *Refutatio Haer.* 6.35.5–7; Tertullian, *Adv. Val.* 4.

17 E.g. *Gospel of Truth, On the Resurrection* and *Tripartite Tractate* from Codex I, the *Gospel of Philip* from Codex II and the Valentinian treatise and liturgical fragments from Codex XI.

18 On Valentinus, see Quispel (1947) and Stead (1969, 1980).

19 Cf. Irenaeus *Adv. haer.* 1.6.2; Clement of Alexandria, *Excerpta ex Theod.* 56.3; Heracleon frag. 46; Tri Trac I 19.16–18.

20 Cf. Pseudo-Hippolytus, *Refutatio Haer.* 5.7.8; 9.7; Epiphanius, *Panarion* 40.2.1–3.

21 For an intriguing linking of the gnostics, Valentinians and Origen see Quispel (1980).

BIBLIOGRAPHY

Bianchi, Ugo (ed.) (1967) *Le origini dello Gnosticismo/The Origins of Gnosticism*. Leiden: E. J. Brill.

Bousset, Wilhelm (1907) *Hauptprobleme der Gnosis*. Göttingen: Vandenhoeck & Ruprecht.

Brent, Allen (1995) *Hippolytus & the Roman Church in the Third Century*. Leiden/New York/Köln: E. J. Brill.

Bultmann, Rudolf (1962) *Primitive Christianity In its Contemporary Setting*. London: Collins.

Doresse, Jean (1960) *The Secret Books of the Egyptian Gnostics*. London: Hollis & Carter.

Foerster, Werner (ed.) (1972) *Gnosis: A Selection of Gnostic Texts: I Patristic Evidence*. Oxford: Clarendon Press.

Frend, William Hugh Clifford (1996) *The Archaeology of Early Christianity*. London: Geoffrey Chapman.

Gero, Stephen (1986) 'With Walter Bauer on the Tigris: Encratite Orthodoxy and Libertine Heresy in Syro-Mesopotamian Christianity', in C. W. Hedrick and Robert Hodgson (eds) *Nag Hammadi, Gnosticism and Early Christianity*. Peabody, Mass.: Hendrickson.

Grant, Robert McQueen (1966) *Gnosticism and Early Christianity*. New York: Harper & Row.

Jonas, Hans (1992) *The Gnostic Religion*. London: Routledge.

Layton, Bentley (1980–1) *The Rediscovery of Gnosticism*, 2 vols. Leiden: E. J. Brill.

—— (1987) *The Gnostic Scriptures*. Garden City, N.Y.: Doubleday & Co.

Logan, Alastair Hendry Black (1994) Review of Markschies 1992 in *Journal of Theological Studies* 45: 310–13.

—— (1996) *Gnostic Truth and Christian Heresy*. Edinburgh: T&T Clark.

—— (1997) 'The Mystery of the Five Seals: Gnostic Initiation Reconsidered', *Vigiliae Christianae* 51: 188–206.

Markschies, Christoph (1992) *Valentinus Gnosticus?* Tübingen: J. C. B. Mohr (Paul Siebeck).

Pagels, Elaine Hiesey (1972) 'The Valentinian Claim to Esoteric Exegesis of Romans as Basis for Anthropological Theory', *Vigiliae Christianae* 26: 241–58.

Pearson, Birger Albert (1990) *Gnosticism, Judaism, and Egyptian Christianity*. Minneapolis, Minn.: Fortress Press.

Pétrement, Simone (1991) *A Separate God*. London: Darton, Longman & Todd.

Quispel, Gilles (1947) 'The Original Doctrine of Valentine', *Vigiliae Christianae* 1: 43–73.

—— (1974) 'L'inscription de Flavia Sophè', *Gnostic Studies 1*. Istanbul: Nederlands Historisch-Archaeologisch Instituut in het Nabije Oosten.

—— (1980) 'Valentinian Gnosis and the Apocryphon of John', in Layton 1980–1: I, 118–32.

Reitzenstein, Richard (1904) *Poimandres*. Leipzig: B. G. Teubner.

—— (1921) *Das iranische erlösungsmysterium*. Bonn: Marcus & Weber.

Roberts, Colin Henderson (1979) *Manuscript, Society and Belief in Early Christian Egypt*. London: Oxford University Press.

Robinson, James M., (ed.) (1977) *The Nag Hammadi Library in English*. San Francisco: Harper & Row.

Rudolph, Kurt (1984) *Gnosis*. Edinburgh: T&T Clark.

Sagnard, François Louis Marie Matthieu (1947) *La gnose valentinienne et le témoignage de saint Irénée*. Paris: J. Vrin.

Schenke, Hans-Martin (1974) 'Das sethianische System nach Nag-Hammadi-Handschriften', in P. Nagel (ed.) *Studia Coptica*. Berlin: Akademie, 165–73.

—— (1981) 'The Phenomenon and Significance of Gnostic Sethianism', in Layton 1980–1: II, 588–616.

Scott, Alan Bruce (1995) 'Churches or Books? Sethian Social Organization', *Journal of Early Christian Studies* 3: 109–22.

Stark, Rodney (1992) 'How Sane People Talk to the Gods: A Rational Theory of Revelations', in Michael A. Williams, Collett Cox and Martin S. Jaffee (eds) *Innovations in Religious Traditions*. Berlin: de Gruyter, 19–34.

—— (1996) *The Rise of Christianity*. Princeton, N.J.: Princeton University Press.

Stark, Rodney and Bainbridge, William Sims (1985) *The Future of Religion*. Berkeley/Los Angeles/London: University of California Press.

Stead, George Christopher (1969) 'The Valentinian Myth of Sophia', *Journal of Theological Studies* 20: 75–104.

—— (1980) 'In Search of Valentinus', in Layton 1980–1: I, 75–102.

Troeltsch, Ernst (1931) *The Social Teaching of the Christian Churches*, Vol. 1. London: Allen & Unwin.

Williams, Michael Allen (1996) *Rethinking "Gnosticism"*. Princeton, N.J.: Princeton University Press.

Wisse, Frederik (1971) 'The Nag Hammadi Library and the Heresiologists', *Vigiliae Christianae* 25: 205–23.

—— (1981) 'Stalking Those Elusive Sethians', in Layton 1980–1: II, 563–78.

MONTANISM

—— •❖• ——

Christine Trevett

ITS NAME AND ITS CHARACTER

'Montanism' appears first in Christian writings in Cyril of Jerusalem's *Catechetical Lectures* (16.8) in the fourth century. Probably its earliest loyalists had called it 'The New Prophecy',[1] which is what Tertullian, its best-known convert, called it also.[2] The term 'Montanism' is anachronistic when used to describe its earliest phase, but it continues to be the designation most widely understood.

It derives from the name of Montanus, a prophet whose second-century activities in Phrygia, along with those of two female prophets Prisca/Priscilla and Maximilla, initiated a prophetic movement within Christianity which spread rapidly and came into conflict with the developing Catholic tradition. Leaders of the Catholic churches in the vicinity closed ranks and after some time New Prophecy believers were rejected from, and were probably also seceding from (the evidence is ambiguous), the mainstream churches.

In Carthage and Rome Montanism had a different history and it is important to distinguish carefully both between Montanism of different areas and between sources reflecting early and later dates of development.

Up to the decade of the 230s we know of New Prophets from the Asian and other sources preserved by Eusebius (an Anonymous source, Apollonius, and reports about Miltiades, Alcibiades, Serapion of Antioch and others), from Epiphanius of Salamis' Anonymous early anti-Montanist source in *Panarion* 48.1–13, from Clement of Alexandria (*Stromateis* 4.13.93.1 and 7.17.108.1), Origen (*De principiis* 2.7.3 and in the *Catenae* on Paul's Epistles to the Corinthians [Heine 1989a: 99]), from Hippolytus in Rome (*Commentary on Daniel* 4.20; *Refutatio omnium haeresium* 8.19; 10.25–6), from a number of writings of Tertullian in Carthage and from Firmilian of Caesarea's letter to Cyprian in Carthage (Cyprian, *Epistula* 75 [74 in some editions]).

They tell of disputes between the New Prophets and the Catholic leadership in several parts of the empire. Catholics deplored the unbridled manner of prophesying and the prophets' states of ecstasy. Such things, they claimed, did not match traditional Christian practice. Also the New Prophets had appropriated to their own age the Johannine promise of the Paraclete.[3] Accusations that Montanus had identified himself as the Paraclete were later ones, however, reflected in spurious 'oracles' more to do with contemporary debate about Trinitarian doctrine than the original teaching of the New Prophecy (Trevett 1996: 80).

Catholic writers were scathing about the New Prophets' so-called 'Jerusalem' communities (*H. E.* 5.18.2 [Apollonius and cf. Cyprian *Ep.* 75.10 from Firmilian]; Epiphanius *Pan.* 49.1), which were to be found in unprepossessing rural settings, and they challenged some Montanists' claims to probity along the following lines: in the second generation of leadership Themiso, a confessor, had allegedly bribed his way from prison and then had dared to pen a 'catholic' epistle. Some scholars see Montanism as a catalyst for the creation of a Christian canon (Walls 1964; Paulsen 1978; Trevett 1996; Robeck 1987), but its importance in that respect has probably been overemphasized. Next Alexander and an unnamed female prophet (*H. E.* 5.18.5–11 [Apollonius]) were castigated, and an opponent recounted the fate of Theodotus who experienced heavenly ascents but had died (so rumour had it) as the result of such hubris and an unspecified accident (*H. E.* 5.16.14 [Anonymous]). Tabbernee (1993: 267–8; 1997a: 21) surmises that Theodotus and Themiso held the distinctive Montanist office of *koinônos*.

No epigraphy exists from this earliest stage but at some point Montanus, Maximilla and Priscilla were commemorated as 'Montanus and the Women' on an inscription destroyed in the sixth century with part of the great marble reliquary at Pepouza. Michael the Syrian recorded this in Book 11 of the *Chronicle*, describing John of Ephesus' response to an edict of Justinian I (527–65 CE). Pepouza had been central to Montanism from its beginnings. Events in the sixth century must have hastened its long and inexorable decline.

The 'newness' of the Prophecy probably related to its understanding of the New Covenant era, distinguishing it from prophetic revelation of the previous dispensation (Klawiter 1975: 64–6). The prophesyings were evidently out of the ordinary – unbridled, noisy and accompanied by unintelligible speech, which may imply glossolalia which would have been rare and misunderstood.[4]

New Prophets were criticized for the rigour of their discipline. In particular there was the teaching about marriage. Montanus' alleged teaching of 'annulment' may have amounted to no more than defending Priscilla's and Maximilla's decisions to leave their husbands on experiencing a call to prophesy (Eusebius, *H. E.* 5.18.2). Remarriage was discouraged and on penance and absolution the New Prophecy took a harder line than its opponents. As for fasting, there was to be more of it.

In Carthage Tertullian, a rigorist by instinct, denied that in essentials there was any novelty. In some respects the New Prophets merely made obligatory what the Catholics left to choice. The discipline of the New Prophecy was a *via media*, he suggested, between the Catholics' tendency to self-gratification and a gnostic or encratite hostility to the gifts of God.[5] The Catholic side saw matters differently.

Another innovation was that perhaps for the first time in Christian history there were *salaried* officials (*H. E.* 5.18.2 [Apollonius]). This would have undercut the pre-eminence of men of good social standing and education (Stewart-Sykes 1999) and it would have diverted money, and gifts in kind, away from the mainstream churches. People of the lower orders, including perhaps even women, would have been empowered through such a change. In addition, collections of the New Prophets' teachings were in circulation and were being treated as authoritative by their followers. They included the utterances of 'these weak females' (in Rome, Hippolytus, *Refut. omn. haer.* 8.19; *Comm. Dan.* 4.20). Consequently Eusebius' Anonymous hesitated to write any treatise against the New Prophecy lest he too be thought to be adding something to the New Covenant writings (*H. E.* 5.16.3). They held the same views about Christ and the creator as did the Catholics, Hippolytus observed, but they also had 'countless books' of their own (*Refut. omn. haer.* 8.19).

Its claims about 'prophetic succession', citing proto-Montanist prophets of the apostolic age and beyond, soon left the New Prophecy vulnerable. Some predictions were unfulfilled and no successor of note followed immediately after the death of Maximilla (Trevett 1997). Nevertheless, prophecy and receipt of visions did not die with the Three (as I call them for brevity's sake), as the witness of Tertullian, Firmilian, Origen and others indicates. Some epigraphy, too, suggests continuity in this repect. Notably there was Quintilla. She was probably a third-century Montanist who left the legacy of the Prophecy's most famous vision, received in Pepouza (Epiphanius was uncertain if she or Priscilla had seen it [*Pan.* 49.1]). It was that of Christ in female form who endowed her with wisdom and spoke of the descent of Jerusalem. The Quintillian branch of the Montanists (Epiphanius, *Pan.* 48.14; 49.1–2; cf. 51.33; Augustine, *De haeresibus* 27) was named after her. They seem to have been somewhat literalistic in their interpretation of eschatological sources (Trevett 1995, and 1996: 167–70; Elm 1996).

The New Prophets' eschatological fervour and zeal for martyrdom has often been overestimated and described as fanatical. The tendency is not dead (Sordi 1983: 72–3, 176–7, 195). In fact we know less about its eschatology than many have assumed. Expectation of the End certainly had figured in its earliest teachings and it owed much to the kinds of millenarian ideas preserved in the book of Revelation, 4 Ezra and other sources (Trevett 1996: 95–105; Stewart-Sykes 1997b, but note Hill 1992). Such expectations, however, were not uncommon.

Tertullian's encouragement to martyrdom (*De fuga in persecutione; Ad Martyras*) has tended to be treated as indicative of the wider New Prophet view, but it is hazardous to assume that Tertullian was typical of the group. Klawiter did regard persecution and the Montanist teaching on martyrdom as key factors in its rise and condemnation and he linked a reverence for confessors and their 'power of the keys' with Montanist women's rise to clerical office (Klawiter 1975, 1980; contrast McGinn-Moorer 1989: 9–11, and Trevett 1996: 190–5). But willingness, indeed eagerness, to embrace death was known amongst Catholics too (Powell 1975; Tabbernee 1985; Trevett 1996: 95–105, 121–9).

After some time of development and fragmentation, the aberrant Trinitarian theology of Montanism became a recurring theme, including accusations of affinity with various brands of Monarchianism (Pelikan 1956: 102–3; Wright 1976: 16; Trevett 1996: 214–23). In its second phase, and in Rome, Hippolytus recounted that early in the third century one (minority?) group of Montanists in Rome had been influenced by the theology of Noetus (*Adv. omn. haer.* 8.19; 10.26; cf. from a later century, Theodoret, *Haereticarum fabularum compendium* 3.2 [PG 83, 401–4]). It is hard to countenance, however, that Tertullian would have aligned himself, just decades after the beginnings of the New Prophecy, with a group which *in general* held to an understanding of God that he would have rejected.

Early Montanism, then, had been in many respects more a determined and discomforting statement of some emphases present already in Asia Minor Christianity than something wholly novel (Aland 1955, 1960a), and it had probably been coloured by distinctively Phrygian religious elements. Opposition had clarified and sharpened its distinctiveness, so that by the time of Pacian of Barcelona (in *Ep. 1 Ad Sympronianum* [PL 13.1053]) Montanists had for long been notorious for their dissenting views about repentance, apostolic and prophetic succession, 'the day of the Passover' (they were probably Quartodeciman in sympathy), authoritative writings, the name 'Catholic', and more. The evidence of Epiphanius, Augustine, Jerome and others suggests that millenarian ideology and respect for the prophetic and other ministries of women had survived, to be part of the teaching of later Montanist groups (Trevett 1995, 1999b; Elm 1996). At this later stage, however, its adherents were referred to variously by names suggestive of their place of origin – Phrygians or Cataphrygians, Pepouzians – or by names which recalled key figures in their past – namely, as Priscillians or Quintillians, as well as Montanists.

Jerome (*Ep. 41 ad Marcellam*) wrote of the revised Montanist order of clergy, with a patriarch (only at Pepouza?) and the other new office of *koinônos* coming next, leaving bishops in third place. It is clear from such developments that order and hierarchy were not foreign to this group, which should not be seen primarily in terms of reaction to increased clericalisation in the churches. The tombstone of Praÿlios (see Figure 36.1), discovered some 15 kilometres from Philadelphia, is one of several items which refer to such a *koinônos*. Other inscriptions speak of a probably Montanist bishop, of a female presbyter, an archdeacon and other office-holders (see e.g. Tabbernee 1997a: 509–18).

The fact that Montanist clerical offices (some at least) were open to women in institutionalized Montanism dismayed the Catholic side. There was 'in Christ neither male nor female' (Gal. 3:28) the Quintillianists observed (Epiphanius, *Pan.* 49.2.1–5). Ambrosiaster mentioned women deacons (*Comm. in Ep. 1 ad Tim.* 3.8–11) and Epiphanius bishops and presbyters (*Pan.* 49.2–3; cf. John of Damascus, *De haeresibus* 87). Among the Quintillians, at least, there was regular formalized prophecy during worship, by appointed lamp-bearing virgins dressed in white (*Pan.* 49.2). The tombstone of Stephania (see Figure 36.2), discovered in Galatia, described her as 'one of the five lamp-bearing virgins, the most God-beloved one of Christ' (Tabbernee 1997a: 518–525), and as the leader (*hêgoumenê*) of them.

The New Prophecy, then, may well have begun in a time of anxiety as a movement of renewal, with emphasis on spiritual gifts and eschatological promises (*H. E.* 5.16.9 [Anonymous]; Epiphanius, *Pan.* 48.13.1 [Maximilla]). But Epiphanius' Anonymous source reported an erroneous claim that 'we too must receive the spiritual gifts' (Epiphanius, *Pan.* 48.1.3). They had 'separated from the church because of spiritual gifts' (*Pan.* 48.12.1), he averred. At first, then, the New Prophecy in Asia had not been divorced from Catholic congregations. It had had the capacity to divide them, nevertheless, and ultimately to win some over (e.g. the accounts about Ancyra in Galatia in *H. E.* 5.16.4 [Anonymous] and Thyatira later according to Epiphanius, *Pan.* 51.33). Given the claims to inspiration and authority which went with the prophecy, it was inevitably perceived as a threat.

The early New Prophecy was next sharpened by opposition, rejection and debate

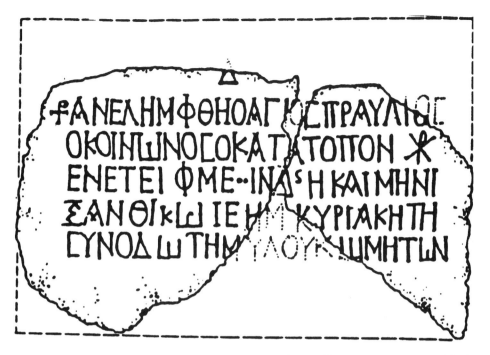

Figure 36.1   Praÿlios, *koinônos* inscription. Drawing from Tabbernee (1997a: 510) with the permission of the author and the publisher, Mercer University Press.

into offering a throughgoing critique of aspects of the developing Catholic tradition. Catholics who had rejected the phenomenon soon came to be labelled 'psychics', by contrast with the New Prophecy's *pneumatikoi*, at least to judge from the witness of Tertullian (*Iei.* 1.1; 3.1; 11.1; 16.8; *Pud.* 21–2; *Marc.* 4.22.5; *Mon.* 1.1) and Clement of Alexandria, who noted that Valentinians too used the derogatory word 'psychics' of the Catholics (*Strom.* 4.13.93.1). Some later epigraphy from 'spiritual' Christians confirms this (Trevett 1996: 203–4; Tabbernee 1997a: 401–6, 544–6, 550–2).

THE DATE OF ITS BEGINNINGS

Eusebius of Caesarea in the *Chronicon* and Epiphanius of Salamis in *Pan.* 48.1.2 offered conflicting dates for the start of the New Prophecy, the latter seeming to suggest *c.* 157 CE, in the nineteenth year of Antoninus Pius, while Eusebius suggested 171–2, the twelfth year of Marcus Aurelius. The issue is confused by both writers being vague or self-contradictory in respect of other dates and events, and by the claim that Thyatira fell to Montanism at some point hard to establish because Epiphanius, *Pan.* 51.33, is so opaque. The matter is complicated further by the possibility that the martyrology of Polycarp (which may refer to events as early as 156 in date) and the account concerning the martyrs of Vienne and Lyon in 177 CE,

Figure 36.2 Stephania tombstone. Drawing from Tabbernee (1997a: 520), with the permission of the author and the publisher, Mercer University Press.

reflect the need to oppose a Montanist understanding of martyrdom (Kraft 1955; Buschmann 1995).

Eusebius' date, I have argued, probably speaks of the time of increased public awareness of the New Prophecy and of more organized opposition to it, rather than of its beginnings. If, as is posited, Maximilla was the last of the leading prophets (which I call the Three) to die, and she was dead *c.* 180 CE, then 172–80 CE seems too short a span of time for the rise, the considerable expansion, the undoubted influence and the condemnation of the New Prophecy. Its origins may indeed go back to the 150s, as Epiphanius claimed, but its rise should be set in the 160s. Second-century Asia Minor provides evidence for the kinds of eschatological hope which fuelled the New Prophecy (including the Revelation and Papias of Hierapolis) and the events of the 160s onward, which included famine, warfare, occasional persecution and plague, and provided cause for concern about that eschatological 'suffering' (*ponos*) of which Maximilla spoke in her oracle (Epiphanius, *Pan.* 48.13.1):

'the Lord has sent me to interpret this suffering, covenant and promise as a partisan, a revealer and interpreter' (Trevett 1997).

THE PLACE OF ITS BEGINNINGS

Montanus had begun his prophesying in a rural backwater. According to Eusebius' Anonymous (*H. E.* 5.16.7) it had been in Phrygian-Mysia at a place known as Ardabau, though the location of that place, like that of Pepouza which was subsequently the centre of Montanism, is hard to establish.[6]

Quite apart from whether the site of Ardabau was in the region of Kallataba, Atyochorion or elsewhere, the name may have had a symbolic significance as the place of Montanus' first prophesying. A not dissimilar name features in a vision in the apocalyptic 4 Ezra (2 Esdras). There a promised city would appear and it was after the vision concerning that place that Ezra had functioned as a prophet (Preuschen 1900; Trevett 1996: 21–6, contrast Tabbernee 1997a: 18). Pepouza, which with Tymion was home to a site (or more probably to an ideal community of people) which Montanus designated 'Jerusalem' (*H. E.* 5.18.2 [Apollonius]), proved to be the 'Mecca' of Montanism for the centuries of its existence. It has been variously located in the vicinity of Hierapolis (modern Pamukkale (see Figure 36.3) or somewhere to the north-west or north-east, towards Philadelphia or Apamea. The present-day villages of Üçkuyu and Bekilli have been suggested as probable sites for both Pepouza and Tymion, but no suggestion has been

Figure 36.3   Remains at Hierapolis (modern Pamukkale), Turkey. Photo Christine Trevett.

verifable. Other scholars have proposed different sites (Tabbernee 1997a: 27–8, 359, 477).

The earliest New Prophecy may have enjoyed some patronage from Christians in the region of Philadelphia, given that some of its emphases echoed prophetic revelation to that region (Revelation 3:7–13, and see Calder 1923; Trevett 1989, contrast Tabbernee 1997a: 53–4). Quadratus and Ammia, who were listed among the prophets who prefigured the Montanists, were associated with Philadelphia (Eusebius, *H. E.* 5.17.4), while the daughters of Philip (or some of them at least), to whose memory the New Prophets also appealed, had been linked with Hierapolis. To judge from the places of origin of those Catholic leaders who first came to confront the New Prophecy the area of its earliest influence must have been within reasonable distance of Otrous, Cumane, Hierapolis, Apamea and Hieropolis (Eusebius *H. E.* 5.16).

The evidence which survives between the beginnings of Montanism and Firmilian's letter to Carthage in the late 250s CE (but concerning the decade of the 230s) offers a picture of expansion. Within a few decades exponents of the New Prophecy were to be found not just in Phrygia, but in Galatia (where the Christian community in Ancyra was deeply divided by it: Eusebius, *H. E.* 5.16.4 [Anonymous]) in Lydia, Cappadocia, eastwards to Antioch as well as westwards in Thrace (where Priscilla was confronted [*H. E.* 5.19.3], indicating a peripatetic element in the activities of the Three). Possibly some New Prophets had reached Gaul too, to judge from some of the language of the letters to Asia and Phrygia about the martyrdoms in Lyon and Vienne (Eusebius, *H. E.* 5.1.1–5.3.4).

In Hierapolis in Phrygia Salutaris opposition to the New Prophecy was spearheaded by bishop Claudius Apolinarius (Eusebius, *H. E.* 4.27; 5.16.1; 5.19.2; cf. Jerome, *De viris illustribus* 26). The bones of some of the daughters of Philip were there and Catholic writers were soon decrying suggestions that those prophesying women had been anything like the New Prophets.[7] Nevertheless, the surviving epigraphy of the fourth century and beyond suggests a continued Montanist presence there, as also in the region of Philadelphia (Tabbernee 1997a: 495–511).

Other writers wrote not only of Pepouza's continued existence, but of its being an administrative and spiritual centre (e.g. Filastrius of Brescia, *Div. haer. lib.* 49) for what were marginalized and now (in a Christian empire) *heretical* Montanists (Montanism was mentioned but not condemned at Nicaea).[8]

Montanism had spread rapidly (Tabbernee 1997a: 53–4). Very soon it was firmly an urban as well as a rural phenomenon and so is not to be explained simply as a rural spasm born of peculiarly Phrygian religiosity, or of alliance with Phrygian paganism generally and the cult of Cybele in particular. This is not to deny, of course, the possible influence of non-Christian and local practices during the history of Montanism in Asia in particular, where it survived longest.[9] Epigraphy provides evidence of communities in Sebaste, Temenothyrai, Dorylaeum/Dorylaeion and the highlands of Phrygia (Tabbernee 1997a: 555–6), but legislation against it must have taken toll of its loyalists and of its vitality. Outside of Asia Minor (Figure 36.4) the most extensive evidence for Montanism has come from North Africa and Rome, though it did not survive so long in those places.

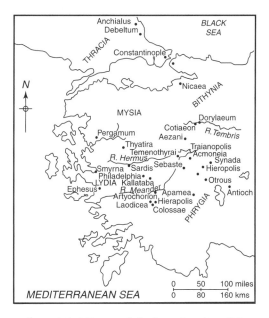

Figure 36.4 Asia Minor and the New Prophecy/Montanism.

MONTANUS, PRISCILLA, MAXIMILLA AND THEIR TEACHINGS

Jensen has tried to show that Montanus was not the originator of this movement but that later writers needed a male heresiarch to append to the New Prophecy. Instead, she maintained, Priscilla should be regarded as its most significant leader and the 'paraclete' Montanus should be seen as literally the 'advocate' (*paraklêtos*) for the two female prophets (Jensen 1996: 135–8; contrast Trevett 1996: 159–62). The case does not convince. Nevertheless, there is no case for their having been other than his equals in leadership and influence, and the attributable prophetic sayings in early anti-Montanist sources and from Tertullian are mostly from the women.

Later anti-Montanist writers did make of the women spiritual dependants or lesser associates of Montanus. He was even described as having 'procured' them, though no sexual impropriety had been alleged at first. Montanism came to be lodged firmly in the register of heresies, and these same women by that time had metamorphosed in Christian rhetoric into mad and dangerous infanticidal whores, or into 'nobles and rich women', who had seduced Christian communities with money before introducing the pollution of heresy (Jerome, *Ep.* 33.4 *Ad Ctesiphon;* see Trevett 1998). The reputation of Montanus fared no better.

From the outset non-Montanists had been offended by the recognition of women's spiritual authority in the New Prophecy. As 'false' prophets afflicted by demons, early Montanist women (but not men it would seem) attracted the attention of exorcizing Asian men. Both Maximilla and the unnamed prophetess (who may be a

937

literary device) described by Firmilian were so confronted (*H. E.* 5.18.13; cf. 5.19.3; Cyprian, *Ep.* 75 [Firmilian]; Trevett 1996: 153–8; 1999a). Montanus, who was probably the first of the Three to die, was accused of lust for leadership (*HE* 5.16.7 [Anonymous]) and of being innovative (*H. E.* 5.18.1 [Apollonius]), but then both he and Maximilla, separately, were said to have committed suicide – further evidence, perhaps, of her demonic possession. This story even the gossipy Eusebian Anonymous doubted, however (*H. E.* 5.16.13).

As for Priscilla, she was jibed at for being titled 'virgin' when she was known to have been married and for receiving gifts of money and clothing (*H. E.* 5.18.3–4 [Apollonius]). But it was left to later writers not only to record unsympathetically later Montanist women's clericalization (McGinn-Moorer 1989; Jensen 1996; Trevett 1996) but also to provide more lurid accounts of the Three, including reference to Montanus' supposed castration (Jerome following Didymus), his former pagan priesthood, Cataphrygians' infant-defiling rites and bloody Eucharistic offerings (Praedestinatus, Epiphanius, Jerome, Augustine and others) and the women's insanity.

The sayings

Given that what we know of these prophets stems almost entirely from hostile sources the extant sayings attributed to them are crucial for any study of Montanism. Past attempts to link Montanism and documents such as the *Didache*, the *Ascension of Isaiah* and the *Odes of Solomon* have made little impact.

The so-called 'oracles' of the Three are in some cases attenuated sayings or mere introductory prophetic self-designation formulae. As we have them they stand divorced from their original context, sometimes seeming to be a riposte from an extended debate, and in the majority of cases (those preserved by Tertullian being exceptions) they are presented as ludicrous, offensive or evidence of hubris. Stewart-Sykes (1999), on the other hand, regards the very lack of wordiness as evidence that in some cases a complete saying *has* been preserved, for the prophets would have been rural types and of little education.

A few sayings are unattributed, notably some preserved by Tertullian: *Pud.* 21.7 on refusal to pardon sin, *Fuga* 9.4 on the Spirit exhorting to martyrdom and *Anima* 55.5. The latter partially echoes the sentiments of *Fuga* 9.4 in advocating martyrdom over death in bed or in the complications of childbearing.

Given that in the past hostile descriptions of the prophesying as bizarre, false, demonically inspired and divorced from the proper Christian kind of prophecy were taken at face value, there was relatively little interest in the likeness of the sayings to Christian and non-Christian prophetic forms or to portions of earlier writings echoed imaginatively for a new situation in 'charismatic exegesis'. Recent study has brought interesting results.[10]

Montanus

An element of 'specialization' may have characterized these early charismatic leaders, each of which also functioned as a prophet for the community. Montanus was said to have the Pauline *charism* of administration, though he was a teacher as well (Eusebius, *H. E.* 5.18.2). He had organized gatherings at Pepouza and Tymion and had organized collectors of offerings from among the sympathetic (Eusebius, *H. E.* 5.18.2; cf. 1 Cor. 12:28).

Extant sayings show Montanus uttering prophetic 'I' sayings designed to establish the source and authority of the inspired speech: 'I am the Lord God, the Almighty dwelling in man' and 'Neither angel nor envoy, but I the Lord God the Father have come' (Epiphanius, *Pan.* 48.11; cf. Isa. 63:9). His best-known utterance (which has parallels elsewhere) suggests a context of debate about the nature of inspiration: 'Behold, man is like a lyre, and I flit about like a plectron; man sleeps, and I awaken him; behold, it is the Lord who changes the hearts of men and gives men a heart' (Epiphanius, *Pan.* 48.4).

Montanus' claims to inspiration and his mode of prophesying created alarm. He seemed possessed and prophesied in a frenzied manner, with ecstasy and strange speech as well. Priscilla and Maximilla similarly prophesied in an inappropriate fashion (*H. E.* 5.16.9 [Anonymous]), or so it was reported. One early anti-Montanist writer claimed that he was a recent convert to Christianity (*H. E.* 5.16.7). In later centuries, as has been indicated, Christian writers seized on every element of the exotic. Jerome maintained that Montanus had been 'a castrated and emasculated man' (*ubscisum et semivirum*: [*Ep.* 41.4]), suggesting devotion to the goddess Cybele. Alternatively, it was suggested that he had been a priest of Apollo (the latter according to the *Dialexis* or *Debate of a Montanist and an Orthodox Christian* [Ficker 1905; Heine 1989a: 123]). Had such claims been correct, the earliest opponents of Montanus would surely have seized on them. Pelikan has discounted all such accusations and has suggested that Montanus had been a presbyter (1971: 97).

The accusation that (some later?) Montanists baptized using an aberrant Trinitarian formula which included Montanus' came from Basil of Caesarea (*Ep.* 188.1). Remarkably, it seemed to be confirmed by a late fourth-century African inscription from Khenchela (ancient Mascula) in Numidia (Figure 36.5). In this a certain Flavius Avus, *domesticus* (which may indicate membership of an elite military corps), had marked the fulfilment of a promise by the setting up of a marble slab, with AW symbols and graffito: *Flavius Avus, domesticus, has fulfilled what he promised in the name of the father and son {and} the lord Muntanus.*

Though most writers have assumed the inscription to be Montanist, Tabbernee (1997a: 445–52, cf. 534–9) has argued to the contrary, pointing to the local cult of the African martyr Montanus (died 259 CE) whose name may have been pronounced locally as Muntanus. The cult, he suggested, may in fact have been Donatist.

Priscilla

Tertullian called her Prisca, the non-diminutive form of the name, and he wrote of her as being a mouthpiece of the Paraclete (*Res.* 11.2). She may have been the deliverer of the unattributed sayings preserved by Tertullian (a) about martyrdom, which has a special relevance for women: 'Do not wish to die in your beds or in miscarriages and mild fevers, but rather in martyrdom', and (b) which exhorts

Figure 36.5 Flavius Avus graffito, from Khenchela (ancient Mascula). Drawing from Tabbernee (1997a: 446), with the permission of the author and the publisher, Mercer University Press.

against fear of exposure to public gaze and praise, for *righteousness* it was which brought such exposure (*Fuga* 9.4).

Priscilla's parenetic words on those who ministered in holiness told of the church rightly guided by the 'spiritual' (*pneumatikos*) rather than 'psychic' individuals: 'For purification produces harmony . . . and they see visions, and when they turn their faces downward they also hear salutary voices, as clear as they are secret' (Tertullian, *Cast.* 10.5, trans. Heine 1989a). It was a view of Montanist experience which Tertullian shared when he wrote of some women's receipt of visions (by ecstasy) during the church's rites. These were afterwards transmitted to a wider audience (*De anima* 9.4; *Virg.* 17).

Prisca's saying, 'They are flesh yet they hate the flesh' (Tertullian, *Res.* 11), may have belonged in an anti-gnostic or anti-docetic context. It would have been such emphasis, which may be discerned elsewhere in the extant oracles (Davies 1955), together with the increased discipline brought by the New Prophecy, that had attracted Tertullian.

Maximilla

Epiphanius' early Anonymous anti-Montanist source pointed to Maximilla's name and that of other Montanists as evidence of their barbarous cradling (*Pan.* 48.12.3). She may have survived longest of the Three and would have had longer to become infamous. Even so, the evidence of the Eusebian Anonymous suggests that she may have been dead by *c.* 179–80. Her death has come to be regarded as an important point of division between the original New Prophecy and subsequent developments.

Maximilla's utterances about eschatology and her interpretation of 'signs of the times' proved troublesome. The saying on being an interpreter of covenant and suffering has been noted already, and the Eusebian Anonymous told of her predictions of future wars and revolutions (*H. E.* 5.16.18). Time had proved her wrong. There had been peace in the 13 years between her death and his writing!

Another prediction could also be shown to be inaccurate: 'After me there will no longer be a prophet but the end', she had said (Epiphanius, *Pan.* 48.2.4), and of course it had not been so. At the time it must have seemed that with her death any expectation of continued prophecy had been thwarted.

Maximilla's best-known saying reflects the tension engendered by the New Prophecy in Asia: 'I am driven away like a wolf from the sheep', she complained in a saying preserved by Asterius Urbanus via the Anonymous (Eusebius, *H. E.* 5.16.17). 'I am not a wolf. I am word and spirit and power.' The language is reminiscent both of Matthew (7:15) and of Paul's words about his own power in weakness (1 Cor. 2:4). Another saying, 'Do not hear me but hear Christ' (Epiphanius, *Pan.* 48.12.4), illustrates her claim to be a prophetic mouthpiece, though she, like the others, functioned as a teacher also. Epiphanius' Anonymous wrote of her dismissively (*Pan.* 48.13.1) as an alleged fount of exhortation (*parakalouthia*) and teaching (*didaskalia*).

Maximilla, 'driven away' as condemnation of the New Prophecy took hold and proved wrong by events, was also the only one of the Three whose name was not appended to some form of the movement (Montanists, Priscillianists, etc.). I have surmised that in course of time Maximilla's reputation declined and she became marginal in Montanist memory. Like many a new religious movement since, the Montanists of the third and fourth generations onwards may have preferred to forget some of the excesses and wrong judgements of their beginnings (Trevett 1997).

MONTANISM IN NORTH AFRICA

The Montanism of North Africa (especially Carthage) was a second phase of the movement and it is not easy to determine whether and to what it extent it resembled the more original Asian kind. Much of what we know of it has been filtered through the idiosyncratic Tertullian, who would have been a loyalist by 207 CE. His witness must be assessed with care before being taken as typical.

Further evidence may be gleaned from the *Passio Perpetuae et Felicitatis*. The account had a Montanist redactor who acknowledged new visions, 'new prophecies' and the promise of Joel 2:28–9, while deploring (*Pass. Perp.* 1) those who would limit to 'times and seasons' the gifts and experiences to be described. Some writers (myself among them) assume that the male and female martyrs themselves (died 203 CE) belonged to the New Prophecy in Carthage (Trevett 1996: 176–84; Tabbernee 1997a: 57–9).

In the arena Perpetua faced the crowd and the beasts 'in spirit and in ecstasy' (*Pass. Perp.* 20.8). She and her circle assumed the availability of dreams and visions and hers included a ladder to heaven (dangerously spiked for the unwary and with a dragon at its base: see Figure 36.6), a dream of becoming male and a gladiator for Christ, and a meeting with a shepherd from whom Perpetua took curds to drink. Some have found this reminiscent of the practice of the Artotyrites or 'bread and *cheesers*' mentioned in later anti-Montanist sources such as Epiphanius (*Pan.* 49.1–2) and Augustine (*Haer.* 28).

Then there is Firmilian's letter to Cyprian in the late 250s CE, with its female prophet who is evidently intended (*pace* Jensen 1996: 182–6) as a description of a Montanist. The account (penned from Caesarea in Cappadocia) may have functioned to promote Asian-type opposition to Montanism in a church (Carthage) where it

Figure 36.6 The Perpetua window from Chester Cathedral. Photo Patricia Jones.

enjoyed a much greater degree of toleration (Trevett 1999a). The Prophecy in Carthage fared differently from elsewhere, perhaps because it *was* different.

Far from being driven out, as had happened in Asia (Fischer 1974, 1977), New Prophets seem to have remained integrated into congregations in Carthage. During and for some time after Tertullian's lifetime there is nothing to suggest their rejection or separation. Tertullian himself remained in the Catholic fold. His descriptions of church life suggest what Powell (1975) called a Montanist *ecclesiola in ecclesia*.[11]

We know little about African Montanism post-Tertullian, however. The writer dubbed 'Praedestinatus', in *De haeresibus* 1.86, claimed that the so-called 'Tertullianists' of Carthage handed over their basilica to the Catholics in Augustine's time, in the fourth century. Augustine himself (*Haer.* 86) claimed that Tertullian had seceded from Montanism as well as from the Catholic faith, and had created his own 'Tertullianist' sect, which is improbable. The 'Tertullianists' have been taken to be synonymous with Montanists in Africa (Barnes 1971: 258–9; cf. Aland 1960b: 161–3; Powell 1975) or perhaps (Tabbernee 1997a: 475–6) a group post-Tertullian and post-Cyprian which *had* left the Catholic mainstream in Carthage.

Augustine's evidence about Cataphrygians and Quintillians confirms there was distinctive Montanist teaching on the Paraclete (*Contra Faustum* 32.170), digamy, and about women in church offices (cf. Epiphanius, *Pan.* 49.2). It includes accusations of Quintillianist bloody rites, involving the pricking of infants.[12] The fourth century may indeed have been the last one for Montanists in the region. In the middle of it Optatus of Milev in Numidia claimed there were no Montanists in Africa (*Schism. Donat.* 1.9.1), though there were plenty of Donatists and some people may have slid soundlessly from one to the other.

Tabbernee itemizes epigraphy of what has been claimed to be Montanist presence in Africa to the sixth century – though perhaps some is Donatist (Frend 1940, 1980; Tabbernee 1997a: 105–23, 444–51, 534–44).

MONTANISM IN ROME

The New Prophecy probably reached Rome at an early stage in its history. Most things gravitated there.[13] It was probably strongest among Asiatics in the city and eventually sparked a debate between Proclus the Montanist and Gaius the Catholic, during the episcopacy of Zephyrinus (*c.* 199–217 CE; Eusebius, *H. E.* 2.25.5–7 and 6.20.3; cf. Pseudo-Tertullian, *Adv. omn. haer.* 7).

Tertullian (*Prax.* 1) claimed that one Roman bishop had recognized the New Prophecy and had penned a peacable letter to Asia and Phrygia before being persuaded of his wrong-headedness by a reminder of his predecessors' different response. Tertullian blamed a *bête noire* nicknamed 'Praxeas' ('busybody'), who had propagandized against the New Prophecy.

Who was the bishop? It is hard to determine. It may have been Eleutherus (174–89), who had received letters of embassy from Gaul in 177 CE. When the Gallic Christians had sent letters of peace to the East, Eleutherus may have decided on similar letters of peace, at least until an Asian anti-Montanist (Praxeas) took action

Figure 36.7   Late second-century statue of Apollo from the arena in Carthage, now in the Bardo Museum in Tunis. Photo Christine Trevett.

on his people's behalf and they were recalled. Both the New Prophets and their enemies may have been canvassing support from many quarters at this time.

In that case it would have been bishop Soter (166–74) who had been among those not recognizing it. Praedestinatus (*Haer.* 1.26) offers some weak and confused evidence in corroboration of this. In any case I find it hard to believe that the tough-minded bishop Victor was the one to give solace to Montanists, albeit briefly (Trevett 1996: 55–60). Other writers have interpreted events quite differently, even in terms of there having been formal excommunication in the past.

As for the New Prophets' teachings in Rome, it seems that their doctrine of the

Paraclete (which Heine took to be a *Roman* Montanist innovation) caused particular concern (Heine 1987, 1989b; contrast Trevett 1996: 62–6). Rome may indeed have become the seat of opposition to Johannine writing, however, such as worried Irenaeus (*Adversus Haereses* 3.11.12). While he deplored those who claimed to have discovered 'more than the truth', he also feared Christians who over-reacted and who would nullify the Spirit's gift and drive prophecy from the church altogether.

It was Epiphanius in *Pan.* 51.3–34 who made the association between the Roman anti-Montanist Gaius and the so-called Alogi who rejected John's Gospel and the Apocalypse.[14] Dionysius bar Salibi, in his twelfth-century *Commentary on the Apocalypse* (*Comm. Apoc.* 1), said that Gaius himself had attributed Gospel and Apocalypse to Cerinthus. There is no consensus, however, as to whether Alogism started in Asia or in Rome, though many writers associate it with response to the New Prophecy.

Questions of authority and heritage were in the air. In Rome the two sides debated the merits of apostolic forebears and apostolic and other writings. Hippolytus (Brent 1995) wrote of Montanists' 'countless books' and of their reverence for even the women's utterances. In response to such things 'they devise new feasts, fasts and the eating of dry food and cabbage' (*Refut. omn. haer.* 18.19). Romans and Asiatics defended their traditions and the merits and memorials of their predecessors (Eusebius, *H. E.* 2.25.6–7; 6.20.3; cf. 3.31.2–5; 5.24; Tabbernee 1997b).

Montanism survived longer in the East than in the West where (Rome excepted perhaps) it had ceased by the end of the fourth century (Aland 1960b: 149–50; Tabbernee 1978: 402). The increasingly Christianized empire could not tolerate it (Trevett 1996: 223–32), and Jerome wrote scathingly of Montanism to the Roman Marcella (*Ep.* 41), naming Sabellianism as its chief fault. Montanists were certainly still in Rome at the end of the fourth century. Praedestinatus (*Haer.* 1.86) told of a 'Tertullianist' priest establishing a *collegium* there, thanks to the patronage of an influential African woman. But they would not have enjoyed peace for long, given that Honorius, the western emperor, passed legislation against Montanists and ordered the burning of books (*Cod. Thod.* 16.5.4). The bishop of Rome, Innocent I (402–17) also allegedly exiled some Cataphrygians to an unnamed monastery.

Some of the Roman epigraphy seems to confirm the existence of Montanist communities in Rome in that long period of silence after Hippolytus, though Tabbernee is sceptical about certain items (Tabbernee 1997a: 124–32; 452–68; 544–52). Some inscriptions used the term *pneumatikos*, and like earlier analysts Tabbernee argued for a thriving Montanist community of Asiatic origin in the late fourth century, and especially in the region of the Via Aurelia.

WHAT WRITERS HAVE SAID ABOUT MONTANISM

The Protestant–Catholic divide, which once characterized scholarship about Montanism, is now much less in evidence. Protestants more readily saw the New Prophecy as promoting renewal or trying to safeguard aspects of 'original' Christianity. *Charismata* were being marginalized, some suggested, even though gifts of the spirit continued to be exercised in many Christian congregations at the time (Campenhausen 1969; Pelikan 1971: 99–100).

Montanism and Gnosticism have been seen as the forces over against which the emerging Catholic tradition defined itself and, in respect of Gnosticism, Catholics and Montanists would have been on the same side (Davies 1955; contrast Froehlich 1973). Since as early as Arnold at the end of the seventeenth century the New Prophecy was seen as a force to stem the tide of secularization in the churches (de Soyres 1878; Bonwetsch 1881 [an important source for information on earlier commentators]; Harnack 1883), while others have written of the struggle of prophetic (including female prophetic) power against that of the clerical kind.

The debt of Montanism to paganism (especially Phrygian paganism) has been a theme since the writing of August Neander (1828), who investigated possible links between the New Prophecy and aspects of the cults of Attis and Cybele. But it was William Ramsay (1895–7) who looked to the possibility of influence from a distinctively Phrygian church, Phrygian society and Phrygian paganism. Anti-Montanist writers may have deliberately hinted at paganization. Klawiter (1975: 129–41) noted parallels between the descriptions of the prophet Montanus and the language and ideas of Lucian's satire of Alexander of Abonuteichos (who was also active in the decade of the 160s). But had pagan influence been thoroughgoing it would surely have been condemned explicitly at an early stage.

These things apart, the firmly *Christian* and more specifically *Asian* Christian, character of the early New Prophecy has been widely acknowledged.[15] Schepelern (1929) found occasional local pagan influences, observable in practices mentioned in later anti-Montanist sources, but the same was true of Asian Christianity generally, he observed.

In nineteenth-century scholarship the tensions between the Montanists and other Christians were sometimes portrayed in terms of a Jewish Christian (Montanist) versus gentile Christian stance. Theories of the debt of Montanism to Ebionism (popularized by the Tübingen school in particular) have been abandoned, but more recently Ford (1966) has pointed to particular parallels with Qumran, the Karaites and the Therapeutae which to her suggest that Montanism was 'Jewish Christian'.

Twentieth-century scholarship has seen more interest in conflicts of culture, in the possibly nationalist or 'rural uneducated' versus 'urban sophisticated' element in the rise of groups such as Montanists and Donatists (Frend 1979, 1988a, 1988b, 1994; Stewart-Sykes 1999) as well as in the political dimension of apocalyptic thought (Grant 1970: 142), in the role of women in Montanism,[16] in analysis of the prophecy and its condemnation, in competing trajectories of Pauline Christianity (McGinn-Moorer 1989) and in the substantial body of possibly Montanist epigraphy.

There are now several collections of disparate literary *Testimonia* and epigraphy. These include the surviving 'oracles' of its prophets which are enumerated differently in different lists (Trevett 1996: 248–9, after Froehlich 1973: 96). They include Labriolle (1913a), Heine's (1989a) compilation and English translation (which omitted 96 items studied by Labriolle), Huber (1985: 218–22) and Aland (1960a) on the oracles. William Tabbernee's substantial study of Montanist and allegedly Montanist epigraphy (1997a, and 1978: 626–724) includes comprehensive references to all earlier important nineteenth- and twentieth-century work, and he finds that the evidence from what is now Turkey, from North Africa and Italy, is in many cases less certainly Montanist than has been claimed.

Finally, several of the studies referred to above include reflections on trends in scholarship (Klawiter 1975; Trevett 1996; Tabbernee 1997). McGinn-Moorer (1989) is the most comprehensive.

NOTES

1 See Eusebius, *Historia Ecclesiastica* 5.16.4; cf. 14 (Anonymous); 5.19.2 (Serapion of Antioch).

2 See *Adversus Marcionem* 3.24.4; 4.22.4; *De resurrectione carnis* 63.9; *Adversus Praxean* 30.5; *De monogamia* 14.4.

3 See Epiphanius' Anonymous in *Pan.* 48.11.5–6; Hippolytus, *Refut. omn. haer.* 8.19; Tertullian, *De anima* 55.5; *De virginibus velandis* 1.8 and 10; *De res. carn.* 11.2; Pseudo Tertullian, *Adv. omn. haer.* 7; Origen, *Princ.* 2.7.3; Didymus, *De trinitate* 3.41.1.

4 See Campenhausen (1969: 18), Ash (1976), Burghardt (1979), McGinn-Moorer (1989: 3–6) and Trevett (1996: 90–1).

5 See e.g. *Virg.* 1.5 and 8; *Res.* 11; *Mon.* 2.1. 4 and 10; 15.1–3; *De pudicitia.* 1; *De Exhortatione Castitatis* 6.2; *De ieiunio* 15.

6 See Strobel (1980: 38–49), Mitchell (1984: 226–7), Trevett (1996: 19–26), and Tabbernee (1997a: 18, 53).

7 See *H. E.* 5.17.2–3 (Alcibiades, but Miltiades is intended); cf. too Origen, *Catenae* (Heine 1989a: 99); Didymus, *Trin.* 3.41.3; Epiphanius, *Pan.* 49.2.

8 See Jerome, *Ep.* 84.4; Socrates, *Historia Ecclesiastica* 1.13.7; Sozomen, *Historia Ecclesiastica* 2.18. See also Sozomen, *H. E.* 2.32.2; Eusebius, *Vita Const.* 3.64–5; Canon 8 of the Council of Laodicea; *Codex Theod.* 16; and Trevett (1996: 198–209; 214–32).

9 See Freeman (1950), Goree (1980), Strobel (1980), Daunton-Fear (1982), Frend (1988b, 1994) and Elm (1996).

10 See Blanchetière (1979), Aune (1983), Groh (1985), Forbes (1986), Elm (1994), Trevett (1996), McGinn (1997) and Stewart-Sykes (1999).

11 See Lawlor (1908), Robeck (1992), van der Lof (1991), Rankin (1995) and Tabbernee (1997a: 54–5, 142).

12 See Augustine, *Haer.* 26–27; cf. Epiphanius, *Pan.* 48.14–15. See Trevett (1995) and Elm (1996).

13 See Klawiter (1975: 191–243), La Piana (1925), Lampe (1989) and Trevett (1996: 55–66).

14 See Labriolle 1913a: lxxii–lxxiii, lxxx, Bludau (1925), Paulsen (1978: 25–7), Heine (1987, 1989b) and Trevett (1996: 139–41).

15 See Kraft (1955), Aland (1955, 1960a), McGinn-Moorer (1989), Tabbernee (1978, 1997b), Trevett (1996) and Stewart-Sykes (1999b).

16 See Fiorenza (1983: 300–3), Huber (1985), McGinn-Moorer (1989) and Trevett (1996).

BIBLIOGRAPHY

Aland, Kurt (1955) 'Der Montanismus und die kleinasiatische Theologie', *Zeitschrift für die neutestamentliche Wissenschaft* 46: 109–16.

—— (1960a) 'Bemerkungen zum Montanismus und zur frühchristlichen Eschatologie', in *Kirchengeschichtliche Entwürfe: Alte Kirche, Reformation und Luthertum, Pietismus und Erweckungsbewegung.* Gütersloh: Gerd Mohn, 105–48.

—— (1960b) 'Augustin und der Montanismus', in Aland 1960a: 149–64.

Arnold, Gottfried (1699, 1700, 1729) *Unparteiische Kirchen-und-Ketzer-Historie*. Frankfurt am Main.

Ash, James L. (1976) 'The Decline of Ecstatic Prophecy in the Early Church', *Theological Studies* 37: 227–52.

Aune, David E. (1983) *Prophecy in Early Christianity and the Ancient Mediterranean World*. Grand Rapids, Mich.: Eerdmans.

Barnes, Timothy D. (1970) 'The Chronology of Montanism', *Journal of Theological Studies* 21: 403–8.

—— (1971) *Tertullian: A Historical and Literary Study*. Oxford: Clarendon.

Blanchetière Françoise (1978, 1979) 'Le montanism originel', *Revue des Sciences Religieuses* 52: 118–34; 53: 1–22.

—— (1981) *Le christianisme asiates aux IIe et IIIe siècles*. Revised production of a 1977 University of Strasbourg doctoral dissertation. Lille: University of Lille.

Bludau, Augustin (1925) *Die ersten Gegner der Johannesschriften* (Bib. St. 22). Freiburg: Herder.

Bonwetsch, G. Nathanael (1881) *Die Geschichte des Montanismus*. Erlangen: Andreas Deichert (1972 reprint Hildesheim: Gersternberg).

Brent, Allen (1995) *Hippolytus and the Roman Church in the Third Century: Communities in Tension Before the Emergence of a Monarch Bishop*. Supplements to *Vigiliae Christianae* 31. Leiden: Brill.

Burghardt, Walter J. (1979) 'Primitive Montanism: Why Condemned?', in Dikran Y. Haddidian (ed.) *From Faith to Faith: Essays in Honor of Donald G. Miller*. Pittsburgh Pa.: The Pickwick Press, 339–56.

Buschmann, Gerd (1995) 'Martyrium Polycarpi 4 und der Montanismus', *Vigiliae Christianae* 49: 105–45.

Calder, William M. (1923) 'Philadelphia and Montanism', *Bulletin of the John Rylands Library* 7: 309–53.

—— (1931) 'The New Jerusalem of the Montanists', *Byzantion* 6: 421–5.

Campenhausen, Hans von (1969) *Ecclesiastical Authority and Spiritual Power in the Church of the First Three Centuries*, ed. and trans. J. A. Baker. London: A. & C. Black.

Daunton-Fear, A. (1982) 'The Ecstasies of Montanus', *Studia Patristica* 17: 648–51.

Davies, J. G. (1955) 'De resurrectione carnis LXIII: a note on the origins of Montanism', *Journal of Theological Studies* 6: 90–4.

Elm, Susannah (1994) 'Montanist Oracles', in Elizabeth S. Fiorenza (ed.) *Searching the Scriptures*. Vol. 2: *A Feminist Commentary*. New York: Crossroad, 131–8.

—— (1996) ' "Pierced by Bronze Needles": Anti-Montanist Charges of Ritual Stigmatization in Their Fourth Century Context', *Journal of Early Christian Studies* 4: 409–40.

Ficker, Gerhard (1905) 'Widerlegung eines Montanisten', *Zeitschrift für Kirchengeschichte* 26: 447–63.

Fiorenza, Elizabeth S. (1983) *In Memory of Her: A Feminist Theological Reconstruction of Christian Origins*. London: SCM Press.

Fischer, Joseph A. (1974) 'Die antimontanistischen Synoden des 2./3. Jahrhunderts', *Annuarium Historiae Conciliorum* 6, 2: 241–73.

—— (1977) 'Angebliche Synoden des 2. Jahrhunderts', *Annuarium Historiae Conciliorum* 9, 2: 231–52.

Forbes, Christopher (1986) 'Early Christian Inspired Speech and Hellenistic Popular Religion', *Novum Testamentum* 28: 257–68.

Ford, Josephine M. (1966) 'Was Montanism a Jewish-Christian Heresy?', *Journal of Ecclesiastical History* 17: 145–58.

Freeman, Greville (1950) 'Montanism and the Pagan Cults of Phrygia', *Dominican Studies* 3: 297–316.

Freeman-Grenville, Greville S. P. (1954) 'The Date of the Outbreak of Montanism', *Journal of Ecclesiastical History* 5: 7–15.

Frend, William H. C. (1940) 'The *memoriae apostolorum* in Roman North Africa', *Journal of Roman Studies* 30: 32–49 (and in Frend 1980).

—— (1964) 'A Note on the Chronology of the Martyrdom of Polycarp and the Outbreak of Montanism', in J. Courcelle *et al.* (eds) *Oikoumene: Studi Paleocristiani pubblicati in onore del Concilio Ecumenico Vaticano II*. Catania: Universitá di Catania.

—— (1979) 'Town and Countryside in Early Christianity', in Derek Baker (ed.) *The Church in Town and Countryside*. Studies in Church History 16. Oxford: Blackwell, 25–42 (and in Frend 1980).

—— (1980) *Town and Country in the Early Christian Centuries*. Collected Series 100. London: Variorum Reprints (includes Frend [1940] and [1979]).

—— (1988a) 'Montanism: Research and Problems', in *Archaeology and History in the Study of Early Christianity*. London: Variorum Reprints, No. 6

—— (1988b) 'Montanism: A Movement of Prophecy and Regional Identity in the Early Church', *Bulletin of the John Rylands Library* 70: 25–34.

—— (1994) 'Montanismus', *Theologische Realenzyklopädie* Band 23: 271–9.

Froehlich, Karlfried (1973) 'Montanism and Gnosis', in David Neiman and Margaret Schatkin (eds) *The Heritage of the Early Church: Essays in Honour of G. V. Florovsky*. Orientalia Christiana Analecta. Rome: Pont. Inst. Stud. Or.: 91–111.

Goree, Balfour W. (1980) 'The Cultural Bases of Montanism'. Waco, Tex.: Baylor University Ph.D. Dissertation.

Grant, Robert M. (1970) *Augustus to Constantine: The Thrust of the Christian Movement into the Roman World*. London: Collins.

Groh, Dennis E. (1985) 'Utterance and Exegesis: Biblical Interpretation in the Montanist Crisis', in D. Groh and R. Jewett (eds) *The Living Text: Essays in Honour of Ernest W. Saunders*. Lanham, Md. and London: University Press of America, 73–95.

Hahneman, Geoffrey M. (1992) *The Muratorian Fragment and the Development of the Canon*. Oxford: Clarendon.

Harnack, Adolf von (1883) 'Montanism', *Encyclopaedia Britannica*, 9th edn, Vol. 16, pp. 774–7.

Heine, Ronald E. (1987) 'The Role of the Gospel of John in the Montanist Controversy', *The Second Century* 6: 1–19.

—— (1989a) *The Montanist Oracles and Testimonia*. Macon, GA.: Mercer University Press.

—— (1989b) 'The Gospel of John and the Montanist Debate at Rome', *Studia Patristica* 21: 95–100.

Hill, Charles E. (1992) *Regnum Caelorum: Patterns of Future Hope in Early Christianity*. Oxford: Clarendon Press.

Huber, Elaine C. (1985) *Women and the Authority of Inspiration: A Re-examination of Two Prophetic Movements from a Contemporary Feminist Perspective*. New York and London: University Press of America.

Jensen, Anne (1996) *God's Self-Confident Daughters: Early Christianity and the Liberation of Women*, trans. O. C. Dean, Jnr. Kampen: Kok Pharos.

Klawiter, Frederick C. (1975) 'The New Prophecy in Early Christianity: The Origin, Nature and Development of Montanism AD 165–220'. Chicago: University of Chicago Ph.D. dissertation.

—— (1980) 'The Role of Martyrdom and Persecution in Developing the Priestly Office of Women in Early Christianty: A Case Study of Montanism', *Church History* 49: 251–61.

Kraft, Heinrich (1955) 'Die altkirchliche Prophetie und die Entstehung des Montanismus', *Theologische Zeitschrift* 11: 249–71.

Labriolle, Pierre H. M. C. de (1913a) *Les Sources de l'Histoire du Montanisme: Textes Grecs, Latins, Syriaques*. Paris: Ernest Leroux.

—— (1913b) *La Crise Montaniste*. Paris: Ernest Leroux.

Lampe, Peter (1989) *Die stadtrömischen Christen in den ersten beiden Jahrhunderten: Untersuchungen zur Socialgeschichte*, 2nd edn. Tübingen: J. C. B. Mohr (Paul Siebeck).

Lawlor, Hugh J. (1908) 'The Heresy of the Phrygians', *Journal of Theological Studies* 9: 481–99.

Lof, L. G. van der (1991) 'The Plebs of the Psychici: Are the Psychics of De Monogamia Fellow-Catholics of Tertullian?', in G. J. M. Bartelink *et al.* (eds) *Eulogia: Mélanges offerts à Antoon A.R. Bastiaensen*. Instrumenta Patristica 24. The Hague: Nijhoff International, 353–63.

McGinn, Sheila E. (1997) 'The "Montanist" Oracles and Prophetic Theology', *Studia Patristica* 31: 128–35.

McGinn-Moorer, Sheila E. (1989) 'The New Prophecy of Asia Minor and the Rise of Ecclesiastical Patriarchy in Second Century Pauline Traditions'. Evanston Ill.: Northwestern University Ph.D. dissertation.

Mitchell, S. (1984) Review of Strobel, *Das heilige Land*, in *Journal of Theological Studies* 35: 225–7.

Neander, August (1828) *Allgemeine Geschichte der christlichen Religion und Kultur*, Vol. 1.3. Hamburg: Friedrich Perthes.

Paulsen, Henning (1978) 'Die Bedeutung des Montanismus für die Herausbildung des Kanons', *Vigiliae Christianae* 32: 19–52.

Pelikan, Jaroslav (1956) 'Montanism and its Trinitarian Significance', *Church History* 25: 99–109.

—— (1971) *The Emergence of the Catholic Tradition (100–600)*. Vol. 1: *The Christian Tradition: A History of the Development of Doctrine*. Chicago and London: University of Chicago Press.

Piana, George La (1925) 'The Roman Church at the End of the Second Century', *Harvard Theological Review* 18: 201–77.

Powell, Douglas (1975) 'Tertullianists and Cataphrygians', *Vigiliae Christianae* 29: 33–54.

Preuschen, Erwin (1900) 'Ardaf IV. Esaia 9, 26 und der Montanismus ', *Zeitschrift für die neutestamentliche Wissenschaft* 1: 265–6.

Ramsay, William M. (1895–7) *The Cities and Bishoprics of Phrygia, Being an Essay on the Local History of Phrygia from the Earliest Times to the Turkish Conquest*, 2 vols. Oxford: Clarendon.

Rankin, David (1995) *Tertullian and the Church*. Cambridge: Cambridge University Press.

Robeck, Cecil M. Jnr. (1987) 'Canon, *regula fidei*, and Continuing Revelation in the Early Church' in James E. Bradley and Richard A. Muller (eds), *Church, Word and Spirit: Historical and Theological Essays in Hon. Geoffrey W. Bromiley*. Grand Rapids Mich.: Eerdmans, 65–91.

—— (1992) *Prophecy in Carthage: Perpetua, Tertullian and Cyprian*. Cleveland Oh.: Pilgrim.

Schepelern, Wilhelm (1929) *Der Montanismus und die phrygische Kulte: Eine religionsgeschichtliche Untersuchung*. Tübingen: J. C. B. Mohr (Paul Siebeck).

Sordi, Marta (1983) *The Christians and The Roman Empire*. London and Bologna: Cappelli.

Soyres, John de (1878) *Montanism and the Primitive Church: A Study in the Ecclesiastical History of the Second Century*. Cambridge: Deighton Bell & Co. (1965 reprint, London: George Bell & Sons).

Stewart-Sykes, Alistair (1997a) 'Papyrus Oxyrhynchus 5: A Prophetic Protest from Second Century Rome', *Studia Patristica* 31: 196–205.

—— (1999) 'The Original Condemnation of Asian Montanism', *Journal of Ecclesiastical History* 50, 1: 1–22.

—— (1997b) 'The Asian Context of the *Epistula Apostolorum* and the New Prophecy', *Vigiliae Christianae* 51: 416–38.

Strobel, August (1980) *Das heilige Land der Montanisten: Eine religions- geographische Untersuchung*. Berlin and New York: de Gruyter.

Tabbernee, William (1978) 'The Opposition to Montanism from Church and State: a Study of the History and Theology of the Montanist Movement as Shown by the Writings and Legislation of the Orthodox Opponents of Montanism'. Melbourne: University of Melbourne Ph.D. Dissertation.

—— (1985) 'Early Montanism and Voluntary Martyrdom', *Colloquium* 17: 33–44.

—— (1993) 'Montanist Regional Bishops: New Evidence from Ancient Inscriptions', *Journal of Early Christian Studies* 1: 249–80.

—— (1997a) *Montanist Inscriptions and Testimonia: Epigraphic Sources Illustrating the History of Montanism*. Macon, Ga.: Mercer University Press.

—— (1997b) '"Our Trophies are Better than Your Trophies": The Appeal to Tombs and Reliquaries in Montanist–Orthodox relations', *Studia Patristica* 31: 206–17.

Trevett, Christine (1989) 'Apocalypse, Ignatius, Montanism: Seeking the Seeds', *Vigiliae Christianae* 43: 313–38.

—— (1995) 'Fingers up Noses and Pricking with Needles: Possible Reminiscences of Revelation in Later Montanism', *Vigiliae Christianae* 49: 258–69.

—— (1996) *Montanism: Gender, Authority and the New Prophecy*. Cambridge: Cambridge University Press.

—— (1997) 'Eschatological Timetabling and the Montanist Prophet Maximilla', *Studia Patristica* 31: 218–24.

—— (1998) 'Gender, Authority and Church History: A Case Study of Montanism', *Feminist Theology* 17: 9–24.

—— (1999a) 'Spiritual Authority and the "Heretical" Woman: Firmilian's Word to the Church in Carthage', in J. W. Watt and J. W. Drijvers (eds) *Portraits of Spiritual Authority: Religious Power in Early Christianity, Byzantium and the Christian Orient*. Leiden: Brill, 45–62.

—— (1999b) '"Angelic Visitations and Speech She Had": Nanas of Kotiaeion', in P. Allen *et al.* (eds) *Prayer and Spirituality in the Early Church*, Vol. 2. Brisbane: Australian Catholic University, 259–78.

Walls, Andrew F. (1964) 'The Montanist "Catholic Epistle" and its New Testament Prototype", *Studia Evangelica* 3, 2 (*Texte und Untersuchungen* 88): 437–46.

Wright, David F. (1976) 'Why were the Montanists Condemned?', *Themelios* 2: 15–22.

DONATISM

——— •✦• ———

James Alexander

INTRODUCTION: THE ORIGINS AND PERSISTENCE OF DONATISM

The history of the schism may be swiftly sketched. It arose from different reactions among Christians in Roman Africa to the last and greatest persecution of the church, under the emperor Diocletian (303–5). A central feature of this persecution was the imperial demand that Christians hand over scriptures to the authorities. Some remained conspicuously loyal to a long-standing tradition of no compromise with pagan religion, which was seen as idolatrous, and provocatively made public their encouragement of those ready to die in defiance of imperial edicts which forbade Christian worship, confiscated bibles, and demanded ritual sacrifice to the gods of Rome. In particular, they refused to engage in *traditio*, 'handing over', of the scriptures. Others, meanwhile, advocated prudence, even at the risk of ostensible compromise, to the extent of becoming actual or apparent *traditores* of scriptures, as the best way for the church to survive this threat to its existence and emerge from the crisis with the least damage done. A vacancy in the see of Carthage, caused by the death of Mensurius (probably early in 307 CE) transformed those two groups into two rival parties, each with its own claimant to Africa's primatial see. Donatus (from whom Donatism gets its name) represented the former, rigorous group, and Caecilian the latter. Constantine, the emperor before whom the case was brought on appeal in 316, ended a long legal wrangle by ruling in favour of Caecilian, thus confirming the earlier decisions of church councils at Rome (313) and Arles (314). However, failure to reconcile the dissidents, ably led by Caecilian's rival Donatus, brought grudging toleration in 321 to the party-in-opposition. So the church in Roman Africa remained divided for over a century.

Eventually, there were few areas without two bishops, each at the head of his own people or congregation, in every city, town and tiny village. Notable among attempts to end the schism was a state-sponsored effort under the emperor Constans in the mid-340s which included a generous distribution of alms, but resulted in the massacre of many Donatists, so making reconciliation of the opposing parties all the more difficult. But Donatism was weakened in 393 by an internal split, when it lost perhaps almost a quarter of its support to the Maximianist schism. Numerically, this now put the two main parties more or less on an equal footing. Attempts towards reunification were, at the same time, given new impetus by the ingenuity and determination of Augustine, bishop of Hippo. These culminated in a full legal inquiry set up by the emperor Honorius in 411, the so-called Conference of Carthage, after which stringent measures of coercion were, as far as the evidence allows us to say, effectively enforced against the Donatists. The Vandal conquest of Africa, not long after, may possibly have been conducive to unity against a common foe but, more likely perhaps, by ending, at least for a century, the Catholic political ascendancy in Africa it may have facilitated the survival of Donatism as a separate entity. At any rate, a rump of Donatist non-conformity appears to have persisted to the time of Gregory the Great.

Donatism raises some important issues, two of which will be considered in turn here. Firstly, the extent to which religious disputes often seem to merge with divisions along ethnic, economic, social or political lines. And secondly, the possibility of the co-existence of alternative views of the nature of the church. Both of those aspects are relevant to what answer we might choose to give to one simple question: why did Donatism last so long?

THE INTERRELATIONSHIP OF RELIGIOUS, ETHNIC, ECONOMIC, SOCIAL AND POLITICAL ISSUES

Special conditions in Roman Africa

Compare the Donatist schism in Africa with the Melitian schism in Egypt (Frend [1952] 1972: 22–4). Both arose in the early fourth century under apparently similar conditions, in the aftermath of the persecution of the church under the emperor Diocletian. Both centred on disagreement over the terms of rehabilitation of church members and particularly of clergy who had lapsed, either by surrendering copies of the scriptures on demand to the persecuting authorities (*traditio*) or by performing some ostensible act of conformity with pagan ceremonial rites (*sacrificatio*, *turificatio*), regrettable, if perhaps necessary, compromises in the circumstances, yet regarded by most Christians as constituting a public betrayal of the faith. Some were quick to cast themselves in the role of upholders of the faith over against those who had betrayed it, insisting that the lapsed could be reinstated to full communion only after a suitably long period among the ranks of the penitent and that lapsed clergy should be reduced to the status of laymen. An apostate priest was no longer worthy of office in the church. If he presumed to continue his duties, his sacraments were null and void and those who remained in communion with him merely implicated themselves in his apostasy by condoning it. Thus, Caecilian of Carthage was held by his critics to have become implicated in apostasy by receiving his consecration as bishop from known apostates. His opponents therefore consecrated another, Majorinus, who was soon succeeded by Donatus, rival bishop of Carthage from *c.* 313 to *c.* 355. But there were others, who did not share the view of the rigorist party and who, in view of the large number of lapsed Christians, urged less delay in their re-admission to the church and were even prepared to excuse compliant clergy by covering up their guilt or explaining it away.

So why, then, was Donatism so long-lived in Africa, while in Egypt the Melitian schism died off within a few years? In each case a similar cause of disagreement on the religious level obviously did not produce similar results, at least in the long term. Part of the explanation for the longevity of Donatism has therefore been sought beyond the religious sphere in the local conditions of Roman Africa. Observing that the main concentration of Donatist churches occurred within a particular area, the high plains of central Numidia, William Frend argued that Donatism represented a reaction of native Berber culture against the process of Romanization, a reassertion of regional identity lost through political absorption in the Roman empire, the protest of an impoverished rural population against the prosperity of the towns and cities, the main centres of Roman culture and influence (Frend [1952] 1972).

Town and country

It seems clear that while its main power-base lay in central Numidia, Donatism was well supported throughout North Africa. Augustine's anti-Donatist polemic stressed that his own side, the North African Catholics, had succeeded in winning official recognition from the rest of the church, whose increasingly world-wide communion could be seen as the fulfilment of the church's promised universality through the preaching of the gospel to all nations. By contrast, the Donatist faction was confined to a corner of Africa. Fortunately, we can check the accuracy of Augustine's characterization of Donatism as essentially a Numidian affair by looking at the lists of bishops from each side attending the Carthage Conference in 411. Already employed by William Frend ([1952] 1972), and again assessed by Serge Lancel, this evidence gives a good picture, since each side wished to demonstrate numerical superiority over the other in terms of their bishops and the congregations they represented — as the roll was called at the opening session of the Conference each bishop identified himself and acknowledged where he had his see (Lancel 1972–91: I, 107–90). The tally of Catholic and Donatist bishops was not much less than three hundred each, with the Donatists marginally in the majority. Although the precise location and the size and importance of a number of sees remains doubtful, the overall picture which emerges shows the Donatists not only in the ascendant in Africa's western provinces, Numidia and Mauretania, but holding their own in the eastern provinces as well, Byzacena and Tripolitana, except for the most important part associated with Carthage itself, the proconsular province, where the Catholics enjoyed a clear majority. In other words, Donatism is not so easily identifiable with its Numidian heartland as Augustine's polemic might lead us to expect. Further, each side at the Conference accused the other of having artificially increased the number of its bishops by a regular policy of subdividing what had formerly been one see into two or even three, upgrading rural congregations to the position of episcopal sees which would normally have been centred in a city or town. What often seems to have happened is that in a town where both parties maintained rival bishops, as changing circumstances enabled one bishop to gain the upper hand, his rival would be obliged to retreat to the country and set up a temporary see in a nearby village, no doubt in the hope of returning to his old see at some more favourable opportunity. Or again, where one side held undisputed sway, the other might be tempted to enter a challenge by installing a bishop or even a presbyter with a token congregation, either in the town itself where the existing bishop had his see or not too far away in the surrounding countryside. The episcopal lists at the Conference show that both sides had sees in country areas, the Donatists probably more than the Catholics, but that the former were as much in evidence as the latter in the towns and cities. The attempt therefore to represent Donatism as the religion of a less Romanized and underprivileged countryside, as opposed to that of the more prosperous centres of urban life and culture, requires qualification. It is also worth noting that in the case of Africa the contrast between town and country should not be exaggerated. Unlike Egypt, where the Greek cities stood out starkly against a native rural background, the process of urbanization had penetrated deeply in Roman Africa, which included a few larger centres of population, such as Carthage itself, the capital, or Hippo Regius, Augustine's see, and a large number of smaller units, most of them enjoying civic status (Février 1966: 235; cf. 1964: 1–47).

Local culture

Urbanization went hand in hand with Romanization, which also seems to have been pretty thorough, even if not quite complete. The suggestion of a native Berber culture reasserting itself against the culture of the conqueror and finding a useful ally in Donatist non-conformity, comes up against two main difficulties. First, the language in which the controversy was conducted was exclusively Latin and the leading protagonists on the Donatist side – Donatus himself; his successor, Parmenian; the biblical exegete Tyconius; Petilian, fifth-century bishop of Cirta in central Numidia; Cresconius the grammarian; Emeritus of Mauretanian Caesarea; Gaudentius of Timgad in Numidia, to name the most notable – even if they lack the rhetorical brilliance of Augustine, are as representative of the Roman culture of their age as their Catholic counterparts. Second, the term 'Berber' is used by modern scholars to refer to what is assumed to be a continuous cultural and linguistic tradition stretching back in North Africa to before the Carthaginian empire. While there is some inscriptional evidence indicating the use in North Africa in Roman times of a script, though not necessarily a spoken language, other than Punic or Latin, it seems clear that Punic, the language of the earlier Carthaginian empire, was the main alternative to Latin in Augustine's time (Millar 1968: 126–34). We hear of Augustine's Donatist counterpart in Hippo having his sermon relayed through an interpreter on one occasion to a congregation which included visiting members who understood Punic but not Latin. We also hear of Augustine's own concern that Catholic clergy in Punic-speaking rural areas should be competent in that language. So Punic at least appears to have presented equal problems of communication for the Romanized leadership of either side. Such evidence suggests that Punic-speakers were, by the time of Augustine, limited to certain rural areas, even perhaps that they represented only a marginal group in North African society, and that Latin was the language of most church members as well as their leaders, whether

Catholic or Donatist, who used it as their principal means of instruction and polemic.

Political disaffection

Politically, fourth-century North Africa was administered through officials responsible to a central government, where overall power was divided between co-emperors based at Constantinople in the East and, successively, at Rome, then Milan, and finally Ravenna in the West, and was exercised through a vast, complex machine of civil servants and military personnel. The principle of dynastic succession provided for most of the fourth century a reasonably successful transference of power from one set of rulers to the next. There were of course opportunities of advancement for good military leaders, who knew that a timely bid for power could often succeed. In Africa two such attempts were made by Roman commanders of Moorish stock, indeed, of the same family: Firmus in the 370s and Gildo in the 390s. The rebellion of Firmus was quickly dealt with, but Gildo ruled Africa for a number of years. Arguing against the Donatists Augustine does not hesitate to suggest – at least for the sake of argument – that their loyalty to the Roman government was compromised through their association with Firmus and Gildo in turn. So was Donatism linked to a reassertion of regional political identity, a reaction led by native military commanders against the Roman empire itself?

There is little evidence that either Firmus or Gildo wished for more than positions of power within the imperial structure (Tengström 1964: 79–90). They do not appear to have wanted to undermine that structure itself. It was rather the case that their self-promotion failed to win the official approval for which they hoped and so they found themselves treated as usurpers. This enabled Augustine to mock Donatist links with Roman military officials who came to be branded as rebels. So what were those links? In the case of Firmus, the Donatist bishop of Rusubbicari, a coastal town in Caesarean Mauretania, was responsible for negotiating its terms of capitulation to Firmus near the start of his campaign: the terms were said to have allowed his soldiers to pillage the property of the Catholics of the town, while sparing its Donatist inhabitants. This incident, Augustine claims, earned for the Donatists the nickname 'Firmiani', for supporting Firmus. This is Augustine's response to the Donatist labelling of Catholics as 'Macariani', followers of Macarius, for their complicity in the notorious massacre of Donatists under that Roman official in the mid-340s. Clearly, Augustine's polemical purpose here must be given due weight in determining the extent to which Donatists may be said to have condoned rebellion against the central Roman authorities through supporting Firmus. Second, in the case of Gildo's revolt, Augustine concentrates on the extent to which the Donatist bishop Optatus of Timgad, in Numidia, was involved. Gildo's control of Africa (386–98) may indeed have favoured the Donatists, at least when compared with the close cooperation which existed a few years later between the representatives of the central government and the Catholic episcopate in implementing a policy of legal repression against the African schismatics. Augustine accuses bishop Optatus of taking unscrupulous advantage of the situation under Gildo to promote Donatist interests by methods of intimidation, involving a class of religious fanatics and trouble-makers known as circumcellions, a phenomenon to be discussed presently. It was rumoured, Augustine informs us, that when Gildo was eventually executed as a rebel, bishop Optatus died in prison as one of his chief satellites. It may be that Optatus was able to exploit the favour of Gildo as chief military official in Africa in his time in much the same way as Augustine himself later fostered a relationship beneficial to the Catholic side with successive Roman officials of high rank who served in Africa. It was unfortunate for the Donatists that the official under whom they benefited most came to be branded a rebel. But this hardly means the Donatists in general were hostile to Rome.

There is in Donatist literature, particularly in their martyr-acts (accounts of the suffering and death of Donatists, with the connivance of their Catholic opponents, at the hands of Roman officials) a fair amount of adverse criticism of the Roman empire. Its rulers, agents of the Devil, have always persecuted the church (*Passio Marculi 3 {Maier 1987: 278}; Passio Isaac et Maximiani* 8 [Maier 1987: 267]). This is really saying no more than earlier accounts of the Christian martyrs, but the Donatists are still making the point when almost everyone else was ready to applaud Eusebius of Caesarea's eulogy of the Christian emperor as a divinely appointed agent in God's plan of salvation for humanity. That was not how things seemed to the Donatists, who claimed to be upholding the authentic tradition of the early church, yet found themselves labelled schismatics and heretics for refusing to conform to the official church. It is worth noting however that, like Tertullian before them, the Donatists were not opposed to the empire as such, but rather to its persecution of the church, and they were even more bitterly opposed to their Catholic opponents, who appeared to encourage such persecution. In an 'open' pastoral letter of about the year 400, Petilian, Augustine's contemporary and a leading protagonist on the Donatist side, tags on to a traditional list of persecuting emperors the names of successive Roman officials responsible for persecuting Donatists. He wishes to show the Donatists in direct succession to the church of old, still fruitful in martyrs. But, like Tertullian, it is the local government agents he takes as the target of criticism. Significantly, he does not directly blame the emperor Constantine and his successors. For Petilian, professedly Christian emperors had been misled by the opponents of Donatism into dismissing their sect as a deviant form of the faith and a threat to unity. It is notable how persistent Donatist leaders were in their efforts to persuade successive emperors of this misapprehension. As the emperors, after all, did not, throughout the fourth century, adhere to a wholly consistent position on Arianism, it was not entirely unreasonable for the Donatist leaders to continue to believe in the possibility of imperial favour for their faction. The nearest they came to it was under the 'apostate' Julian, a fact which led Augustine to respond that the Donatists could find favour only with pagan emperors. Yet in Africa, an important province in political and economic terms, it was the Donatists who probably formed an overall majority of the population. Petilian therefore had some cause for optimism and would no doubt have welcomed a change in imperial policy. So he was careful to speak of Constantine and his successors, if not as Christian, then as wanting to become so. It only required that they should cease to be misled by the hostile critics of Donatism (Augustine, *Contra litteras Petiliani* 2.92.202). In the light of this we can see that the sense in which the Donatists continued an out-dated posture into the post-Constantinian age – that of a church of the martyrs set over against a hostile and persecuting empire – was tempered by a readiness for rapprochement.

Economic grievance, social unrest and the circumcellions

How far did the Donatist schism provide a convenient channel in an autocratic state for the expression of economic and social discontent? To what extent did it embody the protest of an increasingly impoverished rural population against economic exploitation by those, in both church and state, with powerful vested interests in the Roman empire – a protest which was, in the main, couched in the language of religious controversy? Should we, for example, picture the Donatist leaders facing a similar situation to that of Martin Luther, confronted in 1525 with a Peasants' Revolt inspired by the dreams of millenarian religion and the demands of social justice (Büttner and Werner 1959: 52–68)?

North Africa was one of the most prosperous regions of the Roman empire and, after the diversion of the Egyptian corn supply from Rome to Constantinople in the fourth century, it became the main source of cheap food for the older capital, with what appear to have been increasingly disadvantageous consequences for local tenant-farmer and peasant producers. Such conditions would naturally have been conducive to economic and social discontent.

Against the Donatists, Augustine makes a great deal of the fact that they were involved in one way or another with a mysterious class of people known as '*circumcelliones*' to their critics, as '*agonistici*' to their friends. Of the former Augustine provides an etymological explanation: this group got their nickname for 'going around buildings in the countryside seeking the means of their own sustenance' (hoc genus hominum . . . uictus sui causa cellas circumiens rusticanas: *Contra Gaudentium* 1.28.32). His explanation is intended to be derogatory, for he wishes to emphasize their terrorism of the countryside and their irresponsible idleness from agricultural labour. But even if we may perhaps suspect that here Augustine is making up a convenient etymology to suit his case, his derivation of the name presumably still corresponds to some typical aspect of their activity. Optatus, Catholic bishop of Mileu, writing some time between 364 and 367, provides the classic description of the circumcellions. He notes three distinctive features. First, they were always on the move, wandering about from one place to another, though they could be found frequenting the marketplaces. Second, they were disruptive of the social order, intimidating creditors into cancelling debts, sometimes to very large amounts, and on occasion they even reversed the role of master and slave, making it unsafe to travel, when the master might find himself thrown out of his carriage and made to run in front of his own slaves seated in their master's place. Third, they were religious, at least in the sense of being fanatically devoted to the ideal of martyrdom, taking it to suicidal extremes by getting someone to kill them or throwing themselves from cliffs. The much more complimentary title '*agonistici*' given to this group by the Donatists themselves indicates their role as soldiers of Christ engaged in religious warfare, supremely exemplified by the Christian martyrs.[1] Augustine often reiterates Optatus' characterization, but fills it out with a considerable amount of circumstantial detail from the late fourth and early fifth centuries, especially from his experience of the circumcellions in his own diocese around Hippo. Augustine shows their tactics of intimidation were aimed chiefly in reprisal for the legal take-over of Donatist church buildings by their Catholic opponents, or in retaliation against laity and particularly clergy who transferred their allegiance from the Donatist to the Catholic side (Diesner 1960: 497–508). In one typical incident, the circumcellions gave the ex-Donatist and now Catholic bishop of Bagai, a traditional Donatist stronghold in Numidia, such a severe beating that his wounds were still visible for inspection at the emperor's court when he accompanied a delegation of Catholic bishops to Ravenna in Italy to plead for stronger repressive measures against the Donatist church. The story lost nothing in the telling, from the unceremonious smashing of the wooden altar under which the unfortunate bishop of Bagai had taken refuge from attack by circumcellions to the final humiliating disposal of the victim in the middle of the night on a rubbish tip, where he lay unconscious till found by a passer-by (*Contra Cresconium* 3.43.47). In fact, the charge of circumcellion terrorism was influential in bringing about a renewal of anti-Donatist legislation in 405. The edict of 412 which finally confirmed the illegality of Donatism lists the circumcellions near the bottom of the social scale, as liable to a relatively less severe fine than better-off ranks of society if convicted of supporting the Donatist cause – they are placed between the plebeian order and slaves or peasant workers (*Codex Theodosianus* 16.5.52). This suggests that, for the purpose of this edict at least, they were a socially identifiable group of relatively modest means. About ten years later, Augustine claims this legal pressure against Donatism as a whole had had the beneficial result of ridding a significant number of circumcellions both of their name and of the notorious deeds associated with it, by inducing them to take up useful employment in the fields (*Gaud.* 1.29.33).

Who then were the circumcellions? They have been variously understood by modern commentators, with emphasis either on economic grievance or religious fanaticism, although of course those two things need not be taken as mutually exclusive. As a social entity they can be seen either as an economically under-privileged group of agricultural labourers rebelling against harsh conditions or, alternatively, as a religious group, associated with ascetic practices, but especially with fanatical devotion to the ideal of martyrdom. In favour of the former view it is argued that, no longer able to sustain a livelihood by working in the fields, the circumcellions may have taken to roaming the countryside living off what they could steal from one barn after another (Monceaux 1912–23: IV, 180). Or again they may have been farmworkers whose constant mobility was determined by the nature of their seasonal work: they may have gone from farm to farm as casual labourers, who remained unemployed for most of the year, but presented themselves for work at the time of the wheat or olive harvest (Saumagne 1934: 351–64). In either case, the ' buildings' in Augustine's expression, quoted above, 'going around buildings in the countryside', are understood to mean 'farm buildings' or 'barns'. So it is possible to envisage them driven by economic hardship and an excess of apocalyptic zeal to attempt to introduce by violent methods a greater measure of social justice and frequently ending up martyrs for the cause. But while nothing is known of their millenarian views, what has sometimes been interpreted as a laudable concern for social justice may have been no more than skilful tactics of intimidation. Donatist writers sometimes identify their party with the innocent poor who suffer oppression at the hands of the rich. It may therefore have suited them to make common cause with the economically and socially deprived in contemporary North African society (Brisson 1958: 325–410). But it is important to note that the Donatists consistently apply this biblical theme to disparage the Catholic opposition in a very precise sense. Through the deceit of riches the Devil has won his way into their hearts in the form of imperial patronage of the Catholic party and now, having entered the Christian fold as a wolf in sheep's clothing, he persecutes the true Christians, the Donatists, more subtly and effectively than ever before (*Passio Donati* 3 [Maier 1987: 204]).

The second line of interpretation sees the circumcellions primarily, but not necessarily only, in religious terms, whether as ascetics or would-be martyrs. The suggestion that they may have been monks of some sort depends mainly on a passage in which Augustine draws an unfavourable comparison between Donatist circumcellions and Catholic monks. The establishment of monasticism in Africa on an organized basis was something for which Augustine himself seems to have been largely, if not solely, responsible. The Donatists made fun both of the institution and of its name, but this was part of their attempt to discredit Augustine. The so-called '*agonistici*', as the Donatists preferred to call the circumcellions, may indeed, Augustine acknowledges, derive their name from the Bible (2 Tim. 4:7), but they do not live up to it because the 'contest' in which they engage is far from 'good': Donatist cirumcellions are to Catholic monks as drunk men to sober, foolhardy to prudent, the irresponsible to the innocent, vagabonds to a settled community (*Enarrationes in Psalmos* 132.3 and 6; see Calderone 1967: 94–109; Frend 1969: 542–9). Augustine's comparison would gain much in piquancy if the circumcellions did actually make some pretension to ascetic virtue. Elsewhere he mentions them recruiting to their number widows and virgins who had consecrated themselves to a life of continence. Possidius, Augustine's colleague and biographer, in fact refers to the circumcellions' 'supposed profession of continence' (*Vita* 10.1.22). Monks who wandered about from one monastery to the next, sampling the life but never settling down to take it seriously and frequently getting into mischief, were a common object of criticism for Augustine and other church leaders of his time. The circumcellions might therefore be understood as mendicant ascetics and Augustine's description of them 'going about buildings in the countryside' interpreted as 'going the rounds of monastic cells situated in the country'. Some Eastern ascetics are known to have taken self-mortification to suicidal extremes, while others are described as embracing the cause of the socially and economically aggrieved, including arranging the cancellation of debtors' bonds. It should of course be noted that this was always a matter of righting individual wrongs, not of implementing social reforms on a grand scale.

But any ascetic tendencies on the part of the circumcellions may perhaps best be understood in association with their role as martyrs. In that case perhaps they represented the religiously zealous wing of Donatism, disciplined by asceticism and dedicated to martyrdom. A fourth-century inscription from Mauretania including the phrase 'martyrs' shrine' supports the view that Augustine's expression 'going around buildings in the countryside' meant that the circumcellions, for the sake of their own sustenance, went about 'country shrines' dedicated to martyrs. That such shrines existed in the North African countryside is clear from both literary and archaeological evidence. The Catholic bishop Optatus describes whitewashed memorial slabs marking the graves of circumcellion martyrs. These were in the form of altars or tables suitable for the martyrs' commemoration with the traditional anniversary feast. Archaeology confirms examples of altars or tables erected in the open air, usually in cemeteries and confined to a special section, and also of martyrs' tombs in or adjoining churches (Optatus 3.4; Duval 1982: II, 458–64, 525–42). Augustine often describes the orgies of the circumcellions in celebration of the martyrs, so the food and drink available on the occasion of martyrs' festivals may have been one reason for their behaviour – 'going round martyrs' shrines in the country for the sake of their own sustenance'. It is clear that the martyr-cult formed a vital element in popular Christian piety, which was difficult for church leaders to keep within reasonable bounds, and Augustine preached many a sermon against the excesses of revelry which characterized the Catholic observance of this custom (cf. *Ep.* 29.11). The Donatists, of course, who saw themselves pre-eminently as a church of the martyrs, a church which, in their own words, 'suffers but does not inflict persecution', had a special reason for upholding this tradition. While most Christians were content to venerate the martyrs at the safe distance of commemorative festivals, the Donatists, as a persecuted sect, continued to experience martyrdom as a gruesome reality. The line between suicide and martyrdom, between dying in a good cause and a bad, was often hard to draw clearly and depended very much on whose side you happened to be on. The Donatist leaders, however, were not altogether lacking in discrimination. We hear of one occasion when the Donatist veneration of dead cirumcellions as martyrs was officially disallowed and their relics, which had been honoured with burial in church, were duly disinterred (Optatus 3.4.). It seems likely that among Donatists as a whole some at least were critical of the popular practice of according martyr-status, somewhat indiscriminately, to those who had sacrificed their lives, in one way or another, in the cause of religion. The widespread debate in the early church on the question of who truly merited martyr-status did not leave the Donatists untouched. When taken to task for the 'voluntary deaths' of circumcellion martyrs Cresconius could apparently point to conciliar decisions of his own party condemning such suicidal fanaticism (*Cresc.* 3.49.54). That circumcellion atrocities were regularly laid at the door of Donatist bishops suggests a close bond existed between Donatists and circumcellions (*Cresc.* 3.43.47). If the bishops, for their part, protested they could not be held responsible, since as churchmen they had no means of controlling such conduct, the case of Optatus of Timgad, previously mentioned, shows how effectively they could advance their cause by means of circumcellion terrorism. One final and important clue to the identity and motivation of the circumcellions is the fact, reported by Augustine, that their efforts were directed as much against paganism as against African Catholicism, which was of course perceived by them as a deviant form of Christianity. At the cost of their own lives they would attempt to disrupt pagan worship and destroy the sacred objects of the cult as idolatrous (*Ep.* 185.12; *Gaud.* 1.28.32; 1.38.51). It may, then, be concluded that the circumcellion phenomenon makes better sense when viewed against the background of a much more general 'militant tendency' in early Christianity (Chadwick 1985: 9–27). Such anti-pagan and anti-heretical activity on the part of religious zealots was by no means peculiar to the Donatist sect.

DONATISM AND THE AFRICAN THEOLOGICAL TRADITION

There is, of course, no need to deny the importance of the various influences discussed above in order to do adequate justice to the religious aspect of the dispute, to which the ancient sources themselves give prominence. The initial causes of the schism – personal rivalry and ecclesiastical ambition – and the contributory factors which later made themselves felt – a sense, however ill-defined, of African regional identity, political opportunism, the exploitation of economic grievances – warn against over-simplification. The schism cannot be explained in too narrowly religious terms. Nevertheless, it seems likely that the persistence of Donatism owes much to theology.

The Donatists of course were not strictly heretics. The Catholic Optatus clearly distinguished them from those heretics whose deficiencies in Trinitarian or Christo-logical doctrine the church had condemned. Thus he deliberately labels them schis-matics, since, though separated from the official church, they shared the same creed and observed identical sacraments, which Optatus was prepared to accept (Donatists coming over to the Catholic church did not require rebaptism: Optatus 1.10). Augustine too conceded that, apart perhaps from some ambiguous language sug-gestive of Arianism, the Donatists essentially agreed in doctrine with the rest of the church. Wishing however to put an effective end to the schism by bringing the Donatists within range of the anti-heresy laws, he was content to have them officially stigmatized as heretics through their practice of rebaptizing African Catho-lics who transferred to their side (*Ep.* 185.1; *De haeresibus* 69; *Cod. Theod.* 16.6.4). For Augustine, persistent schism amounted to heresy (*Cresc.* 2.7.9). Not surprisingly, these were charges which the Donatists rejected and of which they urged their opponents to provide proof (*Petil.* 2.95.218; *Gesta conlationis Carthaginiensis* 3.193). Yet the Donatists too castigated their rivals as both schismatics and heretics (*Petil.* 2.38.91). In short, each side described the other in similarly dismissive terms, which of course reflected the fact that each side shared a common view of the church as one. They agreed that there could be only one church, clearly identifiable as a social entity in terms of its hierarchical structure and of its carefully regulated membership. The issue, then, was precisely the nature of that church. Thus, a comment from Augustine reveals how this crucial question was eventually reached at the Conference of Carthage, after much preliminary posturing: 'If only our breth-ren on the opposite side had brought forward this letter (introducing the doctrinal question) before all those delaying speeches of theirs, so that we might have got down to the debate on the church, on which the case turns' (ut iam de ecclesia, unde causa uertitur, aliquid ageremus: *Gesta conl. Carthag.* 3.261).

Alternative views of the church

William Frend pertinently identified the underlying issue dividing the two sides as two different ways of seeing the church in relation to the world, a point further

developed by Peter Brown (Frend [1952] 1972: 324; Brown 1969: 214). The Donatists, Brown writes, thought of themselves as a group trying to preserve an alternative to the society around them. 'They felt their identity to be constantly threatened:
first by persecution, later, by compromise. Innocence, ritual purity, meritorious
suffering, predominate in their image of themselves.' With this he contrasts Augustine's Catholicism, reflecting the attitude of a group 'confident of its powers to
absorb the world without losing its identity'. From this point of view it would be
true to say that Donatism, as an example of puritan separatism, was, as Robert
Markus put it, 'the local expression of a permanent religious option'. Markus, however, adds the cautionary remark that expressing this contrast too starkly fails to take
sufficiently into account 'the possible variety of ways in which a religious group
might conceive its place in society' (Markus 1972: 21, 27). Markus is himself
concerned to emphasize how much common ground existed between Augustine and
the Donatists, how extensively both drew on a common African theological tradition reaching back to Tertullian and Cyprian. Markus thus rejects the view of
Augustine as 'the theorist of the Constantinian revolution', who simply, as it were,
endorsed the baptism of the Roman empire by insisting that Augustine retained an
element of healthy scepticism towards the idea of a Christian state, a scepticism he
shared with his Donatist contemporaries (Markus 1970: 114; cf. Brown 1961: 99).
As for Donatism itself, Markus maintains that in its understanding 'of what kind of
community the church was, of what was decisive for its identity in the world . . . it
was representative in the fourth century of an older African theological tradition
with deep roots in its characteristic religious mentality' (Markus 1972: 28).

Donatist theology: the official line

These observations gain precision from what evidence survives of Donatist theology.
Here, for the most part, we have to rely on what can often only be a partial and
tentative reconstruction of the Donatist position from the writings of Catholic
authors whose purpose was refutation. Thus, of Donatus' theology we remain almost
entirely ignorant. According to Jerome he left many writings pertaining to the
Donatist heresy and also a treatise *On the Holy Spirit*. This is perhaps to be identified
with his work *On the Trinity* mentioned by Augustine, since both writers criticize
Donatus' Trinitarian language as subordinationist, in order, it seems, to smear the
author with a suspicion of Arianism (Jerome, *De Viris Illustribus* 93; Augustine,
Haer. 69). It is perhaps more likely that Donatus simply adhered to the Trinitarian
formulae elaborated by Tertullian (Tertullian, *Adversus Praxean* 9; 16; 23; cf. Novatian, *De Trinitate* 27.12). A further work is mentioned by Augustine, a letter of
Donatus he thought worthy of refutation (both letter and refutation are
unfortunately lost). In this letter, however, Augustine all but admits that Donatus,
in defending his party's exclusive claim to baptism, was indebted to Cyprian, while
granting that Donatus did not invent the practice of rebaptism (*Retractationes* 1.2.1
and 3). This former bishop of Carthage (*c.* 248–58) was acknowledged as the African
church's most eminent leader, the authority of whose teaching, preserved in a number of treatises and an extensive correspondence, had been sealed by martyrdom.

It is likely perhaps that Donatus, to whose liberal education and biblical expertise

Augustine pays tribute and whose importance in consolidating the opposition to Caecilian he acknowledges, had already enunciated a doctrine of baptism and of the church somewhat similar to that later propounded by Parmenian (363–93), his successor in the see of Carthage (*Sermo* 37.3.3; *Enarr.* 124.5). For our knowledge of Parmenian's views we are largely dependent on Optatus, his Catholic contemporary, bishop of Mileu in Numidia, who wrote a detailed refutation (traditionally referred to as 'Against Parmenian the Donatist'). It remains a difficult task to try and disentangle Parmenian's argument from Optatus' reply. It appears, however, that Parmenian treated baptism, the church, and the problem of sinners within it, this last only after giving due weight to the pertinent charges of apostasy and persecution made by the Donatists against their African opponents (Optatus, 1, 6.). In fact Optatus found much of which he could approve in his antagonist's portrayal of baptism; for example, his use of traditional images, such as the Flood (cf. 1 Pet. 3:19–21) and Circumcision (cf. Col. 2:11–12; Rom. 4:11). These images had already been employed by Tertullian and Cyprian. Optatus' main criticism is that, in rebaptizing African Catholics, the Donatists wrongly made baptism depend on the personal worth of the priest and so repeated what these images depict as a once-only sacrament (Optatus 1, 5). This provides a striking instance of the way both writers, Catholic and Donatist, shared a common African theological and exegetical tradition, yet it reveals important differences between them. It is worth noting that, on the whole, it is Parmenian who emerges as the conserver of the Cyprianic tradition, Optatus, by contrast, as the innovator. And this no doubt does much to account for the srength of Donatism. In rejecting the sacraments of unworthy priests Parmenian followed Cyprian. Again, in defending the practice of rebaptism by adducing the example of those who first received the baptism of John the Baptist, then, afterwards, baptism in the name of Christ (cf. Acts 19:1–7), Parmenian followed Cyprian (Cyprian, *Epp.* 65.2; 73.24–5). Parmenian further developed Cyprian's teaching based on the imagery of the Song of Songs, by insisting that the church to which Christ is betrothed is one (S. of S. 6:8), so that she alone has rightful possession of his gifts. She may thus be compared to 'a garden enclosed' and to 'a fountain sealed', from which heretics (among whom Parmenian included his African opponents) are excluded (Optatus 2.10; cf. S. of S. 4:12). They possess neither the 'keys' of episcopal authority to unlock the garden nor the 'seal' of baptism, the credal confession, which confers the right to drink from the fountain. Parmenian enumerated six gifts, which may perhaps be indentified as follows: episcopal authority (Cyprian had stressed the importance of one bishop in each see following his predecessor in orderly succession, but to Parmenian any such authority claimed by his opponents was invalidated by their toleration of apostate priests: their episcopal 'seat' (*cathedra*) was the 'seat of pestilence' (cf. Ps. 1:1); the 'angel' of baptism (cf. John 5:4 [longer version]); the divine agency by which water was sanctified for the cleansing of sins; the 'Spirit of God' or Holy Spirit conferred in baptism, which could only be given by a priest who had received it himself (and not lost it through apostasy); the 'fountain sealed' (S. of S. 4:12), the life-giving water, the salvific properties of baptism; the 'seal' of faith or creed confessed in the baptismal ceremony, an essential precondition of benefits received; and finally, the altar, symbolized by the navel of the bride in the Song of Songs (7:2) and representing, perhaps, as the place from which it was dispensed, the Eucharistic rite to which the baptized were admitted (Optatus, 2.2; 2.5–7). In all of this Parmenian can be seen to be elaborating a series of images already used by Tertullian and especially Cyprian. If some of the details of his exposition remain obscure, his intention was to claim for his own party the essential features of the church's endowment by Christ on the ground of superior sanctity. This point is given emphasis by his interpretation of biblical texts, already expounded by Cyprian, concerning the 'oil' (Ps. 140:5) and the 'sacrifice' (Isa. 66:3) of a sinner, to show that unworthy priests (those implicated in apostasy and persecution) could not be tolerated in the church without compromising its holiness (Optatus, 4.1).

We can follow this line of Donatist theological interpretation as the debate between the two sides intensified up to and after the decisive confrontation at the Conference of Carthage of 411. For the most part, it was a matter of consolidating existing positions with additional scriptural texts, but the central issues of the controversy also gradually came to be more sharply defined. For our information we depend mainly on Augustine's refutations of various Donatist writers of his time, such as Cresconius, Gaudentius, Emeritus, and Petilian, the last however especially, since his open pastoral letter of about the year 400 was quoted in full by Augustine in the course of countering it.

In Petilian's pastoral letter the nature of baptism and the church are, once again, discussed, but, once again the twin charges of apostasy and persecution, brought by the Donatists against their opponents, are reiterated throughout. He maintains that priests who are unworthy in this precise sense, when administering baptism, confer their own unworthiness, far less any benefit, on those who receive this sacrament. That was the crux of the matter between the opposing parties. For Petilian the sacrament depends on the holiness of the priest, so that knowingly to receive baptism from a sinful priest involves one in guilt, because so to receive it is to condone the sin and therefore to become implicated (*Petil.* 2.3.6; 2.4.8; 3.22.26). Augustine, for his part, insisted it was possible to receive a sacrament from a known sinner without necessarily consenting to his sin, in which case it did one no harm. But although with reference to sins in general Augustine's response might have seemed reasonable, his opponents did not find it very convincing. It is when the particular sins in question are borne in mind, that is, apostasy issuing in persecution, that the Donatist contention can be seen to have force. Augustine retorts that they focus too narrowly on certain sins to the neglect of others. But for Cresconius too the distinction between sins of such extreme seriousness and others was crucial (*Cresc.* 2.22.27). Some commentators have preferred to speak of ecclesial rather than personal holiness being important to the Donatists, referring in particular to a remark of Cresconius. Discussing Petilian's statement quoted above, Augustine asks what happens in baptism in the case of a sinful priest whose sin is not known. Cresconius replies that the presumption of innocence depends on his being in that church whose essential holiness the Donatists uphold. If sufficiently serious sin were exposed, such a priest would, according to the Donatist contention, be condemned and expelled (*Cresc.* 2.18.22). This observation underlines the principle on which the Donatists so strongly insist, that theirs was a church which had kept itself holy, free of those sins of apostasy and persecution which seemed to be the very contradiction of Christianity itself. As Petilian challenged his opponents: 'What kind of faith do you have, which does not have charity? . . . Charity does not persecute' (*Petil.* 2.77.171).

Petilian also had a hand in drafting the communal Donatist letter presented as a formal reply to the Catholic case at the Carthage Conference in 411. Fortunately, this is preserved intact among the Conference records (*Gesta conlationis Carthaginiensis* 3.258). To the Catholic evocation of a universal and morally mixed church awaiting God's judgement before finally achieving its promised holiness, the Donatists opposed their own conception of the church's holiness presently maintained by a priesthood whose ministry remained unimpaired by the guilt of serious sin. It was not, it seems, that the Donatists rejected the idea of a universal church, although it is true that Optatus and Augustine made the most of the fact that it was their party which was in formal communion through Rome with the rest of the world, while the Donatists were, to all intents and purposes, limited to Africa. Several times during the debate the Donatists challenged their opponents' claim to Catholicity, insisting that whichever party won the argument should be accorded that title (*Gesta conl. Carthag.* 3.146). It is to the church's holiness that they here appealed because their case rested precisely on their claim to maintain that. They therefore introduced themselves, in contrast to their opponents, as 'we who uphold the church's purity' (nos qui defendimus ecclesiae puritatem: *Gesta conl. Carthag.* 3.258). Its holiness, they argued, is foretold in scripture, in Messianic prophecies about a holy city or way, which find their fulfilment in Christ's saving work, the sanctification of the church mediated through baptism (Eph. 5:25–7). They then took up the challenge to reply to their opponents' argument that known offenders (including bishops compromised by apostasy and persecution) may be tolerated in the church for the sake of unity. This argument was based squarely on the four parables of the field (Matt. 13:24–30; 36–43), threshing-floor (Matt. 3:12), sheep and goats (Matt. 25:32–46) and net (Matt. 13:47–50), all of which seemed to sanction the coexistence in the church of saints and sinners, further support for this interpretation being drawn from the examples of the prophets, Christ himself, and the apostles. The Donatists respond that their opponents' argument gains no support from the parables quoted because either, as in the case of the field, it is the world, not the church, that is referred to, or, as in the case of the net, it is purely a question of sinners whose presence in the church escapes detection by the priests: the bad fish remain unknown to the fishermen till the final separation (Matt. 13:48). The Catholic indentification of the field with the church, although in this case following Cyprian, is smartly trumped by the Lord's own interpretation clearly identifying the field as the world (Matt. 13:38). Next come the scriptural examples from which the Catholic side had sought corroboration for their interpretation of the parables, beginning with the prophets, whom they understood as not discriminating in any but a moral sense between themselves and those whose sins they denounced. The Donatists refute this with a formidable array of texts to show that the prophets indeed lived among those whose sins they so harshly condemned, but could not, without being false to their own words, have shared in their religious observances. The apostles too are shown to have expelled sinners from their midst, and even Christ's own toleration of Judas, the archetypal apostate (*traditor*), is neatly turned back against the Catholic side when it is pointed out that Judas remained an unknown sinner as far as the other apostles were concerned: when exposed, he was immediately expelled. The Lord's toleration of Judas does not therefore open the apostolic ministry to apostates.

The Carthage Conference was a defining moment in the Donatist controversy, to which the protagonists on either side afterwards looked back, as Augustine's later anti-Donatist works demonstrate. The Donatists were in no doubt that, although the official verdict at the end of the Conference, which simply reiterated the earlier legal outcome of Constantine's tribunal, went against them, they had nevertheless been defeated not by argument but by force (gesta indicant si uictus sum aut uici, si ueritate uictus sum aut potestate oppressus sum: Emeritus in Augustine, *Gesta cum Emerito* 3). The verdict was swiftly followed up by measures of coercion which eventually, it seems, had their desired effect.

Theological diversity within Donatism

But there is another dimension to Donatist theology which was in some ways more influential than the official party line. This is represented by Parmenian's contemporary, the Donatist exegete Tyconius. The latter was criticized by Parmenian, as party-leader, in a letter later refuted by Augustine, for deviating from the Donatist position. In fact his theological stance is known mainly because his technical manual on biblical interpretation, the so-called *Book of Rules*, survives almost intact (edited by Burkitt 1894). Strangely enough, this has come about because of Augustine's own recommendation, in *De doctrina Christiana* 3.30.42–3.37.56, where the Rules of Tyconius are summarized and evaluated (for discussion of the Rules, see Bright 1988). Despite his Donatism, there was much in Tyconius' writing that Augustine could admire. Unfortunately, his other works, which included a commentary on the book of Revelation, much of it recycled by later Catholic commentators, have not been preserved (Gennadius, *De viris illustribus* 18). Augustine of course was eager to exploit the differences between Tyconius and Parmenian in developing his own arguments against the Donatist schism (*Contra epistolam Parmeniani* 1.1). So we have to take account of this in trying to assess Tyconius' own theological position. When, for example, Augustine contends that Tyconius made two key concessions to the Catholic case – namely, that the church is universal in extent and morally mixed in composition – it is not necessarily true that Tyconius accepted the Catholic position on those points, as expressed by Optatus and Augustine. What seems to have happened is that Augustine took over some central Tyconian themes and made them very much his own, subtly and skilfully adapting them where necessary to his own polemical purpose.

From the *Book of Rules*, although this is designed as a textbook on exegesis, not a theological treatise, we can at least gain some impression of Tyconius' doctrine of the church. Here his discussion has, as its central theme throughout the work, the Pauline idea of the church as the body of Christ (1 Cor. 12:12–26; Eph. 4:16). As already noted, despite their limitation as a sect to Africa, the Donatists did not dispute the fact of the church's universal expansion: Cresconius, for example, comments with approval on the gradual conversion then in progress of the entire world from idolatry to Christ (*Cresc.* 4.61.74). Tyconius also stresses the physical fact of the

Figure 37.1 The eagle gives to the seven angels the vials of the wrath of God (Rev. 16), from a twelfth-century Spanish manuscript of Beatus' *Commentary on Revelation*, which owes much to Tyconius. British Museum MS. Add. 11695, fol. 172r, with the permission of the British Library.

church's presence throughout the world, like the stone in the book of Daniel (Dan. 2:35) which grows into a great mountain and fills the whole world. The stone, he explains, is Christ the head, the mountain his body, the church (Tyconius, *Liber Regularum* {Burkitt 1894: 2–3}). But Tyconius' understanding of the church is also closely bound up with the idea that through scripture the people of God are addressed collectively 'as a body'. Words of praise and blame alike are spoken to the one people of God, sometimes words so sharply critical as to appear incompatible with the words of praise. The problem of inconsistency is solved if we accept that those words are directed at one body made up of two different parts (duo autem corpora mixta sunt uelut unum, et in commune unum corpus laudatur aut crepatur: Burkitt 1894: 26). Such a view conveniently suited the contemporary state of the North African church where two rival parties claimed to be the church, each being, in its polemics against the other, accustomed to reserve biblical commendation for itself while directing the strongest biblical denunciations at the party in opposition. But for Tyconius the entire body of those addressed through the words of scripture is to be indentified with the body of Christ, the church, made up of two parts, the praised and the blamed, the good and the bad, saints and sinners. The novelty of his approach is precisely that, in his view, you belonged to this body, the church, whether you were a Catholic or a Donatist. Clearly, then, Tyconius' conception of the church differs from the traditional identification of it with a given social entity, defined in terms of hierarchy and membership, the identification made by Cyprian, by the Catholic Optatus and by the Donatist Parmenian. Augustine for his part, of course, developed a more complex doctrine of the church in which he tried to reconcile the Cyprianic view with the Tyconian. But the Tyconian view is worth noticing for its own sake.

If, then, for Tyconius, the body of Christ is the physical presence of the church in the world, one people addressed 'as a body', it is necessary to distinguish in principle, even if it is not always possible in practice, between true members of that body and false, between those who belong to it, as Tyconius puts it, only in a 'physical' or 'nominal' sense and those who are united to Christ in 'heart' and 'will'. True Christians are those whose membership of the body of Christ is accompanied by a willing obedience. But how is willing obedience to be defined? Tyconius turns to the question of faith and works which occupies so central a place in Pauline theology. He insists that throughout the Bible the terms of God's relationship with his people remain constant: 'for the same Spirit, the same faith, the same grace through Christ has always been given' (Burkitt 1894: 18–19). 'Let him who glories glory in the Lord' (1 Cor. 1:31), for we have nothing we have not received (cf. 1 Cor. 4:7). The true Christian, he says, is one who is justified 'by grace alone through faith' (sola gratia per fidem: Burkitt 1894: 15; cf. Eph. 2:8.). Our entire work is faith, though faith expresses itself in good works, which God may be said to perform through us by the gift of the Holy Spirit. Augustine, who later insisted that faith itself is God's gift, not something we can take credit for ourselves, felt that in saying our entire work is faith Tyconius had not gone far enough (Burkitt 1894: 19; cf. *De doct. Chr.* 3.33.46). Yet in expressing it even more uncompromisingly, Augustine was surely merely following through Tyconius' intention. Thus, for Tyconius, there is a sense in which the stipulations of the Law found in scripture no longer apply to Christians who do not depend on the Law for justification and whose attitude to God is such as to lead to a willing fulfilment of the same moral duties as the Law requires. Indeed we fall short of perfection, but what counts is our intention and effort, and, if there is always something left for God to forgive, that is to enable us to acknowledge our ultimate dependence on his mercy. And this is true even of the greatest saints and martyrs, as the mother of seven martyred sons confesses in the second book of Maccabees (Burkitt 1894: 20–1; cf. 2 Macc. 7:29). It would probably not be wrong to see Tyconius here as the apologist of Donatism, responding to Catholic criticism that the Donatists as a church of self-styled saints and martyrs prided themselves unduly on their own righteousness.

God promised Abraham 'all nations', a promise fulfilled in the church, but not by the mere physical expansion of the church throughout the world. Rather, the promise applies to Abraham's spiritual descendants, those in the church who are justified by faith, not to Abraham's carnal descendants, those in the church who may still be regarded as the offspring of the Law. For the Law has not been totally replaced by grace, just as grace was not entirely absent when the Law was in full vigour under the old dispensation. So there is, for Tyconius, a sense in which the Law still operates in the church, where Christianity becomes an arid legalism, especially among those whose outward conformity to the Law of God is hypocritically at variance with their persecution of the saints (quid persequitur Verbum in carne? . . . aliud maius est euidentius signum agnoscendi antichristi non esse dixit, quam qui negat Christum in carne, id est odit fratrem: Burkitt 1894: 68; cf. 1 John 4:1–3).

Tyconius tries to makes sense of this state of affairs in the perspective of the final divine judgement. Most Christian writers in the West, in line with Jewish apocalyptic thinking, expected the Messiah to come in power at the end of the age, at the final day of reckoning, which had at first been thought imminent but was now generally considered to have been mercifully delayed. Christ had not only come, but would come again a second time to lay manifest claim to the spiritual victory his earthly ministry had achieved over Satan and the powers of darkness. Tyconius reinterprets the idea of a 'second coming' to give it a twofold sense: it may be understood not only of the final coming in glory of Christ the head, but also of his body, the church, in the rebirth and suffering of whose members Christ may be said to 'come again' now. The same is true of the coming of Antichrist. All who oppose Christ also form a body, with the Devil at their head. They will be fully exposed and defeated only at the end, but their presence now within the church is clearly revealed by the fact of persecution carried out in the Christian name. The church itself therefore is the place where the epic struggle between Christ and the Devil is now carried on through their respective followers and will eventually reach its final outcome. Since this is essentially a moral struggle, however, it is one which brings condemnation and defeat upon the persecutor, but to the victim of persecution a victory continuous with that of Christ himself. Indeed, it is in this sense that Tyconius reinterprets the promised millennium, the reign of Christ and his saints here on earth for a thousand years. The thousand years are taken as symbolic of the present age, of Christ's reign with his saints here and now. In so far as through the saintly members of the church the power and wiles of the Devil are being overcome now, Christ may be said to reign victorious. Christ comes now in glory unseen, but in the end his coming will be revealed in full splendour (Burkitt 1894: 4).

Fundamentally, Tyconius rests his case on a straightforward moral judgement. To him, as to his fellow Donatists, it was a self-evident absurdity that persecutors of Christians could be true Christians themselves. His doctrine of the church appears to

Figure 37.2 Augustine at work, and his two cities, from J. Amerbach's 1489 Basle edition of Augustine's *De civitate Dei*. With the permission of the University of St Andrews Library.

reflect the historical fact that the Donatists found themselves up against a Catholic party officially recognized and supported by the state and prepared to encourage or connive at the use of force in order to establish and maintain that privileged position. Persecutors had commonly been consigned to the Devil. If, like tares, they were now to be found, sown by the Devil, in the field of the church, their membership of the body of Christ was no more than nominal, for, in Tyconius' view, it is by their conduct, not merely their confession, that Christians express their true allegiance, either to Christ or to the Devil. Tertullian had already seen persecution as a foretaste of final judgement. For Tyconius, what was happening in Africa between persecuted Donatists and persecuting Catholics was but a present anticipation of the final definitive separation between good and bad which, according to the book of Revelation, would take place amid persecution on an unprecedented scale and on a global dimension.[2]

Tyconius' large-scale vision and subtle sophistication are equally impressive. It is ironic that his teaching should have been so eagerly listened to by Augustine, yet rejected by the leading spokesmen of his own sect. Parmenian and subsequent Donatist leaders no doubt realized how destructive it could be of a position which depended so much for authentication on the theology of Cyprian. But it was hardly Tyconius' intention to undermine the Donatist case. Tyconius could, as occasion demanded, write sharply in defence of his party, as later Catholic commentators on Revelation, such as Primasius and Bede, freely acknowledged in recording their debt to him.[3] Yet as a theologian and exegete Tyconius may be said to have raised the level of the Catholic–Donatist debate on to a higher plane. His view of the church's universality, as of its incorporation of saints and sinners, in so far as this was put forward as an account of the church's true nature revealed in scripture, may perhaps be seen as an attempt to transcend the sectarian divide in fourth-century Africa. He may even have felt that to do so could help pave the way for a meeting of minds (Chadwick 1989: 54). However, it was left to Augustine to realize the full potential of Tyconius' teaching, as part of his effort to reconcile the Donatists, which included his own, distinctive reformulation of the doctrine of the church.

Why, then, to return to the question with which this discussion began, did Donatism last so long? It may perhaps be concluded that the local conditions of Roman Africa contributed in no small measure to the protracted duration and bitterness of the controversy, but that the persistence of the schism was mainly due, despite some diversity within Donatist theology, to the success with which the Donatists appropriated Cyprian and to the consistency with which they adhered to a clear-cut position. In short, they were able to present themselves convincingly to the majority of their fellow-Africans as the true heirs of the Christian tradition.

NOTES

1 *Circumcelliones agonisticos nuncupans*, Optatus 3.4 (speaking of Parmenian); cf. bonum agonem certaui, 2 Tim. 4:7; Tertullian, *Ad Martyras* 4.2; Cyprian, *Ep.* 10.4; Augustine, *Enarrationes in Psalmos* 132.6.

2 quod autem in Danihel dixit, in Africa geritur (Burkitt 1894: 67; cf. Matt. 24:15–16;

Tertullian, *De praescriptione haereticorum* 4). Bede's commentary on Revelation uses that of Tyconius, 'apart from those places where he attempted to defend the schism of his own party, the Donatists, and deplored the persecution which they suffered . . . speaking of it as martyrdom and glorying in the fact that this had been foretold in the book of Revelation' (*Explanatio Apocalypsis*, PL 93.132–3).

3 Tyconius 'made biting mockery of our church', says Primasius (*Commentarius in Apocalypsin*, Prologus, CChr.SL 92.1); for Bede, see previous note.

BIBLIOGRAPHY

Bright, P. (1988) *The Book of Rules of Tyconius: Its Purpose and Inner Logic*. Notre Dame, Ind: University of Notre Dame Press.

Brisson, J.-P. (1958) *Autonomisme et christianisme dans l'Afrique romaine de Septime Sévère à l'invasion vandale*. Paris: Boccard.

Brown, P. (1961) 'Religious Dissent in the Later Roman Empire: The Case of North Africa', *History* 46: 83–101.

—— (1969) *Augustine of Hippo*. London: Faber.

Burkitt, F. C. (1894) *Liber Regularum Tyconii*. Cambridge Texts and Studies, Vol. 3, Part 1: Cambridge: Cambridge University Press, 1–114.

Büttner, T. and Werner, E. (1959) *Circumcellionen und Adamiten. Zwei Formen mittelalterlicher Haeresie*. Berlin.

Calderone, S. (1967) 'Circumcelliones', *La Parola del Passato: Rivista di studi classici/antichi* 113: 94–109.

Chadwick, H. (1985) 'Augustine on Pagans and Christians: Reflections on Religious and Social Change', in D. Beales and G. Best (eds) *History, Society and the Churches: Essays in Honour of Owen Chadwick*. Cambridge: Cambridge University Press, 9–27.

—— (1989) 'Tyconius and Augustine', in W. Wuellner (ed.) *Center for Hermeneutical Studies in Hellenistic and Modern Culture: Protocol of the 58th Colloquy, 16 October 1988*: 'A Conflict of Christian Hermeneutics in Roman Africa: Tyconius and Augustine', Berkeley, Cal.: Graduate Theological Union and University of California-Berkeley, 49–55.

Congar , Y. *et al.* (1963–65) *Œuvres de Saint Augustin, Traités Anti-donatistes*. Bibliothèque Augustinienne, vols 28–32. Paris: Desclée de Brouwer.

Diesner, H.-J., (1960) 'Die Circumcellionen von Hippo Regius', *Theologische Literaturzeitung* 85: 497–508.

Duval, Y. (1982) *Loca Sanctorum Africae: le culte des martyrs en Afrique du IVe au VIIe siècle*. 2 vols. Rome: Ecole française de Rome.

Février, P. A. (1964) ' Notes sur le developpement urbain en Afrique du Nord', *Cahiers Archaeologiques* 14: 1–47.

—— (1966) 'Toujours le Donatisme', *Rivista di storia e letteratura religiose* 2: 228–40.

Frend, W. H. C. ([1952]. 1972) *The Donatist Church*. Oxford: Clarendon Press.

—— (1969) 'Circumcellions and Monks', *Journal of Theological Studies* 20: 542–9.

Labrousse, M. (1996) *Optat de Milève: Traité contre les Donatistes*, 2 vols. Sources chrétiennes 412, 413. Paris: Editions du Cerf.

Lancel, S. (1972–91) *Actes de la Conférence de Carthage en 411*, 4 vols. Sources chrétiennes 194, 195, 224, 373. Paris: Editions du Cerf.

Maier, J.-L. (1987. 1989) *Le Dossier du Donatisme*, 2 vols. Texte und Untersuchingen, 134 and 135, Berlin: Akademie-Verlag.

Markus, R. A. (1970) *Saeculum: History and Society in the Theology of Augustine*. Cambridge: Cambridge University Press.

—— (1972) 'Christianity and Dissent in Roman North Africa: Changing Perspectives in Recent Work', *Studies in Church History* 9: 21–36.

Millar, F. (1968) 'Local Cultures in the Roman Empire: Libyan Punic and Latin in Roman Africa', *Journal of Roman Studies* 58: 126–34.

Mommsen, Th. and Meyer, T. (eds) (1905) *Codex Theodosianus*. Berlin: Weidmann.

Monceaux, P. (1912–23;) *Histoire littéraire de l'Afrique chrétienne depuis les origines jusqu' à l'invasion arabe*, 7 vols. Paris; (reprint: Impression Anastaltique, Culture et Civilisation, 115 Avenue Gabriel Lebon, Bruxelles, 1966).

Saumagne, Ch. (1934) 'Ouvriers agricoles ou rôdeurs de celliers? Les circoncellions d'Afrique', *Annales d'histoire économique et sociale* 6: 351–64.

Tengström, E. (1964) *Donatisten und Katholiken: Soziale, wirtschlaftliche und politische Aspekte einer nordafrikanischen Kirchenspaltung*. Studia Graeca et Latina Gothoburgensia 18. Göteborg: Elanders Boktryckeri Aktiebolag.

ARIANISM

—— ·✦· ——

David Rankin

CONTEMPORARY INTEREST IN ARIANISM

The charge of espousing 'Arian' views remains a potent and potentially damaging one even in modern times: 1977 saw the publication of the highly controversial *The Myth of God Incarnate* (Hick 1977). Perhaps nothing in the last few decades has generated so much heated theological debate. Within months a counter publication, *The Truth of God Incarnate* (Green 1977), appeared, as did a number of highly critical and influential reviews of *The Myth*. While few of the scholars who responded critically to *The Myth* explicitly accused any of its contributors of 'Arianism' (or of any named heresy), the implication was often clear (Torrance 1981: 132; Heron 1981: 75). John Macquarrie, for example, reflects this – though he is himself more cautious – when he writes that while 'it would be an anachronism to describe the positions [of the contributors to *The Myth*] as Arian, deist or Unitarian, . . . unquestionably there are affinities, and it is hardly likely that an updated Christianity without incarnation will prove any more successful than these dead ends of the past' (in Green 1977: 144). From the late 1970s until the present day the same accusations have also been directed at proponents of some forms of New Age thought present within a number of mainstream Christian churches, as well as at aspects of feminist theological teaching (Toon 1991: 296). The supposed connection between particular expressions of these and the ancient heresy of Arianism is rarely made explicit yet is often implied. 'Arianism', whatever that term might mean in any given context, is apparently ever with us!

ARIUS AND THE EARLY ARIANS

History: the early period (318–37)

The precise order of events surrounding the outbreak of the so-called Arian controversy has been the subject of intense debate for as long as scholars have studied the period. The prevailing consensus would have it that at some time around 320 CE Arius (256–336 CE), a presbyter in Alexandria although a native of Libya, took exception to the teachings of his bishop Alexander concerning the relationship of the Son to the Father. This Arius tradition posits both a Libyan connection (Epiphanius, *Panarion* 69.1) and an association with the Meletian schism of the 310s, although Rowan Williams (1987) has convincingly demonstrated that the latter is impossible given that Athanasius would not have failed to mention it had it been true.

In a letter to Eusebius of Nicomedia (Opitz 1934–5: Urkunde [Document] 1), Arius also refers to himself and Eusebius (died 341/2) as 'fellow-Lucianists' and this has led, not unreasonably, to speculation that Arius was a pupil of Lucian of Antioch (*c.* 240–312). This is, however, now largely discounted and it is assumed that Arius was merely seeking to identify himself, and thereby to establish some sort of alliance with a particular group of powerful ecclesiastical figures. If we accept the ordering of events suggested by Williams (and there seems every reason to do so) – in particular the ordering of the Arian documents of the period (see pp. 979–80) – then in 321 (Opitz suggests 320) Arius wrote to his bishop (Urkunde 6) outlining a distinctly monotheistic position. This he claims clearly to have learned from both tradition and the bishop himself. The Son is described as a distinct hypostasis (as is also the Spirit) but also as the creature (though perfect) and offspring of God (the Father) created before time but implicitly not from eternity; as not *homoousios* ('of the same being') with the Father; as not co-eternal with Him; and as not (that is, not having existence) before his generation. For Arius (according to this letter), 'begotten' must mean 'created'.

Alexander now took formal action against Arius (and some of the latter's associ-

Figure 38.1   Late Roman mosaic representation of Alexandria from Jerash in Jordan. Photo J. C. N. Coulston.

ates) who, within a short time of the letter above, felt constrained to write to Eusebius, bishop of the imperial capital Nicomedia, complaining about his treatment at the hands of Alexander (Urkunde 1: Williams [1987] dates this as 321/2, Opitz as 324). Not a great deal is known about the particular theology of this Eusebius. His own letter to Paulinus of Tyre (Urkunde 8; *c.* 320/1?) suggests that it included the incomparability of God and the impossibility of God communicating his own essence. He nowhere appears to describe the Son as derived from the non-existent. Alexander had, so Arius claims, 'driven us out of the city as atheists' and publicly preached that the Son was eternally existent, was unbegotten along with the Father (no Arian ever distinguished between 'agenetos' and 'agennetos'), and had his existence from the Father (God) himself. Arius then outlines his own position: that the Son is not unbegotten but only-begotten, that he has subsisted from before time (but implicitly not from eternity), that he had a beginning and was created from the non-existent (ex oun onton).

Alexander, by way of an encyclical letter (Urkunde 4b), then notified the wider church that the bishops of Egypt and Libya, meeting in synod, had anathematized Arius for his alleged heresy (Williams 1987 gives 325, while Opitz 1934–5 gives 319; that is, the latter places it before Arius' letter to Alexander, which is no longer tenable given the almost irenic tone of that epistle). In this encyclical, which should precede the Council summoned to Nicaea by a few months and was probably intended to influence events there, Alexander spells out the 'Arian' heresy in much the same way as posterity has come to characterize it. Arius teaches that there was a time when God was not a Father, that his Word was not from eternity, that this Word was made out of nothing (the non-existent), that there was [sc. a time] when he was not, that the Son is a creature and a work, that the Son is not the Father's true Word or Wisdom, that the Son/Word is mutable and that the Son knows accurately neither the Father nor even the nature of his own essence.

Eusebius of Caesarea

After his excommunication Arius fled to Nicomedia. He was not without friends and around this time, at a synod held in Caesarea of Palestine, Arius' teachings were declared orthodox. The bishop of Palestinian Caesarea, the famous church historian Eusebius Pamphili (*c.* 263–337 [or 340]), himself wrote to Alexander pleading Arius' cause. This Eusebius was a pupil of Origen – Young refers to him as a representative of 'popular Origenism' (1983: 1) – and he is identified commonly (and probably unhelpfully, as we shall see later) as semi-Arian. Kelly says that he was 'not really an Arian at heart' (1977: 231) and Young an 'amateur' theologian and philosopher (1983: 17). He did not, maintains Young, actually understand or appreciate many of the dilemmas present in the controversy in which he became so closely involved, he was confused in many of his responses, and his theology was ultimately marked by 'sheer mediocrity and conservatism' (1983: 23). Like Arius, much of Eusebius' theological reflection was as much reactive as proactive. He was deeply involved in the action taken after Nicaea against Eustathius of Antioch and Marcellus of Ancyra against whom Eusebius directed much of his polemical effort. His *De ecclesiastica theologia*, three books written in 337 primarily against Marcellus (he had already written his *Contra Marcellum* the year before), was characterized in part by what Quasten calls an 'advanced subordinationism' (1983: 342) and Kelly 'Origen in his most subordinationist mood' (1977: 225). He could, with Origen (and Paulinus of Tyre), describe the Logos as a 'second God'. Subordinationism was for him the only way to guarantee an appropriate distinction of Persons. The Son is God, but not the one, true God. Eusebius was not, as later events would show, opposed absolutely to the concept of the '*homoousion*' describing the relationship between Father and Son as long as it was understood neither in a Sabellian sense, emphasizing the distinctiveness of the Son from the Father (which was his major concern with Marcellus), nor as implying a division in the substance of the Monad. In a letter written to his congregation after Nicaea, he explained his understanding of its application at Nicaea as declaring that the Son was like the Father and bore no resemblance to the creatures. Eusebius could not accept the notion that the Father had created the Son. The Logos was the first product (*gennema*) of all beings. For Eusebius, as a good Origenist, the Son (and the Holy Spirit) had his own distinct hypostasis. This hypostasis (though not that of the Spirit who was a creation of the Son) is divine, but subordinate to the Supreme God. The Son worships the Father as God; therefore, the Father is God of the Son (Hanson 1988b: 49). The Logos functioned also as the Father's intermediary for creating and governing the universe – Young calls Eusebius' Logos the Neoplatonic Word-Soul, the intermediary between God and creation (1983: 18) – and is God solely as the image of the true God though not in his own right (*De ecclesiastica theologia* 2.23). The Son's mediatorship is connected, however, *not* to the Incarnation but to his status within the Godhead (Hanson 1988b: 39). Unlike Origen, however, for Eusebius there is no eternal begetting. The begetting of the Son is not without beginning. The Son is not co-eternal with the Father (*Demonstratio evangelica* 5.1.20). The Father is alone unoriginated. For Eusebius, however, the Logos was not created 'out of the non-existent' (*De ecclesiastica theologia* 1.10) but is, somewhat vaguely, 'from the Father' (as are not all things surely?). In addition, there is no human soul in Eusebius' Christ (*De ecclesiastica theologia* 1.20.90) – for Eusebius is an early exponent of a Word–flesh Christology – nor is the Logos a mutable creature.

The Council of Nicaea in 325 and its aftermath

In early 325 a synod meeting at Antioch provisionally excommunicated Eusebius for failing to condemn Arius and set this decision for ratification at a subsequent council to be convened by the emperor at Ancyra in Galatia after Easter. Constantine then transferred this meeting to Nicaea near Nicomedia so that he could give it his personal attention. Over 200 eastern bishops attended. At Nicaea came the definitive repudiation of Arius (and the rehabilitation of Eusebius of Caesarea) and both the promulgation of the beginnings perhaps of the famous Creed and the formal declaration of the '*homoousion*'.

Almost immediately the tide began to turn against the radical Nicene/Homoousian 'party'. This was the result partly of the growing influence of Eusebius of Nicomedia (more radical in his support of Arius than his namesake) and, to a lesser extent, of Eusebius of Caesarea himself (who led those favouring recognition of the Son's divinity in purely biblical terms), of the theological extremism of the hyper-Nicenes Eustathius of Antioch and Marcellus of Ancyra (a major target later of the Neo-Arians), and both the theological (although note the view that Athanasius did not become theologically involved until after 339) and, more significantly, the political activities of Athanasius, bishop of Alexandria from 328. Eustathius was deposed by a synod meeting in Antioch in 326, Athanasius by one in Tyre in 335 (but for political more than theological reasons) – Hanson argues that Athanasius took no part in the controversy until 341 (1988b: 272) – and Marcellus at Constantinople in 336. Arius himself had been recalled from exile (but not restored to communion everywhere) in 328. As the tide swung away from the Homoousian – even Athanasius himself apparently thought it impolitic to make any significant use of it until 360/1 – and towards first the Homoiousian and later the Homoian, Arius apparently felt vindicated, although there were no real attempts to rehabilitate him (events, though the controversy was destined to bear his name, had simply passed him by), and legend has it that the rather sad and forlorn figure died in a privy the evening before Constantine was to restore him (*c.* 336). Constantine himself died in 337.

ARIAN DOCUMENTS OF THE EARLY PERIOD

There are a number of extant documents which relate to the early period of the controversy, particularly to those events involving Arius himself. We have looked above at Arius' letter to his bishop preserved by both Athanasius and (thankfully) Epiphanius which Williams (1987) rightly dates to 321 (Opitz 320); at Arius' letter to Eusebius of Nicomedia preserved by both Theodoret and Epiphanius which Williams dates to 321/2 (Opitz 318); and at the encyclical letter of Alexander announcing Arius' anathematization preserved by the historian Socrates which Williams dates to 325 (Opitz 319). There is also Arius' confession of faith addressed to the emperor (Urkunde 30) preserved by both Socrates and Sozomen and dated to 327. In this confession Arius claims both to have been vindicated by recent events and to have held faithfully to the teaching of the church and, more importantly, of the Scriptures.

The actual letters of Arius are, of course, the most helpful when examining the thought of the alleged arch-heretic. Also of considerable value, though to be treated with great caution, are the extracts which Athanasius claims to have lifted from Arius' metrical piece, the so-called *Thalia*, and included in his *De Synodis* (15) and *Orationes contra Arianos* (1.5–6). Though useful, we must remember that these are quoted by Athanasius for polemical purposes and must be read against what we do know that Arius actually wrote. Although Kannengiesser (1983: 467) has argued strongly that the *De Synodis* 15 extracts – those called the *Blasphemies of Arius* by Athanasius – belong to the early 360s and were probably written by a later Arian theologian rather than by Arius himself, the present consensus appears to be that both sets of extracts, however refashioned or represented for polemical purposes by Athanasius or by his immediate source, originated with Arius himself (Williams 1987: 65–6). While differing in particular respects from the verifiable Arian works

– particularly Urkunde 1, Urkunde 6, and Urkunde 30 (the extracts express, for example, a more clearly defined Trinitarian (though heterodox) doctrine than do the letters) – they yet contain significant and telling similarities of language and thought.

What is an Arian?

'"Arian"', says Maurice Wiles, 'as a designation for anyone other than the immediate associates of Arius himself who were excluded from the church of Egypt by Alexander, is a title given by Athanasius to his opponents for a specific polemical purpose of defamation by association' (in Barnes and Williams 1993: 42). Elsewhere he speaks of Arians as 'a loosely allied group of people with overlapping but by no means identical concerns, held together more by their opposition to certain Marcellan and Athanasian tendencies than by a single theological platform' (in Williams 1989: 159). Here lie most of the problems associated with identifying and categorizing Arianism in the fourth century.

Williams (1987: 2–25) gives a more than adequate summary of the history of Arian research and scholarship from the seventeenth century until the present day. Up to the 1830s Arianism was associated primarily with Neoplatonism (1987: 3). Newman, in his celebrated *The Arians of the Fourth Century* (1833), sought to explain Arianism 'in terms of the distinctive theological and exegetical positions of the Antiochene church'. Like Newman, Harnack (*Lehrbuch der Dogmengeschichte*, 4th edn, 1909) saw Aristotelian Rationalism as the obvious background to Arius' system. Knowing only a notion of 'an external obedience to God, in the Logos and in believers alike', says Harnack, 'Arianism provides merely a rationale for heroic asceticism (p. 7). For Gwatkin (*Studies of Arianism*, 1882 and 1900), Arianism was the result of irreverent philosophical speculation (p. 9).

One has to ask the question from the outset whether it is even possible to categorize or describe Arianism as such. Was there such a thing? If Arianism is that which was taught and preached by Arius, the Alexandrian presbyter, were there any other Arians? For we know so little about his teaching and beliefs (though much about what Athanasius alleged he believed and taught) and can see little evidence (indeed the opposite applies) that any contemporary or later group of persons saw themselves as his followers. And if there was a group after Arius' time who could be described as Arian, can Arius himself then properly be called Arian? And with respect to those from later in the century – people like Aetius and Eunomius (the so-called neo-Arians) – who were characterized by their opponents as Arian, could Arius again be numbered among their legitimate forebears? Or, if there was a body of thought (even if only in the mind of Athanasius and others) which has come to be known as Arianism, was there anybody in the fourth century to whom such beliefs could accurately or reasonably be ascribed?

Frameworks for Arius' theology

Arius' monotheism, according to Pollard, was philosophical, not biblical, metaphysical and not ethical, and his God the Absolute of the philosophical schools

(1958: 103f.). This view of early Arianism was a commonplace until recent times but has now been soundly rejected by Wiles (1962: 339f.), Stead (1964: 19) and Gregg and Groh (1981: 87), among others. While Arius, according to Stead, 'placed more reliance on philosophical and dialectical techniques than either of his great critics' (1964: 16), some (like Pollard) have been too ready to assume, from Arius' use of the term *monas*, that he has transformed 'the living God of the Bible' into 'the Absolute of the philosophical schools' (1964: 19). Barnard, however, accepts quite readily the essentially philosophical basis of Arius' position. 'Arius' philosophical presuppositions determined the direction which his theological speculation took' (1970: 186). 'Arius drew on no "proto-Arian" tradition already evolving within the Church. His system was simply philosophical dualism' (1970: 187; cf. Stead 1964: 22). Yet, he concedes, 'for Arius *monas* is a theological rather than a philosophical title' and 'it is unlikely that [he] began from *monas* as the Absolute of the philosophical schools into which he fitted some Christian elements' (1972: 112). The differences between Arius and Athanasius, for example, 'do not lie primarily in their idea of God considered philosophically' (1972: 113). For Dragas, 'Arius [presents] a monistic doctrine of God, who exists in himself and must be existentially differentiated from all things which were made by him out of nothing' (1981: 26f.). 'Arius' starting point is theo-monistic' (1981: 28); what Arius presents is 'an ultimately deistic-philosophical theology against a theistic theology of Athanasius' (1981: 38). The Arian crisis, for Kannengiesser, was essentially one of hermeneutics (1982: 1) and the teachings of Arius of an essentially metaphysical order (1982: 17).

The Trinity

'Arianism was a Trinitarian doctrine which arose out of the difficulty of conceiving of an eternal generation in God in which the Son while remaining distinct from the Father will nevertheless remain equal with him' (Hanson 1988b: 84). Except for a brief mention of 'three hypostases' in the letter of Arius to Eusebius of Nicomedia, however, there is not, in any of the unquestioned writings of Arius himself, any explicitly defined Trinitarian doctrine. Nor does Alexander of Alexandria allude to any such on Arius' part in his encylical. What we do have can be found in the *Thalia* excerpts given by Athanasius which demonstrate why Athanasius and his allies were for so long opposed to the trihypostatic language eventually adopted by orthodoxy. Arius' 'Trinity arises as the creation of distinct and subordinate beings by the original monad' (Stead 1964: 18). The Father (i.e. God), according to the letter to Alexander, is 'Monad and Beginning of all' (presumably including the Son and the Holy Spirit). The *Thalia*, according to *Contra Arianos*, declares that 'the essences of the Father and the Son and the Holy Spirit are separate in nature and estranged and disconnected and alien and without participation of each other' (1.6), and according to *De Synodis* 15, the Son (and presumably the Spirit, too) came 'to be truly only at the Father's will' (38). According to Urkunde 6, the Father is 'one God, alone unbegotten, everlasting, unbegun, true, immortal, wise, good, sovereign, judge'. From the same letter we read that the Son is 'the perfect creature of God', although the Supreme One (the Father) could, according to a *Thalia* extract from *De synodis*, 'begat one equal to the Son but not greater or superior or more excellent' (28f.). The

Son's perfection is then not necessarily, but only historically unique. The notion of Arius that the Son-Logos was created for the purpose of creating the world is attested in Urkunde 6, in the *De Synodis*, and by Alexander. The *De synodis* extract of the *Thalia*, in terms similar to that from the *Contra Arianos*, 'presents Arius' view of the separate and unequal hypostases in the Trinity (Stead 1978: 26) as a 'Trinity of unequal powers' (ibid.: 30). While it is true that 'such a hierarchical Trinity would be perfectly intelligible to anyone familiar with the Origenist tradition' (ibid.), we are reminded, yet again, that the subordination of the Son (and of the Spirit) to the Father in the time before Nicaea was more the rule than the exception, in both East (Origen) and West (Tertullian), among orthodox and heterodox alike. Where Arius does seem to part company (if he ever enjoyed it!) with Origenism is in his emphasis on the separate and alien character of the three hypostases. For Arius, God, rather than the Father, precedes the Son in existence. God, for Arius, (that is, the only true God), only becomes, indeed can only become Father with the creation/begetting of the Son; at least, that is, Arius as represented by Alexander and the *Thalia* excerpts. According to Alexander, Arius declared that 'God was not always a Father' (Urkunde 4b) and Athanasius reports the *Thalia* as declaring that 'God was not always a Father'. This generation of the Son, for Arius, takes place at a point in time and is not – while clearly pre-existent (see Urkunde 1: 'the Son subsisted before time by the Father's will'; Urkunde 6: 'at the will of God [the Son] created before times and before ages'; Urkunde 30: '[the Son] begotten of God the Father before all ages') – from eternity (Urkunde 1: 'the Son had a beginning'; Urkunde 6: '[sc. the Son is] not eternal or co-eternal or co-originate with the Father'; Urkunde 4b: 'the Word [is] not from eternity').

The Logos-Son

The two Logoi/Wisdoms

'For Arius the Logos which is proper to God is an attribute to God and has no separate hypostatical existence of its own' (Pollard 1957: 284). 'Arius [denies] the identity of the Logos and the Son, by dehypostasising the Logos, by reducing the concept of eternal generation to premundane origination, by making the Son a creature, and by interpreting the concept of subordination in the sense of posteriority and inferiority of essence' (ibid.: 286). The evidence for these assertions, particularly for that of the implied notion of the two Logoi, the one an integral attribute of God and the other a separate, hypostasized creature identified with the Son, can be found both among the *Thalia* excerpts from the *Contra Arianos* – where the author speaks of two Wisdoms (= two Logoi): 'one an attribute co-existent with God; the other originated in God, and named as Wisdom and Word as partaking of it [sc. the attribute] . . . not the true power of God' (1.5) – and in Alexander's encyclical, where the Son is described as 'not by nature the Father's true Word or Wisdom' and as having come 'into being by God's own Word and Wisdom'. It is noteworthy that no such sentiments are to be found in any of the 'genuine' writings of Arius himself (Urkunde 1, 6 and 30).

Notwithstanding these reservations, however, whatever disagreements different scholars might properly have with Pollard on other matters relating to Arius and to Arianism, few would today seriously disagree with these particular assessments. Yet, some still question them with respect to their implications for a relatively low status of the Son/created Logos, arguing rather that Arius exhibited a particularly high, even exalted, view of the status of the Son. The Son is described by Arius in Urkunde 1 as 'before ages as God full (*plêrês theos*) [of grace and truth]' and among the *Thalia* excerpts in the *De Synodis* as 'being a mighty God' hymning 'the Supreme [sc. God] in part' – though the latter does imply as an inferior form of deity. A *Thalia* excerpt from *Contra Arianos* suggests this particularly, declaring the Word to be 'not true (*alêthinos*) God', to be 'God only in name . . . by participation'. This does seem to imply two Wisdoms or two Logoi (Athanasius, *Contra Arianos* 1.6); that is, the first Logos/Wisdom (in patristic thought these were often interchangeable terms) as an attribute (from eternity) of God, and the second as the creature of God, pre-existent but not from eternity (see the *Thalia* excerpt from the *Contra Arianos* above). Yet, while it is safe to say that Arius may well have believed in the existence of the two Wisdoms/Logoi, he seems not actually to have expressed himself in such terms in his 'genuine' writings. Perhaps, however, we can trust the evidence of *Contra Arianos* (and possibly that of Alexander's encyclical letter) that Arius viewed only the Reason intrinsic to God as properly and 'truly' termed Word and Wisdom (Gregg and Groh 1981: 56) and speak of the Arian doctrine of God's intrinsic Word, and of the Son as merely named 'Word' (Gregg and Groh 1981: 111); that is, that it is only the Logos or Wisdom being the attribute of God which can properly be termed or regarded as 'God', and the other only as titled 'god' by grace and not by nature; that is, as not truly God (see the credal anti-Arian emphasis on the Son/Logos as 'truly/very God').

The nature of the created Logos: the Logos as creature

The Logos was not, for Arius, generated from the essence of God – this is evidenced both by Urkunde 1 ('the Son [was] not part of the unbegotten . . . nor part of God) and Urkunde 6 ('the Son was not a portion [of God]') and by a *Thalia* excerpt from the *Contra Arianos* – but was created 'ex ouk onton' (out of the non-existent). Given that Arius could apparently understand generation only in a material sense, the notion of God generating or creating the Son/Logos out of his own being was simply unacceptable, implying as it would a diminution of the divine majesty and a division of the divine essence. This is clear in Urkunde 6 where Arius denies the generation of the Son by a Sabellian-like division of the supreme Monad. Another major issue in any consideration of Arius' theology is his position on the mutability of the Son/Logos. For while it is of God's essence to be immutable, some would argue that the very creatureliness of the Son/Logos would render him, of necessity, mutable. The requirement of his active and voluntary obedience, it is claimed, would require it. Yet such claims of the mutability of Arius' Logos are supported only by Alexander's encyclical, where the Son is described as 'by nature mutable and susceptible to change', and by an excerpt from *Contra Arianos* which declares the Word to be 'by nature . . . alterable (as we are) and remains good by his free will': Urkunde 1 and Urkunde 6 – Arius' 'genuine' writings – on the other hand, describe the Son as 'unchangeable' and 'unalterable and unchangeable' respectively.

Alexander describes Arius as depicting the Son as both a 'creature' (*ktisma*) and a 'work' (*poiêma*). In Urkunde 6 Arius himself describes the Son as a 'perfect creature' (*ktisma teleion*) of God, but with the qualifying 'but not as one of the creatures', and as 'an offspring (*gennema*), but not as one of things that have come into existence'. Neither set of *Thalia* excerpts suggests that the Son was explicitly called by Arius a 'creature' or a 'work'. According to Gregg and Groh, however, 'what [the Arians] preach is a creature promoted to the status of a god' (1981: 1). The Arian mediator is not then, for them, an extension of the divine nature but a creation of the divine will (ibid.: 5) – this is evidenced for them by Urkunde 1, Urkunde 6 ('[the Son] subsists at God's will') and the *Thalia* excerpts from *De Synodis* – and the centrality of the Son's dependence on the divine will (ibid.: 7). Gregg and Groh even call this a 'Christology of the Divine Will' (ibid.: 161–91). Arius' God, maintain Gregg and Groh, requires a freely obedient rational creature who responds also by willing (ibid.: 14). To Arius, Jesus, as changeable (mutable), was thereby (morally) improvable along the lines of the Stoic notion of '*prokopê*' (advance) (ibid.: 19). Gregg and Groh speak of a promotional scheme on the part of Arius, of a Christ raised by God to the pinnacle of creaturely exaltation because of his obedient fidelity in a virtuous life (ibid.: 20). Indeed this promotional Christological understanding is fundamental to their reconstruction of Arian soteriology (ibid.: 21). They speak of 'a perfected creature whose nature remained [no matter how exalted] always creaturely and whose position was always subordinate to and dependent upon the Father's will' (ibid.: 24). For Arius the unity of Son with the Father is one of agreement (*sumphonia*) with God, one of harmony rather than of essence (ibid.: 26). Much of this is, again however, too dependent on the unreliable *Thalia* excerpts. Their claim that the Son/Logos is according to the *Thalia* indispensable for creaturely knowledge and reverence of the Father (ibid.: 81) is questionable even there, for the knowledge and vision of the Father on the part of the Son is limited to the Son's own capacity, as it is for us. Indeed, it is questionable to what extent the Arian Christ even knows himself. In both Urkunde 4b and the *Thalia* excerpts Arius is seen to maintain that the Son does not know even his own essence (*ousia*). Gregg and Groh assume this 'advancement' Christology as Arius' own. It is actually the evidence of Alexander or Athanasius which suggests this; we do not have any hard evidence that Arius himself used the language of participation by grace.

For Gregg and Groh the Arian Christ is 'a begraced creature . . . [though] more than others' (1981: 27), a servant like by nature who by grace can call God 'Father' (ibid.: 28). Christ is representative Son, but by no means the only possible Son (ibid.: 30). For this dimension one can observe the statement of the *Thalia* excerpts from *Contra Arianos* that 'the Supreme [God] could begat one equal to the Son but not greater or superior or more excellent'. Here the 'ethical and voluntarist cast of Arius' thought is crucial (ibid.: 57). Yet Gregg and Groh, to my mind, stake far too much on suspect evidence.

The soul of Christ

Arius, according to Wolfson, denied the existence of a rational soul in Jesus (1958: 27). Such an assertion has long been a commonplace in much (uninformed) Arian scholarship. According to Haugaard, while in Arius there is 'an implicit assumption that the Word is the subject of all the actions and words of the Gospel, and that the Word-as-human-soul psychology is consistent with his views, it does not follow that he actually articulated such a psychology' (1960: 256f.). Hanson, however, appears to adopt the earlier view, arguing that it can be plausibly argued that Arius strenuously and steadfastly denied that the Incarnate Word had any human soul at all (1987: 411). Lucian of Antioch, whom Hanson suggests may have been the teacher of Arius, taught the doctrine of the *'soma apsychon'* (1988b: 26). Yet, says Stead and somewhat persuasively, our only firm evidence for it (i.e. Arius' non-acknowledgement of a human soul in Jesus) is Eustathius of Antioch (1994: 33). 'We cannot', Haugaard declares, 'accuse Arius of being any more specific about his doctrine of the union of the Word and the man in Jesus Christ than were his orthodox opponents'. (1960: 261). One only has to read Athanasius himself (Stead 1982b) to sense the possibility that he, too, along with his erstwhile pupil Apollinaris, may have held such a belief, even by default. The fact is that, as Stead has properly noted, there is nothing in the extant writings of Arius, including the alleged excerpts from the *Thalia* provided by Athanasius, to suggest that Arius did so.

The Logos created for creation

In both 'genuine' and suspect Arian texts there exist clear proofs – though probably more clearly so in the latter it must be conceded – that Arius taught that the Son was created for the (sole?) purpose of creating the universe. In Urkunde 4b the Son is said to be 'made for us, so that God might create us by him' and that the Son 'exists only for creation'. In Urkunde 6 the Son is said to be the one 'through whom [God] made both the ages and the universe', but it is not said explicitly that this was the sole purpose for his existence. Wolfson maintains that 'the view that the Logos was used as an intermediary in the creation of the world because of some inability on the part of God to create it directly was introduced by Asterius and adopted by Arius after the Logos had already been transformed by them into a created being' (1958: 10; see also Barnard 1970: 181; Gregg and Groh 1981: 25). Each of these scholars is probably right, but the fact that none of the 'genuine' Arian writings (including Urkunde 6) attest to it explicitly must leave the assertion open to some doubt.

'At the root of Arianism', declares Hanson, 'lay the conviction that God cannot communicate himself, and that ultimately the Son was a means of protecting God from contact with the world rather than a guarantee that he has involved himself in it' (1982: 437). Arius' God needs a mediating creature (Dragas 1981: 33). Only through the mediation of the Logos/Son can God deal with creation and yet maintain his transcendence intact and thus his freedom to be God. Again, speculation to be sure, but with a high probability of being right.

The Logos as the creature-god

Against Pollard and many earlier commentators, Stead argues that Arius took a relatively high view of the Logos, short, however, of making him coeval and consubstantial with the Father (1982a: 287). 'There is no need for us to accept Athanasius' claim that Arius regarded the Logos as merely one of the creatures, but rather as first-born and unique' (1985: 157). Arius argues, maintains Dragas, for a mediator who is half-way between the uncreated God and the created universe, a mythological image of the mediator-creator who is neither eternal, nor temporal, neither true God nor true creature, but a divine-creature (1981: 30). Arius has a doctrine of creation which does not allow the possibility of a divine human person; that is, of a real revelation of God in man (ibid.: 32). For Arius, participation is only a moral concept which leaves the being of God untouched by the being of the creatures (ibid.: 35); that is, God as transcendent and thereby as free to be God. Much of what is claimed here is attractive, but must remain, short of explicit evidence to support it, as speculation. It is clearly what Athanasius and Alexander genuinely believed to be the clear (or logical) implication of what Arius was saying, but this does not make it what he actually said.

The Logos/Son as God

Yet, as Stead properly points out, any notion of the Son/Logos as mere creature in Arius' eyes must contend with the fact that 'in his letter to Alexander [Urkunde 6] Arius apparently called the Son *plêrês theos*, which must exclude any notion of a purely nominal deity' (1978: 38). While the *Thalia* excerpts, as we saw above, concede Arius' Son a conditional and qualified (even second-grade) divinity, the 'genuine' Arian reference has no such explicit condition or qualification. Hanson argues that the Arians wanted a God – though an inferior god, not the High God – to suffer for the sake of humankind (1988b: 112). At the heart of the Arian Gospel, he declares, is a God who suffered; that is, one ontologically capable of enduring human experiences (ibid.: 121). But is such a god truly God? Does this god provide for the genuine self-revelation and self-communication of the true God? Can such a creature-god, neither God nor human, truly save humankind?

Christ as Saviour

While in Urkunde 1 Arius declares the Son to have subsisted before time and before ages 'as God full [of grace and truth]', the *Thalia* excerpts offer a different view. In the *De Synodis* Arius is alleged to have called the Son God, but in a way clearly inferior or subordinate to the Supreme (God); in *Contra Arianos* that the Word is not true God, but rather God only in name and by participation (metoche). It is then only on the basis of the *Thalia* excerpts that it can be said that for Arius, whatever the actual divine status of the Son, salvation may be a form of deification (as for Athanasius) in that the Son is the prototype of '*theoi kata charin*' (Wiles 1962: 339f.) Indeed, says Wiles, 'the most fundamental reasons for the rejection of Arianism and Apollinarianism were soteriological' (1966: 321). This would seem to support, at least implicitly, the notion of Gregg and Groh, exemplified in the title of their controversial book, *Early Arianism: A View of Salvation*, that soteriology is the most significant, even the central feature of the whole Arian scheme. For Gregg and Groh, the Son's identity with the creature is critical for the Arian scheme of salvation (1981: 65); 'in the Arian scheme of salvation (soteriology is) controlled by voluntarist rather than substantialist thinking' (ibid.: 67).

Yet the emphasis given by them to soteriology as the crucial element in Arian Christology is questioned by most, if not all their critics. While recognizing the valuable contribution made by Gregg and Groh to Arian scholarship it is clear that these critics believe that they have claimed too much (see Stead 1982a: 288; Louth 1982: 140; Meijering 1982: 68; Osborn 1984: 54). Few scholars would argue that soteriology is not one of a number of important elements in Arian Christology; they simply argue that Gregg and Groh have gone too far in seeming to claim it as the pre-eminent one.

Williams argues that in this early literature of the controversy 'the distinctiveness of the Arian position is chiefly conditioned by the distinctiveness of the particular assertions which the Arians are denying' (1983: 57). Arius asserts that his involvement in the controversy was in terms of his 'orthodox' reaction to what he perceived to be Alexander's heterodox teaching. He saw his own position, although sound in terms of Christian tradition and Scripture, as essentially reactive and not proactive (and thus not innovative).

Christ as exemplar

Gregg and Groh, as one would expect, argue that the Arians placed particular emphasis on the similarity of the Son's status to ours and on the progress of the Son in ethical behaviour (1981: 6). They speak of the Arian view that Christ shared with other creatures that progress which depends upon the steadfast choice of the good (ibid.: 146). A passage from the *Thalia*, as reported in the *Contra Arianos*, would appear to bear this out; the Word is described there as 'by nature . . . alterable (as we are)' and remaining 'good by his free will'. Yet, against this, Stead argues that the Arians represented Christ as a moral agent, not as the moral norm (1982a: 288) and that it is most unlikely that Arius thought of salvation exclusively in exemplarist terms (1994: 31, 36). It must be said, of course, in defence of Gregg and Groh, that they nowhere explicitly claim this. It must also be said, however, that while the *Thalia* passage in question does seem to suggest an identification of sorts on the part of the Son with us, Urkunde 6 speaks of the Son as a perfect creature of God, but not as one of the creatures. This would appear to negate any suggestion of an identification with the imperfect creature.

Early Arian use of Scripture

On at least three occasions in Urkunde 30 – his post-Nicaea confession of faith – Arius declares that his theology is sourced from the Holy Scriptures. After offering a brief creed-like statement, he declares that 'this faith' has been received by him and his associates from the 'holy Gospels'. He then asserts that they believe and receive the teachings on the Father, Son and Holy Spirit as held by the whole Catholic church and as taught by the Scriptures (in which he affirms they believe in every respect). Towards the end of the letter, he reaffirms that they hold to the faith of the church and of the Holy Scriptures. If nothing else, Arius claimed clearly to have followed both the tradition of the church and the teachings of Scripture on matters Trinitarian and Christological.

The assumption that Arius was a literalist in his approach to biblical exegesis, however, is based primarily on the notion – long accepted without further argument – that he belonged to the 'Antiochene' School. This school, it was claimed, operated on a 'historico-literal' model of exegesis, while the 'Alexandrian' School (following the Origenist lead) was exclusively devoted to allegory. Yet more and more evidence has brought into question the very notion of such fixed schools of exegesis in this period – or in any period for that matter – and in any case whether either Antioch or Alexandria was exclusively committed to a particular exegetical approach. Few now accept that Arius was an actual pupil of Lucian of Antioch, whatever Arius' own words might suggest (see p. 976), and Peter, bishop Alexander's predecessor at Alexandria, and by whom Arius may indeed have been ordained, was a committed literalist. According to Williams, none of the exegetical material available to us in the extant texts supports the notion that Arius was a literalist (1987: 109). The fact that the *Thalia* was 'a hymn to the living God of scriptural narrative' (ibid.: 111) does not in any way require him to have been one. The same epitaph could just as easily have been applied to the arch-allegorist and 'man of the book' Origen. Arius was a theological exegete – with far more sophistication than many more recent scholars appreciate (though some have sought to undermine the ancient and biased view of him as a technologue driven almost exclusively by the demands of philosophical speculation which is true rather of the later Neo-Arians like Aetius) – and one, according to Williams, with no particular interest in epistemology or metaphysics in their own right (1987: 213). Arius' commitment to the Scriptures can be seen in the efforts made by his opponents, however accurately or otherwise they may have portrayed his actual views, to counter his apparently effective use of Scripture. Athanasius' *Contra Arianos*, particularly *Orationes* 2 and 3, are a case in point. Arius' opponents saw the danger – that he was a biblical theologian – and sought simultaneously both to meet him on the ground of scriptural interpretation and to deny his commitment to such an enterprise by portraying him as a philosophical speculator when, in fact, his philosophical grounding was no more or less than theirs. His favourite scriptural texts appear to have included: Phil. 2:5–11; Pss. 44 and 110; Prov. 8:22–31; Heb. 1:4 and 3:1–2; Acts 2:36; and John 14:28.

Influences on Arius

The Alexandrian tradition

Many early scholars accepted, almost without question as we saw above, that the Arian controversy represented, at least in part, an Antiochene/Alexandrian divide. Wiles, however, is critical of these, particularly with respect to the notion that Arius *must* have found influences beyond the church at Alexandria and Origen (1962:

339f.). Stead agrees, arguing persuasively, as always, that an origin for Arius' theory can be found quite readily within the Alexandrian tradition itself (1964: 21). 'Whatever may be true of his adherents, Arius draws upon a Platonic tradition evolving within the Church, rather than representing a violent incursion of alien philosophy' (ibid.), drawing upon Origen, Methodius, Athenagoras, Clement and Dionysius of Alexandria. Lorenz asserts, however, that Arius cannot be explained as just a more radical subordinationist in the line of a traditional Origenist theology (in Kannengiesser 1983: 471). Hanson likewise argues that 'Arius adopted no large nor significant part of Origen's theology . . . his account of the Christian doctrine of God is perhaps fundamentally different from that of Origen' (Hanson 1987: 413). Origen contributed to many sides in the debate. With respect to the present consensus that Arius was not a disciple of Lucian of Antioch, Hanson argues, against the flow, that we must take the 'co-Lucianist' tag seriously and that Lucian may have been the source of Arius' alleged teaching of the '*soma apsychon*' (1988b: 11, 79f.).

Asterius the Sophist

Another probable influence on Arius was Asterius the Sophist. An apostate during the Maximinian persecution, Asterius earned his living as an orator and wrote the *Syntagmation* some time after Nicaea (he died *c.* 341). In it he defended the notion precious to Arian and later Neo-Arian alike that there cannot be two '*agenneta*' (unbegotten entities). The almost-Nicene *Homilies on the Psalms*, which speak of a suffering God, a crucified God and a Son who is not a 'mere man' (*psilos anthropos*), which can, of course, be understood in a distinctly Arian sense, may in fact not be his (see Kinzig 1989). Several undoubtedly genuine fragments of his work have, however, survived in references from both Athanasius and Eusebius of Caesarea: God created the Son/Logos as mediator for creating, for a created nature could not endure to experience God's unmediated hand (fr. viii); the Son and the Father are one (John 10:30) both because there is a consistent and exact correspondence of their teaching and will (fr. xiii) and because there is between them an exact agreement in ideas and activities (fr. xxxii); the genesis of the Son is the Father's will (fr. xviii); it is acceptable to call the Son the 'exact image of the Father's substance' (fr. xxi); the Father and the Son are distinct hypostases (fr. xxvii) and distinct *prosopa* (persons) (fr. xxviii). There is, however, no extant record that Asterius ever claimed, as Arius probably did, that the Son was produced out of the non-existent.

With respect to the much disputed (and in my view over-emphasized) influence of philosophical thought on Arius, Gregg and Groh, according to Hanson, make a good case for the chief philosophical influence on Arius being Stoicism (1982: 433), though not with respect to the particular Stoic notion of advancement or progress in Christ; the Arian Christ cannot example human perfection for he is precisely, as '*soma apsychon*', not a man (1988b: 97). He also sees some appropriateness and sense in the suggestion that Aristotelian rather than Platonic categories lie behind Arius' thought (ibid.: 94). Kannengiesser argues for some measure of influence emanating from the thought of Plotinus. 'Arius' entire effort', he argues, 'consisted precisely in acclimatising Plotinic logic within biblical creationism' (1982: 38f.). Williams argues for the influence of Philo on Arius' notion of divine freedom (1987: 122);

Williams, Young points out, makes out a convincing case for Arius as an intellectual, the prevalent ancient characterization of him (1989: 267), much against the tide of modern opinion which has tended to portray him, against the ancient polemical view, as a rather dull literalist exegete with very little to offer to a sophisticated debate.

ARIANS AND NEO-ARIANS (HOMOIANS, ANOMOIANS AND HETEROOUSIANS)

History: the later period (337–81)

In 337 Constantine died and was succeeded by his sons Constantius II (died 361) in the East and Constantine II (died 340) and Constans (died 350) in the West. Constantius was an undisguised supporter of the anti-Nicene forces, of Eusebius of Nicomedia in particular, while the western emperors generally supported the Nicene cause. Within a few years most of the original protagonists were dead; Alexander by 328; Arius himself in 336; Eusebius of Caesarea by 340; and Eusebius of Nicomedia by 342.

In 341 a synod meeting at Antioch produced a number of credal statements, among them the so-called Second Antiochene or Dedication Creed (possibly seen by its proposers as a substitute (Hanson 1988b: 290) for Nicaea) which repudiated Arius (and especially the notion that the Son was a creature but not as one of the creatures), spoke of three hypostases, and adhered generally to the Nicene position but without the 'homoousian'. For 20 years after Nicaea no-one it seems, not even Athanasius, mentioned the latter (Hanson 1988b: 170). Antioch II was characterized by subordinationism; anti-Sabellianism (= anti-Marcellanism); and the omission of such phrases as 'from the *ousia* of the Father' and 'begotten, not made'. It may properly be called Origenist and its probable influences included Origen, Eusebius of Caesarea and Asterius (Hanson 1988b: 290). It was the last victory for the moderates (semi-Arian is an inappropriate title) in the East for a generation at least. A Fourth Antiochene Creed, traditionally associated with this 341 council but composed later by a smaller group of bishops, strengthened both the anti-Arian and the anti-Marcellan elements of Antioch II (Kopecek 1979: I, 84). In 343, at a western council in Serdica – apparently in an attempt (though abortive) to reconcile East and West (Hanson 1988b: 306), with the Easterners meeting at Philippopolis – the Latin-speaking church received Marcellus of Ancyra and repudiated the trihypostatic language of the anti-Nicene forces. For this the Greek (Origenist) suspected the Latin church of Sabellianism (as the Latin did the Greek of tritheism). Only later, under imperial pressure, did the Latin church appear to abandon Marcellus. The Philippopolis synod strengthened the anti-Marcellan tendencies of Antioch IV (Kopecek 1979: I, 85). At Antioch in 345 the so-called Macrostich (Long-lined) Creed was adopted. It spoke of no eternal generation, implied one hypostasis (but three *prosopa* or *pragmata*), did not mention '*ousia*', was subordinationist, and made certain concessions to western sensibilities but avoided any suggestion of Sabellianism. This creed was anti-Arian, anti-Marcellan and anti-Athanasian (Kopecek 1979:

I, 87). A western synod meeting in Milan later in the same year, however, virtually ignored its existence. In 346 Athanasius returned from exile.

In 350 Constans died and Constantius became sole emperor. The Arian (i.e., the Homoian) ascendancy had begun. Athanasius was condemned yet again at Arles in 355, and in 356 was re-exiled from Alexandria. In both Alexandria and Antioch anti-Nicenes became bishop. At Sirmium in 351 a creed not unlike the so-called (but incorrectly) Antioch IV (341) and with 26 anathemas was adopted. Fourteen of these were anti-Sabellian, five anti-Nicene and three opposed extreme variations of Arianism. In 357 at Sirmium a council explicitly declared the Son to be subordinate to the Father in the so-called Second Creed of Sirmium or 'Blasphemy' (according to the Nicene Hilary of Poitiers in his *De Synodis* 15). Those attending included Valens of Mursa and Ursacius. It was originally written in Latin and declared that *'ousia'* language introduced inappropriate corporeal notions into the Godhead. Hanson regards this council as a landmark in that confusion was now at an end, battle-lines were clearly drawn, and many of those moderates whose fear of the Nicene quasi-Sabellian *'homoousios'* had driven them into anti-Nicene arms now saw the clear danger of the latter (1988b: 347). In 358, for a short time, the Homoiousian Basil of Ancyra convinced the emperor (at Sirmium III) to accept *'homoiousios* (of like substance)' as an acceptable compromise, with the *'homoousian'* being declared anathema. In 358 Basil also convened what Kopecek calls 'the first self-consciously homoiousian assembly' (1979: I, 110). This gathering anathematized the alleged Aetian phrase 'unlike-in-essence' (*anomoion kat'ousian*) depicting the Father–Son relationship. For many Antioch II (341) was something of a benchmark. But this Basilian ascendancy did not last long. We might also note at this point that the associates of Basil of Ancyra (probably wrongly called the Homoiousians, for none actually used the term themselves) were troubled less by Sabellianism than by the emerging Neo-Arians. In 358 the Basilians were wary of, but had not yet rejected the notion of 'ungeneratedness' as the primary designation of God; by 359 they had done so, preferring Father–Son language along with Athanasius. The Basilians opposed the ungenerated/generated language as not properly communicating the intimate relationship between Father and Son. The Basilians now clearly saw the Neo-Arians as their main opponents, while the Homoians and Neo-Arians forged a new (though temporary) alliance against them. In 359, the year before which Athanasius had tactlessly referred to the emperor as the AntiChrist! (*Historia Arianorum*), another council meeting at Sirmium, which was convened under the influence of the new imperial favourite Valens of Mursa (the 'Arian viper' to his opponents), produced the Fourth Creed of Sirmium (called the 'Dated Creed' after the unusual intrusion into its text of the date of its promulgation) which did away with the 'homoiousian' and declared the Son to be 'like the Father in all things' (*homoios kata panta*). Later in the same year synods meeting in the West at Arminium and in the East at Seleucia (described by Kopecek as a mixture of Antioch II and IV, and the Dated Creed [1979: I, 208]) were compelled against their own apparent inclinations, since most preferred the language of Antioch II, to accept the 'like in all things', a formulation clearly susceptible to Neo-Arian interpretation. Their deliberations were presented to the emperor at Nike and at Constantinople in 360 (Kopecek 1979: II, 305 suggests that there were two such councils at Constantinople [one in December 359 and the other in January 360]) and at the latter place, at the dedication of the Sancta Sophia church, a council formally adopted, under pressure from Valens of Mursa and supported by the Neo-Arians Aetius and Eunomius, the 'homoian' option without the qualification 'in all things'. This council, influenced no doubt by Acacius of Caesarea, decreed that no longer could 'ousia' be used to described the divine essence, suggesting as it did a sort of divine matter. Nicaea was clearly repudiated. 'The world groaned', declared Jerome, 'to find itself Arian.' Basil of Ancyra and others of his party were exiled. Aetius was also banished and deposed from the diaconate, but more for his manner than his theology. But from 360 Athanasius and the Basilian moderates (who favoured the trihypostatic language) determined to join in alliance. Eunomius, ordained previously as deacon at Antioch, was distressed at Aetius' exile but chose, for the moment at least, to accept both the Homoian settlement and appointment as bishop at Cyzikos. Soon thereafter he was accused by some of the Cyzikan clergy, possibly for introducing a one-immersion baptism in the name of the death of Christ alone (Kopecek 1979: II, 398), and, though acquitted at trial before Eudoxius of Constantinople, was angered by the latter's alleged failure to keep a promise to expedite the recall of Aetius and went into self-imposed exile. He now began the process of forming a Neo-Arian sect in place of an ecclesiastical party (Kopecek 1979: II, 398, 414). He was summoned by Constantius to defend himself at Antioch in 361 but continued to enjoy considerable clerical and popular support there, including some, though later abandoned, from Eudoxius the Homoian bishop of the city.

In 361 Constantius died and was succeeded by Julian the Apostate (361–3). An adherent of the old paganism, he recalled all exiles (including Aetius, the friend of his brother the Caesar Gallus) and exercised toleration as a way of setting all the Christian protagonists at one another's throats. Basil now began his *Contra Eunomium* as a Neo-Arian synod got under way in Constantinople in 362. Julian was succeeded by Jovian (363–4) who favoured the Nicenes and Athanasius; he was in turn succeeded by Valentinian I (364–75) in the West who was 'neutral in religious differences', and his brother Valens (364–78) in the East who was inclined to the Homoian party. In 367 both Aetius and Eunomius were briefly banished for allegedly supporting the would-be usurper Procopius the previous year. Aetius died soon thereafter. We now enter the period of the Cappadocian Fathers – Basil and the two Gregories – who dealt most resolutely with the issue of the deity of the Holy Spirit and most vigorously with Eunomius. In 370 Eunomius was re-exiled for Neo-Arian activity in Cappadocia and in 378 returned to both Constantinople and Antioch. In the latter he presided over a synod of Neo-Arian metropolitans.

In 378 Valens died in battle against the Goths and was succeeded in the East (Gratian was emperor in the West) by the Spaniard Theodosius. His accession swung the tide the Nicene way and opened the door, beginning at Antioch in 379, to the eventual Nicene settlement at Constantinople in 381, where both the '*homoousion*' was re-established and the deity of the Holy Spirit affirmed. An edict of Theodosius prior to Constantinople had proscribed both Arians and Neo-Arians, by which they were not permitted to use churches within towns of the eastern empire. Canon 1 of the council itself anathematized Neo-Arians, Arians and others. Soon after the council a new edict specifically proscribed the building by Neo-Arians of new churches even in the countryside. Another declared that all existing Arian and Neo-Arian churches must be surrendered to Nicene-faithful parties, and another, after Theodosius' abortive Unity Conference in 383, proscribed their meeting even in private homes, as well as their rituals and ordinations. Neo-Arianism was now effectively illegal. Eunomius was banished for non-compliance with the edicts, and after his death in the early 390s, Neo-Arianism was rent by schism. In the West at Aquileia, under Ambrose, Arianism was also defeated in the Balkan provinces, although as Daniel Williams' (1995) book demonstrates (and Ambrose's own letters reveal), Arianism was far from dead in the West at this time. In 386 Valentinian II, now the western emperor, promulgated a new edict allowing worship to (Homoian) adherents of Rimini (359) and Constantinople (360).

ARIAN AND NEO-ARIAN DOCUMENTS OF THE LATER PERIOD

Like the extant works of Arius himself, those of the later Arians (Homoians) and Neo-Arians are few in number. The *Syntagmation* of Aetius (written towards the end of 359; Hanson 1988b: 600), which defends the alleged Neo-Arian watchword '*anomoios*', probably in response to Athanasius' *De Decretis* (Hanson 1988b: 606), is one. The extant writings of Eunomius of Cyzicus are, thankfully, more voluminous and not only for the extracts to be found in Basil's and Gregory of Nyssa's refutations of his theology. We have his fully extant *First Apology* (written in 359; Hanson 1988b: 618), where he defends the notion, against the Homoiousians, that the proper name for deity is 'Ungenerated', and his *Second Apology* (*Apologia Apologiae*) (written in 378/9 [Books 1 and 2] and 382/3 [Books 3, 4 and 5] against Basil's *Adversus Eunomium*), which is found mainly in Gregory's work directed against it. We also have his *Confession of Faith* (written probably for the emperor Theodosius' 383 unity conference; Hanson 1988b: 618) and snippets of other works preserved in the writings of his opponents.

The Homoians

Hanson (1988b: 557) properly argues that a distinction should be made between Homoianism and what Kopecek has called Neo-Arianism (and others less properly Anomoianism but more appropriately Heteroousianism). (1988: 557). For the Homoians were not 'Unlikers' (as probably the Neo-Arians were not as well). The Homoians (so favoured by Valens) were little interested in philosophical speculation, and were more inclined to engage in a literal than an allegorical exegesis of the biblical text (ibid.: 559). The two main leaders of eastern Homoianism were Acacius of Caesarea and Eudoxius (although he was also, for a time, politically if not theologically supportive of Aetius and Eunomius), and those of the West Ulfilas, the missionary to the Goths, Valens of Mursa, Ursacius of Singidunum, Germinius of Sirmium, Palladius of Ratiaria and Auxentius of Milan.

Their two main credal formulations were those of Sirmium II (357) and Nike-Constantinople (360), although Ulfilas' Rule of Faith and the Creed of Auxentius of

Milan were also significant in the West (Hanson 1988b: 558f.). Their theology was essentially a development of that of Eusebius of Caesarea and is characterized mainly by a profound distaste for the word *'ousia'* and its derivatives with respect to the relationship of Father and Son. Thus, they preferred the term *'homoios'* without further qualification. It can be said that their 'party', as such, dates only from the time of Sirmium II. They saw themselves as deeply attached to the scriptural text; 'what I read, is what I believe', said one. The description of the Father–Son relationship should be restricted to the limits of scriptural language and *'homoousios'*, *'homoiousios'*, and *'heteroousios'* avoided at all costs. They disavowed the name of 'Arian' and claimed to be upholding the traditional faith (ibid.: 561). Their emphases included the ignorance of Jesus; his disvowal of his own goodness; that Jesus was a created being called by divine grace; that the Son was produced wholly from the Father's will; that the Son's praying to the Father demonstrates their inequality; and that the Father is simply incomparable.

For Acacius of Caesarea, the disciple of his predecessor Eusebius (from 341–66), and whose leadership was as much political as doctrinal (Hanson 1988b: 583), the Son is the exact image of the Father in all respects save one; he is not unbegotten. There are two distinct hypostases (much Arian thought was clearly directed against Marcellus of Ancyra), Ingenerate and Son, and while the latter can be called God (and possibly is God) he is not God as the Ingenerate/Father is God. In Eusebius of Emesa (*c.* 300–59; bishop from 340/1), the distinct existence of the Son is maintained against the Sabellians (Marcellus as the new Sabellius?) and the language of obedience is regularly applied to the Son. Palladius, Ambrose' formidable opponent at Aquileia in 381, spoke of a Trinity comprising the one High-God, one demi-god, and one superior angel, and of an ontological distinction between them (Hanson 1988b: 564). The Son was not created out of nothing and his begetting implies that he is from the Father's will. The Incarnation, along the lines of Phil. 2:9, comprises a reduction of divinity. A drastic subordinationism is central to his (and all Homoian) thought. The Father is God of the Son and, for that reason, the Son worships the Father. The Son is properly the High Priest of the Father, as declared in Hebrews 3. Father and Son are alike in energy, power and activity but not in substance. The Homoousians are guilty of both Sabellianism and of tritheism! (Hanson 1988b: 577). Ulfilas reflects a theology which is clearly concerned with subordination and obedience, the Father is God of the Son, the Holy Spirit is not God but only minister of Christ, the Son (like with Origen, Eusebius of Caesarea and Rufinus) is a 'second God', and the Father is creator of our creator. Valens and Ursacius were the main architects of Sirmium II and Germinius one of those who drew up the 359 Dated Creed. Later (in the mid-360s probably) he abandoned the Homoians and went over to those who looked primarily to Antioch II.

Homoianism was less technical and less sophisticated (but more popular) than Neo-Arianism (Hanson 1988b: 597). The areas of difference between the Homoians and the Neo-Arians comprised the comprehensibility of God, the mutability or immutability of the Son, the use of philosophical language, and the formula for describing the Son's likeness to the Father.

The Neo-Arians

With Aetius and Eunomius, it is generally agreed, later Arian theology became a form of technology. It is perhaps true also that 'Anomoian' is not the appropriate title for this party (Hanson 1988b: 598). Many Neo-Arians repudiated any suggestion that the Son is always, without further qualification, 'unlike' the Father.

Aetius was a pupil of both Paulinus of Tyre and Athanasius of Anazarbus. He was famous for his use of syllogisms. He was ordained deacon by the Arian Leontius in Antioch in 346 and then released from the diaconate in order to pursue a teaching career in Antioch and Alexandria (348–50) where he first taught the young Cappadocian Eunomius. In 357 he was reappointed deacon by another Cappadocian, George of Alexandria, an early supporter of the Neo-Arians. For Aetius the real problem was whether or not a created ingenerate (that is, an uncreated Logos) was logically possible. Being caused belonged to the very essence of the Son. God's being named as 'Father' does not imply any participation by the Son in his essence (Kopecek 1979: I, 124). The essential contrast for Aetius was between the Ingenerate One (God) and the (created/generated) Son. For Aetius (and for Eunomius) ingeneracy is the very essence of God that is, is God. Therefore, the Son, not being ingenerate, cannot be God, and not being God, cannot be ingenerate. Therefore, the Son can be neither homoousios nor homoiousios to the Father.

To our knowledge the *Syntagmation* of Aetius does not discuss the Incarnation; what matters primarily to Aetius is 'knowing God' (John 17:3) (Hanson 1988b: 606). For him different names (e.g. Father and Son) indicate different natures. Names express realities and are not mere conventional symbols. The word 'Ingenerate' is not just one name for the Father but his very essence. Neither is it a mere privative, for then the Father would be non-existent, which would be absurd, or there would have to be a prior status – generatedness – which the Father would then lack. He also preferred creator/created language for the Father–Son for it implied both no passion on the part of God and that the created Son is both complete and fixed from the outset and therefore not mutable (Kopecek 1979: I, 171). Aetius rarely mentions either the Bible or Christ (Hanson 1988b: 610) and the *Syntagmation* itself has only one recognizable scriptural reference, John 17:3 in Syllogism 37. God, the true God, cannot beget; therefore, Aetius implies, he cannot have a true Son. God can only be known intellectually; he cannot communicate himself. He is known only by being known as the Ingenerate One. Aetius employs logical analysis to prove his case. He employs neither *'anhomoios'* nor *'heteroousios'*. Philostorgius, the later Arian apologist, preferred the latter term, since for him the Son was unchangeably like the Father in some respects, but not in *ousia*, although he opted for 'incomparable (*asugkriton*) in *ousia*'. All 37 propositions found in the *Syntagmation* concern the relationship of Father and Son, and none the Incarnation. For Kopecek, Syllogism 32 implies even that the Son is significant religiously, however cosmologically so, only as a means through which to approach the one God (1979: II, 95); this is, he says, a 'radical Christian monotheism'. Aetius is a rationalist and his theology is essentially metaphysical (Hanson 1988b: 611).

Eunomius, a pupil of Aetius, was not a strict believer in the Son being *anomoios* ('unlike') the Father; for him the Son is like the Father 'according to the scriptures', but not in *ousia*. He was comfortable with the term '*heteroousios*' (Kopecek [1979: 330] sees this implied at least in Eunomius' *First Apology* 20). As with Aetius, the true name and thus the true nature of divinity is the Ungenerated (*Apologia Apologiae* 382). God is the Ingenerate (*First Apol.* 7) and, therefore, the Incomparable. The Ungenerate does not admit comparison (homoiousion) with the Generate One (*First Apol.* 9; see John 14:28). The Ingenerate is no mere title or privative. The Son is related to God only by the activity that produced him and is similar to this cause. The Son's likeness is to the Father's activity and will and not to his essence (*First Apol.* 24). The Father is God's will. Father and Son are then 'alike'; God and the Son can only be 'unlike'. But this activity of God is temporary and its product will cease when the cause shall cease. No act of begetting goes on forever but comes to an end; therefore, it must have a beginning (*Apol. Apol.* 224). God's will and purpose are not identical with God's essence, for the act of willing has both a beginning and an end (*First Apol.* 23). God exists apart and prior to the Begotten One and therefore the latter was not before his begetting (*Apol. Apol.* 224). Eunomius' theology is established on the principle that God is the cause of all things and a cause *must* pre-exist what it causes (Kopecek 1979: III, 12). Indeed, strictly speaking, God cannot beget – for the '*agennetos*' cannot beget '*gennetos*' (Hanson 1988b: 622) – but only create.

The essence of the Son is begotten(ness) (*First Apol.* 12). To call the Son a '*gennema*' (product) is to describe his *ousia* and hypostasis. The Son was begotten when he was as yet not, but was not one of those things brought into existence '*ex ouk ontôn*' (*First Apol.* 15). The Son is the only essence which exists as a hypostasis by means of the Father's activity; the Son is 'direct' from the Father's hand. The Son is the perfect minister of the whole creativity and purpose of the Father (*First Apol.* 18). The Son is like the Father as to will but not as to essence (*First Apol.* 18) and therefore not a real Son (Hanson 1988b: 625). The Fatherhood of God is an *energeia* and therefore separate from God's essence and temporary. There is a fundamental distinction between the divine *ousia* and the divine *energeia*. Thus the real distinction, as with Aetius, is between the Ingenerate One and the Son, not between Father and Son. Col. 1:15–16 proves that the Son is the image of the Father's activity (Kopecek 1979: II, 340). The Holy Spirit lacks godhead altogether, even of an inferior brand (*First Apol.* 25). The Son is offspring but not as other offspring (*First Apol.* 28). The Son is not made Son or God because of obedience but because he is 'Son' and Only-Begotten (*Expositio fidei* 3). In Eunomius' extant writings there are no references to the Incarnation (as with Aetius). As with Aetius, different names mean different realities. God, for Eunomius, cannot communicate God's own self. Eunomianism is, says Kopecek, 'thoroughgoing Arianism presented in its full consistency and justified with a comprehensive theory of language' (1979: II, 330). For Eunomius, God did not become man, but only the Son/Word did so, being in the form of God. God is 'inactive'; the Son 'acted out God's love' (1979: II, 493).

One interesting notion in Eunomius is that God cannot know more about his own essence than we can; for his essence is his unbegottenness and we can know that (fr. ii). Divine simplicity indeed! Thus God, for Eunomius – unlike for the orthodox or even for Arius – is knowable. For Eunomius Greek philosophy can explain all questions about God (Hanson 1988b: 630). Reason (that is, correct method) is the final court of appeal (Hanson 1988b: 631). And yet, Eunomius has 'a deep, almost

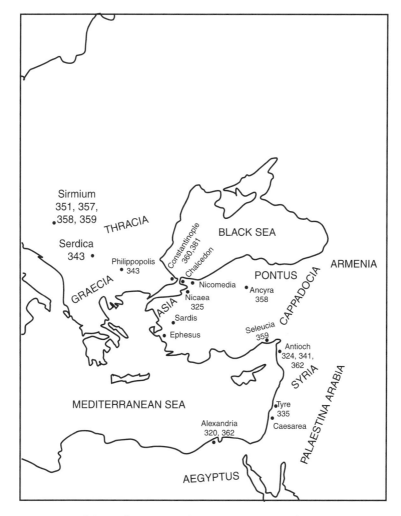

Figure 38.2   Sites and dates of councils and other major centres during the Arian controversy in the eastern empire.

literalist respect for Scripture' (ibid.). Given that Eunomius himself became more and more exegetical over time – as witness the progression from the *First Apology* to the *Apologia Apologiae* to the *Expositio Fidei* – and that much of the schismatic activity after Eunomius' death was exegetically driven, is it true to say that Neo-Arianism was in the end purely dialectic and rationalistic?

CONCLUSION

We now return to the question at the beginning of this chapter. Is there such a thing as fourth-century Arianism? Do the thoughts of Arius, the Eusebeians, the

Figure 38.3   Sites and dates of councils and other major centres during the Arian controversy in the western empire.

Homoians and the Neo-Arians (Eunomians) have much in common? Or was the designation 'Arian' simply a convenient polemical tool? Were there Arians, as such, only in the minds of Athanasius and his allies? The answer is not simple. On the one hand, there is clearly no unified group to which such a designation could readily apply; on the other, there is clearly in the fourth century a movement of thought against which persons like Athanasius and Hilary, and even Marcellus and Eustathius, did react. The various groupings called by history 'Arian' – if not by themselves, for even Arius would have eschewed the title, believing himself only a simple, biblical Christian – do share a number of common beliefs or points of doctrine.

They declared belief in the one God who is absolutely transcendent and who does not, indeed cannot share his essence. They deny the possibility of eternal generation, believing the Son to be a product of the Father's will. For them the *'agennetos'* stands fundamentally over against the *'gennemata'*. For them too, *'gennema'* and *'poiema'* are identical terms. The Father/God is *'agennetos/agenetos'*; the Son/Logos is *'gennetos/genetos'*; to them one 'nu' was as good as another! Father and Son are inherently unequal (Butler 1992: 365).

Yet, while for some God is comprehensible to the human mind as simply and essentially *'agennetos'* (Neo-Arian 'N'), to others he is ultimately incomprehensible (Arius – 'A'). For some the possession of *'epinoiai'*, the human conceptions or human inventions by which we talk indirectly about God,[1] suggests God as composite, and thereby as not simple (N); for others again *'epinoiai'* are a marvellous means of expressing the very richness of God (A). Some repudiated *'homoousios'* and *'homoiousios'* but liked *'heteroousios'*, for God is incomparable; others could bear *'homoiousios'* but never *'homoousios'* (A); others again preferred no *'ousia'* language at all for God's being, opting simply for *'homoios'* (Homoians). For some salvation is purely in knowing God (that is, in knowing God's pure essence as 'Ungenerated' [N]); for others salvation comes through ethical imitation of the Son, the god-creature (A). For some the Son was mutable by nature (A); for the others he could not be mutable and redeemer at the same time (N). Some saw the creation of the Son as for the purpose of creation (A); for others this threatened, even unintentionally, to make the Son inferior to the created order (N). For some, orthodox three-immersion/three-name baptism was appropriate (A); for others, it was to be one immersion in the single name of Christ's death (N).

Arians there were in the fourth century. Arius Arians (at least one of them); Eusebeian Arians; Homoian Arians; Aetian–Eunomian Arians; and even Athanasian Arians (at least in his mind). And none loved the others any more than they were loved by those who feared and hated them.

Likewise in the late twentieth century it is probably unwise to attach such a label too readily, if at all, to any particular theological position. Given that problems of definition and identification, with particular respect here to the notion of 'Arianism', were such major issues in the fourth-century debates, this can hardly be any less so in this century. It is therefore perhaps often inappropriate, not to say simply incorrect, to employ the term as a form of criticism in the context of modern theological disputation.

NOTE

1 Origen, Arius and the Cappadocians favoured them as a way of speaking about the transcendent, unknowable God, while Eunomius believed that they suggested a composite God and denied the notion of God as simply 'Unbegotten'.

BIBLIOGRAPHY

Barnard, Leslie (1970) 'The Antecedents of Arius', *Vigiliae Christianae* 24: 172–88.
—— (1972) 'What was Arius' Philosophy?', *Thelogische Zeitsschrift* 28: 110–17.
Barnes, Michael and Williams, Daniel (eds) (1993) *Arianism after Arius: Essays on the Development of the Fourth Century Trinitarian Conflicts*. Edinburgh: T&T Clark.

Butler, M. E. (1992) 'Neo-Arianism: Its Antecedents and Tenets', *St Vladimir's Theological Quarterly* 36: 355–71.

Dragas, George (1981) 'The Eternal Son', in Thomas F Torrance (ed.) *The Incarnation: Ecumenical Studies in the Niceno-Constantinopolitan Creed AD 381*. Edinburgh: T&T Clark, 16–57.

Green, Michael (ed.) (1977) *The Truth of God Incarnate*. London: Hodder & Stoughton.

Gregg, Robert (1985a) *Arianism: Historical and Theological Reassessments*. Patristic Monograph Series No. 11. Philadelphia Pa.: Philadelphia Patristic Foundation.

—— (1985b) 'Cyril of Jerusalem and the Arians', in Gregg 1985a: 85–109.

Gregg, Robert and Groh, Dennis (1981) *Early Arianism: A View of Salvation*. London: SCM.

Grillmeier, Aloys (1975) *Christ in the Christian Tradition. Vol. 1: From the Apostolic Age to Chalcedon (451)*. 2nd edn. Atlanta, Ga.: John Knox Press.

Hanson, Robert (1982) 'New Light on Arianism', *Journal of Ecclesiastical History* 33: 431–7.

—— (1987) 'The Influence of Origen on the Arian Controversy' in L. Lies (ed.) *Origeniana quarta*: 410–23.

—— (1988a) Review of Williams 1987, *Journal of Ecclesiastical History* 39: 235–7.

—— (1988b) *The Search for the Christian Doctrine of God*. Edinburgh: T&T Clark.

Haugaard, William (1960) 'Arius: Twice a Heretic. Arius and the Human Soul of Jesus Christ', *Church History* 29: 251–63.

Heron, Alasdair (1981) 'Homoousios with the Father', in Thomas F. Torrance (ed.) *The Incarnation. Ecumenical Studies in the Nicene-Constantinopolitan Creed AD 381*. Edinburgh: T&T Clark, 58–87.

Hick, John (ed.) (1977) *The Myth of God Incarnate*. London: SCM Press Ltd.

Kannengiesser, Charles (1982) *Holy Scripture and Hellenistic Hermeneutics in Alexandrian Christology: The Arian Crisis*. Berkeley: Graduate Theological Union and University of California.

—— (1983) 'Current Theology: Arius and the Arians', *Theological Studies* 44: 456–75.

Kelly, John Norman Davidson (1977) *Early Christian Doctrines*, 5th edn. London: A. & C. Black.

Kinzig, Wolfram (1989) *In Search of Asterius: Studies on the Authorship of the Homilies on the Psalms*. Gottingen: Vandenhoeck & Ruprecht.

Kopecek, Thomas A. (1979) *A History of Neo-Arianism*. 2 vols. Philadelphia, Pa.: The Philadelphia Patristic Foundation.

Louth, Andrew (1982) Review of Gregg and Groh 1981, *Theology* 85: 139–41.

Macquarrie, John (1977) 'Christianity without Incarnation: Some Critical Comments', in Michael Green (ed.) *The Truth of God Incarnate*. London: Hodder & Stoughton, 140–4.

Meijering, E. (1982) Review of Gregg and Groh 1981, *Vigiliae Christianae* 36: 67–8.

Opitz, Hans (1934–5) *Urkunden zur Geschichte des arianischen Streites 318–328 (Athanasius' Werkle, Band III, 1)*. Berlin and Leipzig: de Gruyter.

Osborn, Eric Francis (1984) 'Arian Obedience: Scouting for Theologians', *Prudentia* 16: 51–6.

Pollard, T. E. (1957) 'Logos and Son in Origen, Arius and Athanasius', *Studia Patristica* 2: 282–7.

—— (1958) ''The Origins of Arianism', *Journal of Theological Studies* n.s. 9: 103–11.

Quasten, Johannes (1983) *Patrology. Vol. 3: The Golden Age of Greek Patristic Literature*. Westminster: Christian Classics.

Stead, Gregory Christopher (1964) 'The Platonism of Arius', *Journal of Theological Studies* 15: 16–31.

—— (1978) 'The *Thalia* of Arius and the Testimony of Athanasius', *Journal of Theological Studies* n.s. 29: 20–52.

—— (1982a) Review of Gregg and Groh 1981, *Journal of Theological Studies* 33: 285–9.

—— (1982b) 'The Scriptures and the Soul of Christ in Athanasius', *Vigiliae Christianae* 36: 233–50.

—— (1985) 'Arius on God's "Many Words"', *Journal of Theological Studies* n.s. 36: 153–7.

—— (1994) 'Arius in Modern Research', *Journal of Theological Studies* 45: 24–36.

Toon, Peter (1991) 'Inclusive Language: Right or Wrong?', *Evangelical Review of Theology* 15: 292–7.

Torrance, James (1981) 'The Vicarious Humanity of Christ', in Thomas F. Torrance (ed.) *The Incarnation. Ecumenical Studies in the Nicene-Constantinopolitan Creed AD 381*. Edinburgh: T&T Clark, 127–47.

Vaggione, Richard (1987) *Eunomius: the Extant Works*. Text and Translation. Oxford: Oxford University Press.

Wiles, Maurice (1962) 'In Defence of Arius', *Journal of Theological Studies* 13: 339–47.

—— (1966) 'Soteriological Arguments in the Fathers', *Studia Patristica* 9: 321–5.

Williams, Daniel (1995) *Ambrose of Milan and the end of the Nicene-Arian Conflicts*. Oxford: Clarendon Press.

Williams, Rowan (1983) 'The Logic of Arianism', *Journal of Theological Studies* n.s. 34: 56–81.

—— (1987) *Arius: Heresy and Tradition*. London: Darton Longman & Todd.

—— (ed.) (1989) *The Making of Orthodoxy: Essays in Honour of Henry Chadwick*. Cambridge: Cambridge University Press.

Wolfson, Harry (1958) 'Philosophical Implications of Arianism and Apollinarianism', *Dumbarton Oaks Papers* No. 12. Cambridge, Mass.: Harvard University Press, 4–28.

Young, Frances (1983) *From Nicaea to Chalcedon: a Guide to the Literature and its Background*. London: SCM Press.

—— (1989) Review of Williams 1987, *Scottish Journal of Theology* 42: 263–7.

PART IX

PROFILES

———.✦.———

ORIGEN

———·◆·———

Fred Norris

INTRODUCTION: THE ENIGMA OF ORIGEN

Origen (*c.* 185–*c.* 251–4) is always in the eye of the beholder. Although he was the greatest early theologian of the East – only Augustine is comparable in the West – his corpus is remarkably fragmentary and fragile. He warned in his own lifetime that copies of a debate which he had with another theologian had been interpolated and rewritten by his opponent (Jerome, *Apologia Contra Rufinum* 42–4; Hritzu 1965; Laudet 1982; Rufinus, *De alteratione librorum Origenis* 10–13; Dell'Era 1983). In Arabia to serve as a skilled expert in a meeting which was to focus on the questionable positions of a bishop named Heraclides, his own views came under scrutiny when another bishop asked him if the soul is the blood. His response shows how deeply concerned he was with simple believers' understandings of material language used in scripture for things spiritual. It is so clumsy that a third bishop summarizing Origen's views gives the impression that Origen relies more on Platonists than scripture (Origen, *Dialogue with Heraclides*; Scherer 1960; Daly 1992). At home in Alexandria, Demetrius, his bishop, had supported him early in his youth, but became quite angry with him when he was ordained by bishops in Palestine (Eusebius, *Historia Ecclesiastica* 6.8, 19, 23 Schwartz and Mommsen 1903, 1908; Lawlor and Oulton 1927). After Origen's death, his reputation changed with the tides. His scriptural exegesis of whole books and short passages, however, stayed for the most part within various traditions of orthodoxy.

Augustine, particularly in his *Retractiones*, remade himself for posterity on his own terms, but Origen died, probably in the Decian persecution, without rearranging himself. We have possibly three complete letters from him, although Eusebius of Caesarea knew a nine-volume collection of at least one hundred epistles (*H. E.* 6.36.3) and Jerome found at least four different collections of correspondence in Caesarea when he worked in that city. Because Origen left no guide for understanding his works like Augustine's, he provokes more contradictory readings than most ancient Christian figures. Tradition tells us that in the fourth century Basil of Caesarea and Gregory of Nazianzus put together the *Philochalia*, a selection from Origen's writings which attempted to bring together in a favourable light some of his most compelling insights (Junod 1976; Harl 1983). One of the reasons that we

Figure 39.1 Lithograph of Origen, after a relief by Michael Burghers. From Cave (1687: 213)

have only a few examples of sustained biblical commentary from the Cappadocians is probably their dependence upon his brilliant and extensive efforts.

After Origen's death, those who most valued him found it necessary to write in his defence. Gregory Thaumaturgus, one of his students and later bishop of Neocaesarea in Cappadocia, wrote a eulogy to him which gives details of his teacher's approach to Greek literature as a tool for Christian mission and learning (Crouzel 1969; Salmon 1975). Pamphilus (*c.* 240–309), a presbyter at Caesarea in Palestine and a scholar/teacher there, himself transcribed most of Origen's works which Jerome later used (Jerome, *De viris illustribus* 75; in Richardson 1896, 1952; Slusser

1998); he also wrote an *Apologia* for Origen, now only partially extant in a Latin translation (Migne, PG 17: 521–616). His student Eusebius (*c.* 260–*c.* 339), the noted church historian who provides important information on Origen's life, also wrote an *Apologia*, in at least two books, which is no longer preserved.

The debate about Origen's orthodoxy is reflected in other sources. The life of the towering figure in Egyptian monasticism, Pachomius (*c.* 292–346), comes down to us in different language traditions. The Greek one, most often considered a secondary source, has Pachomius condemn Origen, but the Bohairic Coptic biography, the primary source, contains no such reference. Those composing the Greek life evidently were so fearful that monasticism might be tarred with the brush of Origen that they saved Pachomius by making him a critic of the Alexandrian (Goehring 1997: 75–6).

In the fifth century, both Rufinus and Jerome translated Origen's *Peri archôn* (*On First Principles*; Koetschau 1913; Görgemanns and Karpp 1976; Crouzel and Simonetti 1978–84; Butterworth 1966), and fought bitterly over the results. Rufinus tells his readers that he does not render all of Origen's original because the Greek text he possesses suffers from serious interpolations. He also does not want to spoil the Alexandrian's acceptance in the West with unending discussions of unimportant points, but he makes no changes except on the basis of what he has read in other writings from Origen. We have Rufinus' translation. Jerome responded with his own translation and accused Rufinus of taking out or softening the heretical opinions of Origen and thus creating a warped impression. Jerome's full translation is lost. Only a few extracts remain (Quasten 1953: 73–4). They sometimes appear in later efforts to prove that Origenism was wrong and that Origen was a heretic. The *Philochalia* (Junod 1976) contains the fourth book of *Peri archôn* in Greek; some other Greek fragments are available. The fullest text of the work, however, is the translation of Rufinus. The first modern critical edition inserted 43 fragments from the Origenist controversy in places where the editor decided that they belonged, fragments both from Jerome and from later figures or groups who castigated Origen (Koetschau 1913). Two new critical editions in the last quarter century, however, have rejected that practice as misguided in two directions: first, in believing the worst representation of Origen; and second, in deciding where the floating quotations should fit into the piece itself (Görgemanns and Karpp 1976; Crouzel and Simonetti 1978–84; Norris 1994).

As if these developments were not difficult enough, the actual proceedings of the Fifth Ecumenical Council at Constantinople in 553 also leave us in a quandary. In the eleventh anathema of that council, Origen's name is listed as one of seven condemned theologians, but he appears out of chronological order and thus seems to stand as almost a symbol of problems with Origenism, a posture that centred on a style of theological thinking that marked the wider debate of the sixth century (Daley 1995). Yet in the council's 14 anathemas neither his doctrinal errors nor those of later Origenism are specified (*Decrees of the Ecumenical Councils;* Tanner *et al.* 1990, esp. Anathema 11). Theodore Askidas noted that Origen had been condemned after his death, perhaps not first at the 553 council but in an edict of 543 signed by Pope Vigilius and other bishops (*Sacrorum conciliorum;* Mansi *et al.* 1960–1: IX, 272). At the same time 15 anathemas against Origenism, reflecting teachings from Evagrius of Pontus rather than those from Origen himself (Guillaumont 1962), have come down to us as related to the council. There is also a letter from emperor Justinian to Mennas, bishop of Constantinople, which contains a series of extracts from Origen's *Peri archôn* that Justinian found suspect (*Sacrorum conciliorum*; Mansi *et al.* 1960–1: IX, 524–33). We are left with the odd situation that we do not know if the Fifth Ecumenical Council officially discussed or rejected Origenism, but that it listed Origen as an heretical teacher while no mention is made of what he taught that must be condemned (Gray 1979: 70–1; Clark 1992: 249). Thus this formative theologian of the East was adjudged both enigmatic and problematic. The obvious conciliar contrast with the bishop of Hippo appears in the strong defence of Augustine's later positions, as he defined them, by Caesarius of Arles and the 25 canons reflecting his views which were accepted as the definitive western understanding of theology at the Council of Orange in 529.

The central concern of this chapter is a sympathetic reading of this master. The official posthumous condemnation of a teacher over three hundred years after his death smacks of little historical understanding, particularly of the development of doctrine (Drewery 1985; Vogt 1987). About fifty years after Origen's demise, Eusebius elected not to speak of all the inspiring stories about him which were still told by the elders of that era (Eusebius, *H. E.* 6.33.4). Origen, as a monk who probably preached daily and wrote commentaries on nearly every book of the Bible, who wanted to avoid both questionable doctrine and practice, viewed himself as a devoted churchman (Origen, *Homilies on Joshua* 7.6; Baehrens 1921; Jaubert 1960; Origen, *Homilies on Luke* 16.6; Crouzel *et al.* 1962; Lienhard 1992). The church has not continuously embraced him, but the benefits of his work are too many to be cast aside as totally overshadowed by the shortcomings.

ORIGEN'S LIFE

Origen was born in Alexandria in about 185 CE into a Christian family, perhaps of recent converts. Its deep piety is displayed in the martyrdom of his father, Leonides, while his son was still young. Eusebius recounts how Origen himself avoided martyrdom in his teens only because his unnamed mother hid his clothes and thus did not let him go outside the house (*H. E.* 6.2). Eusebius tells us another tale, one that depicts Origen castrating himself in a carefully considered act of piety (*H. E.* 6.8). Whether true or false, the story indicates how hallowed hagiography attributed to him feats of overachieving, perhaps overreaching, holiness.

Such remarkable passions, combined with his intellectual brilliance, made him in his late teens the primary teacher in the Christian school at Alexandria. We should not doubt that a number of the more obvious candidates had been killed in persecutions, but every scrap of information we have about Origen, whether praising or attacking him, demands that we take him seriously as a Christian intellectual and scholar whose greatest interest was in centring the church on its scripture through the rule of faith. From boyhood the Bible had been his mainstay, memorized under his father's urging, deepened in public worship and questioned for its meaning within the loving confines of the home; prayer three times a day was the common practice. His father had also led him through classical Greek texts that formed the regular early education of upper-class children in Alexandria.

On his father's death, which probably entailed the confiscation of family property, a wealthy woman took responsibility for the boy's welfare. Although she had within her entourage an Antiochene teacher of suspect gnostic faith named Paul, Origen supposedly fended off his heretical teachings, did not pray with him and kept to the rule of faith which he had been taught. He evidently used the financial support to study with Ammonius Saccas, a noted Middle Platonist in Alexandria; at the same time he visited Christians in prison. Thus in spite of his age, he was worthy of the catechetical position, not the least because of his lived piety and his deep education in both the church and the academy. Students from both arenas came to study with him. Most took up what he commended as the true philosophic life even to the point of Christian martyrdom; others sought him out initially to learn more about the Greek heritage.

His growing reputation led him to visits with Christian friends and other churches: at least those in Rome, Jerusalem, the Caesareas in Palestine and Cappadocia, Nicomedia, congregations in Greece and others in 'Arabia'. One story tells of his meeting the emperor Alexander Severus' mother, Mamaea, at Antioch when she wanted to find out about this famous fellow. Origen left Alexandria in the early 230s during a dispute with his bishop, Demetrius, and took up permanent residence in Palestinian Caesarea among bishops who highly valued his biblical interpretation. On a previous visit, those bishops had listened intently to his homilies from scripture. Demetrius strongly objected to such preaching by a layman in the hearing of bishops, but the Palestinians leaders found the practice an accepted one within the church. Demetrius was able to recall the teacher on the first occasion, but then was adamant in his rebuke when Origen accepted the priesthood at the hands of those Palestinian bishops.

Origen finally experienced the martyrdom which early called him and had claimed his father. During a period of persecution, perhaps in 251 or a bit later, he succumbed to torture. In his last painful days he wrote letters of encouragement to others, ones unfortunately now lost (Eusebius, *H. E.* 6.1–5, 8, 14–19, 21, 23–32, 36–9; Schwartz and Mommsen 1903; Lawlor and Oulton 1927; Pamphilus, *Apologia pro Origene;* Migne *et al.* 1857)

ORIGEN'S WRITINGS

Origen began his writing career rather early. Another Alexandrian patron, a certain Ambrose, paid for seven scribes who in shifts took dictation from the prodigy. Preaching on scripture and composing commentaries on its text became the core of his intellectual life. Were he to teach on a modern theological faculty, he would probably be a professor of Old Testament, but one with so many interests in all the theological disciplines that in essence he would be a faculty in himself, yet more missionary, holistic and helpful than many.

His *Hexapla* was a piece without peer. He took the trouble to learn Hebrew, according to Eusebius not at all a common undertaking of Christian scholars. Thus his *Hexapla* began with the Hebrew text extant among Jews, probably not represented in Hebrew characters but by a transliteration of the Hebrew into Greek characters. Greek translations by Aquila and Symmachus came next, followed by a column devoted to the Septuagint. Any clause not in the Hebrew but in the Septuagint was set off with an obelus. Any Hebrew clause not in the Greek was designated with an asterisk. A translation into Greek by Theodotian formed the fifth column and a selection of other translations the sixth, although on occasion, as in Psalms, he made use of three more unnamed translations, one found not long before in a jar at Jericho. Apparently for those less concerned with the Hebrew, he also created a *Tetrapla* which was comprised of the four major Greek translations. This is surely one of the most unusual early textual projects of the church, although we do not know how many manuscripts Origen used for either his Hebrew text transliterated in Greek or his Septuagint text. Thus we have little idea how much this work involved the building of a critical text of scripture itself. In many ways he was not as deeply interested in the kind of textual study that fascinated Jerome, i.e., the establishment of the best text. Origen often preferred the richness of the variations as sources for his theological reflections.

Probably only one exemplar of the *Hexapla* ever existed. Now it remains in fragments, a Syriac copy of the fifth column, and in occasional comments in a few manuscripts of the Old Testament and a few extracts in writings of other Church Fathers (Nautin 1977: 303–61; Wright 1988; Munnich 1995).

Origen certainly did not begin commentary on Christian Scripture (Grant 1993). One translator of the Old Testament text, Symmachus, himself a Jewish Christian (Eusebius, *H. E.* 6.17; Schwartz and Mommsen 1903; Lawlor and Oulton 1927) had written a commentary on Matthew. A gnostic, Heracleon (only partially extant: Brooke 1967), mentioned by Origen in his own *eis to kata euaggelion Ioannên exêgêtikôn, (Commentary on John)*, had previously commented on that Gospel. But Origen was considered a master interpreter of scripture. In terms of both homilies and commentaries, he seems to have dealt with almost every book of the Bible. One of the saddest aspects of his career is that so little of that remarkable effort has reached us. Jerome (*Epistle* 33) says that Origen created scholia on Exodus, Leviticus, Isaiah, Psalms 1–15, Ecclesiastes and the Gospel of John. None of them are fully extant (Junod 1995), although certain *catenae* have some of the comments as does the *Philochalia* (Junod 1976; Harl 1983).

Quasten (1953: 46–7) noted that of 574 homilies known to us, only 20 in Greek and others in Latin are extant. Fully 388 are lost. The decision not to copy them, or to suppress them because of the Origenist controversy, leaves us without the many insights into Christian spirituality and mysticism which so richly enhanced much of Origen's corpus. Scripture spoke to him of deeper things than those which capture the attention of many modern historical-critical exegetes. Crouzel (1984: 75) insightfully insists that he preached in ways which remind us of the pastoral skills of a spiritual director.

The commentaries have fared a bit better, but many of them are no longer extant. Not one comes to us complete. Of the 25 books on Matthew, only eight survive in Greek. An anonymous Latin translation contains comments from 22:34–27:65 not contained in the Greek, but both texts lack reflections on 1:1–13:35 (Klostermann

1933, 1935, 1941; Girod 1970). Jerome's *Commentariorum in Matheum* (Hurst and Adriaen 1969; Bonnard 1977, 1979) depends much on Origen's work where the relationship can be checked. But we are left with uncertainty about the rest. Only eight of at least 32 books on John remain. Fifteen books on Romans are now reduced to a few Greek fragments in various sources and a ten-book translation into Latin by Rufinus which uses a Latin biblical text as its base (Bauernfeind 1923). Another Latin translation by Rufinus, this time of a commentary *In Canticum Canticorum* (Baehrens 1925), contains only four of the ten books. Jerome found that work to be the best of Origen's efforts.

Quasten (1953: 51) says that of 291 books of commentary, 275 are lost: 13 on Genesis, evidently some on Kings, 46 on 41 psalms, 30 on Isaiah, five on Lamentations, 25 on Ezekiel, 25 on the minor prophets, 15 on Luke, five on Galatians, three on Ephesians, as well as some on Philippians, Colossians, Thessalonians, Hebrews, Titus and Philemon. Only fragments remain in *catenae*, the margins of biblical manuscripts and quotations by other fathers.

Origen's *Peri archôn* (Koetschau 1913; Görgemanns and Karpp 1976; Crouzel and Simonetti 1978–84; Butterworth 1966) gives us a glimpse into his hermeneutic. The work has been viewed not only as a kind of sounding into the depths of theology, or an early attempt at systematics, but also as a piece itself centred on scriptural exegesis and the themes and questions which emerge when a brilliant scholar comes to the texts with the theological questions of his age (Daley 1998). The introduction carefully sets out both the affirmations and limits of Christian faith in its relationship to biblical interpretation. For Origen the rule of faith directs the church's teaching by leading it into what it will find expressed in the Bible. That is the rock from which Christian faith is hewn. But outside its boundaries there are remarkable areas of speculation which one seeking further knowledge should pursue. Any sound theology depends upon the life reflected in the rule of faith, yet there is no harm in playing with other questions which the interpreter or the world may want to ask. The simplest truths of scripture and the rule of faith will save the simple. The enlightened, however, may, indeed must, look into higher concerns (*Peri archôn*, Introduction; Koetschau 1913; Crouzel and Simonetti 1978–84; Butterworth 1966).

The very structure of scripture itself includes difficulties which alert the true learner to deeper meaning, ones which do not allow the exegete to be absorbed in the study of language alone. Things stated that are unworthy of God induce the student to turn from the letter to hear more from the Spirit. The primary aim of the biblical texts is to connect spiritual events that have already transpired with those that have yet to occur. To do that the Word brought into unity important mystical events and actual historical events. But scripture also tells tales which did not happen, ones that could never have happened, and ones that could have but did not (*Peri archôn* 4.2.9; Koetschau 1913; Görgemanns and Karpp 1976; Crouzel and Simonetti 1978–84; Butterworth 1966).

Picking up such cues by carefully reading scripture frees one's imagination, or, rather, empowers it to consider what would be worthy of God. Origen had been from his youth not only a student of Christian texts but also of texts from Greek philosophy, religion and other subjects. Gregory Thaumaturgus (*The Oration and*

Panegyric Addressed to Origen; Crouzel 1969; Salmon 1975; Slusser 1998) details how he led his students through those texts while he was a teacher in Caesarea of Palestine. He read them as they were being read, allegorically in the best and traditional ways. Hellenistic teachers of his era and earlier had interpreted valued ancient texts through categories of contemporary values. Not only the ancient classics like Homer, but also honoured philosophical, historical and medical texts were read with the sense that within them there were clues as to how their apparently odd stories and truisms were to be taken with seriousness in the third century. Since the Protestant Reformation this type of interpretation has struck many biblical scholars as an uncontrolled, subjective perversion of texts, yet it was the preferred way in which educated Hellenistic intellectuals reclaimed their sacred books. Origen's biblical project seems neither so odd nor so original when it is placed within the communities of readers who populated both Alexandria and Caesarea (Dawson 1992). Indeed, his penchant for offering more than one possible interpretation of a text rather than insisting that each verse has only one meaning alerts us to his sense of theology as a research programme which cannot be easily systematized (Vogt 1980; Crouzel 1984). Various points of his theology are given different, even contradictory expression, but their inclusion demonstrates not only his nimble intellect but also often his humility in knowing that he was unable to specify all aspects of Christian mystery. In his own times and even now he is pressed to consistency by theologians of lesser imagination and suffocating systematic correctness when he best fits within post-modern interests in a plurality of readings (Norris 1994).

His approach both allowed him to study scripture with infinite care and press questions from his immediate context. While in Palestine at Caesarea he visited various places mentioned in the Bible and commented on their locations and their names. He corrected some manuscripts in his possession on the basis of his own observations. He rejected the literal reading of some verses because they did not speak of God in a proper manner, one he had learned not only from the Christian community but also from the developed and detailed criticism of Greek gods which he had gained from Greek philosophers as well as influences in his Egyptian milieu (Bostock 1975). In ways that make one think of a good mission contextualist, he found knowledge of God in many circles and formed his fullest conception from them. Christian revelation was always his centre, but he heard the Word speaking in many places. That ability helped him make scripture available to sophisticated readers, to the elite of his society, at the same time that it did not exclude either the Bible or the liturgy from those who could not read.

ORIGEN'S THEOLOGY

In his earliest work of theology, *Peri archôn*, Origen first laid out what must guide every Christian theologian: the rule of faith. His rule varies to some degree from that found in Tertullian's North Africa and in the missionary Irenaeus' home in Asia Minor or his adopted Gaul. Yet Christian theology had a unity in the midst of its considerable diversity, one to which Origen appealed (Blowers 1997).

Rufinus' translation of the rule (*Peri archôn* 1.4–8; Koetschau 1913; Görgemanns and Karpp 1976; Crouzel and Simonetti 1978–84; Butterworth 1966) begins with God as the creator, both just and good, who was worshipped by all the ancient righteous ones of Israel, both patriarchs and prophets. That same God sent our Lord Jesus Christ to call first Israel and then, after their unbelief, the gentiles. He offered the Law, prophets and gospels. He is the apostle's God, that of both old and new covenants.

Christ Jesus was subordinate to the Father, spoken of either as begotten or created. He was present serving God at creation; all things were made through him. In these last days, he was made man, took on flesh although he remained God. Born of a virgin and the Holy Spirit, he truly suffered, died and was resurrected, lived for a while with his disciples and then was taken up.

The Holy Spirit shared honour and unity with the Father and the Son. Whether he was begotten or a Son of God, is open to investigation, but he is the one Spirit who inspired saints of the old and new covenants.

The human soul has its own life and substance. It will be held accountable for its actions and rewarded either in blessed life or eternal torment. There is a resurrection of the dead when the corruptible body will rise in glory. As a rational being the soul has free will and choice, for humans are not imprisoned in necessity.

The Devil and his angels are real, but exactly what they are and how they exist is not clearly explained. Most Christians, however, think Satan is a fallen angel who persuaded other angels to follow him. The world came into existence; it is not eternal and thus it will be dissolved. But what was before and what comes after this world is not set forth exactly in Christian teaching.

Scriptures are composed by the Spirit of God and have both obvious and hidden meanings.

The apostles delivered the above doctrine in the most simple expressions to the church. Yet they neither looked deeply into the grounds for all those statements nor restricted Christian theology to those beliefs. If the rule of faith determines the scope of scripture, its core, and the letter of scripture can save the simple, then speculation about many subjects only partially suggested by biblical verses may be entertained and developed. At the same time different views of what a particular passage meant or what it means in conjunction with other passages may be held in tension without final resolution.

The resulting theological richness of these views is extraordinary. They have proved quite threatening to many who did not enjoy the ambiguity and often settled the question of what Origen really taught by choosing the suggestion which to them seemed the most heretical. During his lifetime, however, Origen found many within the church who followed the rule of faith and accepted him. Invitations from all over the Mediterranean to preach, teach and serve in debates or discussions indicate that. At the same time he dealt with a series of Christian opponents whose views he contested. Among the simple believers whom he loved and tried to care for, sometimes in a condescending way yet often in a pastoral manner, were anthropomorphists. These folk read or heard scripture literally and thus were willing to insist that God had arms and legs. They also thought that a resurrection body would be the earthly body brought back to life without any sense of the transformation which the apostle Paul had stated (Armantage 1971: 397–414). Origen found both views to be absurd, yet in spite of his anger with such interpretations, he could not bring himself to reject simple believers. They had a place in the church, although their views at times had to be rejected (McGuckin 1995). The letter of the Bible could kill, but it also could save. The church needed to believe, confess and teach the rule, study scripture attentively, and not insist on anthropomorphic readings of texts about God so that the intellectual elite of the Mediterranean would be forced out of its embrace.

If Origen did not want to alienate illiterate believers, he also did not want to succumb to the flights of fancy that he found propagated by certain intellectuals within the church. Modern historians have had great difficulty explaining exactly what Gnosticism was in the early third century (see Chapter 35 of this volume), but such teachings and the people who proposed them were influential. During Origen's lifetime or soon after, Greek philosophers like Plotinus and later Porphyry were attacking some gnostic ideas; thus we may infer that such views were not limited to Christian circles. They appeared within Hellenistic culture and, in mission terms, could easily have been seen as important bridges to educated people outside the church as well as those inside it. Discussions of evil, its relationship to divinity, the nature of the material and spiritual worlds, the purpose of human life now and hereafter marked many communities.

What are sometimes referred to as protognostic themes have been found within the New Testament, but it is not clear that actual gnostic groups with theologians who logically organized the teachings were functioning within Christianity that early. The attempt within Christian congregations to develop coherent patterns of gnostic thought seems to begin in earnest during the second half of the second century, but the extant texts from such teachers and their communities are notoriously fragmentary. Even the richness of the Nag Hammadi documents has only opened up questions about Gnosticism in dramatic new ways. Those proponents and their circles who are most in evidence as opponents of Origen are still not known thoroughly. If he is difficult to systematize, so are they. He is often represented in extracts of his thought chosen by those who take them out of context and use them to prove he is a heretic. Too often Origen's opponents have been treated similarly.

Three such groups stand out in Origen's Alexandrian and Caesarean contexts: followers of Basilides, Valentinus and Marcion. Modern interpreters do not consider Marcion (died *c.* 154) to have been primarily a gnostic. As best we can tell about a man from whom we have no full texts and whose views come to us from opponents who consider him a dangerous heretic, he did not involve himself in speculations about souls and worlds in the ways that many gnostics did. Born in Sinope in Pontus, the son of a rich shipbuilder, he evidently experienced some difficulty with Christian authorities there, went to Rome, studied with the gnostic, Cerdon, and eventually set up his own well-financed and well-organized church which spread throughout the Mediterranean basin and east of Antioch. What brought his work into the debates that concern Origen was his insistence that the creator-God who made the material world was evil. The God of the Old Testament was not to be worshipped because he was not good. Texts of what became the New Testament gospels had been thoroughly interpolated by Judaizers, which is what the apostles actually were. Only the Gospel of Luke, filtered on the basis of Paul's non-Judaizing teachings, could be seen as providing a genuine portrait of Jesus (Harnack 1990; *Second Century* 1987–8). Origen indicates his rejection of Marcion's views directly (*Contra Celsum* 6.53 and 74 *inter alia*; Chadwick 1965; Borret 1967–9, 1976). His extensive allegorical interpretation of the Old Testament and his commentaries and homilies on the gospels indicate that he found the God of Hebrew and Christian scriptures to be the same, good deity. He dealt with difficult passages, not by assuming interpolations of the texts, but by insisting that problematic literal texts were there to alert the reader to the true allegorical meanings underneath.

Basilides, probably a Syrian who taught in Alexandria during the second quarter of the second century, more easily fits a common gnostic definition, but he also is represented to us only by his opponents. Apparently he was neither forced out of the Christian community in Alexandria nor did he choose to leave it. If he had a fully developed system, it is not retrievable from our sources. According to the myths spelled out in contradictory details by his enemies, Irenaeus (*Adversus Haereses* [*Against All Heresies*] 1.24; Roberts and Rambaut 1951; Rousseau *et al.* 1965–82) and Hippolytus (*The Refutation of All Heresies* 7.20–7 [7–15]; Nautin 1949; MacMahon 1951) he taught that the God of the Jews was a lower archon, responsible for much of the misery in creation, an autocrat who needed teaching. The high God, who is totally transcendent and can only be described by negative comments concerning what he is not, attempted to free humans. He sent his *nous* in Jesus Christ who delivered the knowledge necessary to get through the many levels of reality to the final abode of the supreme God. The Christ only appeared to have a material body. He did not suffer on the cross; Simon of Cyrene was crucified. The limited humanity of Christ allowed him to communicate with human souls but not be imprisoned in evil flesh. Some suggested that Basilides could count as many as 365 heavens through which a soul, freed from its material body, had to pass in order to reach home. Like Marcion, Basilides was deeply concerned with Christian scripture. One of his writings, no longer extant, carried the title *Exegetica*. What some consider to be genuine fragments of his work indicate that he knew a few of the Pauline epistles, Matthew, and perhaps wrote commentary on 1 Peter 4. Although Origen did speculate about souls before and after this life, he neither rejected the God of the Old Testament nor made him responsible for the imprisonment of souls in evil bodies.

Valentinus (fl. 120–60), born in Egypt and educated in Alexandria, evidently taught in Rome beginning perhaps as early as 136; he left there in 160 and basically disappeared from view. For years he also was known primarily from descriptions of the early heresiologists, but the *Evangelium Veritatis* (*Gospel of Truth*; MacRae 1977) may actually be a writing from him. It certainly represents his school. The other quotations of him, however, come from epistles and sermons; neither they nor the *Evangelium Veritatis* give us a deep sense of what his system may have been like, if indeed it was a system. Irenaeus claims it was (*Against All Heresies* 1.1; 2.14; Rousseau *et al.* 1965–82; Roberts and Rambout 1951). The myth seems to be similar to that found in the Sethian *Apocryphon of John* (Waldstein and Wisse 1995) and aspects of *Eugnostos* (Parrott 1991), both adjusted to Valentinus' own thinking. There is no way to be certain whether Valentinus belonged to a larger group of Christians in Alexandria who were deeply interested in gnostic themes or whether he was first persuaded by various gnostics and then added Christian elements to their teachings.

What we can glean from Irenaeus' description of Valentinus in particular suggests Platonic features beginning with a differentiation between parallel worlds of ideas and phenomena. Many aeons, existing in pairs, had offspring. The God of the Old Testament, the lowest of those, created the material world. Salvation of humans was procured by the aeon Christ who united with the human Jesus at his baptism and brought the knowledge necessary for salvation. Those created as 'pneumatics' like the Valentinians would receive that gnosis and eventually become part of the pleroma. 'Catholics' were only made 'psychics', who through faith and works could enter a middle level but never the pleroma. Most of humankind were formed as 'hylics', content to be imprisoned in matter and thus doomed.

Valentinus also was an exegete of Christian scripture; evidence for his use of Matthew, John and Romans appears in various fragments. The *Evangelium Veritatis* speaks of the writings of God's church and seems to know Matthew, John, Romans, 1 and 2 Corinthians, Ephesians, Colossians, Hebrews, 1 John and Revelation (Trigg 1983; Pearson 1990). Heracleon (Brooke 1967), a Valentinian leader in Rome, evidently wrote a commentary on John, one to which Origen responded in his John commentary.

Valentinian teachings about the eternal generation of the Son, the Fall, ecclesiology and the Christian life were similar to those which Origen advocated (Scott 1992). We can rather easily imagine at what points Origen would have contested a Valentinian myth by remembering his sense of the rule of faith. He specifically says that Valentinians had changed the gospel. They were wrong to think people were damned or saved on the basis of how they were created; their speculations about circles in circles as well as their understanding that wisdom should be represented as a virgin named Prunicus made no sense (Origen, *Contra Celsum* 2.27; 5.61; 6.34–5; Borret 1967–9, 1976; Chadwick 1965).

Not all of the opponents to whom Origen responded were those from within the broadest definition of the Christian community. Celsus, an intelligent proponent of what he considered to be traditional Graeco-Roman religion, had died before Origen was born. His *Alethês logos* (*On True Doctrine*; Hoffman 1987) was seen as being an important attack on Christianity, one which Origen's patron Ambrose thought was worth answering. Modern historians have debated who this Celsus was: a friend of Lucian of Samosata identified as an Epicurean and opponent of magic, or someone basically unknown from other texts. At present most view him as a Middle Platonist, seeing Origen as labelling him an Epicurean to make him an easier target. He had studied Christian texts, probably Genesis, Matthew, Luke and 1 Corinthians, and had talked or debated with many Christians including Marcionites and an almost endless collection of Christian Gnostics. His work appears to be the first systematic attack on Christianity from outside, at least the first still available in large part because Origen quoted much of the treatise in his *Contra Celsum* (*Against Celsus*; Chadwick 1965; Borret 1967–9, 1976). Although Celsus' effort may be called encyclopaedic, it turns around a series of points. Christians have rejected traditional religion, even their own precursors, the Jews, and thus are a real threat to societal cohesion. They see themselves as a separate nation. Emperors have been correct to outlaw them. Their writings about their leader Jesus are inconsistent; they clearly indicate that they have been redacted many times in attempts to cover up his background as a deceiver and a sorcerer. His death shows he was not immortal. The teaching about resurrection is offensive nonsense. His deeds are no better, in some instances less good, than those of other religious leaders.

Christians themselves are low life: mostly slaves, trades people, women and children. They reject education of the intellect as the way to virtue. They have split into innumerable sects and thus present no unified sense of truth. Their god is evil, an unskilled creator who could not get it right the first time. He is not all powerful, indeed quite inferior to the impassible god of Greek philosophy. It is remarkably silly that these folk, who worship such a deity, can be so exclusive and tribal.

Origen's *Contra Celsum* (Borret 1967–9, 1976; Chadwick 1965) in particular and Gregory Thaumaturgus' *The Oration and Panegyric addressed to Origen (Eis Origenês prosphônêtikos kai panêgurikos logos)* (Crouzel 1969; Salmon 1975; Slusser 1998), well indicate Origen's relationship to Greek philosophy. Although Origen early in his life had sold his library of Greek literature, when he turned his attention to teaching theology, to instructing students in the ascetic, mystical way of Christian life, he found it necessary to have them thoroughly study philosophers. Thaumaturgus tells us that he only excluded writers who denied either that God existed or that divine providence operated in the world. His students were required to read carefully and look for the features of that literature which could be pulled out and appropriated by Christians. As ancient Israel plundered Egypt of its treasures and built them into their liturgy, so intellectual Christians should make the riches of the Graeco-Roman and Egyptian heritages their own and use them for God, for misused riches they surely were (Origen, *Philocalia* 13.2; Harl 1983; Walls 1997). At first glimpse this approach, known as 'the despoliation of the Egyptians', seems a rapacious one; in some ways it is. But it has the distinct advantage that it expects to find truth in Egyptian and Hellenistic philosophy, religion and culture. It follows in the line of earlier apologists who argued vigorously for the ultimate wisdom of Christian revelation and rejected thoughts and practices they found wanting while at the same time they insisted that the entire cultural and religious heritage around them was not false. Origen and his students employed the methods of investigating texts which had been developed in the Greek schools. They studied grammar, rhetoric (Torjesen 1995), logic and dialectic, the natural sciences, geometry and astronomy as well as ethics and theology. For Origen such study had missionary purposes.

The eclectic borrowing from Greek philosophy is so intricate and pervasive that it can be seen rather clearly in a number of Origen's commentaries on scripture. Those works themselves resemble commentaries on Aristotle (Heine 1995). It is probably fair to think of Origen as a Middle Platonist, who gained much from the mystical, idealistic sides of the great Platonic heritage. His interest in logic suggests that despite his rejection of Aristotle's view of the eternity of the world, he made more use of Aristotle than some have thought (Pichler 1980). Origen certainly knew Stoic logic very well; aspects of its developments which are not represented directly in any extant Stoic writings or fragments may be gleaned from his work (Roberts 1971). He uses it unobtrusively in his commentaries (Heine 1993).

No list of opponents would be complete without mention of third-century

Judaism. Origen inherited a tradition of high regard for Philo from Clement of Alexandria (Runia 1992). Probably both in Alexandria and in Caesarea, Origen listened to Jewish rabbis concerning the Old Testament. It is quite likely that whatever facility he had in Hebrew came from the Jewish community. Yet at the same time that he depended upon them, he saw them as adversaries. Apparently Judaism had not ceased to be a missionary religion; it sought proselytes. And in many ways it remained one of the strongest antagonists. Origen knows about Christians who were swayed by Jewish ritual and practice, and indeed of Christians who converted (De Lange 1975; Blowers 1988). The intricate interweaving of his relationships with Jews is probably seen best, not only in his commentaries which indicate his discussions and debates, but also in his *Contra Celsum* where he responded to the construction by Celsus of a dialogue between a Christian and a Jew. There he contests both characterizations.

Working out from the rule of faith through opposition to Christian anthropomorphists and gnostics, traditional Egyptian and Greek religion, Hellenistic philosophy as well as Judaism we can see a deeper understanding of Origen's theology. The nature of God as incorporeal may not be as clear in scripture as it might be, but God is certainly immaterial. There are not two gods as the Marcionites insisted, one demiurge who was evil and created material things as gnostics taught. In a strange and unexpected way Origen took over the biblical insight of God suffering. There was reason to think of divinity as immutable, incorporeal, uncircumscribed, all the many adjectives that could be found in most descriptions which appear in Graeco-Roman and Egyptian religions. At the heart of Christian faith, however, is a suffering Father, one who could through certain aspects of his nature be above such things, yet because of his controlling love could be moved by the prayers and cries of those who sought him out. The pastoral concern of Origen himself, his attempt to be a spiritual director of consequence, both within his teaching and within his relationships with those around him, came from his grasp of God's own compassionate suffering. Celsus was wrong that God the Father sent his Son to suffer because he himself was not capable of suffering, was by nature above and beyond such material and lesser concerns. God was above and beyond, but by choice he was also nearby and within.

Christ Jesus was unclearly subordinate to the Father in Origen's thought. Prayer was not to be offered in the name of Jesus (Origen, *De oratione*; Koetschau 1899a; Greer 1979). The texts we have which deal with the questions of the Son's nature are not symphonic but dissonant (McGuckin 1987). Christ was there at creation, the one through whom everything was created, but he was also the first born of creation. The later careful distinctions between 'made' and 'begotten', which begin in the fourth-century Arian controversy and are most clearly stated by the Cappadocians, do not function in third-century debates. Yet even the Cappadocians are not always consistent in their efforts to distinguish the Greek *genêtos*, 'made', from *gennêtos*, 'begotten', as manuscripts of their works indicate (Norris 1991: 121, 135). Thus we can hardly be astonished that Origen does not have such precisely delineated features in his doctrine of Christ. He gives the Son honour and authority along with the Father and carefully involves the human soul in what later theologians would call the person of Jesus Christ (Williams 1975). Indeed we now know from Origen's

Dialogue with Heraclides (*Origenous dialektoi pros Hêrakleidan kai tous sun autô episkopous*; Scherer 1960; Daly 1992), discovered at Tura, south of Cairo in 1941, that he insisted on a human soul in Jesus for the sake of the Christian economy of salvation. 'What was not assumed was not saved' that stunning formula previously known to us from Gregory Nazianzen (*Epistle* 101; Browne and Swallow 1954; Gallay 1974) in his anti-Apollinarian correspondence of the later fourth century, had been bequeathed to the church by Origen nearly one hundred and fifty years earlier.

The Holy Spirit forms a part of Origen's rule of faith, but the sense of that Spirit in his theology is developed further. Certainly in the view of an exegete like Origen, the inspiration of scripture, the structuring of the texts with literal anomalies that alert the reader to deeper meanings, holds a primary place in the work of the Spirit. That Spirit has separate personal existence and thus may be spoken of as one of three in Trinity. But the reality both goes beyond the limits of human language in any age and does not yet reflect the technical terms that will be employed in particularly the fourth and fifth centuries.

The Spirit is deeply involved in the development of holiness through a life of disciplined virtue. Prayer and everyday living are unthinkable without the Spirit. Communion with, indeed union with, God depends on the work of the Spirit; full indwelling of the Holy Spirit reaches divinization although that goal is also related to the Father and the Son (Berthold 1992).

Origen's understanding of the soul and the body of each human becomes in many ways the focus of much of the controversy concerning his views. He posited pre-existent souls as a way to counter the determinism of astrology as well as the gnostic and Marcionite insistence that an evil demiurge was responsible for the horrors of the material world. Origen was a pastor at heart, one movingly grieved by the pressing problems he and people around him faced. If God was the great creator, both good and just, and there was no other who was responsible for such travesties as people experienced daily, what was a Christian theologian to say? The area of specu-lation, necessary not only for the intelligent, educated questioner but also the sorrowing, illiterate peasant, concerned both what came before and after the creation and the consummation of the world. If souls had existed before the world, if their lives in that existence were marked by their freedom and the consequent responsibility for their actions, then what happened in earthly lives could not be laid solely at the feet of God. He created souls and offered them choices. What they experienced in earthly life was a reward or punishment for their previous deeds.

In his understanding of the rule of Christian faith, this area had not been determined by the church; there was no consensus. The openness for such speculation was important because this was the arena in which he could bring scripture, worship and pastoral care to bear on the daily sadness of life. Even Origen's ideas about stars being alive and with souls, which drew on traditions in Greek philosophy and probably some of his gnostic opponents, focused on particular theological problems raised well outside the bounds of Hellenistic philosophy. He attacked Marcionites and others who demeaned God the Creator on the basis of his sense of theodicy and its relationship to the stars themselves. Their movement pointed not to astrological determinism but to the free and moral will of rational beings, not just humans but all who were led to respond to the unified divine law of God. Stars influenced the natural order, not humans, because they themselves had sinned in their pre-existent forms and were thus doing penance in their reduced status (Scott 1991).

Origen flirted with the possibility of reincarnation when he speculated in his *Commentary on the Gospel according to John* (*eis to kata Ioannên euaggelion exêgêtikôn* 2.180–9; Preuschen 1903; Heine 1989) about who John the Baptist actually was, perhaps an angel, perhaps the Holy Spirit. He denied that the Baptist was the Holy Spirit in his *Homilies on Luke* (*Homiliae in Lucem* 4.4; Rauer 1959; Lienhard 1996) and in his *Commentary on Matthew's Gospel* (*eis to kata Mathaion euaggelion exêgêtikôn* 13.1–2; Klostermann 1933, 1935, 1941; Girod 1970) he vigorously rejected the transmigration of souls (Lienhard 1992). In words that pushed not only towards but into a doctrine of universal salvation, he insisted on the victorious love of God which in the end would overcome all. But in a letter quoted by his proponent Rufinus and his antagonist Jerome, he denied as totally absurd any suggestion that Satan himself ultimately would be saved (Jerome, *Apology against Rufinus* 42–4; Hritzen 1965; Laudet 1982; Rufinus, *De alteratione librorum Origenis* 10–13 [Dell' Era 1983]; Norris 1992).

The impression left in his developed hermeneutic does not sit well with all. The brilliant exegete from an early age was not particularly taken with the prowess of the masses within the church. He did not in any way want to put their salvation in jeopardy. Indeed as he says in his *Contra Celsum* (3.44–55), it is surely true that children and women, some hysterical, can be found within Christian congregations. Since God wanted to save all, they should be there, but they do not teach. Only his growing compassionate heart keeps him from being the type of theologian many church people still fear: haughty, dismissive, ruthless. It is in such light that his numerous readings of scriptural texts without making a final decision, his multiple interpretations of individual biblical passages and thus his sometimes convoluted theological musings, are to be understood. Theology should be imaginative; it should be open where the church has not closed it. But its primary structure lies in the rule of faith, stated literally in scripture for the salvation of the simple and not to be gainsaid by the intellectual as if it demanded the suicide of the mind.

It is fitting to end this chapter with a look at Origen's theology spelled out in his *On Prayer* (*Peri euchês*) and *On Martyrdom* (*Eis marturion protreptikos*), treatises written in Caesarea at the height of his career. The first (Koetschau 1899a; Greer 1979), extant in only one late Greek manuscript with no Latin translation, was known to those of the fourth and fifth centuries who debated Origen's orthodoxy. Three considerations may have been involved in the near catastrophe of losing this piece: first, Origen says that the Son is subordinate; prayer is not to be offered in Jesus' name. Other sentences suggest that all prayer is directed to God through Christ, but the ambiguity left Origen open to frontal attack. Second, there is an odd lack of practicality because the concerns of life in a material body appear at times to be irrelevant. Even praying for daily bread is turned into a request for supersubstantial food for the soul. Third, prayer is treated almost entirely as a private exercise. Its place in the liturgical life of a worshipping church is not emphasized.

Each of these aspects, however, has its own strength. First, Jesus prayed to God; the Son did not demand a place greater than that of the Father. Second, surely the deepest Christian prayer deals daily with more than bread. And the Greek word *epiousios* is not a normal usage for 'daily' as Origen insisted and modern lexicographers agree (Bauer 1979: 296–7). Third, a man who preached regularly, perhaps daily, who worked so diligently within the church of his age and looked forward to its consummation, cannot be faulted as an individualist (Crouzel 1984: 219–66). He here wants prayer to be so much a part of each person's life that it marks those times outside worship together.

The work has considerable merit. The transcendence of God which is basic to his sense of worship receives a prominent place. Prayer in response to grace is the attitude in which reason begins to think clearly about the possibility of knowing impossibilities (Junod 1980). It may be offered to God through the Spirit when we do not know how to word our requests. Four types of prayer are distinguished: adoration, petition, entreaty and thanksgiving, each addressed to God. The last three might be addressed to deceased saints, but adoration can only be expressed to God the Father, not even the Son.

Praying without ceasing is a difficulty, but also a key to how all of life must be a prayer. Directions for prayer at least three times a day, standing and facing east, provide a disciplined routine in which rather oddly for one who does not always find the body a helper, its position in prayer can be of assistance. The growth of the soul occurs not only in deep contemplative prayer but also in practised virtue following Christ (Crouzel 1984: 97–8). The rather discursive commentary on the Lord's Prayer shows both the scholar comparing the texts of Matthew and Luke and the pastor reaching out through scripture to every Christian seeking God's will.

The mature theologian who as a youth wanted to follow his father into a martyr's death now reflected on the theme again in his *Exhortation to Martyrdom* (*Eis marturion protreptikos;* Koetschau 1899a; Greer 1979). His experience had been like that of all other Christians in his era: periods of peace punctuated with times of persecution. The occasion of this rather hurried writing, however, was a request from his patron Ambrose and one named Protoctetus, both of whom faced the possibility of persecution.

As a pastor and son of a martyr Origen knows the pain and fear involved in the government's demand to sacrifice in worship to the emperor. But idolatry and apostasy represent a severe danger to the soul and the person's loved ones. God, the angels and the demons are among the spectators at the martyr's contest. Staying faithful to God in one's inner heart while making the required public sacrifice only strengthens the demons. At all costs each person must face persecution squarely and trust that standing fast through death is the greatest achievement possible in human life, the surest way to union with God and helpfulness to others. Sins committed after baptism, both those of the persecuted one and those who pray to that one, can be forgiven through faithful suffering unto death. The path of martyrdom leads to the throne of God where one not only lives in eternal blessedness but one also can hear the prayers of people on earth. Christian honour given to the martyrs, praying to them, is appropriate.

Origen was forced to consider his own advice. He closed his life as a martyr, both accepting the torment of persecution and calling others to hold fast. Whatever one thinks about his theological speculations, his intellectual imagination, moral activity and spiritual depth were crowned with martyrdom.

CONCLUSION

According to Eusebius (*H. E.* 6.39), Origen was brutally tortured for a man of his age. He thus imitated his Christ, followed his earthly father and wrote encouragement to the community in which he lived and served. Later theologians have always been able to find aspects of his life and theology to be less than they demand. But the positive contribution of this ascetic, exegete, mystic, mission theologian and spiritual director, with all its deficiencies, towers over that of nearly all others.

The development of mystical theology in the Cappadocians, in Maximus the Confessor (Blowers 1992), in a number of orthodox stalwarts of later ages, is impossible to understand without the gifts which Origen gave. Erasmus, now recognized as a theologian of consequence, is inexplicable without his dependence on Origen, the exegete and theologian (Godin 1982). Even in the late nineteenth and early twentieth centuries, figures from different traditions, particularly Roman Catholics, have relied on him for positive themes as well as treating him as a repulsive abrasive who polished them. Crouzel (1984), Daniélou (1959) and De Lubac (1998) in their lives and their scholarship were deeply formed by their encounter with Origen. Balthasar (1984), the only twentieth-century theologian who may surpass Barth, had both heart and head shaped by Origen. Even R. P. C. Hanson (1959), who saw in Origen the precursor of the despised Bultmann, used this father of the church as a template for important contemporary discussion. Andrew Walls, the dean of mission historians, points out that Origen was the first professor of mission studies, the model for remaking missiology for the twenty-first century (Walls 1999). Whatever form ecumenical theology takes in the twenty-first century, it will be better if it can wrestle from Origen the way, the truth and the life which he sought and embodied.

BIBLIOGRAPHY

Primary Sources

Origen

Baehrens, W. A. (ed.) (1921) *Die Homilien zu Numeri, Josua und Judices*. GCS 30.

—— (ed.) (1925) *In Canticum Canticorum*. GCS 33.

Bauernfeind, Otto (1923) *Der Römerbrieftext des Origenes nach dem Codex 184 B 64*. Texte und Üntersuchungen 44, 3.

Blanc, Cécile (ed.) (1966–92) *Commentaire sur saint Jean*. SC 120, 157, 222, 290, 385.

Borret, Marcel (ed.) (1967–9, 1976) *Contre Celse*. SC 132, 136, 147, 150, 227.

Butterworth, George Williams (trans.) (1966) *On First Principles*. New York: Harper & Row.

Chadwick, Henry (trans.) (1965) *Contra Celsum*. Cambridge: Cambridge University Press.

Crouzel, Henri and Simonetti, Manlio (eds) (1978–84) *Traité des Principes*. SC 252, 253, 268, 269, 312.

Crouzel, Henri, Fournier, François, and Périchon, Pierre (eds) (1962) *Homélies sur l'Évangile de saint Luc*. SC 87.

Daly, Robert J. (trans.) (1992) *Treatise on the Passover and Dialogue of Origen with Heraclides*. ACW 54.

Girod, Robert (ed.) (1970) *Commentaire sur l'Évangile selon Matthieu*. SC 162.

Görgemanns, Herwig and Karpp, Heinrich (eds) (1976) *Origenes vier Bücher von den Prinzipien*. Darmstadt: Wissenschaftliche Buchgesellschaft.

Greer, Rowan (ed.) (1979) *Origen: An Exhortation to Martyrdom, Prayer, First Principles: Book IV, Prologue to the Commentary on the Song of Songs, Homily XXVII on Numbers*. The Classics of Western Spirituality. New York: Paulist Press.

Harl, Marguerite (ed.) (1983) *Philocalia 1–20*. SC 302. New York: Harper & Row.

Heine, Ronald E. (ed.) (1989) *Commentary on the Gospel according to John*. FC 80, 89.

Jaubert, Annie (ed.) (1960) *Homélies sur Josué*. SC 71.

Junod, Éric (ed.) (1976) *Philocalia 21–27*. SC 226.

Klostermann, Erich (ed.) (1933, 1935, 1941) *Matthäuserklärung*. GCS 38, 40, 41.

Koetschau, Paul (ed.) (1899a) *De Oratione*. GCS 3, 297–403.

—— (ed.) (1899b) *Exhortatio ad martyrium*. GCS 3, 1–47.

—— (ed.) (1913) *De principiis*. GCS 22.

Lienhard, Joseph T. (trans.) (1996) *Homilies on Luke; Fragments on Luke*. FC 54.

Preuschen, Erich (ed.) (1903) *Johanneserklärung*. GCS 20.

Rauer, Max (ed.) (1959) *Die Homilien zu Lukas in der Übersetzung des Hieronymus und die griechischen Reste der Homilien und des Lucas-Kommentars*. GSC 49 (35).

Scherer, Jean (ed.) (1960) *Entretien avec Héraclide*. SC 67.

Other sources

Bardy, Gustave (ed.) (1950) *Augustine: Les revisions*. Texte de l'édition Bénédictine. Paris: Desclée de Brouwer.

—— (ed.) (1952–8) Eusebius, *Histoire écclesiastique*. SC 31, 41, 55, 73.

Bogan, Mary Inez (ed.) (1968) *Augustine: The Retractions*. FC 60.

Bonnard, Émile (ed.) (1977, 1979) (Jerome) *Commentaire sur Sainte Matthieu*. SC 242, 259.

Brooke, Alan England (ed.) (1967) *Heracleon, The Fragments of*. Theological Studies 1.4. Nendeln, Liechtenstein: Kraus.

Browne, Charles Gordon and Swallow, James Edward (trans.) (1954) 'Letters on the Apollinarian Controversy', in Edward Rochie Hardy, with Cyril C. Richardson (eds) *Christology of the Later Fathers*. LCC 3, 215–32 (Gregory of Nazianzen).

Crouzel, Henri (ed.) (1969) (Gregory Thaumaturgus) *Remerciement à Origène*. SC 148.

Migne, J. P., Delarue, Caroli and Vincentii Caroli (eds) (1857) *Pamphilus: Apologia pro Origene*. PG 17, 521–616.

Dell' Era, Antonia (ed.) (1983) (Rufinus) *De alteratione librorum Origenis*. Collana di testi stoici 15. L'Aquila: L. U. Japadre.

Foerster, W. and Wilson, R. Mcl. (eds) (1972) *Gnosis: A Selection of Gnostic Texts*, Vol. 1. Oxford: Clarendon, 162–83.

Fremantle, W. H., Lewis, G. and Martley, W. G. (trans.) (1952) *Letter 33. The Principal Works of Jerome*. NPNF 6, 46.

Gallay, Paul (ed.) (1974) *Grégoire de Nazianze: Lettres Théologique*. SC 208.

Hilberg, Isidorus (ed.) (1910, 1912, 1918) (Jerome) *Epistulae*. CSEL 54–6.

Hoffman, Joseph (trans.) (1987) (Celsus) *On the True Doctrine*. Oxford: Oxford University Press.

Hritzu, John N. (ed.) (1965) (Jerome) *The Apology Against the Books of Rufinus*. FC 53.

Hurst, D. and Adriaen, M. (eds) (1969) (Jerome) *Commentariorum in Matheum*. CCL 77.

Knöll, Pius (ed.) (1902) *Sancti Aureli Augustini Retractionem libri duo*. CSEL 36.

Laudet, Pierre (ed.) (1982) (Jerome) *Apologia contra Rufinum*. CCL 79.

Lawlor, Hugh Jackson and Oulton, John Ernest Leonard (trans.) (1927) *Eusebius: The Ecclesi-*

astical History and the Martyrs of Palestine. London: Society for Promoting Christian Knowledge.

MacMahon, J. H. (trans.) (1951) *Hippolytus: The Refutation of All Heresies*. ANF 5, 9–153.

MacRae, George W. (trans.) (1977) *Gospel of Truth*. *The Nag Hammadi Library in English*, (ed.) James Robinson. San Francisco: Harper & Row, 37–49.

Malinine, Michel, Puech, Henri-Charles and Quispel, Gilles (eds) (1956–61) *Evangelium Veritatis: Codex Jung*. Studien aus dem C. G. Jung-Institut 6. Zurich: Rasher.

Mansi, J. D., Martin, J. B. and Petit, L. *et al.* (eds) (1960–1) *Sacrorum conciliorum nova et amplissima collectio . . . , nova et amplissima collectio*. Graz: Akademische Druck und Verlagsanstalt.

Nautin, Pierre (ed.) (1949) *Hippolyte: Contre les hérésies, fragment, étude et édition critique*. Études et textes pour l'histoire du dogme de la Trinité 2. Paris: Études du Cerf.

Norris, Frederick W. (1991) *Faith Gives Fullness to Reasoning: The Five Theological Orations of Gregory Nazianzen*, intro. and com. Frederick W. Norris; trans. Lionel Wickham and Frederick Williams. Leiden: E. J. Brill

Parrot, Douglas M. (ed.) (1991) *Eugnostos and the Sophia of Jesus Christ*. Nag Hammadi Studies 27. Leiden: E. J. Brill.

Richardson, Ernest Cushing (ed.) (1896) (Jerome:) *De viris illustribus*. Texte und Üntersuchungen 14.1a.

—— (trans.) (1952) (Jerome) *Lives of Illustrious Men*. NPNF 3, 359–84.

Roberts, A. and Rambaut, W. H. (eds) (1951) *Against All Heresies, Irenaeus: Writings*. T. ANF 1, 309–578.

Rousseau, A., Doutreleau, L. and Mercier, C. (eds) (1965–82) (Irenaeus) *Contre les Heresies*. SC 100, 152, 153, 210, 211, 263, 264, 293, 294.

Salmon, S. D. F. (trans.) (1975) (Gregory Thaumaturgus: *The Oration and Panegyric Addressed to Origen*.) ANF 6, 21–39.

Schwartz, Eduard and Mommsen, Theodor (1903, 1908) *Eusebius' Kirchengeschichte*. Die griecheschen christlichen Schriftsteller.

Slusser, Michael (trans.) (1998) *Address of Thanksgiving to Origen* in *St. Gregory Thaumatungus: Life and Works*. FC 98, 91–126. Washington, DC: Catholic University of America.

Simonetti, Manlio (ed.) (1961) (Rufinus) *De alteratione librorum Origenis*. CCL 20.

Tanner, Norman P., Albergio, G. *et al.* (eds) (1990) *Decrees of the Ecumenical Councils*. London: Sheed & Ward.

Waldstein, Michael and Wisse, Frederick (eds) (1995) *The Apocryphon of John*. Nag Hammadi and Manichaean Studies (formerly Nag Hammadi Studies) 33. Leiden: E. J. Brill.

Secondary literature

Armantage, James (1971) 'Will the Body be Raised? Origen and the Origenist Controversies'. Ph.D. Dissertation, Yale University.

Balthasar, Hans Ur von (1984) *Origen, Spirit and Fire: A Thematic Anthology of His Writings*, trans. Robert Daly. Washington, DC: Catholic University of America Press.

Bauer, Walter (1979) *A Greek–English Lexicon of the New Testament and Other Early Christian Literature*, 2nd edn, trans., rev. and augmented by F. Wilbur Gingrich and Frederick W. Danker. Chicago: University of Chicago Press.

Berthold, Georg C. (1992) 'Origen and the Holy Spirit', *Origeniana Quinta*, 444–8.

Blowers, Paul M. (1988) 'Origen, the Rabbis, and the Bible: Toward a Picture of Judaism and Christianity in the Third Century', *Origen of Alexandria*, 96–116.

—— (1992) 'The Logology of Maximus the Confessor in His Criticism of Origenism', *Origeniana Quinta*, 570–6.

—— (1997) 'The *Regula Fidei* and the Narrative Character of Early Christian Faith', *Pro Ecclesia*, 199–228.

Bostock, D. Gerald (1975) 'Egyptian Influence on Origen', *Origeniana*, 243–56.

Cave, William (1687) *Apostolici: or, the History of the Lives, Acts, Death, and Martyrdoms of Those who were Contemporary with, or immediately succeeded the Apostles, as Also the Most Eminent of the Primitive Fathers for the first Three Hundred Years, to which is added, a Chronology of the Three First Ages of the church*. London: Richard Chiswell.

Clark, Elizabeth (1992) *The Origenist Controversy: The Cultural Construction of an Early Christian Debate*. Princeton, N.J.: Princeton University Press.

Crouzel, Henri (1984) *Origen: The Life and Thought of the First Great Theologian*, Trans. A. S. Worrall. San Francisco: Harper & Row.

Daley, Brian (1995) 'What Did "Origenism" Mean in the Sixth Century?', *Origeniana Sexta*, 627–38.

—— (1998) 'Origen's *De Principiis*: A Guide to the Principles of Christian Scriptural Exegesis', *Nova et Vetera: Patristic Studies in Honor of Thomas Patrick Halton*, ed. John Petruccione. Washington, DC: Catholic University of America Press, 3–21.

Daniælou, Jean (1959) *Origen*, trans. Walter Mitchell. New York: Sheed & Ward.

Dawson, David (1992) *Allegorical Readers and Cultural Revision in Ancient Alexandria*. Berkeley: University of California Press.

De Lange, Nicholas Robert Michael (1975) 'Jewish Influence on Origen', *Origeniana*, 225–42.

De Lubac, Henri (1998) *Medieval Exegesis*, Vol. 1, trans. Mark Sebanc. Edinburgh: T&T Clark.

Drewery, Benjamin (1985) 'The Condemnation of Origen: Should it be Reversed?', *Origeniana Tertia*, 271–7.

Godin, Andræ (1982) *Erasme: lecteur d'Origène*. Geneve: Droz.

Goehring, James (1997) 'Monastic Diversity and Ideological Boundaries in Fourth-Century Christian Egypt', *Journal of Early Christian Studies* 5: 61–84.

Grant, Robert (1993) *Heresy and Criticism: The Search for Authenticity in Early Christian Literature*. Louisville, Ky.: Westminster/John Knox.

Gray, Patrick T. R. (1979) *The Defense of Chalcedon in the East (451–553)*. Leiden: E. J Brill.

Guillaumont, Antoine (1962) *Les 'Kephalaia Gnostica' a'Evagre le Pontique et l'histoire de l'Origénisme chez les Grecs et chez les Syriens*. Patristica Sorbonensia 5. Paris: Éditions du Seuil.

Hanson, Richard P. C. (1959) *Allegory and Event: A Study of the Sources and Significance of Origen's Interpretation of Scripture*. Richmond, Va.: John Knox Press.

Harnack, Adolf (1990) *Marcion: The Gospel of the Alien God*, trans. John E. Steeley and Lyle D. Bierma. Durham, N.C.: Labyrinth Press.

Heine, Ronald (1993) 'Stoic Logic as a Handmaid to Exegesis and Theology in Origen's *Commentary on the Gospel of John*', *Journal of Theological Studies* n.s. 44: 90–117.

—— (1995) 'The Introduction to Origen's *Commentary on John* Compared with the Introductions to the Ancient Philosophical Commentaries on Aristotle', *Origeniana Sexta*, 3–12.

Junod, Éric (1980) 'L'Impossible et le Possible: Étude de la Déclaration préliminaire de *De Oratione*', *Origeniana Secunda*, 81–93.

—— (1995) 'Que savons-nous des "scholies" (*scholia* – *sêmeiôseis*) d'Origène?', *Origeniana Sexta*, 133–49.

Kannengiesser, Charles and Peterson, William L. (eds) (1988) *Origen of Alexandria: His World and His Legacy*. Notre Dame, Ind.: University of Notre Dame Press.

Lienhard, Joseph T. (1992) 'Origen's Speculation on John the Baptist or Was John the Baptist the Holy Spirit?', *Origeniana Quinta*, 449–53.

McGuckin, John (1987) 'The Changing Forms of Jesus', *Origeniana Quarta*, 215–22.

—— (1995) 'Structural Design and Apologetic Intent in Origen's *Commentary on John*', *Origeniana Sexta*, 441–57.

Munnich, Olivier (1995) 'Les *Hexaples* d'Origène à la lumière de la tradition manuscrite la *Bible* grecque', *Origeniana Sexta*, 167–85.

Nautin, Pierre (1977) *Origène: Sa vie et son oeuvre*. Paris: Beauchesne.

Norris, Frederick W. (1992) 'Universal Salvation in Origen and Maximus', *Universalism and the Doctrine of Hell: Papers Presented at the Fourth Edinburgh Conference in Christian Dogmatics, 1991*, ed. Nigel M. de S. Cameron. Carlisle: Paternoster Press, 35–72.

—— (1994) 'Black Marks on the Communities' Manuscripts' (The 1994 North American Patristic Society's Presidential Address), *Journal of Early Christian Studies* 2: 443–66.

Origeniana (1975) Eds Henri Crouzel, Gennaro Lomiento and Josep Rius-Camps. Bari: Instituto di Letteratura Cristiana Antica.

Origeniana Secunda (1980) Eds Henri Crouzel and Antonio Quacquarelli. Rome: Edizioni Dell'Ateneo.

Origeniana Tertia (1985) Eds Richard Hanson and Henri Crouzel. Rome: Edizioni Dell'Ateneo.

Origeniana Quarta (1987) Ed. Lothar Lies. Innsbruck: Tyrolia Verlag.

Origeniana Quinta (1992) Ed. Robert J. Daly. Leuven: Leuven University Press.

Origeniana Sexta (1995) Eds Gilles Dorival and Alain Le Boulluec. Leuven: Leuven University Press.

Pearson, Birger A. (1990) *Gnosticism, Judaism, and Egyptian Christianity*. Minneapolis, Minn.: Fortress Press.

Pichler, Karl (1980) *Streit um das Christentum: Der Angriff des Kelsos und die Antwort des Origenes*. Frankfurt-am-Main: Peter Lang.

Quasten, Johannes (1953) *Patrology*, Vol. 2. Utrecht and Antwerp: Spectrum Publishers.

Roberts, Louis (1971) 'Philosophical Method in Origen's *Contra Celsum*'. Ph.D. Dissertation, State University of New York at Buffalo.

Runia, David T. (1992) 'Philo and Origen: A Preliminary Survey', *Origeniana Quinta*, 333–9.

Scott, Alan B. (1991) *Origen and the Life of the Stars*. Oxford: Clarendon Press.

—— (1992) 'Opposition and Concession: Origen's Relationship to Valentinianism', *Origeniana Quinta*, 79–84.

Second Century (1987–8) Vol. 6.3.

Torjesen, Karen (1995) 'Influence of Rhetoric on Origen's Old Testament Commentaries', *Origeniana Sexta*, 13–25.

Trigg, Joseph W. (1983) *Origen: The Bible and Philosophy in the Third-century Church*. Atlanta, Ga.: John Knox Press.

Vogt, Herman Josef (1980) 'Wie Origenes in seinem Matthäus-Kommentar Fragen offen lässt', *Origeniana Secunda*, 191–8.

—— (1987) 'Warum wurde Origenes zum Häretiker erklärt?', *Origeniana Quarta*, 78–99.

Walls, Andrew (1997) 'Old Athens and New Jerusalem: Some Signposts for Christian Scholarship in the Early History of Mission Studies', *International Bulletin of Missionary Research* 21, 4: 146–54.

—— (1999) 'In Quest of the Father of Mission Studies', *International Bulletin of Missionary Studies* 23: 98–105.

Williams, Rowan (1975) 'Origen on the Soul of Jesus', *Origeniana Tertia*, 131–7.

Wright, John (1988) 'Origen in the Scholar's Den: A Rationale for the Hexapla', in Kannengiesser and Peterson (eds) 1988: 48–62.

CHAPTER FORTY

TERTULLIAN

——— .◆. ———

David Wright

TERTULLIAN'S LIFE AND ACHIEVEMENT

For a writer who was one of the chief creators of the tradition of western Latin Christianity, we know disappointingly little about the life of Quintus Septimius Florens Tertullianus. No contemporary mentions him, not even Cyprian, the bishop of Carthage in the mid-third century, whose indebtedness to some of his works is obvious and who (so Jerome recorded) read him every day. He flourished between about 190 and 220, but the years of his birth and death are unknown. Jerome, in his Who Was Who of early Christian writers, composed in 392/3, could report merely that 'he is said to have lived to a decrepit old age' (*Famous Men* [*De viris illustribus*] 53; Barnes 1985: 3–29, 323–5).

Even some of the meagre biodata Jerome's entry provides have been called into serious doubt by modern scholars. That Tertullian was a presbyter of the Catholic church and the son of an officer in the Roman army (a 'proconsular centurion') is most improbable. His identification with a little-known Roman jurist of the same period and the same name cannot be sustained, and with it wavers also the widespread view that our Tertullian was trained as a lawyer and practised at the bar, perhaps in Rome. No firm evidence places him in Rome at all, or for that matter anywhere outside Carthage. This city (see Figure 40.1) had been founded in the ninth or eighth centuries BCE by settlers from Tyre in Phoenicia (hence the epithet 'Punic' used in relation to it), had grown to great power under rulers like Hannibal (247–183/2 BCE), had been sacked by the Romans (146 BCE) and then recolonized by Augustus, to become the capital of Africa Proconsularis. By the second century CE Carthage had become the second city only to Rome in the western Mediterranean.

It is in well-educated circles in Carthage that Tertullian most securely belongs, although Carthage cannot with certainty be assumed to have been his place of birth.[1] His youthful years as a pagan seem not to have been exceptional, though marked by a love for the amphitheatre and some sensual misdemeanours. When and through what influences he became a Christian can be ascertained, if at all, only by tempting but unsafe deductions from his writings. Perhaps he was impressed by the efficacy of Christian exorcisms, or deeply moved by the steadfastness of Christian martyrs –

Figure 40.1   Remains of Punic Carthage. Photo A. N. S. Lane.

perhaps even the group of Scillitans put to death at Carthage on 17 July 180. As a Christian writer Tertullian advocated the sharpest of demarcations between paganism and Christianity, and much of his literary work was devoted to shaming Christians into emulating this in their personal behaviour and social relations. As he put it in one of his many eminently quotable utterances (invariably more lapidary in his Latin), 'Change, not birth, makes people Christians' (fiunt non nascuntur Christiani: *Apology* 18.4 – modelled on a Stoic saying).[2] Everything suggests that Tertullian himself 'became' a twice-born Christian.

The two books *To My Wife* reveal him married to a Christian. The first urges her not to remarry if he dies first; the second, written after some interval for reconsideration, to make sure to marry a Christian if she has to remarry. (His second thoughts indicate a lack of eligible men in the Christian community in Carthage.) What is not known is whether marriage followed his conversion; his wife may have accompanied or followed him out of paganism. Women and marriage were subjects that preoccupied the Christian Tertullian both before and after his espousal of the New Prophecy – Montanism, as it is known to modern discussion.

Champion of New Prophecy

It was probably around 208 that Tertullian became the most distinguished champion of the adventist prophetic renewal that began a generation or more earlier with the preaching of Montanus in Phrygia. An impressive – but not unchallenged – consensus of recent scholarship no longer believes that Tertullian the Montanist left,

Figure 40.2 Early Christian symbols from Carthage in the Carthage Museum. Photo A. N. S. Lane.

or was expelled from, the catholic church.[3] Even less did he subsequently abandon the Montanist assembly of Carthage to start his own even more exclusive sect of 'Tertullianists'. These were later known to Augustine (*Heresies* [*De haeresibus*] 86), but were probably simply the remnants of African Montanism. But the writings of Tertullian's Montanist years – the last 10–15 years of his active life – became increasingly harsh in their criticism of the compromises of catholic churchmen. Functioning partly as an *ecclesiola in ecclesia* ('a little church within a church') and no doubt increasingly marginalized, Tertullian and his fellow New Prophetists stridently promoted an escalation of the ethical and disciplinary demands of Christianity, as taught by the Paraclete (the Montanists' favoured designation of the Holy Spirit, highlighting the role assigned him in John 14–16) in the latter days through prophetic oracles. In aspiration a force for renewal and reform, they must have been increasingly resented as the awkward squad. No wonder Tertullian was never canonized, even if he was never formally condemned or excommunicated.

Tertullian's adoption of the New Prophecy in mid-career should not be read as marking a significant change of direction in his religious and theological orientation. It simply drove him further along the trajectory of total Christianity which appears to have characterized the church in Roman North Africa for most of its history. Not for nothing did this church first burst into view with the martyrdom of the Scillitans in 180. Although its earliest roots in Carthaginian society remain hotly contested, more than one aspect of Tertullianic Christianity may well reflect the residual influence of the grim child-sacrificing Punic religion of pre-Roman Carthage (Stager and Wolff 1984; Brown 1991; Leglay 1966: 486ff.). The daring blood imagery of the *Passion of Perpetua and Felicity* (203) is all of a piece with a religious ethos which so exalted martyrdom that Tertullian can even surmise that God covets human blood (*Antidote to the Scorpion's Sting* [*Scorpiace*] 6.11; Musurillo 1972: 106–31). Only one or two scholars still credit Tertullian with compiling the *Passion*, but its prologue and epilogue attest the kind of proto-Montanist spirituality which could well have predisposed Tertullian to embrace the New Prophecy. These editorial sections of the Passion evince a vivid sense of the immediacy of the power of the Spirit in the present day, accomplishing greater works than in the past. This Carthaginian Christianity dealt in austere heroics; it was no haven for wimps and softies.

Pioneer of Christian Latin

The *Passion of Perpetua* is uniquely valuable in its contemporary witness to the Christian community of Carthage in Tertullian's lifetime. For apart from the *Acts of the Scillitan Martyrs* (Musurillo 1972: 86–9), which are highly informative despite their documentary brevity, hardly any sources earlier than Tertullian's corpus survive from the Christian church of Roman North Africa. The *Acts* attest the existence of some Latin translations of Paul's letters and probably the Gospels, and some of the Apostolic Fathers were by now available in Latin, but to all intents and purposes Christian literature in Latin begins with Tertullian. Nearly all writers now agree that the *Octavius* of Minucius Felix is dependent on Tertullian and not vice versa, and the attempt of Jean Daniélou in particular to place a handful of Pseudo-Cyprianic treatises in late second-century Africa has not prevailed against post-Tertullian datings.[4] Hence the truly enormous importance of Tertullian's Latin works.

The ones he wrote in Greek have not survived. That Greek was the first language of some Christians in Carthage is evident from the *Passion of Perpetua*. Indeed, one of the sources the *Passion* incorporates, Saturus' account of his vision, was probably originally composed in Greek. The subjects of Tertullian's lost Greek works, such as baptism, the veiling of virgins and a dissuasive against attending public entertainments, suggest that they served a catechetic purpose in Carthage – and point to his serving the Christian community as teacher rather than presbyter. At the same time, their failure to survive supports the conclusion that very soon Latin was the sole language of Christians of Carthage. Greek would remain the public tongue of Roman Christianity for decades to come. Carthage was the cradle of Latin-speaking Christianity, and Tertullian was both parent and midwife. It was his unequalled achievement to translate – both literally and in the metaphorical missiological sense – an almost exclusively Graecophone religion into a vigorous, colourful and long-lasting Latinity.

We should not imagine that Tertullian started completely from scratch. The spoken Latin of Christian worship and conversation and Latin scriptures provided some basic vocabulary. How far the synagogue had already Latininized the Jewish Bible, whether direct from Hebrew or through the Greek Septuagint, cannot easily be determined; the Jewish community in Carthage probably did not go back beyond the second century. Yet none of these factors detracts from Tertullian's accomplishment in being the first to make Jesus Christ speak Latin.

Many terms could, of course, be transliterated straight from Greek into Latin, like baptism, eucharist and church (*ecclesia*). In some cases this was done after an alternative had been tried and found wanting; Tertullian settled for the verb *baptizo* after trying out *tingo*, 'dip'. In other instances, a new career was created for a Latin word, such as *sacramentum* (instead of a transliteration of the Greek *mysterion*). It was especially in the field of Christological and Trinitarian doctrine that Tertullian's

Figure 40.3   An early Christian basilica in Carthage. Photo A. N. S. Lane.

linguistic creativity was most influential, with the coining of *Trinitas* and the enlistment of *persona* and *substantia* into the technical vocabulary of future debate and definition. Hundreds of Latin neologisms appear in Tertullian's writings, but by no means all can confidently be credited to him. Nevertheless it is beyond question that across a wide range of subject-matters Tertullian successfully, even brilliantly, pioneered the cultured Latinization of Christian discourse (Braun 1977).

In one particular area he is frequently indicted for muddying the stream of Latin theology at its source. He certainly used a range of terms which also were at home in the law-courts, such as merit, satisfaction (making good breaches of the law by compensatory acts) and guilt (*culpa*, *reatus*). A standing charge faults him for importing a legalistic strain into western Christian thought, especially in relation to atonement, reward and punishment. There is probably still some truth in this allegation, even when its undergirding assumption of Tertullian's legal formation is dismantled. The legal colouring of his writing has often been exaggerated by failure to examine his actual use of terms which elsewhere have technical judicial force. He frequently turns the language and concepts of the jurists to non-specialized purposes, in a manner at times incongruous with a supposed professional training in law.

Rhetorician of revelation

Whereas earlier writers on Tertullian commonly cast him as a lawyer only imperfectly Christianized (a portrayal that still persists in some systematic theological circles), present-day scholars find in him the consummate rhetorician. Some of the features traditionally ascribed to his legal background are readily understood in terms of his expertise in the ways of rhetoric. This emphasis in turn is part of an enhanced appreciation of his assimilation of classical culture in the cause of Christian argument. This approach to Tertullian sees him as the product of a scholastic environment in Carthage which 'could have provided all the learning that was good for a man' (Barnes 1985: 194 and *passim*). His classical erudition was wide-ranging, and in the case of some authors, such as Plato, ran deep. In respect of rhetorical technique, he exemplifies the elaborateness of the Second Sophistic movement, which loved to parade its learning and to trade in philosophical themes. Tertullian deployed its skills in the service of theology, but in a style that all too often gives the impression that everything is subordinate to oratory (Sider 1972).

One crucial importance of reading Tertullian's intellect predominantly in literary and rhetorical categories is that it gives the lie to a disgracefully common misrepresentation of him as not only anti-philosophical but even as anti-intellectual and an enemy of reason. His name has come to stand for one of the stock positions in the age-old debate between faith and reason. The warrant for his classification as a thoroughgoing fideist is found in two of his famous – or notorious – dicta yanked from their contexts in his arguments. 'I believe it is absurd' (*credo quia absurdum*) turns out to be a distorted version of some words from Tertullian's refutation, rich in irony, of Marcion's docetic denial of the sufferings of the Son of God (Décarie 1961; Osborn 1997: 48–64). Taking his cue from the depiction of the crucifixion by St Paul (a great authority with the Marcionites) as folly to the Greeks (1 Cor. 1–2), Tertullian arrives at a criterion of what is worthy of belief – namely, its foolishness. He plays also on the saying of Jesus in Matt. 10:33 (and parallels), 'Whoever is ashamed of me, of him will I be ashamed', and drives to a resolution:

> The Son of God was crucified; I am not ashamed because others must be ashamed of it. And the Son of God died; it is believable because it is foolish (*ineptum*). And after burial he rose again; it is certain because it is impossible.
>
> (*The Flesh of Christ* [*De carne Christi*] 5.4)

A wooden citation in isolation of one clause which is then misquoted misses out on everything that is Tertullianic in this passage: its biblical seriousness, its rhetorical virtuosity, its teasing glorying in the paradoxical, which here means that he demonstrates the believability of what Marcion denies on grounds that Marcion himself advances in denial!

Even better known is 'What has Athens to do with Jerusalem?' – the type of question that English grammar recognizes as 'rhetorical'; that is, designed not to elicit information but to make an impression. In context it is the first of three: What then has Athens to do with Jerusalem? What the Academy to do with the church? What heretics with Christians? (*Prescriptions against Heretics* [*De praescriptione haereticorum*] 7.9). The clue to interpretation is evident in the first member in the third question, not 'philosophers' (as the parallelism leads us to expect) but 'heretics'. The passage is part of Tertullian's complaint against the philosophical corruptions of the Christian revelation perpetrated by the different heretical sects. It belongs to an argument for the integrity of the revealed faith of Christians, for Tertullian is indeed pre-eminently a theologian of revelation and an opponent of all *curiositas* beyond the church's rule of faith. He is not making an absolute pronouncement outlawing all philosophy from Christian interest. If this were the nuance conveyed by 'What has Athens to do with Jerusalem?', then 'Almost every word he wrote gave the lie to the answer he implies' (Barnes 1985: 210; see Osborn 1997: 27–47).

The Prescription(s) of Heretics is the traditional English rendering but singularly unhelpful. The Latin *praescriptio* has normally been understood of a courtroom procedure: Tertullian 'applies for an injunction to restrain any heretic from trespassing upon holy scripture' (Barnes 1985: 64). The treatise refuses to enter into debate with heretics on the basis of scripture because as the possession of the church they have no right to its use. But a wider examination of the occurrences of the noun and its cognate verb in Tertullian's writings, including this one, discloses that its basic meaning is logical, demonstrative, dialectical, with no more than a legal tint. Indeed it is deployed with a range of meanings according to its context – principle, objection in principle, proof, argument, definition – one kind or other of dialectical procedure (Fredouille 1972: 195–234). This shift in interpretation is a handy illustration of the move away from reading Tertullian in the categories of Roman law. Manuscript evidence may be cited in favour of the plural, *praescriptiones*, in the title, together with 'against all heresies'. The result accords neatly with Tertullian's own concluding summary of what the treatise has accomplished:

> We have now taken up a general position against all heresies, that on definite, just and necessary objections in principle (*praescriptionibus*) they must be debarred from discussion of the scriptures.
>
> (*Prescriptions* 44.13)

ANTI-HERETICAL WRITINGS

In *The Prescriptions*, written around 200, Tertullian finally promises separate treatises against individual heresies. These constitute one of the three main groupings into which we can divide his thirty odd-writings.[5] *Prescriptions* was followed by *Against Hermogenes*, a gnostic in Carthage indebted to Middle Platonism and Stoicism, against whose teaching Tertullian defended the doctrine of creation *ex nihilo*; *The Flesh of Christ* and *The Resurrection of the Dead*, linked by their rejection of the docetic views of gnostics and Marcionites; *Against the Valentinians*, one of the main varieties of Gnosticism, whose adherents' differences Tertullian plays off against each other in a brief discussion offered as a trailer for a full-scale engagement; and *Antidote to the Scorpion's Sting* (Latin *Scorpiace*), a vindication of martyrdom against gnostic objections by a demonstration on biblical grounds that it was ordained by God.

Tertullian's highly important work on *Baptism*, the first Christian treatment of the subject, was occasioned by polemic against the rite by a woman of the Cainite gnostic heresy, and so may be included in this group of his writings. It is abundantly informative on African liturgical practices, shares in the concreteness that characterizes so much of Tertullian's thought by its eulogy of water and displays already that preoccupation with purification before baptism which would prove so distorting to western baptismal usage. It also counsels against the baptism of babies – thereby providing the earliest unambiguous reference to the practice and sparking off still unfinished debate whether it or his objection to it was the real innovation.

The soul and the Trinity

Tertullian's anti-heretical corpus includes three of his weightiest works. *The Soul*, almost his longest, picks up the theme of a lost treatise against Hermogenes on *The Origin of the Soul* (*De censu animae*).[6] It is directed against philosophical and philosophically inspired gnostic errors on the origin and nature of the soul, rejecting Platonic views in favour of an explicitly Stoic understanding of the soul's spiritual essence as material substance. (Tertullian believed the same about the spiritual being of God.) Platonic pre-existence of souls is also refuted as Tertullian opts for traducianism, according to which body and soul alike come into existence simultaneously at conception (which helps to explain Tertullian's rejection of abortion, in accord with early Christianity as a whole). Pythagorean transmigration is also discounted, in a work which illustrates Tertullian's classical learning to great effect – but can also appeal to Perpetua's vision of paradise and to a vision of 'a soul in a bodily shape, . . . offering itself even to be grasped by the hand . . . and in form resembling that of a human being in every respect' reported by a prophetically gifted sister as received during Sunday worship at Carthage (*The Soul* [*De anima*] 9.4). Dreams are also considered at some length, and ecstasy too – which whets our appetite in vain for his lost work on this subject.

It is one of the paradoxes of Tertullian's career that it was during his Montanist years that he produced his greatest refutations of heresy. 'Praxeas did a twofold service for the devil at Rome: he drove away prophecy and introduced heresy; he put to flight the Paraclete and crucified the Father' (*Against Praxeas* [*Adversus Praxean*]1.5). Praxeas is otherwise unattested, and may be Tertullian's pseudonym, 'busy-body', for some better-known Asian teacher who both opposed Montanism and propagated monarchianism, that early and influential but facile resolution of the difficulties of conceiving the Trinity by representing Father, Son and Spirit as impermanent modes of activity of the single undifferentiated God. *Against Praxeas* is by common consent one of Tertullian's most original and influential writings. By laying so mature a foundation for the doctrine of the Trinity, he secured the West against the decades of controversy suffered later in the East over Arius and his successors. His contribution consisted above all in furnishing Latin theology with a technical Trinitarian vocabulary, with his innovative use of *Trinitas*, *substantia* and *persona* in particular. Threeness and oneness are equally safeguarded in a series of quasi-definitions whose economic Latin defies translation with similarly lucid brevity in English. But if the formulae proved durable, the content Tertullian conveyed by them still at one major point betrayed the limiting legacy of the subordinationism of second-century Logos theology. Tertullian conceived of the eternal Wisdom of God being sent forth as Word (Logos) and generated as Son in stages in the course of the divine 'economy' in creation, revelation and redemption. When he talks of 'the sacrament of the economy which distributes the unity into Trinity, setting forth Father, Son and Spirit as three' (*Against Praxeas* 2.4), he reminds us that theological genius always remains a creature of its time.

Intense discussion has enveloped a number of the terms Tertullian uses in his Trinitarian expositions, such as *substantia, persona, gradus, census, status, forma, species*. A legal background has been claimed for several of them, or again a philosophical one, but it is no less possible that Tertullian took some of them from everyday speech. As such, they were well sourced to serve the distinctive thrust of his theological mind, which Daniélou characterizes as:

> making every effort to place concrete data in relationship to one another. He is essentially realistic in his thinking . . . First, there is its descriptive, experiential, concrete quality; it sets out to make an inventory of reality. Second, there is the urge to discriminate, to arrange, to put everything in its proper place. In this respect Tertullian's work . . . is the product of a . . . typically Latin spirit.[7]

Marcion posed a far greater threat to second- and third-century catholic Christianity than Praxeas. By far the longest of Tertullian's works was *Against Marcion*, in five books as we now have it in its third edition (as Tertullian informs readers at the outset). The stages of its textual development are still subject to scholarly refinement. Its value for our knowledge of Marcionism is enhanced by the failure of several other writers' refutations to survive. The five books deal in succession with Marcion's dualism of two Gods, the identity of the creator of the world with the Father of Jesus, Marcion's Christology, and in turn his gospel text and his Apostolikon. From Book 4 onwards, Tertullian drew upon Marcion's *Antitheses* between the writings of old and new covenants. Books 4 and 5 carry special interest for the textual history of parts of the New Testament, but from Book 2 onwards much of the work consists of biblical documentation of his case. The kernel is found in the initial overthrow of Marcion's dualistic theology. What follows, in its relentless rhetorically barbed dissolution of Marcionite positions, attests the seriousness with which Tertullian took his challenge – as well as that addiction to the total demolition of opposing cases which provided such scope for the display of his argumentative genius.

APOLOGETIC WRITINGS

To the Nations

Tertullian was combative by nature, so that the second genre into which his writings fall, apologetic, shows him in his element. Most of these works were produced in his early years as a writer, in the later 190s. First came *To the Nations* (*Ad nationes*), generally regarded as unfinished and unrevised and perhaps never intended, for publication. The *Apology* (*Apologeticum*) would soon cover much the same ground, but far more skilfully and to much greater effect. *To the Nations* may even be viewed as a collection of materials, or in part a first draft, for the *Apology*. It is in the tradition of earlier Greek apologies, on some of which it probably drew, particularly in Book 1, in arguing that Christians were tried under unjust procedures and in ignorance of what they stood for, and in refuting the common allegations of cannibalism, incest and the like. Book 2 moved from defence to attack. Tertullian deployed material from the Roman writer Varro to flesh out the argument that pagan gods were simply deified human beings.

Apology

The *Apology*, by contrast, is often judged Tertullian's masterpiece (meriting an early Greek translation). It is addressed to the governors of the imperial provinces and more precisely the magistrates of Carthage. The work's effectiveness resides partly in the immediacy and directness with which it depicts the experience of Christians in Carthaginian society, but much more in the brilliance of the argument which is still capable of leaving the reader applauding in admiration. In Tertullian's hands *apologia* shifts from the philosophical mode to the rhetorical and even juridical. Tertullian is the apologist as advocate, mingling defence with attack, pulling every rhetorical trick in the book, searching high and low in Christian and pagan sources and even Jewish for the building blocks of his case, which repeatedly by the device of *retorsio* casts back upon the heads of critics the very scandals and follies they fasten on Christians. It abounds in quotable paragraphs and phrases, revelling in irony, in *reductio ad absurdum*, in bathetic pricking of inflated pretentiousness, in breathtakingly sharp swings of mood and style. Christian readers (to whom most apologies are truly directed) would have been hugely enheartened by Tertullian's matchless confidence in the superiority of the Christian religion. In his intellectual vivacity, unflinching defiance and confidence in taking the battle onto enemy territory Tertullian must have been hailed as an invincible champion. His is the virtuosity not merely of dazzling oratory but also of conceptual brilliance, not least in the surprising connections he makes. The images of pagan deities are but human artefacts, produced by processes akin to the tortures inflicted on Christians:

> It might be no small solace to us in all our punishments, suffering as we do because of these same gods, that in their manufacture they suffer as we do themselves. You put Christians on stakes and crosses: what image is not first formed from clay and then set on cross and stake? The body of your god is first consecrated on a gibbet. You tear the sides of Christians with your claws, but to every limb of your gods axes, planes and files are more vigorously applied. We lay our heads on the block; before lead, glue and nails are fetched your gods are headless . . . If this is how a deity is composed, then those who are punished are consecrated and tortures will have to be declared divinities!
>
> (*Apology* 12.3–5)

Nor does the cruelty of the persecutors, however exquisite, achieve its ends. 'Instead it entices others to our school. The more you mow us down, the more we multiply. The blood of Christians is seed' (50.13).

To dispel slanderous gossip, Tertullian explains, soberly but movingly, how Christians conducted themselves in meeting for worship. It is one of our most valuable early descriptions:

Figure 40.4   The Roman amphitheatre in Carthage. Photo A. N. S. Lane.

We assemble together and form a congregation so that by united force we may capture God by our prayers. This is the violence God delights in . . . It is chiefly the quality of our love in action that brands a distinguishing mark upon us in some people's eyes. 'See how they love one another', they say – for they themselves hate one another. 'See how ready they are to die for each other' – for they are more ready to kill each other . . . One in mind and soul, we do not hesitate to share our earthly goods with one another. We have everything in common but our wives.

(Apology 39.2, 7, 11)

If persecutors really believe that Christians engage in cannibalistic feasting, 'then blood is a test that should be applied to identify Christians . . . Let them be proved by their appetite for human blood, just as they are by their refusal to sacrifice' (9.15).

Humanity and religious freedom

Among the profounder threads running through the *Apology* is the appeal to a common humanity. He exposes the absurd incongruity of the enormities alleged against Christians by inviting his readers to picture themselves, in order to gain eternal life, plunging the knife into an innocent baby, saturating their bread with its blood, noting where their mother and sister are sitting so that when the lights are doused they will know where to perpetrate incest. He imagines pagan readers recoiling at the very thought:

Why then can others do it, if you cannot? Why cannot you, if others can? I suppose we Christians are by nature aliens, grotesque monsters, with fangs like aliens and monstrous energies for incestuous lust! If you believe this of a human being, you too can do it. You are human, as a Christian is. If you cannot do it, you ought not to believe it. For a Christian is a human being no less than you.

(*Apology* 8.4–5)

There emerges in the *Apology* the lineaments of a fresh understanding of the state (Campenhausen 1964: 14, and the whole essay, 4–35). Tertullian moves beyond traditional protestations of Christian loyalty and traditional promises of Christian prayer for imperial welfare. He dares to establish the dignity of the emperor on an entirely new basis, by acknowledging in his office God's ordained authority over the nations. Only a true estimation of the emperor's humanity under God offers him due allegiance and respect. 'I might say that Caesar is more ours than yours, for our God has appointed him.' On this proper appreciation of the emperor's place depends the purchase on God that Christians alone gain by their prayers. And pray they will, for 'a large benevolence is enjoined upon us, even so far as to entreat God for our enemies and to beg for blessing on our persecutors' (*Apology* 33.1, 31.2).

Finally, among so much else that invites admiring précis and quotation, Tertullian enters a claim for freedom of religion. If, as the Romans' instincts and behaviour reveal, their gods are nothing but dead human beings deified, refusal to worship them cannot constitute irreligion. 'On the contrary, the taunt will redound on your own head: worshipping a lie, you are really guilty of the crime you charge against us, not merely by rejecting the true religion of the true God but by actually assaulting it' (*Apology* 24.2).

See whether this too may not contribute to the chargesheet of irreligion – removing religious liberty and forbidding free choice of deity, so that I am not allowed to worship whom I will but am forced to worship whom I would not. No one, not even a human being, wants to be worshipped unwillingly . . . Every province and every city has its own god . . . We alone are debarred from our chosen religion. We injure the Romans, we are not reckoned as Romans, because we do not worship the Romans' god. It is well that God belongs to all, and all we to him, whether we will or no. But with you it is lawful to worship anything you wish apart from the true God, as though he was not rather the God of all to whom we all belong.

(*Apology* 24.6, 8, 9–10)

Yet a tone of sober realism pervades the *Apology*. If Christians (who are but of yesterday) now fill every place of public resort and have left the pagans nothing but the temples, Tertullian still regards affairs of state as utterly foreign to them. It was inconceivable that a Christian would aspire to be emperor. He slips instinctively into saying 'Roman' when he means 'non-Christian'. A world-renouncing quietism breaks through: 'Only one thing in this life greatly concerns us, and that is to get quickly out of it' (41.5). And so the work ends on a note of gratitude for the opportunity of gaining full forgiveness by the blood of martyrdom. 'As divine and human reckonings clash, when we are condemned by you, we are absolved by God' (50.16).

Other apologetic works

The *Testimony of the Soul* (*De testimonio animae*) is as brief and precisely focused as the *Apology* is expansive and ambitious. It picks up a paragraph in *Apology* 17.4–6, which, in support of the truth of the one God, cites 'the witness of the soul that by its very nature is Christian' (*testimonium animae naturaliter Christianae*). Eschewing earlier apologists' reliance on the philosophers, Tertullian summons a new witness – the human soul, the soul of common folk, unspoilt by education, which instinctively gives voice to a natural awareness of God in its unguarded cries, 'Good God!', 'God will repay me', 'God bless you'. The soul is of course not Christian (for no one is born a Christian), which makes its testimony the more valuable – 'as simple as it is true, as popular as it is simple, as universal as popular, as natural as universal, as divine as it is natural' (*Testimony* 5.1). The argument, which depends on a commonplace of Hellenistic, especially Stoic, philosophy, is as enchanting as today it is unconvincing, but it is still perhaps Tertullian's most charming book.

To Scapula (Ad Scapulam) is addressed to the African governor of that name who took to persecuting Christians. Written in 212, and possibly the author's last extant treatise, it strikes a menacing note, referring to a recent total eclipse as a warning of divine retribution. Scapula will not succeed, for the Christian community thrives on persecution. If Scapula persists, he might find his door thronged by many thousands of Carthaginians of every sex, age and rank, all eager for martyrdom. Although much here recalls the *Apology*, the more strident tone bespeaks the zeal of a Montanist.

Notably unsuccessful is Tertullian's *Against the Jews*, certainly left unfinished and of doubtful authenticity for some scholars. It was occasioned by an argument between a Christian and a Jewish proselyte, which may have involved Tertullian himself, but the contents of the book are largely traditional. It provides little evidence of close personal engagement with the Jewish community in Carthage on Tertullian's part (Setzer 1997).

Finally, among his apologetic writings may be included his shortest and most enigmatic, *De pallio*. The *pallium* was the mantle or cloak characteristic of philosophers, and this is a defence of the abandonment, by Tertullian presumably, of the Roman toga for the *pallium*. The sole Christian element appears at the very end: 'Rejoice, mantle, and exult! A better philosophy has dignified you since you began to clothe a Christian' (6.2). In difficult Latin (even by Tertullian's standards), clever but affected, recherché in its erudition, viewed variously as the earliest or latest of his works, if it is more than 'a mere "jeu d'esprit" or literary curiosity' what is its message? Perhaps it means that 'a Christian can take his pagan intellectual inheritance with him into his new faith. The antithesis between Athens and Jerusalem . . . has been resolved' (Barnes 1985: 230–1). Others have read it as a summons to Christians to be nonconformists in society, even ascetics. The toga had been a Roman import, ousting the earlier *pallium*, and was the attire of unsavoury characters and behaviours. But if Tertullian here calls for some form of Christian renunciation, he has chosen to cloak it in abstruseness.

MORAL AND DISCIPLINARY WRITINGS

De pallio might well have been included in the largest category of Tertullian's works, the moral and disciplinary. Among them are several others concerned with appropriate dress, as part of a larger concern for a proper correspondence between the inward and the outward. Here we observe Tertullian the instructor of the Christian people, predominantly concerned to foster distinctiveness and even separation, scornful of excuse and compromise, exhorting to martyrdom, tending towards asceticism, and, as he became a champion of the New Prophecy, explicitly escalating the standards expected of spiritual Christians in terms of what may be called a development of ethics (rather than of doctrine).

Examples of Tertullian's shift into a higher Montanist gear will introduce us to some of these fifteen or so writings. *Flight in Persecution* ([*De fuga in persecutione*], commonly dated 212/13) disallows it. Nothing happens without God's will, and if persecution ensues, he intends us to suffer, for our good. Jesus' counsel 'Flee from city to city' (Matt. 10:23) was meant only for his original hearers. Responding repeatedly to objections to his hard line, Tertullian denies that God cherishes the weak – 'he always rejects them, teaching first that we must not flee from persecutors but rather must not fear them' (6.2). What looks like a prophetic oracle clinches it: 'Have no desire to die in bed, in miscarriage, in gentle fever, but in martyrdom, that the one who suffered for you may be glorified' (9.4). Those who have received the Paraclete have one who will speak for them and succour them in suffering.

Thus Tertullian annuls his approval of flight in earlier treatises on *Patience* and *To My Wife* (*Ad uxorem*). His attractive panegyric of patience (*De patientia*), composed near 200, displays Tertullian at his least contentious. Christ himself is its supreme exemplar. Patience bears with the inconveniences of flight (13.6). Writing to his wife, Tertullian is already more grudging: 'even in persecutions it is better with permission "to flee from city to city" than when arrested and tortured to deny the faith' (*To My Wife* 1.3.4). The Paraclete later improved his hermeneutics. So often in these works on Christian behaviour we glimpse debates within the church of Carthage, with scripture bandied to and fro.

Against remarriage

We have already noted the movement of Tertullian's interest between the two books *To My Wife*. The first is essentially a eulogy of celibacy, which widowhood gives a wife a golden second opportunity to grasp. The second insists that remarriage must always be 'in the Lord'. In enlarging on the problems of mixed marriages, Tertullian furnishes illuminating detail on Christian practice and domestic life in contemporary Carthage. The Christian wife

> has by her side a servant of Satan who will act as an agent of his master in obstructing the performance of Christian duties and devotions. Thus, for example, if a fast day (*statio*) is to be kept, her husband will make an early appointment with her to go to the baths; if a fast is to be observed, her husband will, that very day, prepare a feast; if it be necessary to go out on an

errand of Christian charity, never are duties at home more urgent. Who, indeed, would permit his wife to go about the streets to the houses of strangers, calling at every hovel in town in order to visit the brethren? Who would be pleased to permit his wife to be taken from his side, when she is obliged to be present at evening devotions?

(To My Wife 2.4.1–2; trans. Le Saint 1951: 29)

There is much more to similar effect. The stern warning is necessary, for it is hard to find in the house of God unmarried men rich enough to keep wealthy Christian widows in the style to which they have been accustomed. 'Where but from the devil will they get husbands to maintain their sedans, their mules, the outlandishly tall slaves they need to dress their hair?' *(To My Wife* 2.8.3; Le Saint 1951: 34).

But whatever the obstacles in the way of finding a Christian spouse, such a second marriage possesses the beauty of all Christian marriage, which Tertullian movingly portrays in conclusion. Yet in one of his most blatantly Montanist works, *De monogamia*,[8] Tertullian declares the remarriage of the widowed as heinous, as simultaneous bigamy. For the most part he constructs his case from scripture alone, but only after he has laid his cards on the table about the distinctive ministry of the Paraclete. The words of Jesus in John 16:12 show adequately 'that the Holy Spirit will reveal such things as may be considered innovations, since they were not revealed before, and burdensome, since it was for this reason that they were not revealed' *(Monogamy* 2.2; Le Saint 1951: 71). To exclude the possibility that such an argument might justify 'any oppressive obligation' as a new revelation of the Spirit, Tertullian sets up the criterion of the orthodoxy of the Spirit, i.e. the New Prophecy. An evil spirit first perverts the creed before perverting morality. If the prohibition of remarriage is truly new and burdensome, the Paraclete had sufficient grounds in the practice and teaching of Jesus and his apostles to have gone further and forbidden marriage altogether! The Paraclete may indeed be welcomed as our advocate, since he exempts our weakness from the demand of total continence. From this perspective 'it is no novelty the Paraclete reveals. What he foretold, he now fulfils; what he deferred, he now exacts' *(Monogamy* 3:9; Le Saint 1951: 76).

The Paraclete's stricter discipline

One can but admire the rhetorical skill of this Christian sophist. In other Montanist works Tertullian spells out the theoretical basis for the Paraclete's introducing a more stringent discipline, insisting all the time that the New Prophecy adheres unwaveringly to the doctrinal rule of faith. The writer who in the *Apology* made such play of pagan follies and contradictions, now revels in exposing similar absurdities in 'sensualist' catholics. The Montanists are accused not of theological error but of 'plainly teaching more frequent fasting than marrying' *(Fasting* [*De ieunio*] 1.3). Such extended fasts and xerophagy (eating only dry food) attune a Christian to bear the life of prison and martyrdom, while catholics, ever a gullible prey to pseudo-martyrs (as the pagan journalist Lucian of Samosata reported so vividly), pamper their prisoners with every home comfort (the details are revealing of the possibilities of mitigating prospective martyrs' hardships) and even drug them to face death unflinchingly.

The Veiling of Virgins (*De virginibus velandis*) similarly exacts a practice more stringent than Carthaginian custom. The precise difference need not concern us so much as the justification Tertullian presents at length.

> While the rule of faith remains constant, other issues of discipline and conduct allow the novelty of correction, as the grace of God works and makes progress to the very end. How do we understand the work of God if, while the devil is ever working and adding daily to the ingenuities of wickedness, it has either ceased or stopped advancing? This was why the Lord sent the Paraclete, that since human mediocrity was unable to take in everything at once, little by little discipline should be straightened, ordered and carried on to perfection by the Holy Spirit acting in the place of the Lord . . . (John 14:12–13) . . . What then is the Paraclete's service function but this: straightening discipline, revealing Scripture, reforming the understanding, making progress towards better things? Nothing is without its stage of life, everything awaits its time.
>
> (*Veiling* 1.4–5)

Tertullian proceeds to develop the image of growth from seed to fruit.

> So too righteousness (for one and the same is the God of righteousness and of creation) was at first elementary, with a natural fear of God. From that stage it advanced through the law and the prophets to infancy, and thence through the gospel it burst into the ferment of youth. Now through the Paraclete it is settled into maturity.
>
> (*Veiling* 1.7).

Thus Montanism received its most sophisticated formulation at the hands of the rigorist rhetorician of Carthage. On more than one count it was too daring for the catholic bishops. No more than church leadership in any age could they tolerate such a free-range Holy Spirit, and in any case, as the Christian community competed for breathing space in the Mediterranean world, accommodation was the order of the day. The granting of a second, and last, opportunity for repentance for grave lapses after baptism, was carefully hedged around in Tertullian's early work on *Repentance*. It includes a graphic account of the public prostration and humiliation entailed in this demanding 'confession' (Tertullian uses the Greek word *exomologêsis*): groaning, weeping and roaring to God and rolling before the presbyters' feet seem uncannily reminiscent of revivalist phenomena in every century.

But a book of his Montanist years, *De pudicitia*, a title which resists an obvious English translation – *Modesty, Purity, Chastity* are possibilities – lambasts an unnamed bishop who had the effrontery to decree, 'I remit the sins of adultery and fornication to those who have fulfilled repentance.' This 'supreme pontiff' and 'bishop of bishops' is now identified by most interpreters not as a Roman bishop but as a bishop of Carthage, most probably Agrippinus. *De pudicitia* denies that the church hierarchy has authority to forgive the capital sins of apostasy, fornication and murder to the baptized. The power of the keys was granted to Peter in a solely personal capacity as the first to be endued with the Spirit. Thereafter it resides only with the similarly Spirit-endowed who constitute the church, 'which is properly and principally the Spirit himself'. In a passage compacted densely with biblical allusions and echoes, Tertullian envisages the Spirit – 'in whom is the Trinity of the one Godhead' – as creating the church which consists in 'the (two or) three'. This 'church of the Spirit' may forgive grievous sinners after baptism, but it will decline to do so, lest discipline be relaxed (*Modesty* 21).

This treatise is of signal importance for the early history of penitential discipline. It is also the one which, more than any other, has given rise to the image of Tertullian as an anti-episcopal schismatic. Its tone is shrill and the satire biting – but wonderfully effective. In its favour was the *casus belli* – a grotesque innovation in an utterly wrong direction. Why should not change be for 'the better'?

Idolatry

Of Tertullian's other writings in this third ethical-disciplinary grouping only one deserves more than brief mention, *Idolatry*.[9] It has been given widely differing dates by commentators. If nothing in it is unmistakably Montanist, its strictness accords well with the ethos of his undoubted Montanist productions. On the other hand, if an early work, it surely supports that interpretation of Tertullian's progress which tracks in it no abrupt changes of direction but only unrelenting linear movement towards one pole. *Idolatry* is richly instructive on the interaction of Christian and pagan in Carthaginian society, for its main burden so inflates the definition of idolatry as to require the Christian's withdrawal from many areas of communal life. Taking his hermeneutical cue from the Sermon on the Mount, in which Jesus deepened the scope of some of the Decalogue, Tertullian does the same with the prohibition of idolatry. Christians must be on their guard, eternally vigilant, against the long reach of idolatry. Everyone who contributed to the making of an idol is guilty of idolatry: 'what must not be worshipped must not be made ... You worship them when you make them such as can be worshipped' (4.1; 6.2). With the retort 'I have nothing else to live by' Tertullian will have no truck. Throughout the work he ridicules and shames plaintive protests against his rigour. He has no difficulty citing words of Jesus in the face of those who plead lack of livelihood or care of family. 'Faith fears no hunger' (12.4). He proceeds to rule out a wide range of occupations which are intrinsically idolatrous (including astrology: 'A fine astrologer you are, if you did not know you would become a Christian!' [9.8]) or idolatrous by inescapable associations – such as school-teaching, shopkeeping ('It is no defence that the same wares ... imported for sacrifice to idols, are also used by men and women as medicines and by us Christians as aids to burial as well' [11.2]), trainers of gladiators, military service (the subject of Tertullian's *The Soldier's Crown*, dated by some writers close to *Idolatry*), magistrates.

He also surveys the activities of social life. He says little about public entertainments, referring to his volume on *The Shows* (*De spectaculis*), where at a stroke he condemns every place of recreation – circus, stadium, theatre, amphitheatre, and every kind of spectacle they might host. If it is an extravaganza you want, the coming judgement day will furnish a stunning display. Christians may not teach, but Christian children have to learn, because the principles involved in the two activities differ. A pupil does not commend, as a teacher cannot avoid doing, and a pupil can escape a teacher's entanglement with the defilements of school life from festivals and seasonal rituals. But the concession of schooling for children is not uncharacteristic of the book even if it becomes casuistical in the process. Attendance at various family celebrations is permitted: 'I am disposed to think that we are in no danger from the whiff of idolatry which occurs at them' (16.1) – but only so long as the invitation does not mention participation in the sacrifice. One can speak a god's name . . . when directing someone to the temple of Jupiter! But there are no exceptions for the military; for example, no soldier who continues to serve, even in the rank and file with no requirement to offer sacrifices or shed blood, can be admitted to the faith.

Threaded through the pages is a series of axioms: 'At no point ought I to be an indispensable instrument to another person's doing what I may not do myself' (11.4); 'Let us mourn while the world rejoices, and afterwards rejoice when the world mourns' (13.4); 'I wish it were possible for us never to see what we must not do' (16.4). And Tertullian time and again rejects appeal to a scriptural quotation (Paul said 'I please men in all things' {14:3}), thereby reflecting the internal discussions of Christians of Carthage on appropriate Christian behaviour.

Idolatry connects with other works of Tertullian, such as *To the Martyrs* and *Apology*, and in its attention to various kinds of dress, especially forms of the toga, with a constant preoccupation of his, seen in *Women's Dress* (*De cultu feminarum*) for example. Here Tertullian spares readers no detail of current cosmetics, jewellery and

Figure 40.5 The animal exit from the Roman amphitheatre in Carthage. Photo A. N. S. Lane.

fashion. Much is calculated today to raise a gentle smile, but the seriously religious underpinning is never far away and can still inspire an affecting peroration.

> Go forth decked out in the cosmetics and ornaments of prophets and apostle, drawing your whiteness from simplicity, your ruddy hue from modesty, painting your eyes with bashfulness and your lips with reticence, fixing in your ears the word of God, fastening to your neck the yoke of Christ . . . Clothe yourselves with the silk of integrity, the fine linen of holiness, the purple of modesty. Thus arrayed you will have God for lover.
>
> (*Women's Dress* 2.13.7)

Tertullian was never dull, but frequently infuriating, not least in his clipped, elliptical, telegram-style Latin. The richness and freshness of his vocabulary, his dexterity in phraseology and his command of every figure in the rhetorician's book made him a remarkably forceful writer. As Vincent of Lérins put it in the early fifth century, 'the cogency of his argument compelled assent even when it failed to persuade. Almost every word was a sentence; every statement a victory' (*Commonitorium* 18). Rarely did he lay aside the combative vigour of the disputant out to win a case, but he did so in his early treatise on *Prayer (De oratione)*. It contains the earliest extant exposition of the Lord's Prayer, in which Tertullian discerned 'an epitome of the whole gospel' (1.6). The work's practical directness (which may be contrasted with Origen's more speculative interpretation) reflects a quality that stamps all Tertullian's writing. His scriptural exegesis was generally literal and historical rather than allegorical (O'Malley 1967). Everything he wrote had in view the challenging existence of a minority Christian community, for whom fidelity to Christian beliefs and mores could raise issues of life and death. He was a passionate advocate of a Christianity of radical discontinuity. As the churches in the West, not least in Europe, seem set for an experience of living as a minority unparalleled since the early centuries, this ancient Father of Latin Christianity may still prove a prophet for a new day (Bediako 1992: 100–36).

NOTES

1 Barnes (1985), Fredouille (1972). On Roman Africa, see Raven (1993), and on Carthage Picard (1964) and Lancel (1994). For an interesting popular account of Christianity in Roman North Africa, see Daniel (1993).

2 The most complete English translation of Tertullian's works is in four volumes in the *Ante-Nicene Christian Library*, eds Alexander Roberts and James Donaldson (Edinburgh: T&T Clark, 1867–70; with later reprints). In addition to individual translations, smaller or greater selections appear in other series, including *Ancient Christian Writers*, *Library of Christian Classics* and *Fathers of the Church*. A list of translations to 1970 appears in Barnes (1985: 286–90), and fuller details of all works in Quasten (1953: 246–340). The complete Latin text is edited in *Corpus Christianorum Series Latina* 1–2 (Turnholt: Brepols, 1954). Excellent bilingual (Latin–French) editions of many works have been published in the *Sources Chrétiennes* series, and Latin–English of some edited by Ernest Evans. Unless otherwise indicated, translations given in this chapter are the present writer's (with some indebtedness to the *Ante-Nicene Christian Library*).

3 Powell (1975), Braun (1985), Rankin (1995: 27–51), Rives (1995: 273–85); on Montanism, see Robeck (1992) and Trevett (1996).

4 Daniélou (1977: 17–98); among criticisms, Orbán (1976), but support from Quispel (1982).

5 Helpful introductions to each work discussed in this chapter will be found in Quasten (1953: 246–340).

6 For an outstanding commentary, with an edition of the text, see Waszink (1947).

7 Daniélou (1977: 344, and 343–404 generally) for a perceptive characterization of Tertullian's thought.

8 The title is to be translated simply 'monogamy' rather than in a manner that would bring out the treatise's opposition to remarriage, because Tertullian regards second marriage as a breach of monogamy.

9 There is a fine translation in Greenslade (1956), on which the quotations given here are based, and text, translation and commentary in Waszink and Van Winden (1987).

BIBLIOGRAPHY

Barnes, Timothy David (1985) *Tertullian. A Historical and Literary Study.* Oxford: Clarendon Press (corrected reprint of 1971, with added postscript).

Bediako, Kwame (1992) *Theology and Identity. The Impact of Culture upon Christian Thought in the Second Century and in Modern Africa.* Oxford: Regnum Books.

Braun, René (1977) *Deus Christianorum. Recherches sur le vocabulaire doctrinal de Tertullien*, 2nd edn. Paris: Études Augustiniennes.

—— (1985) 'Tertullien et le Montanisme: Église institutionelle et église spirituelle', *Rivista di storia e letteratura religiosa* 21: 245–57.

Brown, Shelby (1991) *Late Carthaginian Child Sacrifice and Sacrificial Monuments in their Mediterranean Context.* JSOT/ASOR Monograph 3. Sheffield: JSOT Press.

Campenhausen, Hans von (1964) *The Fathers of the Latin Church*, trans. Manfred Hoffman. London: Adam & Charles Black.

Daniel, Robin (1993) *This Holy Seed. Faith, Hope and Love in the Early Churches of North Africa.* Harpenden: Tamarisk Publications.

Daniélou, Jean (1977) *The Origins of Latin Christianity (A History of Early Christian Doctrine before the Council of Nicaea 3)*, trans. David Smith and John Austin Baker. London: Darton, Longman & Todd, and Philadelphia: Westminster Press.

Décarie, Vianney (1961) 'Le paradoxe de Tertullien', *Vigiliae Christianae* 15: 23–31.

Fredouille, Jean-Claude (1972) *Tertullien et la conversion de la culture antique.* Paris: Études Augustiniennes.

Greenslade, Stanley L. (1956) *Early Latin Theology*, trans. and ed. Library of Christian Classics 5. London: SCM Press.

Lancel, Serge (1994) *Carthage. A History*, trans. Antonia Nevill. Oxford: Blackwell.

Leglay, Marcel (1966) *Saturne africain: histoire.* Bibliotheque des Écoles françaises d'Athenes et de Rome 205. Paris: E. de Boccard.

Le Saint, William P. (1951) *Tertullian. Treatises on Marriage and Remarriage*, trans. and annot. Ancient Christian Writers 13. New York and Ramsey, N.J.: Newman Press.

Musurillo, Herbert (1972) *The Acts of the Christian Martyrs*, trans. and ed. Oxford Early Christian Texts. Oxford: Clarendon Press.

O'Malley, T. P. (1967) *Tertullian and the Bible. Language–Imagery—Exegesis.* Latinitas Christianorum Primaeva 21. Nijmegen and Utrecht: Dekker & Van de Vegt N.V.

Orbán, Árpád Péter (1976) 'Die Frage der ersten Zeugnisse des Christenlateins', *Vigiliae Christianae* 30: 214–38.

Osborn, Eric (1997) *Tertullian: First Theologian of the West.* Cambridge: Cambridge University Press.

Picard, Gilbert (1964) *Carthage*, trans. Miriam and Lionel Kochan. London: Elek Books.

Powell, Douglas (1975) 'Tertullianists and Cataphrygians', *Vigiliae Christianae* 29: 33–54.

Quasten, Johannes (1953) *Patrology*, Vol. 2. Utrecht and Antwerp: Spectrum Publishers, and Westminster, Md.: Newman Press.

Quispel, Gilles (1982) 'African Christianity before Minucius Felix and Tertullian', in J. den Boeff and A. H. M. Kessels (eds) *Actus. Studies in Honour of H.L.W. Nelson.* Utrecht: Institut voor Klassieke Talen, 257–335.

Rankin, David (1995) *Tertullian and the Church.* Cambridge: Cambridge University Press.

Raven, Susan (1993) *Rome in Africa*, 3rd edn. London and New York: Routledge.

Rives, J. B. (1995) *Religion and Authority in Roman Carthage from Augustus to Constantine.* Oxford: Clarendon Press.

Robeck, Cecil Melvin (1992) *Prophecy in Carthage: Perpetua, Tertullian and Cyprian.* Cleveland, Oh.: Pilgrim Press.

Setzer, Claudia (1997) 'Jews, Jewish Christians and Judaizers in North Africa', in Virginia Wiles, Alexandra Brown and Graydon F. Snyder (eds) *Putting Body & Soul Together. Essays in Honor of Robin Scroggs.* Valley Forge, Pa.: Trinity Press International, 185–200.

Sider, Robert Dick (1972) *Ancient Rhetoric and the Art of Tertullian.* London: Oxford University Press.

Stager, Lawrence E. and Wolff, Samuel R. (1984) 'Child Sacrifice at Carthage – Religious Rite or Population Control?', *Biblical Archaeology Review* 10: 31–51.

Trevett, Christine (1996) *Montanism. Gender, Authority and the New Prophecy.* Cambridge: Cambridge University Press.

Waszink, J. H. (ed. and comm.) (1947) *Tertulliani* De Anima. Amsterdam: North-Holland Publishing Company.

Waszink, J. H. and Van Winden, J. C. M. (ed. and trans.) (1987) *Tertullianus* De Idololatria. Supplements to *Vigiliae Christianae* 1.

PERPETUA AND FELICITAS

—— ·✦· ——

Ross S. Kraemer and Shira L. Lander

INTRODUCTION

Within a series of profiles of prominent early Christians, Perpetua and Felicitas differ from the others considered in this volume for several crucial reasons. First, and perhaps most obviously, they are the only women. Second, and perhaps more importantly, whereas all the men profiled here are well-known through their own extensive writings, or through the detailed writings of others, Perpetua and Felicitas are essentially known only from a work narrating their gruesome martyrdom in North Africa in the early third century CE that claims to incorporate Perpetua's own account of her imprisonment and divinely inspired visions.[1] Third, both women are said to have been extremely young when they died: the so-called *Passio Sanctarum Perpetuae et Felicitatis* (hereafter *Passio*) cares chiefly about their recent conversion to Christianity, their exemplary deaths, and in the case of Perpetua, but not Felicitas, her various visions. It offers only a modicum of biographical data for Perpetua, and virtually none for Felicitas. Thus, writing their 'profiles' becomes a substantially different endeavour from writing a profile of an Origen, an Augustine or an Athanasius.

Perpetua and Felicitas are by no means the only women martyrs in early Christian traditions. The fourth-century church historian, Eusebius of Caesarea, includes a *Letter of the Churches of Lyons and Viennes* narrating the martyrdom of an enslaved woman named Blandina and three male companions in 177 CE (Eusebius, *Historia Ecclesiastica* 6.1.3–63).The so-called *Acts of the Scillitan Martyrs* appears to reproduce the trial account of six Christians, three women and three men, in Carthage, North Africa, in 180 CE. What distinguishes Perpetua, and Felicitas by association, is the claim that a portion of the *Passio* is written by Perpetua herself, *manu sua*, in her own hand.[2] If true, as contemporary scholarship generally takes it to be, Perpetua is the first and only known Christian woman to write in her own name before the fourth century CE.[3] Furthermore, because this portion of the *Passio* (re)presents Perpetua's experiences, emotions and visions, it constitutes, if authentic, the only first-person account of a Christian woman's experiences. Its potential significance, then, is inestimable, and recent feminist scholarship in particular has been much taken with Perpetua for precisely these reasons.[4]

SYNOPSIS OF THE *PASSIO*

After a prologue in defence and praise of recent visions, a brief narrative frame at the beginning of the *Passio* (2.1–2) relates that at an unspecified time and place, for an unspecified reason, a number of catechumens (recent converts who had not yet been baptized) were placed under arrest. Three were men: Revocatus, Saturninus and Secundulus. Two were women: Felicitas, described as the *conserva* (probably co-slave) of Revocatus, and Vibia Perpetua, described as well-educated (*liberaliter instituta*), elite (*honesta*) and properly married (*matronaliter nupta*). Both her parents were still living, as were two brothers, one a catechumen but himself inexplicably not arrested.[5] Although Perpetua had a baby boy still nursing, the entire *Passio* is silent on the identity and whereabouts of her husband.

It is difficult to reconstruct the specific experiences of the catechumens from the portion attributed to Perpetua herself. It appears that between the time she was arrested and the time she and the others were detained in a public prison, Perpetua had occasion both to argue with her father over her Christianity (3.1–3), and to receive formal baptism (3.5a). Once imprisoned, the catechumens were held in a particularly hellish location (3.5b–6), but moved to a more comfortable place after the deacons Tertius and Pomponius bribe the prison guards. Perpetua takes advantage of the respite to nurse her famished baby and then hand him over temporarily to the care of her mother and brother until she receives permission to keep the child with her (3.8–9).

At this point, the first of four visions is related in Perpetua's voice (4.1–10). Prompted by her brother, Perpetua asks for and receives a vision in which she ascends a bronze ladder into heaven, together with Saturus, the catechumens' teacher who was not initially arrested with them but who is also subsequently martyred. At the foot of the ladder lies an enormous dragon; all along the sides of the ladder are sharp weapons. Once safely in heaven, Perpetua encounters a grey-haired man in shepherd's clothing milking sheep in an immense garden populated with thousands of people in white garments. Welcoming Perpetua as his child, the man offers her some of the milk. When she consumes it, all present say 'amen', and Perpetua wakes with a sweet taste in her mouth. Recounting the vision to her brother, Perpetua realizes that the Christians are fated to suffer and die. Shortly thereafter, a rumour spreads that the catechumens are to have a hearing (5.1a). Perpetua's father appears just in time to beg his daughter once again to reconsider (5.1b–5). Although she claims to pity his old age, Perpetua is unmoved (5.6). Abruptly summoned sometime later to a formal hearing in the forum, she resists her father's importuning yet a third time, confesses to being a Christian and is sentenced, along with her companions, to fight with the beasts (6.1–6).

Back in prison, Perpetua sends Pomponius, who seems to have free access to the prisoners, to fetch her baby. He has apparently been returned to her father's care, although the account provides no explanation of when or how (6.7). Her father refuses to yield the child, but conveniently, if not miraculously, the child loses interest in nursing and Perpetua's milk supply dries up without causing her any discomfort (6.8).

Soon thereafter, Perpetua's second vision occurs (7.3–8), in which she sees her deceased younger brother Dinocrates suffering the traditional torments of the unfortunate dead. He is hot, thirsty, pale, and still bears the marks of the facial cancer that killed him. In front of the child she sees a pool of water, but the refreshment the dead seek is beyond his small reach. Perpetua prays for Dinocrates for days, until the prisoners are transferred to a military prison. That night, she has another vision (8.1–4), in which she sees Dinocrates clean and refreshed, a scar where the wound had been, and the rim of the pool now lowered to a height he can reach. Above the rim floats a golden bowl, from which she sees Dinocrates drink his fill and then go off to play. Waking, Perpetua realizes that Dinocrates suffers no more.

As the date of her contest approaches, Perpetua's father returns a fourth time. Perpetua repeats her sorrow for him, but does not relate her reply, if any, to him.

Her fourth and final vision (10.1–13) is set the day before the contest. Led by Pomponius into the arena, Perpetua finds herself to be a man, set to fight a repulsive-looking Egyptian. An immensely tall man clad in a purple tunic and marvellous sandals of gold and silver presides over the fight. Ultimately, Perpetua triumphs over the Egyptian: while her assistants sing psalms, she receives a branch with golden apples from the man. After he kisses her, saying 'Peace be with you, my daughter', she walks out through the Gate of Life. Waking, she understands that she is to fight the Devil and emerge victorious.

With this vision, the portion of the *Passio* ascribed to Perpetua ends and another vision, ascribed to Saturus, follows immediately (11.1–13.8). In this lengthiest of all the visions, Saturus and Perpetua, now dead, are carried by four angels to a heavenly garden, where they meet up with other martyrs not mentioned in the account ascribed to Perpetua, and are greeted and kissed by the Lord himself, an aged man with white hair and a youthful face. Having been told by elders to 'go and play' (*ite et ludite*: 12.6), Perpetua and Saturus find the bishop Optatus and the presbyter Aspasius feuding. When the two men implore them to intervene, Perpetua and Saturus demur, but Perpetua then speaks with them in Greek. Ultimately, angels instruct Optatus and Aspasius to settle their own dispute.

The remainder of the *Passio* (14.1–21.11) recounts the deaths of the martyrs, with the most extensive description reserved for that of Perpetua and Felicitas. Only now does the reader learn that Felicitas was eight months pregnant, and that she and her companions prayed successfully that she might deliver early. Otherwise, she would have had to wait to die until the birth of her child, since Roman law forbid the execution of a pregnant woman.

On the emperor's birthday, the catechumens are sent into the arena. Despite Perpetua's final vision of her combat as a man with the Egyptian, she and Felicitas are stripped naked, clad in netting, and sent to fight a wild heifer, the sex of the animal matching the sex of the martyrs (the men fought an assortment of leopard, bear and wild boar). Yet none of the martyrs dies of these wounds. Instead, all assent to the wishes of the perverse crowd and have their throats cut by the waiting gladiator. Perpetua herself must guide his hand into her throat after he initially misses and strikes a bone. The *Passio* concludes with a brief peroration comparable in style and theme to the more lengthy introduction.

ASSESSING THE HISTORICITY OF THE *PASSIO* AND OTHER PERPETUA TRADITIONS

The accounts of Perpetua's arrest, last days and martyrdom are usually titled *Passio Sanctarum Perpetuae et Felicitatis*: some add their co-martyrs Saturus and Revocatus. The texts exist only in medieval manuscripts dating from the ninth through the seventeenth centuries. Apart from one Greek manuscript, all are Latin. The variety of the manuscripts presents obstacles to reconstructing a literary history for the Perpetua traditions. Moreover, their usefulness for reconstructing a historical account is hampered by conflicting and indeterminate historical references.

The situation is further complicated by the existence of another set of Perpetua materials, the *Acta*.[6] The relative brevity of the *Acta* (approximately one-quarter the length of the *Passio*), suggests they may have been composed for public recitation rather than private reading (LeClercq 1939: 409). Although the earliest extant Perpetua manuscript is of the *Acta*, scholars believe that the traditions contained in these manuscripts but not in the *Passio* are late (not before the fifth century) and unreliable, thereby justifying their omission from historical reconstructions of Perpetua's life and death (Amat 1996: 271; van Beek [1936] 1956: 98).

A majority of scholars believe that Latin is the original language of the Passion text.[7] All the traditions set Perpetua's martyrdom in North Africa, where Latin, Greek, and indigenous Punic were spoken. The texts either situate Perpetua's arrest in a small city about thirty miles south-west of Carthage called 'Thuburbo minor', in what is modern Tunisia, or they give no location for the events of the story (*Passio* 2.1; *Acta* 1.1). Some scholars take the amphitheatre description to refer to Carthage (Figure 41.1), since it would have been the only city large enough to contain an arena fully equipped with soldiers' quarters and a prison, and it was the seat of the provincial governor (Amat 1996: 22–5; Rives 1995: 78).

The texts also do not agree on the precise dates of Perpetua's martyrdom. The title of the Latin *Passio* gives the nones of March (also *Acta* 9.5), while the Greek has early February. The earliest calendar on which Perpetua and Felicitas are listed, the *Feriale Ecclesiae Romanae*, dated 354, lists the March date (Mommsen 1891: IX,71). Scholars have tended to accept the date commemorated on the Roman calendar, 7 March, without historical warrant.[8] The fact that the February date corresponds to Perpetua's commemoration on the eastern calendar suggests that the traditions reflect alternative dates for commemorating Perpetua in different martyrological traditions rather than useful historical evidence for dating her martyrdom (Robinson 1891: 17).

Attempts to date the text are based on the assumption that Perpetua's martyrdom itself can be securely dated, accepting the historicity of the events as they are presented in the narrative. The only contemporaneous evidence for Perpetua outside the *Passio* is from the North African Christian writer, Tertullian, who adduces the heavenly vision of Perpetua, 'the most heroic martyr', as evidence that only the privileged few can enter heaven before the Final Resurrection (Tertullian, *De anima* 55.4). Since Tertullian had died by the Valerian persecution, he could not have known a Perpetua tradition which placed the martyrdom in the mid-third century.

External verification of Perpetua's martyrdom relies both on Tertullian's witness

Figure 41.1   The amphitheatre at Carthage. Photo J. C. N. Coulston.

and on historical evidence for persecutions that occurred during his lifetime. Thus, most scholars date the martyrdom to the reign of Septimius Severus.[9] The fourth-century church historian Eusebius relates a Severan persecution in Alexandria, yet he mentions neither North Africa nor Perpetua and her companions (Eusebius, *H. E.* 6.4–5). The late and suspect *Historia Augusta*, a compilation of Roman history, relates a Severan edict that puts Christianity in the same category as Judaism: 'it is forbidden to become Jews', but a prohibition against proselytism seems likely to be anachronistic.[10] Thus, even accepting the martyrdom's historicity, attempts to explain Perpetua's death as punishment for her conversion are probably misguided.

If Severus had not issued a recent ban on conversion, he might have encouraged a climate of episodic persecution of Christians, similar to the situation reported by Pliny the Younger, governor of Bithynia-Pontus in the early second century CE, in his letter to Trajan (Pliny, *Epistles* 10.96–7). The *Passio* conveys a sense of random-ness about Perpetua's arrest which would comport with such a climate. The arrest of the 'young catechumens' occurs without context or explanation and the passive construction (*Passio* 2.1) conceals those who may have ordered the arrest and why. There is no mention of mass arrests or widespread executions.[11] The friends and family who visit the martyrs in prison are not afraid to be associated with them. People are not fleeing to avoid arrest and persecution, or to avoid appearing before makeshift outdoor courts to prove their allegiance to the Roman deities, as we have in other representations of more systematic persecution (*pace* Cyprian, Lactantius and Eusebius). When this group of Christians 'suddenly' receives a hearing at the forum

(*Passio* 6.1), the governor merely asks Perpetua to perform a sacrifice on behalf of the emperors. When she demurs, he then asks, 'Christiana es?' to which she replies affirmatively (*Passio* 6.3–4). The crime of being Christian, in so far as it prevents this upper-class Roman matron from performing her civic duty, is Hilarianus' reason for condemning her to the beasts (*Passio* 6.6). Like the court accounts of Pliny, the martyr's hearing seems to indicate that admitting to being Christian and refusing to sacrifice were sufficient to incur punishment.[12]

An early dating (for the martyrdom and the *Passio*) does not depend only on demonstrating the historical plausibility of these events.[13] It depends also on how one interprets seemingly historical references in the *Passio*. Many scholars identify the governor Hilarianus, successor of Minucius Timinianus (*Passio* 6.3–5, 18.8), with the P. Aelius Hilarianus mentioned by Tertullian (*Ad Scapulam {To Scapula}* 3.1), and the Caesar in celebration of whose birthday the martyrs are to be ceremonially killed (*Passio* 7.9) as Geta, the emperor's son (later rejected for the throne and ostracized by his brother, Caracalla). Each piece of evidence has problems rendering them inconclusive at best as support for a Severan date.[14]

The problem of dating by itself should alert the careful reader to the difficulty of identifying the extant medieval manuscripts with a literary tradition dating back to the early third century. Tertullian mentions Perpetua only in a passing reference and refers neither to a text nor to a commemoration. No other third-century literature, inscription, or author mentions her. Despite the fact that Tertullian and Cyprian, the mid-third-century bishop of Carthage, both mention offerings and prayers on behalf of the departed (Tertullian, *De corona militis* 3; Cyprian, *Epistles* 12.2.1), neither mentions the practice of reading a Passion text on the anniversary of a martyr's death. By itself, Tertullian's reference may merely evidence a local oral tradition and not acquaintance with the *Passio*, although many scholars read it this way. It is not until the fourth century that these artefacts of Perpetua's martyrdom, text and commemoration, can be securely identified.

The earliest evidence of Perpetua's commemoration appears on the liturgical Calendar of Rome in 354.[15] Canon 47 of the Council of Carthage which took place in 397 permits such commemorative texts to be read even though they are not canonical writings,[16] reflecting a trend also apparent in Palestine and Asia Minor towards a containment of saint veneration within the physical and temporal boundaries of the church.

This institutionalization of saint devotion converges with the evidence provided by three sermons of Augustine, bishop of Hippo, at the end of the fourth century. Augustine marks the occasion as the anniversary of the martyrdoms (*dies natales*: literally birthdays) of Perpetua and Felicitas, and provides the first known reference to an actual text of the Passion which was read in his basilica.[17] Augustine's homilies contain many of the traditions preserved by the medieval manuscripts of the *Passio*. There are, however, unexplained ambiguities which suggest that his text is not identical to the *Passio*. Details of Augustine's discussion and those found in a fifth-century sermon, now referred to as 'pseudo-Augustine', conflict with what has been preserved as the *Passio* text.[18]

According to Pseudo-Augustine, Felicitas accompanies Perpetua up the ladder to the heavenly garden, not Saturus as in the *Passio*. Two of the images they see, the simultaneously old and young shepherd and the surrounding vessels of milk, differ from the extant *Passio*. In Pseudo-Augustine, Perpetua and Felicitas see 'a shepherd both young and old' who shows them vessels of milk. In the *Passio*, it is Saturus who sees in his vision 'an aged man with white hair and a youthful face' (12.3), an image evoking Rev. 1.13–14 and Dan. 7.9. The heavenly visions of both Saturus and Perpetua in the *Passio* use the pronoun 'we' to indicate Saturus and Perpetua. Pseudo-Augustine and Augustine use the plural to refer to Felicitas and Perpetua (Augustine, *Sermo* 280). It seems that either our texts have emended the original company of Felicitas to Saturus, or an earlier tradition, no longer extant, had replaced Saturus with Felicitas.

Rather than suggesting these ancient commentators made a 'mistake' in their references to a Perpetua tradition, the evidence suggests that the attribution of the visions was not a consistent tradition.[19] All the visions of heavenly ascents may have originally been assigned to Perpetua and Felicitas alone, since the day of commemoration bears their names. Felicitas may have become a problematic figure for the post-Constantinian church. A pregnant slave who seemingly wills the life-threatening premature delivery of her own child so that she too may win the crown of martyrdom may have been written out of the vision by later editors or scribes.[20] As Brent Shaw has argued, the *Acta* give her a plebeian husband, whom she publicly rejects (5.2–6.1), to mitigate the scandal of her circumstances (Shaw 1993: 33–42).

In its final form, The *Passio* of Perpetua and Felicitas consists of three narrative layers. The middle core claims to be the original account of the martyr Perpetua herself, just as written by her hand and from her point of view: *sicut conscriptum manu sua et suo sensu* (*Passio* 2.3). This core relates the events from the arrest of Perpetua and her companions up to the day of her martyrdom, including the visions or dreams she has during this time. An editorial framework surrounds this core, which introduces the prison section, then continues the account of Perpetua's martyrdom from where she left off as well as that of her companions (presented as the editor's eyewitness account), and concludes with a doxological exhortation. An anomalous insertion after Perpetua's diary claims to be Saturus' account of his prison vision; as we have previously seen, this dream, or some form of it, might well have been originally attributed to Perpetua herself. The differences in style and theme between this vision and those of Perpetua within the prison narrative may suggest, though, that the vision has undergone significant revision in the process of reassignment.

The identity of the editor remains obscure as does his or her religious perspective, which we shall consider further (pp. 1061–2). The more interesting question, from the perspective of women's authorship and self-representation in antiquity, is whether Perpetua actually wrote the prison section of the *Passio*.

Writing something in someone else's name is a widespread practice in the ancient world, whether understood as intentional fraud or pious fiction. Tertullian himself denounces an anonymous presbyter in Asia Minor whom, he says, forged the story of Paul and Thecla, although he concedes that the presbyter claimed to do so out of love for Paul.[21] (Whether Tertullian is here correct is irrelevant for present purposes: *De baptismo* 17.5). Further, the editor's claim, that Perpetua wrote it in her own hand, does not ensure its authenticity for the modern scholar. The same assertion occurs, for instance, not only in several undisputed letters of Paul (1 Cor. 16:21; Gal. 6:11; Philem. 19) but in letters now thought to be pseudonymous (Col. 4:18 and 2 Thess. 3:17, where the author's insistence on this point seems particularly telling).

Recently, Thomas Heffernan has critiqued the characterization of the prison narrative as a diary, the term regularly used by recent scholarship, and questioned the authenticity of Perpetua's section on philological grounds.[22] Heffernan examines the prison narrative as *hypomnemata*, a catch-all genre which encompassed many types of non-rhetorical writing, including 'memoir, memorandum, note, diary, or commentary on an author' (Heffernan 1995: 321). Perpetua's dreams in particular, he argues, reflect a new emphasis on self-revelation emerging in the late second century. Heffernan points out that the text violates an essential aspect of the diary form: it provides 'deliberate temporal continuity . . . [using] such expressions as "after a few days", or "many days", "a few hours later", to indicate the passage of time and to introduce a new narrative sequence' (Heffernan 1995: 322). Furthermore, he points out, the grammar lacks an additional feature typical of diary writing: the verbs are mainly not conjugated in the present tense. Heffernan proposes instead that the prison narrative is a mediated account from one of Perpetua's visitors, to whom she revealed her dreams and the circumstances of her imprisonment (Heffernan 1995: 323–4).

Contemporary claims about the authenticity of the prison narrative often appeal to the controversial notion of a female rhetoric.[23] Emotional, personal, fragmented, and colloquial, the style of Perpetua's account is thought to prove the trustworthiness of the editor's claim. However, we are less confident that this style can be identified specifically with Perpetua herself and consider just as likely the possibility that this style is purposefully constructed by an ancient author to appear as a (female) martyr's diary. The essentialist claim that women in antiquity wrote in a distinctive and detectable form and voice collapses in view of ancient sources. Pliny the Younger, for instance, writes about

> some letters which he [Pliny's friend, Pompeius Saturninus] said were written by his wife, but sounded to me [Pliny] like Plautus or Terence being read in prose. Whether they are really his wife's, as he says, or his own (which he denies) one can only admire him either for what he writes, or the way he has cultivated and refined the taste of the girl he married.
>
> (Pliny *Ep.* 1.16.6, in Fantham *et al.* 1994: 349)

Pliny's identification of the style of the letters with that of Plautus and Terence, two male authors, leads him to conclude that either his friend's wife did not write them, or that she learned how to write in male rhetorical style from her husband. Implicit in Pliny's judgement may be a notion of a distinctive female writing style, to which these letters do not conform. Pliny ultimately concedes, despite his preconceptions, that a woman could be trained to write 'like a man'.

That, further, a man could write like a woman, in a voice recognizable as female, is evident from the majority of ancient playwrights and novelists who devoted much of their work to constructing gendered representations not only of characters, but of their speeches and letters as well. In so doing, they appealed to assumptions about gendered language that may also be reflected in Pliny's remarks. Chariton, in his novel *Chaereas and Callirhoe*, has Callirhoe write a letter, which he has, of course, composed himself. Chariton writes in the letter, 'this letter is written in my own hand' (Reardon 1989: 116). Likewise, Xenophon has Manto write a love letter in which she exclaims that she 'can no longer contain herself, improperly, perhaps for a girl' (Reardon 1989: 141). Additional evidence may be found in the intriguing but generally ignored pseudepigraphic correspondence allegedly between one Mary of Cassabola and Ignatius of Antioch (Kraemer 1991: 236–9). Both letters are clearly written by the same author, so either a woman has written in both male and female voices, or a man has done so. In either case, our dilemma is apparent, if its solution is not.

Thus, attempts to verify the authenticity of Perpetua's narrative on gendered stylistic grounds prove troubling.[24] Furthermore, the similarity of the section to other autobiographical narratives which are considered authentic but heavily edited and rewritten, such as Aelius Aristides' *The Sacred Tales*, should give us pause about identifying stylistic features as a sign of authenticity rather than as self-consciously constructed rhetorical devices. As Glen Bowersock has aptly stated, 'Whether Perpetua's words, in whatever language, allow us to hear an authentic and distinctive woman's voice . . . is much more doubtful. How would we tell?' (Bowersock 1995: 34).

Our scepticism about the diary's authorship draws further support from a comment made by Augustine in a discussion of infant baptism. He mentions Perpetua's ability to intervene on behalf of her deceased brother's soul, citing the *Passio* text which 'is not itself a canonical writing, whether she herself wrote it or whether anyone else wrote it' (*De natura et origine animae* 4.10.12; our translation). Augustine doubts that Perpetua wrote this account, yet his concerns pass unremarked through centuries of transmission.

Finally, the startling degree to which the specifics of the *Passio* conform to the biblical citation of Joel 2:28–9/Acts 2:17–18 contributes to our concerns. It is possible, indeed perhaps tempting, to read the *Passio* in its present form as a narrative dramatization of this citation, as it appears here:

> For in the last [literally newest] days, says the Lord, I will pour out my spirit over all flesh and their sons and daughters will prophesy; and I will pour my spirit over my male servants and female servants (*servos et ancillas meas*) and the young shall see visions and the old shall dream dreams.
>
> (*Passio* 1.4)

Many elements of the *Passio* conform closely to the specifics of this prophecy. As the prologue makes clear, the events of the *Passio* take place in these newest days (1.1–3). The outpouring of the divine spirit over all flesh may be depicted in the catechumens as a whole, or even in the larger phenomenon of conversion to Christianity which they may represent, although admittedly, the *Passio* is not terribly specific on this point. Perpetua and probably Saturus demonstrate the prophesying sons and daughters. The extraordinary emphasis on Perpetua's role as a daughter, primarily through her relationship with her father, coheres exceedingly well with the characterization of the female prophets as daughters.

The precise citation of the biblical verses in the *Passio* does not correspond exactly to any other known ancient Latin translations of either Joel 2:28–9 or Acts 2:17–18. Where the Hebrew, Greek and Vulgate all modify the sons, daughters, male servants and female servants, with the possessive 'your', the *Passio* applies the third-person plural 'theirs' (*eorum*) to the sons and daughters, and lacks any possessive for the young visionaries and the old dreamers.[25] Applied to Perpetua, this adjective seems particularly apt. Born to pagan parents, she is 'their' daughter in at least two senses: she is not only of the gentiles, but the daughter of two living parents. Such a reading provides one way of making sense of the limited presence of her mother. The emphasis on Perpetua's noble birth and elite social status may also stem from the redactor's desire to characterize her as the daughter distinct from the female servants (*ancillae*).

While Acts 2:18 predicts that the servants will also prophesy, Joel limits this activity to the sons and daughters, as does the citation in the *Passio*. And not surprisingly, none of the slaves prophesy. They appear only to receive the Spirit, most notably perhaps in the response to their prayers for Felicitas' early delivery, and probably also in their baptism. Their very presence in the story enhances the conformity of the *Passio* to the biblical verses. Interestingly, apart from her description as the *conserva* of Revocatus, there is no reason to think that Felicitas is a slave.[26] Yet the characterization of Felicitas and Revocatus as *conservi*, construed as co-slaves, enhances the correspondence of the prophecy and the *Passio*, which requires examples of slaves who receive the spirit, if not also who prophesy.

At several points, the redactor emphasizes both the youth of the catechumens as a whole, and that of Perpetua in particular. They are described as *adolescentes* (2.1), while she is 22 (2.3) and still called *puella* (20.1–2). The attention to her age and the emphasis on her visions coheres with the prediction of the young seeing visions. While the cultivation of visionary experience seems to have characterized much of North African Christianity, one might wonder whether the correspondence results from an existing tradition about Perpetua, or from the prophecy itself.

Admittedly, several components of the biblical prophecy, as quoted in the *Passio*, are less apparent, including the pouring out of the divine spirit 'over all flesh', the prophesying sons and the aged dreamers. The awkward integration of the figure and vision of Saturus into the text, which we noted earlier, may represent an attempt to offer an example of the prophesying son. It may also supply the old dreaming dreams, since his age is not specified, and he is not among the adolescent catechumens, but is rather their teacher, and therefore presumably somewhat older. Alternatively, the author of the *Passio* may find it sufficient to demonstrate partial fulfilment of the biblical text. In any case, the collective prophecies, visions and reception of the divine spirit in the *Passio* clearly represent fulfilment of this particular phrasing of ancient divine prophecy.

Thus, yet another explanation for the formation of the *Passio* is that its original core is an account of the imprisonment and visions of a martyr, Perpetua, with or without Felicitas, and that many of the additions function, intentionally, to demonstrate the fulfilment of the prophecy. If this reading has merit, it points to an author who looks for the fulfilment of biblical prophecies in the details of historical experience. Our discussion of the probable history of the traditions about Perpetua, and of the *Passio* itself, suggests that it is unlikely that the entire martyrdom of Perpetua is generated out of the biblical passage(s), but it seems quite possible that both the general outline and many of the details of the prison narrative and the remaining sections are shaped to conform to the biblical text.[27]

In consideration of the myriad challenges the *Passio* poses to historical claims about the martyrdom of Perpetua, and the serious questions raised about the authenticity of the prison section, we consider it impossible to identify the original source of this martyrdom account. At some level, the account may reflect the experience of a young Carthaginian woman, an elite Roman matron, who was possibly executed for her adherence to Christianity, yet historical certainty is simply unattainable. While recent scholarship generally considers the prison account of Perpetua to be authentic and accurate, and the *Passio* as a whole to be a reasonably trustworthy representation of the martyrdom of Perpetua, Felicitas, and their male associates, it is our assessment that the hagiographic tradition may not be historically reliable to a sufficient degree to permit a profile of Perpetua and Felicitas comparable to what may be possible for other persons in the current section of this volume. Rather, what we may have is a 'representation' whose correspondence to actual persons and events cannot be determined. Nevertheless, if we assume for the sake of discussion that a sufficient amount of the *Passio* is rooted in actual historical events, we may explore a number of questions pertinent to a profile of the two women. The remainder of this chapter will endeavour to do just this.

PERPETUA AND FELICITAS: A PROVISIONAL PROFILE

As we noted at the outset, the *Passio* as a whole is not much interested in the lives of these martyrs prior to their conversion to Christianity and their consequent arrest. In this regard, it appears to differ markedly from the genre of Christian biographies, or *Lives*, itself modelled on Graeco-Roman forms, that flourishes from the fourth century on.[28] While hagiographic interests shape the use of biographic details in those accounts, the *Lives* nevertheless typically not only narrate birth, education and familial relationships, but also offer extended examples of piety and self-abnegation.

Scholars have heavily mined the significant amount of apparent biographical data about Perpetua condensed into the brief lines of *Passio* 2.1–3. Perpetua was a member of an old established family of Roman citizens, the Vibii, well-documented in North Africa.[29] According to one family of Latin manuscripts (identified by the Greek letter gamma) and the only extant Greek manuscript, she came from a town called Thuburbo Minus west of Carthage.[30] Shaw concludes that '[s]he came, therefore, from a solid municipal family, no doubt of some local wealth and prestige' (Shaw 1993: 11).

The narrator claims that Perpetua was not only born into the *honestiores*, but was the recipient of a liberal education (*liberaliter instituta*) that would have included training in Latin grammar and rhetoric. Citing Ovid, Amat proposes that young women would also have been schooled in music and singing (Amat 1996: 193; Ovid, *Ars Amatoria* 3.35). Because the vision attributed to Saturus depicts Perpetua addressing the quarrelling church leaders in Greek, some scholars have argued that she was literate in Greek as well, but the scepticism of both Amat and Shaw on this point seems well-taken (Amat 1996: 193; Shaw 1993: 12, n. 34).

That the daughters of citizen families would have been formally educated is substantiated by numerous ancient sources.[31] If Perpetua is indeed the author of the prison narrative, she was obviously sufficiently well-educated to compose it, and to write it in her own hand. In that portion of the *Passio*, scholars have seen allusions to Latin literature that bolster these claims.[32] The description of Perpetua as *liberaliter instituta* functions to affirm the claim that she is the writer of the prison account: it is precisely what we might expect from an author who wished to 'authenticate' the representation of a woman writer.

The narrator informs readers that Perpetua was *matronaliter nupta*, a phrase that appears to indicate that by virtue of her marriage Perpetua attained the status of *matrona* (Amat 1996: 193). As numerous commentators have observed, neither the narrative frame nor the prison account provides any information regarding the identity or whereabouts of Perpetua's husband. Since she is not described as a widow, many scholars have assumed that her husband opposed her conversion to Christianity, and that this opposition accounts for his absence throughout the *Passio*. Such an interpretation accords well with numerous other early Christian representations of the dynamics of women's conversion to Christianity, from the story in Justin Martyr of the unnamed woman whose acceptance of ascetic Christianity causes her husband to bring charges against her and her Christian teachers (2 *Apology* 2.4ff.), to the numerous tales in the Apocryphal Acts from Thecla on. Conceivably, then, the absent (and here anonymous) husband may be understood as a standard type in early Christian conversion narratives whose opposition requires no explanation. But equally possible, however, the troublingly absent husband may be viewed as evidence for some historical core of the narrative, on the logic that his absence creates more problems than it solves, and is thus unlikely to be fictive.

According to the narrator, Perpetua's parents are both still living, as are two brothers, one of whom is said to be a catechumen as well. She is herself 22, and the mother of a son young enough to be still nursing, which would probably make him less than three years old. Assuming the boy to be her first child, or at least her first living child, this would accord well with a marriage at about age 18, consistent with other evidence for the age at first marriage for elite Roman women (Shaw 1987).

This portrait of Perpetua is generally consistent with that of the account attributed to the martyr herself, although not completely. The prison narrative itself mentions (but never names) the father, the mother, and the baby boy. The catechumen brother is more problematic. Within the prison narrative, Perpetua at one point entrusts her baby to the care of her mother and brother, which suggests that he is not imprisoned, nor is there any particular reason to think he is also a Christian (3.8). In 4.1, however, Perpetua relates that 'her brother' told her to ask for a vision about her fate (but not their fate), which she does. Coming to, Perpetua relates the vision of Saturus and the ladder to her 'brother'. Although the language of 4.10 suggests that this 'brother' is also a Christian, it is impossible to say whether the brother is with Perpetua in prison, or a visitor. As Amat notes, 'brother' may signify both a true sibling, or a fellow Christian. Perpetua's description of Dinocrates (the only member of her family to be named) as her brother 'in the flesh' (7.5) may suggest that we should understand the unnamed brother in chapter 4 as simply another Christian.[33]

As many scholars have recently considered, the portrait of Perpetua's relationship with her father in the prison narrative is particularly fascinating. Of all Perpetua's familial relationships, this one receives the most extensive articulation. Perpetua's four visions are interwoven with four confrontations in which her father begs her to renounce her Christianity. The visions and the confrontations may well be inter-related: aspects of the father may be seen not only in the grey-haired old man milking sheep in the first vision, but in the enormous dragon in the same vision and the hideous Egyptian in the third vision, both of whose heads Perpetua steps on (4.7; 10.11; Lefkowitz 1976).

By comparison, Perpetua's relationship with her mother receives short shrift. Only in 3.8 does Perpetua speak with her mother, concerning her anxiety for her infant son and arrangements for his care. How Perpetua's mother felt about her conversion and impending martyrdom is never explicit. Nowhere does her mother implore her to desist, although in 5.3 Perpetua's father begs her to think of the pain her death will cause her mother. Shaw takes Perpetua's statement in 5.6 to mean that Perpetua's family in general opposed her Christianity, and thought her impend-ing death appropriate punishment, but the words 'he [the father] alone of all my family would not rejoice to see me suffer' (*solus de passione mea gauisurus non esset de toto genere meo*) could easily be construed to mean that Perpetua's other relatives would rejoice in her suffering because they knew that it would lead to her immediate glorification (Amat 1996: 31, 209). Whether this means that the mother and other relatives may have been Christians themselves, it seems at least that they sympa-thized with Perpetua's Christianity.

If the prison narrative is indeed autobiographical, it alludes to a complex father–daughter relationship common to the dynamics of elite citizen families, in which fathers lavished devotion and attention on their daughters, while the relationships of mothers and daughters were relatively minimal.[34] Imploring her to abandon her Christianity, Perpetua's father reminds her of how he favoured her above all her brothers. Shaw, Elm and Perkins, in particular, have demonstrated the extent to which the interactions between father and daughter function as an apt expression of the Christian critique and inversion of Roman power relations.[35] They focus in particular on the exchange in chapter 5, where Perpetua's father calls her no longer *filia* (daughter) but *domina* (5.5), the feminine form of *dominus*, lord or master.[36] While Shaw and Elm (and many others) take these scenes to be more or less accurate, the utility of these interactions might suggest that their representation is a more deliberate artifice than might initially appear.

Virtually no biographical data is offered for Felicitas, who figures only in the narrative sections, and is never mentioned in the account attributed to Perpetua. All that we are told of her is that she was a slave, the *conserva*, or co-slave, of Revocatus,[37] and was many months pregnant at the time of her arrest. With Perpetua, she is described as *puella* (20.1) which may signify her relative youth. Nothing suggests that she and Perpetua had any relationship prior to their shared martyrdom, or at least to their conversion to Christianity. No visions are attributed to Felicitas, nor any exercise of leadership or authority. Since, as we noted earlier, the fifth-century homily falsely attributed to Augustine has Felicitas, not Saturus, ascend the ladder to heaven with Perpetua, it may be that Felicitas' status as a slave lies behind eventual suppression of earlier traditions in which Felicitas fills a role subsequently co-opted by Saturus.[38] Interestingly, though, neither Augustine, Pseudo-Augustine nor Quodvultdeus characterize Felicitas as enslaved, and we have already raised questions about the historicity of the claim that Felicitas was a slave.

What kind of Christian might Perpetua (and perhaps Felicitas) have been? The language of the prologue, with its citation of Joel 2:28–9/Acts 2:17–18, and its praise of new prophecies and visions, has long suggested an association with the Christian revivalist movement known as the New Prophecy, or Montanism (see Chapter 36 in this volume). Originating in Phrygia (in ancient Asia Minor; modern Turkey) around the third quarter of the second century CE, the movement appears to have been founded by a male prophet named Montanus, and two women prophets named Priscilla and Maximilla. It attracted significant support not only in Asia Minor but also in North Africa at the end of the second century: Tertullian himself was a Montanist for a some significant period of his life.[39] Characteristic of the movement was a resurgence of charismatic activity, including prophecy, leadership roles for women based on such activity, and heightened eschatological expectation. Although the New Prophecy encountered considerable opposition from proto-orthodox Christians, it seems to have survived well into the fourth century.[40]

Numerous elements of the *Passio* would be consistent with what we know of the New Prophecy. Among these are Saturus' own vision, the authority Perpetua exercises there, the visions reported in her own voice, and even the citation of Joel 2:28–9/Acts 2:17–18. Numerous scholars have remarked on the possible correlation between Perpetua's consumption of a Eucharistic cheese-like substance in her first vision, and reports that the Montanists celebrated a Eucharist of bread and cheese.[41]

Yet the Montanist character of the *Passio* is not without problems. Nothing in the text is unambiguously Montanist. Precisely the elements often adduced as indicators of Montanism, including an emphasis on prophecy and heightened eschatological interest, appear typical of much Christianity in North Africa in this period. So, too, the interpretation of dreams as divine revelations and an emphasis on their power, particularly for confessors (those prisoners waiting to be martyred), appears to have been commonplace.[42] Cyprian describes his own actions as 'prompted by the Holy Spirit and counselled by the Lord through many explicit visions' (Cyprian, *Ep.* 57.5.1). He equates visions and revelations, and maintains their power to predict the future (Cyprian, *Ep.* 11.4.1–5.1). Furthermore, Maureen Tilley offers strong arguments that 'The *Passion* lacks the central and distinctive attributes of Montanist literature'; namely, asceticism, millenarianism, and ecstatic prophecies (Tilley 1994: 835).

The question of martyrdom is particularly troublesome. Opponents of the New Prophecy accused its members of avoiding martyrdom, which, if true, would certainly weaken the identification of the *Passio* as Montanist. On the other hand, if members of the New Prophecy wished to represent themselves as exemplary martyrs, the *Passio* would certainly constitute an effective means of doing so.

Although one of us has earlier analysed Perpetua and the *Passio* from the vantage point of Montanism, it seems wise to conclude that the matter cannot be resolved with any certainty (Kraemer 1992: 157–73). It is certainly possible that whoever composed the prologue was indeed a Montanist, and even intended both the quotation of Joel 2:28–9/Acts 2:17–18 and the defence of contemporary prophecy to signal this identity. Such an author may also have understood Perpetua to have been a member of the movement, as evidenced in particular by her consumption of the Eucharistic cheese in her vision. If the visions are authentic, Perpetua may indeed have been a member of the New Prophecy. Were this to be the case, it might account for a puzzling aspect of the *Passio* that has never been adequately explained; namely, why only a small group of catechumens were arrested, while other Christians, including the deacons Pomponius and Tertius, apparently came and went unhindered and unconcerned that they, too, might be arrested and condemned. Perhaps Perpetua and her companions could be construed as members of the New Prophecy, whose affiliation singled them, but not other Christians, out for prosecution. This hypothesis, however, has serious problems, not the least of which is its attempt to offer a historical explanation for a feature of a literary production.

Certain specific Christian characteristics may be deduced from the prison portion by itself, although these are not without problems. Manifestly obvious is the emphasis on martyrdom, while less remarked is a noteworthy absence of miracles suspending the natural order common to other second- and third-century Christian literature such as the Apocryphal Acts. Martyrdom appears to ensure immediate entrance to heaven, consistent with a view Tertullian himself attests. Although this is clearer in the vision of Saturus, it is also discernible in Perpetua's first vision, where she and Saturus ascend the ladder to heaven and are welcomed by the aged shepherd and the saints, a vision that, as many scholars have observed, appears grounded in the predictions of Revelation (e.g. 7:9–17). Implicit in this dream may be precisely the belief that Christians who die ordinary deaths cannot ascend into heaven until the second coming.

The prison portion affords little insight into authoritative and organizational church structures. The only church leaders mentioned are the two male deacons, unless perhaps we include the reference to Saturus as a teacher. No women leaders appear, nor do any male presbyters or bishops. Nevertheless, Perpetua's effective prayers for the salvation of her brother, Dinocrates, have led at least one scholar to suggest that she effectively held the rank of presbyter (Klawiter 1980). In this period, Christians awaiting martyrdom (confessors) were thought to have great powers, a perception expressed in the prison account at 4.1 and 9.1.[43] Among these powers was the ability to forgive those who had denied their faith under pressure. Since this power was otherwise arrogated to bishops and presbyters, the ability of confessors such as Perpetua to effect the forgiveness of others apparently entitled them to the equivalent ecclesiastical rank. Klawiter points out that since women as well as men were arrested in anticipation of martyrdom, the assignment of ministerial rank to confessors had the potential to enable women to attain offices otherwise prohibited.[44]

Apart from her intercession for Dinocrates, Perpetua exercises no leadership within the prison account. In the separate vision of Saturus, Perpetua finds herself mediating a dispute between a presbyter and a bishop said to be those of her own church (although one might suggest that the presence of these officials represents a deliberate attempt to respond to the absence of such authorities in the prison narrative). In the narration of the martyrdom itself, Perpetua twice intervened effectively with the Roman tribune, once to secure better treatment for the prisoners, and once to prevent them from having to wear the garments of the priests of Saturn and priestesses of Ceres (16.2–4; 18.4–6).

Seen through the multiple prismatic lenses supplied by the additional layers of the *Passio*, a fuller version of Perpetua's Christianity becomes visible, although whether it says more about the subsequent redactors than about any historical Perpetua remains an important question. The *Passio* as a whole attests a Christianity steeped in the cosmic framework of the Apocalypse of John, enamoured of martyrdom, apparently positioned at the end of time (although the language of the prologue seems ambivalent on this point when it predicts that 'these [new manifestations] will one day become ancient and needful for the ages to come').

CONCLUSION

By the fourth century, Perpetua's fame had spread beyond Carthage. Her image as martyred mother, unlike the Maccabean mother who exhorted her sons to martyrdom, uniquely exemplified the choice between the Roman family and the family of Christ, which was only paralleled in accounts of female asceticism. Whereas sexual abstinence had forced a wedge between Christian wives and non-Christian husbands, Perpetua's faith required her to give up her human father and son in exchange for a divine father and son (Tilley 1994: 839–40). The *Passio* shows how the conflict between Roman civic authority, which was mirrored microcosmically in the institution of the *domus*, and the church can be resolved in self-sacrifice, or death. As this political struggle dissipated, the story of Perpetua's martyrdom came to represent the rejection of whatever interpreters deemed to be less worthy. For these Latin interpreters, the choice of martyrdom symbolized obedience to those values represented by the Church.

In the fifth century, the remains of Perpetua and Felicitas were believed to be located in the main Basilica of Carthage, attested by both inscriptions and the comments of Victor Vitensis. Sixth-century cameo mosaics commemorate the martyrs in the church of Ravenna. As can be seen in Figure 36.6 of this volume, a photograph of The Perpetua window from Chester Cathedral,[45] these monuments suggest that independent of the historical details of Perpetua's death, her martyrdom was a powerful symbol and her story continued to be read, translated, edited, and interpreted by Christians in the East as well as in the West.

NOTES

1 Perpetua receives some notice in the writings of Tertullian: as discussed on p. 1051, it is unclear whether Tertullian knows the text of the martyrdom or some other version, oral or written, but in any case, he does not provide independent attestion of the life of either woman.

2 *Passio* 2.3. All citations of the text follow the edition of Amat (1996). English translations

are generally our own. The standard English translation is that of Musurillo (1972: 106–31), reproduced in Kraemer (1988: 96–107).

3 Kraemer (1991), Rader (1981), Snyder (1989).

4 E.g., Elm (forthcoming), Kraemer (1992), Maitland (1996), Miles (1989), Perkins (1995), Rader (1981), Salisbury (1997), Shaw (1993) and Tilley (1994).

5 Amat thinks the text is ambiguous on this point: 'One of the two [brothers] is also a catechumen, the redactor tells us, but without specifying whether he was arrested or not' (1996: 31, our translation from the French).

6 Text and French translation in Amat (1996).

7 Amat (1996: 66), Barnes (1968b: 521), Dronke (1984: 1) and Fridh (1968: 80–3), who maintains the original of the Saturus vision was Greek.

8 Robeck (1992: 13), Barnes (1968b: 523–5) and Shaw (1993: 3).

9 Barnes (1968b: 522–3), Frend ([1978] 1993: 87), Dronke (1984: 1), Amat (1997: 20–1), LeClercq (1939: 421) and van Beek (1938: 3).

10 Barnes (1968a: 40–1). For the opposite perspective, see Frend (1975).

11 That Perpetua is not presented as having been killed in a wave of systematic persecution supports an earlier date, before the mid-third century, since the later persecutions were widespread.

12 The editor of the *Passio* relates that the guard had received 'warnings from false witnesses (*homines uanissimores*)' about the prisoners (16.2), like Pliny's complaint that 'others who were named by the informer said that they were Christians and then denied it, explaining that they had been, but had ceased to be such, some three years ago' (*Ep.* 10.96; trans. H. M. Gwatkin in Stevenson 1987: 19).

13 Other martyr traditions present alternative dynamics of persecution. For example, the *Acts of the Scillitan Martyrs* presents the martyrdom of these six women and six men as essentially voluntary and initiated by the martyrs themselves. The proconsul Saturninus entreats the Christians to 'return to their senses [so that they might] obtain the pardon of our lord the emperor' (*Acts of the Scillitan Martyrs* 2; trans. in Musurillo 1972: 87). Although Perpetua is not portrayed as an eager volunteer for martyrdom, the vague description of her arrest leaves open the possibility that she, like her predecessors, came forward to publicly bear witness.

14 Roman prosopographies do not link the prenomen 'Minucius' with the nomen Timinianus: see Harris and Gifford (1890: 9). Hilarianus is also a common name for North African procurators. Only one version of the *Passio* contains the name Geta, which actually appears in the manuscript as 'ceta' (Amat 1996: 130). That this tradition is historically unreliable can be inferred from a note in the Latin historian Spartianus that Geta's birthday was in May, not February or March (Barnes 1968b: 523).

15 Thurston and Attwater (1956: I, 493). Barnes' attempt to verify the authenticity of the eyewitness account of the *Passio* relies solely on Roman dates for Geta's birth. He never considers the lack of textual evidence for the Geta reference itself, or the problems of competing dates in other calendars and versions (1968b: 521–5).

16 *Concilium Carthagensis* III.47, quoted in Delehaye (1912: 423, n. 3): *Ut praeter scripturas canonicas nihil in ecclesia legatur sub nomine divinarum scriptarum . . . Liceat etiam legi passiones martyrum quum anniversarii dies eorum celebrantur.*

17 Augustine, *Sermo* 280.1. Since the moment of death was equivalent to second baptism, or rebirth into the Spirit, these days were called *dies natalis*. The custom of referring to the acts of saints and martyrs as *gesta* makes more explicit the parallel between the Christian commemorations and the Roman celebration of the emperors' birthdays. In his commentary on Psalms, Augustine cites the text as *The Passion of Blessed Perpetua* which 'we know and read' (*Enarrationes in Psalmos* 47.13).

18 Amat (1996: 271). The sermon is tentatively identified by Shewring as authentic Augustine, yet he admits 'Whether it may in fact be genuine I lack the competence to say' (1931: xxix).

19 Braun (1979: 105), Frend (1965: 363, 365), Fridh (1968: 9–10) and Harris and Gifford (1890: 8). It is presumptuous to suggest that Augustine and Pseudo-Augustine could have made a mistake in their sermons just after the text had been read aloud before their congregations.

20 Augustine, *Sermo* 281.3; trans. in Hill (1994). Subsequent quotations for Augustine's sermons are from this translation

21 For an English translation of the *Acts of (Paul and) Thecla*, see Kraemer (1988: 280–8); for a feminist commentary with helpful bibliography, see McGinn (1994).

22 Heffernan (1995: 315–25) and Habermehl (1992: 241–8), who raises concerns but ultimately does not resolve the question of the authenticity of the diary.

23 Dronke (1984: 1–17), Petroff (1986: 63) and Shaw (1993: 19).

24 See e.g. Shaw (1993), Dronke (1984) and Petroff (1986), all of whom argue for a distinctive female style.

25 Interestingly, the possessive *eorum* does occur in Tertullian's citation of these verses, which itself differs from other ancient attestations: *in novissimis temporibus effundam de Spiritu meo in omnem carnem et prophetabunt filii filiae que eorum et super servos et ancillas meas de meo Spiritus {sic?} effundam* (*Adversus Marcionem* 5.8).

26 For the thesis that she was not, see Poirier (1970). Neither Augustine nor Pseudo-Augustine nor Quodvultdeus describes Felicitas as a slave.

27 In a manner not unlike that Kugel (1990) argues for the rabbinic Joseph traditions, and Kraemer (1998) explores with regard to the Greek tales of Joseph and Aseneth. For the view that the citation of this passage represents self-conscious Montanist exegesis, see Atkinson (1982).

28 Examples of women's lives include the *Life of Macrina*, the *Life of Melania the Younger*, and the *Life of Olympias*.

29 See Shaw (1993: 10–11) for more detailed discussion of the issues such as the antiquity of the Vibii, whether or not they were of senatorial status, and so forth.

30 See again Shaw (1993: 10, esp. n. 28) for details; see also critical apparatus to 2.1 in Amat (1996: 104), and her commentary (pp. 192–3).

31 Snyder (1989), Kraemer (1991), Harris (1989) and Hallett (1999).

32 Shaw (1993: 12), citing Harris (1989) and Dronke (1984: 107–11).

33 Amat (1996: 32, 200) where she asks whether the *frater* is here Saturus, presumably because it is Saturus who appears in the requested vision. In 5.3, Perpetua's father implores her to think of her brothers (*aspice fratres tuos*) who will be devastated by her death. Were it not for the claim of the narrator that one of her brothers was a catechumen as well, we might read this to suggest that however many brothers she had they were not Christians, any more than her mother, aunt, or father were Christians.

34 On which, see Hallett (1984) and Kraemer (1993).

35 Shaw (1993), Elm (forthcoming) and Perkins (1995).

36 In 4.1, the 'brother' also addresses Perpetua as *domina soror*.

37 See Amat (1996: 193) for brief treatment of the possibility that *conserva* designates a spouse.

38 But see also the possibility discussed on p. 1056–7 that a desire to conform to the biblical citation of Joel 2:28–9/Acts 2:17–18 also affects the representation of Felicitas.

39 The chronology of Tertullian's life, including his period as a Montanist, is quite complex: for discussion, see Barnes (1971).

40 Ancient evidence is collected in Heine (1989) and Tabbernee (1997). For a recent

treatment, see Trevett (1996); for briefer overviews of the movement, particularly with reference to women, see Kraemer (1992: 157–73) and Elm (1994).

41 Epiphanius, *Panarion* 49.2; Kraemer (1992: 163–5).

42 An important study on this topic is Robeck (1992). Cf. Tabbernee (1997: 56–7).

43 According to Tertullian, Christians visited confessors to ask for intercessions of various sorts: adulterers and 'fornicators' flocked to those imprisoned to ask for absolution, bring with them food and drink for the martyrs, reminiscent of *Passio* 9.1 (*De pudicitia* [*On Modesty*] 22.1).

44 For further discussion of this, and of women's leadership in early Christian churches, see Kraemer (1992: 174–98, esp. 179–81) and Cardman (1999).

45 Perpetua is even listed on the Syriac calendar, yet her co-martyr there is Saturnilus ('l' and 'n' are easily confused in Syriac), not Felicitas (W. Wright in Robinson 1891: 23).

BIBLIOGRAPHY

Amat, Jacqueline (1996) *Passion de Perpétue at de Félicité suivi des Acts: Introduction, Texte Critique, Traduction, Commentaire et Index.* Source Chrétiennes, 417. Paris: Éditions du Cerf.

Atkinson, P. C. (1982) 'The Montanist Interpretation of Joel 2: 28, 29 (LXX 3: 1,2)', *Studia Evangelica* 126, 7: 11–15.

Barnes, Timothy D. (1968a) 'Legislation Against the Christians', *Journal of Roman Studies* 58: 32–50.

—— (1968b) 'Pre-Decian *Acta Martyrum*', *Journal of Theological Studies* 19, 2: 509–31.

—— (1971) *Tertullian: A Historical and Literary Study.* Oxford: Clarendon Press.

Bowersock, Glen (1995) *Martyrdom and Rome.* Cambridge: Cambridge University Press.

Braun, R. (1979) 'Nouvelles observations linguistiques sur le rédacteur de la 'Passio Perpetuae', *Vigiliae Christianae* 33: 105–17.

Cardman, Francine (1999) 'Women, Ministry and Church Order in Early Christianity', in Ross Shepard Kraemer and Mary Rose D'Angelo (eds) *Women and Christian Origins.* New York: Oxford University Press, 300–29.

Delehaye, P. (1912) *Les origines du culte des martyrs.* Brussels: Bureaux de la Sociètè des Bollandistes.

Dronke, Peter (1984) *Women Writers of the Middle Ages: A Critical Study of Texts from Perpetua (†203) to Marguerite Porete (†1310).* Cambridge: Cambridge University Press.

Elm, Susanna (1994) 'Montanist Oracles', in Elisabeth Schüssler Fiorenza (ed.) *Searching the Scriptures: A Feminist Commentary.* New York: Crossroad, II, 131–8.

—— (forthcoming) 'Perpetua the Martyr – Perpetua the Saint: The Cultural Context of an Early Christian Phenomenon', in M. Behrman and F. Schiffauer (eds) *Martyrdom Religious/ Political: The Rhetoric of Fundamentalism in the Age of Globalization.* Amsterdam: Amsterdam Institute for Religion and Society.

Fantham, Elaine, Foley, Helen Peet, Kampen, Natalie Boymel, Pomeroy, Sarah B. and Shapiro, H. Alan (1994) *Women in the Classical World.* New York: Oxford University Press.

Frend, W. H. C. (1965) *Martyrdom and Persecution in the Early Church from the Maccabees to Donatus.* Oxford: Basil Blackwell.

—— (1975) 'A Severan Persecution? Evidence of the *Historia Augusta*', *Forma Futuri. Studi in onore del Cardinale Michele Pellegrino.* Turin: Bottega D'Erasmo, 470–80.

—— (1978) 'Blandina and Perpetua: Two Early Christian Heroines', in M. Leglay (ed.) *Les Martyrs de Lyons (177).* Paris: Éditions du Centre nationale de la recherche scientifique. Reprinted in David N. Scholer (ed.) (1993) *Women in Early Christianity 14.* New York: Garland, 87–115.

Fridh, A. (1968) *Le problème de la passion des saintes Perpétue et Félicité* Studia Graeca et Latina Gothoburgensia 26. Göteborg: Acta Universitatis Gothoburgensis.

Habermehl, P. (1992) *Perpetua und der Ägypter oder Bilder des Bösen im frühen afrikanischen Christentum. Ein Versuch zur Passio Sanctarum Perpetuae et Felicitatis.* Berlin: Akademie Verlag.

Hallett, Judith (1984) *Fathers and Daughters in Roman Society: Women and the Elite Family.* Princeton, N. J.: Princeton University Press.

—— (1999) 'Women's Lives in the Ancient Mediterranean', in Ross Shepard Kraemer and Mary Rose D'Angelo, (eds) *Women and Christian Origins.* New York: Oxford University Press, 13–34.

Harris, Rendel and Gifford, Seth (1890) *The Acts of the Martyrdom of Perpetua and Felicity. The original Greek text now first edited from a ms. in the library of the Convent of the Holy Sepulchre at Jerusalem.* London: C. J. Clay & Sons.

Harris, William V. (1989) *Ancient Literacy.* Cambridge, Mass.: Harvard University Press.

Heffernan, Thomas (1995) 'Philology and Authorship in the *Passio Sanctarum Perpetuae et Felicitatis*', *Traditio: Studies in Ancient and Medieval History, Thought, and Religion* 50: 315–25.

Heine, Ronald J. (1989) *Montanist Oracles and Testimonia.* North American Patristic Society 14. Macon, Ga.: Mercer University Press.

Hill, Edmund (1994) *The Works of Saint Augustine: A Translation for the 21st Century 3.* Hyde Park, N.Y.: New City Press.

Klawiter, Frederick (1980) 'The Role of Martyrdom and Persecution in Developing the Priestly Authority of Women in Early Christianity: A Case Study of Montanism', *Church History* 49, 3: 251–61.

Kraemer, Ross S. (1988) *Maenads, Martyrs, Matrons, Monastics: A Sourcebook of Women's Religions in the Greco-Roman World.* Philadelphia, Pa.: Fortress Press.

—— (1991) 'Women's Authorship of Jewish and Christian Literature in the Greco-Roman Period', in Amy-Jill Levine (ed.), *'Women Like This': New Perspectives on Jewish Women in the Greco-Roman Period.* Early Judaism and its Literature 1. Atlanta, Ga.: Scholars Press, 221–42.

—— (1992) *Her Share of the Blessings: Women's Religions Among Pagans, Jews and Christians in the Greco-Roman World.* New York: Oxford University Press.

—— (1993) 'Jewish Mothers and Daughters in the Greco-Roman World', in Shaye J. D. Cohen (ed.) *The Jewish Family in Antiquity.* Brown Judaic Studies 289. Atlanta, Ga.: Scholars Press, 89–112.

—— (1998) *When Aseneth Met Joseph. A Late Antique Tale of the Biblical Patriarch and His Egyptian Wife, Reconsidered.* New York: Oxford University Press.

Kugel, James (1990) *In Potiphar's House: The Interpretive Life of Biblical Texts.* San Francisco: HarperCollins.

LeClercq, Henri (1939) 'Perpétue et Félicité (Stes)', in F. Cabrol and H. Leclercq (eds), *Dictionnaire d'Archéologie Chrétienne et de Liturgie.* Paris: Letouzey et Ané, 14, 1: 393–444.

Lefkowitz, Mary (1976) 'Motivations for St. Perpetua's Martyrdom', *JAAR* 44: 417–21.

McGinn, Sheila E. (1994) 'The Acts of Thecla', in Elisabeth Schüssler (ed.) *Searching the Scriptures: A Feminist Commentary.* New York: Crossroad, II, 800–28.

Maitland, Sarah (1996) *The Martyrdom of Perpetua.* Visionary Women 3, (ed. Monica Furlong). Evesham: Arthur James.

Miles, Margaret (1989) *Carnal Knowing: Female Nakedness and Religious Meaning in the Christian West.* New York: Random House.

Mommsen, Theodor (ed.) (1891) *Monumenta Germaniae Historica. Auctores Antiquissimi.* Berlin: Weidmann.

Musurillo, Herbert (1972) *The Acts of the Christian Martyrs.* Oxford: Clarendon Press.

Perkins, Judith (1995) *The Suffering Self. Pain and Narrative Representation in the Early Christian Era*. London: Routledge.

Petroff, Elizabeth A. (1986) *Medieval Women's Visionary Literature*. New York: Oxford University Press.

Poirier, M. (1970) 'Note sur la Passio Sanctarum Perpetuae et Felicitatis: Félicité était-elle vraiment l'esclave de Perpétue?', *Studia Patristica* 10, 1: 306–9.

Rader, Rosemary (1981) 'Perpetua', in Patricia Wilson-Kastner *et al.*, *A Lost Tradition: Women Writers of the Early Church*. Lanham, Md.: University Press of America, 1–32.

Reardon, B. P. (1989) *Collected Ancient Greek Novels*. Berkeley: University of California Press.

Rives, J. B. (1995) *Religion and Authority in Roman Carthage from Augustus to Constantine*. Oxford: Clarendon Press.

Robeck, Cecil Jnr. (1992) *Prophecy in Carthage. Perpetua, Tertullian, and Cyprian*. Cleveland, Oh.: Pilgrim Press.

Robinson, J. A. (1891) *The Passion of S. Perpetua. Newly Edited from the Mss. with an introduction and notes*. Cambridge Theological Studies 1.2. Cambridge: Cambridge University Press.

Salisbury, Joyce E. (1997) *Perpetua's Passion. The Death and Memory of a Young Roman Woman*. New York: Routledge.

Shaw, Brent (1987) 'The Age of Roman Girls at Marriage: Some Reconsiderations', *Journal of Roman Studies* 77: 30–46.

—— (1993) 'The Passion of Perpetua', *Past and Present* 139: 3–45.

Shewring, W. H. (1931) *The Passion of Perpetua and Felicity. A New Edition and Translation of the Latin Text Together with the Sermons of Saint Augustine*. London: Sheed & Ward.

Snyder, Jane (1989) *The Woman and the Lyre: Women Writers in Classical Greece and Rome*. Carbondale: Southern Illinois University Press.

Thurston, Herbert and Attwater, Donald (1956) *Butler's Lives of the Saints*. New York: P. J. Kennedy & Sons.

Stevenson, J. (1987) *A New Eusebius. Documents Illustrating the History of the Church to* AD 337. London: SPCK (reprint of 1957 edition).

Tabbernee, William (1997) *Montanist Inscriptions and Testimonia. Epigraphic Sources Illustrating the History of Montanism*. North American Patristic Society Patristic Monograph Series 16. Macon, Ga.: Mercer University Press.

Tilley, Maureen (1994) 'The Passion of Perpetua and Felicity', in Elisabeth Schüssler (ed.) *Searching the Scriptures: A Feminist Commentary*. New York: Crossroad, II, 829–58.

Trevett, Christine (1996) *Montanism. Gender, Authority and the New Prophecy*. Cambridge: Cambridge University Press.

van Beek, C. J. M. J. ([1936] 1956) *Passio Sanctarum Perpetuae et Felicitatis. Vol 1. Textum Graecum et Latinum ad fidem codicum MSS*. Nijmegen: Noviomagi, Deker & Van de Vegt.

—— (1938) *Passio Sanctarum Perpetuae et Felicitatis. Latine et Graece*. Florilegium Patristicum 43 (eds B. Geyer and J. Zellinger). Bonn: Peter Hanstein.

Wypustek, Andrezej (1997) 'Magic, Montanism, Perpetua, and The Severan Persecution', *Vigiliae Christianae* 51: 276–97.

CHAPTER FORTY-TWO

CONSTANTINE

——— .◆. ———

Bill Leadbetter

INTRODUCTION

Constantine remains a figure of controversy. He is one of those people who seem by their personality, their acumen, and their ability both to take the opportunities offered and to leave the world markedly changed by their presence in it. He bequeaths a series of paradoxes: an autocrat who never ruled alone; a firm legislator for the Roman family, yet who slew his wife and eldest son and was, himself, illegitimate; a dynastic puppet-master, who left no clear successor; a soldier whose legacy was far more spiritual than temporal.

Constantine's origins

His origins lay within the ruling Roman military caste. By the late third century, the traditional Roman landed aristocracy had given way to a new class of men distinguished by their military merits. Constantine's father, Constantius, was one such. Of Pannonian origin (Aurelius Victor, *De Caesaribus* 39.26), he followed a career within the senior echelons of the army. One source lists his posts, in ascending order, as protector, tribune, governor of Dalmatia (*Origo Constantini imperatoris* 1.2). At some point during Constantius' rise through the senior ranks he acquired Helena, a concubine of humble origins (Leadbetter 1998b). In about 272, their son Constantine was born in the Pannonian town of Naissus, the modern Nish (Barnes 1982: 39–42).

If, as has been conjectured (Barnes 1982:36) Constantius' governorship of Dalmatia belonged to the reign of Carinus (283–5), then his support will have been critical to Diocletian, victor over Carinus in a civil war. The final battle in that war occurred at the Margus river, in a region adjacent to Constantius' own province. Diocletian's victory certainly brought Constantius within the small circle of those who really ruled the empire.

The dyarchy and the tetrarchy

Diocletian's accession to unchallenged power marked a change in the way in which the Roman world was ruled. Beset by pressure on the frontiers, separatist revolt, and the pressing need for administrative change, he appointed a deputy with whom he formally shared power, thus creating the 'dyarchy' ('rule by two'). The person whom he appointed, Maximian, was another Pannonian military man (*Epitome de Caesaribus* 40.10). Diocletian was careful to preserve both the trappings and the reality of seniority (Leadbetter 1998c), but the junior emperor was still a formidable figure.

A cryptic passage in a panegyric to Maximian, delivered in 289, has led many scholars to accept that, by that time Constantius was Maximian's praetorian prefect (Barnes 1982: 37, 125f.; Nixon and Rodgers 1994: 70f.; Leadbetter 1998b: 75–7). The passage (*Panegyrici Latini* 10[2] 11.4) celebrates a marriage, in all likelihood the marriage of Constantius and Maximian's daughter Theodora. At this point, then, Constantius put his concubine aside for the sake of a highly advantageous dynastic match.

In 293, Diocletian expanded the imperial college still further. While he and Maximian retained their ranks as emperors of more senior status (*Augusti*) two deputies, each with the title of 'most noble (*nobilissimus*) Caesar', were appointed. This arrangement is referred to as the 'Tetrarchy' ('rule by four') and was commemorated in imperial statuary (see Chapter 10, and Figures 10.1, 10.2). Diocletian's deputy was his own son-in-law, Galerius. Maximian's was Constantius. The principal task for the Caesars was to assert imperial authority on the frontiers and win back separatist regions. As generals they were extremely successful. Constantius recaptured Britain from the separatist emperors Carausius and Allectus; Galerius shattered the power of Rome's ancient enemy, Persia.

Constantine's early career

Like his father, Constantine pursued a military career. He was assisted by his father's rank, but all of his early military service was in the armies of Galerius and Diocletian (Barnes 1982: 41f.). While it is legitimate to conjecture that he was hostage for his father's loyalty during this period, he was also an active and valiant warrior. He was in the army of Galerius which invaded Persia, and fought with distinction against Sarmatian bands on the Danube frontier. Soon afterwards, he was transferred to Diocletian's personal staff, where he served until 305.

In May 305, Diocletian and Maximian abdicated. Diocletian's abdication was voluntary (although it followed upon a long illness); Maximian was less willing, but he complied with his senior colleague's wishes. Both retired to country houses, Diocletian to the cultivation of his garden (*Epitome de Caesaribus* 39.6). They were succeeded by their deputies: Constantius replaced Maximian and Galerius took the place of Diocletian. Constantius, however, was the senior of the two, and his name appears first in inscriptions of the period. One source suggests that it was expected that the new Caesars would be Constantine and Maxentius, the son of Maximian (Lactantius, *On the Deaths of the Persecutors* 18.8). Instead, they were Maximin Daia and Severus, both men loyal to Galerius.

Galerius had benefited immensely from the transfer of power. While he could not inherit Diocletian's formal seniority, he sought to exercise Diocletian's station. Constantius, for his part, seems to have accepted the situation. It may be that he had no desire to risk open conflict with Galerius; it may be that he was mindful that Constantine was now posted to the court of Galerius. Constantius certainly sent to Galerius, asking that his son be returned to him (Lactantius, *On the Deaths of the Persecutors* 23.3–4; *Origo Constantini imperatoris* 2.2). Galerius, unable to decline such a request, acceded, and Constantine returned to his father's side in time to accompany him on campaign against the Picts (*Panegyrici Latini* 6[7]7.5). On 25 July, 306, however, Constantius died and Constantine was proclaimed emperor by the troops in York (for the dates, see Barnes 1982: 61).

CONSTANTINE THE POLITICIAN

Constantine did not immediately set himself up as a rival to Galerius. Rather, he preferred to accept Galerius' verdict. His opportunism was swiftly imitated. In late October 306, Maximian's son Maxentius, then resident in Rome, was proclaimed emperor by the remnants of the Praetorian Guard still resident there. He was careful to claim no title, striking coins instead as *princeps* rather than *Augustus* or *Caesar* (Cullhed 1994, 32–4). This did not suffice to appease Galerius, who might reward audacity when there was an imperial vacancy to fill, but would not countenance disloyalty otherwise. Severus, Constantius' successor in the West, marched against

Figure 42.1 Head of Constantine from the Basilica of Constantine in Rome. Photo J. C. N. Coulston.

the rebel, who sat securely behind the walls of Rome. Maxentius called upon his father for aid. Maximian had commanded the troops now serving under Severus, and it was a simple matter for him to recall them to their old loyalty. Deserted by his army, Severus fled to Ravenna, where he was handed over to Maximian and compelled to abdicate (Lactantius, *On the Deaths of the Persecutors* 26.6–11; *Origo Constantini Imperatoris* 3.6–4.10). The vacancy which Maxentius required had been created, but not in any way calculated to endear him to Galerius. The senior emperor himself now marched on the rebel, but with only marginally more success. Galerius escaped from Italy with his life and his army, but Maxentius still remained, unscathed, behind the walls of Rome.

Maxentius' successful revolt was a piece of extraordinary good fortune for Constantine. It reintroduced Maximian into the affairs of the empire, and robbed effective control of the West from Galerius, thus effectively leaving Constantine a free hand in his own lands. Constantine used his opportunity to cement his position through dynastic arrangements of his own. He had previously enjoyed a relationship with a concubine, Minervina, who had borne him a son, Crispus (*Epitome de Caesaribus* 41.4), Zosimus (*New History* 2.20.2) and Zonaras (13.2.37) all call Minervina a concubine. There is no reason to dispute their testimony, although Jones *et al.* (1971: 602–3) suggest otherwise. This was now put aside for a grand match.

As the armies of Galerius trudged wearily eastwards in the winter on 307, a grand celebration was taking place in Gaul. Constantine was marrying Maximian's daughter Fausta. An orator celebrated the occasion in a panegyric, which also noted a further development. Constantine accepted promotion to the rank of Augustus from the hands of Maximian (*Panegyrici Latini* 7[6]5.3). Constantine's claim to the rank was attractive and plausible. Following the death of Severus there was no Augustus in the West; Constantine had been his Caesar and so therefore next in line. It was also confirmed by the one who had bestowed the rank of Augustus upon Constantine's father. This last point was not lost on the panegyrist who made much of it.

The promotion was, however, in open defiance of Galerius, who claimed the right to nominate Severus' successor. In order to add lustre to his decisions, he nominated himself and the retired Diocletian as consuls for the following year (308) and summoned an imperial conference at Carnuntum in Pannonia. Diocletian's presence added due weight to its deliberations. He prevailed upon Maximian to return to private life; the two, together with Galerius, nominated a new Augustus for the West, Licinius, an old friend and ally of Galerius (*Origo Constantini imperatoris* 5.13). Constantine was not rejected from this scheme; instead, he retained the insignia of Caesar.

This arrangement was hardly satisfactory to Constantine, who ignored the decision of Carnuntum and retained the title of Augustus. He was, after all, the effective ruler of Britain, Gaul and Spain. His nominal superior, Licinius, controlled a patch of Pannonia, and had the task of recovering Italy and Africa from Maxentius. Constantine also took his responsibilities seriously. When not engaged in high politics, he was on campaign (Barnes 1982:70). In 310, Maximian, excluded from power by Maxentius and reduced to the pathetic status of vexatious mendicant, sought to depose Constantine. The coup was ludicrous; the aged Augustus, its only casualty, was forced to suicide. Constantine's condign treatment of his father-in-law illustrates the limits of his *pietas*. Another panegyric, delivered in Autun in 310, sets out the official version (Nixon and Rodgers 1994: 237–43).

The panegyrist of 310 was also entrusted to deploy a hitherto undisclosed fact about Constantine's family. In praising the emperor, he also praises his ancestry: not merely his father Constantius, but also more remote antecedents. A link is drawn between Constantine and the emperor Claudius II Gothicus, a hero of the Roman recovery, mythologized for the defeat of a Gothic horde and premature death from plague (*Panegyrici Latini* 6[7]2; Nixon and Rodgers 1994: 219; Syme 1974). Although the precise nature of Constantine's kinship with Claudius is never elucidated by the panegyrist, it is nevertheless clear that a new shot in a propaganda war has been fired.

Hitherto, Constantine had rested his claims to legitimacy as much upon his recognition by Galerius and Constantine as upon his proclamation by Constantius' army in 306. He now cast aside the mantle of tetrarch, and seized that of dynast. One reason for his change of strategy may well have lain with Galerius. The senior Augustus had already begun making plans for his retirement. A palatial villa was being constructed for him at Romuliana, the place of his birth (Srejovic *et al.* 1983; Srejovic 1985, 1992/3). Lactantius states that he had already commenced amassing state resources for the celebration of his *vicennalia* (Lactantius *On the Deaths of the Persecutors* 31.2). This year-long celebration of his accomplishment and longevity was due to commence in March 312 and conclude with his abdication 12 months later.

Constantine was probably therefore preparing the ground for his own claim to seniority within the empire. If so, then his anticipation was rewarded when Galerius died prematurely in May 311. No successor was proclaimed. Rather, Licinius and Maximinus partitioned the territories which he had occupied: Licinius ruled in the Balkan provinces; Maximinus in Asia Minor, Syria and Egypt; Constantine in Britain, Gaul and Spain; Maxentius in Africa and Italy. Whereas Diocletian's tetrarchs had been united by patronage and their loyalty to the senior ruler, this group of four was divided by mutual suspicion and rivalry.

War with Maxentius

Images of Maxentius have largely been crafted by Constantine's propagandists. From them emerges the picture of a greedy and wanton ruler who dabbled in the magic arts. But Maxentius was not so wicked. He was a conscientious ruler who retained the loyalty of his troops. He tolerated Christianity, although he also exiled two popes whose elections had occasioned disorder (Cullhed 1994: 72–3). Constantine, however, felt the need to blacken his memory, in all likelihood because the war which he waged against Maxentius was unprovoked.

In the summer of 312, Constantine invaded Italy. His army defeated a large force led by Maxentius' general, Pompeianus, at Verona, and then marched on Rome. Maxentius, responsive to criticism from within Rome, abandoned his earlier policy of sitting behind Rome's mighty walls and subverting his opponent's army. Instead, he marched out to oppose Constantine. The armies met in battle at the still extant Milvian Bridge, outside Rome.

Eusebius, writing in his *Life of Constantine* (composed soon after the emperor's death in 337), states that Constantine himself had told him that one afternoon before this battle while marching with his army he saw with his own eyes, as did all his army, a cross of light written in the sky, together with the words 'In this conquer'. The following night Christ appeared to him in a vision with the sign seen in the sky and told him to make a copy of it to serve as his standard in war. Next day Constantine summoned his craftsmen and produced such a standard, consisting of a tall pole and a cross-bar, with the now familiar chi–rho monogram ☧ (symbolizing Jesus Christ, chi and rho being the first two letters of *Christos*) embellished with gold and jewels at the top of the pole, and a banner carrying the image of Constantine hanging from the cross-bar. Thus was created the famous *Labarum*. Constantine also had his soldiers paint the *chi–rho* monogram on their shields. Under this sign his army conquered (Jones 1972: 98–101).

Maxentius was defeated. Thousands of his men drowned in the Tiber as they were forced back by Constantine's army. Fleeing across the bridge with a large crowd, Maxentius himself was pushed into the river and drowned (Jones 1972: 83). Rome, Italy and Africa were now Constantine's. His subsequent triumphal entry into Rome is celebrated on the Arch of Constantine later erected in the city (see Figure 42.2).

THE CONVERSION OF CONSTANTINE

The question of the conversion of Constantine has continued to excite controversy. Its authenticity has been questioned and asserted with equal ferocity. The degree of vigour with which the partisans of either side (e.g. Kerestzes 1981; Kee 1982) have approached this question is enduring testimony to the historical significance of the religious policies embarked upon by Constantine. Despite attempts to demonstrate otherwise, the nature of Constantine's personal religious beliefs will always be a mystery precisely because they remained private. What does matter, however, is the way in which Constantine came to frame a religious policy which did more than merely tolerate Christianity.

Immediately following his defeat of Maxentius, Constantine confirmed his policy of toleration in an edict issued from Rome in which he ordered the cessation of persecution everywhere (Corcoran 1996: 187). This order was principally directed at Maximinus, who initially complied. Some months afterwards, Constantine met with Licinius in the city of Milan. There, the alliance between the two was sealed by the marriage of Licinius to Constantine's sister Constantia (Pohlsander 1993). They also produced a document, 'The Edict of Milan', which was enforced in the territory which they ruled directly. This granted universal toleration and the restitution of all Christian property.

Licinius' new-found toleration of Christianity was one substantial policy difference which he had with Maximinus, who had recommenced a persecution which he had been reluctant to abandon in the first place (Castritius 1969: 63–86; Mitchell 1988: 115; Nicholson 1991). Other counsels prevailed. Before a blow was struck in the war between the two, Maximinus ordered the toleration of Christianity in terms identical with those of the Edict of Milan (Eusebius, *Historia Ecclesiastica* 9.10.7–11;

Corcoran 1996: 152, 188). It did not help him. Before the two armies of Maximinus and Licinius met in battle at Adrianople, that of Licinius recited a prayer to 'the supreme God', the words of which were (according to the emperor) dictated to him in a dream by an angel. The battle necessarily took on a religious dimension; Licinius, the champion of 'the supreme God' was challenging Maximinus, publically zealous for the traditional deities. In this religious trial by combat, Licinius was victorious and Maximinus fled to Tarsus and there took his own life. Licinius was the master of the East; the last vestiges of persecution eradicated.

Licinius' alliance with Constantine guaranteed peace for the Christians under his direct rule. He expressed a degree of appreciation for the faith which Constantine favoured. His wife was Christian and places were found for bishops at his court (Pohlsander 1993: 156–7). The political relationship between the two was uneasy, however. A war broke out in 316 and Licinius was defeated, losing most of his European possessions to Constantine. It was only after this that Licinius revived a policy of hostility towards the Christians. He only slowly became an active persecutor, instead preferring to cancel legal privileges which Christians had gained and regulate the affairs of the churches (Barnes 1981: 70–1). Licinius sought to suppress the churches in his last years, when his confrontation with Constantine had become intolerable. No doubt he feared the Christians as the fifth column of his rival and acted accordingly. Licinius' anti-Christian measures then became the substantive cause of the final war between himself and Constantine, who was, no doubt, glad of the excuse which they provided for him (Barnes 1981: 72–3). In 324, Licinius was defeated and deposed by Constantine. The empire was now united under his authority. Persecution had gasped itself out and the Constantinian church reigned triumphant.

CONSTANTINE AND THE CHURCH

Introduction

When Constantine entered Rome in October 312, he brought with him an entirely new approach to Christianity. His predecessors had been hostile or ambivalent. He became an active patron and benefactor. In so doing, he was not careless of the sensitivities of those in the empire who were not Christians. Constantine was not a crass triumphalist. In the city of Rome itself, the only image of him which referred to the new faith was the great statue in the basilica which bore his name (see Figure 42.1). This statue depicted him holding the *Labarum*, his own symbol of Christianity (see p. 1074). Otherwise he expressed a dutiful traditionalism. The inscription on his triumphal arch in Rome refers coyly to 'the divinity' (*Inscriptiones Latinae Selectae* 694 = *Corpus Inscriptionum Latinarum* 6. 1139). For five years or more after his victory at the Milvian Bridge his coinage retained traditional pagan images, such as Hercules the Victorious, Mars the Destroyer, Jupiter the Preserver and, above all, Sol Invictus, 'the Unconquered Sun' (Jones 1972: 97; Bruun 1966: 61–4), which also features on his triumphal arch (see Figure 42.2).

These ought not to be taken as uncertainty in Constantine's own mind or policy.

Figure 42.2 Relief of Constantine's triumphal entry into Rome, from the Arch of Constantine, showing Sol Invictus over the emperor and also in a chariot. Photo J. C. N. Coulston.

It was mere courtesy to the considerable numbers of people in the empire with different religious beliefs. Taken as a whole, Constantine's actions make his preference for Christianity perfectly clear. This is most clearly seen in the nature of some of his legislation; his patronage of the church, which was on a vast scale; and his involvement in its internal disputes, particularly the Donatist and Arian schisms. Christians in turn made their own preference for Constantine clear. A new theology of empire emerged which exalted the Christian emperor, a development with which Constantine was pleased to cooperate.

Legislative acts

Constantine's patronage of Christianity was expressed soon after his victory over Maxentius through a series of legislative acts. There is evidence of imperial subsidy of the church and the exemption of Christian clergy from civic duties as early as 313 (Eusebius, *H. E.* 10.6, 7). These acts of favour towards the church reflect a general policy of legitimation of it by Constantine. Because the Christians had hitherto formed a fringe or clandestine community, the church had no clear public role. Throughout his legislation, Constantine sought to provide such a role. The exemption of clergy from civic duties, already flagged in a letter to the governor of Africa, was made more explicit in later mandates (*Theodosian Code* 16.2.1, 2). Such directives encouraged the view that bishops and other clergy were already, by virtue of their office, men in public life. The Christian congregation, too, found a place in law. Slaves could now be manumitted by declaration before a gathering, in the presence of a bishop (*Theodosian Code* 4.7.1; 2.8.1; *Code of Justinian* 1.13.1); episcopal courts were given official legal status (*Code of Justinian* 1.27.1; *Sirmondian Constitutions* 1); clergy became exempt from taxation (*Theodosian Code* 16.2.10); and the Christian day of worship (Sunday) declared a day of rest (*Code of Justinian* 3.12.2). Moreover, Constantine removed one legal impediment to Christian practice when he rescinded the old Augustan penalties against celibacy and childlessness (*Theodosian Code* 8.16.1) and sought to privilege Christians over Jews for the first time.

Constantine's legislation pertaining to the Jews of the empire is most revealing of the degree to which he favoured Christianity. While relieving Christian clergy of curial duty, for example, he reversed an ancient principle and ordered that Jews should now be subject to nomination to town councils (*Theodosian Code* 16.8.3; Lindner 1987: 120–4). Moreover, he ordained that Jews be restrained from attacking members of their communities who converted to Christianity (*Theodosian Code* 16.8.1; *Code of Justinian* 1.9.3; Lindner 1987: 124–32; *Sirmondian Constitutions* 4; Lindner 1987: 138–44). These laws are not as innocuous as they might appear. They provide legal privileges for Christians and remove traditional privileges enjoyed by Jews.

The most controversial question relating to Constantine's legislation is that relating to traditional sacrifice. Eusebius makes a remark to the effect that Constantine abolished it altogether (*Life of Constantine* 2.45). This statement has been variously believed and disbelieved (Barnes 1981: 210–12; Drake 1983: 462–6). Endeavours to harmonize the evidence have been offered (Errington 1988; Bradbury 1994). Certainly if Constantine ever did forbid traditional sacrifice, such an order was never enforced during his lifetime. Constantine's abhorrence of blood sacrifice, however, is clear from his own statements. His preference for Christian governors ensured that the public sacrifices normally performed by imperial officials would be discontinued (Eusebius, *Life of Constantine* 2.44; Bradbury 1994: 129–30).

Constantine as imperial patron

The most obvious and enduring consequence of Constantine's patronage of the Christian church is in the monumental construction of vast new buildings for public gathering and worship. Christians had not developed a singular architecture for their public buildings for the simple reason that they did not have many. Those which they did possess were, by and large, private dwellings converted for the purpose like the third-century church building at Dura-Europos (Krautheimer 1965: 4–8). There are 25 known pre-Constantinian Christian communities in Rome (Kirsch 1935; Lampe 1989). They are known from the names (or *tituli*) of the apartment houses, in which they worshipped and which they probably owned. In all likelihood, they were confiscated by the state during the Great Persecution. Constantine unconditionally restored all Christian property very soon after his victory over Maxentius (Eusebius, *H. E.* 10.2. 15–17).

It may have been less than two weeks after the battle of the Milvian Bridge that Constantine took a further step, donating to the church an imperial villa on the outskirts of Rome (Krautheimer 1979: 89–90; 1983: 13–15). Constantine's gift was not, however, of a mere house. Out of its old buildings, and sprawling into the gardens, there slowly arose the great hall which we know today as St John Lateran. Across the Tiber, in the Vatican fields, the entire side of a hill was levelled, the spoil tumbling into, and filling up, a gully in which a pagan cemetery was located. Also in that gully was the shrine upon which the new church was constructed: the presumed grave of St Peter (Toynbee and Ward-Perkins 1956). Elswhere in Rome at the Sessorian Palace, Constantine's mother Helena resided, with her precious relic, a piece of the True Cross from Jerusalem. This in turn became another great Constantinian basilica, Santa Croce in Gerusalemme. The shrine of St Lawrence too received imperial attention. The deacon who, legend had it, had been executed at the order of the emperor Valerian, had a tomb beyond the walls of Aurelian. Like the bones of St Peter, those of St Lawrence were the object of particular veneration by Rome's Christians. A great basilica soon arose over his grave, to attract pilgrims and worshippers to partake of his sanctity.

Temple-building had always been a major feature of imperial euergetism. When Constantine ordered the construction of the new Christian basilicas within Rome itself he was extending imperial benificence to the new faith. It certainly accorded the Christian church a status which it had never possessed before, and permitted it to express a new grandeur of display in ritual and self-advertisement.

It was a cautious kind of euergetism, concentrating upon the outskirts of the city of Rome itself, and upon Christianity's holiest sites. Upon the site of Helena's discovery of the True Cross, now interpreted as the place where both the Crucifixion and Resurrection occurred, there was constructed a grand new Basilica of the Holy Sepulchre. Likewise, at Bethlehem, the church of the Holy Nativity was built around the supposed scene of Christ's birth. These grand basilicas neatly annexed to the empire the sacred stories which lie at the heart of the Christian gospel: the narratives of Jesus himself, and of his apostles and those who died for the faith.

Such properties were maintained by a generous endowment (Janes 1998: 54–6). The *Liber Pontificalis*, an early chronicle of the papacy, lists an extraordinary amount of property which Constantine donated to the church. The well of Constantine's financial generosity to the various sees was both deep and wide. In taking on the role of imperial patron of the church, however, Constantine also necessarily involved himself in its internal disputes.

Moreover, the level of imperial generosity made the price of schism necessarily high. It was now not merely the fracturing of the Christian community, but also the consequent privileging of one segment of that community over the other, since one received imperial largesse and the other did not. It also forced the emperor into the role of arbiter and judge of doctrine, a role which Constantine did not assume with any degree of comfort.

Constantine's new city

Although Constantine embellished Rome with great cathedrals, perhaps the most enduring of his architectural legacies lay on the Bosporus. There, after the defeat of Licinius in 324, he laid the foundations of a new city – Constantinople. This was to be a Christian city, uncontaminated by pagan cult or tradition (Barnes 1981: 212). Constantine, at first, did not spend much time in his new foundation. Over the following years, he preferred to base himself at Nicomedia while his newest city was being constructed. Occasionally he made tours of inspection, but it was not until 330, when the city was formally dedicated, that he finally based himself there (Dagron 1974: 33; Barnes 1982: 69, 75–8). The city which he created was embellished with art plundered from Greece, and was endowed with a hippodrome, baths, and a Senate house (Dagron 1974: 36–7; Krautheimer 1983: 45–50). No temples were built by Constantine, however. Rather, a series of great churches were constructed, the most notable being the Church of the Holy Wisdom – a vast and lofty basilica attached to the imperial palace (Krautheimer 1983: 50–5). This landmark cathedral was located in the ceremonial heart of the new city. It proclaimed the solid institutional identification between emperor and church.

The only church in the city which was completed during Constantine's lifetime was of equal significance. The Church of the Holy Apostles (*Apostoleion*) was endowed with memorials of all 12 apostles, and was intended to be Constantine's tomb (Krautheimer 1983: 55–60). There he would lie as the thirteenth and last of the messengers of God.

When Constantine founded this city, it was less to found the new capital of the empire than to found a new capital. Rome had long ceased to be the centre of the imperial world. Rather, the capital was where the emperor was (Millar 1977: 15–53). But he certainly intended this to be a great city. He attracted a population there through great incentives, according to one critic stripping neighbouring cities bare of people (Eunapius, *Lives of the Sophists* 462). He endowed a senatorial class. But this senatorial class was not equivalent to their venerable western colleagues. Their titles and entitlements differed. This new town was, however, constructed in Constantine's image. As such, it became the metropolitan city of the Christian empire – simultaneously a museum of the pagan past and an aggressive assertion of the Christian future.

Constantine and Christian dissent

The Donatist controversy

Constantine's involvement in the doctrinal and disciplinary affairs of the church commenced with an appeal for his intervention in the Donatist dispute. This was not without precedent. In 270, over forty years before Christians were to win religious toleration, a dispute over the tenure of the see of Antioch led to an appeal to the judgement of the emperor Aurelian. On that occasion, Aurelian had referred the appellants to the bishop of Rome (Eusebius, *H. E.* 7.30.19–21). On this occasion, the Donatists appealed to Constantine to rule in their dispute with Caecilian. Constantine followed the precedent of Aurelian in referring the matter to Miltiades, the bishop of Rome (Eusebius, *H. E.* 10.5.18).

Miltiades' response was to call a wider council of bishops to Rome to resolve the matter. They judged in favour of Caecilian, and the response of the Donatists was, again, to appeal to the judgement of Constantine. Constantine ordered a council of bishops to be held at Arles, a city in which he was sometimes resident, in order to hear the appeal. The Donatists again lost their suit, and sought a third time for Constantine's intervention. Somewhat exasperated by their persistence, Constantine finally relented and himself took a stand, rejecting the Donatist appeal and aligning himself firmly with the previous judgements of Miltiades and the Council of Arles.

Constantine's involvement in the Donatist dispute had been unwilling, forced by the intransigence of the Donatists themselves. Nevertheless, it taught him a valuable lesson about the relationship between himself and the Christians. When the next controversy arose, his approach was far more interventionist.

The Arian controversy

For some years, a dispute had been brewing between two Alexandrian clergy about the nature of the godhead. A presbyter, Arius, who had been a student of Lucian of Antioch, asserted a theological view which emphasized the transcendence of the Father, and within which the Son was conceived of as a subsquent and therefore neither co-eternal nor co-valent with the Father. Arius was a popular preacher whose views found ready acceptance, both within his own community in Alexandria and also within the wider Christian world. He also encountered considerable opposition, not the least from his own bishop, Alexander.

When Constantine took control of the Eastern provinces, after the final defeat of Licinius in 324, he was presented with this controversy. Unlike the Donatist schism, this was over a matter of theological doctrine rather than church order. Constantine's first instinct was to seek to negotiate an agreement between the disputants. Accordingly, he sent Ossius of Cordova, his theological adviser, to Alexandria to mediate a solution. With him, Ossius took a letter from Constantine which characterized the whole matter a triviality; an inconsequential conflict over an unnecessary question. He urged forbearance and forgiveness (Eusebius *Life of Constantine* 2.63–72).

For the participants, however, such a dispute had far greater weight than mere philosophical hair-splitting. Neither could simply beg to differ. Ossius himself sought to resolve the conflict by resort to church order: Alexander was bishop; Arius a presbyter who owed him obedience. A subsequent gathering of bishops in Antioch likewise supported episcopal authority over priestly inspiration. At this council three of Arius' sympathizers, including Eusebius of Caesarea, were excommunicated (Barnes 1981: 213–14). Their excommunication was temporary and was to be reviewed at a council which was determined would be held later in the year at Ancyra. In the event, no such council was called. Constantine, perhaps dismayed by the failure of the bishops to agree amongst themselves, intervened and called a council at Nicaea.

Constantine at Nicaea

Nicaea was the most comprehensive church council called to that point, with representatives from all parts of the empire, and also from dioceses outside the empire. Constantine's patronage of the Council was apparent from its inception. The bishops were transported, housed and fed at public expense. The sessions were not held in an ecclesiastical building but on imperial property, in a structure described by Euse-bius as a 'palace'. In its initial session, Constantine addressed the bishops, exhorting them to reach agreement. When he withdrew, Ossius of Cordova assumed the role of president of the Council. Although Constantine was never formally a member of the Council, his stamp was upon it, and all of the participants were aware of his own determination to reach a satisfactory settlement.

In this, he seems to have been let down. As with the Donatists, Constantine was disappointed by the incapacity of the bishops to reach an agreement. In his various interventions, Constantine himself sought to be an eirenic voice for moderation. Final resolution upon a credal statement, however, could only be enforced by Con-stantine's own insistence that it would be the final word on the matter, and dissent meant exile.

Following the transaction of further ecclesiastical business, the Council wound up at a grand banquet to celebrate the twentieth anniversary of Constantine's accession to power. It was a remarkable occasion, in which Constantine's alliance with the church was proclaimed to the world at large, and its price to episcopal participants who dined surrounded by the armed guards who enforced the imperial will.

CONSTANTINE AND THE EMPIRE

Constantine's reforms

Constantine's adoption and championing of Christianity affected much of the imperial policy which he pursued. While many of his administrative reforms do not appear, at least overtly, to be Christian, it was impossible for Constantine not to nuance them somehow in favour of the church. Military chaplains appeared, for example, for the first time (Jones 1953); Christians were preferred for administrative posts; bishops were entrusted with juridical responsibilities.

In general, Constantine continued the tenor of administrative reform com-menced by Diocletian. An enduring achievement was the stabilization of the coin-age. The standard silver coinage had become heavily debased in the course of the third century, and Diocletian's attempt to re-tariff it had not been completely successful. In producing a high denomination standard coinage, Constantine aban-doned silver and instead struck a gold coinage (the *solidus*) which became a highly prized and stable means of storing and transferring value (Jones 1964: 107–9). Within the structure of the imperial administration, he created new offices and orders which completed a process, begun in the time of Augustus, of the trans-formation of the emperor's private household into a stratified, hierarchical imperial court.

He also made changes to the structure of the army. Significantly, he sup-plemented its numbers by recruitment from outside the empire. Constantine's later pagan critic Zosimus charged him with barbarizing the army (*New History* 2.34). While the charge is exaggerated and rhetorical, it is certainly true that in the generations which immediately followed even senior commanders could be drawn from the ranks of non-Roman communities. The static arrangements of the first two imperial centuries had been slowly dispensed with. Between them, Diocletian and Constantine remodelled the imperial army so that it was, in essence, two forces. There were troops on permanent garrison duty (the *limitanei*), who acted as a police and intelligence service. Then there were the mobile field armies (*comitatenses*), flexible enough to act as a defensive force when occasion arose, and as an offensive force without denuding the garrisons of necessary troops. This arrangement has been called 'defence in depth' by one military historian (Luttwak 1976: 127–90), although this thesis has been (properly) criticized by subsequent scholars (notably Isaac 1992: 372–418). It was not always a defensive arrangement.

Constantine's wars

Constant campaigning on the frontiers by Constantine and his predecessors had created a measure of peace and security. The necessity for such skirmishing continued in his later years. Campaigns are attested against Danubian peoples (particularly the Sarmatians: Barnes 1982: 75–9, 258). Towards the end of his reign, he mounted a successful campaign in Dacia (modern Transylvania), in which he claimed to have recovered territory which had been given up in the time of Aurelian (Julian, *The Caesars* 329b–d; Barnes 1982: 80).

Relations with the great rival empire of Sassanid Persia were less successful. When Armenia became a Christian nation, Rome's position in the East was strengthened. Some time later, he received Hormisdas, a Sassanid prince, as a refugee from the rule of the Great King, Shapur II. At some point, he personally wrote a letter to Shapur, asserting a role as protector of Shapur's Christian subjects (Barnes 1985: 130–3). War between the two states broke out during the last years of Constantine's reign. Persian troops invaded Armenia and expelled its Christian king. Constantine responded by making his own disposition for the rule of Armenia: his nephew Hannibalianus was proclaimed as its king, and an army was sent under his son Constantius to enforce this claim (*Epitome de Caesaribus* 41.20; *Origo Constantini imperatoris* 6.35). The initial campaigning was a success. Constantius drove the Persians from the key fortress town of Amida, and in the course of the fighting Narses, another of Shapur II's brothers, was slain (Dodgeon and Lieu 1991: 153–5). Emboldened by success, Constantine was preparing a further assault when he was overtaken by illness and died in May 337. His death left the Persian War as a long and bloody inheritance for his successors.

Constantine's dynasty

Constantine's family was a large one. His father's marriage to Theodora had produced six children, three of whom (his sisters) were deployed in dynastic matches (Barnes 1982: 37). His half-brothers, on the other hand, he preferred to keep away from the centre of power (Leadbetter 1998b: 80). Julian complained that this was at the behest of Constantine's mother who wished to see her own grandchildren exalted (Libanius, *Oration* 14.30). Like his father, Constantine fathered a son by a concubine. Minervina, the mother of his oldest son Crispus, is described in a number of sources as Constantine's concubine (Jones *et al.* 1971: 602–3). Crispus himself was a bright and engaging prince. Tutored by Lactantius himself, he was raised to the rank of Caesar in 317, and played an active role in Constantine's victory over Licinius in 324 (Jones *et al.* 1971: 233). Shortly after, however, he was executed, probably a victim of the clumsy intrigues of his stepmother Fausta. Soon afterwards, she too was executed (Jones *et al.* 1971: 326).

The death of Crispus, together with the relegation of Constantine's half-brothers, left the succession clear for Constantine's sons by Fausta. There were three of these, Constantine, Constantius and Constans (Barnes 1982: 43). Each of these was raised to the rank of Caesar in the lifetime of their father: Constantine in 317, Constantius in 324 and Constans in 333 (Barnes 1982: 7–8; Kienast 1990: 305, 307, 309). In 335, however, Constantine complicated this neat arrangement. His nephew Flavius Dematius was raised to the rank of Caesar also (Kienast 1990: 303). This, together with the new prominence of Constantius I's children, occasioned a succession crisis after the death of Constantine. The consequence was a long interregnum. Uncertainty was only resolved by the intervention of the army, which proclaimed Constantine's sons his legitimate successors and killed everyone else.

Constantine never ruled alone. He successfully safeguarded his own position through the deployment of members of his family as nominal colleagues. While this was of great political benefit to Constantine, it left an ambiguous legacy. His sons came to rule after his death through violence rather than a peaceful transition. Their own relationship was marked by mutual suspicion. In 340, Constantine was eliminated by Constans, who was in turn removed by a usurper. Constantius II, himself childless was forced to turn to the two surviving grandsons of Constantius I. Of these, he executed one (Gallus), while the other rebelled against him (Julian). Julian's own reign was ephemeral. His death in 363 marks the end of a dynasty which had, only one generation previously, been richly populated.

BIBLIOGRAPHY

Alföldi, Andrew (1948) *The Conversion of Constantine and Pagan Rome*, trans. Harold Mattingly. Oxford: Clarendon Press.

Arnheim, M. T. W. (1972) *The Senatorial Aristocracy in the Later Roman Empire*. Oxford: Clarendon Press.

Barnes, Timothy D. (1973) 'Porphyry "Against the Christians": Date and Attribution of Fragments', *Journal of Theological Studies* n.s. 24: 424–42.

—— (1975) 'The Beginnings of Donatism', *Journal of Theological Studies* n.s. 26: 13–22 (= T. D. Barnes, *Early Christianity and the Roman Empire* no. 8, London: Variorum).

—— (1976a) 'Sossianus Hierocles and the Antecedents of the Great Persecution', *Harvard Studies in Classical Philology* 80: 239–52.

—— (1976b) 'The Emperor Constantine's Good Friday Sermon', *Journal of Theological Studies* n.s. 27: 414–423.

—— (1981) *Eusebius and Constantine*. Cambridge, Mass. and London: Harvard University Press.

—— (1982) *The New Empire of Diocletian and Constantine*. Cambridge, Mass. and London: Harvard University Press.

—— (1985) 'Constantine and the Christians of Persia', *Journal of Roman Studies* 75: 126–36.

—— (1993) *Athanasius and Constantius: Theology and Politics in the Constantinian Empire.* Cambridge, Mass. and London: Harvard University Press.

Baynes, Norman H. (1934) 'Eusebius and the Christian Empire', *Annuaire de l'Institut de Philologie et d'Histoire Orientales (Mélanges Bidez)* 2: 13–18.

—— (1972) *Constantine the Great and the Christian Church.* 2nd edn. Oxford: Oxford University Press.

Blockley, Roger (1981) *The Fragmentary Classicising Historians of the Later Roman Empire: Eunapius, Olympiodorus, Priscus and Malchus.* Liverpool: Francis Cairns.

Bowder, Diana (1978) *The Age of Constantine and Julian.* London: Paul Elek.

Bradbury, Scott (1994) 'Constantine and Pagan Legislation in the Fourth Century', *Classical Philology* 89: 120–39.

Brown, Peter (1961) 'Aspects of the Christianization of the Roman Aristocracy', *Journal of Roman Studies* 51: 1–11.

—— (1971) 'The Rise and Function of the Holy Man in Late Antiquity', *Journal of Roman Studies* 61: 80–101.

—— (1978) *The Making of Late Antiquity.* Cambridge, Mass.: Harvard University Press.

—— (1981) *The Cult of the Saints.* Chicago: University of Chicago Press.

—— (1995) *Authority and the Sacred: Aspects of the Christianisation of the Roman World.* Cambridge: Cambridge University Press.

Bruun, Patrick M. (1958) 'The Disappearance of Sol from the Coins of Constantine', *Arctos* 2: 15–37.

—— (1962) 'The Christian Signs on the Coins of Constantine', *Arctos* 3: 5–35.

—— (1966) *The Roman Imperial Coinage Volume 7: Constantine and Licinius A.D. 313–337.* London: Spink & Son Ltd.

Cameron, Averil (1991) *Christianity and the Rhetoric of Empire: the Development of Christian Discourse.* Berkeley, Los Angeles and London: University of California Press.

Castritius, Helmut (1969) *Studien zu Maximinus Daia: Frankfurter Althistorische Studien 2.* Kallmünz: Verlag Michael Lassleben.

Chitty, Derwas J. (1966) *The Desert a City.* Oxford: Basil Blackwell and Mott.

Chuvin, Pierre (1990) *A Chronicle of the Last Pagans.* trans. B. A. Archer. Cambridge, Mass. and London: Harvard University Press.

Corcoran, Simon (1996) *Empire of the Tetrarchs: Imperial Pronouncements and Government AD 284–324.* Oxford: Clarendon Press.

Cullhed, Mats (1994) *Conservator Urbis Suae: Studies in the Politics and Propaganda of the Emperor Maxentius.* Stockholm: Acta Instituti Romani Regni Sueciae, Series in 8°, 20.

Dagron, Gilbert (1974) *Naissance d'une Capitale. Constantinople et ses institutions de 330 à 451.* Paris: Bibliothèque Byzantine, Études 7.

Decker, D. de (1968) 'La politique religieuse de Maxence', *Byzantion* 38: 472–562.

Dodgeon, Michael H. and Lieu, Samuel N. C. (1991) *The Roman Eastern Frontier and the Persian Wars A.D. 226–363. A Documentary History.* London: Routledge.

Drake, H. A. (1975) *In Praise of Constantine: A Historical Study and New Translation of Eusebius' Trecennial Orations.* Berkeley, Los Angeles and London: University of California Press.

—— (1983) Review of T. D. Barnes, 'Constantine and Eusebius', *American Journal of Philology* 103: 462–6.

Elliot, Thomas B. (1987) 'Constantine's Conversion: do we really need it?', *Phoenix* 41:420–38.

—— (1989) 'Constantine's Early Religious Development', *Journal of Religious History* 15: 283–91.

—— (1992) 'Constantine's Explanation of his Career', *Byzantion* 62: 212–34.

Errington, R. Malcolm (1988) 'Constantine and the Pagans', *Greek, Roman and Byzantine Studies* 29: 309–318.

Fowden, Garth (1993) *Empire to Commonwealth: Consequences of Monotheism in Late Antiquity.* Princeton, N. J.: Princeton University Press.

Frankfurter, David (1998) *Religion in Roman Egypt: Assimilation and Resistance.* Princeton, N. J.: Princeton University Press.

Frend, W. H. C. (1952) *The Donatist Church.* Oxford: Clarendon Press.

—— (1965) *Martyrdom and Persecution in the Early Church.* Oxford: Basil Blackwell.

—— (1984) *The Rise of Christianity.* Philadelphia, Pa.: Fortress Press.

Frend, W. H. C. and Clancy, K. (1977) 'When did the Donatists Schism Begin?', *Journal of Theological Studies* n.s. 28: 104–9.

Helgeland, John (1978) 'Christians and the Roman Army', in H. Temporini (ed.) *Aufstieg und Niedergang der Römischen Welt.* Berlin: de Gruyter, 725–834.

Hunt, E. D. (1982) *Holy Land and Pilgrimage in the Later Roman Empire A.D. 312–460.* Oxford: Clarendon Press.

—— (1993) 'Christianising the Roman Empire: the Evidence of the Code', in Jill Harries and Ian Wood (eds) *The Theodosian Code.* Ithaca, N. Y.: Cornell University Press, 143–158.

Isaac, Benjamin (1992) *The Limits of Empire: the Roman Army in the East*, rev. edn. Oxford: Clarendon Press.

Janes, Dominic (1998) *God and Gold in Late Antiquity.* Cambridge: Cambridge University Press.

Jones, A. H. M. (1953) 'Military Chaplains in the Roman Army', *Harvard Theological Review* 46: 239–40.

—— (1963) 'The Social Background of the Struggle Between Paganism and Christianity', in A. Momigliano, (ed.) *The Conflict Between Paganism and Christianity in the Fourth Century.* Oxford: Clarendon Press, 17–37.

—— (1964) *The Later Roman Empire.* Oxford: Basil Blackwell.

—— (1972) *Constantine and the Conversion of Europe.* Harmondsworth: Penguin.

Jones, A. H. M., Martindale, J. R. and Morris, J. (1971) *The Prosopography of the Later Roman Empire I.* Oxford: Clarendon Press.

Judge, Edwin. A. (1983) 'Christian Innovation and its Contemporary Observers', in B. Croke and A. M. Emmet, (eds) *History and Historians in Late Antiquity.* Sydney: Pergamon, 13–29.

Kee, Alistair (1982) *Constantine Versus Christ.* London: SCM Press.

Keresztes, Paul (1981) *Constantine: A Great Christian Monarch and Apostle.* Amsterdam: J. C. Gieben.

Kienast, Dietmar (1990) *Römische Kaisertabelle: Gundzüge einer römischen Kaiserchronologie.* Darmstadt: Wissenschaftliche Buchgesellschaft.

Kirsch, G. P. (1935) 'Origine e carattere degli antichi Titoli ecclesiatici a Roma' *Atti Dell III Congresso Nationzionale di Studi Romani*, Vol. I. Bologna: Instituto di Studi Romani, 39–47.

Krautheimer, Richard (1965) *Early Christian and Byzantine Architecture.* Harmondsworth: Penguin.

—— (1979) *Corpus Basilicorum Christianum Romae.* Vatican City: Pontifical Institute of Christian Archaeology.

—— (1983) *Three Christian Capitals: Topography and Politics.* Berkeley, Los Angeles and London: University of California Press.

Labriolle, Pierre de (1942) *La Réaction Païenne.* Paris: L'artisan du Livre.

Lampe, Peter (1989) *Die Stadtrömischen Christen in den ersten beiden Jahrhundert.*

Wissenschaftliche Untersuchungen zum neuen Testament 2 Reihe 18. Tübingen: J. C. B. Mohr.

Lane Fox, Robin (1986) *Pagans and Christians*. Harmondsworth: Viking.

Leadbetter, Bill (1998a) 'Lactantius and Paideia in the Latin West', in T. W. Hillard, R. A. Kearsley, C. E. V. Nixon, and A. M. Nobbs, (eds) *Ancient History in a Modern University*. Vol. II. Grand Rapids, Mich.: Eeerdmans, 245–52.

—— (1998b) 'The Legitimacy of Constantine', in S. N. C. Lieu and Dominic Montserrat (eds) *Constantine: History, Historiography and Legend*. London: Routledge, 74–85.

—— (1998c) 'Patrimonium Indivisum? The Empire of Diocletian and Maximian 285–289', *Chiron* 28: 213–28.

Lindner, Amnon (1987) *The Jews in Roman Imperial Legislation*. Detroit: Wayne State University Press.

Luttwak, Edward N. (1976) *The Grand Stategy of the Roman Empire: From the First Century A.D. to the Third*. Baltimore, M. D.: Johns Hopkins University Press.

MacMullen, Ramsey (1984) *Christianizing the Roman Empire*. New Haven, Conn. and London: Yale University Press.

—— (1990) *Changes in the Roman Empire: Essays in the Ordinary*. Princeton, N. J.: Princeton University Press.

Markus, Robert (1974) 'Paganism, Christianity and the Latin Classics', in J. W. Binns (ed.) *Latin Literature of the Fourth Century*. London and Boston: Routledge & Kegan Paul.

—— (1990) *The End of Ancient Christianity*. Cambridge: Cambridge University Press.

Maier, Jean-Louis (1987) *Le Dossier du Donatisme*. Berlin: Akademie Verlag.

Millar, Fergus (1977) *The Emperor in the Roman World (31 BC–AD 337)*. London: Duckworth.

Mitchell, S. W. (1988) 'Maximus and the Christians in 312: A New Latin Inscription', *Journal of Roman Studies* 78: 103–20.

Nicholson, Oliver (1991) 'The Pagan Churches of Maximus and Julian the Apostle', *J. E. H.* 45: 1–10.

Nixon, C. E. V. and Rodgers, Barbara Saylor (1994) *In Praise of Later Roman Emperors: the Panegyrici Latini*. Berkeley, Los Angeles and Oxford: University of California Press.

Novak, D. M. (1979) 'Constantine and the Senate. An Early Phase in the Christianization of the Aristocracy', *Ancient Society* 10: 271–310.

Pohlsander, Hans. A. (1993) 'Constantia', *Ancient Society* 24: 151–67.

—— (1996) *The Emperor Constantine*. London and New York: Routledge.

Ste. Croix, G. E. M. de. (1954) 'Aspects of the Great Persecution', *Harvard Theological Review* 47: 75–109.

Srejovic, Dragoslav (1985) 'Felix Romuliana, le palais de Galère à Gamzigrad' (French abstract), *Starinar* 36: 65–7.

—— (1992/3) 'A Porphyry Head of a Tetrarch from Romuliana (Gamzigrad)', *Starinar* 43–44: 41–7.

Srejovic, Dragoslav, Jankovic, D., Lalovic, A. and Jovic, V. (1983) *Gamzigrad: An Imperial Palace of the Late Classical Times*. Belgrade: Serbian Academy of Arts and Sciences.

Stevenson, J. (1987) *A New Eusebius: New Edition*, Rev. W. H. C. Frend. London: SPCK.

Syme, Sir Ronald (1974) 'The Ancestry of Constantine', *Bonner Historia Augusta Colloquium* 11: 237–53.

Tomlin, R. S. O. (1998) 'Christianity and the Late Roman Army', in S. N. C. Lieu and Dominic Montserrat (eds) *Constantine: History, Historiography and Legend*. London: Routledge, 21–51.

Toynbee, Jocelyn and Ward-Perkins, John (1956) *The Shrine of St Peter and the Vatican Excavations*. London, New York and Toronto: Longmans Green & Co.

Vogt, J. (1963) 'Pagans and Christians in the Family of Constantine the Great', in A. Momigliano, (ed.) *The Conflict Between Paganism and Christianity in the Fourth Century*. Oxford: Clarendon Press, 38–55.

Wilken, Robert L. (1992) *The Land Called Holy: Palestine in Christian History and Thought*. New Haven, Conn.: Yale University Press.

Williams, Rowan (1987) *Arius*. London: Darton, Longman & Todd.

ANTHONY OF THE DESERT

——— •◆• ———

Columba Stewart, OSB

WHOSE ANTHONY?

We are beginning to let go of our assumption that we can recover 'history' as if it were something awaiting discovery by the proper tools. In the case of someone like Anthony, it is harder to surrender our desire to know about the 'real' person. However, written documents cannot resuscitate historical figures. Once pen was put to papyrus a gap opened between the subject and the resulting text, reflecting the interval of perspective between observer and observed. Therefore no form of narrative is immune from the distorting effects, benign or insidious, of characterization. When the subject is famous, immensely famous, like Anthony, and the literary portraits are numerous, the approach becomes very tricky indeed. The 'quest for the historical Anthony' has consumed students of monasticism just as their colleagues in New Testament studies have circled round and round in their quest for another, and even more famous, maker – and product – of history.

We can be confident on the basis of many written sources, and of so many different kinds, that Anthony was a major, even dominant, presence in early fourth-century Egyptian monasticism. Although texts may not resuscitate, they do propagate, and it was Anthony's fortune not only to *be* great but also to have a masterful and highly placed biographer intent on keeping him so. The *Life of Anthony* (hereafter '*Life*') written by the controversial bishop Athanasius of Alexandria within a year of the monk's death at his retreat in the Eastern desert, has been the most successful and widely imitated hagiographical text of all time. It evoked competition from Jerome, who wrote a rival *Life of Paul the First Hermit*. It prompted Augustine's crisis of conversion when he heard of the spiritual triumphs of an uneducated Copt. The *Life* inspired remarkable paintings by Bosch, Breughel and others. Breughel's version sparked the literary imagination of the nineteenth-century French novelist Gustave Flaubert, who in his *La Tentation de Saint Antoine* took it upon himself to supplement the dialogue provided by the more discreet Athanasius. Anthony provoked scorn from Gibbon but fascinated other scholars, who have not ceased from producing study after study about him, especially in the last century and a half. What is perhaps most remarkable is that Anthony's life and teaching, however mediated, remain an inspiration to men and women claiming to follow him in the monastic life. This monk, and the traditions surrounding him, must indeed be reckoned with.

PRINCIPAL SOURCES

Athanasius' portrait of Anthony has been the most important one for both monastic audiences and other readers. The longest and most detailed account, it is the predictable mix of factual information gathered from those who knew Anthony, idealized scenarios about Anthony's life and teaching, and Athanasius' own agenda. The question of authorship has been settled in Athanasius' favour, though without excluding the possibility that he worked with some earlier documents about Anthony (Brakke 1994; Bartelink 1994: 27–42). He certainly wrote with earlier literary models in mind, establishing Anthony as a Christian (and superior) counterpart to the philosopher-heroes whose biographies circulated widely in the Hellenistic world.

Opinions vary, however, about the reliability of Athanasius' version of Anthony and his teaching. Attempts have been made to test the *Life* by checking its data against other extant information about Anthony (Rubenson 1995: 126–91). As is generally the case with such assessments, the peculiarities of the sources themselves tend to make any conclusions about them impressionistic. The position taken here is that Athanasius' portrait does resemble the Anthony found in the other sources, though the biographer has exercised his power to emphasize and to de-emphasize certain traits. These traits and Athanasius' handling of them will be considered below. The important point to note here is that the *Life* was an immediate success, soon translated into Latin (in two versions) and several other languages, widely distributed, and eagerly read in both the Christian East and West (Bartelink 1994: 37–42, 68–70, 95–108). It is arguable that no other non-biblical Christian text has enjoyed so wide a circulation or been so influential a model for spiritual biographies of other notable figures such as Martin of Tours, Syncletica of Alexandria or the monks remembered by Cyril of Scythopolis.

Next in importance to the *Life* are the many sayings, or *apophthegmata*, attributed to Anthony or about him (Dörries 1949; Rubenson 1995: 145–62). The textual history and editorial complexities of the sayings are notorious, and using them as a check against other texts becomes a scholarly hall of mirrors. On the other hand, they can provide broad-stroke portraits of their subjects, as is immediately evident when reading sayings of or about major figures such as Arsenius, John Kolobos, or Poemen. One gains a sense of these monks even though the details cannot be pressed too closely. The sayings about Anthony, especially the most frequently repeated ones, are important evidence for how Anthony's monastic heirs chose to remember him. While surely preserving some actual dicta and historical information, they in any case illustrate the place accorded Anthony in the tradition and highlight what later monks found most constructive or memorable about his teaching.

Athanasius' *Life* was not the only narrative portrait of Anthony in early monastic literature. Palladius (*c.* 364–*c.* 425), an educated monk sympathetic to the controversial spiritual theology of Origen and his heir Evagrius Ponticus, has several stories about Anthony in his *Lausiac History* (c. 419). This work was actually written almost seventy years after Athanasius' *Life*, though it was based on the author's sojourn in Egypt at the end of the fourth century. Palladius had read the *Life of Anthony* – so had virtually everyone of his social class and religious interests – but he also had access to other sources from his own visits to various Egyptian monasteries including Anthony's at Pispir near the Nile (Figure 14.4). Palladius' Anthony sounds more like a classic desert elder than does Athanasius', perhaps because Palladius wrote from inside the monastic tradition and was more interested in Anthony's interactions with other monks than with the non-monastic luminaries highlighted by Athanasius. Palladius also wrote after Anthony's legacy and 'official' monastic reputation were firmly established.

In the *Lausiac History* we find Anthony capable of severity towards other monks in the name of spiritual discipline (*LH* 21–2), a quality absent from Athanasius' portrayal. Palladius also notes Anthony's stratagem for screening visitors (*LH* 21.8), another indication that however holy he may have been he did not suffer fools gladly. Similar in tone to Palladius' accounts are the references to Anthony in the *History of the Monks of Egypt*, a travelogue roughly contemporary to the *Lausiac History*. Both works are most significant for the information they provide about Anthony's network of disciples and their descendants, who were leaders of the Origenist party to which Palladius belonged (Rubenson 1995: 178–82).

The last major source of information about Anthony from the early period comes from the hagiography of the 'other' Egyptian monastic tradition, Pachomian cenobitism. Two versions of the *Life of Pachomius*, a kind of biography-cum-institutional history, describe a visit to Anthony by Pachomian monks shortly after their leader's death in 346 (*Bohairic Life of Pachomius* 126–33; *Greek Life* 120). The upshot of the interview is Anthony's praise of Pachomius and his communal form of monastic life. The Coptic *Life* even includes Anthony's regrets that he had been unable to become a cenobite himself! Setting aside questions of historical accuracy, the significance of the accounts lies in the importance accorded to Anthony's validation of the Pachomian movement as authentically monastic.

Thus the principal sources *about* Anthony. There remain the writings *by* Anthony. The *Life* by Athanasius mentions Anthony's correspondence with emperors (*Life* 81) and with an Arian official (*Life* 86). In the *Life of Pachomius* there are references to letters sent by Anthony to monks and to Athanasius; the Coptic version quotes from these letters (*Bohairic Life of Pachomius* 126–33; *Greek Life* 120). Seven other letters by Anthony, all addressed to monks and pertaining to the spiritual life, have survived in various states. Jerome notes the existence of the letters and their translation into Greek, though it is unclear whether he himself had read them (*De viris illustribus* 88). Obviously the *Letters* are of great importance for any study of Anthony since they are the most direct evidence we have of his own teaching (Rubenson 1995: 35–42). They contain no biographical information, though their affinities with Origen's theology and their use of philosophical language have important consequences for assessment of Anthony's educational background. Only one contains information about its addressees, who were monks at Arsinoë (*Letter* 6).

The *Letters* bear notable similarities of style and *Letters* 2–7 have close parallels of structure and content. This means that at least those six were probably written at about the same time; a reference to Arius in *Letter* 4 suggests a date in the late 330s, i.e., about twenty years before Anthony's death (Rubenson 1995: 42–6). The *Letters*, then, offer snapshots of Anthony's concerns for particular audiences at a particular time. The letters quoted in the *Life of Pachomius* are later (346, the year of Pachomius' death); they provide no information about Anthony himself though the use of the epithet 'Israelite', interpreted as 'one who sees God', is a stylistic parallel with the earlier letters (*Letters* 3.6; cf. 5.1–2; 6.2, 78, 93; 7.5, 58).

The influence of Anthony's *Letters* on later monastic tradition has been much less than that of the *Life*. The Coptic original survives only in one seventh-century fragment. The Greek translation of the *Letters*, the earliest and also the most useful for wide distribution, has been lost. The Syriac version seems to have been early but partial (by 534, only one letter), and the Latin version is relatively modern (1475, from the now-lost Greek text). The best surviving witness is the Georgian translation. Much of the material is preserved in a thirteenth-century Arabic translation made from the lost Coptic original; according to a recent study of the *Letters*, the Arabic appears to be the only version based on the Coptic (Rubenson 1995: 15–34). This curious legacy suggests that even monks found the *Life* and the sayings to be more useful to them than the *Letters*. There are also aspects of the letters, particularly their more speculative passages, which would have made later readers nervous after the traumas of the Origenist Controversy. It has been suggested that the Anthony of the letters differs rather considerably from Athanasius' hero (Rubenson 1995); to assess this claim we will look at the teaching of the *Letters* in more detail below.

It is clear from even this brief review of the sources that we have to approach Anthony through the impressions, memories, and agenda of others except in so far as we can use the *Letters* to nuance those perspectives. To evaluate Anthony's role in monastic tradition, however, is a somewhat different matter than seeking the historical person. To begin to see Anthony as the greater number of his followers have seen him means working with all of the sources available. The resulting construct may not be 'historical', but it is arguably 'authentic' as a monastic archetype in which we can see the genesis of practices and teaching which would become central to monastic spirituality.

THE STORY

The basic plot of Anthony's life as presented by Athanasius is easily told. Born a Christian to prosperous landowning parents, he was orphaned with his younger sister when he was 18. Following a call to the ascetic life manifested externally in a dramatically literal obedience to Jesus' commands to leave all for his sake and to renounce all cares, Anthony disposed of his property, placed his sister in the care of local virgins and apprenticed himself to a village ascetic. Subject to the usual struggles of disengagement from the past and from alternative ways of life, Anthony showed a marked eagerness to confront the challenges directly, spending time in solitude in tombs at the edge of the nearby desert. After severe and frightening trials he resolved to pursue greater solitude and made the move that would bring him fame.

Going deeper into the desert, away from the security offered by proximity to settled land, he lived 20 years as a recluse in an abandoned fort at Pispir. After his protracted retreat he became available to both monks and seculars for advice. Many followed his example and settled around his retreat. He made at least two trips to Alexandria, one in the first decade of the fourth century to show his solidarity with Christian martyrs, the second (in 337 or 338) to fight Arianism.

In time he sought greater solitude and journeyed deeper into the Eastern desert, where he found a site remarkable for its beauty and its fresh spring. There he established his so-called 'Inner Mountain', from which he would commute periodically to the 'Outer Mountain', his first retreat at Pispir, to offer advice and teaching. He died at the Inner Mountain in 356 at an advanced age (Athanasius claims 105) and his *Life* was written the following year.

To this sketch we can add a few important elements from other sources. First, the *Letters* prove that Athanasius' references to Anthony's lack of letters (*Life* 1.2; 3.7; 73.3; 85.5; 93.4) are not to be taken as suggesting illiteracy but rather a Christian education instead of a primarily philosophical one (cf. *Life* 4.1; 44.2). Even Athanasius' Anthony, depicted as refuting the arguments of visiting philosophers by virtue of his faith in Christ and knowledge of the Bible (*Life* 74–80), urges his disciples to write down their thoughts as a technique of self-knowledge and discipline (*Life* 55.9–12). Study of the *Letters* reveals an acquaintance with the writings of Origen and a familiarity with the Hellenistic thought-world of the time. Despite his use of interpreters when meeting Greek-speakers (*Life* 74.2; 77.1; cf. 81.4), Anthony must have known some Greek himself (Rubenson 1995: 41–2); in any case Coptic is saturated with Greek loanwords.

Second, other sources provide the names of Anthony's closest associates. Athanasius names only two monks, Amoun of Nitria (*Life* 60) and Paphnutius 'the monk and confessor', bishop of the Upper Thebaid (*Life* 58.3). Neither was Anthony's disciple. Palladius and the *apophthegmata*, however, identify as Anthony's close followers Paul the Simple and Macarius the Egyptian ('the Great') (Palladius, *Dialogue* 17), and the *History of the Monks of Egypt* names Anthony's successors at Pispir, Ammonas and then Pityrion (*HM* 15.1–2). This lineage connects Anthony to major figures in later Egyptian monasticism. In sayings and letters attributed to these monks we can see the development of Anthony's teaching. Those texts both verify the monastic authenticity of Athanasius' presentation of Anthony and confirm Anthony's links to theologically sophisticated members of the Egyptian monastic scene.

SACRED GEOGRAPHY

Anthony was not the first monk, nor even the first hermit. What set him apart in the eyes of his contemporaries was his commitment to *anachoresis*, 'withdrawal'. Anthony's practice of *anachoresis* was expressed physically by greater and greater distance from settled regions. The stages of physical withdrawal were mirrored psychologically in his progressively deeper encounter with himself, a theme we will return to later.

Athanasius presents the physical journey in a somewhat stylized manner, but other sources confirm Anthony's withdrawal into deeper solitude at greater distances from human settlement. The move to the edge of the village as an ascetic was followed by brief periods spent in the tombs in the near desert. The spiritual symbolism of being sealed within a tomb is obvious, but for Anthony, an Egyptian, the move from the realm of the living to the abode of the dead had even more significance. The geographical distinction between life and death was clear in a land dependent on the river for sustenance. One did not have to go far to find the desert, to leave the zone of safety. But the difference was dramatic. The abode of the dead was also the home of the demons, spiritual counter-forces to human progress.

For Anthony to spend time in tombs was more than *Schadenfreude*. It was a challenge to all within him and beyond him that was opposed to life. Athanasius plays up this aspect of Anthony's story, using him as an exemplar of the fully divine Christ's victory over evil and death, a victory shared with those who believe in him. Although Athanasius' theological agenda is plain, there is no indication that he is betraying or even greatly distorting Anthony's own struggles or his reliance on faith in Christ. The direct literary parallels between the *Life of Anthony* and Athanasius' other writings are largely confined to the sections describing Anthony's debates with visiting philosophers (*Life* 74–9; see Bartelink 1994: 36–7). Furthermore, Anthony himself attacks Arius in *Letter* 4.17–18. As we shall see, battle against the demons was the principal focus of Anthony's ascetic teaching as recorded in both the *Life* and the *Letters*.

Anthony's decision to become a solitary in the desert was regarded by his peers as something novel (*Life* 3.2; 11.1–2). A link with civilization remained, for he settled in an abandoned fort 'in the mountain' (i.e., above the river valley) 'across the river' (*Life* 12.3) at the site known as Pispir. Nor was it the end of human contact, for he relied on others to bring him bread every six months and acquired disciples who would visit him there, though Athanasius claims he would only speak to them through the door and not actually see them (*Life* 12–13). A definitive break with ordinary society and with ascetic custom had nonetheless been made, and this became the basis for his extraordinary reputation. After 20 years he became available for consultation and would leave his hermitage to visit other monks, including those who settled around him. The scope of his pastoral activity will receive more attention below.

After an unspecified time he established a further retreat at what became known as the 'Inner Mountain' to distinguish it from the 'Outer Mountain' at Pispir. This move into the deep desert required both divine guidance and reliance on a Saracen caravan. Together they led him to a remote but beautiful location distinguished by a striking mountain and a vigorous fresh water spring (*Life* 49–50). The site traditionally considered that of the Inner Mountain, where the Coptic Monastery of Saint Anthony (Deir Amba Antonios; see Figure 43.1) can be visited to this day, was three days' journey east of the river towards the Red Sea.

Athanasius records that Anthony 'loved' his mountain. There he spent most of his time for the rest of his life, though he continued to visit Pispir for pastoral purposes (*Life* 57–8; 84.3–5; 85.1–4). Occasionally he would receive visitors at the Inner Mountain, but the distance and harsh conditions of the journey would have

Figure 43.1 The Monastery of Saint Anthony today, with his 'Inner Mountain' rising behind. Photo C. Stewart.

Figure 43.2 Entrance to Anthony's Cave near the top of the 'Inner Mountain'. Photo C. Stewart.

discouraged all but the most intent (*Life* 50.7; 59.2; 82.3). Tended in extreme old age by two disciples, Anthony died at the Inner Mountain in 356 at the age of 105 and was buried, claims Athanasius, in a secret location (*Life* 92).

Athanasius depicts Anthony's move into the desert as the beginning of monastic colonization of demon-held territory, threatening Satan's domination of lifeless regions (*Life* 14.7; 41.1–4). He complements this hyperbolic, propagandist stance with a more attractive vision of the desert as an alternative, truly Christian, society where prayer, love and ascetic discipline ensured peace (*Life* 44.2–4). Anthony himself was able to re-establish the paradisiacal harmony between human beings and animals (*Life* 50.8–9). The notion of an ideal society in the desert was not new; Philo had said the same of the Therapeutae in his treatise *On the Contemplative Life*. In the Christian and monastic context, however, there was an added theological dimension of establishing a kind of intermediate zone between earth and heaven in which human beings (and all of nature) were restored to their intended condition in preparation for eschatological glorification.

ANTHROPOLOGY AND ASCETICISM

The anthropology found in both *Life* and *Letters* presumes the essential goodness of human beings created with freedom of the will (*Life* 20; *Letters* 7). The decision to listen to evil insinuations by fallen spiritual essences (Satan, demons) led humans to an irrationality in which the body escaped the control of the intellect (Greek *nous*) and was subject to domination by the passions and constant suggestions from the demons (e.g., *Letters* 2). Alongside this basically biblical model there are elements of Origen's cosmological perspective emphasizing a fall from the original unity of spiritual essence to the present multiplicity of creatures (see *Letters* 6.5–6, 56–62, 84; cf. Rubenson 1995: 64–8). The Incarnation and Resurrection of Christ made 'resurrection of the mind' possible (*Letters* 2.23, etc.), to be realized through ascetic discipline prompted and supported by the Holy Spirit, who teaches knowledge and discernment (*Letters* 1.18–34).

The *Life* offers a generally holistic view of the interaction of body and spirit (*Life* 14.3–4; 67.6–8) while being suspicious of allowing the body too much in the way of concession (*Life* 45.2–7). This latter point is stressed in the *Letters*, which emphasize the captivity of the body to the passions and to evil spirits (e.g., *Letters* 6.51–3). Even so, the body is not scorned or ignored, but is involved in the ascetic process and transformative work of the Spirit (*Letters* 1.46–71; *Life* 22.3; *Sayings* Anthony 8 and 13). The powerful pneumatology of the *Letters* is all the more striking when compared with the *Life*'s almost entirely Christological orientation. It may be here particularly that one sees the anti-Arian agenda of Athanasius, for whom a potent pneumatology would not have been nearly as helpful as an emphasis on the divine power of Christ. The *Letters* present a more balanced perspective that is both centred on Christ and dynamically pneumatological.

As Athanasius describes it, Anthony's asceticism was typical of what we know about Egyptian anchoritic monasticism. It was a severe but, in relative terms, not an excessive regimen (*Life* 7.6; 47.2; 51.1). He ate once daily, relying on bread, salt, vegetables, olives and oil but excluding meat and wine (*Life* 7.6; 51.1). Often he would extend his fast and eat less frequently (*Life* 7.6; 47.2). He never bathed or used oil on his body (*Life* 7.6; 47.2; 93.1). He wore a goatskin garment with the hair turned inside, and slept on a mat or sometimes on the bare ground using a cloak given him by Athanasius (*Life* 4.1; 7.6; 47.2; 91.8–9). The basic elements of his spiritual discipline were dedication to prayer, especially in night-time vigil, memorization of biblical texts, and manual labour (*Life* 4.1; 30.2; 44.2; 55; *Letters* 1.77). He worked both for personal economic support and to help the poor; it is noted in the *Life* that Anthony made rope to earn money for food (*Life* 30.2; 44.2; 53.1). The exhortatory nature of the *Letters* means that they have little to say about ascetic practices.

The distinctive traits of Anthony's ascetic teaching were his emphasis on focused intention and self-knowledge. The first is most prominent in the *Life*, the second pervades both *Life* and *Letters*. He cautioned against dwelling on memories of the past (*Life* 7.11; 20.1–2; cf. Anthony, *Sayings* 6). Monastic life means daily recommitment to the discipline (*Life* 7.12; 16.3; 47.1; 91.2) in awareness of the brevity of life (*Life* 16.4–8; 19.2–3; 45.1; 89.4; 91.3). In the *Letters*, self-knowledge is the overarching theme, set within the broadly 'gnostic' framework of those texts (Rubenson 1995: 59–64). In the *Life*, however, the Stoic language of 'paying heed (*prosechein*) to the self' is preferred (*Life* 3.1–2; 55.5–13; 91.3) and 'knowledge' language is absent. This could be owing to anxiety on Athanasius' part that such language would be construed in a heterodox manner despite its roots in both biblical

Figure 43.3 View from Anthony's Cave near the top of the 'Inner Mountain'. Photo C. Stewart.

(especially Johannine) and Alexandrian tradition. In ascetic terms the difference is minimal, though theologically in the *Letters* the gnostic terminology is tied closely to the pneumatological emphasis equally absent in the *Life*. In later monastic texts the terminology of the *Life* would prevail.

THOUGHTS AND DEMONS

The practical application of self-knowledge is learning to 'discern spirits', i.e., to understand the activity of one's thoughts (*logismoi*) and the manipulation of them by demonic counter-forces. In the *Life of Anthony*, the terms 'demon', 'spirit', and 'thought' are used synonymously for these counter-forces, with a preference for 'demon' (60 instances, versus 16 for 'thought' and two for 'spirit'). In the *Letters* the proportions are equal (about six each), and the term 'passion' occurs alongside them to describe the human faculty stirred by demonic suggestion. Athanasius claims that Anthony learned how to understand and combat the demons from the Bible (*Life* 7.3; 16.1); the key text, Eph. 6:11–17, is cited or alluded to five times in the *Life*.

Athanasius describes Anthony's personal struggles with memories and temptations, especially in the early stages of his monastic life, as a progression from issues about external material and social issues (possessions, family, money, fame) to bodily ones (food, leisure, lust), and finally to emotional issues such as struggle with sadness and discouragement (see *Life* 5). The descriptions in the *Life* are vivid: he experienced physical traumata (to the point of unconsciousness, *Life* 8), heard voices, and saw apparitions (*Life* 6; 8–9; 13; 35; 51.2–5).

These descriptions are fascinating but disturbing to the reader. To help the reader understand their significance, Athanasius includes a lengthy discourse (28 chapters) attributed to Anthony summarizing his teaching about how the demons play on human weakness to discourage hopes for progress (*Life* 16–43; see Guillaumont 1957: 189–96). Although we cannot know how much of the address is actually attributable to Anthony, its basic teaching clearly derives from considerable ascetic experience and must have come to Athanasius from within the monastic movement. This text, or perhaps one should say the teaching contained in it, was the basis for later development by ascetic theologians such as Evagrius Ponticus (d. 399). In the *Letters* the appeal for self-knowledge is directed in the first place towards understanding the inner confusion caused by sin and demonic influence; one could see *Letters* 1 and 6 as counterparts to the discourse in the *Life*.

Anthony is more interested in providing practical directives than in developing a demonology as such (see *Life* 21.5, and cf. the emphasis on Anthony's experience in 22.4, 39–41, 51–3). The general theological framework is the conventional one, articulated and developed by Origen, that demons are fallen spiritual creatures motivated by jealousy to retard human recovery of original goodness (*Life* 21–2; *Letters* 6.30–62; see Daniélou 1957: 182–9). In both *Life* and *Letters* the ascetic's confrontation with the demons is placed within a cosmic salvation history that regards the Incarnation, Death and Resurrection of Christ as a definitive turning point in the human struggle against sin. Since Christ's coming, the demons have

Figure 43.4 The temptations of Anthony as imagined by late sixteenth-century artists. From *Solitudo, sive vitae patrum eremicolarum*, by Jan and Raphael Sadeler, after figures by Maarten de Vos, *c.* 1590.

been robbed of their real power and must do what they can through deception and pretence (*Life* 28–9).

The ascetic's task is to see through the schemes of the demons and to claim the power that comes through invoking the name of Christ (as in the *Life*) or receiving the Spirit (as in the *Letters*). Indeed, Athanasius uses Anthony's triumph over the demons as a case in point that Christians serve the true God and tread the false gods (the demons) of the pagans underfoot (*Life* 94). Demons have no bodies of their own, which makes them invisible (*Letters* 6.50), impossible to exclude (*Life* 28.3–5), and able to move so quickly from place to place that they can seem to predict the future on the basis of what they have seen somewhere else (*Life* 33.2–6). Their lack of bodies means that they work within the human soul ('we are their bodies': *Letters* 6.51) and have direct access to thoughts. Therefore they can pattern themselves according to what they find, playing on anxiety or despair or pride: if one avoids such states, the demons have less room for manoeuvre (*Life* 27.4; 42). More dangerously, they can also masquerade as angels promising glory (*Life* 35.1), or as exemplary monks shaming one into despair (*Life* 25).

The best technique for discerning the activity of the demons is awareness of one's feelings: fear or distress are signs of demonic instigation, while joy and calm are good spirits (*Life* 35–6). Any intrusive thought or apparition is to be interrogated (*Life* 11.3–4; 43; cf. 41.2), and thoughts can be written down as an aid to self awareness (*Life* 55.9). The *Letters* repeat incessantly the imperative to know oneself. To block the corrosive work of the demons, Anthony used and recommended the use of biblical texts, especially the Psalms (*Life* 9.3; 13.7; 37.4; 39.3, 6; 40.5; 52.3). This practice, known in later tradition as 'antirrhetic' (literally, 'counter-suggestive') prayer, was a basic component of monastic discipline. He recommends invocation of the name of Christ (*Life* 39.2; 40.2; 41.6; 63.3) and use of the Sign of the Cross as defensive tactics (*Life* 13.5; 35.2; 53.2; 80.4). All of these techniques require the ability to be aware of what is happening and to achieve some distance from the immediacy of the experience. Such perspective is what 'discernment of spirits' means in practice; Anthony regards it as a divine grace given in answer to much prayer (*Life* 22.3; 38.5; *Letters* 1 and 6, *passim*).

MONK AND MINISTER

Anthony is famous as ascetic and hermit, but he was extraordinarily available to others. Athanasius notes how much he was loved in his early days as a village ascetic (*Life* 4.4) and emphasizes his grace of speech and presence (*Life* 14.6; 73.4; 87). In a crowd of monks Anthony was unmistakable because of the calm and joy he radiated to others (*Life* 67.4–8). The calm was contagious: Anthony was a 'physician given to Egypt by God' (*Life* 87.3). One of the most striking sayings attributed to him contains the line: 'our life and death is with our neighbour' (Anthony, *Sayings* 9). He emphasized love for others (*Life* 4.1; 17.7; 44.2; 81.5–6; *Letters* 6.91–2; Anthony, *Sayings* 21) and the dangers of anger (*Life* 4.1; 17.2; 30.2; 55; *Letters* 6.33–9). The latter theme would be of central importance in later monastic writings.

In the *Life*, Anthony's 20 years of reclusion at the Outer Mountain ended when disciples broke down the door and called him forth to minister to them (*Life* 14.2). He handled such demands without apparent resentment (*Life* 14.4; 70.4), though he guarded his solitude; his most famous dictum is that a monk away from his cell is like a fish out of water (*Life* 85.3–4; Anthony, *Sayings* 10). As noted earlier, after his withdrawal to the Inner Mountain he preferred to see visitors only at the Outer Mountain of Pispir. Palladius records that even at Pispir he used a receptionist, Brother Macarius, to screen visitors. If they were announced as coming 'from Egypt' they received a meal and a blessing; if 'from Jerusalem', Anthony would stay up all night talking with them (*LH* 21.8).

Naturally enough, his primary ministry was to other monks through teaching and counselling. This work is mentioned several times in the *Life* and was the context for the sayings preserved in the *apophthegmata* and for the *Letters*. However, monks were not his only audience. Many lay people came to him for healing. When health was granted he attributed it to the power of Christ called upon in prayer; when healing did not occur, Athanasius observes, the suppliants benefited from his words of encouragement (*Life* 48; 56–8; 84.1). According to the *Life*, Anthony visited Alexandria at least twice. The first time was to show solidarity with Christian martyrs during the fierce persecutions of early fourth-century Egypt. After visiting the imprisoned and practising a form of civil disobedience, he returned to the desert intent on sharing the suffering of the martyrs through his own ascesis (*Life* 46–7). About twenty years later (*c.* 337–8) he returned to Alexandria to battle Arianism in support of the Nicene cause (*Life* 69–70).

In addition to the letters mentioned earlier, he wrote to an Arian official in protest of his treatment of Nicene Christians (*Life* 86) and was consulted by emperors (*Life* 81.1; cf. Anthony, *Sayings* 31). One should note that these events and the extant collection of *Letters* appear to date from around the 330s, a period when Anthony's fame was well established and he was still active in his various ministries (if Athanasius' chronology is accurate, he would have been in his eighties). It is clear from the ubiquity of Anthony in monastic and other literary sources that Athanasius gives us a faithful portrait of this monk very much involved in the lives of other people.

LEGACY

Anthony was both exemplar and exception. Later tradition venerated his example while cautioning his imitators to do nothing without counsel: Anthony's largely solitary formation was not to be the prevailing model (cf. Anthony, *Sayings* 1 for his angelic spiritual director). The psychological experiences Athanasius describes present the array – and even the stages – of struggles against forces of gluttony, lust, avarice, anger, sadness, accidie, vainglory and pride that would be systematized by Evagrius Ponticus at the end of the fourth century. The transformed, peaceful and inviting Anthony of the *Life* (e.g., *Life* 14; 67) is the perfect embodiment of the ideal Evagrius would describe as *apatheia* or Cassian as 'purity of heart'. We cannot draw the lines of spiritual descent as precisely as we would like, but Anthony's influence on Ammonas, his successor at Pispir, and Macarius the Great, teacher of Evagrius, placed him at the origins of the most important theological tradition of the Egyptian desert.

Perhaps most significant is that Anthony was a force not only of that extraordinary period of early monastic fervour. His story has endured better than those of most of his contemporaries, and perhaps best of them all. A 'physician given to Egypt by God', indeed, but not to Egypt only.

BIBLIOGRAPHY

Note: References to the *Life of Anthony* are to chapter and sections as in Bartelink (1994); the same chapter divisions are found in Migne, *PG* 26: 837–976, and in modern translations. References to the *Letters* are to the English translation in Rubenson (1995: 197–231); for differences of numbering among the versions, see Rubenson (1995: 15). References to the *Sayings* are to the Alphabetical Collection to be found in Migne, *Patrologia Graeca* 65: 72–440, translated in Ward (1975).

Bartelink, Gerhardus J. M. (1994) *Athanase d'Alexandrie. Vie d'Antoine*. Sources chrétiennes 400. Paris: Cerf.
Brakke, David (1994) 'The Greek and Syriac Versions of the *Life of Antony*', *Le Muséon* 107: 17–56.

Daniélou, Jean (1957) 'Démon II.3: Le combat spirituel chez Origène', *Dictionnaire de spiritualité* 3: 182–9.

Dörries, Hermann (1949) 'Die Vita Antonii als Geschichtsquelle', *Nachrichten der Akademie der Wissenschaften in Göttingen, Philologisch-historische Klasse* 14: 359–410.

Guillaumont, Antoine and Claire (1957) 'Démon III.1: Les vies des moines du 4ᵉ siècle', *Dictionnaire de spiritualité* 3: 189–96.

History of the Monks of Egypt. Greek text and French trans. André-Jean Festugière. Subsidia hagiographica 53. Brussels: Société des Bollandistes, 1961. (English trans. Norman Russell, *The Lives of the Desert Fathers.* Oxford: Mowbray, 1981.

Pachomius. *Bohairic Life.* Bohairic text and French trans. Louis Theodore Lefort. *S. Pachomii vita Bohairice scripta.* Corpus scriptorum christianorum orientalium 89 and 107. Louvain: L. Durbecq, 1952–3. (English trans. Armand Veilleux, *Pachomian Koinonia I: The Life of Saint Pachomius.* Cistercian Studies Series 45. Kalamazoo, Mich.: Cistercian Publications, 1980.)

—— *Greek Life.* Greek text: François Halkin, *Sancti Pachomii vitae Graecae.* Subsidia hagiographica 19. Brussels: Société des Bollandistes, 1932. (English trans. Armand Veilleux, *Pachomian Koinonia I: The Life of Saint Pachomius.* Cistercian Studies Series 45. Kalamazoo, Mich.: Cistercian Publications, 1980.)

Palladius, *Dialogue on the Life of John Chrysostom.* Greek text ed. Anne-Marie Malingrey. Sources chrétiennes 341–2. Paris: Les Éditions du Cerf, 1988. (English trans. Robert T. Meyer, Ancient Christian Writers 45. New York: Newman Press, 1985.)

—— *Lausiac History.* Greek text ed. Cuthbert Butler, *The Lausiac History of Palladius . . . with Notes.* Texts and Studies 6.1–2. Cambridge: Cambridge University Press, 1898 and 1904. (Chapter subheadings as in the English trans. by Robert T. Meyer. Ancient Christian Writers 34. Westminster, Md.: Newman Press, 1964.)

Rubenson, Samuel (1995) *The Letters of St. Anthony. Monasticism and the Making of a Saint.* Minneapolis, Minn.: Fortress Press.

Sadeler, Jan and Sadeler, Raphael (*c.* 1590) *Solitudo, sive vitae patrum eremicolarum.*

Ward, Benedicta (1975) *The Sayings of the Desert Fathers. The Alphabetical Collection.* London: Mowbray, and Kalamazoo, Mich.: Cistercian Publications.

CHAPTER FORTY-FOUR

ATHANASIUS

—— ·✦· ——

David Brakke

From his election as bishop of Alexandria in 328, until his death in 373, and to the present day, Athanasius has aroused passionate and polarized reactions. While admirers have praised his courageous defence of Nicene orthodoxy, even imputing to him 'a total lack of self-interest' (Robertson 1892: lxvii), others have condemned his violent personality, even comparing him to 'a modern American gangster' (Barnes 1987: 397). If today's ordinary Christians have any impression of him, it may be an unpleasant one, based on something Athanasius did not write (but would surely endorse): the so-called Athanasian Creed, which consigns to eternal torment anyone who does not share its uncompromising Trinitarian theology (Kelly 1964). Athanasius' dual identity as saint and gangster stems from his more basic identity as a Christian bishop in the post-Constantinian imperially favoured church: the fourth-century bishop's roles as preacher, theologian, patron, and administrator render hopeless any modern attempt to separate 'religion' from 'politics' or 'thought' from 'action'.

For Athanasius, 'the Incarnation [of the Word of God] was the clarifying and compelling key to alienation and disorder, chaos and death' (Lyman 1993: 131). His political and theological efforts find their focus in the attempt to bring stability, unity, and divine power out of the instability, fragmentation, and human frailty that characterized fallen individuals, the divided Christian church, and the tumultuous ancient Mediterranean world. Just as it was necessary for a fully divine Word of God to become incarnate in a human body in order to bring healing transformation to the disordered human personality, so too it appeared necessary for a fully authoritative bishop of Alexandria to use all the means at his disposal to bring salvific unity to the chaotic Egyptian church. If the resulting Athanasius seems less appealing than, say, the Augustine who sanctioned coercive actions against the Donatists, it is perhaps because, unlike Augustine, Athanasius has left us few glimpses of the inner life of a man burdened with such weighty responsibilities. The public Athanasius, Athanasius the bishop of Alexandria and patriarch of Egypt, is the only Athanasius we can know.

CONFLICTS AND CONTROVERSIES (299–335 CE)

Athanasius was born around 299 CE, received a Christian (but not classical) education, and as a young man became the protégé of Alexander, the bishop of Alexandria from 312 to 328. As Alexander's secretary and a deacon, Athanasius drafted writings for the bishop (Stead 1988) and accompanied him to the Council of Nicaea in 325 (Severus, *Historia patrum Alexandrinorum* 1.8; Sozomen, *Historia ecclesiastica* 2.17; Socrates, *Historia ecclesiastica* 1.14). While Athanasius was on a mission to the imperial court on the bishop's behalf (Epiphanius, *Panarion* 68.7.2; 69.11.4; Barnes 1993: 18), Alexander died on 17 April 328. Athanasius, whom Alexander had designated as his successor, returned to Alexandria, where, in circumstances so disputed that the actual truth may never be known, he was consecrated bishop on 8 June. Athanasius immediately faced opposition to his election from Christians both inside and outside Egypt, eventually was charged with a variety of crimes (including murder), and by 335 was in exile in Trier, the first of five times he would be forced to leave the city. These tumultuous events early in Athanasius' episcopal career reflect the disordered state of Christianity in Egypt and elsewhere in the early fourth century, to which the beleaguered bishop tried to bring unity and coherence.[1] They are also rooted in the agonistic, group-oriented culture of the late ancient Mediterranean, in which social and political ties counted for more than theological ideas (Malina 1993: 28–116).

Figure 44.1 Icon of Athanasius, by the contemporary Greek artist Ralles Kopsides and owned by Professor Thomas Torrance. Photo reproduced from Torrance (1988) with the permission of the author and T&T Clark.

The 'Melitian' and 'Arian' conflicts

First of all, there were two Christian churches in Egypt, each with its own hierarchy of bishops and priests, a situation known as 'the Melitian schism'. This conflict began during the persecutions that Christians suffered in the first decade of the fourth century (the 'Great Persecution'). In 304, Peter, the bishop of Alexandria, was forced to go into hiding to avoid arrest and likely execution and thus was not able easily to carry out his duties, which had traditionally included appointing bishops throughout Egypt and Libya. Peter's absence created an opportunity for the bishops of Upper Egypt (south of Alexandria but upstream on the Nile) to assert some independence from the Alexandrian patriarch, and thus bishop Melitius of Lycopolis began ordaining priests for Alexandria and installing bishops and priests in other sees. Peter and other hiding bishops denounced what they considered an illegitimate intervention into their spheres of authority and had Melitius excommunicated before Peter was martyred in 311. By the time of the Council of Nicaea in 325, long after Peter's death, there were then two Christian churches in Egypt, a Petrine one and a Melitian one, each claiming to be the true single Christian church. Although later interpreters presented the conflict as one between the 'rigorist' Melitius and the 'moderate' Peter over how severely Christians who lapsed in persecution should be treated, the real issue originally appears to have been the authority of the Alexandrian bishop over the rest of Egypt, which in some ways was socially and culturally different from the great metropolis (Martin 1996: 217–98; Bagnall 1993).

Meanwhile, during Alexander's term as bishop of Alexandria, the Petrine church itself became divided over issues of theology and episcopal authority (Williams 1987; Marrou 1976). Since the earliest expansion of Christianity out of the city to the rest of Egypt in the second and third centuries, the bishop of Alexandria had exercised great power over the bishops and clergy in Egypt and Libya, but within the city the bishop was traditionally seen merely as the first among his equals, the priests, who were accustomed to electing the bishop from among themselves and to preaching and teaching in the city's local churches and Christian schools with autonomy. Values associated with 'intellectual freedom' were deep-rooted in Alexandrian Christianity, which had a long tradition of educated Christianity centred around brilliant teachers and scholars, such as Clement, Origen, and Valentinus. In the late 310s bishop Alexander became concerned about the preaching of Arius, the popular priest of the church of Baucalis, who taught that the Word of God who became incarnate in Jesus Christ was not divine in the same sense as God the Father was, but rather became worthy of the title 'Son of God' based on his exceptional advance in virtue, which human beings could now imitate. In contrast, Alexander believed that the Word was as eternal, divine, and unchanging as the Father. Despite the insistence of Arius and sympathetic Alexandrian clergy that his views were traditional, Alexander convened a synod of Egyptian and Libyan bishops (whose appointments he had approved), which rejected the teachings of Arius and excommunicated all who adhered to them. Here Alexander tried to use his patriarchal authority outside Alexandria to trump his weaker position with respect to the Alexandrian clergy. (The Melitians, by the way, insisted on their 'orthodoxy' on this

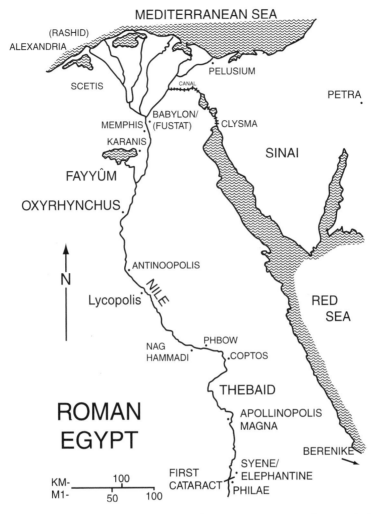

MEDITERRANEAN SEA

(RASHID)
ALEXANDRIA
PELUSIUM
SCETIS
CANAL
PETRA
BABYLON/
MEMPHIS (FUSTAT)
CLYSMA
KARANIS
SINAI
FAYYÛM
OXYRHYNCHUS
N
ANTINOOPOLIS
NILE
Lycopolis
RED
SEA
PHBOW
NAG
HAMMADI
COPTOS
THEBAID
ROMAN
EGYPT
APOLLINOPOLIS
MAGNA
BERENIKE
SYENE/
FIRST   ELEPHANTINE
KM-   100   CATARACT PHILAE
M1-   50   100

Figure 44.2   Map of Roman Egypt. Adapted from Haas (1997: 4), by permission of The Johns Hopkins University Press.[2]

matter, so much so that they later falsely claimed that Melitius himself had condemned Arius long before Alexander did!)

Alexander's actions did not end the controversy, however, because Arius had numerous followers in the city of Alexandria. These included priests and deacons who considered his teachings acceptable or who resented Alexander's heavy-handed response (which was not in keeping with either the historically collegial role of the bishop within the city or Alexandria's traditions of intellectual freedom); local parishioners who found Arius' eloquent preaching inspiring; and numerous ascetic Christians, male and female, for whom Arius' theology and spirituality were congenial with their own efforts at disciplined improvement in virtue. Arius found additional support outside Egypt, among bishops in Asia Minor, Syria, and Palestine, who shared his theological views (or at least regarded them within the range of acceptable diversity), who saw an opportunity to reduce the international prestige of the bishop of Alexandria, or both. Councils in Asia Minor and Palestine found Arius' views orthodox and urged Alexander to accept him into his church. Alexander refused, and thus the stage was set for an international resolution of the controversy at the Council of Nicaea.

It is important to note that both the 'Melitian' and the 'Arian' conflicts were not about theological doctrine or pastoral policies alone, but raised the issue of the authority of the bishop, whose role as centre of church unity and guarantor of 'orthodoxy' was growing markedly in the new imperially favoured church, but not without resistance. 'At the level of patriarchs', that is of Alexander and his successor Athanasius, 'questions of authority and appropriate governance cannot be disassociated from issues of doctrine' (Elm 1998: 83).

At Nicaea the young Athanasius saw his mentor Alexander vindicated on the questions both of Melitius and Arius. The Council recognized the Petrine organization, headed by Alexander, as the legitimate church in Egypt. It commanded Melitius, who was still alive, to retire to Lycopolis and not to involve himself in ecclesiastical affairs, but it recognized Melitian ordinations and allowed for Melitian bishops and priests to be integrated into the Petrine hierarchy by submitting to the authority of the bishop of Alexandria. Meanwhile, the Council excommunicated Arius and exiled several bishops who had embraced his cause. It adopted a theological statement that heavily emphasized the unity of the Father and Son as one God: the Son is 'begotten, not created', and 'of one substance' (*homoousios*) with the Father. It was a good meeting for Alexander and Athanasius. It is possible that it was in the wake of these successes that Athanasius wrote his impressive two-volume work, *Against the Nations* and *On the Incarnation of the Word*, without any explicit mention of Arius or his teachings (Barnes 1993: 12–13).[3]

But the years that followed did not see these conflicts lessened. Soon even bishops who had signed the creed adopted at Nicaea began to worry that it supported the views of a theologian like Marcellus of Ancyra, who saw little if any distinction between the Father and Son. The emperor Constantine, eager to bring unity to the church, allowed exiled bishops to return to their posts and urged Alexander to re-admit a supposedly repentant Arius to communion. This Alexander refused to do. Meanwhile, Nicaea's Melitian policy created awkward problems in cities and villages where there were now two bishops (Martin 1996: 313–17) and did not address the underlying dissatisfaction of Upper Egyptian bishops with submitting to Alexandrian authority. Such was the situation when Alexander died in April 328, with Athanasius on a mission to the imperial court to explain the patriarch's policy on Arius.

A disputed election and criminal accusations

Although Alexander had designated Athanasius as his choice to succeed him, matters were not so simple. For one thing, it appears that Athanasius was just shy of thirty, the minimum age for bishops according to canons adopted at Nicaea, and he was only a deacon, not yet a priest, the rank from which bishops were traditionally chosen in Alexandria (although not elsewhere). Moreover, an early practice in which the priests of Alexandria elected the bishop and then the bishops of Egypt consecrated him had only recently given way to election by the bishops, and at least one ancient source recalls that priests were still involved in Athanasius' election (*Apophthegmata Patrum* Poemen 78 [PG 65: 341]). Finally, this was the first election in which both Petrine and reconciled Melitian bishops would participate, raising the question of whether even former Melitian bishops who now shared a see with a Petrine one could vote (Martin 1996: 331–2) and making the achievement of consensus very difficult. It appears that, before any decision had been reached, a small minority of the gathered bishops went ahead and consecrated Athanasius: while many (if not most) of the other bishops accepted this development, numerous others did not, particularly the 'reconciled' Melitians, who elected their own bishop of Alexandria. The Melitian schism returned in a new, more dramatic form: for the first time even Alexandria itself had rival bishops, a situation repeated numerous times in the following century.

Thus, Athanasius' position as bishop and patriarch was precarious from the start. In addition to the ongoing political controversies over Arius and Petrine-Melitian relations, the unity of Egyptian Christianity under the Alexandrian patriarch was rendered fragile in more subtle ways, especially by the rapid growth of monastic movements (Brakke 1995). Ascetic Christians had long been a part of Christian communities in Alexandria and Egypt, but in the late third and early fourth centuries the number of such persons increased dramatically. In cities like Alexandria, 'renouncers', whether male 'solitaries' or female 'virgins', practised such disciplines as fasting, celibacy, and meditation, and lived in a variety of settings: at home with their families, in small single-sex communities, or in male-female celibate partnerships. It was not clear to what extent these Christians were under the authority of bishops and priests, whether Athanasian or Melitian. In Leontopolis, for example, a brilliant scholar named Hieracas led a community of celibate men and women who studied scripture under his direction and worshipped apart from ordinary Christians, sometimes singing songs composed by Hieracas. Could the local bishop tell Hieracas and his followers what to believe and how to worship? In and near the villages of Upper Egypt, a monk named Pachomius was founding a series of communal estates, where male or female monks lived, worked, and prayed together. Some more solitary monks, especially those who braved the heat and dangers of the desert, exemplified by the famous Anthony, became Christian superstars, to whom other Christians looked for spiritual guidance and miraculous deeds, such as healings and exorcisms. These charismatic Christians and their followers posed challenges to the idea of Christianity as centred around local churches, led by bishops and priests.

After his election, Athanasius tried to meet these challenges directly. It was the custom of the Alexandrian patriarch annually to announce the date of Easter in a *Festal Letter*, which he could use also to exhort his followers throughout Egypt and Libya. In his first such letter, written in the winter of 329, Athanasius makes no mention of his disputed election. Instead, he praises the benefits of fasting before Easter and declares that both ascetic and married Christians are following calls to virtue; he then turns to a traditional if distasteful way of promoting cohesion among

Christians: disparaging the Jews, whom he derides as 'ignorant' (*Epistulae festales* 1.3, 7 [ed. Cureton 1848: 14, 17]). He also made a trip through the Thebaid (Upper Egypt), much of which was Melitian territory, to consolidate his support. Such a tour of the Alexandrian patriarch was an impressive display of power, akin to an imperial *adventus* (the elaborately staged and celebrated arrival of a touring emperor in a city): 'He was mounted on a donkey and countless people were following him, including bishops, innumerable clerics with lamps and candles, and also monks from various places who were preceding him chanting psalms and canticles' (*Bohairic Life of Pachomius* 201 [trans. Veilleux 1980: 249], describing a later tour). One local bishop, Sarapion of Tentyra, had hoped that during his visit Athanasius would resolve a conflict between himself and the monastic leader Pachomius by ordaining Pachomius a priest and thus making him subordinate to Bishop Sarapion. Nothing came of this request, but it illustrated the growing tensions between monks and clergy that Athanasius would eventually have to address (Brakke 1995: 113–20). Athanasius made at least two more episcopal tours of regions under his patriarchal authority in the next four years (*Festal Index* 4, 6 [ed. Martin and Albert 1985: 230–2]).

Back in Alexandria, however, events began to turn against Athanasius, as an alliance formed between his Melitian enemies within Egypt and his pro-Arius enemies outside Egypt. The latter, led by Eusebius of Nicomedia, wished to see Arius restored to communion and were alarmed by the absence in the creed of Nicaea of any way to understand the separateness of the Father and the Son. The Melitians supplied Eusebius and his allies with criminal charges against Athanasius that could be the basis for his removal from office. These ranged from financial improprieties (bribery, forced requisition of linen tunics), to violence (beatings, imprisonments, even murder), to sacrilege (the destruction of a consecrated chalice used by a Melitian priest). A complicated series of events led to an international council of bishops at Tyre in 335, which found convincing evidence for the chalice incident, admitted Arius and the Melitians to communion, deposed Athanasius from his office, and appointed a new bishop of Alexandria. Since it was then up to Constantine to enforce these decisions, Athanasius secretly fled Tyre and raced to meet the emperor in Constantinople. Constantine agreed to set aside the Council's decisions, but the temperamental Athanasius managed to insult the emperor, who then sent the bishop into exile in Trier in November 335 (Barnes 1993: 19–33). Although Constantine had set aside the verdict of the Council of Tyre, the criminal accusations of violence and extortion would haunt Athanasius for the rest of his career.

Was Athanasius guilty of the charges made against him? Some, like the charge of murder, were disproved at the time, but others have remained unresolved, Athanasius' writings being the only surviving evidence. But in 1924 H. I. Bell published a papyrus letter written in 335 by a Melitian named Callistus to two priests in a Melitian monastery (*P. Lond.* 1914 [ed. Bell 1924: 53–71]). In this letter Callistus reports how 'partisans of Athanasius' tried to seize the Melitian bishop of Alexandria, Heraiscus, and his guests, and when they could not, beat four Melitian monks nearly to death. Callistus vividly describes Athanasius' anxiety as he faced the Council of Tyre: the 'despondent' bishop would send his baggage to the boat and then nervously call it back. He says that Athanasius tried to prevent opponents from travelling to the Council by imprisoning Melitian clergy in various prisons and even the meat-market. Although Callistus' letter does not corroborate any specific charge made against Athanasius at Tyre, it has been viewed by most scholars as the smoking gun that demonstrates that 'Athanasius exercised power and protected his position in Alexandria by the systematic use of violence and intimidation' (Barnes 1993: 32). Defenders of Athanasius' saintly character have had to work very hard to cast doubts on this first-hand evidence (Arnold 1991).

Late ancient Alexandria, it must be remembered, was a multicultural city, in which ongoing tensions between and within ethnic and religious communities at times burst into acts of violence, such as riots, lynchings, destruction of property, and outright warfare (Haas 1997). During the fourth century, not only in Alexandria but throughout the empire, violence and intimidation, whether by rioting mobs or by small groups of professionals, became one of the tools available to Christian bishops in their efforts to secure both their own power and the solidarity of their communities (Brown 1992: 90–1; MacMullen 1990; McLynn 1992). It would indeed be a miraculous instance of saintliness had Athanasius been able to exempt himself from his society and culture in this regard. Despite his many protests of innocence of the charges against him, it is not clear that Athanasius' definition of saintliness required such pacific restraint. To his mind, people's orthodox belief and ultimate salvation were not separable from their obedience to himself as head of the Catholic church in Egypt. In 369, confronted with Christians who promoted martyr cults that were not under his authority, Athanasius declared that just as Christ had violently forced the money-changers out of the Temple, so these disobedient Christians should be 'driven out by whippings . . . for those who commit such a sin must receive the same punishment' (*Ep. fest.* 41 [ed. Lefort 1955: 26]; Brakke 1998: 480–1). The analogy of 'a modern American gangster' fails to capture this volatile combination of genuine religious conviction and brute political force, which may better be compared to that of a modern Iranian ayatollah.

INTERNATIONAL POLITICS (335–73 CE)

The remaining four decades of Athanasius' episcopal career were as tumultuous as the first seven years. His changing fortunes reflected not only the ebb and flow of theological debates over the doctrine of God (Hanson 1988) but also the vicissitudes of imperial politics, which now became closely intertwined with ecclesiastical affairs (Barnes 1993). Controversy over Athanasius always centred ostensibly on allegations of professional misconduct, while the bishop himself consistently (and not groundlessly) claimed that hostility to his theological beliefs was the real motivation behind the actions of his opponents.

Intrigues with the sons of Constantine (337–53 CE)

Athanasius' exile in Trier came to an end not long after the death of Constantine on 22 May 337; within a month, the new emperors – Constantinus, Constantius and

Constans, sons of Constantine – allowed all exiled bishops to return to their homes. Athanasius did not enter Alexandria until November, for he travelled through the eastern empire lending assistance to his political allies before reclaiming his own see. The bishop did not have long to enjoy his homecoming: a council (probably in Antioch) in the winter of 337–8 yet again deposed Athanasius, who travelled to Cappadocia to plead his case before Constantius (Barnes 1993: 36–45). This mission forestalled enforcement of the deposition, and in the summer of 338 Athanasius arranged for the famous monk Anthony to make a highly publicized visit to Alexandria as a show of support for the Athanasian cause (*Festal Index* 10 [ed. Martin and Albert 1985: 236]; *Life of Anthony* (*Vita Antonii*) 69–71 [ed. Bartelink 1994: 314–20]). His *Festal Letter* for this year encourages his followers in the face of 'afflictions' from 'the Ario-maniacs' (*Ep. fest.* 10.1, 9 [ed. Cureton 1848: 45, 49–50]), and it is likely that at this time he also wrote a letter to Alexandrian virgins that exhorts them to avoid the teachings of Arius and Hieracas (*Ep. virg.* 1 [ed. Lefort 1955: 73–99; trans. Brakke 1995: 274–91]; Brakke 1994a: 24–5). The following winter yet another council at Antioch found Athanasius guilty of the chalice incident and additional acts of violence: he was deposed, and a Gregory of Cappadocia was named as his replacement. Constantius enforced this decision through his imperial officers in Egypt. Gregory entered Alexandria on 22 March 339. Athanasius had already gone into hiding to avoid arrest, and on 16 April he left Egypt for Rome, which was in Constans' territory and thus out of the reach of Constantius.

In Rome Athanasius undertook a vigorous campaign to win back his see (Barnes 1993: 47–55). On the political front, he wrote an *Encyclical Letter* to numerous bishops giving his version of the events that had led to his expulsion. He gained the support of bishop Julius of Rome, wrote pleading letters to the emperors Constans and Constantius, and recruited to his side prominent Christians in the Roman aristocracy. Theologically, he began his rich and substantive *Orations Against the Arians*, which eventually ran to three books. This work begins by mocking Arius and his teachings as 'effeminate' (*Ar.* 1.5 [*PG* 26: 20]; Burrus 1991: 235–9), but then turns to a vigorous defence of the essential unity and likeness of the Father and Son and to exegesis of biblical passages such as Prov. 8:22, which his opponents cited as evidence of the Word's created status.

Athanasius' efforts paid off, but at some cost. On the one hand, a council of western bishops at Serdica in the autumn of 343 found Athanasius innocent of charges against him (a parallel council of Eastern bishops conspicuously did not do the same); and in 345 Constantius allowed him to return from exile after his brother Constans threatened civil war over the matter and the rival bishop Gregory had died (Barnes 1993: 89–91). Athanasius arrived in Alexandria in October 346. On the other hand, Athanasius' aggressive courtship of Constans would later lead to the charge that he had sowed enmity between the two brother emperors, and during this period his political case and theological views became yoked to those of another eastern bishop exiled to the West, Marcellus of Ancyra. Marcellus' theology stressed the unity of God to such an extent that he appeared to grant no independent existence to the Son at all: this extreme version of pro-Nicene thought alarmed nearly everyone in the Greek-speaking East, and Athanasius' association with Marcellus became a liability for him.

The nearly ten years between October 346 and February 356 form the longest period of time in which Athanasius enjoyed possession of his see in Alexandria, and thus they have come to be called the 'Golden Decade' by Athanasian scholars. In truth Athanasius' troubles and triumphs on the international political scene continued unabated, and his real theological influence began to fade as discussion among even bishops inclined to accept Nicaea began to turn to how to speak of the separateness of Father, Son and Holy Spirit within the context of their unity. In 349 a council at Antioch, for which Athanasius prepared a brief that is now basically the *Defence Against the Arians* (Barnes 1993: 98–100, 192–5), condemned and deposed him once again and appointed George of Cappadocia as bishop of Alexandria in his place. But before Constantius could enforce this decision, a more urgent problem confronted the emperor: in the West a revolt by the general Magnentius, whose troops proclaimed him Augustus on 18 January 350, led to the death of his brother Constans. Both Constantius and Magnentius sought Athanasius' support, the former by giving up on enforcing the deposition of Athanasius (and sending Athanasius a prized letter expressing his support for him), the latter by sending envoys to meet with the patriarch in Alexandria. In public at least Athanasius rebuffed Magnentius' overtures, but insinuations that he privately courted the usurper would later surface. It took Constantius until the summer of 353 to put down Magnentius' revolt decisively. That both of these contestants for imperial power found it expedient to

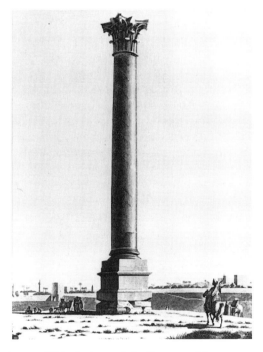

Figure 44.3   The column of Diocletian, originally topped by a statue, erected on a hill in Alexandria to commemorate the emperor's victory over a rebellion in Egypt in 298 CE. Photo from the Napoleonic *Description de l'Égypte*, Paris, 1808–28.

gain the support of Athanasius testifies to the power and prestige that the Alexandrian patriarch commanded.

Urban violence and literary productivity (353–62 CE)

Once Constantius was firmly in control of the entire empire, East and West, he could more effectively enforce the ecclesiastical policies that he favoured. In a series of councils held at Sirmium, Arles and Milan from 351–5, the emperor coerced even western bishops into condemning and deposing Athanasius. In the midst of these prolonged struggles, Athanasius wrote *On the Council of Nicaea*, in which for the first time he placed that council's term *homoousios* ('of the same essence') at the centre of the debate. Orthodoxy, Athanasius asserted, is adherence to the creed of that council and its language. Still, Constantius moved to enforce the decisions of his councils. In January 356 the military commander Syrianus entered Alexandria with a large number of troops. Brandishing the letter of support that Constantius had written him during Magnentius' revolt, Athanasius denied that the emperor would now wish to remove him. But Syrianus looked for an opportune moment, and on the night of 8–9 February he stormed the Church of Theonas where Athanasius was leading prayers. The bishop escaped, however, with the aid of local monks.

Athanasius spent the next six years in hiding, moving among monastic settlements and local churches in Egypt, Libya, and at times even Alexandria itself. Provided secure cover by his supporters, he was able to able to intensify his campaign of literary propaganda. He augmented his *Defence Before Constantius*, first composed in 353 (Barnes 1993: 196–7), and wrote a *Defence of His Flight*, the highly invective *History of the Arians*, and his *Letters to Serapion* (the bishop of Thmuis), which defend the full divinity of the Holy Spirit. Ascetic Christians formed an important target of these works: the bishop wrote letters warning them to give no hospitality to his opponents and spreading a grisly account of the death of Arius. He composed the *Life of Anthony*, which portrayed the recently deceased monk as an implacable foe of Arians, Melitians, and all 'heretics', whose spiritual achievements illustrated Athanasius' doctrine of the incarnation of the Word (Brakke 1995: 129–38; Roldanus 1983; Gregg and Groh 1981: 142–53). A masterpiece of Christian literature, the *Life* was soon translated into Latin and many other languages, inspiring imitation of two kinds: subsequent hagiographers used it as a model for their own literary endeavours, and subsequent ascetics used Athanasius' Anthony as a model for their spiritual disciplines (see Chapter 43 of this volume).

If Athanasius' ability to elude arrest and to carry on such literary endeavours for six years represents a noble demonstration of the support he enjoyed among the Christians of Egypt, events in Alexandria provide less edifying evidence of Athanasian strength. The city was plagued with violence. It took the imperial government four months to wrest control of the church buildings from the Athanasian clergy and hand them over to supporters of Athanasius' replacement, George. Bishop George did not feel confident enough to enter the city until February 357; once there he tried to build up a non-Athanasian community, for instance by patronizing the anti-Nicene theologian Aetius, whose student Eunomius became a famous defender of the separateness of the Father and the Son. But George's efforts were in vain: in

August 358 a mob nearly killed him at the Church of Dionysius, and in October he fled the city. The Athanasians regained control of the churches, but by December they were forced out again. It was not until November 361 that George returned to Alexandria, but when news of the death of Constantius, George's supporter, reached the city, he was imprisoned. On 24 December a mob attacked the prison and lynched George.

A gradual withdrawal from the international scene (362–73 CE)

The death of Constantius and the accession of the pagan emperor Julian allowed Athanasius to return to Alexandria in February 362. Shortly thereafter he chaired a small council of bishops, the goal of which was to articulate a basis for unity among supporters of Nicene theology. The divisions among this group were exemplified by the situation in Antioch, where pro-Nicene Christians were divided into moderate and hard-line factions, each with its own bishop. In a document addressed to the Christians in Antioch (*Tomus ad Antiochenos*) in 362, the assembled bishops proposed that adherence to the creed of Nicaea be the sufficient basis for unity and addressed themselves to the controversial term *hypostasis*, which Nicaea had rejected as a way of speaking about the separateness of the Father and Son. They suggested that it was acceptable for pro-Nicene Christians to speak of 'three *hypostaseis*' ('three substances or persons') if they also spoke of the Trinity as *homoousios* ('of one substance or essence') (*Tom.* 5 [*PG* 26: 800–1]). This point was a major concession on the part of Athanasius, who had dedicated his career to refuting language that spoke of the separate identity of the Son from the Father in such blunt terms. It is likely, as a modern scholar has suggested, that Athanasius accepted this point 'with his teeth clenched' (Barnes 1998: 67, n. 49), but accept it he did and so contributed in a small way to the consensus on the doctrine of God that began to emerge in the 360s and 370s.

After the 362 Council of Alexandria, Athanasius' prominence on the international scene faded as younger men began to do the cutting-edge theology and almost everyone lost interest in matters like chalices broken 30 years earlier. He was forced to retire to the Thebaid briefly under Julian in 362–3 and again under Valens in 365–6. The schism among the Nicenes at Antioch continued, and Athanasius' stubborn loyalty to the smaller hard-line faction became more a hindrance than a help to the Nicene cause in the East. Repeated pleas from Basil of Caesarea in the late 360s and early 370s that Athanasius moderate his position on the Antiochene situation met with silence, for the aged bishop's attention had turned to vexing problems in his Egyptian church, as the *Festal Letters* of 367–70 (see below) and a second letter to virgins demonstrate (*Ep. virg.* 2 [Lebon 1928; trans. Brakke 1995: 292–302]; Brakke 1994a: 27). However, alerted by bishop Epictetus of Corinth that some Christians took the divinity of the Son so seriously that they suggested that even Christ's body was not really human, but *homoousios* with the Word's divine nature, Athanasius eagerly took pen in hand to denounce any such distortion of his position (*Epistula ad Epictetum* [*PG* 26: 1050–70]). On 2 May 373 the patriarch died.

Athanasius the international politician presents an imposing figure on the stage of late Roman imperial history, so much so that even the hard-headed Edward Gibbon attributed to him 'a superiority of character and abilities which would have qualified him, far better than the degenerate sons of Constantine, for the government of a great monarchy' (Barnard 1985). The elements for such a picture can be discerned in Athanasius' brilliant deployment of polemics in defence of his case, from which only meticulous scholarship can extract the truth (Barnes 1993); his willingness to use (and then to cover up) violence against his enemies; his courting of and by emperors and would-be emperors; his success in identifying attacks on himself with attacks on Christian orthodoxy; and, above all, his ability to hold onto his episcopal office through nearly forty years of attempts to unseat him. But traces of a less confident, more insecure Athanasius remain: the *Festal Letters'* frequent ruminations on the role of 'afflictions' in the believer's life; the portrayal of Anthony in the *Life* as treating the emperors Constantine, Constans and Constantius with a diffidence that Athanasius could only envy (*V. Ant.* 91 [ed. Bartelink 1994: 366–70]); and the Melitian Callistus' picture of a nervous Athanasius vacillating over whether to depart for the Council of Tyre in 335. In this last instance we may catch a rare glimpse of a young bishop, not yet forty years old, the golden boy of the Alexandrian clergy, caught in an ecclesiastical game in which, thanks to the use of imperial force to enforce conciliar decisions, the stakes had become much higher than they had ever been. Although Athanasius would in this instance be a loser, he eventually learned to play the new game of Constantinian imperial Christianity, and to play it well. But that should not totally erase the image of the 'despondent' young bishop calling for his luggage to be returned in the hope that he could avoid what lay ahead.

THE POWER OF A BISHOP AND THE CREATION OF A CATHOLIC CHURCH

While a player in imperial and ecclesiastical politics on the world stage, Athanasius was always bishop of Alexandria and thus patriarch of Egypt. As other bishops did in their own environments, Athanasius worked to form a unified and dominant church in Egypt, a 'Catholic' church that would be inclusive of diverse persons and dependent on the clerical hierarchy. Both Alexandria and Egypt were the objects of the bishop's efforts as he established and displayed episcopal authority. We have already seen at least three methods of doing this: the annual *Festal Letter* announcing the date of Easter, tours of visitation through the region, and the use of violence and intimidation.

The bishop as patron and ascetic

Within the city of Alexandria (see Figure 44.4) Athanasius worked to establish a dominant presence in the civic space through buildings, rituals, and patronage. Benefiting from the new wealth that came with imperial favour, the church built impressive new buildings in the city, augmented old ones, and took over pagan structures (Haas 1997: 208–12). Under Alexander, the temple of Kronos (Saturn)

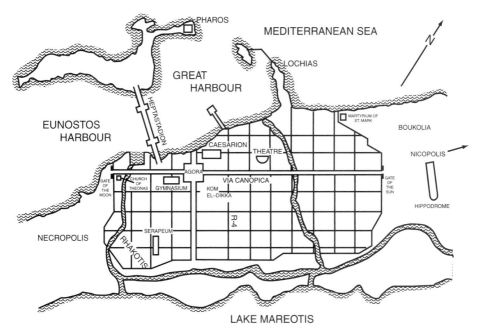

Figure 44.4 Map of Alexandria. Athanasius' headquarters, the Church of Theonas, lay near the western gate. Adapted from Haas (1997: 4), by permission of The Johns Hopkins University Press.

was converted into a church dedicated to St Michael the Archangel, the first major Christian building at the city centre; and the pre-existing Church of Theonas, which was situated just inside the western gate on the Via Canopica, Alexandria's main thoroughfare, was enlarged and ornamented, and became the bishop's headquarters.

In the middle of Athanasius' career (339–46, actually while he was in exile and Gregory was in residence as bishop), Constantius gave to the Christians the Caesarion, a huge complex originally built by Cleopatra (died 30 BCE) that was marked by tall twin obelisks plundered from an ancient Egyptian temple (one of which was still standing when French scholars visited Egypt at the turn of the nineteenth century). The Caesarion had served as the centre for the imperial cult for over three hundred years. This dominating structure became the Great church, the new seat for the bishop. Disgruntled pagans did not take this lightly, however, and treated the chaotic events of 356 as an opportunity to attack the church and try to reclaim it as their own ritual space (Haas 1997: 283–6). Another such attack in 366 required extensive rebuilding with imperial support in 368. Athanasius' final major building project was a church in the north-west section of the city, which he dedicated on 7 August 370 and was later called by his name (*Festal Index* 41–2 [ed. Martin and Albert 1985: 272–4]). Once again it was a pagan temple that was converted to Christian use and was strategically positioned near where sea travellers entered the

Figure 44.5 The Caesarion in Alexandria at the turn of the nineteenth century. From the Napoleonic *Description de l'Égypte*, Paris, 1808–28.

city. The built landscape of Alexandria began to reflect the prestige and wealth of the church and its bishop.

In these impressive major buildings and in the numerous local parish churches, a regular ritual calendar bound Christians together and broadcast their communal life to others. The annual celebration of Holy Week and Easter, the Christian *Pasch*, was the most important of these liturgical events. Athanasius expended considerable energy trying to standardize Alexandrian practices associated with Lent and Easter (Brakke 1998: 460–2). The numbers of worshippers at Easter became so large that Athanasius had to move services into the new Great church before it was dedicated: the press of the crowds in the smaller buildings caused not only children and old women, but even young men to faint (*Apologia ad Constantium* 14–15 [Szymuziak 1958: 102–4]).

These buildings were also headquarters for the bishop's system of patronage, which formed only one aspect of a complicated socio-economic web in which the fourth-century bishop played a leading role. In a society marked by extreme disparities in wealth and social power, patron-client relationships promoted social cohesion and secured patterns of inequality as powerful persons dispensed benefits to their inferiors, who in turn owed their patrons honour through publicly expressed gratitude and concrete political support (Saller 1982). The Christian bishop bestowed not only material, but also spiritual benefits on ordinary Christians (Bobertz 1993), and at times acted as a 'broker' between them and even higher powers, the emperor and God (Moxnes 1991: 248–9).

In the case of Athanasius, imperial subsidies for the church and the needy in Egypt and Libya, such as allotments of grain, were channelled through the bishop of Alexandria, who in turn enjoyed some ability to requisition supplies for charitable purposes. Some of the charges against Athanasius revolved around his powers in this area (Barnes 1993: 178–9). In addition to imperial funds, contributions from wealthier church members went to the bishop, who then distributed them to the poor, widows, and ascetic Christians. Local bishops and clergy were tied to the patriarch not only by this welfare system, but also by their exemptions from costly civic offices: one way the government could coerce clergy into supporting either Athanasius or one of his rivals was by determining to which patriarch clergy must adhere in order to receive the exemption. In turn, it was the patriarch who determined what adherence to him meant practically. Athanasius, then, stood at the centre of a complex system of financial dependencies and privileges that bound together lay and clergy, prosperous and poor Christians.

Such day-to-day power rarely surfaces in the historical record, but the few instances are revealing. Athanasius reports being charged that he threatened to prevent grain from being shipped from Alexandria to Constantinople (*Apologia contra Arianos* 87.1 [*PG* 25: 405]), and there are indeed indications that the patriarch enjoyed a special patron-client relationship with Christian ship captains and sailors, who were engaged in intense rivalry with Jewish competitors (Haas 1997: 116–18). New regulations under Constantine gave the patriarch some control over the city's guilds (Brown 1992: 102). When the government turned over Alexandrian churches to rivals of Athanasius in 339 and 356, conflicts over the welfare system turned violent. In 356, according to Athanasius, when his supporters lost control of the churches, they tried to keep supplying widows and poor with food and money in other locations, while the opposing clergy tried to force the aid recipients back into the churches and onto their dole by 'striking them on their feet' (*Historia Arianorum* 61 [ed. Opitz 1935–41: 217]; Brakke 1995: 190–1). What these rival clerical organizations were after was not only the political support of the indigent themselves, but the ability to present themselves to the governing elite and the wider populace as the protectors of and spokesmen for 'the poor' (Brown 1992: 89–103).

Often among those dependent on the bishop for economic aid were ascetic Christians: forging strong connections between the institutional church and the diverse ascetic movements was one of Athanasius' most important goals in creating a unified Egyptian church (Brakke 1995). The variety of ascetic Christians required a variety of strategies. Many of the Alexandrian virgins of his day were literate and independent women who formed celibate relationships with ascetic men, made pilgrimages to Jerusalem, and became involved in the theological discussions surrounding 'Arianism'; thus, Athanasius urged them to reject 'Arian' teachings and to model their lives after the reclusive and submissive young Virgin Mary. As 'brides of Christ', they were to behave like wives: silent, withdrawn, and obedient to male authority figures. In contrast, he tried to rally the male monks of Upper Egypt to a more politicized pro-Athanasian disposition: he recruited monks to serve in his clergy, and he exhorted them to withhold hospitality and communion from anti-Athanasian monks. He wrote letters to monks instructing them on proper ascetic practices and occasionally intervened in the sometimes confused authority structure of the huge Pachomian monastic federation. The *Life of Anthony* was his definitive portrait of ascetic Christianity in league with Athanasian teachings and institutions. Athanasius positioned himself as the patron of ordinary Christians and the leader of ascetic Christians.

Continuing conflicts

Athanasius' relentless and persuasive propaganda, his theological clarity and embrace of monasticism, and his financial clout enabled him to achieve a great deal of success in creating a unified Egyptian church out of the divisions that confronted him at the beginning of his episcopate. After the bloody clashes of the late 350s, the anti-Athanasian forces in the city of Alexandria (the 'Arians', he would say) appear to have been greatly weakened. In Upper Egypt, the Melitian church steadily lost ground, so that by the late 360s Melitian clergy and monks had no real ecclesiastical organization to speak of (Barnes 1993: 95–6; Camplani 1989: 262–82). But the aspects of Egyptian Christianity from which these conflicts stemmed – a rich tradition of intellectual speculation in the cities, and a tendency among Upper Egyptian Christians to develop their own modes of spirituality without Alexandrian control – did not disappear. In *Festal Letters* from late in his career (367–70), Athanasius confronts these problematic trends and tries to stigmatize them by labelling them with the old epithets 'Arian' and 'Melitian'.

The 39th *Festal Letter* for 367 addressed the issue of scripture in the official church by enumerating a list of 'canonical' books that are 'inspired by God', sketching a short list of early Christian works that are 'useful for instruction' (e.g., the popular *Shepherd of Hermas*), and denouncing certain 'apocryphal' books attributed to Enoch, Moses and Isaiah (Joannou 1963: 2.71–6; Lefort 1955: 16–22, 58–62; Coquin 1984: 135–58; trans. Brakke 1995: 326–32). The letter, famous because it is the first Christian document to list precisely the 27 books that now comprise the New Testament, promulgated a biblical canon suited to the hierarchical episcopate as a means of attacking two competing modes of authority (Brakke 1994b). On the one hand, Athanasius assailed Christian 'teachers' who offered their own 'evil thoughts' rather than repeating only the doctrines of 'Christ the Teacher', found in the canonical books. In this way the bishop attacked yet again the kind of independent teaching authority that Arius had exercised and his predecessor Alexander had tried to squash. On the other hand, Athanasius accused 'the Melitians' of publishing such fraudulent works as the *Testament of Moses*, which promoted revelations to martyrs as means of access to truth apart from Christ. The promotion of a set canon bolstered episcopal authority based in parish churches.

In his letter for 368 (no. 40), Athanasius complained about irregular ordinations of priests and bishops in Upper Egypt (Lefort 1955: 22–3; Coquin 1984: 144–6; trans. Brakke 1995: 332–4, cf. 100–2). Some Christians, he claimed, were 'electing clergy for other dioceses that are not theirs'. What appears to have been in dispute was the balance between local and Alexandrian interests in the election of bishops. This problem lay at the origin of the Melitian schism: despite the decline of an organized Melitian network, Egyptian bishops still sought a greater role in the

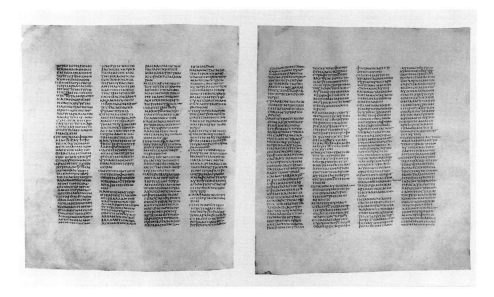

Figure 44.6   Codex Sinaiticus, the earliest surviving manuscript of the complete New Testament, dated to the fourth century and possibly produced in Alexandria. By permission of the British Library, Add. MS. 43725.ff.244v–245.

selection of their neighbouring colleagues, at the expense of patriarchal control and thus, in Athanasius' view, of 'good order'.

Finally, in 369–70, Athanasius used his 41st and 42nd *Festal Letters* to condemn a number of practices associated with the developing cult of the martyrs (Lefort 1955: 23–6, 62–4; Coquin 1984: 146–52; trans. Brakke 1998: 486–93). Certain Christians ('Melitians') were, according to Athanasius, exhuming the bodies of martyrs and carrying them out of 'the cemeteries of the catholic church' to set up independent martyr shrines. At these shrines, demons were exorcised, and divination was offered, as the martyrs' spirits would answer people's questions by speaking through a possessed person or forcing a demon to speak. Christians who availed themselves of these services made financial contributions to the shrine. Such activity infuriated Athanasius, who insisted that all power to combat the demonic and to reveal the truth belonged to Christ alone. To his mind, these shrines were a deceptive means to 'lead astray' Christians, to seduce them from the Catholic church where 'the Word of God speaks from heaven' to follow merely 'those who speak from earth'.

These letters, written at a time when Athanasius' involvement in international politics had waned considerably, reveal that even at the end of his episcopate the patriarch had to work hard to create a unified, dominant, and episcopally centred church in Egypt. His efforts, ranging from building new churches to distributing aid to the needy to establishing a canon of the Bible, illustrate the ways in which fourth-century bishops created a new 'catholic' church in the era between Constantine and Theodosius.

THE POWER OF THE WORD AND THE CREATION OF A CATHOLIC THEOLOGY

Such a catholic church, one that embraced society and culture rather than stood in opposition to them, required a theology that was also 'catholic', that is, inclusive of and intelligible to persons of a wide variety of social roles and at diverse levels of spiritual perfection. It is usual to characterize Athanasius' theology as 'biblical' or 'dogmatic', rather than 'philosophical' or 'systematic'. 'There was', one scholar has written, 'something un-Greek about him' (von Campenhausen 1959: 70). What this means is that, unlike such versatile theologians as Gregory of Nyssa and Augustine, Athanasius' thought is not wide-ranging or considered in its use of philosophical distinctions and concepts. Instead, Athanasius focused with laser-beam intensity on a single idea: the fully divine Word of God became incarnate in human flesh to save humanity from sin and death. In his justly famous formulation, the Word 'became human, so that we may become divine' (*de Incarnatione* 54 [ed. Thomson 1971: 268]). His theological writings, forged mostly in the heat of ecclesiastical conflict, defend and expound this fundamental conviction by specifying the identity of this Word and the necessity and benefits of his incarnation.

If there is any philosophical concept at the heart of Athanasius' thought, it is the distinction between Creator and created, between the eternal, unchanging God and his contingent, changeable creation.[4] He was a relentless critic of traditional Egyptian religiosity, such as that centring on the Nile, which was the heart of the social, economic, and religious life of ancient Egypt (see Figure 44.7): 'If a person sinks to the nature of the waters and reckons them to be a god, as the Egyptians worship the water, let him see their nature being transformed by him (the Word of God) and recognize that the Lord is their creator' (*de Incarnatione* 45 [ed. Thomson 1971: 248], referring to Mark 4:35–41).

For Athanasius, moreover, there are no gradations of divine being: thus, the Son of God must be either fully divine or fully created. As Son, however, God's Word is not created, but 'begotten', of the same 'essence' (*ousia*) or 'nature' (*physis*) as the Father's, just as human fathers do not create sons that are of a different nature from themselves, but beget them as like themselves in every way. But God the Father, as eternal and unchanging, could not have become a father at some point in time: rather, God is always Father of the Son (*Ep. Serap.* 1.16 [*PG* 26: 568–9]). It is of God's nature as life-giving fountain and source to be Father and Son (*Ar.* 1.14, 19, 24; 2.32; *Ep. Serap.* 2.2 [*PG* 26: 40–1, 49–53, 213–17, 611–12]). The Word of God, in turn, does not become a son based on his exceptional virtue or his perseverance in clinging to the Father: he is eternally the Son, the Word, Wisdom, Power, and Will of the Father. God does not choose to be Father, Son, or Spirit: the Trinity is a matter of God's nature, not of his will, for God cannot be anything other than who and what he is. The Father, Son, and Holy Spirit are 'indivisible' (*Ep. Serap.* 1.17 [*PG* 26: 569]). Athanasius has little to say about how they are different.

Human beings, in contrast, were created by God out of nothing and have bodies that are vulnerable to corruption and death. Although Athanasius took over his Alexandrian predecessor Origen's notion of the eternal begetting of the Son, he eschewed Origen's idea that human beings originated as 'intellects', which became

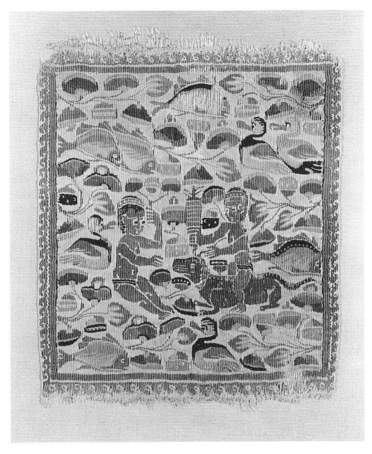

Figure 44.7 Egyptian tapestry of the Nile, from the fourth or fifth century, showing two putti, part of the entourage of the river god Nilos and symbolic of the river's fertility, playing among fish and ducks. By permission of the Metropolitan Museum of Art, New York, Gift of George F. Baker, 1890, 90.5.825.

souls and acquired bodies when they turned away from God. Instead, Athanasius' original human beings were already embodied intellects (Brakke 1995: 148–9). Because the original human beings had rational faculties, they could contemplate God through his Word, thanks to God's grace; but because they also had bodies, which were corruptible and the sources of 'pleasure' and 'desire', they were changeable and could fall away from this attention to God. This, of course, they did: people failed to persevere in renunciation of the body and adherence to God. Instead, through a 'lack of attention' to God, human beings became subject to the now disordered pleasures of the body, inclined towards selfish desires, and vulnerable to the corruption and death that was natural to their bodies. Fear of death and the loss of pleasures resulted in an accelerating inclination towards sin and an inability to reverse course and return to virtue and contemplation of God (*Contra Gentes* 2–4; *de Incarnatione* 4–5 [ed. Thomson 1971: 4–12, 142–6]).

It is crucial to note the ascetic character of Athanasius' vision, which places the proper control of the body and its passions at the centre of the human plight. Human beings could have enjoyed blessed immortality if they had persevered in attention to God and discipline of the body. Fallen human beings, however, are enslaved to the passions of the body, unable to know God truly, and vulnerable to the devil and his demons. Only the incarnation of the fully divine Word of God could solve these problems. By assuming an ordinary human body, the incarnate Word, unchangeable in virtue and invulnerable to the passions, conquered the destabilizing 'movements' of the body, such as lust, avarice and fear (Badger 1990). As the Word perfectly controlled his assumed body and remained unaffected by its passions, he transformed the body itself, rendering it incorruptible, both morally and physically: the Word's unwavering guidance divinized the flesh. Moral courage and disciplined control of the body were now possible for human beings because they shared a 'kinship of the flesh' with the Word's assumed body (*Ar.* 2.69 [*PG* 26: 293]). The key mechanism of salvation is not, as it had been with Origen (*Exhortation to Martyrdom* 47; *de Principiis* 1.1.7), the human intellect or soul's 'kinship' with the eternal Word, but the human body's 'kinship' with the incarnate Word's flesh.

Still, the Word's role as teacher of humanity has not disappeared. The incarnation was necessary also because humanity's knowledge of God had to be renewed. Since people were now attuned to their bodily senses, only the appearance of the unchanging image of God in a body could re-educate them about God (*Inc.* 13–16 [ed. Thomson 1971: 164–72]). This renewed knowledge of God remains available in the scriptures, in which the unmediated voice of the Word continues to speak his teachings (*Ep. fest.* 39 [ed. Lefort 1955: 16]). But in Athanasius the element of struggle and resistance is always present: the climax of the incarnation is the death and resurrection of the Word's body, which made manifest Christ's triumph over the corrupting passions of the body and represented the definitive victory over Satan and his airborne demons: 'The Lord came to cast down the devil, clear the air, and prepare our way up to heaven' (*Inc.* 25 [ed. Thomson 1971: 194]).[5] Christians now could advance towards heaven by resisting the demons through determined moral effort (*Life of Anthony* 65–6 [ed. Bartelink 1994: 304–10]).

One of the most controversial features of Athanasius' theology is precisely how he imagined the union of humanity and divinity in Christ. Towards the end of his career and in the years following his death, an admirer of Athanasius, Apollinaris of Laodicea, taught that the Word of God simply replaced the human mind and soul in the incarnate Christ: what was human about Christ was only his body. At the Council of Alexandria in 362, Athanasius agreed in contrast that Christ had a human body and soul (*Tom.* 7 [*PG* 26: 804–5]), but his usual instinct was to attribute the passions – not only desires like lust, but also emotions like fear – to the body and thus to the flesh that the Word of God assumed. The logic seems to be that, while in ordinary human beings the body's passions affect and disorient the soul, in Christ they were powerless against the embodied Word and thus were 'extinguished'. Any human soul that Christ may have possessed plays little if any role. Rather than assessing Athanasius' thought on this point against some later standard of orthodoxy, it may be best to appreciate his distinctive views on the body, the passions, and the benefits of the incarnation within his own symbolic world-view.

Since they have free will, human beings are able to appropriate the benefits of the Word's incarnation in a disciplined life of 'thanksgiving' (*Epp. fest.* 3.2–5; 6.3; 10.5 [ed. Cureton 1848: 27–31, 42–3, 47]): 'We sail on this sea by our own free will, as though by a wind, for everyone is carried where it his will [to go]. Either, when the Word is navigating, one enters into rest, or, when pleasure is in control, one suffers shipwreck and is endangered by the storm' (*Ep. fest.* 19.7 [ed. Cureton 1848: 45*]). Christians achieve a 'withdrawal' from the pleasures of the world and ascend to heaven through acts of bodily renunciation, attention to the scriptures, and reception of the sacraments (*Epp. fest.* 6.11–12 [ed. Cureton 1848: 5*-6*]; 24 [=2] [ed. Lefort 1955: 37–42]). Thus, all Christians, in Athanasius' view, are ascetics, but at different levels of intensity. The monk Anthony was so 'navigated by the Word' that his body already displayed the divinizing transformation that the incarnation made possible (*V. Ant.* 14 [ed. Bartelink 1994: 172–4]). Monks and virgins could imitate Anthony's perfectionism: their complete virginity exemplified the freedom to pursue virtue that the Word enables (*Gent.* 26; *Inc.* 48, 50, 51 [ed. Thomson 1971: 68, 254, 260, 262]; *Ep. virg.* 1.8, 23 [ed. Lefort 1955: 76, 84]). But most Christians disciplined their bodies in a much more moderate way: through occasional fasting and sexual abstinence, through charity to the poor, and through study of the scriptures (*Epp. fest. passim*; Brakke 1995: 182–98). The parish-centred, episcopal Christianity that Athanasius promoted was an inclusive, diverse community: like the hundredfold, sixtyfold, and thirtyfold produce of the field in the Parable of the Sower (Matt. 13:1–8), the faithful Christians nourished by the Word were not 'uniform', but 'various and rich' (*Ep. fest.* 10.4 [ed. Cureton, in Burgess 1854: 146]).

Athanasius' thought, then, is best not thought of as 'biblical' in contrast to 'philosophical' or 'Platonist'; rather, it is social, ecclesiastical, and 'Catholic' in the sense of articulating the shared life of an imperially favoured church made up of diverse people and guided by the bishop (Lyman 1993: 159). It is in the church, in its rituals, teachings, scriptures, and social practices, that the power of the incarnate Word to transform sinful humanity is mediated to believers.

A TRANSITIONAL FIGURE

Although many of his modern students admire Athanasius without reservation, most approach this giant of the fourth century with ambivalence. His courage and perseverance in defending what he believed to be Christian truth cannot be denied, but these noble qualities were accompanied by a violence in his thought and action that are at the very least disquieting. Few theologians have articulated so eloquently the Christian conviction that God became human in the incarnation of Christ, but the details of his exposition and his inability to speak convincingly of how the Father and Son are separate leave much of his thought unsatisfying. His ecclesiastical policies within Egypt aimed to produce a church inclusive of persons with diverse social roles and identities, but at the cost of certain attractive traditions of Egyptian religious life, such as intellectual freedom. The ambiguities of Athanasius' legacy may best be understood in terms of his own position as a liminal figure in Christian history, temporally and geographically.

Temporally, Athanasius' career spanned the tumultuous decades between Constantine's decision to legalize and patronize the Christian church and Theodosius' establishment of Christianity as the official religion of the Roman empire (Barnes 1993: 165–82). Although imperial and ecclesiastical politics intertwined during this period, they were not identical. Thanks in part to privileges granted by Constantine, bishops enjoyed their own sources of power, independent of that of the emperor. Councils of bishops met at times under the aegis of the emperor, at other times not; the emperor enforced the decisions of such councils, but usually did not make them. How exactly church and state should interact were, in many ways, up for grabs in this period. For his part, Athanasius scrambled to take full advantage of the possibilities and ambiguities opened up by the post-Constantinian situation, exercising his new episcopal powers with a desperate roughness that reflects their novelty. The clarity of Theodosian Nicene orthodoxy did not yet exist.

Likewise, Athanasius stood between East and West at a time when these two traditions in Christianity were increasingly going their separate ways. A Greek speaker and writer, trained in the Origenist tradition of Alexandrian Christian thought, Athanasius none the less found support for his theological views mainly in the Latin West. He would leave a complicated theological legacy to both Greek and Latin Christianity. His conception of salvation as divinization of the flesh and exercise of humanity's free will in pursuit of virtue would eventually fail to resonate with Latin theologians indebted to Augustine, but became a hallmark of eastern orthodox thought. Similarly, in the West Athanasius' emphasis on the unity of God and thus the full divinity of the Son became synonymous with orthodox faith, as the Athanasian Creed demonstrates, but the logic of his incarnational thought, as followed by his Alexandrian successors like Cyril and Dioscorus, would become the focus of heated controversy in the East (while his reputation remained intact). Athanasius, this man of contradictions, may be the last great Church Father to whom both the Latin West and the Greek East may lay claim with equal justice.

NOTES

1   Most of the dates and movements of Athanasius are supplied by two ancient sources: an index to the Syriac translation of Athanasius' *Festal Letters* and a chronicle of Athanasius' career compiled by the Alexandrian see called the *Historia acephela* (both found in Martin and Albert 1985). Still, many of the facts of Athanasius' career, including the dates, locations, and even reality of many events, are notoriously difficult to recover out of a tangled web of contradictory and tendentious sources. For the most part I have followed the judgements of two recent studies: Martin (1996) and especially Barnes (1993), a brilliant and painstaking reconstruction of Athanasius' political career. Readers interested in the documentation and evaluation of the primary evidence that lies behind my narrative should consult these works.

2   Alexandria was geographically and socially distinct from the rest of Roman Egypt. The Melitian Schism originated in efforts by bishops of Upper Egypt (that is, southern Egypt, upstream on the Nile), led by Melitius of Lycopolis, to gain some independence

from the patriarch of Alexandria. When he became bishop in 328, Athanasius made tours of Egyptian churches to solidify support for himself in the face of Melitian opposition.

3 The dating of this masterpiece is highly controversial among Athanasian scholars. In truth, any date between 325 and 337 seems possible.

4 I use masculine pronouns to refer to God advisedly, since in my view they reflect how Athanasius thought. The best recent succinct exposition of Athanasius' theology is Lyman (1993: 124–59); see also Petterson (1995) and Roldanus (1968).

5 The idea that Christ's death was a substitutionary sacrifice for the guilt of sin is present in Athanasius (e.g., *Inc.* 37; *Ar.* 1.60), but it is by no means central to his thought, which sees the entire incarnation event as salvific.

BIBLIOGRAPHY

Arnold, Duane W.-H. (1991) *The Early Episcopal Career of Athanasius of Alexandria.* Notre Dame, Ind., and London: University of Notre Dame Press.

Badger, Carlton M. (1990) 'The New Man Created in God: Christology, Congregation and Asceticism in Athanasius of Alexandria', Ph.D. thesis, Duke University.

Bagnall, Roger S. (1993) *Egypt in Late Antiquity.* Princeton, N.J.: Princeton University Press.

Barnard, Leslie W. (1985) 'Edward Gibbon on Athanasius', in *Arianism: Historical and Theological Reassessments*, Philadelphia, Pa.: Philadelphia Patristic Foundation.

Barnes, Michel René (1998) 'The Fourth Century as Trinitarian Canon', in Lewis Ayres and Gareth Jones (eds), *Christian Origins: Theology, Rhetoric and Community.* London and New York: Routledge.

Barnes, Timothy D. (1987) 'The Career of Athanasius', *Studia Patristica* 21: 390–401.

—— (1993) *Athanasius and Constantius: Theology and Politics in the Constantinian Empire.* Cambridge, Mass., and London: Harvard University Press.

Bartelink, G. J. M. (ed.) (1994) *Vie d'Antoine.* Paris: Éditions du Cerf.

Bell, H. Idris (1924) *Jews and Christians in Egypt: The Jewish Troubles in Alexandria and the Athanasian Controversy Illustrated by Texts from Greek Papyri in the British Museum.* (Rpt. 1976.) Westport, Conn.: Greenwood Press.

Bobertz, Charles (1993) 'Patronage Networks and the Study of Ancient Christianity', *Studia Patristica* 24: 20–7.

Brakke, David (1994a) 'The Authenticity of the Ascetic Athanasiana', *Orientalia* 63: 17–56.

—— (1994b) 'Canon Formation and Social Conflict in Fourth-Century Egypt: Athanasius of Alexandria's Thirty-Ninth *Festal Letter*', *Harvard Theological Review* 87: 395–419.

—— (1995) *Athanasius and the Politics of Asceticism.* Oxford: Clarendon. (Reprinted in 1998 as *Athanasius and Asceticism.* Baltimore and London: Johns Hopkins University Press.)

—— (1998) '"Outside the Places, Within the Truth": Athanasius of Alexandria and the Localization of the Holy', in David Frankfurter (ed.) *Pilgrimage and Holy Space in Late Antique Egypt.* Leiden: Brill.

Brown, Peter (1992) *Power and Persuasion in Late Antiquity: Towards a Christian Empire.* Madison and London: University of Wisconsin Press.

Burgess, Henry (1854) *The Festal Epistles of S. Athanasius.* Oxford: Clarendon.

Burrus, Virginia (1991) 'The Heretical Woman as Symbol in Alexander, Athanasius, Epiphanius, and Jerome', *Harvard Theological Review* 84: 229–48.

Camplani, Alberto (1989) *Le Lettere festali di Atanasio di Alessandria: Studio storico-critico.* Rome: C.I.M.

Coquin, R.-G. (1984) 'Les Lettres festales d'Athanase (CPG 2102), Un nouveau complément: Le manuscrit IFAO copte 25', *Orientalia Lovanensia Periodica* 15: 133–58.

Cureton, William (ed.) (1848) *The Festal Letters of Athanasius*. London: Society for the Publication of Oriental Texts.

Gregg, Robert C. and Groh, Dennis E. (1981) *Early Arianism – A View of Salvation*. Philadelphia, Pa.: Fortress.

Elm, Susanna (1998) 'The Dog That Did Not Bark: Doctrine and Patriarchal Authority in the Conflict Between Theophilus of Alexandria and John Chrysostom of Constantinople', in Lewis Ayres and Gareth Jones (eds), *Christian Origins: Theology, Rhetoric and Community*. London and New York: Routledge.

Haas, Christopher (1997) *Alexandria in Late Antiquity: Topography and Social Conflict*. Baltimore and London: Johns Hopkins University Press.

Hanson, R. P. C. (1988) *The Search for the Christian Doctrine of God: The Arian Controversy 318–381*. Edinburgh: T&T Clark.

Joannou, Périclés-Pierre (ed.) (1963) *Les canons des pères grecs*. Vol. 2 of *Fonti: Discipline générale antique (IVe-IXe s.)*. Rome: Grottaferrata.

Kelly, J. N. D. (1964) *The Athanasian Creed*. New York: Harper & Row.

Lebon, J. (1928) 'Athanasiana Syriaca II: Une lettre attribuée à saint Athanase d'Alexandrie', *Le Muséon* 41: 169–216.

Lefort, L. Th. (ed.) (1955) *S. Athanase. Lettres festales et pastorales en copte*. Louvain: Durbecq.

Lyman, J. Rebecca (1993) *Christology and Cosmology: Models of Divine Activity in Origen, Eusebius, and Athanasius*. Oxford: Clarendon.

McLynn, Neil (1992) 'Christian Controversy and Violence in the Fourth Century', *Kodai* 3: 15–44.

MacMullen, Ramsay (1990) 'The Social Role of the Masses in Late antiquity', in Ramsay MacMullen, *Changes in the Roman Empire: Essays in the Ordinary*. Princeton, N.J.: Princeton University Press.

Malina, Bruce J. (1993) *The New Testament World: Insights from Cultural Anthropology*. Louisville, Ky.: Westminster/John Knox.

Marrou, Henri-Irénée (1976) 'L'Arianisme comme phénomène alexandrien', in Henri-Irénée Marrou, *Patristique et humanisme*. Paris: Seuil.

Martin, Annick (1996) *Athanase d'Alexandrie et l'église d'Égypte au IVe siècle (328–373)*. Rome: École français de Rome.

Martin, Annick and Albert, Micheline, (eds) (1985) *Histoire 'acéphale' et index syriaque des lettres festales d'Athanase d'Alexandrie*. Paris: Éditions du Cerf.

Moxnes, Halvor (1991) 'Patron-Client Relationships and the New Community in Luke-Acts', in Jerome H. Neyrey (ed.) *The Social World of Luke-Acts: Models for Interpretation*. Peabody, Mass.: Hendrickson.

Opitz, Hans-Georg (ed.) (1935–41) *Athanasius Werke*. Berlin: Akademie.

Petterson, Alvyn (1995) *Athanasius*. Ridgefield, Conn.: Morehouse Publishing.

Robertson, Archibald (1892) *Select Writings and Letters of Athanasius, Bishop of Alexandria, Nicene and Post-Nicene Fathers of the Church*, 2nd Series, 4. (Reprinted 1987, Edinburgh-T&T Clark.)

Roldanus, Johannes R. (1968) *Le Christ et l'homme dans le théologie d'Athanase d'Alexandrie*. Leiden: Brill.

—— (1983) 'Die *Vita Antonii* als Spiegel der Theologie des Athanasius und ihr Weiterwirken bis ins 5. Jahrhundert', *Theologie und Philosophie* 58: 194–216.

Saller, Richard (1982) *Personal Patronage in the Early Empire*. Cambridge: Cambridge University Press.

Stead, G. C. (1988) 'Athanasius' Earliest Written Work', *Journal of Theological Studies* n.s. 39: 76–91.

Szymusiak, J. M. (1958) *Deux apologies*. Paris: Éditions du Cerf.

Thomson, Robert W. (ed.) (1971) *Athanasius: 'Contra Gentes' and 'De Incarnatione'*. Oxford: Clarendon.

Torrance, Thomas F. (1988) *The Trinitarian Faith: The Evangelical Theology of the Ancient Catholic Faith*. Edinburgh: T&T Clark.

Veilleux, Armand (ed. and trans.) (1980) *Pachomian Koinonia I*. Kalamazoo, Mich.: Cistercian.

von Campenhausen, Hans (1959) *The Fathers of the Greek Church*. New York: Pantheon.

Williams, Rowan (1987) *Arius: Heresy and Tradition*. London: Darton, Longman & Todd.

JOHN CHRYSOSTOM

—— •✦• ——

Pauline Allen and Wendy Mayer

JOHN IN CONTEXT: A STUDY IN COMPLEXITY

Biographic outline

For a figure of the importance of John Chrysostom, it is surprising that although we know that he was born in Syrian Antioch (see Figure 45.1), on the Orontes, his birthdate is unknown, although it fell some time in the period 340–50 CE (Kelly 1995: 296–8). He was from a well-off family and in his youth studied philosophy, and probably learned rhetoric from the famous sophist Libanius. At the age of 18, however, he transferred his attentions for three years to Meletius the Confessor, an Armenian then in charge of one faction of the Nicene Antiochene church, who saw in him promise of great things to come. During this period he also began studying asceticism and theology. Hankering after a more extreme ascetic life, he then withdrew to the mountains outside Antioch and lived with an old hermit for four years, before spending two years of even more rigorous mortification in a cave, largely on his own (Palladius, *Dialogue* 5). He returned to Antioch and was ordained a deacon in 381 by Meletius and a priest in 386 by bishop Flavian. He held this second office from 386–97, in the process establishing a reputation as one of the greatest orators the church has ever known. For much of this period Theodosius I was emperor in Constantinople. Indeed, in 387, when the actions of a mob in mutilating the statues of the imperial family in Antioch had led Theodosius to consider destroying the city entirely, Chrysostom delivered a particularly magnificent series of homilies (*De statuis*) to strengthen the Antiochene faithful.

This happy phase of his life ended in September 397, when Nectarius, the patriarch of Constantinople, died and John was chosen to succeed him. An apparently unwilling Chrysostom was eventually installed in Constantinople and set about reforming the city and the clergy. He proved to be a round peg in a square hole, not always operating according to the imperial realities of the capital and alienating many of the clergy, monks and members of the elite through his fiery temper and strong language and action. The empress Eudoxia, the real power behind Arcadius' throne, alternately supported and became alienated from him. His actions in 401 in having six Asian bishops who had been guilty of simony deposed intensified the

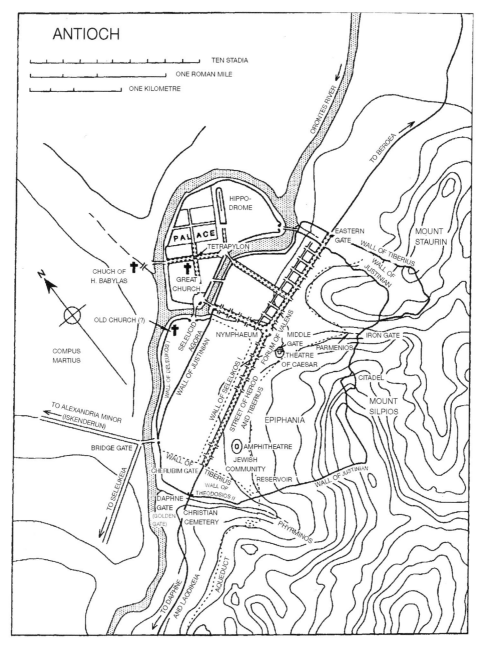

Figure 45.1 Antioch-on-the-Orontes, although in John's time the walls of Theodosius II and Justinian did not exist. From Downey, (1961). Reprinted by permission of Princeton University Press (as adapted in Kelly 1995).

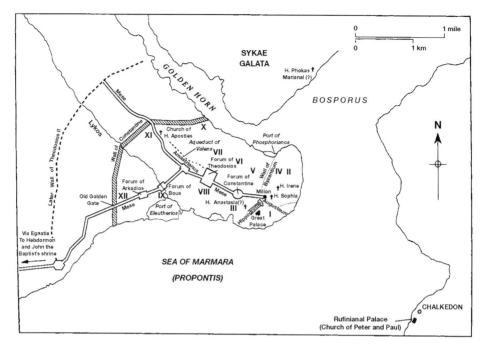

Figure 45.2   Constantinople *c.* 400 CE. From Kelly (1995), with the permission of the publisher, Gerald Duckworth & Co.

pressure to get rid of him. After various other developments, too numerous to mention here, he was, on 20 June 404, exiled from Constantinople to Cucusus in Lesser Armenia, where he remained for three years. But his troubles were not over. Since many of his former flock from Antioch visited him in Cucusus, his enemies in Constantinople saw to it that he was exiled to a more remote place, Pityus on the Eastern shore of the Black Sea. As it turned out, however, he died on the journey there, at Comana in Pontus, on 14 September 407.

Understanding John Chrysostom

John Chrysostom, who has left a more extensive literary legacy than any of the other Greek Fathers, has been one of the most studied figures in early Christianity. Mostly, however, he has been approached from a theological/spiritual standpoint (for example, Meyer 1933), or historical/chronological perspective, as demonstrated by two influential twentieth-century biographies, those by Chrysostomus Baur (1929–30) and Kelly (1995). The latter approach has resulted in a compartmentalized treatment, whereby John is considered against the background of Antioch, where he was monk and presbyter, and then in the context of Constantinople, where he was bishop from 398–404 CE; he is viewed from various perspectives as ascetic, preacher, bishop, pastor, and master of the spiritual life, without a systematic attempt to integrate all these facets; or his homilies and letters are used for establishing the chronology of political and other events of the late fourth century and early fifth. The main profiles of John Chrysostom which have appeared before this have usually one of two failings. Either, in the case of Baur's biography, we find a hagiographic slant in which he is presented as a saintly man much wronged by his time – a view heavily influenced by the fact that John Chrysostom was in later centuries elevated to the status of a saint of the Eastern church, or else there is a failure to address adequately the psychology of the subject, who then, as in Kelly's study, becomes a politically naive and harsh authoritarian who alienated the nobility, the empress Eudoxia, and many of his clergy in Constantinople. There have also been charges of misogyny levelled against him. It is our aim in this chapter to cut through some of these characterizations and to approach John Chrysostom in an integrated fashion, such that his profile will be that of an individual in his cultural setting, and of a complex man in a complex society. In order to allow the person to come to the fore, John will be viewed through his interactions with different individuals and levels in the society in which he operated during various phases of his life and in various capacities or roles (cf. Mayer and Allen 2000).

JOHN CHRYSOSTOM'S SOCIAL INTERACTIONS

A preliminary note about sources

At the outset a word needs to be said about the considerable literary sources at our disposal for this view of John. Not only have nearly one thousand of his homilies survived whole or in part, but over two hundred and forty letters of his have come down to us, the great bulk of which he wrote during his time in exile (Delmaire 1991). In the case of the homilies it is often impossible to determine whether they were delivered during his presbyterate in Antioch or during his patriarchate in Constantinople (Allen and Mayer 1994, 1995a, 1995b; Mayer 1996), many of them are available only in editions which date back to the seventeenth and eighteenth centuries (see Malingrey 1973), and the definition of the corpus of homilies authentic to John is still not absolute (Voicu 1996). The preponderance of other evidence illustrates John's life in the capital and in exile: the church histories of Socrates and Sozomen, the anonymous *Life of Olympias*, selected orations of Gregory Nazianzen and the same author's *Carmen de vita sua*, the homilies of Severian of Gabala, the biography of John by a so-called Martyrius, and Palladius' *Dialogus de vita Iohannis Chrysostomi* (see Kelly 1995: 291–5). Incidental information from liturgical or archaeological sources can also be used with caution to supplement the literary sources. Despite this plethora of material, which also includes ten or more treatises that survive from the period of his diaconate, there is very little evidence that would enable us to draw a responsible portrait of John prior to his ordination as presbyter and even for much of his presbyterate.

John Chrysostom's close relationships

Women deacons

We consider first his interactions in close relationships, as bishop John seems to have worked closely with a surprising number of women deacons attached to the churches in Constantinople (Mayer 1999: 270–4). The most famous of these, because the relationship is the best documented, was the aristocratic ascetic, Olympias, who had founded a monastery at some point during the episcopate of John's predecessor, Nectarius. The closeness which existed between John and Olympias is attested in the 17 surviving letters which John wrote to her (*Epistulae* 1–17; SC 13 bis) – unfortunately hers have not come down to us – and in her anonymous biography (*Vita Olympiadis*) and Palladius' biography of Chrysostom. John is said to have been the only male allowed to enter the premises of Olympias' ascetic establishment, which abutted the Great church and had its own private passage feeding directly into the church's narthex. His visits are said to have been made regularly, perhaps even on a daily basis, for the purpose of instructing her and her ascetic companions (*Vita Olymp.* 6, 8; SC 13 bis.418.1–7, 422.5–9). Indeed we know that three sisters, Palladia, Elisanthia and Martyria, relatives of Olympias, were ordained by John as deaconesses, which implies some form of prior instruction and ongoing supervision by the bishop (*Vita Olymp.* 7; SC 13 bis.420.6–9). Olympias sent across to John in the *patriarcheion* or bishop's palace the monies required for his day-to-day expenses (*Vita Olymp.* 8; SC 13 bis.422.12–6). She may also have had meals sent across to him, and either arranged to have his laundry done or did it herself (Nicephorus Callistus, in Eusebius, *Historia Ecclesiastica* 13.24. PG 146, 1012).

When, in 404, John was about to depart for exile the second time, although he farewelled the assembled bishops in the bishop's palace, he moved into the *baptisterion* to take his leave separately of all the deaconesses – Olympias, Pentadia and Procla, with the widow Silvina, according to Palladius (*Dialogue* 10; SC 341.206.34–208. 67; see Liebeschuetz 1984: 108). John arranged to have a presbyter lead the weeping women from the premises in order to prevent them stirring up the crowd, a precaution which suggests that, in the minds of the people of Constantinople, the women were intimately associated with the bishop. It is noteworthy, too, that it was not just Olympias but also Pentadia who was arrested and charged with setting fire to the Great church as a protest against John's departure into exile (see *Ep.* 94); the inference is that his relationship with these women was perceived by the hostile authorities too as being particularly close (Mayer 1999: 272–3). From Letter 104 we learn that Pentadia had intended to make the arduous journey to see John in exile at Cucusus, but that John dissuaded her because he seemed to have regarded her presence in Constantinople as vital to his own rehabilitation in the city. Similarly, Sabiniana, John's elderly aunt, a much-respected deaconess from Antioch, in fact arrives at Cucusus on the same day as John, declaring her intention to follow him wherever he is sent: she had heard rumours that he was being deported to Scythia, and would have gone there, if necessary, as we learn from Letter 6 (13). The relationship with Sabiniana proves that John had close contact with at least one woman of similar ecclesiastical status and character to Olympias prior to his arrival in Constantinople. Furthermore, the correspondence which he conducted in exile with Adolia, Carteria, Asyncritia, Chalcidia and Bassiana (e.g., *Epp.* 33, 52, 18, 227, 232, 29, 60, 43), all Antiochene women of some wealth and status, leads one to suspect that when he arrived in Constantinople in late 397 John was not without experience of the kind of wealthy, aristocratic women whom he was to encounter there. The attentions of Carteria, in particular, can be said in some ways to rival those of Olympias: she sends John medication, which she herself has prepared (*Ep.* 34; PG 52.629.5–15 *a.i.*), and another gift, which may have been monetary (*Ep.* 232; PG 52.738–9), while John himself is at greater pains than usual to assure her that in refusing the gift he holds her in no lesser esteem (see further Delmaire 1997: 305).

The clergy

While we are not informed in such detail about John's close relationships with his clergy, the manuscript tradition of the homilies on Paul's letter to the Hebrews attributes to the Antiochene presbyter Constantius their reworking into a published series on the basis of notes taken in shorthand, and we know that Constantius travelled to Cucusus to be with John in his exile (*Ep.* 6 [13]). In fact, Constantius seems to have spent a great deal of time with John there, and to have been instrumental in supervising John's concerns in his absence, at least outside Constantinople (Delmaire 1997: 304). Like Olympias, Constantius rates a special mention in Palladius' *Dialogue* (*Dial.* 16; SC 341.308.64–312.109), and it is clear in Letter 62 that he has just been with John and is on his way back to the Antiochene presbyters to whom John is writing. Among these presbyters there is a group around Diophantes to whom John writes several warm letters from exile, which suggests a close relationship of long standing between them (*Epp.* 222, 239–41). Delmaire (1997: 306–9) provides useful detail concerning John's correspondence also with non-clerical men and women at both Constantinople and in Syria during the period of his exile and concludes that, with rare exceptions, the relationships with individuals in Syria were of longer standing and therefore more enduring.

Here we see Chrysostom most closely associated with family, and with select men from among the clergy at Antioch and select women from among the deacons with whom he worked at Constantinople. There is also some suggestion of long-standing relationships with lay men and women in Syria. Since the available sources regarding this aspect of his person date predominantly from the period of his exile and from his episcopate at Constantinople, however, it is difficult to determine to what extent this picture is representative. Kelly (1995: 16–7, 57) would also have the younger John working and associating closely at Antioch with both bishop Meletius and bishop Flavian, when lector and presbyter. He suggests too that in his late teens or early twenties John was part of a close circle of young men of like background who experimented with the ascetic life (1995: 18–20). Several of the members of this circle seem to have entered the monastic life or the priesthood. Given that the greater portion of his life was spent in the service of the Nicene church it is not unreasonable to suppose that John's closest and most enduring relationships were with men and women who were either themselves ordained or who worked closely with him in his ministry.

The royal court

As bishop of the imperial capital John had *ex officio* contacts with the royal couple, the emperor Arcadius and the empress Eudoxia (*Nov. hom.* 2–3 [CPG 4441.1–2]; Kelly 1995: 128). We know that on a state occasion, the anniversary of the death of Theodosius I, John delivered a panegyric in the church of the Holy Apostles in the presence of Arcadius and Eudoxia (*Nov. hom.* 6). It is also probable that in a solemn ceremony on 6 January 402 he baptized the couple's only son, Theodosius II (*Sermo post reditum* [PG 52.445.37–52]; Wenger 1952: 52–4). In the third Homily on Acts he suggests that as bishop he was treated at court with special reverence (PG 60.41.6–10). About the relations between bishop and empress we have a substantial amount of complex information, but John's interaction with Arcadius cannot be gauged with any certainty, whether because of the emperor's alleged lack of character and decisiveness, or his carefully managed and therefore anonymous role, or the bias of the sources. We know, however, that John was not afraid to make his opinion known to the emperor regarding certain decisions (Socrates, *Historia Ecclesiastica* 6.6; Sozomen, *Historia Ecclesiastica* 8.4; Theodoret of Cyprus, *Historia Ecclesiastica* 5.32), or to resist the soldiers sent to carry out Arcadius' decree when it conflicted with the authority of the church to grant asylum (*In Eutropium*; *De capto Eutropio* [referring not to Eutropius but to Count John; see Cameron 1988]). All the information with which the historians supply us suggests that in her relationship with Chrysostom Eudoxia vacillated between reverence, even superstitious awe for his position and person as bishop, and exploitation of his position, as the following episode indicates. In order to settle the clash between John and his locum Severian of Gabala, who had seemingly usurped the bishop's position during his absence in Asia during 402, Eudoxia sought John out in the church of the Holy Apostles (Socrates, *H. E.* 6.11; Sozomen, *H. E.* 8.10), put her baby son on his lap, and insisted that he swear on the baby's head that he would be reconciled with Severian. Much to his annoyance, John was obliged to accede. Such annoyance at her interventions in delicate matters seems, however, to have been balanced on John's part by respect and gratitude for Eudoxia's support of Nicene Christianity, as evidenced by his eulogistic homily on the occasion of her participation in the nocturnal procession of martyrs' remains to a martyrium some miles outside the city (*Nov. Hom.* 2; CPG 4441.1). We know that the nocturnal processions introduced by the bishop to counter those of the Arian party received support from the empress in the form of large silver crosses and the participation of her chamberlain Brison (Socrates, *H. E.* 6.8; Sozomen, *H. E.* 8.8). That the empress was ultimately the more powerful partner in the imperial marriage appears to have been recognized not only by John, but also by most clergy and ascetics who arrived in Constantinople seeking imperial favours, the monks of Nitria and bishop Porphyrius of Gaza being cases in point. While it is true that Eudoxia provided hospitality for those hostile to John's interests, notably Theophilus of Alexandria and Epiphanius of Salamis, it must also be acknowledged that Olympias herself cheerfully and impartially provided hospitality for Theophilus and others (Mayer 1999: 276).

In his dealings with the palace at Constantinople, then, the sources reveal John almost exclusively in relation to the empress, Eudoxia. There exists only the occa-

Figure 45.3   Solidus of Theodosius I (a) and solidus of Eudoxia (b). Photo by permission of Byzantine Collection, Dunbarton Oaks, Washington, DC.

sional hint of his relationship with the emperor Arcadius. Likewise he is only rarely to be observed in contact with their children. That he had relatively frequent contact with the imperial couple and family, their intimates and with palace officials, however, is almost certain. For instance, the widow Silvina, one of the four intimates John farewells on his departure for exile, is essentially a resident of the palace, as is John's 'enemy' Marsa (Mayer 1999: 271–5). The subtle indications of a more complex set of interactions with the palace and its individuals suggest that this aspect of John's life would benefit from a more nuanced reading (see Liebeschuetz 1984, 1985).

Congregations and laity

As far as his relationships with his congregations and with the laity in them is concerned, Chrysostom had the ability to inspire either great loyalty or great disaffection. Both of these reactions we find on the occasion at Constantinople when John had a visiting bishop from Galatia preach in his stead, a courtesy to which his congregation reacted very negatively because they had wanted John to preach and had expected John (*In illud: Pater meus usque modo operatur*; CPG 4441.10). At

Constantinople the laity, in particular women, grew hostile towards him, and attended synaxis elsewhere presided over, it seems, by another bishop, who trod a fine line with respect to John's authority (*In Eph. hom.* 11; Mayer 1996: 345–50). It is difficult, however, to determine the extent to which Chrysostom and other bishops in Late antiquity had direct contact with people outside of their relationship with them as preachers, because we do not yet know how much pastoral work they did in person. It is prima facie possible that a great deal of it was delegated (Rentinck 1970: 180–3). None the less, John seems to have had direct and private contact with wealthy elite women at Constantinople, even if these women did not belong to the class of deacons who came under his responsibility with regard to the clergy (Synod of the Oak, Charge 15 {SC 342.104.36–7}; Mayer 1999: 273–4). Whether he had the same intimate contact with laymen of this status is uncertain and perhaps unlikely.

At Antioch, whether by virtue of his private contact with the laity, or simply as a result of the relationship which he forged with them as an entertaining preacher, Palladius suggests that John was kidnapped in 397 in order to avoid a riot, or at least civil unrest (*Dial.* 5; SC 341.112–14). In other words, Chrysostom enjoyed a high degree of popularity amongst a sufficiently large sector of the Antiochene community for the authorities to fear the consequences of their displeasure. In Antioch too we have a suggestion of John's relationship with individual congregations in *In illud: In faciem ei restiti*, where it is clear that at that point he was assigned to the congregation at the Old church (Palaia), and had the opportunity to build up a particular rapport with the group of Christians who regularly worshipped there. At both cities, since a much larger number of Christians or nominal Christians tended to attend worship only at times of major festivals (particularly when they involved spectacular processions), his relationship with such irregular attendees is likely to have been less close. This hypothesis is borne out by *In Eph. hom.* 11, where he talks of different strata of attendees (PG 62.88.17–23); John himself points out that the majority of those who are presently disaffected with him came from those who used to attend regularly, which suggests that they had previously been particularly attached to him. John's effect on his audiences varied markedly, however, since in *De proph. obsc. hom.* 2 he refers to members of the audience pushing and shoving to get close to the ambo from which he was preaching (PG 56.176.22–31), while in *In Heb. hom.* 15 it is clear that people are chatting and making amusing comments to each other or else openly laughing while he is preaching his sermon (Mayer 1997: 113–14; 1998a: 132–3).

With regard, then, to the laity and the members of the various congregations which he served in each city, John seems to have inspired a complex range of emotions. The level of attachment to his preaching and degree of loyalty to his person appears to have varied. So too did the level of interaction differ from individual to individual within each congregation. While recent research has enabled us to some degree to recover what occurred between John and his audiences within worship, his contact with individuals and families in the street, business or home has yet to be investigated.

Figure 45.4   Eleventh-century mosaic depicting John Chrysostom, lower apse, Cathedral of Sancta Sophia, Kiev. Photo by permission of Yuri Koszaryez.

The clergy

Also, in John's relationships with clergy, whether of the same status as himself, of a more elevated status or subordinate, we observe a variety of interactions. In Antioch his relations with his bishop, Flavian, and with Meletius, Flavian's successor, have traditionally been thought to have been close (see e.g. Kelly 1995: 57, 103), to the point where Flavian deputized John to take over many of his duties during the latter part of John's presbyterate. There is no clear evidence for this, however, beyond John's obvious popularity as a preacher and the suggestion in *In illud: In faciem ei restiti* that Flavian on at least one occasion took John away from his regular duties to accompany him on some official occasion. The fact that John preached as one of a number of presbyters or in conjunction with Flavian on festival occasions (e.g., *De b.*

Philogonio, De s. Babyla, In diem natalem) merely reflects routine procedure during this time. Again, John's warm encomia on Flavian and Meletius in *Cum presbyter ordinatus fuit, In Meletium* and *De statuis hom.* 3 and 21 could owe as much to rhetoric as to a genuinely close and warm relationship between John and these bishops. His relations with other clergy, male and female, in Antioch have yet to be explored properly and documented. None the less, we know that he had more or less annual contact with a group of rural Syriac-speaking monk-priests who came in from the surrounding countryside to consult with Flavian and appeared in John's own congregation on occasion (*De statuis hom.* 19, *Catechesis* 8; van de Paverd 1991: 260–89), and, as we have seen, there is also evidence in his letters of his continuing contact with various clergy from Antioch after his transfer to Constantinople.

We are much better informed about John's relations with the clergy in the imperial capital, although these are not usually highlighted in the biographies. Regarding the clergy John inherited at Constantinople, Palladius (*Dial.* 5, SC 341.118–24) makes it clear that on his arrival the new bishop conducted a major review of their activities and lifestyles, alienating many of them in the process because of his stricter views (Liebeschuetz 1984: 88–90). On the other hand, John was not averse to ordaining and promoting his own candidates to positions. This was demonstrated most notably by his interference in church affairs in Ephesus which resulted in the consecration of Heracleides as bishop there (Liebeschuetz 1984: 94–5), and by the promotion of Serapion the deacon to the post of supervisor of the church administration in Constantinople, despite Serapion's poor human resource management skills, which are discussed at length by both Baur (1959–60: II, 97, 158–9) and Kelly (1995: 121, 182–4). Chrysostom's relations with visiting clergy were not always smooth, as is evidenced by the visit of Theophilus of Alexandria and Epiphanius of Salamis, who eventually snubbed him (Palladius, *Dial.* 8, SC 341.158–62; Socrates, *H. E.* 6.14; Sozomen, *H. E.* 8.14). Despite John's initially pleasant contact with Severian of Gabala, empress Eudoxia, as we have seen, had to intervene in order to reconcile the two, and the homilies *De pace* imply an interim public reconciliation. On the other hand, if we may believe that around forty bishops were with Chrysostom at the time of his exile (Palladius, *Dial.* 8; SC 341.164), it seems that a large number of visiting bishops supported his authority and activities. Palladius' partisan account of John's life and trials is witness to the strength of attachment to John on the part of at least one fellow bishop. John's authority over and pastoral care of his clergy in Constantinople are revealed by his letters to the presbyters Theophilus and Sallustius (*Epp.* 212, 203), in which he dwells on their failure to continue their duties bravely immediately after his exile. An important part of John's interaction and relations with the clergy involves the female deacons, especially in Constantinople. His private farewell to Olympias, Pentadia, Procla and Silvina (if the latter was in fact ordained) suggests that he worked with these deacons directly, not through male deacons or presbyters, and that the Johnites in Constantinople considered them to be particularly close to the bishop. In the case of Olympias' female relatives, as we have seen, John not only ordains them but possibly also instructs them, and he continues to supervise their activities within Olympias' monastery.

As is evident from this brief discussion of John's relations with other clergy the evidence for his experiences at Antioch both during and prior to his presbyterate are poor in comparison to the amount of information available for Constantinople and the period of his exile. A view of his relations with women deacons and other church workers during this earlier period is noticeably absent. Yet if, as Kelly posits, in the latter years of his presbyterate at Antioch John took on *de facto* oversight of the Nicene church in that city, one must then ask whether he acted in the same authoritarian and unrelenting manner towardss the clergy of that city as he is supposed to have done at Constantinople. Likewise, did he work equally closely with female deacons? Whatever the answers to these questions, it is clear that the nature of his interactions with fellow clergy is again more complex than is usually supposed and that the current view presents only a small part of the possible picture.

Ascetics

John's six-year experimentation with the ascetic life during his twenties in Antioch gave him first-hand experience of various ascetic lifestyles and their devotees (Brown 1988: 305–22; Mayer 1998b). He trained with several companions in the urban *asketerion* of Diodore and Carterius, and spent four years in the mountains behind Antioch with an elderly Syrian ascetic mentor prior to living supposedly for two years on his own in a cave (Palladius, *Dial.* 5; SC 341.108–10). Bishop Flavian of Antioch, to whom John was responsible as presbyter, was himself an ascetic. Whether on his return to Antioch John continued to visit the ascetics with whom he had spent time in the mountains is difficult to determine: he instructs his congregation to visit them (e.g., *In Matt. hom.* 69/70, 72/3; *In I Tim. hom.* 14), but there is no evidence that he himself did. However, the presence of the monks in the city on the day of the trial of the decurions after the riots (*De statuis hom.* 17) may have meant that he had a brief contact with men whom he had encountered during those earlier years. Of the various female ascetical establishments in Antioch John may have known from his childhood the group of *parthenoi* who lived under the supervision of the female deacon Publia (Theodoret, *H. E.* 3.14). In Constantinople it is possible that he had frequent contact with ascetics, not just through the bishops and monks who visited the city, but also since he appointed various ascetic persons to staff the hospital which he established out of church funds (Palladius, *Dial.* 5; SC 341.122). He certainly had a heated dispute with the large numbers of monks he found in the capital, who were led by the influential Syrian, Isaac, and over whose loose organization the local bishop had little control (Sozomen, *H. E.* 8.9; Dagron 1970; Liebeschuetz 1984: 90–3; Mayer 1998b). John's clash with Isaac seems also to have been personal (Palladius, *Dial.* 6; SC 341.126–8), and the monk adduced charges against him at his trial (Kelly 1995: 123–5). John's close contact with Olympias and her convent in Constantinople is, as we have seen, well attested. In terms of women who had chosen not to enter into a second marriage, his own mother was such a person and probably led a celibate life (*ad viduam iuniorem* 2; SC 138.120) his aunt Sabiniana seems to have been a celibate as well as a deacon, and at Constantinople the women closest to him were all widows who had renounced a second marriage and who were either deacons or were involved in charitable activities as lay individuals (Mayer 1999: 269–74).

As a result of his own ascetic leanings and as a consequence of the state of the ascetic movement in Eastern cities in the latter part of the fourth century, John is found in close association with a number of ascetic individuals and communities throughout the course of his adult life. It is possible that the degree to which he associated with men and women attracted to the ascetic life owed something, too, to his family's position in Antiochene society and to the circles in which he moved as a cleric at both Antioch and Constantinople. Unlike many of the other spheres of interaction examined in this chapter, the ascetic arena is one of the few for which the sources are broadly distributed.

Administrative officials

Both in Antioch and in Constantinople Chrysostom had ample opportunity to observe the work of administrative officials and to become acquainted with them personally. In Antioch, for example, the *consularis Syriae* came into the church to calm the people in the period of intense fear after the riots (*De statuis hom.* 16; see van de Paverd 1991: 55), while it is possible that an official of similar status, who is simply termed 'the archon', led the procession occasionally in Antioch on the feast-day of certain martyrs (*Hom. in martyres*). When John was carried off from Antioch with the intention of conveying him to Constantinople for consecration as bishop of that city, it was a *comes* who was entrusted with the task of summoning him and informing him of his candidature (Palladius, *Dial.* 5; SC 341.112–14). Officials who were Christians, such as the *magister militum per Orientem* Ellebichus, may also have been encountered by him when he assisted in distributing the Eucharist. In Constantinople contact with high-level officials also occurred outside of the domain of worship. John alludes to the long-standing hostility between himself and the powerful eunuch and chief chamberlain Eutropius (*In Eutropium*): the consul has constantly waged war against the church, most notably in his laws restricting the right of asylum and restricting the right of the church to provide sanctuary, while John for his part has apparently had frequent clashes with Eutropius in which he has criticized his behaviour and materialistic motives. Later, at imperial behest, John was involved in negotiations with the Gothic general, Gainas, who had demanded of the emperor that his three chief political enemies, the ex-consul Aurelianus, the general Saturninus and Eudoxia's favourite, Count John, be handed over to him as hostages. Count John, who managed to escape being handed over to Gainas, none the less conceived a great dislike for Chrysostom because of John's failure to support him adequately, while Saturninus' widow, Castricia, was left with an enduring dislike of the bishop as well (Liebeschuetz 1984: 97–8). Close contact must have developed between John and Eudoxia's chamberlain, Brison, who trained the church choir and assisted with the nocturnal processions which John instituted to combat the influence of the Arians in the capital. John also encountered Brison when he was recalled from his first exile, in that the chamberlain was the official entrusted with the letter of recall (Socrates, *H. E.* 6.16, Sozomen, *H. E.* 8.18), and the bishop continued to write to him from exile, which suggests an ongoing relationship (*Epp.* 190, 234). While travelling into exile a second time Chrysostom met various officials from other cities, perhaps at Caesarea (Delmaire 1997: 306), and most obviously consorted constantly with the military escort (*praefectiani*) who accompanied him and prevented him from too close contact with various persons along the way. John writes to several officials from his place of exile (Delmaire 1997: 306–8): to Gemellus (*Epp.* 79, 132, 124, 194), who was elevated to a prefecture in 405 (Delmaire 1991: 128–9); to Paeanius (*Epp.* 95, 193, 204, 220), who seems to have been a close supporter and is clearly promoted to a relatively high position shortly after John's exile (Delmaire 1991: 148–51); and to a certain Studius (*Epp.* 197), who is *eparch tes poleos*, on the subject of the death of his brother. The latter correspondence, however, does not necessarily indicate a relationship; it may be simply that John thinks it expedient to send his condolences.

Because of the close connection between church, city and state in the second half of the fourth century it is not surprising to find John consorting with various high-ranking administrative officials, especially when he was bishop of Constantinople, the imperial capital. While the evidence for Antioch is more limited it is reasonable to suppose that there too he had some degree of interaction with provincial and city officials outside of the domain of worship.

Relations with non-Christians

We come now to how John Chrysostom conducted himself with people of other faiths. The prominence of Jews in Antiochene society in Late antiquity is well known (Wilken 1983), and, while there is little evidence to support the assumption, they doubtless played a part in the society of Constantinople too. As a consequence, the anti-Jewish rhetoric which we find in John's writings, particularly in his homilies, is to be taken largely as reflecting some of the ecclesiastical agendas of the time, rather than as evidence of John's own attitude. While his general comments with regard to Jews can be polemical in the classical manner, when he is speaking in specific rather than general terms his comments can be admiring or even warm. For example, he claims that the local Jews in Antioch put Christians to shame by their assiduous observance of the Sabbath, in that they stop all business dealings immediately as soon as they see the sun setting on Friday (*In illud: Si esurierit inimicus*; PG 51.176.31–45). Again, in contradistinction to Christians, the local Jews obey their priests and do not complain about desisting from all physical labour for a designated number of days (*In princ. Actorum hom.* 1; PG 51.70.1–11).

The fact that John spent seven discourses in Antioch preaching against the tendency of some of his parishioners to Judaize suggests that he was well aware of the seductiveness of the alleged healing properties of the cave of Matrona at Daphne outside Antioch (Vinson 1994: 180–6), and of the attraction for the general population of the dancing and public festivities at Jewish festivals (Wilken 1983: 93). In Antioch the Jewish sector clearly had a long history within the city, and John's disgust at the preference exhibited by Christians for sealing business deals in the local synagogue (*Adv. Iud. hom.* 1; PG 48. 847–8) shows how central it was to his task as preacher to teach his audience to distinguish between proper Christian practices and certain Judaizing habits which were of long standing and held priority. *In illud: Vidi dom. hom.* 3 (SC 277.110.74–7), where the more overt devotional practices of certain Jews are described, indicates that the public behaviour of Jews was a familiar part of the Antiochene community.

In terms of pagan communities and Chrysostom's relationship with them, we again have better information for Antioch. Like the rhythms of Jewish life and worship which were an integral part of life in that city, pagan rituals and events had an equally integral role, regardless of the religious affiliations of the inhabitants (Wilken 1983: 16–26; MacMullen 1997). Thus we learn from *In II Tim. hom.* 8 that Chrysostom's parishioners prefer to consult pagan priests when they have lost a valuable animal (PG 62.649–50), and from *In Col. hom.* 8 it appears that women in Antioch automatically resort to amulets for the cure of sick children, and consult old women in the hope of a cure (PG 62. 357–8). In *De statuis hom.* 19 we are told that women and small children tend to wear pieces of the Gospel text hanging from their necks for apotropaic purposes (PG 49.196 37–40). Pagan superstition in general played a large role in the life of John's parishioners in Antioch (*Cat. ad illuminandos* 2; cf. *In Eph. hom.* 12 [provenance uncertain]): the rhythms of the city, its calendar, theatrical performances and horse races were intimately linked to long-standing celebrations, including the local Olympic games. In *In S. Iulianum* he expresses his concerns about the established custom among the Antiochene citizenry of retiring to Daphne on the following day for some kind of meal or picnic, which was accompanied by male choruses and other lewd festivities (PG 50.672–4). In *In kalendas*, too, he indicates some of the alcoholic celebrations with which the church had to compete at that time of year. With the exception of the latter, the influence of pagan activities undoubtedly obtained to a large degree in Constantinople as well, but there the impact of the imperial cult, despite the overt Christianization of the imperial family, would have been more in evidence. In the capital both the hippodrome and festivities associated with the imperial cult physically disturbed church services, either through the noise or through the competition for attendance (*Contra ludos et theatra*; PG 56.263), and the church historians Sozomen and Socrates describe the celebrations associated with the new statue erected in honour of the empress Eudoxia, which was apparently the last straw for John (Sozomen, *HE* 8.20 and Socrates, *HE* 6.18). As was the case with Judaism, here too it must have been John's constant concern to instruct his parishioners to differentiate Christian civic obligations from pagan or paganising activities. Not to be forgotten in the context of the paganism of his day are John's personal dealings with pagan or paganizing officials, such as the *consularis Syriae* in Antioch, Celsus, who presented himself at the church to calm the populace after the riots concerned with the imperial statues, and with urban prefects and other prominent figures at Constantinople who were obliged to preside over the civic and imperial cults regardless of their personal conviction (Dagron 1974: 292). At Antioch, too, it is important to remember that John received his more advanced education from the pagan rhetorician Libanius as well as from the ascetic Christians Diodore and Carterius.

For once, with respect to John's encounters with individuals and communities of other faiths, the bias of the evidence permits a clearer reconstruction of what occurred at Antioch. At Constantinople the picture is much obscured in the sources by the imperial presence and interest in John's own uneasy relationships with various groups in the capital, his trial and exile. While Antioch emerges clearly as a city with complex religious dynamics – that is, a city in which Christianity was still much in competition with other cults – it should not be assumed that conversely at Constantinople Christianity was dominant. Quite apart from the inherently pagan character of the civic calendar and imperial cult, private non-Christian beliefs and practices were tenacious (MacMullen 1997) and it is likely that John was obliged to preach and counsel against their persistence in the daily lives of his parishioners there also. In addition, too little is known about the presence of Jews at Constantinople during this period to ignore the possibility of their influence.

Relations with heterodox and schismatic Christians

Not to be neglected in any study of John Chrysostom is his interaction with heterodox Christians and schismatics. After all, as a young man he grew up in Antioch in a church that was divided between at least three factions within Christianity, including the Arian Christians and two schismatic Nicene factions (Wilken 1983: 10–16; Kelly 1995: 10–13). For a brief period around 375 the city also boasted a fourth bishop, an Apollinarian. John himself was appointed lector in one of the two schismatic factions, the one that was led by Bishop Meletius, neither of which was in particular favour at the time (Kelly 1995: 16–17). John's experience among that group of Christians involved services in the open air on the *campus martius* across the river from the city, because that faction had been banned from the city itself and its churches placed in the hands of the Arians by the emperor Valens. It is likely that the *asketerion* run by Diodore and Carterius, both adherents of the Meletian faction, was situated across the river in the same vicinity (*Laus Diodori*; PG 52.764.26–8). It was only when John was ordained deacon that his Christian church became prominent in Antioch. The schism between his group of Nicene Christians and the other persisted, however, during the entire length of his presbyterate there, and it was only after his elevation to the see of Constantinople that the issue was resolved (Kelly 1995: 116–18). Consequently, when John speaks of the Christians in Antioch he is always talking about a confused and divided community, just as when he talks of processions with the whole city in attendance on days of martyrial festivals his comments must be viewed with a degree of scepticism. The techniques which he learnt during those years in Antioch for promoting the Christian faction to which he was attached, techniques which would have included careful phrasing of doxologies and the conduct of nocturnal processions and of litanies, would have prepared him for the situation which he found on his arrival in Constantinople. There the Arians, who had dominated the city until the accession of Theodosius, still exerted a degree of influence over the populace, and various ascetic or monastic communities living within and immediately outside the city had Arian leanings (Dagron 1970, and 1974: 419–53; Miller 1985: 74–85). In a series of sermons attacking the Anomoeans, the most radical of the Arian parties, he himself suggests that the Nicene Christians of Constantinople are in the minority (*Contra Anomoeos homilae* 11). The presence of the Novatians within the city, with their own churches and imperial protection, is likely to have struck him as contributing to a situation which bore marked parallels with that with which he had been familiar in Antioch (Kelly 1995: 125–7).

Relationships with members of various social strata

Lower status groups?

When we consider John's relationships with the various social strata in Antioch and Constantinople, it is interesting to speculate in the first instance whether the monks and ascetics with whom he associated as a young man in his ascetic phase came from markedly different social backgrounds from those with which he was used to associating, or whether they were of a similar social standing. For instance, the elderly Syrian who was John's ascetic mentor ought, according to Brown's theory (Brown 1971), to have come from a poor, uneducated background; but this is by no means certain. It is, in fact, questionable when we consider that in Antioch Bishop Flavian, himself clearly from the upper class (*Sermo cum presbyter* [PG 48.696.46–9]; *In Gen. sermo* 1 [PG 54.585.47–67]), was an ascetic, and that the young men with whom John lived when experimenting with urban asceticism in the *asketerion* of Diodore and Carterius were all from the same comfortable social background as John (Kelly 1995: 18–23). On the other hand, the Syriac-speaking rural monk-presbyters whom John encounters every year or so are less educated and probably of a much lower social status (van de Paverd 1991: 281). In Antioch, the site for which we have more information on social strata during John's preaching career, it is likely that at least one of the congregations with which he was involved contained middle-class persons, including artisans, and possibly also soldiers (*De baptismo Christi* [PG 49.365. 5–14]; *De paen. hom.* 3 [PG 49.291.31–5 *a.i.*]). In general, however, the bulk of the evidence points to audiences comprised of the wealthy to the very wealthy, in particular the aristocratic elite (MacMullen 1989; Leyerle 1997; Mayer 1998a).

Upper status groups

In Constantinople, John seems to have moved to a large extent in the circles of the rich and influential; that is, the senatorial and curial classes (Liebeschuetz 1984; Mayer 1999). Here he had some negative experiences, for instance with the three widows whom Palladius describes as being particularly hostile to John and who also had intimate connection with the palace: Marsa, the widow of Promotus, who had been a distinguished military commander and consul; Castricia, the widow of the ex-consul Saturninus; and Eugraphia, who provided hospitality to Theophilus, bishop of Alexandria, when he should have accepted the hospitality of John (*Dial.* 4; SC 341.94.89–94; and *Dial.* 8; SC 341.162.76–9). As foster-mother of Eudoxia Marsa had influence on, and an especially close connection with, the empress. On his travels in exile, it is the wealthy who offer hospitality in particular and assist him in whatever way possible. For example, Seleucia, the wife of Rufinus in Caesarea, offers him her suburban estate and gives instructions for her manager to gather farmers from her various estates to defend John, if the monks should threaten him there (*Epp.* 9 [14]). It is the senatorial class who engage in pastoral work and generally support the charitable activities of the church. Sozomen (*H. E.* 8.23) tells of the elderly noblewoman, Nicarete, from Bithynia, who, despite confiscation of a large portion of her patrimony, still cares for the sick and poor in Constantinople during John's episcopate, and resists John's attempts to ordain her as a deacon or as a catechist of female ascetics. John's networks extended beyond the Eastern capital to Rome and elsewhere, as evidenced by Letters 168–9, written to Proba and Juliana in Rome asking for their patronage of certain of his clergy, and Letter 170 to the Roman matron Italica, in which he persuades her to use her connections on his behalf.

It is difficult to say whether John ever had any direct interaction with lower social classes. Certainly he passed beggars and the homeless in the streets of Antioch (*De eleemosyne*) and encountered them outside the churches and martyria there (*De paen. hom.* 3; PG 49.294); it is also possible that he was accosted by beggars in the agoras of Constantinople (*In Acta apost. hom.* 3; PG 60.39.27–8). While, according to Palladius (*Dial.* 5; SC 341.122), John organized the hospitals in Constantinople, including one specializing in the care of lepers (Ps. Martyrius; see Kelly 1995: 119–20), there is no evidence that he visited these institutions or involved himself in the day-to-day care of the inmates. Again, it is valid to wonder what he means when, as in *In princ. Actorum hom.* 1 (PG 51.69.51–61), he says that the poor are absent from the church on that occasion because they have to earn their living. Is this perhaps a similar social group to the one he refers to in *De mutatione nom. hom.* 3 (PG 51.136. 21–7), where he says that married males who spend their lives in daily toil or are caught up in business affairs can only manage to attend the liturgy once a week? From John's other homilies it is patent that the poverty which he discusses on many occasions is relative, possibly because the truly poor may not have taken part in the synaxis, but waited outside the church to beg (Cunningham and Allen 1998: intro.; Mayer 1998a).

As we have seen, it is at present difficult to determine the identity of the social classes with which John had direct interaction throughout the course of his life and ecclesiastical career, apart from the aristocracy and the wealthy. While he himself was probably a member of the curial class at Antioch and associated with citizens of the same or higher status during his youth, the real question lies with the degree to which he interacted with persons outside of his own class as a result of his pastoral and preaching duties. At Constantinople the bulk of the evidence points likewise towards senatorial women and other members of the elite. Careful investigation of the sources, particularly John's sermons, is required before it can be determined with any confidence whether members of the lower classes and the very poor attended the different churches at which he preached, or came under his personal care in their homes or in the church-run welfare institutions.

Different ethnic and language groups

While the city of Constantinople must have struck John in many ways as similar to Antioch in that both were large, wealthy, influential and Hellenized cities, there was not only similarity but also difference in the two locations with regard to the different language groups and ethnic communities with which he came into contact. In Antioch he regularly encountered Syriac-speaking laypeople and ascetics on the occasion of martyrial festivals which drew such people to the city from the surrounding countryside, particularly when a market-day was associated with it (*De b.*

Philogonio [PG 48.749–50]; *De ss martyribus* [PG 50.705–7]). In the case of Syriac-speaking ascetics who also operated as priests, such occasions apparently also provided an opportunity for consultation with their bishop. Since such persons appear not to have spoken Greek, and it is probable that Flavian, who grew up in Antioch as a member of the wealthy upper classes, did not speak Syriac, the episcopal entourage must have incorporated bilingual interpreters. The same may also have been the case on the occasions when such persons attended worship (*Cat.* 8; *De statuis hom.* 19), although it may be that worship continued in Greek as usual and the Syriac-speaking visitors were expected to cope as best they were able. The regular influxes of beggars and the rural poor into Antioch at times of famine would also have exposed John and his fellow citizens to non-Greek speakers (Libanius, *Oration* 1.205–11; Downey 1961: 383–4, 419–20). The extent to which Syriac speakers lived within the city of Antioch and comprised a normal sector of the community is unknown. By contrast, at Constantinople there was a relatively large Gothic-speaking community because of the strong representation of ethnic Goths in the armed forces. The Nicene members of this community had their own church, in which John preached in Greek on at least one occasion (*Cum presbyter Gothus*; CPG 4441.9). While he preached in Greek, the lessons were read in Gothic, and a homily was also preached by a presbyter in Gothic. The extent to which the liturgy itself was conducted in Gothic is unknown. John also encountered a range of languages simply because Constantinople was the capital of the eastern empire and the residence of the imperial couple, a factor which drew people from all over the East who were seeking patronage and influence. Severian of Gabala was a native speaker of Syriac who arrived during John's tenure and to whom John entrusted the task of preaching while he himself was absent on a trip to Ephesus (Socrates, *H. E.* 6.11; Sozomen, *H. E.* 8.10). Acacius of Berrhoea, a semi-permanent resident of Constantinople at this period, was likewise a Syrian native, although presumably both he and Severian were capable of conversing in Greek. By the same token John Cassian, whom John ordained to the priesthood while he resided in Constantinople (Palladius, *Dial.* 3.83–4), came from the West and presumably spoke Latin by preference, as did the aristocratic widow Silvina, with whom John was closely associated. On the occasion of the translation of martyrial remains to a martyrium outside Constantinople, John states explicitly that during the nocturnal procession the Psalm was sung in Greek, Latin, Syriac and Gothic (*Nov. hom.* 2 [CPG 4441.1]; PG 63.472.10–13). The capital was evidently a more diverse community ethnically and linguistically than the city of his childhood and youth.

Relations with visitors

Firmly fixed as John Chrysostom was in the context of his communities, there were numerous occasions when he was called upon to interact with people who were not a permanent part of the communities in Antioch or Constantinople. Here we have to think of visitors, itinerants, country people, and clergy from elsewhere in the same district as well as from other districts. In Antioch John had, for example, periodic contact with the rural Syrian monk-priests when they came to town for consultation with their bishop, Flavian (van de Paverd 1991: 290). Then again, Antioch was a major see in Syria and the East, and synods of varying dimensions were frequently held there (see e.g., *De incompr. dei nat. hom.* 2; SC 28bis.142.20–5), a fact which would explain why occasionally a number of bishops were in attendance on Flavian when John was preaching (*In Gen. sermo* 8; PG 54.616.7–13 *a.i.*). Because of seasonal factors Antioch was also particularly susceptible to the influx of homeless and beggars, who were greeted with deep suspicion by the permanent residents (*De eleemosyna*). These same people are probably some of the homeless whom John has passed in the street on his way to the church. In Constantinople the semi-permanent presence of a number of bishops during John's episcopate is striking. Often these men were in residence for reasons of personal advantage, as the cases of Acacius of Beroea, Severian of Gabala and Antioch of Ptolemais illustrate. Others, like Theophilus of Alexandria, were summoned to the capital for reasons of ecclesiastical politics, while Epiphanius of Salamis travelled there to teach John a lesson with regard to the condemnation of Origenism: in his misplaced zeal he attempted to ordain on John's territory, held a synaxis without permission, and had the intention of denouncing the local bishop during synaxis in the church of the Holy Apostles (Socrates, *H. E.* 6.12–14; Sozomen, *H. E.* 8.14). On one occasion we hear of a bishop from Galatia who, on account of his status, was given licence by John to preach in his stead (*In illud: Pater meus usque modo operatur*; CPG 4441.10), and in his letter to Pope Innocent John tells us that on the night of Easter Saturday, 404, there were more than forty bishops with him for the baptism of the female catechisands (SC 342.86.166–9). Monks too came to Constantinople, such as those from Nitria who sought arbitration between themselves and Theophilus of Alexandria. John, however, avoided this issue, rather than making a stand, but organized various noble women to feed the monks and help them support themselves. Ultimately the men bypassed the bishop's authority and went directly to empress Eudoxia for help (Sozomen, *H. E.* 8.13; Palladius, *Dial.* 7–8).

By virtue of their status both cities thus attracted a diverse range of visitors which constantly swelled and diminished the population of each city in accord with seasonal and periodic factors. As we have seen, various of these groups and individuals would attend church and were encountered by John also in an official capacity. The existence and unpredictability of this factor adds considerably to the complexity of John's relationships.

Women

At the beginning of this study we pointed out that Chrysostom has been charged with misogyny. While far too little comprehensive research has been done on this question, the subject itself is currently gaining momentum, and for the sake of the completeness of our short treatment of John, based as it is on his relationships within his society, it is important to discuss briefly his relationships with women. What has been done (Clark 1979; Ford 1989; Rousseau 1995; Mayer 1999) suggests that, although in his rhetoric John did inveigh heavily against women and their foibles, in his actual relations with them he was one of the more liberal of the Church Fathers and one of the most appreciative of their value to the promotion of the Nicene Christian church and its ministries. It should also be borne in mind that

John inveighed in an equally heated way against the rich (*De eleemosyna*; In *Heb. hom.* 11 *et al.*), against teenage males (*In Matt. hom.* 49/50), and against adult men (*In Matt. hom.* 7; *In I Thess. hom.* 5 *et al.*). That is, when his invective is viewed across the entire body of his homilies and writings, it can be seen that he directed his strictures against all who behaved offensively, without bias towards gender, economic or social status, or age group. Furthermore, as in the cases of Julia, Italica and Proba at Rome, the sisters of bishop Pergamius at Nicaea (*Epp.* 4 [12]) and others, he seems to have appreciated that wealthy, aristocratic women, especially widows, were in a unique position in Late Antique society, which made their contacts as valuable to an ecclesiastic of the curial class as those of rich, aristocratic men, and to have had no qualms about encouraging such women to use their networks and resources in support of his own ecclesiastical agenda. In at least a few instances, involving Olympias, Pentadia, Carteria, Adolia and perhaps others of his female correspondents, he appears to have enjoyed a particularly friendly and close relationship with women from this elevated level of Antiochene and Constantinopolitan society (Liebeschuetz 1984; Mayer 1999). A careful, systematic study of both his rhetoric and his factual relations with both men and women is likely to produce a more complete and balanced picture than has hitherto been accepted.

CONCLUSION

What we begin to observe when we view the person of John from these different perspectives is an array of interconnecting pieces which together reinforce the picture of a complex man in a complex society. For instance, the blurred boundaries between church and city and state at this time, in conjunction with his own background, see him interacting throughout his life with a range of administrative officials both within the ecclesiastical sphere and outside of it. We begin to observe, too, in a number of areas – for instance, that of other faiths, other Christian factions and his relations with women – a discrepancy between his rhetoric and reality. When the bias of the sources towardss his episcopacy – the years at Constantinople and subsequently in exile – are taken into consideration it becomes evident that in fleshing out a profile of the man we need to exercise a great deal of caution. In particular, much careful work has yet to be done before a reliable psychological study of John can be arrived at.

Even so, there are some tentative conclusions which can be drawn at this preliminary stage of the investigation. When John Chrysostom is studied from the perspective of his personal relationships and interactions, the culture and society in which he lived, and the circles in which he moved, there emerges a man who spent a great deal of his time in association with the urban class above that into which he was born. This is seen most clearly at the time of his exile, both because of the extraordinary circumstances which it created and because this is the only period of his life from which there survives communication between John and individuals on a personal level. These letters proclaim his need to maintain his networks with both men and women in Antioch, Constantinople, Rome and along the route at a time when the favours which could be performed by his contacts were vital to him. The complaints which permeate the later letters indicate, too, the strong feelings of frustration which he felt at being cut off in the long winter months from direct and frequent communication. John was very much a man of the large, wealthy, bustling, Hellenized city. His reactions to the circumstances of his exile serve to underline the intelligence with which the route and manner of his deportation were selected. Few other punishments could have been more painful to a man of his particular background, status and generation.

BIBLIOGRAPHY

Allen, Pauline and Mayer, Wendy (1994) 'Chrysostom and the Preaching of Homilies in Series: A New Approach to the Twelve Homilies *In epistulam ad Colossenses* (CPG 4433)', *Orientalia Christiana Periodica* 60: 21–39.

—— (1995a) 'Chrysostom and the Preaching of Homilies in Series: A Re-examination of the Fifteen Homilies *In epistulam ad Philippenses* (CPG 4432)', *Vigiliae Christianae* 49: 270–89.

—— (1995b) 'The Thirty-Four Homilies on Hebrews: The Last Series Delivered by Chrysostom in Constantinople?', *Byzantion* 65: 309–48.

Baur, Chrysostomus (1929–30) *Johannes Chrysostomus und seine Zeit*, 2 vols. Munich: Hueber = (1959–60) *John Chrysostom and His Time*, Sr M. Gonzaga (trans.), 2 vols. Westminster, Md.: Newman Press.

Broc, Catherine (1993) 'Le rôle des femmes dans l'église de Constantinople d'après la correspondance de Jean Chrysostome', *Studia Patristica* 27: 150–4.

Brown, Peter (1971) 'The Rise and Function of the Holy Man in Late Antiquity', *Journal of Roman Studies* 61: 80–101.

—— (1988) *The Body and Society. Men, Women, and Sexual Renunciation in Early Christianity*. New York: Columbia University Press.

Cameron, Alan (1988) 'A Misidentified Homily of Chrysostom', *Nottingham Medieval Studies* 32: 34–48.

Clark, Elizabeth (1979) 'Friendship Between the Sexes: Classical Theory and Christian Practice', in Elizabeth Clark, *Jerome, Chrysostom and Friends. Essays and Translations*, New York: The Edwin Mellen Press.

Cunningham, Mary and Allen, Pauline (eds) (1998) *Preacher and Audience. Studies in Early Christian and Byzantine Homiletics*. Leiden: Brill.

Dagron, Gilbert (1970) 'Les moines et la ville. Le monachisme à Constantinople jusqu'au concile de Chalcédoine (451)', *Travaux et Mémoires* 4: 229–76.

—— (1974) *Naissance d'une capitale. Constantinople et ses institutions de 330 à 451*, Paris: Presses universitaires de France.

Delmaire, Roland (1991) 'Les «lettres d'exil» de Jean Chrysostome. Études de chronologie et de prosopographie', *Recherches Augustiniennes* 25: 71–180.

—— (1997) 'Jean Chrysostome et ses "amis" d'après le nouveau classement de sa Correspondance', *Studia Patristica* 33: 302–13.

Downey, Glanville (1961) *A History of Antioch in Syria from Seleucus to the Arab Conquest*. Princeton, N.J.: Princeton University Press.

Ford, David (1989) 'Misogynist or Advocate? St. John Chrysostom and his Views on Women', Unpubl. Ph.D. dissertation, Drew University, Madison, N.J.

Kelly, J. N. D. (1995) *Golden Mouth. The Story of John Chrysostom – Ascetic, Preacher, Bishop*. London: Gerald Duckworth and Co. Ltd.

Leyerle, Blake (1997) 'Appealing to Children', *Journal for Early Christian Studies* 5: 243–70.

Liebeschuetz, Wolfgang (1984) 'Friends and Enemies of John Chrysostom', in Ann Moffatt (ed.), *Maistor. Classical, Byzantine and Renaissance Studies for Robert Browning*. Canberra: Australian Association for Byzantine Studies.

—— (1985) 'The Fall of John Chrysostom', *Nottingham Medieval Studies* 29: 1–31.

MacMullen, Ramsay (1989) 'The Preacher's Audience (AD 350–400)', *Journal of Theological Studies* n.s. 40: 503–11.

—— (1997) *Christianity and Paganism in the Fourth to Eighth Centuries*. New Haven, Conn.: Yale University Press.

Malingrey, Anne-Marie (1973) 'L'édition critique de Jean Chrysostome. Actualité de son oeuvre. Volumes parus. Projects', in *Symposion. Studies on St John Chrysostom*, Thessalonika: Patriarchal Institute for Patristic Studies.

Mayer, Wendy (1996) 'The Provenance of the Homilies of St John Chrysostom. Towards a New Assessment of Where he Preached What', Unpublished Ph.D. dissertation, University of Queensland, Brisbane.

—— (1997) 'The Dynamics of Liturgical Space. Aspects of the Interaction between John Chrysostom and his Audiences', *Ephemerides Liturgicae* 111: 104–15.

—— (1998a) 'John Chrysostom: Extraordinary Preacher, Ordinary Audience', in Mary Cunningham and Pauline Allen (eds) *Preacher and Audience. Studies in Early Christian and Byzantine Homiletics*. Leiden: Brill.

—— (1998b) 'Monasticism at Antioch and Constantinople in the Late Fourth Century. A Case of Exclusivity or Diversity?', in Pauline Allen, Raymond Canning and Lawrence Cross (eds), with B. Janelle Caiger, *Prayer and Spirituality in the Early church*. Brisbane: Centre for Early Christian Studies, Australian Catholic University.

—— (1999), 'Constantinopolitan Women in Chrysostom's Circle', *Vigiliae Christianae* 53: 265–88.

Mayer, Wendy and Allen, Pauline (2000) *John Chrysostom. Preacher and Carer of Souls*. London: Routledge.

Meyer, Louis (1933) *Saint Jean Chrysostome. Maître de perfection chrétienne*. Paris: Beauchesne et fils.

Miller, Timothy (1985) *The Birth of the Hospital in the Byzantine Empire*. Baltimore, Md.: Johns Hopkins University Press.

Rentinck, Pietro (1970) *La cura pastorale in Antiochia nel IV secolo*. Roma: Università Gregoriana Editrice.

Rousseau, Philip (1995) ' "Learned Women" and the Development of a Christian Culture in Late Antiquity', *Symbolae Osloenses* 70: 116–47.

Van de Paverd, Frans (1991) *St. John Chysostom. The Homilies on the Statues. An Introduction*. Roma: Pont. Institutum Studiorum Orientalium.

Vinson, Martha (1994) 'Gregory Nazianzen's Homily 15 and the Genesis of the Christian Cult of the Maccabean Martyrs', *Byzantion* 64: 166–92.

Voicu, Sever (1996) 'Pseudo-Giovanni Crisostomo: I confini del corpus', *Jahrbuch für Antike und Christentum* 39: 105–15.

Wenger, Antoine (1952) 'Notes inédites sur les empereurs Théodose I, Arcadius, Théodose II, Léon I', *Revue des études byzantines* 10: 47–59.

Wilken, Robert (1983) *John Chrysostom and the Jews: Rhetoric and Reality in the Late Fourth Century*. Berkeley: University of California Press.

JEROME

—— ·◆· ——

Dennis Brown

LIFE AND CONTEXT

St Jerome, in many quarters 'the greatest doctor of the church', is chiefly remembered as one of the most forceful personalities and one of the most important interpreters of the Bible in the early centuries of Christianity. Jerome was probably born sometime in the early 340s CE in the town of Stridon, in Dalmatia, modern Yugoslavia. He died in 420, renowned for his exegetical activity and for living a holy and ascetic life.

Jerome was born into a well-off Christian family. In one of his early letters, (*Epistle* 3.5), Jerome recalls running through the slave quarters of his home and being looked after by foster-nurses and a personal attendant. In Stridon, he attended the *ludus litterarius* or elementary school, the normal age for which was 6 to 11 or 12 years old. Jerome would have learned to read and write here, and have been instructed in simple arithmetic. He may also have picked up the rudiments of Greek. It must also have been at Stridon where Jerome began to train his astonishingly retentive memory, which was, in later life, to prove so very useful in his scholarship.

Jerome was sent to Rome for his secondary education, to one of the most famous teachers of the age – Aelius Donatus. The curriculum here would have included some mathematics, science and music, but was principally concerned with the rules of grammar, particularly the correct analysis and use of language, and classical literature. The favourite authors were Virgil, the poet and founder of liberal Latin culture; Terence, the comic playwright; Sallust the historian; and Cicero the stylist, orator and philosopher. Jerome obviously loved his time in Rome, for his works are full of quotations and allusions to classical literature.[1] When he was about 15 or 16, Jerome would have graduated to a Roman school of rhetoric, where he would have learned the art of public speaking, with a view, perhaps, to entering a career in advocacy or the civil service. Jerome's later writings show how well he learned the art of rhetoric, for instance, its stylized procedures, its stock emotional phrases and its tendency to exaggeration (*Commentary on Galatians* 2.1). His education provided the foundation upon which he was to base all his work in the coming years.[2]

Figure 46.1 Jerome, the greatest doctor of the church. From Siguenza (1595), reproduced in the 1907 English translation.

Though education was perhaps the single most important aspect of Jerome's personality, it was not the only one. He was a fervent supporter of asceticism. After finishing his Roman education, Jerome travelled widely. He seems to have become interested in the ascetic life at Trier, which had become an important centre for monasticism. He soon decided to withdraw to the desert of Chalcis in northern Syria, to experience first-hand the spiritual life offered by a colony of hermits. His sojourn in the desert lasted only two or three years, but the desire to lead a holy and ascetic life stayed with him and became part of his life-long quest.

He moved to Aquileia in *c.*375 CE, but left there in 377 and travelled widely for the next five years. At this point he returned to Rome, taking up residence in the city under the patronage of Pope Damasus. He served as secretary to Damasus from 382 to 385. During this time Jerome became widely known for his advocacy of monasticism, and he gathered a number of disciples, some of whom were noble women. He studied the Bible and asceticism with them, meeting in the house of Marcella on the Aventine. His association with this group of women met a deep-seated need in his personality. His correspondence with them reveals a great deal about his warm sympathies, his skill at adapting himself to their different interests, and his ability to gain a strong hold over several of them, and particularly the wealthy widow Paula and her daughter Eustochium.

After the death of Damasus in 385, Jerome's influence in Rome waned and he was forced to leave, but he was accompanied by Paula and Eustochium. The group visited many of the sacred sites in the Holy land and Egypt. The route taken by the group is recorded by Jerome in *Epistle* 108 and in his *Apology against Rufinus*.[3] In these travels, Jerome learned much about the topography of the important sites in biblical history, and this information was to be very useful to him in his exegesis of both Testaments, particularly when he interpreted the literal sense of texts. He also wrote a trilogy of books, in part based on his travels and which informed and influenced his exegetical studies. These were the *Book of the Interpretations of Hebrew Names*, the *On Sites and Names of Hebrew Places*, and the *Hebrew Questions on the Book of Genesis*. These were largely etymological works, which had a long history, not only in Christianity but also in Judaism and paganism.

Jerome and the group of women finally settled at Bethlehem after their travels. Paula provided the finance to build two monasteries, one for men under the guidance of Jerome, and one for women, over which Paula presided. Jerome formulated rules of monastic living for both institutions, and he remained here for the rest of his long life. Jerome became a champion of the idea of virginity, not just for monks but for lay Christians also. He died there in 420 and his remains rest in St Catherine's church in the city (Figure 46.2).

JEROME AND ASCETICISM

Jerome's interest in asceticism deserves further attention. He probably first became interested in the ascetic life because of the unworthiness of the church in his native Dalmatia. As he writes in the *Life of Malchus*, an essay composed *c.* 390: 'The Church after it had arrived at [the existence of] Christian princes became greater in power by its wealth, but lesser in virtue' (*Life of Malchus* 1). His own bishop, whom Jerome describes as 'an ailing pilot of a sinking ship' disgusted him, as did his fellow townspeople, who were Christians who thought only of their stomachs (*Epistle* 7.5)! When he moved to Aquileia *c.* 375, Jerome was able to establish a community where secular ambitions were renounced and spiritual simplicities embraced. This allowed him the space to live a detached life of abstinence, and the contemplation of divine truths.

At this early stage, the practice of asceticism was still seen as an eccentricity by many Christians, but Jerome's zeal, his controversial personality and the theology of asceticism which he developed over the years, were to make this way of life into the

Figure 46.2; Jerome's tomb in St Catherine's church in Bethlehem. Photo Catherine Brown.

representative movement among Christians in the West. Jerome travelled east, to the desert of Chalcis, to experience what he expected to be the challenging and spiritually uplifting conditions of solitary asceticism. He was to be disappointed in this, however, for the place was overcrowded with quarrelsome monks and he left the place, as previously noted, in 377.

It was at Rome, on his return to the city in the early 380s, that Jerome's ideas on asceticism became more clearly focused. This was partly achieved by the group of wealthy women with whom Jerome became close, and partly as a result of controversy. He became the spiritual adviser to the Christian noble house of the Aemilii which included Paula, and her daughters Eustochium and Blesilla. He instructed them in asceticism as well as Bible study. Jerome described Paula as mourning and fasting, squalid with dirt, her eyes dim with weeping, praying for divine mercy all night (*Epistle* 108.26). The women in Jerome's group lived, in many ways, like nuns. They withdrew, in varying degrees, from ordinary society, practised prolonged fasting, wore coarse clothing, neglected their personal appearance, and avoided comforts like baths. Above all, they practised chastity – the elimination as far as possible of the sexual element of life. Jerome urged Eustochium, for instance (*Epistle* 22),[4] to repress sexual ideas as soon as they arose in the mind. Wine was to be avoided because it stimulated sexual desire; rich or abundant food could be equally exciting and should be avoided. Virgins should not associate with married men or women, as their company would only remind them of what they had renounced. A virgin should have a dedicated woman as a companion, and ought to keep to her own room as much as possible, filling her days and nights with prayer and Bible reading. She should be thoughtful and humble in her conduct and dress, and should always take the Blessed Virgin as her example.

Jerome had a great victory over the lay theologian Helvidius, who taught that Mary had enjoyed a normal family life after the birth of Jesus, and therefore that marriage was just as high a state as celibacy. Helvidius was thus attacking the key argument of those who propounded celibacy as a valid way of Christian life; namely, that Mary was perpetually virgin. Jerome maintained, in *Against Helvidius on the Perpetual Virginity of Mary* (composed in Rome in 383), that all the biblical passages concerning the 'brothers' of Jesus did not imply a blood relationship, but rather that they were his 'cousins'. As for the celibate state, its superiority over marriage was proven by the fact that not only Mary but Joseph also was a life-long virgin. This superiority is confirmed both by Paul's warning that married people cannot give God their undivided attention, and by the everyday observation that married people are distracted by mundane things. This was the earliest work by a Latin writer specifically on Mariology, and Jerome's teaching became the official orthodoxy, with celibacy hailed as the noblest state.

Later, in 393, Jerome wrote a treatise, *Against Jovinian*, an apostate Roman monk who held views similar to those of Helvidius. Jovinian taught four theses: first, that virginity was not a higher state than marriage; second, that those who were baptized could not be influenced by the Devil to sin; third, that fasting brought no special reward; and finally, that those who remained faithful to their baptism all enjoyed the same heavenly rewards. Jerome's reply to these theses is contained in two books, the whole of the first of which is concerned with Jovinian's first proposition. The other three are answered in the second book. Once again, Jerome skilfully deployed arguments based on scriptural exegesis to counter his opponent. Jerome pointed out that Adam and Eve embarked upon marriage only after their sin, and that, while marriage was intended to 'replenish the earth' (Gen. 1:28), 'virginity replenishes paradise' (*Against Jovinian* 1.16). He claims that the figures closest to God in the Bible were all virgins (e.g. Joshua, Elijah, John the Baptist), that Peter was married before he heard the Gospel; his statement in Matt. 19:27 that 'We have left all and followed you' proved that, once he became a disciple of Jesus, he abandoned it (*Against Jovinian* 1.26). This powerful and sustained defence of virginity probably did more than anything else Jerome wrote on this subject to establish asceticism as the norm of Christian life in the West.

Another aspect of his asceticism was the need he felt to give up his intense interest in, and love for, classical literature to concentrate on scripture and Christian writings. In one famous letter (*Epistle* 22) he recounts a dream in which he was taken before God in heaven; asked to say who he was he replied, *Christianus sum* ('I am a

Christian') only to be contradicted with the words, 'Non es Christianus, tu es Ciceronianus' ('You are not a Christian, you are a Ciceronian'). Many European paintings of Jerome depict him in the desert beating himself with a stone to drive the temptation to classical literature from his breast.

JEROME AS BIBLICAL INTERPRETER AND TRANSLATOR

The Roman empire into which Jerome was born had been changing rapidly. The Christian emperor, Constantine the Great, had pushed through policies that favoured Christianity, and many churches were built throughout the empire. Constantine's benevolent actions, and those of his successors, had a dramatic effect on the church. Instead of being persecuted, the church now enjoyed many privileges and it was increasingly to have an influential role in society. Christianity was becoming more and more popular and respectable and, consequently, people were streaming into the church. One result of this was that the church population wanted to learn more about the scriptures, and scholars like Jerome had an important function to fulfil by writing commentaries to explain the biblical books.

Jewish Bible interpretation

Jerome inherited a long tradition of biblical interpretation, both Jewish and Christian. In Judaism, rabbinic scholars had developed a system of interpretative rules and techniques for studying biblical texts. These may be broadly classified under two headings: haggadah and halakhah. Haggadah ('information' or 'anecdote') is seen largely in collections of midrash (a kind of commentary on scripture) and often takes the form of moralizing exegesis. Various techniques were used to achieve this, including juxtaposing originally discrete biblical texts, creative elaboration of the biblical narrative and the use of parable. This midrashic method could provide profound theological insights. Jerome used a great deal of haggadic material in his works, and he was the main source through which echoes of the haggadah reached some of the western Church Fathers. Halakhah ('procedure') was concerned with the implementation of the Torah, the Jewish law, in relation to practical matters, and with ensuring that the Torah could be successfully adapted to the changing conditions in the life of Jews. Jerome often used this halakhic principle in his own exegesis of scripture.

One Jewish scholar who found favour with Jerome was Philo of Alexandria. He calls Philo an 'ecclesiastical' writer, on the grounds that Philo praises Christians at Alexandria and mentions that Christianity is present in other provinces (Jerome, *De viris illustribus* 11). Philo had been aware of haggadic and halakhic traditions, but found that the 'impossibilities' and 'absurdities' produced by a literal reading of scripture could be unravelled by using an allegorical method based on Stoic ethics and Platonic cosmology. By searching carefully in scripture for clues like contradictions, strange expressions, word derivations and mysterious numbers, the interpreter could discover the 'real' message which God intended to convey.

Alexandria and Antioch

This allegorical interpretation of biblical texts spread from Philo to Christianity and became widely used by the catechetical school at Alexandria, particularly by its two greatest scholars, Clement and Origen. For Clement, most of scripture was expressed in enigmas, and it was the task of the interpreter who had received the deeper knowledge (*gnosis*) given by Christ to his apostles after the resurrection, to unlock the spiritual truth of biblical language to those capable of understanding. Following Philo, Clement allegorized the Old Testament freely. His hermeneutical principle for identifying true meaning was an eclectic mixture of Hellenistic (and gnostic) cosmology, soteriology and morality, combined with the conviction that, in the Logos-Christ, all foreshadowing of truth had found its goal.

Although Jerome spoke approvingly of Clement, it is clear that he was much more profoundly influenced by the other great Alexandrian exegete, Origen. Much of Origen's huge literary output was devoted to the interpretation of the Bible. Jerome classified Origen's works into three categories: scholia (short explanatory glosses), commentaries and homilies. Most of the biblical books were dealt with by Origen in one or more of these forms. In his treatise, *De Principiis*, Origen had set out to show systematically how the diversity of the world came about, and how it would eventually return to a divine unity. Fundamental to this structure was the role of scripture and its interpretation. The divinely inspired scriptures had a spiritual purpose; therefore to give them a simplistic understanding was to insult the divine author of the writings. Origen argued that texts like Prov. 22:20f. suggested a threefold sense of scripture analogous to the tripartite anthropology of the philosophers: just as humans consisted of body, soul and spirit, so scripture had a literal, moral and spiritual sense. All biblical texts had a spiritual sense, though not all had a literal one. If no spiritual sense was apparent on the surface, the interpreter must understand the surface sense symbolically. Allegory was the method which would provide the key to unlock the hidden, symbolic meaning of texts, and it was Origen whose influence made allegory the dominant method of biblical interpretation down to the Middle Ages. Jerome was responsible, to an extent, for ensuring that Origen's writings were transmitted to the western church, thus disseminating more widely Origen's allegorizing exegesis.

Not all Christian scholars were convinced, however, that allegorical exegesis was the best method of discovering the truth of scripture. The 'school' of Antioch developed in reaction against the allegorising tendencies of Alexandria. The school's early history is associated with the name of Lucian, the teacher of Arius, but the most influential Antiochenes were Diodore of Tarsus, Theodore of Mopsuestia and John Chrysostom. The Antiochenes insisted on the historical basis of the text of scripture and that, wherever possible, it should be interpreted literally. Only where this could not be done was the typological or allegorical sense to be explored. The Antiochene emphasis on the literal or historical sense is seen in Lucian's emphasis on the details of the text of scripture. He knew Hebrew and corrected the Septuagint from the original Hebrew. Jerome praised this recension and used it widely in his own work on the biblical text.

Jerome and Hebrew

Before it was possible to interpret the text properly, it was necessary to have the best text available. The inescapable conclusion for Jerome was that he had to learn the original biblical languages. As far as the New Testament was concerned, Jerome encountered no problems, for he had learnt Greek at school, and had attended the lectures of Gregory of Nazianzus in Constantinople. But for the text of the Old Testament, Jerome was faced with a considerable hurdle for, apart from Origen, very few other Christian scholars had any knowledge of Hebrew. Jerome took lessons in Hebrew from a Jewish convert to Christianity, and it is clear that he found it a difficult language to master. It must be remembered that no grammars or concordances were available, so he had to learn the language orally, memorizing the sounds of the consonants and vocabulary. Presumably, he practised writing the Hebrew characters by copying out manuscripts. Of his Hebrew studies, Jerome says: 'What labour I spent on this task, what difficulties I went through, how often I despaired and how often I gave up and in my eagerness to learn, started again' (*Epistle* 125.12).

Jerome believed, along with the rest of the ancient Jewish and Christian world, that Hebrew was the world's original language. Despite its antiquity, however, Jerome found Hebrew a barbarous language, which affected his Latin style. In the preface to his *Commentary on Galatians*, Jerome apologizes for his unliterary style, blaming it partly on eye trouble and problems with copyists, but also on his study of Hebrew: 'I leave it to others to judge how far my unflagging study of Hebrew has profited me; what I have lost in my own language, I can tell.'

It is clear that Jerome had a much more extensive and profound knowledge of Hebrew than did any other Christian scholar, including Origen. Jerome had the same quantitative use of Hebrew as did Origen, but he added to it a qualitative use of Hebrew as a guide to the right *meanings* (Barr 1966: 282). This qualitative use of Hebrew manifests itself in various ways. The very fact, for instance, that Jerome undertook the task of translating the Old Testament from Hebrew points towards his possessing a high degree of ability in Hebrew. Ever bearing in mind that he had the previous Greek translations of Theodotion, Symmachus and especially of Aquila, which must have been of considerable value to him, Jerome's own translation from the Hebrew was a quite remarkable achievement, especially when it is seen to be a generally accurate and faithful translation. A second way of showing Jerome's extensive understanding of Hebrew is to look at his vocalizations of Hebrew. The Hebrew text with which Jerome worked would have been unpointed (that is, without vowels). This means that distinctions in meaning could be brought about by different vocalizations of the same consonants. The following example comes from Jerome's *Commentary on Jeremiah*:

> The Hebrew word, which is written with the three letters 'd-b-r' (it has no vowels in it) according to the natural progression of the passage and the judgement of the reader, if 'dabar' is read it means 'word'; if 'deber', it means 'death'; and if 'dabber', it means 'speak' (9.22).

In an unvocalized text, all three words ('dabar', 'deber' and 'dabber') would have been identical in Hebrew. It would only have been possible to discern the correct grammatical construction (the first two are nouns, the third is a verb) and the meaning of the word by studying its position in the sentence. In this example, Jerome is combating the incorrect translations of this word which had appeared in the Greek versions, which implied different vocalizations. The Septuagint omitted the word; Origen's *Hexapla* had interpreted it as 'death'; Aquila had understood it as 'speak', as had Symmachus. It has been suggested that Jerome may have been influenced here by the Jewish *al-tiqre* interpretation (Barr 1966: 282). This means 'do not read [the word in the text] but [another similar one]'. It was a midrashic technique used to introduce alternative readings to a text for purely homiletical purposes. It was understood as a legitimate extension of the literal exegesis of a passage. It seems unlikely in this case, as, if Jerome had been using this technique, he would have used the different possibilities of vocalization in his own interpretation. It is more likely that Jerome is merely revelling in his good knowledge of Hebrew and showing off to his Christian readers by exhibiting his mastery of the language. It was this extensive knowledge of Hebrew that helped Jerome so much in his major task of translating the Bible from its original languages.

Textual criticism

As an essential part of producing an accurate translation of the Bible, Jerome had to be assured that he was working with the best possible text. Jerome, more than any other Church Father of the first five centuries, was very well versed in the principles and techniques of textual criticism (Hulley 1944). It is largely due to his labours in this area that scholars today can ascertain accurately the state of the text of the Old Testament, Septuagint, Hexapla and New Testament in the fourth century.

Jerome acquired an interest in manuscripts and books early in his adult life. Before the end of his formal education, he had made copies of classical authors, and soon after he left Rome, he labouriously copied out Hilary of Poitier's commentaries on the Psalms and the *De Synodis*.[5] During his travels, Jerome collected many manuscripts of biblical and other material. One of the most advantageous from this point of view was his visit to the famous library at Caesarea, which had been assembled by the priest and martyr Pamphilus, friend of Eusebius of Caesarea. Jerome relates that Pamphilus was 'so impassioned with sacred literature that he himself transcribed the greater part of the works of Origen, and these are still preserved today in the library at Caesarea' (*De viris Illustribus* 3).

Jerome became very attached to the manuscripts he had collected, and took them with him when he moved from place to place. In a letter to Paul of Concordia, Jerome suggested that they could make a mutually beneficial arrangement, whereby Jerome would send Paul a copy of his newly composed treatise, the *Life of Paul the Hermit*, if, in return, Paul – who owned a substantial library himself – would provide Jerome with copies of several books, including the commentaries of Fortunatian, the *History* of Aurelius Victor and the letters of Novatian, so that Jerome might increase his personal collection. Unfortunately, we do not know whether the deal was closed and the books exchanged (see *Ep.* 22.30 and *Ep.* 10.3).

Textual criticism is fundamentally concerned with variant readings in texts.

Jerome realized this and asked where these variant readings came from and why they arose. As far as Jerome was concerned, the text critic's task was to remove any errors in a text and to establish a trustworthy one. Many errors were produced – either accidentally or intentionally – by careless or incompetent copyists. Jerome observed that some copyists did not pay attention to their work and even went to sleep over it, or they carelessly changed the reading, writing not what was in front of them, but what they understood. So, at *Commentary on Matthew* 13:35, Jerome noted that the copyist wrote 'Isaiah' instead of 'Asaph', because the former name was more familiar to him and he believed the previous copyist to have been mistaken. In addition to general comments about the causes of errors in texts, Jerome frequently mentioned detailed causes of corruption. Punctuation, for example, was very important for understanding a passage correctly, and faulty punctuation may be a cause of error. The confusion of number symbols was another cause of error. Jerome made the interesting suggestion that the reason why the evangelist Mark seems to disagree with Matthew and John about the exact time of Jesus' crucifixion was due to a copyist's error. Jerome says that the copyist confused the number symbols *S'* and *Y'* and therefore produced an error in the text (*Tractatus in Psalmos* 77). Jerome also mentions that copyists could easily confuse similar letters. Most of his references to this relate to the confusion of Hebrew letters by the translators of the Septuagint, especially the letters *resh* and *daleth*, distinguished only by a small stroke, and the letters *yod* and *vau*, which differ, he says, only in size. Also noticed by Jerome are occasional examples of dittography and haplography, metathesis of letters, assimilation, omission of words and transposition (Brown 1993: 36–7).

One of the areas Jerome would have to approach in writing a commentary on a biblical book was that of authorship, and the authenticity or otherwise of sections of particular books. Although he does not use the terms, Jerome utilizes two criteria for deciding on these issues: internal and external evidence.

With regard to external evidence, one method of ensuring the authenticity of a writing is the *subscriptio*. The apostle Paul, Jerome reported, had used his signature, along with a few words, to take away from false teachers any opportunity of tampering with his own doctrines (*Commentary on Galatians* 6:11). The subscription, however, was not a very good criterion by which to judge a book's authenticity. The signature could be forged or imitated. Another criterion was the *anulus signatorius*, or 'seal' which one put on letters or other works.

Jerome attaches great value to the internal evidence in a work when it comes to verifying its authenticity. First, one must determine whether the contents are consistent with those of its supposed author. For instance, with a book by the Pythagorean author and philosopher, Sixtus, whom Jerome's erstwhile friend Rufinus equates with the Christian martyr, Sixtus, Jerome applies this criterion and establishes that in the entire volume there is no mention of Christ or the apostles. How, then, could it have been written by a Christian martyr (see the preface to his *Commentary on Philemon*)?

When Jerome discusses the suspicions concerning the authorship of the Letter to Philemon, he again uses the criterion of internal evidence. Certain contemporary critics held that it was not Pauline because of its brevity, its seemingly inferior subject matter, and its mundane tone. Jerome, however, argues strongly that if this letter is rejected because of its brevity, then others must also be rejected – for instance Obadiah, Nahum and Zephaniah. He also states that brevity in a document which has in it so much of the beauty of the gospel, is a sign of its inspiration. Further, many of the other (undisputed) epistles mention mundane, worldly matters, like the cloak left at Troas (2 Tim. 4:13). To suppose that common life is distinct and separate from God is to approach the heresy of Manichaeanism, Jerome warns. Should these powerful arguments based on internal evidence not be enough to convince some people, Jerome also uses one piece of external evidence – he says that Marcion, who altered many of the epistles of Paul, did not touch the letter to Philemon, believing it to be genuinely by Paul. If even Marcion believed it to be authentic, Jerome says, then no orthodox Christian should have any reason to doubt it (Preface to the *Commentary on Philemon*).

Jerome never discusses systematically his principles of textual criticism, and this is really because he saw the text critic's task to be a practical one – to establish the correct text. Without the correct text, it was impossible to have any real understanding of its meaning, and this was of paramount importance for Jerome. For his understanding of scripture, this meant that textual criticism preceded the task of translating the biblical texts, and it was only when both of these had been accomplished that true understanding would be achieved.

The Vulgate translation

Jerome was, as he himself says, a *vir trilinguis*, knowing Hebrew, Greek and Latin. One of the greatest achievements for which Jerome is remembered is the translation of the Bible known as the 'Vulgate'. This term comes from the Latin 'vulgata', meaning 'common'. It is used of the Latin version of the Bible followed by the Roman Catholic church, often attributed to Jerome. Jerome used the term himself to refer to his own translation of the Bible, because he wanted to make the scriptural texts available to everyone, not just to scholars who could understand Greek and Hebrew (Sutcliffe 1948: 250). Jerome, more than any other single person, was responsible for fixing the literary form of the Bible of the entire western church. The complicated history of the Vulgate translation and Jerome's involvement in it began in 383, when Pope Damasus came to the conclusion that, because of the proliferation of variant readings in the Latin Bible of the day, a thorough revision was a *desideratum*. For this task, he commissioned Jerome. Although we do not have the actual words of his commission, we get a very clear idea of his wishes from Jerome's *Preface to the Four Gospels*. He says:

> You urge me to compose a new work from the old, and, as it were, to sit in judgement on the copies of the scriptures which are now scattered throughout the world; and, insofar as they differ from one another, you would have me decide which of them agree with the Greek original. The labour is one of love, but at the same time dangerous and presumptuous; for in judging others I must in turn be judged by all; and how can I change the language of the world at this late stage, and carry it back to its early childhood? Is there a man, learned or otherwise, who, when he takes the volume in his hands and sees that

what he reads does not suit his settled tastes, will not break out immediately into violent language and call me a forger and a profane person for having had the audacity to add anything to the ancient books, or to make any changes or corrections to them?

Jerome, however, was prepared to risk castigation in this way for two reasons. First, he explains, is the pope's command. Second, was the great diversity of Old Latin manuscripts. He exclaims that there were 'almost as many forms of text as there are manuscripts'. Jerome's younger contemporary, Augustine, confirms this fact when he laments:

> Those who translated the scriptures from Hebrew into Greek may be counted, but the Latin translators are without number. For in the early days of the faith, every man who happened to get hold of a Greek manuscript (of the New Testament) and who imagined he had any facility in both languages, however slight that might have been, dared to make a translation.
>
> *De doctrina Christiana* 2.16).

Jerome's and Augustine's statements were not mere hyperbole, but based on sound factual information. The Old Latin version was begun in the second century, simultaneously in Africa and western Europe. By the fourth century, it existed in a bewildering number of forms, showing a huge number of variant readings. This was partly because the task of translation had been undertaken by different scholars at different times in different areas, and partly because of errors in translation and careless transcription. The Latin of these early versions was very odd, as the language was adapted to Christian usage, with special vocabulary created for the new translation (Brown 1993: 98–9). The idiom of this form of Latin often recalled the Greek on which the Christian vocabulary was based, and, because it was written for uneducated people, it had a strongly colloquial feel (Metzger 1977: 285–330).

Jerome's statement concerning the many text-types of the Old Latin version would also seem to be substantiated, for the modern scholarly consensus distinguishes four main text-types among Old Latin manuscripts: African, European, Italian and Spanish.[6]

Faced with a bewildering array of variant readings and different text-types, Jerome prepared to carry out Pope Damasus' wish to revise the Latin Bible and create (or re-create) a uniform text. Naturally enough, he began his revision with the four gospels. Pope Damasus did not commission Jerome to make a *fresh translation* of the Bible, but Jerome found himself checking the accuracy of the Latin text by referring constantly to the Greek original. He was conscious, however, of his commission to *revise* the existing Old Latin version, and changed this text only when it was necessary. He finished his revision of the four gospels and presented it to the pope in 384, shortly before the latter's death.

That Jerome revised the four gospels is certain. Less certain, however, is how much of the remainder of the Old Latin New Testament Jerome revised. In *On Famous Men* and elsewhere, he claims to have 'restored the New Testament to its Greek original'. Scholars have expressed opposing views on Jerome's statement. Some, notably Dom J. Chapman (1923), believed that Jerome did, in fact, revise the whole of the New Testament. Chapman argued that Jerome's quotations from Paul in *Epistle* 27 show his intention of publishing soon a revision of the Pauline epistles, that the lack of prefaces to the New Testament other than the gospels can be explained easily – because the pope, for whom Jerome was making the revision, died soon after the gospels had been revised, Jerome did not wish to write prefaces to anyone else. Chapman also attempts to explain why Jerome's quotations from the Pauline epistles often differ from those in the Vulgate: he often quotes readings with which he disagrees and he may have thought a certain reading to be a fairly good one, his own suggestion being meant only to explain the real force of the Greek, not to serve as a tolerable Latin rendering. Jerome is often inconsistent anyway, and the differences between the Vulgate readings and those found in Jerome's works do not necessarily prove that he was not the author of the Vulgate of the Pauline epistles. Chapman cites examples from the gospels which vary from the Vulgate. Those who argue that Jerome did not revise the text of the Pauline epistles because his quotations differ from the Vulgate, must also conclude that he did not revise the text of the gospels, which is absurd. Stylistically, he says, the Vulgate New Testament is the work of a single author and that author must be Jerome. Furthermore, Jerome is always accurate when enumerating his own works, so when he says he had revised the whole New Testament, he must have done. Chapman dates the revision of the complete New Testament to 391.

This traditional belief that Jerome revised the text of the complete New Testament has been seriously questioned by other scholars. F. Cavallera made a detailed study of the Vulgate of Acts, the Pauline epistles and Revelation and noted especially the discrepancies between the Vulgate and quotations in Jerome's works (1922). Sometimes Jerome employs a text which coincides more or less with the Vulgate, but more often he quotes one which differs. Sometimes he rejects readings which are found in the Vulgate. It is very important in this context that, in his commentaries on Galatians, Ephesians, Philemon and Titus, written *c.* 387, shortly after his supposed revision of these letters, he never attributes the Latin text he uses to himself, but, on the contrary, often uses the phrase '*Latinus interpres*' of the translator. He sometimes disagrees with their readings. More recently, J. N. D. Kelly has stated his opinion that the style of the Vulgate of Acts is against Jerome's authorship. Kelly has also asserted categorically that 'the only tenable conclusion is that Jerome, for whatever reason, abandoned the idea of revising the rest of the New Testament (if indeed he ever entertained it at all) once he had completed the gospels' (1975: 88).

Before he left Rome in 385, after having revised the text of the gospels, Jerome revised the Latin text of the Psalter according to the Septuagint. He says that he revised this book very quickly, but made substantial changes. This revision used to be identified as the 'Roman Psalter', but recent work has indicated that, while the Roman Psalter is not the version which Jerome made at Rome in 384, it may well represent the text on which he worked and which he corrected. A few years later (*c.* 387–8), Jerome made another translation of the Psalms, this time using Origen's Hexaplaric Septuagint text as his basis. This version is known as the 'Gallican Psalter', as it was first accepted for use in the churches of Gaul. It also remained in greater use than his later translation of the Psalms from Hebrew, and so became included in the official Vulgate edition of the Bible, ratified by the Council of Trent. In this 'Gallican Psalter', Jerome included Origen's diacritical signs, which were intended to show where the Septuagint text differed from the Hebrew original.

In the same period, Jerome also translated the books of Job, 1 and 2 Chronicles, Proverbs, Ecclesiastes and Song of Songs. The Psalter, Job (in two manuscripts) and (in only one manuscript) Song of Songs, are all that remain of this translation of parts of the Old Testament from Origen's critical Hexaplaric Septuagint text. The other books are not now extant. In 416, when Augustine asked to consult Jerome's revised Septuagint, the latter had to inform the African bishop that, due to someone's deceit, he no longer had a copy of the other books.

By 390, Jerome had become convinced of the necessity to make a fresh translation of the Old Testament from the Hebrew text, and, encouraged by friends and the desire to demolish the arguments of the Jews, he began to translate each of the books of the Hebrew canon, a task which was not completed until 406. It is probable that Jerome began this new translation with the books of Samuel and Kings. After explaining that the Hebrew canon has three divisions, Law, Prophets and 'Hagiographa', Jerome goes on to say:

> This preface to the scriptures may serve as a 'helmeted' introduction to all the books which I translate from Hebrew into Latin . . . Read first, then, my Samuel and Kings; mine, I say, mine. For whatever by careful translation and cautious correction I have learnt and comprehended, is my very own. And when you understand anything of which you were ignorant before, either (if you are grateful) consider me a translator, or (if ungrateful) a paraphraser, although I am not at all conscious of having deviated from the Hebrew original.
>
> (*Preface to Samuel and Kings*)

It sounds as if Jerome is writing this preface as a general introduction to his whole translation of the Old Testament, discussing the contents and limits of the Old Testament canon. He refers to the preface as 'helmeted' (*galeatus*) because he arms himself in advance to defend himself from the critics he knows will rise up against him.

Soon after he had finished the translation of Samuel and Kings, Jerome started on Job, the Psalter and the Prophets. His friend Sophronius made an 'elegant Greek translation' of Jerome's rendering of Job and the Psalter, and in *Epistle* 49, composed in 393–4, he informs Pammachius that he has translated the 16 prophets (thus including Daniel) and Job, of which he will be able to borrow a copy from his cousin Marcella. Of this book, Jerome says: 'Read it both in Greek and Latin, and compare the old version with my rendering. You will then see clearly that the difference between them is that between truth and falsehood.' He also tells Pammachius that he has translated Samuel and Kings. The omission of Psalms must have been an oversight on Jerome's part. Ezra, Nahum and Chronicles were translated in 394–5.

It was not until late 404 and early 405 that Jerome translated any more of the Hebrew Old Testament. He gives no reason for the long delay in completing the project, but it is very probably due to his involvement in the Origenist controversy from 393 till 402–3, and also to the fact that he wrote several commentaries in this period. He first translated the Pentateuch, having been asked to by his friend Desiderius. His preface makes it clear that he thinks there is still a good deal to be done before his translation of the Old Testament would be complete.

Next, he translated Joshua, Judges and Ruth, in early 405. In the preface, he expresses his relief at having finished the Pentateuch: 'Having at last finished Moses' Pentateuch, I feel like a man released from a crippling load of debt.' The rest of the Old Testament books were completed by early 406, thus bringing a labour of some 14 years to an end.

Implications for the canon

One of the major results of Jerome's translations of biblical books was the resolution (to his own satisfaction) of the question of the canon of scripture. In Jerome's early works, he often quotes from 'apocryphal' books; that is, books which were not in the Hebrew Bible, but were accepted by Christians because they were included in the Septuagint version. The Greek Septuagint had been the accepted Christian version of the Old Testament since the second century, and it had taken on the mantle of divine inspiration. Several different versions of the Greek Old Testament existed in Jerome's day, and this diversity was one of the main reasons that he undertook the long task of translating the biblical books from the original languages. His most balanced statement on the relation between his translation from Hebrew and the older versions is seen in the *Preface to Samuel and Kings*:

> I beg you, brother, not to think that my work is in any way meant to debase the old translators. Each one offers what he can to the service of the tabernacle of God; some gold and silver and precious stones, others linen and blue and purple and scarlet; we shall do well if we offer skins and goats' hair.

There are several lists of canonical books in Jerome's writings. One such is found in *Epistle* 53.8, where Jerome includes all the books in the Hebrew Bible, but the order in which they are recorded is influenced by the Septuagint canon in two ways. First, the Minor Prophets are placed before the other prophetic books, and second, Daniel is placed at the end of the Prophets, ostensibly as one of them. This is a good example of the ambivalent attitude Jerome showed towards the canon; the serious scholar is influenced by the Hebrew canon, while the churchman cannot stray too far from the revered tradition of the Septuagint canon (Brown 1993: 62–71).

As regards the New Testament canon, Jerome's views are relatively straightforward. He affirms the books which are now in the New Testament canon, with the possible exception of 2 and 3 John, concerning which he expresses some doubt about whether they were composed by John the apostle or John the presbyter. However, he includes both in the canon (*de viris illustribus* 9). He did much to stabilize the opinion of the western church concerning the position of the epistle to the Hebrews and the book of Revelation. He recognized that various sections of the church rejected these books because of doubt concerning their apostolic authorship, but says:

The epistle called 'to the Hebrews' is received not only by the churches in the east, but also by all church writers of the Greek language before our own time, as being written by Paul the apostle, though many think that it is by Barnabas or Clement. And it makes no difference whose it is, since it is from a church-man, and is celebrated in the daily readings of the churches. And if the usage of the Latins does not receive it among the canonical scriptures, neither do the Greek churches receive the Revelation of John. And yet we receive both, because we do not follow today's habit, but the authority of ancient writers, who for the most part quote each of them . . . . as canonical and churchly.[7]

Other translation work

Jerome did not restrict his translation activities solely to scripture. He is also responsible for translating into Latin a considerable number of Greek theological works (Brown 1993: 91–6; Kelly 1975: 73–7). The first of these translations was made in 380, when he rendered Eusebius of Caesarea's *Chronicle* into Latin. Having spent several years studying the works of Greek theologians, Jerome was apparently anxious that the Latin-speaking world should have the opportunity of benefiting from their scholarship. Interestingly enough, Jerome was not content, with this particular work, simply to translate; he omitted sections he thought unnecessary and added a new section, bringing the *Chronicle* up to date and thereby providing the western world with a history of the world from Abraham to 379.

Jerome then turned to translating into Latin the works of Origen, from whose exegetical writings he had learned so much. Jerome was interested in translating most, if not all, of Origen's works, but was prevented from doing so by a painful eye irritation caused by constant reading, and by a lack of copyists owing to a shortage of money. Jerome did succeed, however, in translating quite a number of Origen's homilies. He also translated a work of Didymus the Blind, *On the Holy Spirit*, from Greek into Latin. This work, along with some of Origen's homilies, is now lost in Greek, and Jerome's translation is the only way we can know these important works today.

Biblical commentaries

By far the major part of Jerome's literary output is in commentary form. He states that the purpose of a commentary is 'to discuss what is obscure, to touch on the obvious, to dwell at length on what is doubtful' (*Commentary on Galatians* 4.6). Scripture, for Jerome, was full of obscurities and a reliable guide is needed. A commentary ought to 'repeat the opinions of the many . . . so that the judicious reader, when he has perused the different explanations . . . . may judge which is the best and, like a good banker, reject the money from a spurious mint' (*Apology against Rufinus* 1.16).

In most of his commentaries, Jerome acknowledges the previous authors from whom he has borrowed, and they are valuable because they transmit a great wealth of comments from other scholars, some of which would otherwise have been lost.

Jerome wrote commentaries on almost all the books of the Old Testament, and on some of the New Testament. One of Jerome's earliest works was the *Hebrew Questions on Genesis*, which was more a grammatical and etymological study of some passages in Genesis. He paid special attention to the (supposed) meaning and etymology of Hebrew words, and intended it to be the first of a series of such volumes. He dropped this project, however, when he began his translation of the Hebrew text of the Old Testament. The work dates from about 390 (Hayward 1995: 23–7). A little earlier, in 386–7, Jerome wrote his *Commentary on Ecclesiastes*, dedicated to the young widow Blesilla, whom Jerome had taught in Rome. He used Origen as his main source, but the short work shows some traces of originality. It is based on the Hebrew text.

During the period 391 and 406, Jerome wrote commentaries on all the Minor Prophets. Most notable among these is the *Commentary on Jonah*. It is interesting because it follows earlier Christian exegesis of this story in seeing in Jonah a pre-figurement of Christ and his resurrection. He translated it first from the Hebrew and then from the Greek text, and gave a double exegesis, first literal then spiritual. Jerome treated the story as genuinely historical and argued strongly that Jonah really did spend three days in the belly of the whale. On the spiritual level, he argued for Jonah as a 'type' of Christ, and interpreted many of the details of the story in this light. Thus Jonah's fleeing from the Lord's face points to the Son's descent from the heavenly realm, and his preaching to Nineveh points to Christ's post-resurrection command to preach to the nations (Duval 1973).

The *Commentary on Daniel*, composed in 407, is a study of selected passages from Daniel, based on Jerome's own translation from the Hebrew. This is one of Jerome's most interesting commentaries, for he spends much of the book criticizing the anti-Christian polemic of the third century Neoplatonist philosopher, Porphyry. The latter had argued (correctly) that Daniel was not a prophecy dating from the sixth century BCE, but rather a tract for the times, written to encourage Jews who were suffering persecution at the hands of Antiochus IV Epiphanes in 167–164 BCE. Jerome, on the other hand, rejected this interpretation and argued that the revelation of Christ was to be found throughout the book. So, for instance, he suggests that 'the stone . . . cut from a mountain by no human hand' (Dan. 2:45), was none other than the Saviour who was conceived without human intercourse.[8]

Jerome's most extensive commentary was on Isaiah, finished in 410, and consisting of 18 books, each with its own preface. Jerome laboured under the false impression that Isaiah was the work of one man, but followed his normal practice of alternating literal and spiritual exegesis, although he reproduced the Greek version only where it differed significantly from the Hebrew, in order to avoid excessive length (Jay 1985).

Jerome's final commentary on the Old Testament was his unfinished work on Jeremiah. This was begun in 414 or 415, and was interrupted by Jerome's involvement in the Pelagian controversy. The commentary covers only 32 of Jeremiah's 52 chapters, but contains several interesting features. There is an increasing emphasis on the Hebrew text, and he argues that the LXX text was unreliable as it had been corrupted by copyists (*Commentary on Jeremiah* 17:1–4). Also interesting is the fact that Jerome criticizes his former hero, Origen, very severely. This is probably because of the Pelagians (who considered themselves to be the disciples of Origen), against whose beliefs Jerome wrote a treatise at this time (*Dialogue against the Pelagians*). A third point of interest in this commentary is the fact that Jerome concentrates on the straight forward, literal interpretation of the text, rather than on allegorical exegesis. This may be partly because of the nature of Jeremiah's text and partly because Jerome was writing for his friend Eusebius of Cremona, who preferred the literal sense (Kelly 1975: 316).

Literal and allegorical exegesis

Jerome assigned great value to the literal sense of scripture. Even in his very first piece of exegesis on the call of Isaiah, Jerome begins with a strictly literal historical exposition of 'who this Uzziah was, how many years he had reigned and who among the other kings were his contemporaries' (*Epistle* 18A.1). Only after this does he move on to the spiritual interpretation of the passage.

Again, in his *Commentary on Ephesians*, composed in 388, Jerome interprets 'Therefore it is said, "Awake, O sleeper, and arise from the dead, and Christ shall give you light"' by explaining that the words were spoken to Adam who was buried at Calvary where Christ was crucified. The place was called Calvary because the head of some ancient man had been buried there and because, when Christ was crucified, he was hanging directly above the place where it was buried. It is likely, though Jerome does not acknowledge it, that he was mainly dependent here on a work by Apollinarius of Laodicea.[9]

While Jerome followed the Antiochene school's emphasis on the priority of the historical sense, he nevertheless believed that Christians must go beyond this to discover the fuller, deeper meaning of a passage. It was possible to understand this deeper meaning only with the aid of the allegorical or spiritual method.

When we study Jerome's allegorical exegesis, we see that he takes many of the specific interpretations directly from Origen, even to the extent of verbal borrowing. This is the case both before the Origenist controversy, in which Jerome played a leading part (393–402), and later on, when Jerome had renounced Origen's theology as heretical. The influence of Origen, whom Jerome had once proudly called 'my master', can be seen on almost every page of Jerome's writings.

One example of the influence of Origen is seen in the *Commentary on Matthew*. This is an interesting example because Origen's comments on this gospel are also extant. Jerome wrote his *Commentary on Matthew* in just 14 days, in order to provide a friend with some reading matter on a long sea voyage. In his interpretation of the parable of the hidden treasure (*Commentary on Matthew* 13:44ff.) Jerome has clearly followed Origen, though not slavishly. The main points of their respective interpretations are set out below:

> *Jerome*: The treasure is the word of God which appears to be hidden in the body of Christ, or the holy scriptures in which rests the knowledge of the Saviour. When the treasure is discovered, one must give up al other benefits in order to possess it.
>
> *Origen*: This is not a parable but a similitude. The field is the scripture. The

treasure is the mysteries lying within the scripture, and finding the treasure a man hides it, thinking it dangerous tо reveal to all and sundry the secrets of scripture. He goes, sells all his possessions, and works until he can buy the field, in order that he may possess the great treasure.

Jerome's interpretation appears to have links with Origen, in addition to the similarities one would expect in the interpretation of this parable. Yet Jerome's interpretation is simpler and more direct than that of Origen in its application of the meaning of the parable. Jerome is not interested in Origen's distinction between a parable and a similitude, the latter being a generic term, the former a particular form of similitude. Jerome sets down two different interpretations of the treasure – it is either the word of God hidden in the body of Christ, or it is the knowledge of the Saviour hidden in scripture. His first interpretation does not stem from Origen, but comes rather from Jerome's characteristic ascetic interests.

It is not only specific passages of spiritual interpretation which Jerome borrows from Origen in the *Commentary on Matthew*, but, more significantly, certain themes. One of these, very important for Origen, was the goodness of God, which he used to combat the Gnosticism of the day. This theme is seen running through Jerome's own *Commentary on Matthew*, even though Gnosticism was not a problem against which Jerome had to fight in his own situation.

Towards the end of his life, after the trauma of the Origenist controversy, it is interesting to note that Jerome was more critical of some of Origen's contentious exegetical interpretations, though he continued to use several specific examples of Origen's exegesis. This trend may be seen most clearly in his *Commentary on Jeremiah*, where Origen is denounced as 'that allegorist!', his unorthodox views are fiercely attacked, and where Jerome relies less than in any other commentary on Origen's allegorical interpretations.

Jerome, then, used to his own advantage specific interpretations from representatives of both the Alexandrian and Antiochene schools. He was also the only church Father in the fourth century to learn Hebrew, having taken lessons from leading Jewish scholars.

Use of Jewish interpretations

One of the reasons Jerome is important in the history of biblical interpretation is because he used many Jewish interpretations of scriptural passages. Jerome believed that Jewish traditions of exegesis were of great importance for Christians in their interpretation of the Old Testament, so long as they were consistent with the teaching of the Bible.

In his *Commentary on Daniel* 5:2, Jerome records the following Jewish tradition concerning Belshazzar:

> The Hebrews hand down a story of this sort: Belshazzar, thinking that God's promise had remained without effect until the 70th. year, by which Jeremiah had said that the captivity of the Jewish people would have to be ended [cf. Jer. 25:12; 29:10ff.] – a matter of which Zechariah also speaks in the first part of his book [cf. Zech. 1:12ff.] – and turning the occasion of the failed promise

into a celebration, gave a great banquet by way of mocking the expectation of the Jews and the vessels of the Temple of God.

Jeremiah had promised Israel that their exile would be temporary. After 70 years they would return to their own land and glory in the destruction of their oppressors, the Babylonians. The chronological problem is to determine which year begins the 70-year period. In *Megillah* 11b it is explained that Belshazzar began his count with the first year of Nebuchadnezzar's reign (605 BCE). This Rabbinic source explicitly says that Belshazzar was mistaken in his calculations, a point which is implicit in Jerome's statement. The 70-year period should have begun from the second year of Nebuchadnezzar's reign, not the first (cf. 2 Kgs. 24:1).

Scholars studying Jerome's use of rabbinic traditions have usually assumed that he had taken those traditions direct from Jewish sources. There are, however, a few instances where it is clear that he has copied out the Jewish material from the writings of Origen, who also made some use of Jewish traditions.[10] One example is seen in one of his early letters (*Epistle* 18A.15), dealing with the topic of the two Seraphim in Isa. 6:6–9, where Jerome makes a comparison between Isaiah and Moses. He says that he had discussed this with some Jews, and reassures his reader that this tradition comes from an excellent (Jewish) source and should be accepted. Jerome gives the impression that he has gleaned this tradition from direct conversation and study with Jews. In fact, however, he borrowed it from Origen who had reported it in his sixth *Homily on Isaiah*, saying that both Isaiah and Moses had refused God's command at first, on the basis of their unworthiness, but had subsequently accepted.

JEROME THE CONTROVERSIALIST

Jerome several times became involved in theological controversies. As we have seen, he wrote two treatises on virginity, *Against Helvidius on the Perpetual Virginity of Mary*, where he argues against the monk Helvidius that Mary remained a virgin after the birth of Jesus, and *Against Jovinian*, combating the claim that matrimony is a higher state than virginity. He also wrote *Against Vigilantius*, where he vigorously defends the cult of the saints; *Against John of Jerusalem*, in which Jerome became involved in the Origenist controversy; *Apology against Rufinus*, in which Jerome hurls abuse against one of his former friends, following a dispute over the works of Origen; and the *Dialogue against the Pelagians*, Jerome's last polemic, in which he argues against the Pelagian notion that man could live without sin, and on the need for infant baptism.

Some of Jerome's controversies were relatively good-natured. Jerome's younger contemporary, Augustine, initiated a correspondence between the two. Augustine criticized Jerome for taking the position (in *Commentary on Galatians* 2:11) that, when Paul chastised Peter at Antioch over eating food with gentile converts, there was really no difference of opinion between the two apostles. Augustine argued that Jerome's interpretation of this passage showed Paul's rebuke of Peter to have been deliberately simulated. This, according to Augustine, meant that a passage of scripture contained a falsehood, and this meant that the truth of the *whole* Bible was put in jeopardy. The vagaries of the postal system meant that Jerome did not receive Augustine's criticisms until years later (see Kelly 1975: 265–7). When he did finally reply, Jerome essentially ignored Augustine's criticism, but made a veiled warning that, if the younger man persisted in criticizing his exegesis, he could expect much harsher treatment in future.

Jerome's other 'controversial' writings were more bitter. These polemical works do not reveal Jerome as a deeply speculative or innovative thinker, but rather as a vigorous and vitriolic defender of the faith and of his own reputation. The most important theologically was his involvement in the 'Origenist' controversy. Jerome had been an admirer of Origen, but, when the dispute between Epiphanius, the fanatical bishop of Salamis in Cyprus, and bishop John of Jerusalem broke, Jerome sided with the former, while Jerome's old friend Rufinus took the side of the latter. Jerome was more concerned to justify his own reputation as an orthodox thinker rather than with the question of Origen's orthodoxy. Jerome wrote:

> I revered him [Origen] as an exegete, not as a theologian – for his genius not his faith, as a philosopher rather than an apostle; believe me I have never been an Origenist.
>
> *(Epistle 46)*

Early in 397, Jerome wrote a ferocious attack on bishop John of Jerusalem (*Against John of Jerusalem*) in which he demolished John's arguments in favour of Origen, and heaped numerous insults on John personally. Jerome found the bishop's beliefs dangerously ambiguous, avoiding the real issues in the dispute and riddled with heresy. On the crucial issue of the state of the body of Christ and of Christians after the resurrection, Jerome was at pains to show, in an extended analytical passage, that John's teaching was hopelessly inadequate; he had always spoken of the resurrection of the body, never of the resurrection of the flesh (*Against John of Jerusalem* 23–6). Jerome ridiculed John on a personal level, labelling him as grovelling, arrogant and insufferably proud.

Jerome and John of Jerusalem were finally reconciled later in 397 in the Church of the Resurrection in Jerusalem. He was never to be reconciled with his erstwhile friend, Rufinus, however. In 398, Rufinus translated Origen's *On First Principles*, and composed *The Falsification of the Works of Origen*, in which he propounded the thesis that Origen's writings had been interpolated wholesale by heretics, and that this accounted for all the unorthodox passages. Jerome was incensed both by the translation and by Rufinus' support for Origen. He immediately produced his own literal translation of *On First Principles* and wrote a scathing letter (*Epistle 84*) in which he set out his own attitude to Origen, playing down his early enthusiasm, and appealing to some of his own commentaries to justify his acceptance of some of Origen's judgements and interpretations, but not his doctrines. Rufinus countered with the *Apology against Jerome* in 401, charging Jerome with adapting and reproducing uncritically some of Origen's worst theses. Rufinus argued that, if Jerome was denouncing Origen, he was really denouncing himself.

Jerome's reply came immediately and was full of indignant rage. This two part invective firstly justified Jerome's own actions, and then launched into a violent castigation of Rufinus. In the following year, Jerome added a third part to this tirade against Rufinus. This has been described as 'quite extreme in its violence' (Murphy 1952: 153). It added little to what he had already written in the *Apology against Rufinus*, reinforcing the charges of heresy, falsehood and provocative translations. It is a bitter, malicious and spiteful attack on Rufinus' person. Rufinus did not reply to this work, but Jerome continued to direct abuse at him even after Rufinus' death.

What Jerome's part in the Origenist controversy shows is the depths to which he was prepared to sink in order to uphold what he believed to be orthodox Christian beliefs as well as his own reputation as a biblical scholar and orthodox believer.

JEROME THE PERSON AND HIS LEGACY

As a man, Jerome was prodigiously hard-working, often studying or writing into the early hours, labouring, even when ill, to finish letters or larger works. He composed the *Commentary on Matthew* in just two weeks, for instance, so that his friend Eusebius of Cremona would have something to read on an imminent sea voyage. He had to work at astonishing speed to get this finished on time, and it should be no surprise that he made historical errors, and that some parts of the gospel are given very cursory treatment. In many ways, Jerome was not a perfectionist; he did not work and re-work material until it was perfect. Rather, he responded to the immediate needs of his friends, who often asked for advice or help of one sort or another.

Jerome could be, as with Eusebius of Cremona, extremely generous, both with his time and talents. He could also be extremely vicious in his attacks on former friends or teachers. Rufinus, as we have seen, had been a very close friend in Jerome's youth, but Jerome turned against him viciously after the Origenist controversy. Jerome's malicious temperament is also seen during the Origenist controversy in the open hostility he shows towards Origen, the man he had formerly called 'The greatest teacher of the church after the apostles' (Preface to the *Book of the Interpretations of Hebrew Names*). Jerome summarizes the heretical views put forward in *On First Principles* but often distorts Origen's opinions. He unjustly accuses Origen of having denied the Incarnation, misrepresents Origen's views on the salvation of the Devil, the transmigration of souls, and the resurrection (*Epistle* 124.2, 4, 8, 11).

As a scholar, Jerome was essentially eclectic. He searched diligently in the works of others and drew the best points from each, while avoiding their errors. This holds true also of the different 'schools' of interpretation accessible to Jerome – Alexandrian, Antiochene and Jewish.

From the Antiochene school, Jerome learned that an interpreter of the Bible must first study and explain the literal, plain sense and only after this has been accomplished should he venture beyond this to the deeper, spiritual interpretation. From the Alexandrian school, especially from Origen, Jerome borrowed many specific allegorical interpretations. Jerome cites Alexandrian authors much more frequently than he does Antiochenes, but the reason for this is not necessarily that he was more in tune with the principles of the former, but rather that the works of Alexandrian exegetes were more readily accessible to him, and also that the Antiochene school was still in its youth when Jerome was writing, and had produced a relatively small collection of commentaries from which he could borrow. From Jewish exegesis, Jerome learned the primary importance of the original text of the Old Testament, so that he was unique among the early Church Fathers in his use of the Hebrew text as the basis of his exegesis of the Old Testament.

Even during his lifetime, Jerome was held by many to be a great authority on the interpretation of the Bible. Jerome's contemporary Sulpicius Severus wrote in 405: 'I would be surprised if he [Jerome] were not already known to you through his writings since he is read throughout the world' (*Dialogues* 1.8).

In the centuries following Jerome's death, he was universally acknowledged as the prince of Christian biblical scholars, and his works became a fertile ground for the labours of subsequent exegetes. The reasons for this fame were twofold. First, Jerome's translation of the Bible became accepted everywhere as the standard biblical text in the western church; second, Jerome's immense and intimate knowledge and understanding of the Bible surpassed that of any other Christian scholar for centuries.

Although Jerome wrote commentaries on several of the Pauline letters and on Matthew's gospel, it is for his Old Testament commentaries that he is chiefly remembered. He is the only ancient author who commented on *all* the books of the Major and Minor Prophets. Jerome saw it as his special task to explain these Old Testament books, because they were more difficult to understand than the books of the New Testament. Jerome's enormous erudition is exhibited on every page of his writings. He quotes frequently from classical authors, as well as from the Bible and other Christian writers. In addition, Jerome, with his highly developed powers of observation, makes many suggestive and original contributions to the understanding of the biblical text.

The writings of Jerome are of lasting value to Christians today because they offer a splendid example of the state of biblical interpretation in the West in the fourth century, because they give us an interesting insight into relations between Christians and Jews in the generations after Christianity became the religion of the state, and also because they paint for us, in vivid colours, a picture of the 'irascible monk' who devoted his life to the study of the sacred scriptures – in his own words: 'What other life can there be without the knowledge of the scriptures, for through these Christ himself, who is the life of the faithful, becomes known' (*Epistle* 30.7).

NOTES

1 On Jerome's use of classical authors, see Hagendahl (1974).

2 For fuller information on Jerome's education, see Kelly: (1975: 10–17).

3 On this, see Kelly (1975: 104–23); *Apology* 3.22; *Epistle* 108: 7–14.

4 Epistle 22 is a long treatise on the virtues of virginity, and the rules by which virgins should organize their daily lives.

5 *Ep.* 22.30; *Ep.* 5.2. On Jerome's knowledge of textual critical methods, see Brown (1993: 21–54).

6 Hort (1881: 81–2); Metzger (1963: 121–41); for versions of the Old Latin texts, see Metzger (1977: 321–2).

7 *Ep.* 129.3. On Jerome and the canon, see Howarth (1908–12).
8 *Comm. Dan.* 2:45. See Braverman (1978).
9 *Commentary on Ephesians* 5:18. See Grützmacher (1901: 40).
10 On these, see Braverman (1978), Penna (1950) and Jay (1985).

BIBLIOGRAPHY

Barr , James (1966) 'St. Jerome's Appreciation of Hebrew', *Bulletin of the John Rylands Library* 49: 280–302.

Braverman, Jay (1978) *Jerome's Commentary on Daniel. A Study of Comparative Jewish and Christian Interpretations of the Hebrew Bible.* Catholic Biblical Quarterly Monograph Series, 7. Washington, DC: Catholic University Press.

Brown, Dennis (1993) *Vir Trilinguis: A Study in the biblical Exegesis of Saint Jerome.* Kampen: Kok Pharos.

Cavallera, Frederic (1922) *Saint Jérôme. Sa Vie et son oeuvre.* 2 vols. Leuven: Peeters.

Chapman, John (1923) 'St. Jerome and the Vulgate New Testament' *Journal of Theological Studies* 24: 33–51, 113–25, 282–99.

Duval, Yves–Marie (1973) *Le Livre de Jonas dans la littérature chretienne grecque et latine: sources et influence du commentaire sur Jonas de saint Jérôme,* 2 vols. Paris: Etudes Augustiniennes.

Grützmacher, Georg (1901*) Hieronymus: Eine biographische Studie zur alten Kirchengeschichte,* Vol. 1. Leipzig: Scientia Verlag Aalen.

Hagendahl, Hans (1974) 'Jerome and the Latin Classics', *Vigiliae Christianae* 28: 216–27.

Hayward, Robert (1995*) Jerome's Hebrew Questions on Genesis.* Oxford: Clarendon Press.

Hort, Fenton John (with Westcott, Brooke Foss) (1881) *The New Testament in the Original Greek. Vol. ii Introduction.* Cambridge: Cambridge University Press.

Howarth, Harold (1908–12) 'The Influence of St. Jerome on the Canon of the Western Church', *Journal of Theological Studies* 10: 481–96; 11: 321–47; 13: 1–18.

Hulley, Karl (1944) 'Principles of Textual Criticism known to St. Jerome', *Harvard Studies in Classical Philology* 55: 87–109.

Jay, Pierre (1985) *L'Exégèse de saint Jérôme d'après son Commentaire sur Isaie.* Paris: Etudes Augustiniennes.

Kelly, John (1975*) Jerome. His Life, Writings and Controversies.* London: Duckworth.

Metzger, Bruce (1963) 'Recent Spanish Contributions to the Textual Criticism of the New Testament', in Bruce Metzger, *Chapters in the History of New Testament Textual Criticism* Leiden: E. J. Brill, 121–41.

—— (1977) *The Early Versions of the New Testament.* Oxford: Oxford University Press.

Murphy, Francis Xavier (ed.) (1952) *A Monument to Saint Jerome.* New York: Sheed & Ward.

Penna, Alphonse (1950) *Principi e carattere dell' esegesi di S. Gerolamo.* Rome: Gregorian University.

Siguenza, Fray José (1907) *The Life of Saint Jerome.* trans. of 1595 Spanish original by Mariana Monteiro. London: Sands & Co.

Sutcliffe, Edward (1948) 'The Name "Vulgate"', *Biblica* 29: 245–52.

CHAPTER FORTY-SEVEN

AMBROSE

——— •✦• ———

Ivor Davidson

Books profiling the leading figures of the early church tend to commit one of three crimes against Ambrose, bishop of Milan from 374 to 397. Very often they trivialize him, reducing his significance to that of supporting actor to the real protagonist of the later West, Augustine, whose creative genius and theological influence more or less totally eclipse the gifts of the one under whose spell he took his decisive steps towards Christianity in the first place. At best, Ambrose merits a bland paragraph or two outlining his impact upon Augustine, with a few predictable phrases explaining that he was in any case first and foremost a 'man of action', which (however true) is apparently intended to suggest that his intellectual abilities were slight. In other surveys, conversely, Ambrose is idolized, depicted as the stained-glass saint, other-worldly to the core, staunch champion of truth against error and sponsor of the rights of the church against every hubristic claim from secular authority. Icon of holiness and fearless defender of the faith, he appears to have scarcely a shortcoming at all. Third, worst of all, and remarkably often, Ambrose has been ignored altogether. The assumption apparently is that, *doctor* of the church or no, he holds little interest for those concerned to trace the big picture of Christianity's development. In far too many undergraduate church history syllabuses, and in the textbooks which they spawn, Ambrose scarcely merits a mention.

Each of these treatments is, wittingly or unwittingly, an injustice to an individual whose role in the formation of Christianity in the West was in fact both remarkable and complex. Ambrose deserves far better. Thankfully, there are signs that he is starting to receive it. Recent years have witnessed the publication of a number of sophisticated studies which seek to explore the man in his own context and to appreciate and critique his achievements in the light of the significant advances that have taken place in our understanding of the social and political world to which he belonged (especially McLynn 1994; Williams 1995; see also Markschies 1995: 84–212; Savon 1997). It is increasingly acknowledged (a) that Ambrose does merit a serious place in the history books, and (b) that he can only be accessed by reading between the narrow lines of a hagiography which has deftly but dangerously abstracted him from the realities of his time. We now know that his successes were far harder won than a good deal of earlier scholarship (e.g. de Labriolle 1928; von Campenhausen 1929; Palanque 1933; Homes Dudden 1935; Paredi 1964a) could or would perceive; that Ambrose struggled against considerable opposition for much of his episcopal career, and often survived not just by dint of an unbending spiritual fidelity but also because of his ability to improvise in tight corners. Sanctity of character and steadfastness of doctrine are undoubtedly relevant categories in any summary of Ambrose's qualities, but they are not the only ones: words like 'brinkmanship', 'chutzpah', and 'effrontery' might also be deployed. The shrewdness of the political operator, the theatricality of the demagogue, and the evocative powers of the image-maker all had a part in his make-up and contributed to his ultimate achievement.

In the attempt to escape both patronizing dismissal and uncritical veneration, however, it is easy to fall prey to yet another danger. If we are not careful, we can create the impression that Ambrose's significance was little more than political, and that his political success in itself should be interpreted with a strong dose of cynicism (cf. Ramsey 1997: ix). The quest for the historical Ambrose, the attempt to strip away the accretions of a reverential portraiture which left the real man buried beneath the weight of his own glory, can equally readily fashion an individual after its own image: reconstructions of Ambrose the saint can, with little difficulty, be replaced by reconstructions of Ambrose the Machiavellian. Either way, the enigma,

Figure 47.1   Icon of St Ambrose. Copyright the Holy Transfiguration Monastery, Boston.

the opacity of his actual motives, drives, and successes may remain untouched. Naturally, no sketch of Ambrose or of any other historical figure can in the end be anything other than a fictive attempt to capture its subject's personality; all that any canvas presents is an interpreted image, the individual as seen from one perspective or another. But the task for the sensitive historian must be to steer a *via media* between the equal and opposite extremes of seeing Ambrose only as an idol to be venerated or as a political phantom whose inner personality is obscure to the point of unreality.

Mindful of the pitfalls that lurk around our path, we shall in this sketch seek to explore Ambrose in a three-pronged approach. First, we shall look at his context, the kind of influences and perspectives which formed him, and the circumstances of his elevation to the episcopate. Second, we shall consider his quest to find his own role as a Christian leader, as one catapulted out of a civil career, with little or no spiritual or theological preparation, and charged with stabilizing an ecclesiastical situation fraught with factional tensions. This must involve us in an examination of developments which belong in the political realm, for although Ambrose was more than just a politician it was through his participation in many of the public events of his time that he carved out his distinctive niche as a churchman. Even in an age when politics and theology were exceptionally intertwined, Ambrose exercised an unparalleled influence upon political affairs. Finally, we shall try to evaluate the larger-scale results of that quest for self-definition as seen in the ecclesial community which Ambrose laboured to construct, both in Milan and further afield. In the end, his legacy is the specific character that he created for the public face of the Nicene faith on the stage of the western empire.

CONTEXT, FORMATION AND ELECTION

Ambrose's early life

Aurelius Ambrosius did not come from the top drawer of senatorial society, but he did hail from a privileged background. He was born at Trier, probably early in 339 (Palanque 1933: 480–2, 542–3), while his father served at the court of Constantine II, almost certainly as praetorian prefect of the Gauls, a high-level role which carried administrative responsibility for a vast area of Western Europe (Fischer 1984; Mazzarino 1989: 75–82). Ambrose senior died young, leaving his widow with three children: a girl, Marcellina, and two boys, Uranius Satyrus, and Ambrose junior. The family moved to Rome (probably returning to a property they already held), and the metropolis became the future bishop's adopted home. His late father's office did not afford him an automatic entrée into patrician society; he and his brother had to earn their place among an aristocratic set by cultivating the appropriate social *mores*. They passed through an education in 'the liberal arts', receiving the standard training in classical literature, rhetoric, and law which equipped young men for a career in the imperial civil service. Ambrose's schooling in the *quadriga* of Cicero, Virgil, Terence and Sallust remained with him for the rest of his days, profoundly influencing the style and texture of his speech and writing.

Their household established itself firmly in Roman Christian society. Marcellina took vows of chastity and received the veil from Pope Liberius in the new basilica of St Peter's, probably on the festival of Epiphany in 353. Marcellina adopted a life of domestic piety, residing in semi-seclusion with her family and a virginal companion, occupied in the kind of spiritual activities described so memorably by Jerome in his sketches of Lea, Paula and Marcella (*Epistles* 23, 108, 127) and above all in his famous *Epistle* 22 to Eustochium. Ambrose spent his youth in a household in which visits from clergymen were a regular event, and where talk of ecclesiastical affairs (such as news from the Council of Milan in 355) was part of regular conversation. Like plenty of other scions of Christian parentage, however, he and Satyrus remained unbaptized in childhood.

On completing their education, the brothers became advocates at the court of the praetorian prefect of Italy, Volcacius Rufinus, at Sirmium on the Danube. This choice of career path would not have been the fastest track to promotion for full-blooded aristocrats, who could count on their connections to open doors for them more directly, but it was a promising appointment for young men whose natural place was on the margins rather than at the core of the senatorial elite. As it turned out, both distinguished themselves as orators, and recognition was not long in coming. The fabulously wealthy Sextus Anicius Petronius Probus was appointed as Rufinus' successor in 368. Like many men of his type, Probus was a largely nominal Christian, but he had (particularly through his wife) significant connections with the church at Rome, and for the Ambrosii the associations were fortuitous. Ambrose soon became an assessor in Probus' *consiliarium*; then, in *c.* 372/3, he was raised to the rank of *consularis* and made governor of Aemilia-Liguria (Satyrus evidently received parallel favours, though the location of his governorship is unknown). This was a prestigious post which carried the title of *clarissimus* and brought jurisdiction – a responsibility for enforcing law and order, administering justice, and collecting taxes – over a considerable tract of north-west Italy. His headquarters were in Milan, which since the beginning of the century had steadily emerged as the principal urban centre in the western empire, now far more important in political terms than the mother-city, Rome.

The see of Milan had been occupied since 355 by Auxentius, a homoian Arian, or subscriber to the position that Christ the Son was not, as the Council of Nicaea had said, 'of the same substance' (*homoousios*) with God the Father, but 'like' (*homoios*) him (Hanson 1988: 557–97). A Cappadocian by birth, Auxentius had been appointed following the deposition of a pro-Nicene bishop, Dionysius, and he had survived more than one attempt from Nicene dissidents to remove him from office, including some serious broadsides from combatants as able as Hilary of Poitiers and Eusebius of Vercelli (Williams 1995: 38–68). He was a popular preacher, well-read in contemporary Greek theology, and a skilful player of church politics. He presided in an immense basilica, seating up to 3,000, the magnificence of which could hardly have failed to impress his parishioners.

Most importantly of all, Auxentius enjoyed the support of Valentinian I (emperor 364–75). A devout Christian, Valentinian aspired to religious neutrality, but while he resided in Milan in 364–5 he had issued an edict calling upon the city to rally behind the man who was after all its official bishop, and he had banished Hilary for protesting that Auxentius' heretical views debarred him from such support. The homoians constituted a clear majority within the Milanese church; the Nicenes could only observe and disapprove of Auxentius' hegemony from without, maintaining a separatist identity by meeting in private houses or by congregating at outdoor conventicles, typically held around the cemetery areas outside the city where their forebears of similar doctrinal sympathies were buried.

The appointment of Ambrose as bishop of Milan

In the autumn of 374 Auxentius died, and the city was thrown into turmoil. The pro-Nicenes demanded a say in the appointment of a successor, and infiltrated an official gathering of homoian clergy and people in Auxentius' basilica to press their case. There is no evidence that the dispute had turned violent, but Ambrose chose to intervene, arriving at the cathedral in person to deliver a stern official's speech on the necessity of keeping the peace. On the face of things, his motives were formal and juridical, an attempt to defuse a dangerous situation and forestall public disorder. In reality, he was seen to be endorsing the legitimacy of the Nicenes' effort to disrupt an official ceremony being held for the purposes of acclaiming a new, and inevitably homoian, candidate. As a son of the Roman church, and by now a catechumen, Ambrose's sympathies undoubtedly lay with the Nicene camp, but he could hardly have anticipated the outcome of his actions. According to Paulinus, his secretary-biographer, all of a sudden, in the midst of the uproar a child's voice was heard to cry, '*Ambrosius episcopus!*' ('Ambrose for bishop!'). At this sound, the story goes, the whole mood of the gathering changed: Arians and Catholics forgot their differences and united in a plea for their *consularis*, truly a wild-card candidate, to become bishop himself (Paulinus, *Vita Ambrosii* 6).

But Ambrose, by his actions seeking to distance himself from the unexpected outcome of the meeting (Paulinus, *Vita Ambros.* 6–9; Rufinus, *Historia Ecclesiastica* 2.11; Duval 1976), immediately left the church and resumed his administrative duties, deliberately ignoring the clamour for his election. He returned to his tribunal and, contrary to his usual practice (or so it is said – implausibly), passed a sentence of public torture on a number of people, in a bid to compromise his image as a just and humane adjudicator. His supporters, however, having followed him from the basilica, cried out that, as far as they were concerned, his sin could fall upon their heads; it made no difference to their wish that he be bishop. Ambrose had now received public acclamation to bolster the attestation already afforded him at the church gathering.

Retreating to his own home, he resorted to some more desperate expedients, this time entering into direct negotiation with his crowd of pursuers. First, he professed that he wished to devote himself to the life of a philosopher. Judging by the later evidence of his reading in philosophical texts, this may have been a genuine plea, but it too failed. Next he tried once more to disqualify himself morally by inviting prostitutes under his roof, but this elicited the same response as his previous attempt to compromise himself: 'Your sin be upon us.' Finally, he resolved to flee Milan. He left the city by night, destined for Pavia, but was discovered the next morning at the Porta Romana, the main triumphal route into Milan. From there he was escorted back into the city. It is improbable that the governor did not know which road to take; Ambrose appears to have deliberately staged the spectacle of a triumphal return, simultaneously frustrated in his attempt to escape yet buoyed up by a clear display of public support. Nevertheless, he still resisted ordination. An appeal was sent to Valentinian, but the accompanying report of Ambrose's attempts to escape was probably intercepted by the prefect Petronius Probus himself, who, as Ambrose's patron, had his own interests in engineering the right outcome. By the time the plea reached the emperor, it doubtless seemed a clear-cut case of sanctioning a candidate for whom there was unanimous popular approval. There is nothing to support the once-standard idea that Ambrose's election was an example of ordination purely by public acclamation (Gryson 1980: 269–73), but it is easy to imagine Valentinian's readiness to rubber-stamp the appointment of an able administrator whose candidacy was presented to him, however tendentiously, as a potential cure for Milan's doctrinal divisions. Meantime, Ambrose sought to flee once more, going into hiding at the estate of Leontius, one of his aristocratic friends. His aim was probably to ensure that if he was to be appointed bishop it would be with the express endorsement of the emperor, and not simply as the partisan choice of the pro-Nicenes. On the arrival of the appropriate response from Valentinian, the *vicarius*, Probus' deputy in Milan and Ambrose's immediate superior, issued an edict threatening severe punishment for anyone found harbouring the fugitive governor, and Leontius wasted no time in handing him over. In the end, we are told, Ambrose gave in, realizing that he could no longer resist the destiny that providence had in store for him (Paulinus, *Vita Ambros.* 9).

To modern eyes, the whole process appears bizarre. Ambrose had no theological training for a clerical role, and had not even been baptized. There is little reason to doubt his reluctance to accept the future being thrust upon him. It was common in the late Roman world for those elected to high public office formally to decline preferment, pleading unworthiness and inability, and the same convention became widespread in church life. Ambrose's refusal, though, must have been genuine enough. A talented young administrator with influential connections, security of tenure, and healthy prospects, he had little reason to desire the invidious task of holding together a community riven by conflicting tribal loyalties. However devout his background in Rome, he must scarcely have considered it likely that this could be his calling.

Nevertheless, his flair for stage-managing events was obvious in his handling of the circumstances in which he found himself. The episodes narrated by Paulinus are not hagiographical embellishments, designed merely to bolster an image of Ambrose's self-effacement. Rather, they reveal the earliest indications that the new bishop had a keen sense of the importance of public gestures (McLynn 1994: 44–52). Ambrose had been faced with a situation which must have surprised him and a prospect which he quickly realized he could not in the end escape. He turned it into a series of steps which ensured that he established his inherently shaky credentials on the best footing possible. First, he insisted upon receiving baptism only at the hands of a Catholic bishop. This was a clear gesture to the Nicenes, for whom baptism by any other brand of cleric would have been invalid. At the same time, he made sure that he was seen to identify with a clerical body that was firmly homoian. After baptism on Sunday, 1 December 374, he was ceremonially passed through each of the clerical grades, from doorkeeper to presbyter, in the course of one week, before being consecrated the following Sunday, 7 December (for a defence of the traditional date, see Faller 1942). This strategy was not a formal satisfaction of the canonical rule that a novice ought not to be elevated to the episcopate overnight (*pace* Gryson 1968: 225, n. 18; Williams 1995: 114–15, n. 48), nor is the account of it an apologetic fabrication by Paulinus (*pace* Fischer 1970; cf. Ramsey 1997: 20–1); rather, it provided a deliberate build-up to the finale of Ambrose's consecration. It successively associated him with each of the ranks in his church, and pre-empted a lengthy examination of his qualifications prior to the formal nomination ceremony on 7 December (McLynn 1994: 51).

As part of the final display, he publicly handed over his gold and silver to the church and to the poor (Paulinus, *Vita Ambros.* 38). This was no naive relinquishing of all his wealth, for the family estates, centred particularly in Africa (plus, it seems, some lands in Sicily), remained in his control, and his sister's needs at Rome were well provided for by the donation of a regular income from the property. It was designed, rather, to signal his new role as civic benefactor and patron of those in need. What must have happened in reality was that a proportion of the family assets were invested in Milan in order to help finance Ambrose's future strategy for managing his diocese.

Ambrose's qualifications and preparation for the episcopacy

Ambrose brought to the episcopate a specific complex of social, intellectual, and practical perspectives. Thanks to natural talent, hard work, and some assiduous networking, he had managed by his early thirties to attain high office in an imperial system which could well have passed over men of his background in favour of those whose *Romanitas* was of more venerable standing.

He had been shaped by the kind of opinions, pretensions and prejudices which typify those who have worked their way to a position of influence and power rather than enjoyed it by direct birthright. He remained profoundly affected by a concern for what 'men of the first rank' would think, for the sort of standards of public behaviour deemed appropriate for gentlemen, and the need to preserve a proper assurance and *gravitas* in social interaction – all of which are expected features in a culture where honour was a central value (see Chapter 1 of this volume). Traditional aristocratic assumptions about race, class, and social dignity are never far beneath the surface of his moralizing, despite all his altruistic language.

Ambrose also possessed a mind steeped in the literature and mythology of the classical world. Acutely conscious of his lack of preparation for his new role and the sudden obligation that it brought to teach and learn at the same time (*De officiis* 1.1–4; *De virginibus* 1.1–4; 2.1–5), he had to learn to apply his gifts to mastering a whole new field. His greatest asset in this area was that he had been trained to read Greek fluently. This skill proved invaluable as he set out to educate himself in the complexities of contemporary Christological discourse and the conventions of how to exegete biblical texts. He set himself a rigorous programme of reading in Philo, Origen, Basil, Didymus, Athanasius, and others, rapidly assimilating the Alexandrians' techniques of allegory and typology and learning to imitate standard moralizing expositions of biblical exemplars. Besides these authorities, he also studied Platonist texts, familiarizing himself with a philosophical literature which was popular among Milan's intelligentsia. Within a few years, his sermons would evince vestiges from Apuleius, Porphyry, and Plotinus, and his spirituality would be configured around the theme of a spiritual ascent towards wisdom – albeit conceptualized in new guise as a journey initiated in the waters of baptism and climaxing in an eschatological union with the God of Jesus Christ (Courcelle 1968: 93–138). Habitually, it seems, Ambrose made sure that his study was *visible* to his people: Augustine tells of how the Milanese would watch their bishop as he pored in silence over his books in whatever precious intervals he could snatch from an administrative and pastoral workload which must from the start have been very heavy (*Confessions* 6.3.3).

In addition, Ambrose had proved himself to be an accomplished rhetorician: his abilities in this field had helped to win him early distinction as an advocate at Sirmium. He would learn to harness these gifts to his new knowledge of theology, and his powerful and learned pulpit performances would soon mark him out as one of the most effective preachers of the patristic age, revered for the eloquent charm of his style (Augustine, *Conf.* 5.13.23). Ambrose played a large part in Augustine's conversion, so that it was by Ambrose that Augustine was eventually baptized, in 387 CE.

He had also acquired invaluable experience as an administrator and adjudicator. In an age when bishops, particularly in metropolitan sees like Milan, had become linchpins in the system of imperial bureaucracy (Hobbs and Wuellner 1980), he would require all of his organizational skills and all of his flair for negotiation and bargaining. Ambrose would find himself not only in charge of considerable financial and material assets, and responsible not just for (often fractious) human resources both in his own city and across North Italy, but would also become a hearer of civil disputes (the onerous work of the *audientia episcopalis*), a vital go-between and sponsor of diverse interests and causes at an imperial court, and a mediator and ambassador on political business. He always looked back on his life as a provincial governor in negative terms (*De paenitentia* 2.67, 72–3; *Off.* 1.4; cf. *Epistle extra collectionem* 14[63].65: Lenox-Conyngham 1982a), but without the training and expertise he had developed in his former career it is highly unlikely that he would have become the kind of episcopal leader that he proved to be.

DEVISING AN EPISCOPAL ROLE

The achievements of preaching, pastoring and leading, however, lay somewhat down the track: first, Ambrose had to work out a basic *modus operandi*. He had inherited a clerical body which remained dominated by homoian officials, and it was not practicable for him to make sweeping changes in his staff. His congregation, too, was predominantly loyal to the memory of Auxentius. He possessed neither the knowledge nor the experience necessary to take on those with whom he disagreed. Prudently, he chose to avoid confrontation, and concentrated on building up his profile

Figure 47.2 'The Saint [i.e. Augustine] baptized by Ambrose'. Painting by Niccolò di Pietro (fl. Venice 1394–1430) in the Vatican. Copyright the Pontifical Monuments, Museums and Galleries, the Vatican.

as bishop of the whole see, rather than playing directly to a pro-Nicene constituency. There is possible evidence that he sought the help of Basil of Caesarea to return to Milan the bones of Auxentius' Nicene predecessor, Dionysius, who had died in exile in Armenia, but it is uncertain whether the information (Basil, *Ep.* 197.2) is authentic: Ambrose may or may not have been able to venture such a gesture. What he did do was show favour to at least one notable former Catholic dissident, the venerable presbyter Simplicianus, who returned from Rome to become his baptismal instructor, and perhaps continued to act as a theological mentor beyond the initiation process (at an advanced age, Simplicianus would one day be nominated by his pupil as his successor in the see).

Ambrose's earliest attentions were devoted to the acquisition of theological knowledge, and he waited more than two years before he published his first written work. When it came, its subject was significant: *De virginibus*. The theme neatly avoided the doctrinal tensions in his church, and gave Ambrose an opportunity to establish a distinctive didactic voice of his own. He speaks as the brother of a consecrated virgin (the work is dedicated to Marcellina), and the son of a pious widow. His family associations with female asceticism are presented as implicitly qualifying him to give instruction on this subject at least, however unprepared he still is for a general teaching role. He draws particularly upon Athanasius and Cyprian, though the debts are barely signalled (Duval 1974). The Italian churches already had plenty of women consecrated to a life of domestic asceticism, but Ambrose preached a new variant on the theme. He called upon the young women of Milan to devote themselves to Christ and his church as a public dedication of their desire to escape the game of being used as financial pawns in marriages arranged by wealthy parents. In a bid to persuade their families to encourage such commitment, he argued that the presence of a consecrated virgin in a household would bring merit to cover the family's sins (*Virg.* 1.32). This kind of strategy provoked some resentment, for the bishop was interfering in the private affairs of the family; but it also won results (Riggi 1980; Brown 1988: 341–65; Savon 1989). Ambrose was able to stage impressive processions of young candidates coming forward in large numbers to receive the veil, some of them from as far afield as North Africa. The spectacle of these parades can only have boosted the fledgling bishop's prestige in the eyes of his public.

Preoccupation with outward form characterized other moves as well. Encountering a cleric who happened to walk in a fashion that displeased him, Ambrose set about dealing with him: the man was summoned before the bishop's tribunal, whereupon he promptly deserted the clergy rather than face the ire of his superior (*Off.* 1.72). The concern for correctness of gait nicely illustrates Ambrose's concern to ensure standards of public behaviour which would commend the church to the eyes of discerning onlookers; he could not institute a wholesale restaffing schedule, but he could make a few changes indirectly which would improve the appearance of his clerical body by raising its proficiency in the semiotics of classical good conduct. He himself adopted a lifestyle which combined these polite manners with a self-conscious austerity, devoting himself not only to study and prayer but also to frugality of dress and diet, including the observance of regular fasts (Paulinus, *Vita Ambros.* 38, speaks of his body being wasted by 'daily fasts'), all designed to demonstrate his consecration to asceticism (Augustine thought his chastity his one obvious hardship: *Conf.* 6.3.3).

Most strikingly of all in terms of public display, he set about a major church-building programme. In time, it would transform the religious landscape of Milan, as the city's suburbs came to be dominated by a series of towering edifices epitomizing the style of Ambrose's regime (see pp. 1198–9). Most of the construction took place in the 380s, but there is evidence that the work had begun as early as the late 370s (*De excessu fratris* 1.20). There are signs, too, that the homoian majority soon came to see the scheme for what it was: an audacious policy of imposing Ambrose's presence, and with it his increasingly open doctrinal alignment, upon the city and its hinterland. Some of the funds for the projects came from the private moneys which Ambrose had invested in the church; but not all. In order to ransom prisoners of war caught up in the Gothic ravages after the Roman wipe-out at the battle of Adrianople in 378 (Burns 1974), Ambrose opted to melt down and sell church plate to provide extra financial resources (*Off.* 2.70–5, 136–43). In itself, this might not have been especially problematic: there were reasonable precedents for such measures. In this case, however, Ambrose evidently made sure that the chalices in question were ones which had been donated to the church by homoian bene-factors. He also seems to have diverted some of the proceeds from the sale of the plate to boost his building-fund, on the grounds that the cemetery basilicas being constructed were providing burial plots for needy Christians. In short, he appears to have been practising opportunism of a conspicuous kind – clearing his attic of assets which to him were tainted by association, while furthering his scheme to extend the physical presence of his church, all in the name of public sacrifice in the interests of a good cause (Brown 1992: 96).

At the time of his consecration, Ambrose's brother Satyrus had abandoned his career in order to devote his life to assisting with the administration of the see, renouncing all his own rights to marry or to make a will – a huge sacrifice. Satyrus undertook the supervision of the family estates, with a view to maximizing the income accrued by the Milanese church. He had, it appears, always been of delicate constitution, and on a return trip from Africa in the late summer of 378 he fell ill and died. His death was undoubtedly a major blow to Ambrose. The brothers had always been close, and their working lives had been intertwined to an unusual degree. But Ambrose did not miss the opportunity to define Satyrus' importance to the Milanese community, and by implication to signal his own significance as civic leader as well. His funeral sermon offered a highly wrought lament, sketching Satyrus' character throughout with reference to the supporting role he played to the bishop. The personal grief is clearly intense, but the formal conventions of the classical *consolatio* genre also shine through unmistakably (Duval 1977; Savon 1980). However acute his loss, it provided scope for him to impress his authority upon his people through the art of rhetorical performance (Biermann 1995).

All the while, Ambrose faced increasingly serious hostility within his community. His footsteps were dogged in particular by the presence of one Iulianus Valens, a homoian bishop who (presumably because of the barbarian invasions) had fled to Milan from his native Pettau in Noricum. Valens established a rival community in direct opposition to Ambrose. In addition, the anti-pope Ursinus seems to have stirred up some hard-line Nicenes to protest against what they perceived to be the compromising pragmatism of Ambrose's refusal to reform the overall structure of Auxentius' clergy. Ursinus himself was not a homoian (he was primarily interested in making life difficult for his real *bête noire*, Damasus), but Ambrose pictures Valens and him in an unholy alliance, for his activities lent added weight to the cause of the Arian opposition (*Ep. extra coll.* 5[11].3). Although the strength of these hostile forces continues to be underestimated by one or two scholars (e.g. Kaufman 1997), it was in fact considerable. Dissident household meetings seem to have been held, with distinct liturgies and apparent plots against Ambrose. Ursinus was exiled to Cologne in 375/6, but this was probably in punishment for the behaviour of his supporters at Rome rather than as a consequence of the trouble he had caused in Milan; evidently there was no official sanction of his activities there. Ambrose made matters considerably worse for himself with the homoians by intervening in a synod in his former base of Sirmium, more than five hundred miles away, to ensure the election of a Nicene candidate as bishop in late 377 or early 378. This highly questionable involvement in the ecclesiastical affairs of a territory quite outside of his jurisdiction (which implied that Ambrose was prepared to take a heavier hand outside Milan than he was yet in a position to do on his own patch) provoked a furious protest locally in Illyricum, where the homoian community were strongly entrenched.

Most ominously of all, it incurred the wrath of the strongly pro-Arian Justina, mother of another son of Valentian I, the young man who would become Valentinian II; her influence over the church at Sirmium was considerable. By forcing the result, Ambrose had directly insulted Justina. It would only be a matter of time before she sought her revenge, in collusion with the homoians of Milan.

Valentinian I died in 375, having arranged his succession so that his brother Valens would rule in the East and his teenage son Gratian in the West. When Valentinian's half-brother, the young Gratian, arrived in Sirmium after the disastrous defeat by the Goths at Adrianople in 378, where Valens himself was killed, it appears that he was met with warnings from the local homoian clergy that Ambrose's theology deserved to be investigated more closely. Probably they feared that his coup in the recent election would lead to further cross-border activities. Gratian was a devout youth, but he clearly lacked the theological knowledge to decide for himself. He opted to request from Ambrose a statement of his faith (Nautin 1974). Ambrose did not respond at once, perhaps because he knew that Gratian was due to visit Milan soon afterwards on his return to Gaul. When they subsequently met, in the summer of 379, Ambrose managed to impress the emperor and his entourage sufficiently to prevail upon Gratian to silence the homoians (*Ep. extra coll.* 12[1].2). Evidently the pressure upon Ambrose from these opponents was serious: in a number of references stemming from this period he warns of the dangers of false prophets leading the faithful astray or, fox-like, stealing sheep from the true fold (e.g. *Expositio evangelii secundum Lucam* 7.28–31, 44–53). When Gratian returned to Milan in the spring of the following year, he was presented with the initial stages in Ambrose's first public manifesto against Arianism, the opening two books of his *De fide* (Williams 1995: 128–53).

Ambrose's argument amounted to a full-scale attack on the theology of the homoians. With remarkable boldness, it is presented not as a defence of the bishop's personal beliefs but as a specially commissioned articulation of a doctrinal position already espoused by the emperor. Ambrose does everything in his power to dissuade Gratian from becoming attracted to homoian ideas while on his forthcoming campaign against the Goths, but he poses not as an apologist but as a spiritual spokesman. As the first serious evidence of his reading in Greek authorities, the work amounts at one level to a pretty dismal piece of intellectual endeavour (Hanson 1988: 669–75). Ambrose refuses to differentiate between the various strands of

Arianism. The homoians are lumped in with those of far more extreme beliefs, such as Aetius and Eunomius, who denied any similarity at all between God the Father and God the Son (Kopecek 1979). At another level, however, the text carries a poignant political message which gives an important clue to the bishop's ideological strategy. The Gothic triumph at Adrianople and the ensuing ravages of the Danubian provinces are depicted in the last paragraphs (*Fid.* 2.136–43) as a divine judgement on Arian strongholds; fidelity to the true faith, conversely, would guarantee a resounding Roman victory this time around. Ambrose was sounding a note that would become a familiar refrain: theological orthodoxy and the security of the empire are all of a piece (Palanque 1933: 325–35; Meslin 1964; Sordi 1988; Inglebert 1996: 297–309).

On his return to Illyricum, Gratian showed the work to Palladius of Ratiaria, the most senior and the ablest of the local bishops (Meslin 1967: 111–34). Palladius issued a sharp rejoinder, refuting Ambrose's misrepresentation of the homoian position and inviting him to engage in a direct debate (Palladius, *Apology* 81–7: McLynn 1991). Palladius was aware that Gratian had decided to convene a general council at Aquileia the following year, intended to resolve the differences between the Nicene and homoian parties, and on the basis of the shoddy logic evidenced in *De fide* 1–2 he must have been confident of his own chances of victory in an open encounter with Ambrose. Probably at his encouragement, Gratian requested further clarification from Ambrose, who opted to wait until the emperor had left Illyricum and was safely back at Trier, far from Palladius' influence, before he replied. He promised to fulfil the emperor's request, and once again deliberately turned around Gratian's plea for further information to make it sound as if the emperor's doctrine was confirmedly in line with his own (*Ep. extra coll.* 12[1]). He rushed off a further three books to *De fide* and followed these up with another three *De Spiritu Sancto*, the first treatise on the Holy Spirit in the West. Once again, the theological quality of the arguments is unimpressive. Notably, Ambrose declines to engage directly with Palladius' criticisms of his earlier work.

Throughout this time, Ambrose's position in Milan remained precarious. One illustration of this can be glimpsed in his reference in *De Spiritu Sancto* 1 to a (presumably recent) attempt to sequestrate a basilica in Milan in the name of the emperor (*Spir.* 1.19–21). The episode may well have been orchestrated by Justina, who had arrived in the city at some point after Adrianople. If so, it was a clear act of revenge for Ambrose's earlier humiliation of her at Sirmium, and a direct plea on behalf of the Milanese homoians (Williams 1994). Even if Justina was not directly behind it, her presence would undoubtedly have emboldened the homoians to press their case that worship in private was no longer good enough: they wanted churches of their own, where they could establish their presence publicly as an official opposition to Ambrose. In this particular case, the order was rescinded, perhaps when Gratian himself arrived in the city, but it reflects tensions which were all too real. The quest for territory was to prove an enduring concern in the years that followed (Maier 1994).

A reversal of Ambrose's fortunes, however, lay around the corner. The catalyst was Gratian's plan for a theological council. Late in 378, Gratian had issued an edict of toleration for the East, proclaiming the right of free worship for all religious groups except the Manichaeans, the Photinians (who denied the pre-existence of Christ), and the Eunomians (*Codex Theodosianus* 16.5.5). However, shortly after his accession to the purple in January of 379, his new colleague Theodosius for his part had expressly proclaimed that 'all peoples' should follow the 'catholic' faith as articulated by Pope Damasus and Peter of Alexandria (*C.Th.* 16.1.2). There is considerable dispute surrounding this edict: was it a binding legal injunction, implicitly threatening imperial retribution for those who refused to comply, or was it simply a manifesto statement, setting out the new emperor's personal preferences – preferences shaped by minority Nicene pressure from the bishop of Theodosius' base at Thessalonica, Acholius? The latter is more likely; but at any rate the edict reflected Theodosius' concern to have his own say in the theological affairs of the East. In a bid to assert his authority over his junior colleague, Gratian announced that a general council would meet in 381 at Aquileia (a place convenient for both western and eastern delegates), but Theodosius was again not to be outdone. He summoned the bishop of Constantinople, Demophilus, and required him to subscribe to the Nicene faith; Demophilus refused, and opted to take his congregation into effective exile beyond the city walls. At the beginning of 381, Theodosius then issued a now-famous decree outlawing Arianism along with other sects (*C.Th.* 16.5.6), and in May of that year he convened his own assembly at Constantinople to elect a successor to Demophilus. It looked as if there was little point in Gratian's general council going ahead.

Ambrose, however, had other ideas. First, he saved Gratian the embarrassment of cancelling his council by insisting that the meeting should be held. But, crucially, he also persuaded the emperor that there was no need to call another large-scale gathering of eastern bishops so soon after Constantinople, for the dispute was, after all, a private one between himself and a few of his brethren from Illyricum. The upshot was that Aquileia proved to be a mere shadow of what Gratian had originally planned. Ambrose ensured that he was surrounded by a group of staunchly loyal supporters from North Italy and Gaul, while Palladius enjoyed far more limited support. In such a fiercely partisan environment, Ambrose orchestrated an overwhelming condemnation of Palladius, and of his prominent colleague, Secundianus, bishop of Singidunum. He swiftly followed it up with conciliar appeals, not only to Gratian but also to Theodosius himself, to act decisively against the Arians, first by legally enforcing the deposition of Palladius and Secundianus from their sees, and then by removing other menaces, such as the presence of Iulianus Valens in North Italy (*Epp. extra coll.* 4[10]–6[12]). A potentially awkward theological *contretemps* had been turned into a major political advantage. The Ambrose who had been struggling for so long had at last, by sheer opportunism and ruthlessness, succeeded in establishing a decisive Nicene bridgehead (Williams 1995: 154–84).

A matter of months before Aquileia, Gratian had officially transferred the western court from Trier to Milan. Ambrose found himself with unprecedented access to the machinery of government, and he exploited it to the full. He became an effective lobbyist not only for his own causes but also on behalf of the careers and aspirations of friends and contacts from the local area and beyond, and a giver of strategic hospitality to assorted officials and visiting dignitaries. Such activity called for a delicate balancing-act, for his own rhetoric insisted that the affairs of a corrupt world were none of the church's concern (*Off.* 1.185), and that clerics were not to involve themselves in financial disputes (*Off.* 2.125; 3.59), or go around attending the power-dinners of the rich (*Off.* 1.86). Ambrose seemed to manage it, nevertheless, and in the process he reinforced his position as a key player in the political affairs of metropolitan society (Matthews 1975: 191–203).

Palladius, meanwhile, continued to protest against the treatment he had received at Aquileia, but to little avail. The details of his argument were apparently relayed to Ambrose, who happened to be publishing a sermon preached against two Arian courtiers who had criticized him (and had ominously managed to get themselves killed when they had failed to turn up to engage in a debate with him which they themselves had requested: Paulinus, *Vita Ambros.* 18); he was able to add a special section responding to Palladius (*De incarnatione* 79–116), in terms as shallow as before. Ambrose never did (Gottlieb 1973) enjoy the kind of ascendancy over Gratian that he duped his biographers into positing; incidents such as the controversy surrounding the Spanish ascetic, Priscillian of Avila, in which Ambrose's antipathy was drowned out by the agencies of Priscillian's supporter, the *magister officiorum* Macedonius (Chadwick 1976: 111–69), illustrate that. Nevertheless, in the latter days of a regime marked by indecisiveness, his influence over an essentially bored and impressionistic emperor was not inconsiderable. Gratian's weak grasp on power was met with the revolt of the British commander Maximus in 383, and death at the hands of one of Maximus' subordinates at Lyon; it was easy for Ambrose to portray him as an innocent victim of betrayal, fostering the assumption that Gratian had been under his wing all along, and that he had even died with the word 'Ambrose!' on his lips (*In Ps.* 61 *enarratio* 23–6; *De obitu Valentiniani consolatio* 78–81).

The political significance which Ambrose's agencies had come to assume also brought him a remarkable role in the checking of Maximus' rebellion. In order to gain time for the forces loyal to Valentinian who were gathering under the Frankish general, Bauto, the bishop went in person to Trier to appeal to Maximus for peace (*Epistle* 30[24]). Valentinian's supporters at Milan also proclaimed their independence from the coup, and urged Theodosius to muster forces against the usurper. In the end, no fighting actually took place, for Theodosius was finally persuaded to grant recognition to Maximus in return for the assurance that Valentinian's court was legitimate. But Ambrose, for his part, soon called in the debt for his diplomatic efforts. In 384, the urban prefect of Rome, the distinguished Quintus Aurelius Symmachus, formulated a legal petition seeking the restoration of the altar of Victory, a potent symbol of Rome's traditional religion, to the Senate-house, an incident related in detail by Bill Leadbetter in Chapter 10 of this volume. Ambrose led the attack on Symmachus. He guaranteed that the direst of consequences would ensue if the altar were restored, for this would symbolize a capitulation on the part of a Christian emperor to the old religious order. Reminding the court of its personal debt to him in his embassy to Trier, he warned Valentinian II, who was a teenage ruler of obvious vulnerability, that he would face the full opposition of his bishop if he chose to heed the pagans' case. Not surprisingly, the threats worked, and Symmachus' petition was rejected (Wytzes 1936; Klein 1972; Matthews 1975: 203–11).

Valentinian's relations with Ambrose were, however, destined to run anything but smoothly. In part, this was because of the influence of Justina, forever characterized by the bishop as the Jezebel of the fourth century (or by Palanque 1933: 140 as the Catherine de Medici of Arianism). But it took more than the will of the queen-mother to make any onslaught (*infestatio*, as Ambrose would call it: *Off.* 1.72) against the bishop and his church a reality, particularly when the pursuit of such a vendetta would conceivably jeopardize political stability. Justina's machinations must have been only part of a tenuous but sinister alliance of hostile forces, in which the lead was taken by the homoians themselves. Chief among the latter was one Mercurinus Auxentius (Williams 1995: 202–10), a former protégé of Ulfila, the homoian 'apostle' to the Goths during the reign of Constantius II (Heather and Matthews 1991: 133–53). As bishop of Durostorum on the Lower Danube, Auxentius had been recognized by Palladius as a potential challenger to Ambrose, and after being removed from his see by Theodosius he found refuge in Milan, probably in the second half of 384. The ensuing period witnessed a revival of the homoians' prospects (Williams 1995: 185–217). Its climax, in the years 385–6, amounted to the most serious crisis of Ambrose's episcopate. Yet that crisis would also become the defining moment in his effort to assert his authority over his own territory once and for all, and to establish the Catholics as the definitive Christian community of Milan.

The pretext for battle was, once again, the vexed issue of space for worship. In the spring of 385, Ambrose was summoned to the imperial palace to be informed that the emperor wished to have a cathedral in which the court's worship could be led by homoian clergy: one of the bishop's basilicas, probably the Basilica Portiana, just outside the city-walls, was to be handed over forthwith (*Ep.* 75a [*C. Aux.*].29). This ultimatum was a direct rebuttal of Ambrose's earlier attempt to dominate Valentinian (though, by way of diplomacy, it was delivered courtesy of a special invitation to the bishop to attend the imperial consistory). Ambrose had, however, apparently informed his supporters that he had been called to the palace, and the meeting was interrupted by a crowd clamouring that the churches of God must remain inviolate. Fearing a public riot, the court had little option but to back down.

On 23 January of the following year, a law was issued (*C.Th.* 16.1.4) requiring freedom of worship for those who followed the (Arian) faith as specified at the councils of Rimini (359) and Constantinople (360). The language of the directive warned that there would be firm retaliation against any who resisted or claimed that such freedom was theirs alone; any such responses would be treated as treasonous. The law was a clear violation of the spirit of Theodosius' edict of 380, and in so far as it was designed to prevent another popular uprising against the right of homoians to worship in their own space it was equally clearly targeted at Ambrose. In all probability, it was framed with the direct involvement of Auxentius, as Ambrose himself contended (*Ep.* 75a [*C. Aux.*].16, 22, 24). The issue now was not just about a private site for the liturgical use of the emperor and his retinue; this time there was an implicit validation of the entire homoian community which had existed in opposition to Ambrose from the start.

In late March, just prior to Easter, Ambrose was once again issued with a request for a church. Now it was no longer the Basilica Portiana, but the central Basilica Nova itself that was sought (the chronology and topography of the affair are both subject to considerable scholarly dispute: see in particular van Haeringen 1937;

largely followed by Lenox-Conygham 1982b; Gottlieb 1985; McLynn 1994: 158–219; cf. Nauroy 1988). This demand for the bishop to give up his own cathedral can hardly have been fully serious, but Ambrose was reminded of the sanctions destined to follow upon any violation of the January law. He replied that a bishop had no power to surrender a 'temple of God', and implicitly appealed to his people to back him in his resistance of any infringement upon their rights (*Ep.* 76[20].2). At a meeting in his church next day, proceedings were interrupted by the arrival of the praetorian prefect, who came with new orders. It was not the Basilica Nova that was being sought for the emperor's use after all, it was said, but the Basilica Portiana. Ambrose's congregation themselves shouted a firm refusal. On Palm Sunday, the bishop was celebrating worship in his church when news came that the Basilica Portiana was being decked with imperial banners, evidently in preparation for use by the emperor and his entourage. It was also reported that a group from his own congregation, going to occupy the church for themselves, had violently assaulted a homoian presbyter (probably a court chaplain). He managed to send some of his men to rescue the unfortunate priest, but it was clear that the situation had taken an unpleasant turn. A severe fine was imposed on the *corpus negotiatorum* from which the rioters had come, and a number of them were imprisoned. It now seemed entirely possible that the court would deploy force to evict the Catholics.

Nevertheless, emboldened by the persistence of his supporters, Ambrose refused to comply with a further demand to persuade them to give up the Basilica Portiana, arguing that he was bound by a higher obligation than any human law not to betray 'divine' property (*Ep.* 76[20].8); he could not, however, challenge the actual legality of the state's claim in the circumstances. Troops were sent to blockade the church, and things threatened to turn nasty when a contingent of them also entered the Basilica Nova while Ambrose was conducting a service. In the event, the latter group, Nicene sympathizers themselves, were induced to desert. Strengthened by this, Ambrose proceeded to deliver a passionate sermon, urging his congregation to remain steadfast in the cause of truth, and asserting that the basilicas were not Caesar's but God's (*Ep.* 76[20].19). At the news that the imperial hangings had been removed from the Basilica Portiana, he dispatched some clergy to join the occupiers of the church. This was a tactical mistake: it now appeared incontrovertible that he was supporting the sedition of the people directly. The news that the imperial hangings had been damaged worsened matters further. Ambrose denied any involvement in the affray, but fearing that he might be arrested he opted to remain in his church with his congregation during the night of Wednesday of Holy Week. It was during this vigil that he made one of his most successful and ultimately enduring moves: he introduced his congregation to the eastern practice of antiphonal singing. The process fostered a sense of solidarity in tense circumstances, and provided a stunningly effective channel for popularizing the idioms of Nicene theology, for Ambrose's followers were given not just psalms to sing, but hymns of his own composition. The faithful stood together and sang together while Satan's forces – or the devotees of a lesser theology – prowled at the doors (cf. Augustine, *Conf.* 9.7.15). The 'Ambrosian hymn', typically eight stanzas of basic iambic dimeters, was to become a widely imitated form: brilliantly, yet almost by accident, Ambrose had devised a formula which would revolutionize western liturgical practice

(Fontaine 1992). Hilary of Poitiers before him had sought to develop the metrical hymn as a medium for doctrinal teaching in the West, but it took Ambrose's delicate poetic gift, the spell of his charisma, and the intensity of his followers' emotions in an hour of crisis to make congregational singing really catch on.

On Maundy Thursday, while the bishop addressed his people, news arrived that the emperor had ordered the withdrawal of the soldiers from the Basilica Portiana and the repayment of the fines imposed on the businessmen. But the affair was not entirely over. After Easter, Ambrose was summoned before the imperial consistory to engage in a debate with Auxentius, the outcome of which was to be decided by a panel of judges nominated by the contestants and chaired by the emperor himself. The bishop would be less confident, it was assumed, off his own ground. He declined to comply, and withdrew to his church in the company of his congregation. The arrival of troops outside provided him with the opportunity to create another (this time imaginary) siege environment. In reality, the government had presumably sent some soldiers merely to forestall further public disturbances, but the scenario allowed Ambrose to argue that he was in no position to come to the palace. Once again, the singing and liturgy went on day and night, this time for a number of days. A final summons was then issued: the bishop must either nominate his arbiters for the debate or else leave the city. Evidently his congregation feared that he might take the latter course, and he had to reassure them that he would face martyrdom rather than abandon his church. To the court's demands, he responded with a sermon against Auxentius (*Ep.* 75a [*C. Aux.*]), a brilliant appeal to his people's sense of outrage that a man of God should yield to the will of evil schemers. He deliberately conflates the January law with Valentinian's orders to engage in dialogue with Auxentius. In an official letter of reply to the emperor (*Ep.* 75[21]), he paints Auxentius as a dangerous upstart, not fit to debate with one such as himself. He contends that the January law would have to be rescinded in its entirety before any such debate could take place, for if Auxentius were to be defeated this would logically invalidate it. He would, he claimed, be most willing to come and discuss matters of the faith – only his clergy and congregation would not let him.

Faced with such skilful evasion, such obstinacy in the guise of reasonableness, Valentinian had few choices left, particularly since there were veiled threats from Maximus and renewed problems on the Danube frontier. Ambrose had gained the upper hand by a combination of audacity, legal posturing, and a fortuitous turn of political events. He wasted no time in pressing his advantage. In June of 386, construction was completed on a magnificent new cathedral, to be known as the Basilica Ambrosiana, where the bishop himself intended to be buried, in the Hortus Philippi west of the city-centre, close by the resting place of the martyr Victor and of his own brother Satyrus (Mirabella Roberti 1984: 120–4). At the dedication ceremony, Ambrose pledged that the building would be decorated appropriately if the remains of some martyrs could be discovered. Next day, he led his people to the memorial to the celebrated martyrs Nabor and Felix, and gave his clerics orders to start digging nearby. Not surprisingly, they soon discovered remains, which were claimed to be those of another two martyrs, Gervasius and Protasius, who were believed to have suffered under Nero; the names were attested by a 'demon' being exorcized from an elderly woman. Amidst great rejoicing from the bishop's supporters, the skeletons were solemnly transported to the new church for re-interment; *en route*, even fleeting contact with the bones is said to have proved sufficient to heal all sorts of diseases among the attending crowds (Doignon 1956; Zangara 1981).

Ambrose's opponents are said to have made accusations that the whole thing was staged by the bishop (Paulinus, *Vita Ambros.* 15), and for all his protests about their impiety (*Ep.* 77[22].16–23) they were doubtless right. But whatever the identity of the relics, what mattered was the impact that the discovery and ceremonial transference of them had upon the volatile Milanese community. Ambrose had provided a spectacular distraction from the tensions of the previous weeks; he had also signalled that, even if his foes had him killed, they would not be able to remove what he stood for: a martyred bishop would be commemorated in noble company in a vast new shrine. His tactics presupposed the growing significance of the cult of the martyrs in the late fourth century, and its ability to evoke powerful passions in a people already stirred by religous fervour (Brown 1981: 36–7). It was not hard for him to connect the *inventio*, the demonic testimonies, and the miraculous healings with fidelity to a theological cause, and to foster the idea that here was reward for spiritual steadfastness (Dassmann 1975). In the end, hopelessly outstaged by the excitement the bishop had inspired, the court gave up in its pursuit of its cause. The January law may or may not have been formally repealed; either way, it was dropped in practice. Rather than risk a further outbreak of potentially more serious anarchy, and increasingly preoccupied elsewhere with the problem of Maximus, Valentinian was advised to abandon the campaign his mother had supported. There were various gestures of reconciliation: Ambrose, for his part, undertook another mission to Maximus at Trier, which in the event did little or nothing to help the cause of peace. Valentinian's regime was nevertheless left fatally wounded by its encounter with Ambrose's intransigence, and within a matter of months the emperor and his retinue were in flight from Maximus' invading forces.

Nothing served to define Ambrose's style so much as this struggle with the forces of Arianism. His victory was won only through his gift for creating the impression that he was always in control, most of all when it must have been anything but true, and for portraying the sense that God was on his side. That is not to denigrate his personal courage, for the possibility of suffering violence or even martyrdom was, at points in the crisis, real for him as well as for his supporters. But the whole episode revealed his ability to exploit mass emotion, and to use his own networks to achieve vital leverage in desperate circumstances. Much of his assurance, for example, only made sense if he had contacts able to supply him with information about developments in his enemies' ranks, and much of his ability to persuade others to support his cause depended on his knack of extracting all the compliance that episcopal *auctoritas* could muster. Ambrose knew how to manipulate crowds while remaining aloof from the uglier side of their actions; he could seem to be one with the sufferers while pleading his willingness to be reasonable with the authorities responsible for the peril to which they were exposed (MacMullen 1990).

Ambrose's initial relations with Theodosius, the swift victor over Maximus' forces in the summer of 388, were conditioned by his existing standing with Valentinian. While in retreat at Thessalonica, Valentinian had repudiated his past homoian allegiances, perhaps in the wake of his mother's death. Ambrose was happy to welcome him back to Milan, and to glory in the triumph of orthodoxy in yet another military confrontation. Theodosius, who accompanied him home, had clear Nicene credentials, but Ambrose lacked the kind of diplomatic history with his inner circle that he had built up with Valentinian's. His strategy, instead, was to use the political profile he had already secured to impress Theodosius with the authoritative grandeur he saw as attaching to his episcopal role.

A famous incident illustrates his approach. At the end of 388 there occcurred a riot in the city of Callinicum, on the Euphrates, in which a Christian mob, led by the local bishop, plundered and burned down a synagogue. Theodosius, consulted by regional officialdom, responded by ordering that the perpetrators be punished and the bishop made to bear the cost of rebuilding the synagogue in person. When Ambrose got wind of this, he reacted sternly, urging Theodosius to revoke his orders, on the grounds that no bishop could with a good conscience be responsible for the construction of a synagogue, a place of 'idolatry'. He even claimed that he himself had validated the Callinicum mob's activities (*Ep.* 74[40].8). Theodosius decided to rescind the fine, but Ambrose wanted more. He argued that the whole case should be dropped. His logic, set out in a skilfully crafted letter to the emperor (*Ep.* 74[40]), reflects some starkly anti-Semitic sentiment, from which even his least critical admirers have felt obliged to recoil (e.g. Homes Dudden 1935: II, 372–9; on these tendencies generally in this period, see Wilken 1983; Millar 1992). It also raised enduring questions about the legitimacy of violence in a religious cause. On the next occasion when he preached in the presence of Theodosius, Ambrose went further, and directly appealed for a pardon to be extended to the rioters. When the emperor and his party protested that, having commuted the original sentence, they still had every right to punish those who had defied law and order, Ambrose refused to continue with the service until he got his own way. Theodosius elected to give in. The situation is depicted by the bishop (*Ep. extra coll.* 1[41]) as a personal triumph, and it has traditionally been interpreted as a daring confrontation – a bold churchman reducing an emperor to a humiliating climb-down, an episcopal Nathan rebuking an imperial David (Paulinus, *Vita Ambros.* 23, influencing, e.g., Palanque 1933: 219). In fact, it is likelier that Theodosius recognized the political capital to be made out of a measured gesture of beneficence: by exercising clemency, he guaranteed himself the affection and gratitude of the Italian Nicenes, whom his advisers had been working hard to win over.

Another incident which reflects the same abilities on the part of Ambrose occurred in the summer of 390 in the city of Thessalonica and is described by Bill Leadbetter in Chapter 10 of this volume. A popular charioteer was arrested and put in prison for allegedly making sexual advances to one of the attendants of Botheric, the commander of the local garrison. The people rioted, and Botheric was killed, along with other officials. When news of this serious outrage reached Theodosius, extreme retaliation was ordered. It is improbable that Theodosius acted simply in anger, without serious consideration of the consequences; but however the decision was made, he endorsed a punitive plan that yielded nothing to clemency (McLynn 1994: 315–23). The garrison at Thessalonica was given orders to execute the faction responsible for the revolt. The details of the order may well have been misunderstood, or the troops were determined to wreak much severer vengeance than had been mandated, for in the space of a few hours a considerable number of innocent residents of the city, possibly up to 7,000 in all (Theodoret, *Historia Ecclesiastica* 5.17), were brutally massacred. The true perpetrators of the murder of Botheric may well have escaped. Although Theodosius, faced with public outrage on a large scale, attempted to distance himself from the atrocity, implying that it was an act of bloodlust by an army stationed far from his immediate control, he was obliged to bear ultimate responsibility. Ambrose saw to it that Theodosius did public penance for this massacre by threatening, in effect, excommunication if he did not.

Ambrose never did cement the kind of dominant relationship with Theodosius that many historians have imagined. His prevarication in dealing with Eugenius, Valentinian's successor in 392–3, reflected an enduring sense of uncertainty as to what would be politically expedient. Ambrose was caught between an initial attitude of warmth towards Arbogast's new Augustus and a desire to wait and see which way Theodosius himself would go. When Eugenius invaded Italy in the spring of 393, Ambrose opted to leave Milan (while away, he managed to preside over the exhumation of further martyr-relics at Bologna: *Exh. virg.* 1–10; Paulinus, *Vita Ambros.* 29), returning only when Eugenius' forces had vacated the city the following year. He himself presents this as a measured decision to rebuff one who, for all his Christian professions, had given in to demands from his pagan supporters for subsidies for their cults (*Ep. extra coll.* 10[57]; cf. Paulinus, *Vita Ambros.* 26.3); more probably, he anticipated the embarrassment of meeting Eugenius after finally opting to side with Theodosius against him. Theodosius' triumph was naturally greeted by Ambrose with rejoicing, and the emperor's death not long afterwards, in January 395, gave him the final opportunity to claim Theodosius as his own. The ebbs and flows which had marked their relations were speedily forgotten, and the bishop's eloquent funeral eulogy (*De obitu Theodosii oratio*) proclaimed Theodosius as model Christian ruler and patron of a Nicene faith that had now definitively captured the West (Duval 1977: 274–91). Ambrose was himself to die just over two years later, on 4 April 397, from an illness incurred after a trip to Pavia, before the imperial dream was shattered, when Stilicho, the Vandal general whom Theodosius had appointed regent over his sons Honorius and Arcadius, lost control, and Milan itself became a potential prey to the invading Goths. His political prominence in these last years, under a governor whose Christianity was nominal, had not been so great, and he had been spared the turmoil of the cataclysmic times which lay ahead.

Ambrose had served his episcopate as a remarkably political figure, in close proximity to a succession of emperors and their courts, over a critical period in the history of the later western empire. Against a disparate but powerful range of opponents (Cracco Ruggini 1974, who nevertheless overstates the degree to which they constituted an organized alliance), and in the face of often considerable tensions with the imperial powers, he had learned to develop a style which, for all its ambiguities, was outstandingly effective. Almost nothing about the process had been as straightforward as Ambrose had managed to make it seem; but manage he had. At once a kind of fusion of Old Testament prophet and judge and the epitome of the classical public man, he had skilfully succeeded in presenting himself as power-broker and spiritual mentor to the highest authorities, one capable of moving with assurance and impact at the ultimate levels of political influence, articulating a message which combined intellectual conviction and social respectability. It was a *persona* designed to reflect an unswerving belief that his version of truth would inevitably prevail, and that a Christianized empire meant the sure triumph of the Nicene faith, not just over the impieties of every theological alternative but over the social and ethical structures of its cultural inheritance.

CREATING AN ECCLESIAL COMMUNITY

When Ambrose assumed office, the Nicene–Arian divisions were only part of the problems afflicting the church in North Italy. The region's bishoprics, each with its own traditions and practices, were spread across a considerable area; Milan, for all its political significance, still needed to evolve an ecclesial identity distinct from Rome's by weaving its independent customs into a tighter and more confident package. The smaller sees required their larger neighbour to provide them with a kind of symbolic leadership; Milan had to find a way of being both the chief mediator of Rome's authority and the figurehead for a proudly particular northern church. The obvious political instability of the 370s and 380s made the need for social cohesion within these communities all the greater. Ambrose was able to capitalize on a *Zeitgeist* which reflected both a sense of uncertainty and a growing perception of the need to consolidate the North Italian church within its own sphere.

His spirituality presupposed a dialectical tension between two worlds, the seen and the unseen, the literal and the spiritual, the temporal and the eternal (Seibel 1958). He carefully engendered what has aptly been described as a 'siege mentality', whereby the church, devoted to the service of Christ, the true 'emperor', was to be seen as surrounded by the evil forces of the *saeculum* (epitomized variously by Manichees, pagans, and Arians of every kind), whose constant determination, satanically inspired, was to bring about its downfall (Meslin 1967: 51, cited by Brown 1988: 347–8). He combined this rhetorical image of a spiritual warfare against the powers of darkness with a pragmatic exploitation of all the leverage that a Christianized imperial system could secure. His dream was for a church that would simultaneously dominate and transcend its social world. Catholic faith and Roman empire were bound together, but the church was to exercise a prophetic vocation to act as the critic and purifier of the residual corruption of the empire's ethos, for it had an eschatological destiny to surpass any merely human moral configurations. The sensualism, the self-absorption, and the material iniquities which characterized the unregenerate human condition were to be decried then remedied in the ascesis of devotion to Christ (Dassmann 1965). The social distinctions presupposed by the world were to be overridden: rich and poor, court officials and illiterate peasants, would come together; the emperor was to worship alongside the most vulnerable members of society. To enter this community by baptism was to leave behind the pollution of the world, and to become privy to the deep things of God, which only spiritual eyes could see. Sacramental initiation was a profoundly mystical process, a *disciplina arcani* hedged about by solemn warnings about privilege and responsibility, and presided over by a sacerdotal class who were to be seen as the guardians of secret rites as awe-inspiring as those over which the Levites of old presided (Jacob 1990). Through the strictures of the system of public penance, the clerical hierarchy acted not only as gatekeepers but also as guarantors of in-house discipline. To be the *populus Dei* in Milan in the 380s was to be the spiritual offspring of patriarchs, prophets, and apostles, in direct continuity with the elect of every age who had been summoned into a life which ascended beyond the standards accepted by a godless world; it was to be destined, at last, for a reward that was heavenly (Hahn 1969; Toscani 1974).

To be effective, the religous mystery of this 'true philosophy' required to be presented in a way that conveyed a powerful sense of cultural assurance. Ambrose's intellectual message was one plank in that strategy. Doubtless a large proportion of his hearers never identified the allusions to Greek texts which he paraded in his sermons, or the evocations of classical literature which lurked in his narratives of biblical stories, when phrases from Virgil and Terence slipped out almost sub-consciously, or stereotyped characterizations of money-lenders, legacy-hunters, or greedy merchants crept into his generalized moral disquisitions on contemporary social evils (Vasey 1982). Reading the transcripts or reworked versions of these homilies today, his spontaneous, discursive articulations of scriptural texts often seem unappealing: they are not systematic expositions in any obvious sense. But the density of their style impressed those who first listened to them. When Ambrose preached (as he usually did) on the Old Testament narratives, the sheer range of his textual reference (which regularly included allusions to the Septuagint, his preferred version, and to variant readings gleaned from authorities such as Origen's *Hexapla*) and the intensity of his delivery seemed to convey authority and passion, and a mind soaked in the idioms of a scriptural spirituality (Nauroy 1985; Graumann 1994). To the cultivated critics of court society, and to judges like Augustine who understood very well what to look for in an orator, Ambrose came across as a pastor and teacher who knew what he was about. In any overall appraisal of his substance, Ambrose was not an original thinker. He did anticipate and shape some significant aspects of later western thinking on original sin (Homes Dudden 1935: II, 612–24), the transform-ation of the Eucharistic elements (Johanny 1968), the veneration of Mary (Neumann 1962), and the idea of a holy war (Swift 1970), but his theological ideas were on the whole derivative, and his grasp of many doctrinal nuances was frequently far poorer than his opponents'. This does not mean, however, that Ambrose was a lightweight. As it happens, modern scholarship has shown that his personal role in reshaping the ideas he imbibed from his exegetical sources was often quite significant (Lazzati 1960; Pizzolato 1965, 1978; Lucchesi 1977; Savon 1977; auf der Maur 1977). Ambrose was a creative synthesizer, driven by pragmatic concerns. Enemies like Jerome may have mocked him as a plagiarist (Paredi 1964b), but what mattered in the end was that Ambrose's intellectual showmanship worked for those whom he needed to sway most – the movers and shakers of his own city, and their social peers within a wider Italian radius (embracing Rome itself), who needed to be either convinced or reminded that the philosophy of the *saeculum* had been vanquished by a definitive revealed truth (Madec 1974; Lenox-Conygham 1993). By publishing redacted versions of his sermons as written treatises, he was able to drive the message home to as wide a literary public as possible.

Another vital element in Ambrose's mission was his programme to dominate the physical landscape of his city (Krautheimer 1983: 69–92; Mirabella Roberti 1984). At the very time when he was most under pressure to yield official space to his opponents, he was also most intent on extending the presence of his own community through the rapid construction of churches. Milan came to be encircled by a string of massive new buildings outside the city walls: the Basilica Ambrosiana (Sant' Ambrogio), dedicated with such ceremony in 386, the emblem of Ambrose's claim to an ineradicable entry in the religious history of his city; the strikingly impressive Basilica Apostolorum (San Nazaro), the first cruciform basilica to appear in the West, modelled, like a number of its eastern contemporaries, on Constantine's Apostoleion in Constantinople, and built strategically on the route taken into Milan by Theodosius, who seems to have donated relics of the evangelists to be housed inside the church; and the Basilica Virginum (San Simpliciano), a smaller cruciform building constructed to the north of the city. (A fourth church, the Basilica Salvatoris [San Donighi] is attributed to Ambrose by later tradition and marked on Krautheimer's plan of the city [Figure 47.3], but it is improbable that it is as old as the fourth century.) The new churches were designed to symbolize that the social triumph of the Nicene cultus was irreversible. They were consecrated using liturgical language which was deliberately anti-Arian, and their architectural and decorative elaborations were intended to placard the wealth and status of the Nicene community's benefactors. The ecclesiastical establishment had traditionally been

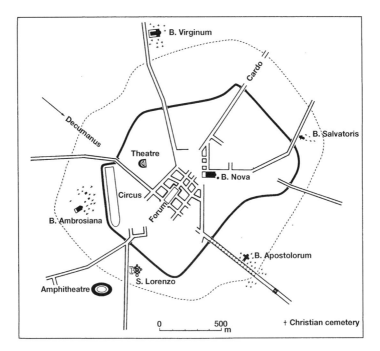

Figure 47.3 Milan *c.* 400, showing location of fourth-century churches. From Krautheimer (1983: 73), by permission of the University of California Press.

concentrated in the area around the central cathedral; now it had colonized suburbia.

The third element in Ambrose's master-plan was the reformation of the ecclesiastical hierarchy. In his early years, as we saw, his options in this area were very limited; but by the second half of the 380s his retinue looked very different. Some of his clergy had perhaps been successfully converted to their leader's theological stance; a large proportion were very probably weeded out and replaced by younger men carefully selected for their malleability (it is also clear that there had been some attrition of supporters during the Arian crisis: cf. *Off.* 1.72). Ambrose's most famous literary legacy, penned in the late 380s, is his *De officiis*, a treatise on moral responsibilities based upon Cicero's famous text of the same name, and significantly influenced by his version of Stoic ethics (Testard 1984–92). As Cicero wrote for his son, Marcus, and for a politically ambitious class of young Roman gentlemen living amidst the débâcle of the Republic in 44 BCE, Ambrose writes for his spiritual 'sons', the clergy of Milan. His aim is not to build bridges between the gospel and secular philosophy, or to create a systematic parody of a celebrated classical exemplar, but to adapt the Ciceronian paradigms to a new, Christian context, and to show that the old account of duties has been superseded by a moral framework which goes much further (Davidson 1995). His anticipated readers are not only ecclesiastics; he also intends the work to be perused by non-Christians, who will be able to compare his exposition of biblical morality with the details of the Ciceronian text around which it is structured. For both classes of reader, his message is that a new elite has emerged, one that is concerned no longer with the service of the *saeculum* but with a nobler end, which it must realize by profounder means. To be in the service of God is to be called to a higher path of 'perfect duty', modelled on Christ's self-sacrifice and oriented towards conformity to his image. Many of the assumptions of the classical patterns of correct behaviour are still regarded as critical – clerics are to be paragons of 'seemliness', walking, talking, and conducting themselves in a way which reveals a true self-mastery, and thus impressing a watching world with their social finesse. Some aspects of the cardinal virtues, notably of mental fortitude and temperance, remain very close to the Roman Stoic ideals. But others are quite different. Prudence is no longer viewed simply as practical good sense: it is, in an ultimate sense, the fear and knowledge of God. Justice is not just about giving to each his or her own; it is also, supremely, about Christian charity, which has replaced civic euergetism as the prerogative of a new, spiritually commissioned officialdom (Becker 1994). The 'effeminacy' and uncouthness traditionally abhorred in the public figure no longer reflect mere ill-breeding; they now bespeak compromise with the defilements of the corrupt world of the flesh. The *athleta Christi* or the *Dei miles* is to be seen to be a conqueror over tendencies that are both aesthetically distasteful and repugnant to God; he is to be chaste, self-denying, altruistic, pure, heavenly minded, and conscious of his ultimate accountability to a divine judge. Virtue and expediency, rightly conceived, are the same thing precisely because each of them is directed towards and determined by the prospect of eschatological reward.

De officiis represents a literary dissemination of a vision which was also expressed through preaching, personal example, and letter-writing, and backed up locally by a strict code of discipline. Ambrose succeeded in surrounding himself with subordinates who followed the very norms which he himself had laboured to polish; his own priestly ideal, a distinctive synthesis of images drawn from the Hebrew cultus, the classical tradition, and the Pastoral Epistles (Gryson 1968; Bonato 1987; Coppa 1992), was passed on. Evidently he had no shortage of clerical candidates: as a metropolitan see, regarded as a valuable springboard for ecclesiastical promotion, Milan attracted plenty of young men ready and willing to be schooled in the bishop's ways. From this mini-seminary environment, a number of his trainees went on to episcopal office elsewhere, sometimes directly (and controversially) through Ambrose's engineering. Through regular correspondence and personal contacts with these and other brethren whom he deemed worthy of direct encouragement and instruction, Ambrose built up a considerable network of loyal supporters throughout North Italy and beyond. By ensuring that these satellites looked to him as their leader and remained faithful to the standards he strove to inculcate, he saw to it that the next generation of leaders were equipped to reinforce the social dominance of their church as the new century dawned (Lizzi 1990). The *episcopi* of the future, having learned to style themselves in the same basic way as the patrons, guides, and regulators of their communities, would head up an ecclesial hierarchy fashioned after their mentor's example.

For Ambrose, in the end, the whole of life was about image, his own and his church's, and the one was intrinsically bound up with the other. That is not to cast doubt on his sincerity, or to suggest that everything about him was a façade. In an age increasingly prone to privatize beliefs and morals, we might even learn from his passionate concern to demonstrate the public validity of his Christian message, and to work out intellectual, social, and political routes by which to commend it to its critics. Ambrose lived in a time and culture uniquely susceptible to the potency of the particular image he laboured to present, and by styling his ministry as he did he proved to be the chief architect of Catholicism's victory in the fourth-century West. There are, at the same time, many areas in which few if any of us would wish to invoke his behaviour as a model. We may admire the dexterity with which he created his dream, without ignoring the dark realities of some of his methods. No doubt the tantalizing complexities of Ambrose's psychological make-up will remain to intrigue us. But if we can hold in our mind's eye both the outstanding achievements and the questionable tactics for which he was responsible, we may at least avoid some of the mistakes into which earlier historians have fallen. We may, in fact, have begun to glimpse the only Ambrose who ultimately matters.

BIBLIOGRAPHY

Becker, Maria (1994) *Die Kardinaltugenden bei Cicero und Ambrosius: De officiis*. Chrêsis 4. Basel: Schwabe.

Biermann, Martin (1995) *Die Leichenrede des Ambrosius von Mailand: Rhetorik, Predigt, Politik*. Stuttgart: Steiner.

Bonato, Antonio (1987) 'L'idea del sacerdozio in S. Ambrogio', *Augustinianum* 27: 423–64.

Brown, Peter R. L. (1981) *The Cult of the Saints: its Rise and Function in Latin Christianity*. London: SCM Press.

—— (1988) *The Body and Society: Men, Women and Sexual Renunciation in Early Christianity.* New York: Columbia University Press.

—— *Power and Persuasion in Late Antiquity: Towards a Christian Empire.* Madison: University of Wisconsin Press.

Burns, Thomas S. (1974) 'The Battle of Adrianople: A Reconsideration', *Historia* 22: 336–45.

Campenhausen, Hans F. von (1929) *Ambrosius von Mailand als Kirchenpolitiker.* Berlin and Leipzig: Walter de Gruyter.

Chadwick, Henry (1976) *Priscillian of Avila: The Occult and the Charismatic in the Early Church.* Oxford: Clarendon Press.

Coppa, Giovanni (1992) 'Istanze formative e pastorali del presbitero nella vita e nelle opere di Sant' Ambrogio', in F. Sergio (ed.) *La formazione al sacerdozio ministeriale nella catechesi e nella testimonianza di vita dei Padri: Convegno di studio e aggiornamento, Facoltà di Lettere cristiane e classiche (Pontificium Institutum Altioris Latinitatis), Roma 15–17 marzo 1990.* Rome: LAS, 95–132.

Courcelle, Pierre (1968) *Recherches sur les 'Confessions' de saint Augustin*, 2nd edn. Paris: Études Augustiniennes.

—— (1973) *Recherches sur saint Ambroise. 'Vies' anciennes, culture, iconographie.* Paris: Études Augustiniennes.

Cracco Ruggini, Lellia (1974) 'Ambrogio e le opposizioni anticattoliche fra il 383 e il 390', *Augustinianum* 14: 409–49.

Dassmann, Ernst (1965) *Die Frömmigkeit des Kirchenvaters Ambrosius von Mailand. Quellen und Entfaltung.* Münster: Aschendorff.

—— (1975) 'Ambrosius und die Märtyrer', *Jahrbuch für Antike und Christentum* 18: 49–68.

Davidson, Ivor J. (1995) 'Ambrose's *De Officiis* and the intellectual climate of the late fourth century', *Vigiliae Christianae* 49: 313–33.

Doignon, Jean (1956) 'Perspectives ambrosiennes: SS. Gervais et Protais, génies de Milan', *Revue des Études Augustiniennes* 2: 313–34.

Duval, Yves-Marie (1974) 'L'originalité du "de virginibus" dans le mouvement ascétique occidental: Ambroise, Cyprien, Athanase', in Y.-M. Duval (ed.) *Ambroise de Milan dix études.* Paris: Études Augustainiennes, 9–66.

—— (1976) 'Ambroise, de son élection à sa consécration', in G. Lazzati (ed.) *Ambrosius Episcopus: Atti del Congresso internazionale di studi ambrosiani nel XVI centenario della elevazione di Sant' Ambrogio alla cattedra episcopale (Milano, 2–7 dec. 1974).* Milan: Vita e Pensiero, II, 235–83.

—— (1977) 'Formes profanes et formes bibliques dans les oraisons funèbres de saint Ambroise', in M. Fuhrmann (ed.) *Christianisme et formes littéraires de l'Antiquité tardive en Occident.* Geneva: Fondation Hardt, 235–301.

Faller, Otto (1942) 'La data della consecrazione vescovile di Sant' Ambrogio', in *Ambrosiana: scritti di storia, archeologia ed arte pubblicati nel XVI centenario della nascita di Sant' Ambrogio, CCXL–MCMXL.* Milan: Arturo Faccioli, 97–112.

Fischer, Balthasar (1970) 'Hat Ambrosius von Mailand in der Woche zwischen seiner Taufe und seiner Bischofskonsekration andere Weihen empfangen?', in P. Granfield and J. A. Jungman (eds) *Kyriakon: Festschrift Johannes Quasten*, 2 vols. Münster: Aschendorff, 2: 527–31.

—— (1984) 'Ist Ambrosius wirklich in Trier geboren?', in E. Dassmann and K. Thraede (eds) *Vivarium: Festschrift Theodor Klauser zum 90. Geburtstag.* Münster: Aschendorff, 132–5.

Fontaine, Jacques (1992) *Saint Ambroise: Hymnes, texte établi, traduit et annoté.* Paris: du Cerf.

Gottlieb, Gunther (1973) *Ambrosius von Mailand und Kaiser Gratian.* Göttingen: Vandenhoeck & Ruprecht.

—— (1985) 'Der Mailänder Kirchenstreit von 385/386: Datierung, Verlauf, Deutung', *Museum Helveticum* 42: 37–55.

Graumann, Thomas (1994) *Christus Interpres. Die Einheit von Auslegung und Verkündigung in der Lukaserklärung des Ambrosius von Mailand.* Berlin & New York: Walter de Gruyter.

Gryson, Roger (1968) *Le prêtre selon saint Ambroise.* Louvain: Edition Orientaliste.

—— (1980) 'Les élections épiscopales en Occident au IVe siècle', *Revue d'histoire ecclésiastique* 75: 257–83.

Hahn, Viktor (1969) *Das wahre Gesetz: Eine Untersuchung der Auffassung des Ambrosius von Mailand vom Verhältnis der beiden Testamente.* Münster: Aschendorff.

Hanson, R. P. C. (1988) *The Search for the Christian Doctrine of God: The Arian Controversy, 318–381.* Edinburgh: T&T Clark.

Heather, Peter J. and Matthews, John F. (1991) *The Goths in the Fourth Century.* Liverpool: Liverpool University Press.

Hobbs, H. C. and Wuellner, W. (eds) (1980) *The Role of the Christian Bishop in Ancient Society.* Protocol of the 35th Colloquy, Center for Hermeneutical Studies. Berkeley and Los Angeles: University of California Press.

Homes Dudden, F. (1935) *The Life and Times of St. Ambrose,* 2 vols. Oxford: Clarendon Press.

Inglebert, Hervé (1996) *Les romains chrétiens face à l'histoire de Rome. Histoire, christianisme et romanités en Occident dans l'Antiquité tardive (IIIe–IVe siècles).* Paris: Etudes Augustiniennes.

Jacob, Christoph (1990) *'Arkandisziplin', Allegorese, Mystagogie: ein neuer Zugang zur Theologie des Ambrosius von Mailand.* Frankfurt-am-Main: Hain.

Johanny, Raymond (1968) *L'Eucharistie, centre de l'histoire du salut chez saint Ambroise de Milan.* Paris: Beauchesne.

Kaufman, Peter Iver (1997) 'Diehard Homoians and the Election of Ambrose', *Journal of Early Christian Studies* 5: 421–40.

Klein, Richard (1972) *Der Streit um dem Victoriaaltar: Die Dritte Relatio des Symmachus und die Briefe 17, 18 und 57 des Mailänder Bischofs Ambrosius.* Darmstadt: Wiss. Buchgesch.

Kopecek, Thomas A. (1979) *A History of Neo-Arianism,* 2 vols. Cambridge, Mass.: Philadelphia Patristic Foundation.

Krautheimer, Richard (1983) *Three Christian Capitals: Topography and Politics.* Berkeley and Los Angeles: University of California Press.

de Labriolle, Pierre (1928) *The Life and Times of St. Ambrose.* (English trans.). St Louis, Mo. and London: Herder.

Lazzati, Giuseppe (1960) *Il valore letterario della esegesi Ambrosiana.* Milan: Archivio Ambrosiano.

Lenox-Conyngham, Andrew (1982a) 'The Judgement of Ambrose the Bishop on Ambrose the Roman Governor', *Studia Patristica* 17: 62–5.

—— (1982b) 'The Topography of the Basilica Conflict of AD 385/6 in Milan', *Historia* 31: 353–63.

—— (1993) 'Ambrose and Philosophy', in L. R. Wickham and C. P. Bammel (eds) *Christian Faith and Greek Philosophy in Late Antiquity: Essays in Tribute to George Christopher Stead. Vigiliae Christianae* suppl. 19. Leiden: Brill, 112–28.

Lizzi, Rita (1990) 'Ambrose's Contemporaries and the Christianization of Northern Italy', *Journal of Roman Studies* 80: 156–73.

Lucchesi, Enzo (1977) *L'usage de Philon dans l'oeuvre exégétique de saint Ambroise. Une 'Quellenforschung' relative aux commentaires d'Ambroise sur la Genèse.* Leiden: Brill.

McLynn, Neil B. (1991) 'The "Apology" of Palladius: Nature and Purpose', *Journal of Theological Studies* n.s. 42: 52–76.

—— (1994) *Ambrose of Milan: Church and Court in a Christian Capital.* Berkeley and Los Angeles: University of California Press.

MacMullen, Ramsay (1990) 'The Historical Role of the Masses in Late Antiquity', in *Changes in the Roman Empire: Essays in the Ordinary*. Princeton, N. J.: Princeton University Press, 250–76, 385–93.

Madec, Goulven (1974) *Saint Ambroise et la philosophie*. Paris: Études Augustiniennes.

Maier, Harry O. (1994) 'Private Space as the Social Context of Arianism in Ambrose's Milan', *Journal of Theological Studies* 45: 72–93.

Markschies, Christoph (1995) *Ambrosius von Mailand und die Trinitätstheologie: kirchen- und theologiegeschichtliche Studie zur Antiarianismus and Neunizänismus bei Ambrosius und an lateinischen Westen (364–381 n. Chr.)*. Tübingen: Mohn.

Matthews, John (1975) *Western Aristocracies and Imperial Court, AD 364–425*. Oxford: Clarendon Press.

Maur, H. J. auf der (1977) *Das Psalmenverständnis des Ambrosius von Mailand: Ein Beitrag zum Deutungshintergrund der Psalmenverwendung im Gottesdienst der alten Kirche*. Leiden: Brill.

Mazzarino, Santo (1989) *Storia sociale del vescovo Ambrogio*. Rome: Bretschneider.

Meslin, Michel (1964) 'Nationalisme, Etat et religions à la fin du IVe siècle', *Archives de sociologie des religions* 18: 3–20.

—— (1967) *Les Ariens d'Occident, 335–430*. Paris: de Seuil.

Millar, Fergus G. B. (1992) 'The Jews of the Graeco-Roman Diaspora, AD 312–438', in J. Lieu, J. North and T. Rajak (eds) *The Jews among Pagans and Christians in the Roman Empire*. London: Routledge, 97–123.

Mirabella Roberti, M. (1984) *Milano Romano*. Milan: Rusconi.

Nauroy, Gérard (1985) 'L'Ecriture dans la pastorale d'Ambroise de Milan', in J. Fontaine and E. Pietri (eds) *La Bible de tous les temps*. 2: *Le monde latin antique et la Bible*. Paris: Beauchesne, 371–408.

—— (1988) 'Le fouet et le miel. Le combat d'Ambroise en 386 contre l'Arianisme Milanais', *Recherches Augustiniennes* 23: 3–86.

Nautin, Pierre (1974) 'Les premières relations d'Ambroise avec l'empereur Gratien', in Y.-M. Duval (ed.) *Ambroise de Milan: Dix études*. Paris: Études Augustiniennes, 229–44.

Neumann, C. W. (1962) *The Virgin Mary in the Works of Saint Ambrose*. Fribourg: Fribourg University Press.

Palanque, Jean-Rémy (1933) *Saint Ambroise et l'Empire romain. Contribution à l'histoire des rapports de l'Eglise et de l'Etat à la fin du quatrième siècle*. Paris: de Boccard.

Paredi, Angelo (1964a) *Saint Ambrose: His Life and Times* (English trans.). Notre Dame, Ind.: University of Notre Dame Press.

—— (1964b) 'Gerolamo e S. Ambrogio', in *Mélanges E. Tisserant 5. Studi e Testi 235*. Vatican City: Biblioteca Apostolica Vaticana, 183–98.

Pizzolato, Luigi Franco (1965) *La 'Explanatio Psalmorum XII'. Studio letterario sulla esegesi di Sant' Ambrogio*. Milan: Archivio Ambrosiano.

—— (1978) *La dottrina esegetica di Sant' Ambrogio*. Milan: Vita e Pensiero.

Ramsey, Boniface (1997) *Ambrose*. London and New York: Routledge.

Riggi, Calgero (1980) 'La verginità nel pensiero di S. Ambrogio', *Salesianum* 42: 789–806.

Savon, Hervé (1977) *Saint Ambroise devant l'exégèse de Philon le Juif*. Paris: Études Augustiniennes.

—— (1980) 'La première oraison funèbre de saint Ambroise (De excessu fratris I) et les deux sources de la consolation chrétienne', *Revue des études latines* 58: 370–402.

—— (1989) 'Un modèle de sainteté à la fin du IVe siècle: la virginité dans l'oeuvre de saint Ambroise', in J. Marx (ed.) *Sainteté et martyre dans les religions du Livre*. Brussels: Editions de l'Université des Bruxelles, 21–31.

—— (1997) *Ambroise de Milan (340–397)*. Paris: Desclée.

Seibel, Wolfgang (1958) *Fleisch und Geist beim heiligen Ambrosius*. Munich: Zink.

Sordi, Marta (1988) 'La concezione politica di Ambrogio', in *I Christiani e l'Impero nel IV secolo. Atti del congresso di Macerata (17–18 decembro 1987)*. Macerata: Università degli Studi, 143–54.

Swift, Louis J. (1970) 'St. Ambrose on Violence and War', *Transactions and Proceedings of the American Philological Association* 101: 533–43.

Testard, Maurice (1984–92) *Saint Ambroise: Les Devoirs*, 2 vols. Paris: Les Belles Lettres.

Toscani, Giuseppe (1974) *Teologia della Chiesa in Sant' Ambrogio*. Milan: Vita e Pensiero.

Van Haeringen, J. H. (1937) 'De Valentiniano II et Ambrosio. Illustrantur et digeruntur res anno 386 gestae: Valentinianus II basilicam adornitur (De Ambrosii Epistula XX)', *Mnemosyne* ser. 3, 5: 152–8, 28–33, 229–40.

Vasey, Vincent R. (1982) *The Social Ideas in the Works of St. Ambrose: A Study on De Nabuthe*. Rome: Institutum Patristicum Augustinianum.

Wilken, Robert L. (1983) *John Chrysostom and the Jews: Rhetoric and Reality in the Late 4th Century*. Berkeley and Los Angeles: University of California Press.

Williams, Daniel H. (1994) 'When did the Emperor Gratian Return the Basilica to the Pro-Nicenes in Milan?', *Studia Patristica* 24: 208–15.

—— (1995) *Ambrose of Milan and the End of the Nicene–Arian Conflicts*. Oxford: Clarendon Press.

Wytzes, J. (1936) *Der Streit um den Altar der Viktoria. Die Texte der betreffenden Schriften des Symmachus und Ambrosius*. Amsterdam and Paris.

Zangara, Vincenza (1981) 'L'*inventio* dei martiri Gervasio e Protasio. Testimonianze di Agostino su un fenomeno di religiosita popolare', *Augustinianum* 21: 119–33.

Zelzer, Michaela (1987) 'Ambrosius von Mailand und das Erbe der klassischen Tradition', *Wiener Studien* 100: 201–26.

CHAPTER FORTY-EIGHT

AUGUSTINE

—— ·✦· ——

Carol Harrison

North Africa, where Augustine[1] was born in 354 and where he was to spend almost half of his life as bishop of the large seaport of Hippo Regius (modern Anaba), lay at the heart of the Roman empire. The coastal region, which possessed the greatest concentration of towns – Hippo was second only to Carthage, the capital – contrasted sharply with the less Romanized, village, agrarian culture of the inland olive and wheat plains. These were, however, central to the Roman economy and provided Rome with at least two-thirds of its grain supply: Africa was known as the breadbasket of Italy.

Figure 48.1 Mosaic from Utica in North Africa depicting olive cultivation. Photo J. C. N. Coulston.

Augustine's birthplace was the small, traditionally Berber town of Thagaste (modern Souk Ahras) in the Eastern part of Numidia. His father, Patrick, belonged to that class of modest landowners who were permanently impoverished by the enormous tax burdens imposed by the emperor, which, as a town councillor (*decurion* or *curiale*) he was either obliged to collect from peasant tenants (*coloni*) or pay himself (see Chapter 1 of this volume). Patrick obviously entertained higher aspirations for his son and was aware that the best means to advance his prospects was to ensure that he obtained that universally recognized, exclusive and distinguishing marker of social prestige and office: a traditional Roman education. This began with the school of grammar in Thagaste where he would have learnt to read a text and study the disciplines of the liberal arts, and then, thanks to a wealthy patron, he went to the school of rhetoric, the art of public speaking, at Madura and Carthage.

The office of rhetor was the highest goal of Late Antique education; thus, in deciding to become a teacher of rhetoric Augustine entered an aristocracy, not of birth, but of educational formation.[2] He taught at Carthage (376–83) and Rome (383–4) and was eventually appointed to the municipal chair of rhetoric in Milan (384), the imperial capital. From here he could well have aspired to a provincial governorship and to senatorial rank. Instead, in 386, at the age of 32, he abandoned his career, broke off his arranged marriage, relinquished any future hope of financial security or worldly status, and converted to Christianity.

Why? Augustine's answer is to be found in his well-known *Confessions*. Here we can read his own account of his life (from infancy, childhood, school, adolescence . . .) and his intellectual journey in search of wisdom, the true philosophy. His autobiographical account of his conversion to Christianity in Books 1–9 is presented as a microcosm of the conversion of creation towards God in Books 11–13, where he comments upon Genesis 1–3. (Book 10 reflects upon his present life as a fallen human being in a fallen world, and therefore on how conversion is not so much the end, as the beginning of his search for God.)

The problem with the *Confessions* is that, like all autobiographies, it was written with the benefit of retrospective reflection and interpretation at least ten years after the events he recounts (397–401). They are therefore fundamentally anachronistic and frustrate any attempt to find out what really happened: Augustine had too many critics, too much to defend and justify, too much to teach and recommend to his readers, too much cultural 'baggage', for this. The *Confessions* must therefore be read on his terms.

CONVERSION OF THE MIND, HEART AND WILL

He would obviously like to portray himself as a rather dissolute youth: fighting for milk at his mother's breast, failing to learn Greek at school, stealing pears, enjoying adolescent sexual adventures, deceiving his despairing mother, unable to remain chaste – all this to demonstrate his own sinfulness and the operation of God's grace in bringing him willingly to embrace Christianity.

He also conveys a sense of intellectual earnestness: he read and understood Aristotle's *Ten Categories* at an early age, was tormented by the question of evil, and at the age of 19 was fired by Cicero's *Exhortation to Philosophy* (a textbook he read while studying rhetoric) to seek for wisdom, the true philosophy. Turning to the Christian scriptures his cultured sensibilities found them quite rebarbative – they were 'unworthy to be compared to the majesty of Cicero'. Instead, he became a member of a dualistic, ascetic, gnostic-type religious sect, founded upon the teaching of the prophet Mani (born in Babylonia in 216 CE). For a time the Manichees[3] seemed to offer Augustine everything for which he had been searching: they claimed to represent a true and purified form of Christianity and criticized precisely those aspects of it which Augustine too had found problematic (contradictory, seemingly immoral scriptures; an anthropomorphic conception of God; an emphasis on faith and authority). He found the communal nature of the sect, its extensive, lavishly illustrated scriptures and, above all, its attempt to distance itself from evil matter by extreme asceticism in its 'elect' deeply attractive, even though he himself felt unable to embrace celibacy and joined the lower rank of 'hearers'. At some stage during the nine years he remained in the sect disillusionment began to set in: their claim to possess truth was revealed as mere pseudo-science, their asceticism proved to be more a matter of words than of practice, their dualism raised more problems than it solved, and the much-acclaimed Manichee, Faustus, failed to answer any of these problems. On finally breaking with them Augustine despaired of ever finding the truth, and hints at a period of scepticism in the *Confessions*.

During this period Augustine moved from Rome to the imperial capital, Milan, to take up the municipal chair of rhetoric, secured for him through the influence of Manichaean friends, and it was while he was in Milan that two decisive encounters occurred which completely transformed his thought. The first was with what he describes as 'some books of the Platonists, translated from Greek into Latin' (*Confessions* 7.9.13). It is unclear what exactly Augustine read; scholars generally conclude that it was probably some Latin translations of Plotinus' (204–70 CE) *Enneads* (he could not read Greek with any great facility) and maybe some translations of Plotinus' editor and disciple, Porphyry (232–300).[4] Whatever the works were they revolutionized his thought, in particular, their insight that the true nature of reality was spiritual. Augustine was finally able to free himself from the prevailing materialism of the thinkers of his day, including the Manichees, to find a convincing alternative to anthropomorphic conceptions of God, finally to discover an answer to the problem of evil (as a privation of the good), and to understand himself as a spiritual being who might find truth in the God who is both the foundation of himself and who transcends him.

The second encounter was with Ambrose, bishop of Milan, whom Augustine heard preach. Part of Augustine's acquaintance with Neoplatonism no doubt came through his sermons, but what especially struck him at this time was Ambrose's allegorical, spiritual exegesis of scripture, which overcame all the objections which the Manichees' literal, rationalisitic exegesis had posed.

In recounting these events in his *Confessions* Augustine obviously wishes to persuade his reader (and, of course, himself) of the rational, logical force of the religion he had embraced. In doing so he would have in mind his own critics, who doubted the genuineness of his conversion, and questioned, for example, whether he had really left Manichaeism behind, and also his intellectual peers, to whom Christianity (and especially its scriptures) appeared somewhat illogical, absurd, crude and rather distasteful, and who criticized its credulity in putting faith in authority before reason.

The final dramatic moment of conversion is, however, not a scene of intellectual argument and proof but a highly emotional turning of his heart and will towards God. The *Confessions* are, in fact, one of the first works of antiquity to reveal a keen sense, and candid portrait of the writer's inner self; his emotions, affections, the intricate and confusing workings of his mind and the depths of his subconscious. This is reflected in their highly charged, vivid poetic language, in dialogue with God.

Describing his gradual ascent towards God in Neoplatonic terms in Book 10 Augustine concludes with the realization that in fact he had no need to seek for Him, since God had always been graciously present, calling to him, as seen in the almost rhapsodic twenty-seventh chapter:

> Late have I loved you, Beauty so ancient and so new, late have I loved you. Yes, you were inside me while I was outside myself. I sought you there and – in my deformity – rushed upon the lovely things of your creation. You were with me, but I was not with you. Holding me far from you were objects which would have had no existence if they did not exist in you. You called! You cried! You shattered my deafness. You glistened! You shone! You put my blindness to flight. You gave off your fragrance and I drew in breath, so now I breathe for you. I tasted you and now I hunger and thirst for you. You touched me, and I am afire for your peace.
>
> (Augustine, *The Confessions* 10.27; trans. Philip F. Esler)

In *Confessions* 8 he describes the actual moment of his conversion as inspired by a divinely graced reading of a passage from the Apostle Paul: hearing a voice chanting 'take up and read' he opened the copy of Paul's epistles which he had been reading in the garden of his lodgings at Milan and his eyes fell upon Rom. 13:13, 'Not in rioting and drunkenness, not in chambering and impurities, not in contention and envy, but put on the Lord Jesus Christ and make not provision for the flesh in its concupiscences' (*Confessions* 8.12.29). Augustine's final conversion was one of his will, away from the temptations, distractions and allurements of the world to true celibacy (*continentia*) – a single-minded, single-hearted devotion to God.

Conversion from Christianity to Christianity

Perhaps most importantly (and most anachronistically?) he describes his search for truth against the ever-present backdrop of Christianity, as if he was never not a Christian but was merely seeking to reconcile himself to it: he had drunk it in with his mother Monica's milk; he had been dedicated to it as a child; when he read Cicero the only thing he found lacking was the name of Christ; the Manichees attracted him because they claimed to be true Christians (*integri Christiani*); the Sceptics he rejected because Christ was absent from their thought; the Platonists he measured against Christian thought and found wanting. Obviously this way of presenting his conversion again serves to demonstrate the insuperable operation of

God's grace, this time in a rather errant intellectual, but more to the point it passes judgement upon the philosophers and religious cults of Augustine's day and vindicates Christianity as the 'true philosophy' and 'true religion', with Christ as the 'one mediator' between God and man. Whereas the philosophers would proudly maintain that truth is accessible to reason or through the cult of the gods,[5] Augustine affirms in the *Confessions* that it is only accessible through the revelation and mediatorship of Christ, and that it is only appropriated by humble faith, hope and love in him. Augustine often uses Rom. 1:19–23 to demonstrate the philosophers' insight into the truth, 'For what can be known about God is plain to them; because God has shown it to them. Ever since the creation of the world, his invisible nature, namely, his eternal power and deity, has been clearly perceived in the things that have been made'. But the verses which follow demonstrate the philosophers' pride and guilt, because, although they thereby knew God, they 'did not give thanks to him as God, but became futile in their thinking, and their senseless minds were darkened. Claiming to be wise they became fools and exchanged the glory of the immortal God for images resembling mortal man or birds or animals or reptiles.'

The doctrine of the fall

What was it that brought about this decisive break with his own past life and habits on the one hand, and with ancient philosophy on the other, to precipitate his conversion to such a distinctive form of Christianity? The apostle Paul provides a clue.

Paul was being read and commented upon by many of Augustine's contemporaries and in the early years of the 390s Augustine undertook a series of works on Romans and Galatians.[6] It was here that he found the material to articulate his understanding of the nature of moral evil, free will and grace. The question of evil had haunted Augustine from the very beginning of his search for truth, because it, more than anything else, militated against the Christian belief in an omnipotent, just and loving creator-God. The Manichees' dualistic explanation, which attributed evil to matter, but not to the transcendent God, for a while satisfied him, but later raised more problems than it solved: how could God be omnipotent if an independent force of evil could overcome the good? He found an answer to these problems in the notion (probably discovered in Plotinus) that evil is a privation of the good: that everything that exists is good, but in so far as it turns away from the good, it moves towards non-being, and thereby becomes evil. Reflecting on his own experience of evil by characteristically turning within in order to analyse his own inner experiences, emotions and passions, he vividly depicts the vitiated, flawed operation of his will, alienated and dissociated from itself, knowing the good but unable to act upon it, and thus locates the origin of evil in the turning of man's will away from the good. This was confirmed for him by Paul's portrait of his divided will in Rom. 7:15: 'For that which I do I allow not: for what I would, that do I not: but what I hate, that do I' (although this is very much Paul interpreted by Augustine: as Krister Stendahl [1963] has suggested, the sense of agonized interiority which Augustine describes was probably not Paul's own experience).

In the earlier commentaries on Paul he seems to have entertained the possibility that God's election of sinful man was based on merit, on man's choice of faith and anticipation of God's grace, and that it was in this way that man moved from being under the law to being under grace. In a letter written to his friend, the priest Simplicianus, in 396, however, he sets forth explicitly, for the first time, a doctrine of original sin which leaves no room for merit, but makes everything hinge upon the operation of God's grace.

In response to Simplicianus' question concerning the fates of Esau and Jacob, which seem to have been determined before their birth, he expounds an uncompromising doctrine of the fallenness of man – of mankind as a *massa peccati*, 'one lump in which the original guilt [of Adam] remains throughout' (*Letter to Simplicianus* 2.17, 20) – of the culpability of all men, the impotence of man's will to do the good and the unmerited grace of God which can alone, regardless of faith, reason or works, inspire in man a delight in the good. These reflections mark a watershed in Augustine's thought which was to profoundly affect its future course. Romans 7 now became a portrait of man under grace, unable to do anything but sin without the inspiration of God's grace which moves his will to delight in the good, 'if these things delight us which serve our advancement towards God, that is due not to our own whim or industry or meritorious works, but to the inspiration of God and to the grace he bestows' (*To Simplicianus* 2.21).

The doctrine of original sin was not, however, Augustine's invention; rather, he was able to draw upon African tradition, not least Cyprian (who also used it to justify the baptism of infants) and Ambrose. He also appeals to a number of scriptural texts, especially 1 Cor. 15:22, 'As in Adam all die, so in Christ all will be given life', and Rom. 5:12, 'in whom [sc. Adam] all sinned' (though, in fact, they are all probably either mistranslated or misconstrued.)[7] The doctrine of original sin also makes him incline towards a traducianist (that all souls are derived from that of the first man and are handed on from one generation to the next) rather than a creationist (that a particular soul is created for each individual) explanation of the soul's origin. But it is his own experience of man's inveterate sinfulness, of the inner conflicts and incapacity of his will, which seems to have provided him with decisive proof of man's falleness. Most especially, it is man's concupiscence, his disordered lust, evidenced most forcefully in sexual intercourse, which provides, for Augustine, decisive proof of his subjection to original sin. The will or reason no longer controls man's body in the ordered and harmonious fashion which would have characterized all its operations, including intercourse,[8] before the fall; rather his actions are now characterized by disordered and uncontrolled concupiscence.

In the texts where he discusses the fall,[9] however, Augustine is at a loss as to how to explain why Adam's will first turned away from his Creator and disobeyed His commandment. He suggests that perhaps the defection of Adam's will was attributable to his original creation from nothing, so that he is liable to move back to nothingness; that Eve, who was the first to be seduced by the serpent, was not yet as advanced in knowledge as Adam; that Adam, in 'friendly benevolence', went along with Eve, rather than abandon her; that he did not think God would deal with him so harshly; that Adam and Eve were already beginning to turn towards themselves in pride; that God foreknew the greater good he would bring from their sin and allowed the serpent to tempt them.

Whatever the reason for the fall, it meant that Adam and Eve, already mortal, were no longer on the path to immortality but justly subject to death. They no longer enjoyed a direct, intuitive knowledge of God or of each other, but became dependent upon language and signs in order to communicate, a means fraught with difficulties and open to misrepresentation, deception and ambiguity. In turning away from God they abandoned the source of their existence, that which gave it order, unity and harmony, and thereby found their attention fragmented, scattered and dispersed, attached and held as with glue to the temporal, mutable things to which they had turned. They became aliens and exiles from their true home; deaf and blind to the truth, subject to the whims of their vitiated will. They were wholly dependent upon the work of God's grace to heal their faculties and to enable them to desire, and move towards, their lost homeland. Such is Augustine's depiction of all men in this life.

Augustine's reflections on original sin in *To Simplicianus* are also the context for the near contemporary work, the *Confessions*, and provide the real key to understanding the way in which he interpreted, and chose to present, his conversion as the working of God's grace upon a mind which was, in fact, fundamentally alienated and dissociated from itself, which could not apprehend the truth, or will to act, without the revelation of God's grace in the incarnate Son to inspire his faith, hope and love. They also explain his rather daunting post-conversion portrait of himself in *Confessions* 10, as someone still subject to temptation, still prone to sin and still wholly dependent upon the grace of Christ, the mediator between God and man.[10]

PRIEST, BISHOP AND MONK

For Augustine, conversion to Christianity meant embracing celibacy. Obviously this was not a strict requirement, but it seems that he would be satisfied with nothing less than what he regarded as the acme of the Christian life. Why this was the case is difficult to establish. The highest rank of the Manichees, Augustine's former co-religionists, were distinguished by their celibacy. Asceticism, frequently expressed as celibacy, had long been the ideal of the philosophic life. The ascetic spirit, fostered by the likes of Tertullian, Cyprian and Ambrose in the West, had made significant inroads into Christian life and practice following the conversion of Constantine in 312, as an effective means of keeping alive the martyr spirit and of resisting 'secularization'. Augustine's first encounter with the famous *Life of Antony*, the Egyptian ascetic, and the story of two civil servants who had embraced celibacy on reading it for the first time, had been very influential in precipitating his conversion. Above all, Augustine seems to have possessed a natural monastic spirit,[11] which found its true home in a community of like-minded individuals, pursuing a common life, in friendship and love. After his baptism in Milan in 387 he immediately set about realizing this ideal in a retreat with family and friends at a country villa in the north Italian village of Cassiciacum, where he also began a series of predominantly philosophical works on such classical subjects as the nature of wisdom, scepticism, the happy life and order.

Although intending to return to his native town of Thagaste with his mother,

Monica, and friends to carry out their 'holy enterprise' (*Confessions* 9.9.2), presumably establishing a community, he was forced to spend a year in Rome, due to a blockade of the Mediterranean in 387–8. Here he no doubt became better acquainted with the vigorous ascetic movements and debates which characterized fourth-century Rome, and encountered for the first time male and female monastic houses organized following Eastern models.[12]

In Thagaste he established a lay community of *servi dei*, or servants of God, spending his time in fasting, prayer, study and good works,[13] and completed a number of works which are more distinctively Christian in their concern with exegesis of scripture, the church, faith and the Incarnation, than those written at Cassiciacum.[14] Although he tells us that he was careful not to visit towns which needed a bishop, it was while visiting a possible recruit for the Thagaste community in Hippo, in 392, that he was laid hold of by the congregation and forcibly ordained priest in order to help their own ageing bishop, Valerius. Quickly realizing the exceptional qualities of his priest, Valerius ensured he could not be snatched away by a neighbouring diocese, by (somewhat irregularly) ordaining him co-adjutor bishop to succeed him on his death. Thus Augustine was to spend the rest of his life as priest and from 396 as bishop of Hippo.

He also continued to pursue a communal life, first in a lay monastery in the garden of the basilica, and then, as bishop, in a clerical monastery established in the bishop's house.[15] His *Rule*[16] is explicitly modelled on the first Christian communities of Acts in its emphasis on the unity in charity of the common life of its members, with 'one heart and soul' directed towards God, putting the interests of the community before personal interest. Its primary concern is not with asceticism, 'holiness' or celibacy, but with the social, ethical aspects of life lived in common. The monastic vocation was the closest Augustine thought man might come, in this life, to overcoming the self-referential pride which had fractured society in the fall, and of approximating to the social life of the saints – even though, in practice, the community fell far short of such ideals and inevitably shared the unavoidable ambiguity of Christian life in a fallen, vitiated world.

From the moment of his ordination Augustine was never again free to pursue the life of a scholar. He was immediately obliged to preach, to address the assembled African bishops in council, to refute the Manichees, to battle against the Donatist schism which had torn the African church apart, as well as attempting to pursue his own writing. The latter was to become increasingly circumstantial, responding to needs, questions, challenges and demands as they arose.

As bishop these demands intensified, for not only was he expected to preach, celebrate and baptize (the first two often daily) but he also assumed the role of administrator and legal arbitrator which had fallen to the bishops following the conversion of Constantine. The church was now a legally recognized institution able to receive gifts, donations and bequests. It was the bishop's duty to administer these goods, which often included land and estates, for the benefit of the church and the needy to whom it had traditionally ministered. More importantly, the bishop could now arbitrate between any two parties who chose to consult him and who agreed to abide by his judgement. In an empire with no organized police force and no organized system of legal advice or representation this episcopal jurisdiction was tremendously popular: it was free, quick and impartial. Augustine heard cases each weekday, frequently from morning until late afternoon – tedious, petty cases of family quarrels and disputes over land, property, debts, children. He also found himself interceding for members of his congregation to higher officials – with little success, to his enormous frustration.

SCRIPTURE AND PREACHING

Although Augustine would have preached almost every day – and therefore in all about eight thousand times – we possess only 546 extant sermons as well as the 124 *Tractates on John's Gospel*, the ten *Homilies on the First Epistle of John* and a series of sermons on all 150 Psalms. He was a very popular preacher, had an enthusiastic congregation at home and was often invited as a visiting preacher, especially at Carthage (see Figure 48.2). This was no doubt due to his simple, straightforward style, which, combined with his finely honed rhetorical skills and his training and experience as a teacher, enabled his congregation to build up a solid knowledge of scripture and to follow even the most difficult theological argument.

Augustine, however, as we have seen, regarded language as a result of the fall: before the fall man would have known and communicated intuitively, without the need for words. His awareness of the problems, and techniques, of teaching and

Figure 48.2   Remains of the Church of St Cyprian in Carthage where Augustine once preached. Photo J. C. N. Coulston.

communicating are cogently presented in *On Teaching the Uninstructed* and in a number of works on language and exegesis.[17] Most especially, he is clear that for teaching to be rightly communicated and understood it must be motivated by, and received in, love.[18] Thus, one of his favourite analogies for the role of the preacher is the descent of Christ to become incarnate in order to lead man back to Himself. Language, too, then, like the common life of the monastic community, when rooted in love, has a social function in enabling the Christian community to cohere, understand and live its faith. And for Augustine the language of Christianity was its scriptures.

When he had first examined the Christian scriptures as a student of rhetoric, fired by Cicero's *Exhortation to Philosophy*, they had jarred with his cultured sensibilites. They appeared crude, badly written and full of vulgarisms and solecisms, unworthy when compared with 'the dignity of Cicero' (*Confessions* 3.5.9). The early third-century Old Latin translation which Augustine no doubt consulted was indeed an extremely literal, rather poor translation, but scripture's defects were a notorious feature of pagan criticism of Christianity which any educated person, pagan or Christian, could not but be sensitive to. Augustine's attitude to them is therefore unavoidably ambiguous. To an extent, he was able to reconcile himself to them by finding features which could be accommodated to cultured, Late Antique taste: Ambrose had shown him that they were full of mysteries and could be interpreted allegorically in order to sound their spiritual depths; they could be analysed according to the rules of rhetoric and not found wanting (*On Christian Doctrine* 4).

Augustine was sensitive to questions of exegetical method. In some passages he outlines a fourfold sense (the historical, analogical, aetiological and allegorical), which necessitates a consideration of the author's intention, his culture and thought forms, his initial inspiration and also of the readers' possible interpretation and re-application of what he has said. He seems to allow for a multiplicity of meaning and interpretation on the part of author and reader, so long as neither contradict the basic rule of love of God and neighbour. Similarly, he allows for discrepancies between the authors of scripture (for example, in *On the Harmony of the Gospels*) on the basis that what matters is not the details each remembers and has presented in his own fashion, but their shared intention, which is unified because of their common inspiration by the Holy Spirit. It is in this context that he explains and justifies his frequent use of allegory as an exegetical tool, especially in sermons: it allows him to investigate the spiritual sense of the literal text of scripture; to present its truth to his hearers at their various levels; to meet the criticisms of scripture's sensitive, erudite pagan critics; to deal with obviously symbolic, figurative or otherwise offensive or absurd passages; to delight the hearer and inspire him to seek for, and delight in finding, the truth.

Most important was what the scriptures had to teach: humility not pride; confession not presumption; grace not self-reliance. These lessons of the Incarnation to fallen man were as relevant to the cultured critic as to the self-sufficient philosopher, and it is the commandment of love of God and neighbour, and the doctrine of the Incarnation, which provides the rules and method for Augustine's interpretation, rather than those of classical grammar and rhetoric.

Nevertheless, Augustine, like most of the Fathers, was a product of a classical education; he had been formed by it, and to a large extent, even as a Christian, it determined his mind-set. It could not simply be dispensed with. It is with the rather ambiguous, but often fruitful, relation between classical culture and Christianity that we find Augustine coming to terms in *On Christian Doctrine* (*De doctrina Christiana*) which is both a work on Christian exegesis and preaching and also a detailed examination of the place and use of secular culture. Of course, pagan religious practice – idolatry, sacrifice, the mysteries – was wholly rejected, but other aspects of pagan culture – the disciplines, philosophy, moral rules, monotheist affirmations and aspirations – had so much in common with Christianity that they were often thought to be derived from earlier teaching in Moses and the prophets. These were 'seeds of the Logos' and could be legitimately appropriated and used by Christians who, like the Israelites, spoiled the Egyptians of their treasure.[19] For Augustine, they are to be used in so far as they facilitate the interpretation, and expression in preaching, of the truth of scripture.

CHRISTIANITY AND PAGANISM

Secular culture was an issue for Augustine and his contemporaries, not just at a cultural, literary level, but also, as our comments about the social function of scripture above might suggest, at a social level too. Although the empire became officially Christian in the course of the fourth century, following Constantine's conversion, the society in which the church found itself was still more than vestigially pagan. Indeed, some scholars suggest that the church made very little impact indeed on the municipal life of the towns of the empire which remained, if not pagan, at least secular and 'unchristianized': it showed no interest in those institutions and offices of state which had traditionally been grounded in paganism; provided no alternatives to the pagan civic rites; did not erect Christian civic buildings or establish Christian schools.[20] But Augustine could not but be aware of the 'vestigial' paganism of his congregation. As his sermons witness, they still carried charms, wore amulets, consulted diviners, swore oaths, used the pagan religious calendar, observed the old funerary customs, and, most especially, took part in the processions and attended the theatre, games, spectacles and shows which were still a central part of civic life. In a very real way it was the duty of the bishop to define just what being a Christian meant in this shadowy and confusing overlap of sacred and secular in the lives of his congregation.[21] Indeed, Augustine and his fellow bishops were forced into making very clear-cut distinctions when imperial policy turned from toleration to the proscription of paganism under Theodosius.

THE UNATTAINABILITY OF PERFECTION

Augustine's understanding of man's fall, of original sin, and of the operation of divine grace meant that any school or doctrine which claimed to be able to attain perfection in this life was, in his eyes, fundamentally unsound and contradictory to Christian doctrine and experience. In the course of his episcopate he encountered three such schools of thought which each, in different ways, challenged his under-standing of the Christian life and forced him to defend and elaborate the basic principles of his faith. The first, which proclaimed itself to be the true, holy and untainted Catholic church in Africa, was the Donatist schism. The second, which upheld the individual's freedom to will to do the good unhindered by original sin, was represented by the school of Pelagius. The third was the classical idea of a wholly just and peaceful society realizable in this life.

Donatism

The Donatist church[22] (so called after its main founder, Donatus, bishop of Carthage [313–55]) was a schism within the African church which arose during the Great Persecution of 303–5 among those who had taken a rigorous, separatist, uncompromising stance towards other Catholics, who, for whatever reason or by whatever means, seemed to have compromised with the Roman authorities, by, for example, handing over the sacred scriptures (see Chapter 37 in this volume). The rigourists refused to accept as bishop of Carthage someone whom they regarded as tainted by the sin of such compromise. Thus two churches were formed, and over the years, despite fierce imperial opposition, the Donatist faction became deeply estab-lished in African tradition and custom, so much so that by Augustine's day it was larger than the Catholic church and for many had become very much the Catholic church in Africa.

The Donatists represented an attempt to preserve the true identity of the African church – the church of the martyrs, of Cyprian and Tertullian – and also a movement of opposition to the world which they regarded as hostile and demonic. They were prepared to defend their faith to the death, to preserve the church without spot or wrinkle. In their opposition to the state the Donatist schismatics seem to have attracted the support of its other disaffected critics, who, whether for economic, political or strategic reasons, wished to defy Imperial policy. Some scholars have identified the origins of the Donatist schism in these varied non-religious griev-ances, but even their most extreme wing, the violent, criminal gangs of martyr-seeking circumcellions, were primarily religious in their self-understanding.

The schism was one Augustine had to counter from the moment of his ordination. He did so in a characteristically thorough and dedicated manner, even though it necessarily distracted him from more congenial, and often more pressing, concerns. He meticulously and painstakingly established the history and facts of the schism for himself, compiling huge dossiers of evidence with which he corrected Optatus' earlier version of the schism; he ensured that his own clergy were beyond reproach by taking energetic measures to enforce clerical discipline, preached innumerable sermons, attempted to organize public debates, and composed numerous treatises and letters to Donatist leaders and bishops.[23] However, his efforts would probably have been in vain without the aid of imperial legislation.

In 405 the emperor Honorius issued an Edict of Unity which for the first time branded the Donatists not only as schismatics but as heretics, and therefore subject to strict and punitive laws. The final, official blow to a weakened Donatist church came in 411 following the momentous Conference of Carthage, when Donatist and

Catholic bishops from throughout Africa faced each other under the presidency of the imperial representative, Marcellinus. In 412 the Edict of Unity was renewed and Donatism became a criminal offence, with a scale of fines according to rank. Clergy were exiled and property was to be surrendered. Although the Donatists did not give in, they were inevitably weakened and their future restricted.

The controversy raised a number of practical, as well as theological issues for Augustine, which were to shape his understanding of the nature of the church and its sacraments, as well as its relation to the state.

His attitude to the persecution and coercion of heretics was at first an ambiguous one, but faced with the violence of the circumcellions, who were not above theft, arson, assault or murder, and the Donatists' deep-rooted, defiant hostility which his own efforts had done little to counter, he seems to have become increasingly supportive of state intervention. He buttressed his acceptance with arguments for the necessity of loving discipline, correction and punishment in order to persuade the sinner of his fault, convert him to the truth, and, perhaps, eventually to even change his inner attitude and bring about a genuine conversion. However, he unfailingly intervened to moderate what he regarded as excessive punishment and to avert the death penalty.

The Donatists regarded themselves as the true Catholic church in Africa, which had stood firm during the persecutions and which was untainted by the sins of apostasy or compromise with the state authorities. They had preserved the church as a pure and holy congregation of the saints. Augustine ridicules their position: is anyone without sin? Who are they to judge the whole of the rest of the church throughout the world, which is largely unaware of them, and to condemn it? Do they not also suffer internal schisms and sinful behaviour? Have they not appealed to the authorities when it suited them? Obviously his theology of the fall, original sin, the operation of divine grace and election led him to cut incisively through the Donatists' all too circumstantial and convenient arguments to demonstrate that the most heinous sin is not that of compromise but of schism, whereby they had cut themselves off from the unity of charity in the universally recognized Catholic church; that all men are unavoidably sinful; that the church necessarily comprehends righteous and unrighteous and will remain a mixture of wheat and tares until the Last Judgement; that no one merits salvation; that the only source of holiness and purity within the church is Christ in His Holy Spirit.

The last point was the crux of Augustine's argument against the Donatists' insistence that the priestly orders of the clergy of the Catholic church were invalidated and rendered ineffective by sin and that therefore the sacraments they administered were likewise tainted, invalid and ineffective. The one source of sanctification, holiness, purity and sacramental effectiveness, Augustine argued, was Christ, through his Holy Spirit, irrespective of the moral character of the minister; the sacraments are 'holy in themselves' (*On Baptism* 4.18). Furthermore, the sacraments were valid, wherever they were administered, if they were performed in the name of Christ who instituted them, following the correct form of words. There was therefore no need for rebaptism, as the Donatists argued: even Donatist baptism, in these terms, was valid. But to be effective for salvation, however, the baptized needed to be reconciled to the unity of the Catholic church, as it was only here that the Spirit can be given and received. The Donatists' separation from the church is a sign of their lack of charity, the absence of the Holy Spirit, and without this, like a tree without roots, everything they did would be fruitless.

Pelagianism

The movement which has become known as 'Pelagianism'[24] does not just refer to the thought of Pelagius, but to a number of authors throughout the empire, from Britain to Sicily, Spain to the Holy Land, whose thought varied according to their specific contexts and concerns but who together possess a certain homogeneity, either through their acquaintance with Pelagius or because of the basic perfectionist thrust of their ideas.

Pelagius (350–425) himself was a British monk who first lived in Bethlehem and then in Rome, whose teaching proved especially popular with a group of influential, extremely conservative, Roman aristocrats because of its asceticism and call for perfection through a strict moral code. Its uncompromisingly high standards allowed them to set themselves apart from 'institutional' Christianity and become true Christians, *integri Christiani*. (Augustine's insistence upon celibacy in embracing Christianity can, strangely, be placed in the same context.)

Pelagius and his followers stood in a tradition firmly rooted in classical moral reflection, which insisted upon individual self-determination, moral responsibility, autonomy of will, and the realization of perfection through knowledge. Apart from a commentary on Romans, Pelagius' work consists largely of letters of ascetic advice and moral exhortation to converts, penitents, virgins, celibates and widows. Advising Demetrias, the daughter of an eminent noble family who wanted to pursue a vocation of virginity, he was emphatic that the choice of good or evil is 'voluntary and independent, not bound by necessity' (*To Demetrias* 3.2); that man possesses natural goodness, reason and wisdom, an inner law, which enables him to recognize and serve God. Although sin might obscure this natural state, he urged that it is not a fault in our nature but our will, and that man's original state can be restored by the remission of sin and Christ's new law appropriated in baptism. It is baptism, above all else, which marks the decisive break with man's past life for it remits his sins, and which allows the new law to operate and restores his original, natural state of knowledge and freedom.

Pelagius had encountered criticism and hostility well before his encounter with Augustine and had already engaged in fierce controversy with Jerome. His arrival in North Africa as an exile, following the fall of Rome in 410, brought him into a context where his teaching, and that of his followers, almost immediately faced censure. Foremost among the latter was Caelestius, who remained in Carthage while Pelagius went on to Palestine. His open denial of Adam's original sin, its transmission to his descendants, of the necessity of infant baptism and his conviction that it was possible for man to be sinless, led to his condemnation and excommunication. The issues were brought to Augustine's notice by letter and from then on, in a number of early treatises and letters, we find Augustine rebutting Pelagianist ideas.[25]

But it was only in 415 that he began to attack Pelagius himself in *On Nature and*

Grace. From that moment on Pelagian teaching was condemned by councils, imperial rescripts and church canons, and its proponents relentlessly pursued. As a result 'Pelagianism' was definitively identified and its details defined. It was a heresy which Augustine used all his powers to counter in numerous treatises, in particular against the southern Italian bishop, Julian of Eclanum, on the subjects of original sin, infant baptism, grace, free will, marriage and concupiscence, until the end of his life.[26]

To Augustine the effects of Adam's fall and the inheritance of his sin (original sin) were abundantly clear in man's vitiated will, his inability to will or to do the good, and in the lust (concupiscence) which overcame his reason. He therefore argued for the necessity of baptism, even for new-born infants, in order to remit the guilt of original sin. Even so, he was aware that the effects of original sin remained after baptism: no one can do anything of himself but sin; in order to do the good he stands in continual need of God's grace. Whereas for Pelagius grace was found in the power which enables man freely to will and to act, in man's created nature and in the 'new law' introduced by Christ's teaching and example which restored that nature, for Augustine the law was of no avail without the aid of God's Spirit. Without the life-giving Spirit the law is the 'letter that kills'. It is not enough for man to obey simply through fear of punishment or hope of reward, he must be moved to desire, love and delight in it – and this is the work of grace.

Reflections such as these made it difficult for Augustine to speak meaningfully of freedom in relation to man's will. In some contexts he speaks of God as helper, as preparing the will, of man cooperating with God, and resists the idea of compulsion in the operation of the will under grace. Many passages do, however, seem to suggest that divine election is irresistible. The reader needs to be aware that what Augustine has in mind is not the power of grace to coerce, override or control the will but rather its ability to unfailingly call forth a response which corresponds with man's true identity as a creature of God, a response of freely willed subjection, delight, desire for, and love of God's revelation. This is effected by God making what is good at the same time attractive, pleasing and delightful to man: 'the good begins to be desired when it begins to be sweet . . . therefore the blessing of sweetness is the grace of God, whereby we are made to delight in and to desire, that is, to love, what he commands us' (*Against the Letters of Pelagius* 2.21). God does not thereby deny man his freedom but enables him to attain it.

The fact that some are not saved, however, raised and continues to raise, intractable problems for Augustine's theory of grace. Why do some believe, while others do not? For Augustine, this is a matter of God's election, not human merit. But if so, why does he choose some but not others? What occupied Augustine, however, was not so much why some are left to damnation but rather why, when all men justly deserve damnation, God has shown mercy by electing some to be saved. His doctrine of original sin, divine election, foreknowledge and predestination was unable to answer why some were not saved, but was nevertheless able to demonstrate that the fact that they were not was wholly just. To the monks of Hadrumetum,[27] in North Africa, and those in Marseilles,[28] in southern Gaul, for whom this theology seemed to undermine their *raison d'être* and to leave no room for human responsibility or initiative, he argues forcibly that both the beginning of faith (which the monks at

Marseilles wished to attribute to man's free choice) and the perseverance to continue in faith, are wholly the work of grace.

The two cities[29]

When Rome fell to Alaric and his Gothic troops in 410 the future of a number of long-held ideals was also threatened. Since Constantine's conversion in 312 there had been a strong current of Christian thought, beginning with Eusebius of Caesarea, which regarded the empire as God's chosen vehicle to establish the Christian church throughout the earth, and the emperor as an almost Messianic figure, providentially appointed to deliver the empire from the forces of paganism and to ensure its salvation in the Christian church. This 'imperial theology' suffered a tremendous blow when Rome, the heart of the empire, fell to barbarian forces. The pagans, of course, as they had always done in times of crisis, blamed the catastrophe on the Christians' neglect of the gods, who could now be seen wreaking their revenge.

Augustine responded to the pagans' charges by addressing them – or at least, the cultured, aristocratic intellectuals who voiced these charges – in the first half of his *City of God*. Arguing from the same pagan classics as his opponents, he demonstrated that Rome had suffered similar crises well before the advent of Christianity; that this was not the judgement of the gods, who were mere jumped-up mortals, but the judgement of divine providence on their vicious subjection of others, not for the sake of peace or justice, but for personal glory and the desire to dominate. As Cicero had made clear, the Romans had long ago ceased to be a commonwealth in any real sense, because they failed to give to everyone their due.

Although Augustine's earliest work shows some leaning towards an 'imperial theology' it is obvious that after 410 he decisively broke with any conception of living in 'Christian times'. Rather, as Robert Markus has demonstrated,[30] he seems to regard the empire as 'theologically neutral', as having no role to play in the work of divine providence, for good or evil, but merely as part of the temporal, as it were, secular, context (*saeculum*), in which Christians and pagans alike lead their lives in the world. Instead, he increasingly drew upon Tyconius, earlier Christian tradition (especially early Jewish-Christian works), scripture, and themes first sketched within his own earlier works, to develop the idea of two cities – the city of God and the city of the world. He understood these cities to be societies made up of individuals united by a common goal or aim. The city of God included all those predestined by God for salvation, whose goal was not earthly goods or glory, but obedience to, and love of God and the common good. The city of this world, on the other hand, comprehends all those who have turned away from God to temporal goods, who seek their own selfish ends and who are therefore destined for damnation.

In developing the theme of the two cities, one of Augustine's main preoccupations is polemical: to refute those philosophers, and those Christian idealists, who thought that man's ultimate good, the happy life, the ideal city, true justice and peace could be attained in this life.[31] He regards such thought as 'amazing folly' which, given the wretched necessities of life in society, everyone, without exception, encounters and suffers at every level of human existence: in the family, the city, the world; they exist even among the angels. Experience underlines the fundamentally flawed and vitiated nature of the human will, the essentially selfish, self-seeking nature of human society, the impossibility of ever attaining peace or realizing true justice. All of this, for Augustine, is a sign of man's fallenness, of the outworkings of original sin.

In this life, therefore, where true peace and justice are unattainable, the two cities are inextricably interwoven; their members share the same society, the same city, the same occupations and laws, and, in some cases, the same family and worship. Because the city of God can only be fully realized in the life to come, its divinely elected and predestined citizens are separated from the city of the world only in will and their desire for their ultimate goal. In this world they are pilgrims, resident aliens, using and abiding by the powers, institutions and laws that be. They take part in government, the administration of the law and military service, in order to maintain whatever degree of peace and justice is possible after the fall, aware that its effects need to be delimited and controlled.

Even the church cannot be identified with the city of God. Although he believed that membership of it, through baptism, was necessary to belong to the city of God, Augustine was well aware, as he made clear during the Donatist controversy, that it in fact contained wheat and tares, righteous and unrighteous, the predestined elect and the damned, and that they will only finally be separated in the life to come.

The last four books of the *City of God* deal with the consummation and fulfilment of history in eternity, in the Last Judgement, Heaven and Hell. Asserting the original and eternal unity of the body and soul Augustine takes a distinctly anti-Platonic stand in defending a doctrine of the resurrection of the body, and discussing the problems which arise from it. In heaven there will be no longer be any need for communication by language and signs, there will be no time or mutability, no need for faith and hope, no need to 'use' and refer things to God; rather, there will be eternal contemplation, love and possession of God Himself, giving rise to eternal praise. Whereas now we can only see 'through a glass darkly', there we shall see 'face to face'.

DOCTRINE

Faith and reason

The crucial role which philosophy, and especially Neoplatonism, played in Augustine's conversion means that his early reflection on the Christian faith takes place very much within a rational, philosophically inspired context, in which the emphasis was placed upon the attainment of truth through the exercise of the mind in the liberal disciplines. These intellectual arts, he thought, enabled man to extricate himself from the temporal, mutable and deceptive reality experienced by the senses and to attain the eternal, immutable truth which can only be grasped by the highest, spiritual part of man: his mind, soul or intellect.

Augustine, was, however, moved to fundamentally revise and temper his early confidence in reason in a number of decisive ways. First of all, his polemic against the Manichees, which became more urgent when he returned to Africa, led him to emphasize and defend the important role of faith in apprehending the truth, as opposed to their claim to be able to explain everything by reason.[32] Second, his attempts to communicate the Christian faith to his largely illiterate, uneducated congregation could not but make him acutely conscious of the incongruence between traditional, philosophically based classical culture and their simple devotion and insight into the faith. His attempts to adapt his teaching to their various levels led to a deeper appreciation of the necessity and usefulness of faith. Whilst faith and reason are complementary, and reason enables us to decide between authorities, we must believe in order to understand.

It was his developed doctrine of the fall, however, with its conviction that the truth is inaccessible to man's darkened mind, and unattainable by his vitiated will, which confirmed for Augustine the indispensability of faith in God's temporal revelation of Himself to fallen man within the very temporal, mutable realm in which man's fragmented self has become imprisoned. It is in this context that Augustine's mature understanding of the scriptures, and his doctrines of creation, salvation history and, most especially, of the Incarnation are fully worked out.

Incarnation

Augustine did not write a work specifically on the Incarnation; rather, his reflections on God becoming man are found in a number of different contexts.[33] Most of these are pastoral, where he is primarily concerned to make clear the exemplary, healing, pedagogic, salvific and sacramental role of the Incarnation. In other contexts Augustine's intention is obviously polemical, and he expounds orthodox doctrine against Docetists, Apollinarians, Arians, Photinians and Sabellians. He also often seems to expound Christological doctrine with the philosophers in mind. This was not least because, although he was prepared to concede (following Rom. 1:19–20) that some philosphers had been able, through reason, to see the truth, he is convinced that they cannot understand or attain it because the only way to truth is a confession of humble faith which follows the way which is Christ; the proud presumption of the philosophers who think they can grasp the truth through their own powers is merely a symptom of their failure to do so.

Although he was largely ignorant of eastern Christological debates and terminology, Augustine does attempt to emphasize the unity of the Word, soul and body, of Godhead and manhood in Christ, partly in order to oppose the philosophers' denigration of the flesh and partly to counter their repugnance at the idea of the resurrection of the body. Perhaps most importantly, however, the unity of Godhead and manhood in Christ forms the basis for Augustine's emphasis upon Christ as the One Mediator between God and man, who was able to effect what the demonic mediators of pagan theurgy could never achieve. As God and man, as both the wisdom (*sapientia*) and the knowledge (*scientia*) of God, he is uniquely able to lead man from the temporal realm (of *scientia*) into which he has fallen to the realm (of *sapientia*) from which he has fallen. In this sense, Christianity offers the 'Universal Way' to salvation which the philosophers had sought but never found (*City of God* 10.32).

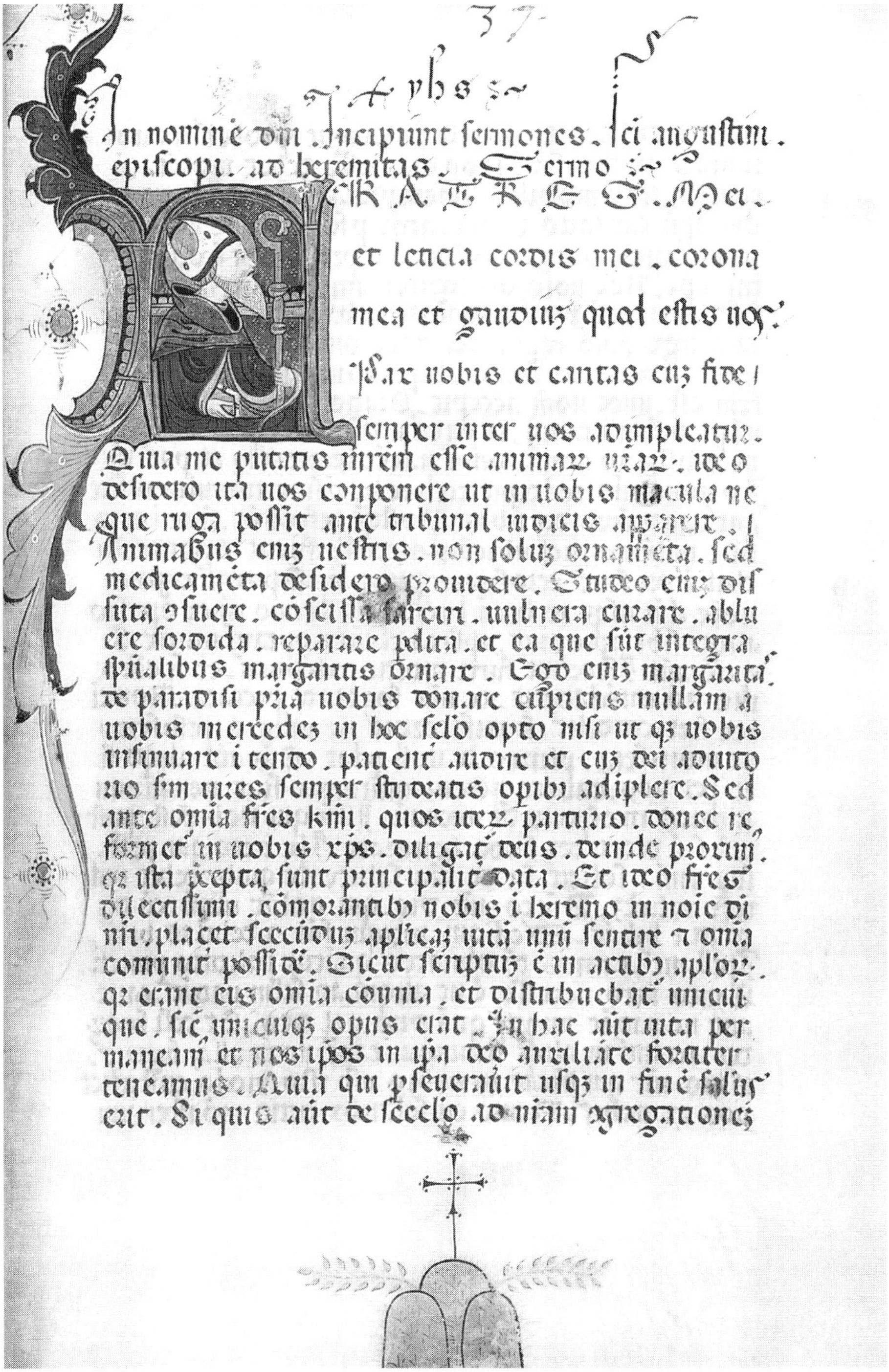
yhs
In nomine domini. Incipiunt sermones. sancti augustini.
episcopi. ad heremitas. Sermo
FRATRES. Mei
et leticia cordis mei. corona
mea et gaudium quam estis nos.
Pax nobis et caritas cum fide
semper inter nos adimpleatur.
Quia me putatis rectorem esse animarum vestrarum. ideo
desidero ita nos componere ut in nobis macula ne
que ruga possit ante tribunal iudicis apparere.
Animabus enim vestris. non solum ornamenta. sed
medicamenta desidero promovere. Studeo enim dis
suta consuere. conscissa sarcire. vulnera curare. ablu
ere sordida. reparare perdita. et ea que sunt integra
spiritualibus margaritis ornare. Ego enim margaritas
de paradisi preciosa nobis donare cupiens nullam a
nobis mercedem in hoc seculo opto nisi ut quod nobis
insinuare intendo. patienter audire et cum dei adiuto
rio secundum vires semper studeatis operibus adimplere. Sed
ante omnia fratres karissimi. quos iterum parturio. donec re
formetur in nobis christus. diligatur deus. deinde proximus.
quia ista precepta sunt principaliter data. Et ideo fratres
dilectissimi. commorantibus nobis in heremo in nomine do
mini. placet secundum apostolicam vitam unum sentire et omnia
communiter possidere. Sicut scriptum est in actibus apostolorum.
quia erant eis omnia communia. et distribuebatur unicui
que. sicut unicuique opus erat. In hac autem vita per
maneam et nos ipsos in ipsa deo auxiliante fortiter
teneamus. Anima qui perseveraverit usque in finem salvus
erit. Si quis autem de seculo ad nostram congregationem

Figure 48.3 First folio of a fourteenth-century Italian manuscript of the *Sermones ad Eremitas* of St Augustine, showing a portrait of St Augustine. Courtesy of St Andrews University Library, MS BR65.A9S2.

The Trinity

Aware that there was very little reflection on the Trinity within the Latin tradition and that much Greek thought was inaccessible to Latin speakers, Augustine worked on his 15-book *On the Trinity* over a period of 20 years (399–419). Although polemical considerations do not predominate, he was aware of the threat which Arianism and Sabellianism, in particular, posed to Trinitarian doctrine, and at various points seeks to refute them. His main concern, however, seems to have been to define and illustrate the traditional, orthodox doctrine of the equality of substance within the Trinity and the inseparable operation of its persons. He establishes the basis for this doctrine, and therefore its authority, in the scriptural account of the Incarnation of the Son and the revelation of the Holy Spirit at Pentecost.[34]

In examining the traditional, philosophical terminology which had been used to articulate the doctrine of the Trinity he is aware that the simple transposition of Greek terms, such as *ousia* and *hypostaseis*, into Latin would be misleading and confusing, since they could only be translated as one essence and three substances. Although he himself preferred the term 'essence' or 'nature' to refer to the One Trinity, he acknowledges the traditional use of 'substance', and therefore endorses the traditional Latin terminology of one substance and (in order not to remain silent, though aware of the inadequacies of language) three persons. He stresses, however, that despite the language of three persons, the only way in which we can meaningfully talk of distinction within the Trinity is in terms of relation: of the unbegotten Father, the begotten Son, and the Holy Spirit who proceeds from the Father and the Son. In every other respect, in mind, will, substance and attributes, they are identical. In describing the procession of the Holy Spirit from the Father and the Son Augustine's intention was not polemical. He was simply drawing upon Latin precedents and was unaware of the Greek creed of Constantinople (381) which stated that the Spirit proceeded from the Father.

In Books 8–15 Augustine proceeds to examine various similitudes to illustrate the inseparable operation and identical nature of the three persons of the Trinity. In a rather original way, he derives his similitudes from the image of God in man, assuming, on the basis of Gen. 1:26 ('Let us make man in our image and our likeness') that it is a Trinitarian image. In man's capacity for self-awareness, reason and love (which he at one point defines as memory, understanding and love) he locates that which sets him apart from the rest of creation and enables him to come closest to his Creator. Most especially, in man's awareness, knowledge and love of the Trinity as revealed in the incarnate Christ, he finds the means whereby the deformed, fragmented, fallen image of God in man might be reformed and ultimately come to full knowledge and love of the Trinity.

It is clear, however, that the reformation of the image of God in man will never be fulfilled in this life: it is a gradual, progressive process of faith, hope and love, whereby the operation of God's grace and the revelation of His love in the incarnate Christ enables man's response, to bring him to ultimate perfection in the life to come.

CONCLUSION

Augustine remained bishop of Hippo until his death in 430 CE. As he recited the penitential psalms on his death bed, and wept for his sins, Hippo was being besieged by the Vandals, Alans and Goths under their leader Geiseric. They finally took the town, and, after an orgy of looting, pillage, murder, rape and torture, evacuated it and burnt it to the ground in 431. A whole world came to an end with Augustine's passing.

What survived, quite extraordinarily, was Augustine's library in the *secretarium* of the basilica at Hippo, which contained, amongst other things, the vast body of his own works, which he had spent the last years of his life carefully annotating, correcting and commenting upon in his *Retractations*. Through these, he continues to give us one of our closest insights into the history and theology of the West in Late antiquity.

NOTES

1 The most accessible general books on Augustine in English are Bonner (1963, 1987), Brown (1967), Chadwick (1995), Clark (1993), O'Donnell (1992) and Rist (1994). Madec (1994), in French, should not, however, be missed.
2 See Brown (1992) and Kaster (1988).
3 On Manichaeism see Brown (1972: 94–118), Lieu (1985: 117–53) and Bonner (1963: 157–236).
4 See Madec (1996) and O'Donnell (1992: II, 421–4).
5 That is, theurgy. Augustine has Porphyry, in particular, in mind. Cf. *City of God* 10.
6 See Frederiksen (1986).
7 Kirwan (1989: 131–2).
8 Augustine is a rare exception to the Fathers' general teaching that sexual intercourse is a result of the fall. See *Literal Commentary on Genesis* 9.3.6.
9 *City of God* 14; *Literal Commentary on Genesis* 11.
10 1 John 2.16.
11 Lawless (1987: 36).
12 See *On the Morals of the Catholic Church and the Manichees*.
13 *Vita* 3.
14 *The Teacher*; *83 Diverse Questions*; *On the Morals of the Catholic Church*; *On True Religion*; *On Genesis against the Manichees*.
15 He probably didn't know of Eusebius of Vercelli's (363) similar arrangement in northern Italy.
16 The male version (*Praeceptum*) was written *c*. 395/6 and was probably soon after re-edited in a form for nuns (*Regularis informatio*) in the convent where Augustine's own sister was superior (Verheijen 1967).
17 *On Dialectic*; *The Teacher*; *On Christian Doctrine*.
18 *On Christian Doctrine*, prologue 6; *On Teaching the Uninstructed* 10.15.
19 *On Christian Doctrine* 2.40.60.
20 Lepelley (1975).
21 Brown (1995) and Markus (1997).
22 On Donatism see Brown (1972: 237–59, 279–300), Crespin (1965), Frend (1952),

Monceaux (1922: IV, VII) and Tengström (1964).

23 Including *Psalm against the Donatists*; *Against Cresconius*; *Against the Letter of Parmenianus*; *Against the Writings of Petilianus*; *On Baptism against the Donatists*; *Against Gaudentius*.

24 On Pelagianism see Bonner (1987), Brown (1972), Evans (1968) and Rees (1991).

25 *On the Consequences of Sins and their Forgiveness; On the Spirit and the Letter; Epistle 157.*

26 *Against the Letters of Pelagius; On Marriage and Concupiscence; Against Julian; Unfinished Refutation of Julian's Second Response.*

27 *On Grace and Free Will; On Correction and Grace.*

28 *On the Predestination of the Saints; On the Gift of Perseverance.*

29 On the *City of God* and Augustine's social and political thought see Markus (1970), Ruokanen (1993) and Van Oort (1991).

30 Markus (1970: 42–51).

31 See especially Book 19.

32 For example, in *On True Religion* and *On the Usefulness of Belief.*

33 For secondary literature see van Bavel (1954), Rémy (1979), Verwilghen (1985) and Madec (1989).

34 For secondary literature see Sullivan (1963), Schindler (1965) and, more recently, Barnes (1995).

BIBLIOGRAPHY

Translations of Augustine's works can be found in *Library of the Fathers*, the *Nicene and Post-Nicene Fathers*, the *Ancient Christian Writers*, the *Library of Christian Classics* and the New City Press *Works of Saint Augustine* series.

Barnes, M. R. (1995) 'De Régnon Reconsidered', *Augustinian Studies* 26: 51–79.

Bonner, G. (1963) *Augustine, Life and Controversies.* London: SCM Press.

—— (1987) *God's Decree and Man's Destiny.* London: Variorum.

Brown, P. (1967) *Augustine.* London: Faber & Faber.

—— (1972) *Religion and Society in the Age of Saint Augustine.* London: Faber.

—— (1992) *Power and Persuasion in Late Antiquity.* Madison, Wis.: University of Wisconsin Press.

—— (1995) *Authority and the Sacred.* Cambridge: Cambridge University Press.

Chadwick, H. (1995) *Augustine.* Oxford: Oxford University Press.

Clark, G. (1993) *The Confessions.* Cambridge: Cambridge University Press.

Crespin, R. (1965) *Ministère et Sainteté – Pastorale du Clergé et Solution de la Crise Donatiste dans la Vie et la Doctrine de saint Augustin.* Paris: Études Augustiniennes.

Evans, R. F. (1968) *Pelagius: Inquiries and Reappraisals.* New York: Seabury Press.

Frederiksen, P. (1986) 'Paul and Augustine: Conversion Narratives, Orthodox Traditions and the Retrospective Self', *Journal of Theological Studies* 37: 3–34.

Frend, W. H. C. (1952) *The Donatist Church.* Oxford: Clarendon Press.

Kaster, R. A. (1988) *Guardians of Language: The Grammarian and Society in Late Antiquity.* Berkeley: University of California Press.

Kirwan, C. (1989) *Augustine.* London: Routledge.

Lawless, G. (1987) *Augustine of Hippo and his Monastic Rule.* Oxford: Clarendon Press.

Lepelley, C. (1975) 'Saint Augustin et la Cité Romano-Africaine', in C. Kannengiesser (ed.) *Jean Chrysostome et Augustin.* Théologie Historique 35. Paris: Beauchesne, 13–41.

Lieu, S. N. C. (1985) *Manichaeism*. Manchester: University of Manchester Press.

Madec, G. (1989) *La Patrie et la Voie*. Paris: Desclée.

—— (1994) *Petites Études Augustiniennes*. Paris: Études Augustiniennes.

—— (1996) *Saint Augustin et la Philosophie*. Paris: Études Augustiniennes.

Markus, R. (1970) *Saeculum: History and Society in the Theology of Saint Augustine*. Cambridge: Cambridge University Press.

—— (1997) 'L'autorité Épiscopale et la définition de la chrétienté', *Studia Ephemeridis Augustinianum* 58: 37–43.

Monceaux, P. (1922) *Histoire Littéraire de l'Afrique Chrétienne*, IV and VII. Paris.

O'Donnell, J. J. (1992) *Augustine: Confessions I–III (Introduction, Text and Commentary)*. Oxford: Clarendon Press.

Rees, B. R. (1991) *The Letters of Pelagius and his Followers*. Woodbridge, Suffolk: Boydell Press.

Rist, J. M. (1994) *Augustine: Ancient Thought Baptized*. Cambridge: Cambridge University Press.

Ruokanen, M. (1993) *Theology of Social Life in Augustine's City of God*. Göttingen: Vandenhoek & Ruprecht.

Schindler, A. (1965) *Wört und Analogie in Augustins Trinitätslehre* Tübingen: Siebeck.

Stendahl, Krister (1963) 'The Apostle Paul and the Introspective Conscience of the West', *Harvard Theological Review* 56: 199–215. (Reprinted in Stendahl 1977: 78–96.)

—— (1977) *Paul Among Jews and Gentiles*. London: SCM Press (first published in the USA by Fortress, 1976).

Sullivan, J. E. (1963) *The Image of God. The Doctrine of Saint Augustine and its Influence*. Dubuque: The Priory Press.

Tengström, E. (1964) *Donatisten und Katholiken: soziale, wirtschaftliche und politische Aspekte einer nordafrikanischen Kirchenspaltung*. Studia Graeca et Latina Gothburgensia XVIII. Göteburg: Elanders Boktryckeri Aktiebolag.

Van Bavel, T. (1954) *Recherches sur la Christologie de saint Augustin: L'Humain et le Divin dans Le Christ d'après saint Augustin*. Fribourg: Paradosis.

Van Oort, J. (1991) *Jerusalem and Babylon. A Study into Augustine's City of God and the Sources of his Doctrine of the Two Cities*. Leiden: Brill.

Verheijen, L. M. J. (1967) *La règle de saint Augustin*. Paris: Études Augustiniennes.

Verwilghen, A. (1985) *Christologie et spiritualité selon saint Augustin: L'Hymne aux Philippiens*. Paris: Études Augustiniennes.

EPHREM THE SYRIAN[1]

—— •✦• ——

Kathleen E. McVey

EPHREM: LIFE, CHARACTER AND IMPORTANCE

Ephrem the Syrian, the foremost writer in the Syriac tradition of Christianity, was born in Nisibis *c.* 306 CE. He came from a Christian family, as he himself affirms in a famous passage in his *Hymns against Heresies* 26.10:

> In the way of truth was I born
> even though I as a child did not yet perceive it.
> Examining, I acquired it for myself, as I perceived it.
> My faith despised the confusing paths that came toward me.

There are many possible interpretations of 'the confusing paths' among which the young Ephrem found himself. Nisibis was a very ancient city with great commercial, political and military significance in his time. After a century of struggle between the Roman and Persian empires, Syro-Mesopotamia had been restored to Roman control by a treaty of 298 CE, which specified Nisibis as the only place for commercial exchange between these two mighty empires. Its population and hence its cultural environment were constituted by a mix of many diverse peoples: Arameans, Arabs, Parthians, Iranians, Greeks, Jews and Romans.

There had been Christians in Nisibis since at least the late second century, as the epitaph of bishop Abercios of Hierapolis attests. This earliest community of Nisibene Christians may have been heterodox by western Christian standards. Scholars are divided in their views since the sources are scarce and difficult to place chronologically, geographically and theologically. Some consider works such as the *Odes of Solomon*, Tatian's *Diatessaron*, the *Gospel of Thomas* or the *Acts of Thomas*, as witnesses to an ascetic, encratite, form of Jewish Christianity, brought to Syro-Mesopotamia by converts to Christianity from a sectarian Jewish group like those at Qumran. Others believe the first Christians in this area are more properly understood to be gnostics or Marcionites.

No doubt the multicultural environment and the theological diversity of Syro-Mesopotamian Christianity caused some confusion for Christians there in the early fourth century. Further, the relation of Christians to the Roman imperial power was equally bewildering. Immediately after the restoration of Nisibis to Rome, the brutal Diocletianic persecution had claimed at least three men and four women martyrs from among Nisibene Christians: Hermas, a confessor; Adelphos, a soldier; and Gaios, Olivia, Eutropia, Leonis and Febronia. In his childhood, Ephrem saw the establishment of Christian Rome under Constantine, and his bishop, Jacob of Nisibis, attended the Council of Nicaea in 325.

When bishop Jacob returned from the Council, he appointed Ephrem as 'interpreter' or 'exegete' in Nisibis. Although this is not a title or office known elsewhere, it apparently entailed the composition of hymns, homilies and commentaries for the instruction of the Christian people of the town.

Ephrem is one of the first Syriac writers to emerge into the light of history with a large body of extant writings intact. Whatever the nature of the pre-Constantinian Christianity in his home, Ephrem himself was deeply committed to Nicene orthodoxy and to its defence and propagation. We know him almost exclusively through the writings he composed for this purpose with the endorsement of a succession of orthodox bishops.

As Rome and Persia continued the struggle for domination of Mesopotamia, Ephrem's homeland became a battleground, and he became a passionate chronicler of the religious and political dimensions of the war. Here, too, his allegiance was clearly to Rome, as the divinely ordained Christian power. He was an eyewitness to the Roman military procession into Nisibis with the corpse of the defeated emperor, Julian 'the Apostate'. He mourned, not the faithless emperor but the tribulations of the Nisibene Christians who were forced to abandon their native city and move westward in order to remain within the Roman empire. He, too, went to Edessa, where he continued to write and where he is said to have established a school of biblical and theological studies and women's choirs to sing his hymns. Ordained to the diaconate there, he died while ministering to victims of famine in 373 CE.[2]

In his hymns and other writings it is evident that, despite his passionate commitment to orthodoxy, Ephrem appreciated the beauty and usefulness of the ante-Nicene Syriac Christian literature. Thus he wrote commentaries not only on the canonical scripture but also on Tatian's *Diatessaron*. He often utilizes graphic feminine imagery for God, as some of the *Odes of Solomon* had done. In his *Hymns on the Pearl* he explores the image of salvation as a precious pearl, an image which has roots not only in the New Testament but also in the gnostic *Hymn of the Pearl* in the *Acts of Thomas*. Yet his *Hymns against Heresies* are harshly polemical, attacking Mani, Marcion, Bardaisan and the astrologers.

Similarly, he is a well-informed but often contentious critic of Judaism. His *Hymns on Paradise* and his *Commentary on Genesis and Exodus* are permeated with non-canonical Jewish traditions. His *Carmina Nisibena* represent a Christian appropriation of the prophetic tradition of the Old Testament. Yet in many of his compositions each positive theological statement seems to evoke propositions for refutation. The unseen opponent may be Jewish as often as pagan or heretical. Consequently, as he expounds his Trinitarian doctrine in the *Sermons on Faith*, he also argues against Judaizing Christians as well as against Arians. In his *Paschal Hymns* he elaborates a theology of redemption in the midst of polemics against Jewish ritual. The incarnation theology of his *Nativity Hymns* is commingled with arguments in defence of Mary's virginity against those – apparently Jewish critics – who would deny it.

In the complex and uncertain world of fourth-century Mesopotamia, Ephrem's emphatic belligerence is comprehensible. In the Graeco-Roman context, moreover, where virtuoso displays of rhetoric in what was a highly competitive culture (see Chapter 1 of this volume) were highly prized, his compositions were stunningly successful. His ability to couch his polemics in richly symbolic verse and to set them to familiar melodies made his efforts all the more memorable and thus more effective. Having seen the damage done over centuries by hostile inter-religious rhetoric, so easily translated into violent acts, most Christians today rightly hesitate to wield the rhetorical rapier against heretics, pagans and adherents to Judaism as Late Antique Christians did. Clearly a passionate man, deeply persuaded that God's love and redemption are present and on display for all who open their eyes and ears, Ephrem had little patience for those who saw things differently. It is a challenge to his contemporary readers to disentangle the beauty of his symbolic theology from his recurrent polemics.

Ephrem's importance for the history of Syriac literature, and for the history of Christianity in the Syriac-speaking context, is immense. His hymns, incorporated early into the liturgy, have remained central in both the East and West Syrian

Figure 49.1 St Ephrem, as portrayed in a twelfth-century manuscript belonging to the Syrian Orthodox Patriarch of Antioch, Moran Mor Ignatius Zakka I Iwas (Dam. Pat. 12/15, folio 5b). Photo Kathleen McVey.

liturgical traditions. The literary and hymnic forms that he used, some of which he may have invented, became the standard forms of all subsequent Syriac literature and hymnography. The success of his hymns helped to make hymnody a central teaching method of his church from his own time down to the present. Although his works incorporate many of the themes found in the Jewish-Christian or gnostic writings of the earliest Syriac Christianity, Ephrem's commitment to Nicene orthodoxy set the subsequent direction of the Syriac church. He lived almost exactly the same years as Athanasius, and in his own way Ephrem was just as dedicated to the Nicene *homoousion* (the idea that Christ was 'of the same being' with the Father) as Athanasius. In his own lifetime and for a half-century thereafter, his method of biblical interpretation was the sole standard among Syriac writers. Even after the formal introduction of Greek hermeneutical methods in the fifth century, Ephrem's interpretations continued to be studied and held in esteem. Despite uncertainty over the precise lines of his contact with Greek culture, not only a concept of orthodoxy but also many philosophical presuppositions and literary forms analogous to those of Greek Christian theological literature are to be found in his work, and through him they descend in the Syriac heritage.[3]

Appreciation of Ephrem's hymns was not limited to those who spoke Syriac. Writing within decades of his death, Jerome attests his fame in the Latin church. The fifth-century Greek church historians portray him as a model of the ascetic life and extol his extraordinary poetic gift. Both Jerome and the Greek writers assert that even in translation they were able to appreciate his eloquence. The translation of his works into Greek had begun even during his lifetime, and in the following centuries they were translated into virtually every language known to Christianity.[4] Although study of the nature and extent of his influence on later western Christianity is still in a fairly rudimentary stage, it is clear that he played a significant role in the development of both Byzantine hymnography and western medieval religious drama.[5]

The extant writings attributed to Ephrem in Greek, Coptic, Ethiopic, Armenian, Georgian, Arabic, Latin and Slavonic constitute a rich and significant body of materials. But the problem of sorting out his legacy to the universal church is complicated by the fact that his authentic writings in Syriac are scarcely represented in the vast body of writings ascribed to him in most of these other languages. There is a nearly complete mismatch between the texts considered by Syriac scholars to be authentic and those which survive in various other languages under Ephrem's name. The latter body of literature is interesting in itself and well deserves the attention it is just beginning to receive from scholars. It will probably not, however, tell us much about Ephrem himself and about the ways in which the 'historical Ephrem' so to speak, may have influenced Christians beyond the confines of the Syriac-speaking world. That actual influence is more likely to be found through the study of the theological themes and imagery traced through the homilists and hymnographers who postdate him in all these varied linguistic traditions. One aspect of his thought that is of enduring interest and continuous importance for all the orthodox traditions as well as for western Christian spirituality is the presence of God in the world.

EPHREM'S THEOLOGY OF THE PRESENCE OF
GOD IN THE WORLD

Ephrem's world is permeated by the divine presence. His poetry is based upon a vision of the created order as a vast system of symbols or mysteries.[6] No person, thing or event in the world exists without a mysterious relation to the whole. History and nature constitute the warp and woof of reality. To divorce an individual person, event or thing from its context in either direction would destroy the handiwork of God in time and space. Each moment of life is governed by the Lord of Life and is an opportunity to see oneself and the community in relation to that Lord. So all historical events must have profound religious significance, not just those described in scripture.

Nature, too, is replete with intimations of the presence of God. In creating the world, God deliberately presented us not only with examples of beauty and order but also with symbols that allude more richly to the identity of their Creator:

> In every place, if you look, His symbol is there,
> and when you read, you will find His prototypes.
> For by Him were created all creatures,
> and he imprinted His symbols upon His possessions.
> When He created the world,
> He gazed at it and adorned it with His images.
> Streams of His symbols opened, flowed and poured forth
> His symbols on its members.
>
> (*Hymns on Virginity* 20.12)

At the centre of all is Jesus Christ, the Incarnate Word, who is at once the apex of history and the metaphysical Mediator between the ineffable Creator and the creation. Ephrem sets forth this notion most succinctly in the *Hymns on Virginity* 28–30, where he speaks of the three harps of God:

> The Word of the Most High came down and put on
> a weak body with hands,
> and He took two harps [Old and New Testaments]
> in His right and left hands.
> The third [Nature] He set before Himself
> to be a witness to the [other] two,
> for the middle harp taught
> that their Lord is playing them.
>
> (*Virg.* 29.1)

This strophe shows clearly not only that scripture and nature play complementary roles in Ephrem's theology but also that the linchpin of his theological system is the Incarnate Word of God, through whom God has revealed the relation of the two Testaments to one another and to nature.

In examining his theology of divine presence, we will begin with his understanding of the Incarnation and proceed to the closely related notions of spiritual progress and sanctification or *theosis*/divinization. Next we will turn to God's presence in history, first considering scripture as the record of salvation history, especially as understood through typological exegesis, and then addressing the sacred dimension of the rest of history, specifically the events which Ephrem himself witnessed and contemplated. Finally, we will consider nature as God's domain, first in human beings created in the divine image, then in the sacraments, and finally in the rest of the creation.

THE INCARNATION: LINCHPIN OF EPHREM'S THEOLOGY

A central theme of Ephrem's *Hymns on the Nativity* is the wonder of the Incarnation, conceived as a paradoxical entry of the ineffable, infinite and omnipotent God into the limitations of human life. It is a theological concept that evokes profound questions: for example, how can the Ruler of the Universe, whom the entire created order is unable to contain, have been contained in a single, small human womb?

> The Power that governs all dwelt in a small womb.
> While dwelling there, He was holding the reins of the universe.
> His Parent was ready for His will to be fulfilled.
> The heavens and all the creation were filled by Him.
> The Sun entered the womb, and in the height and depth
> His rays were dwelling.
>
> (*Hymns on the Nativity* 21.6)

Not only the bare fact of the Incarnation but also its specific circumstances are miraculous and paradoxical: '[God] deprived the married womb: / He made fruitful the virgin womb' (*Hymns on the Nativity* 21.17). Far from showing a weakness, these apparent contradictions show the majesty of the Creator, the 'Lord of natures'.

Yet these are not pointless displays of might; instead they are the concessions of a loving God to human frailty:

> God had seen that we worshiped creatures.
> He put on a created body to catch us by our habit.
> Behold by this fashioned one our Fashioner healed us,
> and by this creature our Creator revived us.
>
> (*Nat.*, 21.12)

Thus this miraculous and paradoxical self-abasement of God is clearly motivated by love for humankind. Ephrem often associates the language and imagery of divine compassion, mercy and maternal love with the Incarnation. Among his many epithets for Christ is *Ḥanânâ*, the Compassionate One, a title which he applies in virtually every moment in the life of Christ. The feast of the Incarnation, the Nativity, is the day on which 'the Compassionate One came out to sinners' (*Nat.* 4.23). Even before his birth, 'He dwelt [in Mary's womb] because of His compassion' (*Nat.* 21.8). The Compassionate One, he says, put on the garment of the body to rescue Adam:

He was wrapped in swaddling clothes . . .
He put on the garments of youth . . .
[and] the water of baptism . . .
[and] the linen garments in death:
All these [garments] are changes
that the Compassionate One first shed and then put on again
when He contrived to put on Adam the glory he had shed.
He entwined swaddling clothes with [Adam's] figleaves,
and he put on garments in place of his skins.
He was baptized for [Adam's] wrongdoing and embalmed for his death.
He rose and raised him up in glory.

(*Nat.* 23.12–13)

That same Compassionate One 'bore our pain' (*Nat.* 3.2). 'He endured spitting and scourging, thorns and nails for our sake' (*Nat.* 18.35).

Out of compassion and mercy, Christ freed human beings and all creation from the slavery of idolatry (*Nat.* 22.4–7). Ephrem relates this theme to the Roman tradition of temporarily releasing slaves for the Saturnalia:

The mercy of the High One was revealed,
and he came down to free His creation.
In this blessed month in which manumission takes place,
the Lord came to slavery to call the slaves to freedom.
Blessed is He Who brought manumission!

(*Nat.* 22.5)

Finally, Christians are expected to imitate the merciful condescension of their redeemer. Addressing Christ in his own voice, Ephrem says:

O [You] Greater than measure Who became immeasurably small,
from glorious splendor you humbled Yourself to ignominy.
Your indwelling mercy inclined You to all this.
Let Your compassion incline me to become praiseworthy in [spite of] my evil.

(*Nat.* 21.13)

The same is expected of all Christians since their baptism is a rebirth from the side of Christ, 'the Compassionate One who . . . came to take up / the body that would be struck so that by the opening of his side / he might break through the way into Paradise' (*Nat.* 8.4).

We are all expected to reciprocate, as Ephrem reminds his congregation once again on the feast of the nativity:

On this day on which God came into the presence of sinners, let not the just man exalt himself in his mind over the sinner.
On this day on which the Lord of all came among servants, let the lords also bow down to their servants lovingly.
On this day when the Rich One was made poor for our sake, let the rich man also make the poor man a sharer at his table.
On this day a gift came out to us without our asking for it; let us then give alms to those who cry out and beg from us.

This is the day when the high gate opened to us for our prayers; let us also open the gates to the seekers who have strayed but sought [forgiveness].

(Nat. 1.92–6)

Finally, Ephrem explicitly binds this imitation of Christ, the Compassionate One, to non-violent behaviour.

> Glorious is the Compassionate One
> Who did not use violence, and without force, by wisdom,
> He was victorious. He gave a type to human beings
> that by power and wisdom they might conquer discerningly.

(Nat. 8.5)

The divine condescension to humankind in the Incarnation has brought about a permanent change in the relationship between human beings and their Creator:

> . . . the Deity imprinted Itself on humanity,
> so that humanity might also be cut into the seal of the Deity.

(Nat. 1.99)

In addition to this language of seals and stamps, which he shares with the Logos theology of Greek Christianity, Ephrem expresses the intimate union of divine and human with the language of painting, likening it to the artist's blending of pigments:

> Glorious is the Wise One Who allied and joined
> Divinity with humanity,
> One from the height and the other from below.
> He mingled the natures like pigments,
> and an image came into being: the God-man!

(Nat. 8.2)

The similarity of Ephrem's thought here to Athanasius' dictum, 'The Word of God became human so that we might become divine' has been noted.[7] But the difference in Ephrem's view needs also to be stressed. For him the Incarnation not only opens up the way to *theosis* but it also brings a humanization of God. He explores the dimensions of that humanization of God especially through images of birth and suckling. In the Incarnation:

> Christ entered [Mary's] womb a mighty warrior, and inside her womb He put on fear.
> He entered Nourisher of all and He acquired hunger.
> He entered the One who gives drink to all, and He acquired thirst.
> Stripped and laid bare, He emerged from [her womb] the One who clothes all.

(Nat. 11.8).

The image of the suckling child provides a radical image of divine love for humankind. To the infant Christ Ephrem says:

> it is as if your love hungers for human beings
> . . . what moves you so to bestow yourself
> upon each who has seen you? . . .

Whence did it come to you so to hunger for human beings?

(*Nat.* 13.12–14)

On the one hand, the Son freely chose to become incarnate: 'By His will He clothed himself with a body' (*Nat.* 3.5). Yet this choice is clearly prompted by love, and it has the result that He became truly needy by this mingling of divinity with humanity:

> Glory to Him Who never needs us to thank Him.
> Yet He [became] needy for He loves us, and He thirsted for He cherishes us.
> And He asks us to give to Him so that He may give us even more.
> His Fruit was mingled with our human nature
> to draw us out toward Him Who bent down to us.
> By the Fruit of the Root He will graft us onto His Tree.
>
> (*Nat.* 3.17)

Perhaps the strongest image of the reciprocity which results from God's condescension to us occurs in a context not of the Incarnation but rather in its figurative equivalent, God's willingness to be clothed in human language; that is to say, the existence of revealed scripture.[8] In this regard Ephrem characterizes the Deity as like a nursing mother or wet nurse:

> Attuned to us is the Deity like a nursing mother to an infant,
> watching the time for his benefits, knowing the time for weaning him,
> both when to rear him on milk and when to feed him with solid food,
> weighing and offering benefits according to the measure of his maturity.
>
> (*Hymns on the Church* 25.18)[9]

This image of the Triune God pondering the right moment to move each human being from milk to solid food provides the perfect transition from Ephrem's understanding of the Incarnation as a singular historical event, the culmination of the history of salvation, to his notion that it is an ongoing reality accessible to each human being according to the level of his or her spiritual advancement.

THE ONGOING, INDIVIDUALIZED PRESENCE OF GOD TO EACH HUMAN BEING

Although God's grand concession to human frailty took place uniquely in the Incarnation, it also continues to take place in every time and place for each individual human being. God is revealed to each according to his or her capacity to perceive:

> He was cheerful among the infants as a baby;
> awesome was He among the Watchers[10] as a commander.
> Too awesome was He for John to loosen His sandals;
> accessible was He for sinners who kissed His feet.
> The Watchers as Watchers saw Him;
> according to the degree of his knowledge each person saw Him.

Everyone according to the measure of his discernment
thus perceived Him, that One greater than all.

(Nat. 4.197–200)

The encounter between Jesus and the Samaritan woman (John 4)

For Ephrem Jesus' encounter with the Samaritan woman at the well in John 4 is especially symbolic of the individualized relationship God conducts with each human being:

> The glorious fount of Him Who was sitting
> at the well as Giver of drink to all,
> flows to each according to His will:
> different springs according to those who drink.
> From the well a single undifferentiated drink
> came up each time for those who drank.
> The Living Fount lets distinct blessings
> flow to distinct people.

(Hymns on Virginity 23.3)

But, not satisfied merely to meet each of us at our present level of spiritual discernment, God leads each of us step by step to higher levels of understanding. Again, the Samaritan woman is paradigmatic of this process:

> Because she in her love said, 'The Messiah will come,'
> He revealed to her with love, 'I am He.'
> That He was a prophet she believed already,
> soon after, that He was the Messiah . . .
> . . . she is a type of our humanity
> that He leads step by step.

(Virg. 22.21)

Most ancient commentators on the story of the Samaritan woman saw her as an immoral woman, one who had been divorced many times or who had simply lived with several men without benefit of marriage. Dipping into the non-canonical books of the Old Testament, Ephrem found another solution to her having had five husbands and a sixth who was not really her husband: like Sarah in the Book of Tobit, she had been unlucky in marriage: all her husbands had died, so no man was brave enough to marry her. Thus her sixth husband did not share her marriage bed. This little detail is not only indicative of Ephrem's style of commentary (one that is narrative, literary and based on a broad familiarity with scripture), it is also significant that, having removed the cloud of opprobrium from over her head, Ephrem moves on to portray the Samaritan woman as an apostle, prophet and type of the *Theotokos*, the Mother of God. He praises her for her readiness to share her insight into Jesus' Messianic identity:

> Blessed are you, O woman, for not suppressing
> your judgement about what you discovered.

(Virg. 23.1.1–2)

Ephrem notes that just as Jesus' love for her led him to meet her need, her love for her neighbours led her to share her news with them:

> The glorious Treasury was Himself present
> for your need because of His love.
> Your love was zealous
> to share your treasure with your city.
> Blessed woman, your discovery became
> the Discoverer of the lost.

(Virg. 23.1.3–8)

Also laudable is the immediacy of her response to one small sign, to be contrasted with the obstinacy of those who refused to accept even the greater evidence of miracles.

In her revelation to others of what she had heard, she is like Mary who conceived by her ear and thereby brought the Son to the world:

> [Praise] to you, o woman in whom I see
> a wonder as great as in Mary!
> For she from within her womb
> in Bethlehem brought forth His body as a child,
> but you by your mouth made Him manifest
> as an adult in Shechem, the town of His father's household.
> Blessed are you, woman, who brought forth by your mouth
> light for those in darkness.
> Mary, the thirsty land in Nazareth,
> conceived our Lord by her ear.
> You, too, O woman thirsting for water,
> conceived the Son by your hearing.
> Blessed are your ears that drank the source
> that gave drink to the world.
> Mary planted Him in the manger,
> but you [planted him] in the ears of His hearers.

(Virg. 23.4–5)

Like the words of the prophets, what she spoke became reality:

> Your word, O woman, became a mirror
> in which He might see your hidden heart.
> 'The Messiah,' you had said, 'will come,
> and when He comes, He will give us everything.'
> Behold the Messiah for Whom you waited, modest woman!
> Through your voice . . . prophecy was fulfilled.

(Virg. 23.6)

She is comparable to the apostles since even before the Twelve were permitted to do so, she preached the good news of salvation to the gentiles:

> Your voice, O woman, first brought forth fruit,

even before the apostles {brought fruit] with their preaching.
The apostles were forbidden to announce Him
among pagans and Samaritans.
Blessed is your mouth that He opened and confirmed.
The Storehouse of life took and gave you to sow.
[Your] city, dead as Sheol,
You entered, and you revived your dead [land].

(Virg. 23.7)

SPIRITUAL PROGRESS AND SANCTIFICATION OR *THEOSIS*

Mary and the Beloved Disciple at the foot of the Cross (John 19:25–7)

Mary, the mother of Jesus, and the Beloved Disciple are also especially significant in Ephrem's understanding of the ongoing process of the Incarnation in sanctification or *theosis*, the full restoration in each human being of the lost *imago dei*. Mary and John (with whom the Beloved Disciple has often been identified) see in each other the complementary mysteries of God's condescending love for us and the bold access to divine love now open to human beings. Through them we, too, may see this twofold mystery of the Saviour. John and Mary, the mother of Jesus, are 'types' through whom we are able to see Christ as in a mirror while they themselves saw Him in one another. Ephrem begins by evoking the scene at the foot of the cross as it is portrayed in John's gospel, where Jesus invites Mary and John to regard one another as mother and son:

Blessed are you, O woman, whose Lord and son
entrusted you to one fashioned in His image.
The Son of your womb did not wrong your love,
but to the son of His bosom He entrusted you.
Upon your bosom you caressed Him when He was small,
and upon His bosom He also caressed [John],
so that when He was crucified
He repaid all you had advanced to Him,
the debt of His upbringing.
For, the Crucified repaid debts;
even yours was repaid by Him.
He drank from your breast visible milk,
but [John drank] from His bosom hidden mysteries.
Confidently He approached your breast;
confidently [John] approached and lay upon His bosom.
Since you missed the sound of His voice,
He gave you his harp
to be a consolation to you.

(Virg. 25.2–3)

The love and care which flowed from Mary to her Son are echoed by the love of Jesus for John and repaid by entrusting her to his care. John shows a special resemblance to Jesus, Ephrem assumes, because he takes his place as Mary's son. But a deeper ethical mystery is contained here: the love of John for his Lord led him to imitate him, thus bringing into higher relief in him the *imago dei* engraved on each human being:

> The youth who loved our Lord very much,
> who portrayed [and] put Him on and resembled Him,
> was zealous in all these matters to resemble Him:
> in his speech, his aspect and his ways.
> The creature put on his Creator,
> and he resembled Him although indeed he did not resemble what He was.
> It is amazing how much the clay is able to be imprinted
> with the beauty of its sculptor.
>
> (*Virg.* 25.4)

By meditating on the relationship of Jesus to His mother, John was better able to understand the Incarnation:

> The youth in the woman was seeing
> how much that Exalted One was lowered,
> how He entered [and] dwelt in a weak womb
> and emerged [and] was suckled with weak milk.
>
> (*Virg.* 25.8.1–4)

Meanwhile, by observing the behaviour of the Beloved Disciple Mary learned about the possibility of spiritual growth and the boldness it encourages:

> The woman also wondered at how much he grew
> that he went up and lay upon the bosom of God.
> The two of them were amazed at one another,
> how much they were able to grow by grace.
> [It is] You, Lord, Whom they saw . . .
> while observing one another:
> Your mother saw You in Your disciple;
> And he saw You in Your mother.
>
> (*Virg.* 25.8.5–9.4)

Nor does the benefit of this insight stop with these two privileged
and holy people, it extends to all who are willing to look deeply into
their fellow human beings:

> O the seers who at every moment
> see You, Lord, in a mirror
> manifest a type so that we, too, in one another
> may see You, our Savior.
>
> (*Virg.* 25.9.5–8)

Consecrated virginity

For Ephrem, thinking of the story of Martha and Mary, Mary Magdalen exemplifies perfectly the concentration on the inner presence of Christ which leads to the full restoration of the *imago dei*:

> She turned her face away from everything
> to gaze on one beauty alone.
> Blessed is her love that was intoxicated, not sober,
> so that she sat at His feet to gaze at Him.
> Let you also portray the Messiah in your heart
> and love Him in your mind.
>
> (*Virg.* 24.7.3–8)

More broadly speaking, for Ephrem it is the consecrated virgin who has most fully stripped off the old Adam to put on the new at baptism. Her body is clothed in a new garment; it is the Temple of God and His royal Palace.

But however strongly Ephrem admonishes the virgin to preserve her sexual innocence, it is clear that this is not an end in itself, but rather it is symbolic of the full dedication of self to God which is the goal of every Christian life:[11]

> Let chastity be portrayed in your eyes and in your ears the sound of truth.
> Imprint your tongue with the word of life and upon your hands [imprint] all alms.
> Stamp your footsteps with visiting the sick,
> and let the image of your Lord be portrayed in your heart.
> Tablets are honored because of the image of kings.
> How much more will one be honored who has portrayed the Lord in all the senses.
>
> (*Virg.* 2.15)

BIBLICAL SYMBOLS AND THE PRESENCE OF GOD IN HISTORICAL EVENTS

Among the historical symbols, biblical typology plays the central role. The events in the history of Israel narrated in Hebrew scripture have religious significance for all people. Like most early Christian writers, however, Ephrem saw the Hebrew scripture as preliminary sketches, as shadows, when compared with the realities of the New Testament:

> [Christ's] power perfected the types,
> and His truth the mysteries,
> His interpretation the similes,
> His explanation the sayings,
> and His assurances the difficulties.

By His sacrifice He abolished sacrifices,
and libations by His incense,
and the [passover] lambs by His slaughter,
the unleavened [bread] by His bread,
and the bitter [herbs] by His Passion.

By His healthy meal
He weaned [and] took away the milk.
By His baptism were abolished
the bathing and sprinkling
that the elders of the People taught.

(Virg. 8.8–10)

Despite the intrinsic importance of the events and persons of the 'Old Testament', they are only 'antitypes' which were fulfilled in the 'types' of the New Testament. On the one hand, the Passover Lamb is an anticipation of Christ and of the salvation gained through Him. To attempt to understand Christ without knowing about the Passover would be to deprive oneself of the depth and richness of meaning placed in human history by God Himself. Yet conversely, in Ephrem's view, to stop with the Passover Lamb rather than interpreting it as a symbol of Christ would mean missing the fullness of God's revelation and accepting a truncated version of the meaning of history.

Ephrem's hymns are permeated with typological exegesis. The central figures of this typology are Jesus and Mary. Ephrem presents a rich variety of Old Testament types for Christ. In the second of his Nativity Hymns he systematically presents Jesus as the prophet, priest and king. His selection of Old Testament figures as forerunners of Christ is similar to many other early Christian writers, but he adds unexpected interpretations as well. For example, Jesus is anticipated not only by Isaac, Melchizedek, Moses and David, but also by Jacob, who is kicked by Esau but does not retaliate.

Ephrem's Mariology is central to his understanding of the incarnation. Mary was chosen because she was most pleasing to God. Yet she who gave birth to the Son of the Most High was given birth by Him in baptism. Paradoxically, Mary gave birth to and nourished and cared for the Incarnate One who gave life, nourishment and care to her. In this she represents all humans and indeed all creation:

By power from Him Mary's womb became able
to bear the One Who bears all.
From the great treasury of all creation
Mary gave to Him every thing that she gave.
She gave Him milk from what He made exist.
She gave Him food from what He had created.
As God, He gave milk to Mary.
In turn, as human, He was given suck by her.

(Nat. 4.182–5)

Her theological importance is confirmed by the wealth of Ephrem's typology for Mary. She is not only the second Eve, but she is also a second Sarah, Rachel and

Anna; she is favourably compared and contrasted with Tamar, Ruth and Rahab (*Hymns on the Nativity* 8.13, 13.2–5, 9.7–16, 15.8 and 16.12). Most unusual is Ephrem's imagery drawn from the Jewish priestly cult to provide a typology for Mary's role. The virginity of Mary and of all the 'daughters of the covenant' is the vestment of the High Priest, who is Christ:

> May all the evidences of virginity of Your brides
> be preserved by You. They are the purple [robes]
> and no one may touch them
> except our King. For virginity
> is like a vestment for You, the High Priest.
>
> (*Nat.* 16.13)

Like the Ark of the Covenant, Mary is honoured not for herself but for the Divine presence within her:

> Joseph rose
> to serve in the presence of his Lord
> Who was within Mary. The priest serves
> in the presence of Your Ark because of Your holiness.
>
> (*Nat.* 16.16)

The Tablets containing the teachings of the Mosaic Law also constitute an antitype which is fulfilled in Mary:

> Moses bore the tablets of stone
> that His Lord had written. And Joseph escorted
> the pure tablet in whom was dwelling
> the Son of the Creator. The tablets were left behind
> since the world was filled with Your teaching.
>
> (*Nat.* 16.17)

These unusual typologies are all based on the premise that in the Incarnation Mary became the dwelling place of God on earth.

To grasp more fully the significance for Ephrem of these metaphors one must be aware that in Syriac 'virginity' (*bethulutha*) is synonymous with 'chastity' (*qaddishutha*), which also means 'holiness'. Behind the coincidence in meanings between 'chastity' and 'holiness' is ultimately a notion of mysterious power, untouchable sacral presence. Mary as the virgin *par excellence* is uniquely suited to be the holy one in whom – or perhaps better the holy place in which – God deigns to be present.

THE SACRED DIMENSION OF ALL OF HISTORY

All historical events have profound religious significance, not just those described in scripture. Ephrem's *Hymns against Julian*, along with the *Nisibene Hymns*, display his kinship with the Jewish prophets. Like them, he contemplates the political and military events of his time in the light of his ethical and theological tenets, looking for evidence of divine activity, rewards, punishments and edifying moral lessons.

Living as he did in an area at the Easternmost edge of the Roman empire constantly under the pressure of Sassanid Persia, Ephrem was presented with dramatic historical events for his contemplation. When the Persian army besieged his town of Nisibis for the third time and it was spared even after its protecting city wall had been broken down, he composed poetry about salvation and grace:

> [God] saved us without a wall and taught that He is our wall.
> He saved us without a king and made known that He is our king.
> He saved us in all from all and showed He is all.
> He saved us by His grace and again revealed
> that He is freely gracious and life-giving. From each who boasts
> He takes away the boast and gives to him His grace.
>
> (*Nisibene Hymns* 2.2)

Warnings against idolatry and encouragement in adversity are as prominent in his hymns as in the pronouncements of Jeremiah and Isaiah. When the apostate Roman emperor Julian brought his army into Mesopotamia, ostentatiously offering sacrifice to the old pagan deities, pressuring the Christians of Mesopotamia to join in that worship, but finally dying in battle (in June 363 CE), Ephrem was not at a loss for words. He elaborated the view that God had made the apostate emperor Julian the representative and symbol of all who hold erroneous views – not only pagans but also heretics and Jews. His defeat was a sign to all nations of the ultimate fate of those who oppose God.

The first of Ephrem's five *Hymns against Julian* stands apart from the rest since it was written prior to the emperor's death in battle. Here the poet offers a message of hope and perseverance to the people of Nisibis, threatened with persecution. The other four hymns reiterate and develop that message in the light of subsequent events. Rather than focusing on the loss of their city to the Persians, a catastrophe caused by Nisibene acquiescence to Julian's re-establishment of paganism there, Ephrem emphasizes that the claims of paganism have been proved false by the fate of the apostate emperor. The political events provide a larger-than-life drama of the cosmic conflict between good and evil. God's partisans, the true members of the church of Nisibis, with the encouragement of the watching angels, withstood the onslaughts of Satan in the form of imperial persecution and Persian military attacks.

Using a favourite metaphor, the mirror as the instrument of Divine ethical lessons, Ephrem takes the apostate emperor as the model of human pride as well as of political promotion of religious error. His policies unmasked the false Christians within the church; his ignominious death demonstrates the folly of his pride as well as the falsity of his beliefs. The divine purpose in the defeat and death of the Roman emperor was to present to all people a model of the vanity of idolatry. At the same time the fidelity of Christians has been tested and many have been found wanting during the pagan emperor's brief reign. Weak or false Christians have returned openly to paganism, or they have attacked their Creator in the contentious error of the Arian heresy. The Jewish people, he contends, have also returned to idolatrous worship. On the other hand, the city of Nisibis presents, again as if in a mirror, a model for fidelity to God, its rewards, and the consequences of its lapse. Reinforcing this primary imagery is the symbol of the church as the true vine, beneficially pruned by the rigours of persecution:

> Rely on the truth, my brothers, and be not afraid
> for our Lord is not so weak as to fail us in the test.
> He is the power on which the world and its inhabitants depend.
> The hope of His Church depends on Him.
> Who is able to sever its heavenly roots?
>
> (*Hymns against Julian* 1.1)

> Although the branch is living, on it are dead fruits
> blooming only outwardly.
> The wind tried them and cast off the wild grapes.
>
> (*Jul.* 1.5)

Several other metaphors serve to teach the same lesson: separation of the wheat from the tares, the purification of gold in the furnace, and separation of the curds and whey in cheesemaking (*Jul.* 1.10–13, 2.10–11; 1.13, 2.24, 4.1; 4.2).

To these symbols current in both biblical and general Hellenistic contexts, Ephrem adds biblical examples of faithless sovereigns and the consequences of their erroneous ways: Nebuchadnezzar, Jeroboam, Ahab, Jotham, Manasseh, Jezebel, Athaliah and Saul provide precedents for Julian's errors as well as his fate (*Jul.* 1.8, 1.20, 2.2, 4.5, 4.8). The attendant notions of true and false prophecy provide a context for his contention that in this case the church has followed the course of Daniel, confronting the pagan ruler, whereas the Jewish people have followed the precedent of the Israelites under Jeroboam, worshipping the golden calf (*Jul.* 1.16–20, 2.2). While this general approach, aptly named 'prophetic anti-Judaism' by Ruether (1974: 117–82), is typical of patristic writers, Ephrem pursues his view with tenacious originality, accompanied, one suspects, by a modicum of perverse misrepresentation. In support of the parallel with the Israelite worship of the golden calf, for example, he associates Julian's bull coinage with his attempt to rebuild the Temple in Jerusalem as well as claiming that the music and sacrifice of traditional Jewish worship resemble pagan worship in its raucousness. Likewise to the established argument that Daniel prophesied the permanent destruction of the Jewish Temple, he adds the claim implicit in Constantine's building programme but not generally stated in theological polemics that Christian pilgrimage functions as a substitute for the Jewish cult of Jerusalem (*Jul.* 4.23–5).

Throughout these hymns, he exploits an extensive variety of animal imagery. The Orphic and broadly Hellenistic notion of a philanthropic shepherd king, already well-established as a model for Christ, is presented as a foil for Julian, the bad king (*Jul.* 1.1–2). Rather than a good shepherd, he is a wolf in sheep's clothing, or a he-goat, favouring the goats rather than the sheep (*Jul.* 2.1–4). The latter image has the added punch of alluding to Julian's unpopular beard as well as intimating lasciviousness (*Jul.* 2.6–9). Ephrem's almost apocalyptic description of the conflict between the forces of good and evil is enhanced by his association of the pagans with vermin, dragons and the primal chaos as well as with the more mundane insults of association with hogs and filth (*Jul.* 1.3, 1.5, 2.13).

Finally, Ephrem's symbolic imagination provides several examples of the ironic outcome of Julian's efforts. Considering it suitable that 'the punishment should fit the crime', he finds numerous coincidences to confirm this view. For example, the emperor's death near Babylon in conjunction with his 'denial' of Daniel's prophecy cements the parallel of Julian with Nebuchadnezzar (*Jul.* 1.18–20). Moreover, Ephrem spins out in elaborate detail the inherent contradiction of Julian's attempt to use Chaldean religion to defeat Persians, and the paradox that he was misled by the oracles to become himself the sacrificial goat (*Jul.* 2.4–25, 4.5–14). The coincidental features of his uncle Julian's fate should have astonished the emperor as they did Ephrem (*Jul.* 4.3). Likewise laden with significance is the similarity of Julian's death by a lance to the death of his sacrificial animals, both of which are implicitly contrasted with the death of the True Lamb who, being pierced, released humankind from the curse of the lance that barred the gate to Paradise (*Jul.* 3.14).

After the death of Julian, the Roman army had chosen a new emperor, Jovian, an orthodox Christian. Seeing no alternative to surrender under the disadvantageous terms offered him by Shapur, Jovian accepted them. These terms included cession to Persia of the city of Nisibis without its inhabitants. The city was, in Ephrem's eyes, the sacrificial lamb that saved the Roman army (*Jul.* 2.15.6). Unlike Ammianus Marcellinus, however, who portrays the fate of Nisibis in exclusively negative terms, Ephrem stresses that, although the city itself was ceded to Persia, the Persian ruler showed respect for its Christian churches and permitted its citizens to depart for Roman territory rather than executing them, enslaving them or exiling them into the Eastern reaches of the Persian empire, as had been the fate of the inhabitants of other recalcitrant Mesopotamian cities (*Jul.* 2.22–7). To celebrate his victory and show appropriate disdain for the religion of the Roman army that had attacked his empire, the Persian king was apparently satisfied to destroy the pagan temples associated specifically with Julian (*Jul.* 2.22). Still, the entire Christian population of this fortress city migrated within a short time to the adjacent cities of the Roman empire. Ephrem was among those who went to first to Amida, then to Edessa, where he would spend his last ten years. Thus the heroic struggle of his native city, a symbol of Rome and of Christianity, against the mighty Persian empire, a struggle which had occupied most of his adult life, ended in defeat and disgrace. The 'constant, unwearying herald' was surrendered to the Persians (*Jul.* 2.16.6). As he meditates on these events in his *Nisibene Hymns* and in his *Hymns against Julian*, Ephrem again shows himself to be a genuine heir to the Jewish prophetic tradition, interpreting historical events as directed by divine Providence towardss the attainment of justice in this world.[12] There must be a reason for God's allowing Nisibis to be taken. For him that reason is clear: the apostasy of the Christian Roman emperor and of those who followed him in reinstating pagan worship:

> Who else has so multiplied altars?
> Who else has so honored all the evil spirits?
> Who else has so pleased all the demons?
> He angered only the One, and he was broken.
> In him was confuted the entire faction of wrong,
> a force unable to support its worshipers!

> (*Jul.* 4.6)

HUMAN BEINGS IN THE DIVINE IMAGE AND DIVINE PRESENCE IN ALL OF NATURE

Ephrem's emphasis on the Incarnation and his extension of that historical moment into the process of sanctification show clearly that human beings have a special place in the created order:

> Blessed is He Who engraved our soul and adorned and betrothed her to Him[self].
> Blessed is He Who made our body a Tabernacle for His hiddenness.
> Blessed is He Who with our tongue interpreted His secrets.
> Let us give thanks to that Voice Whose praise on our lyre
> and Whose power on our kithara are sung.
>
> (*Nat.* 3.7.1–5)

> He is He Who Himself constructed the senses of our minds
> so that we might sing on our lyre something that the mouth of the bird
> is unable to sing in its melodies.
> Glory to the One Who saw that we had been pleased
> to resemble the animals in our rage and greed,
> and [so] He descended and became one of us that we might become heavenly.
>
> (*Nat.* 3.16)

Although it is clear that human beings, with the *imago dei*, enjoy a unique position in the world, certain material things enjoy a privileged place since they link the world of nature to the world of scripture. That privileged place is rooted in nature, in their physical properties and their names. So oil is symbolic of Christ and the salvation brought by Him, not only because He is literally, 'the Anointed One' Who fulfils the roles of priest, prophet and king, but also due to the natural properties of oil: its healing and strengthening properties, its capacity to provide light, its use with pigments for painting an image, its ability to ease forces in conflict, and even its property of floating on water, as Jesus walked on the water (*Virg.* 4–7)! All these properties resonate in the baptismal anointing in which the *imago dei* is restored to us:

> The lamp returned our lost things, and the Anointed also [returned] our treasures.
> The lamp found the coin, and the Anointed [found] the image of Adam.
>
> (*Virg.* 5.8.5–6)

The bread and wine of the Eucharist, although they provide a less fertile field for Ephrem's imagination, play a similar role:[13]

> Blessed is the Shepherd Who became the sheep for our absolution.
> Blessed is the Vineshoot that became the cup of our salvation.
> Blessed also is the Cluster, the source of the medicine of life.
> Blessed also is the Ploughman Who Himself became
> the grain of wheat that was sown and the sheaf that was reaped.
> He is the Master Builder Who became a tower for our refuge.
>
> (*Nat.* 3.15)

Not only the elements of the sacraments, however, but other material things and concepts are symbolic of Christ. So Satan's temptations of Jesus have ironic appropriateness: he tempted with bread the 'Sustainer of all', with stones, 'the perfect Stone', with kingship the true King (*Virg.* 14). Even things without a symbolic tradition in scripture may be seen as representative of Christ's altruistic suffering. In one of his *Virginity* hymns he considers a long series of minerals, plants and animals all worked by human craft on our behalf despite the harm done to them. Like a Buddhist or Manichaean sage, Ephrem notes that they all suffer for our benefit, making them symbolic of Christ, as the following excerpt from the list shows:

> Iron and a sharp stake, indeed, pierce the pearl
> like that One Who was pierced by nails and on the cross.
> It becomes by its suffering an adornment for humankind.

> When a fruit is eaten, by means of its suffering its taste
> pours out in the mouth. This is a symbol of that Fruit
> that brings to life His eaters when His body is eaten.

> The sheep in its shame strips off its garment and cloak
> and gives all of it to its shearers,
> like the Lamb Who divided His garments for His crucifiers.

> All these things teach by their symbols:
> they open by their sufferings the treasure of their riches,
> and the suffering of the Son of the Gracious One is the key of His treasures.
> (*Hymns on Virginity* 11.9, 12, 17, 20)

Finally, every beauty of daily life is a tangible reminder of the graciousness of God:

> But remaining are all those things the Gracious One made in His mercy.
> Let us see those things that He does for us every day!
> How many tastes for the mouth! How many beauties for the eye!
> How many melodies for the ear! How many scents for the nostrils!
> Who can be compared to the goodness of these little things!
> (*Virg.* 31.16)

NOTES

1 Some segments of this chapter have appeared previously in the general introduction, introductions to individual hymns and notes to McVey (1989).

2 For a more detailed account of Ephrem's life, see McVey (1989: 5–28). In addition to allusions within Ephrem's genuine literary corpus, ancient sources for Ephrem's life include Sozomen, *Church History* 3.16; Palladius, *Lausiac History* 40; Jerome, *On Illustrious Men* 115; Theodoret, *Church History* 4.26; a Syriac *vita* tradition; and a Syriac homily

by Jacob of Sarug. For a concise overview of these materials and the recent scholarship, cf. Sebastian Brock (1999).

3 On Ephrem's use of Greek philosophical concepts, see Possekel (1999).

4 On the corpus of translations and their authenticity, see McVey (1989: 4, n. 6). Further, see the excellent collection of conference papers (published as Palmer 1998, 1999).

5 For bibliography on this subject, see McVey (1989: 5, n. 7).

6 On Ephrem's use of symbols, see Bou Mansour (1988).

7 Observed by Brock (1990a: 72–4), with regard to *Hymns on Faith* 5.17; with regard to *Hymns on the Nativity* 1.99, in McVey (1989: 74, n. 66).

8 Brock characterizes this as another sort of 'incarnation' of the Word (1990a: 45–9).

9 The translation is Brock's (1990b).

10 On 'Watchers', a class of angels often mentioned by Ephrem, see McVey (1989: 229, n. 36).

11 On Ephrem's understanding of virginity and of 'singleness' in the context of early Syriac tradition, see Koonammakal (1999).

12 See Martikainen (1974) and Griffith (1987).

13 For example, see *Hymns on Virginity* 16.2.4.5 and 31.13–14. Further on Ephrem's understanding of the Eucharist, see Yousif (1984).

BIBLIOGRAPHY

Note: Recent English translations from Syriac of writings by or about St Ephrem include Amar (1995), Brock (1984, 1990a), Lieu (1989), Mathews and Amar (1995), and McVey (1989).

Amar, Joseph (ed. and trans.) (1995) *A Metrical Homily on Holy Mar Ephrem by Mar Jacob of Serugh*. Patrologia Orientalis 47.1. Turnhout: Brepols.

Bou Mansour, Tanios (1988) *La Pensée symbolique de Saint Ephrem le Syrien*. Bibliothèque de l'Université Saint-Esprit 16. Kaslik: Université Saint-Esprit.

Brock, Sebastian, (ed. and trans.) (1984) *The Harp of the Spirit: Eighteen Poems of Saint Ephrem*, 2nd edn. Studies Supplementary to *Sobornost* 4. San Bernardino, Calif.: Borg Press.

—— (trans.) (1990a) *St Ephrem the Syrian. Hymns on Paradise*. Crestwood, N.Y.: St Vladimir's Seminary Press.

—— (1990b) 'The Holy Spirit as Feminine in Early Syriac Literature', in Janet Martin Soskice (ed.) *After Eve: Women, Theology and the Christian Tradition*. London: Marshall Pickering, Collins, 73–88.

—— (1992) *The Luminous Eye: the Spiritual World Vision of St Ephrem*, rev. edn. Cistercian Studies 124. Kalamazoo, Mich.: Cistercian Publications.

—— (1999) 'St Ephrem in the Eyes of Later Syriac Liturgical Tradition', *Hugoye: Journal of Syriac Studies* 2.1. [http://www.acad.cua.edu/syrcom/Hugoye]

Griffith, Sidney H. (1987) 'Ephraem the Syrian's Hymns "Against Julian": Meditations on History and Imperial Power', *Vigiliae Christianae* 4: 238–66.

—— (1997) *Faith Adoring the Mystery: Reading the Bible with St Ephrem the Syrian*. Milwaukee: Marquette University Press.

Hogan, Martin (1999) *The Sermon on the Mount in St Ephrem's Commentary on the Diatessaron*. New York: P. Lang.

Koonammakkal, Thomas (1999) 'Ephrem's Ideas on Singleness', *Hugoye: Journal of Syriac Studies* 2.1. [http://www.acad.cua.edu/syrcom/Hugoye]

Lieu, Samuel N.C. (ed. and trans.) (1989) *The Emperor Julian: Panegyric and Polemic*, 2nd edn. Liverpool: Liverpool University Press.

McVey, Kathleen E. (trans.) (1989) *Ephrem the Syrian. Hymns on the Nativity, Hymns Against Julian, Hymns on Virginity and on the Symbols of the Lord*. Classics of Western Spirituality. New York: Paulist.

Martikainen, Jouko (1974) 'Some Remarks about the Carmina Nisibena as a Literary and a Theological Source', *Orientalia Christiana Analecta* 197: 345–52.

Mathews, Edward G. and Amar, Joseph P. (trans.) (1995) *St. Ephrem the Syrian. Selected Prose Works*. Fathers of the Church 91. Washington, DC: Catholic University of America.

Murray, Robert (1975) *Symbols of Church and Kingdom: A Study in Early Syriac Tradition*, Cambridge: Cambridge University Press.

Palmer, Andrew (ed.) (1998, 1999) *The Influence of Saint Ephraim the Syrian.Hugoye: Journal of Syriac Studies*, 1.2 and 2.1 [http://www.acad.cua.edu/syrcom/Hugoye].

Petersen, William (1986) *The Diatessaron and Ephrem Syrus as Sources of Romanos the Melodist*. Corpus Scriptorum Christianorum Orientalium 466, Subsidia 73. Louvain: Peeters.

Possekel, Ute (1999) *Evidence of Greek Philosophical Concepts in the Writings of Ephrem the Syrian*. Corpus Scriptorum Christianorum Orientalium 580, Subsidia 102. Louvain: Peeters.

Ruether, Rosemary (1974) *Faith and Fratricide*. New York: Seabury.

Valavanolickal, Kuriakose A. (1996) *The Use of Gospel Parables in the Writings of Aphrahat and Ephrem*. Studies in the Religion and History of Early Christianity 2. New York: P. Lang.

Yousif, P. (1984) *L'Eucharistie chez S Ephrem de Nisibe*. Orientalia Christiana Analecta 224. Rome: Pontificium Institutum Orientalium Studiorum.

JULIAN THE APOSTATE

—— •✦• ——

Michael Bland Simmons

In this chapter I offer a profile of a man whose ambition, if it had been realized, would probably have meant this volume would never have been written. Whereas the other profiles which precede this speak of men and women whose lives contributed to the establishment of Christianity in its first few centuries, Julian lived the last years of his short life determined upon restraining it in favour of a resurgence of pagan religion.

Flavius Claudius Julianus (*c.* 331–63 CE) was born at Constantinople. His grandfather was Constantius Chlorus, a member of Diocletian's Tetrarchy, and his uncle was Constantine.[1] After Constantine's death in 337, his son Constantius II may have ordered the execution of Julian's father, Julius Constantius, and several of his male relatives. During this period Constantius II was ruling the Eastern provinces of the empire. Julian's mother Basilina died when he was an infant, and her family assumed the responsibility of the young orphan and his half-brother Gallus, who was five years his senior. Basilinas' former Scythian tutor, Mardonius, taught Julian in Nicomedia, and inculcated in him a great reverence for Greek culture. Eusebius the Arian bishop of the same city was his principal teacher.[2] It was during these formative years of his life that the basic attributes of Julian's disposition were being developed. Our sources inform us that he was eloquent, studious, shy, often inconsistent, very talkative, prone to nervousness, sexually chaste, extremely superstitious, and loved the applause of the masses.[3]

In 342 Constantius II sent Gallus and Julian to Macellum in central Turkey where they lived for six years.[4] Julian received a good education in Christian literature, including the scriptures, and we are told that eunuchs were assigned to prevent his wavering from the faith.[5] His love of Hellenism, which had been inspired by Mardonius, continued to develop from his studies in Greek literature. It would be unreasonable to question the sincerity of his faith at this time, or the assertion that he became a reader in the church at Nicomedia.[6] Indeed, Christian writers of the period lament the emperor who had once been a dedicated Christian, and pagans confirm his apostasy from a genuine faith.[7]

Constantius II recalled Gallus and Julian from Macellum in 348 to the capital. Julian studied rhetoric there and at Nicomedia until 351, often attending the lectures of Libanius, who became his life-long friend and dedicated several orations to him after he became emperor (Sozomen, *H. E.* 5.2; Smith 1995: 2). It was also during this time (348–51) that Julian met Maximus of Ephesus, who exerted a significant philosophical and religious (especially mystical) influence on the young man, and played a role in Julian's apostasy.[8] Constantius II appointed Gallus Caesar in 351, and Julian was given freedom to continue his studies in western Asia Minor at Pergamum and Ephesus under the Neoplatonic philosophers Aedesius, the disciple of Iamblichus, Eusebius, and Chrysanthius, in addition to Maximus (Bowersock 1978: 28–30; Smith 1995: 2–4). The Iamblichean Neoplatonism espoused by these profoundly impacted his intellectual and spiritual development. Writing from Gaul in 358–9 to his fellow Neoplatonist Priscus, Julian referred to Iamblichus as a god-like man ranking next to Plato and Pythagoras.[9] Neoplatonism by this time was characterized by a combination of religious philosophy and a mystical experience often referred to as theurgy. The latter was associated with the Chaldean theology and oracles which also had a significant influence on Porphyry. In 351 Julian had made the decision to apostasize from Christianity, and he was initiated into the Chaldean theurgical rites by Maximus of Ephesus. From then on, Maximus continued to have a great influence on Julian, persuaded him to convert to paganism, and was a moving force behind Julian's later attempts to revive Hellenism in the Eastern provinces.[10] He was by his side when the emperor died during the Persian campaign in 363 (see p. 1259). Julian continued his studies in Asia Minor until Constantius II ordered the execution of Gallus for treason in 354, at which time the younger brother was summoned to the imperial court at Milan. He was saved from execution on the charge of complicity by the intervention of the empress Eusebia.[11] The following year (355) Julian went to Athens to study, and here he met the great Cappadocian father, St Basil.[12] It proved to be a short stay because Constantius II summoned him to Milan and appointed him Caesar on 6 November (Sozomen, *H. E.* 3.1; 5.2; Socrates, *H. E.* 2.34; Eunapius, *Lives of the Philosophers* 476). By December he was dispatched to Gaul to begin a campaign against the Germanic tribes.[13] After Julian's decisive victory over the Goths at Strasbourg in 357, Constantius II became increasingly suspicious of his growing power[14] and eventually ordered the bulk of Julian's army to be transferred to the East to help in the Persian campaign against Shapur II (Ammianus Marcellinus 20.4.1–2; Libanius, *Or.* 28.92–117). Receiving the imperial order in Paris early in 360, Julian's army mutinied and at once proclaimed their general the new emperor (Ammianus Marcellinus 20.4.14). By the next year (361) both armies were preparing for war, but Constantius II became ill and died in November. Now recognized as the sole emperor, Julian and his troops entered Constantinople in December.[15]

One of his first acts as emperor was the promulgation of an Edict on Religious Toleration which provided for the raising of temples, construction of altars, the restoration of sacrifices, and the reorganization of the pagan priesthood.[16] The major objective of this legislation was to promote the cultural revival of the Eastern cities on the basis of Hellenic *paideia* (Libanius, *Or.* 15.67; 18.23, 161). Libanius tells us that Julian very zealously participated in the programme. He sacrificed animals at dawn and at dusk, and turned his imperial gardens and palace into a pagan temple (Libanius, *Or.* 12.80–2, 17.4; Socrates, *H. E.* 3.17). His fingers were stained red by the blood of so many sacrificed animals (Libanius, *Or.* 12.82). Julian moved quickly to reform the court at Constantinople (Socrates, *H. E.* 3.1; Ammianus Marcellinus 22.5.1–5). After expelling a large surplus of barbers, eunuchs and cooks from the palace, he turned to reducing the number of secretaries in the civil service. He also restricted the mode of imperial transportation and the conveyance of necessities (Socrates, *H. E.* 3.1). Gregory of Nazianzus interpreted these actions as an attempt to eliminate Christians who had served under Constantius II.[17] Although he was careful not to begin an official state persecution of the Christians for fear that this would produce martyrs,[18] Julian none the less systematically began to move against the religion that had been favoured since the conversion of Constantine.[19]

Early in his reign Julian recalled the bishops who had been exiled by Constantius II, which appeared to be an act of benevolence, but the true motives were most probably to cause internal dissension in the Eastern churches.[20] This interpretation is tenable in light of legislation which deprived Christian clergy of the immunities, honours, and provisions granted by Constantine (Theodoret, *H. E.* 3.3; Lieu 1986: 40–6). We must remember that Julian was familiar with the internal disputes of the Christians and could therefore distinguish between orthodox, Arian, and heretical (e.g., gnostic) believers (Julian, *Ep.* 40, to Hecebolus in later 362/early 363 from Antioch). Widows of clergy had to pay back money formerly supplied by imperial funds (Sozomen, *H.E.* 5.5). The emperor publicly ridiculed Christian bishops.[21] We are told that he refused to receive Christian embassies, did not send military aid to the Christian city Nisibis during the Persian invasion, and made another Christian city, Constantia, a tributary of the pagan stronghold Gaza. Christians in Caesarea in Cappadocia were heavily taxed (Sozomen, *HE* 5.3, 4; Balty 1974; Fowden 1978). Even though the emperor did not overtly persecute the Christians, he attempted to make it as difficult as possible for them, especially in the Eastern provinces.[22]

Martyrdom, however, did occur, sometimes tolerated by the emperor himself. At Palestinian Askalon and Gaza, Christian priests and virgins were tortured and executed, while at Sebaste a martyr's bones were burned and scattered.[23] Open persecutions (including executions) of Christians broke out at Heliopolis and Emesa in Phoenicia, in the Thracian city of Dorystolum, and Arethusa in Syria (Theodoret, *H. E.* 3.3; Sozomen, *H. E.* 5.10). Sozomen informs us that Eusebius, Nestabus, and Zeno became martyrs at Gaza, and unlike bishop George's murder at Alexandria, which was met with a letter of rebuke from the emperor, Julian's only response was to depose the governor of the province (Sozomen, *H. E.* 5.9).

In addition to a change in imperial policies towards the newly favoured religion of the empire, one of the major goals of Julian was to bring about the revival of paganism in the urban centres of the East. The heart of his programme was expressed in the ancient ideal of Greek *paideia*, which included all the elements of high culture from literature, art, drama, music, and the art of government, to science, philosophy, and religion. Julian perceived Greek *paideia* to be a synthesis of the outstanding attributes of Hellenism combined with *Romanitas*, which collectively revealed salvation to humanity and civilization to the world because it had been the product of divine revelation.[24] While its spiritual legacy was soteriological and revelatory, in a political and civic sense it was the only hope for the restoration of the former greatness of the empire which began to diminish with the rise of the Galilean superstition.[25] In light of this conviction to resurrect the old cults of the cities, it should not surprise us that Julian set out to reorganize paganism, often in the midst of pagan apathy towards the gods (see Julian, *Ep.* 20), according to the structure and practices of the church. For example, high priests were appointed over areas with the authority to appoint priests in every city and assign them various responsibilities (Julian, *Ep.* 20). Writing to Arsacius, the high priest of Galatia, Julian demanded a higher ethical standard for all priests. They must not enter theatres, he advises, drink in taverns, nor involve themselves in disrespectable trade (Julian, *Ep.* 22). In another epistle he laments that the Galilean folly has 'overturned almost everything'(Julian, *Ep.* 37). After ordering a high priest to make provisions in every city to help the poor, Julian adds that the Galileans are helping not only their own poor, but 'ours' as well (Julian, *Ep.* 22). He commands priests to be benevolent towards humanity because this was the practice of the ancient Hellenic religion.[26]

Julian systematically continued to move against the Christians by the implementation of new legislation. The edict of 17 June 362 which forbade Christian teachers to teach classical literature in the schools was considered a harsh measure even by the pagan historian Ammianus Marcellinus (25.4.20; Banchich 1993; Averil Cameron 1993: 4). The rescript issued later directed provincial magistrates to exclude Christians from educational employment (Julian, *Ep.* 36, after 17 June 362, at Antioch; Hardy 1968: 131). Julian defines the Galilean religion as a mental disease, and emphasizes that literary culture has been revealed to civilization by the gods through men like Homer, Hesiod, Demosthenes and Herodotus (*Ep.* 36). Christian theologians had for many years been using classical works to show how it served God's plan as a preparation for the definitive revelation in Christ. Julian's concept of *paideia*, based on the religious *mos maiorum* of ancient polytheism, affirmed the superiority of Graeco-Roman culture to the man-made myths of the Galileans. The edict therefore had a twofold purpose: it aimed at reviving Hellenism in the cities, and it was a part of imperial policies related to Christianity which were becoming increasingly antagonistic.[27]

Julian moved his court to Antioch during July 362 to prepare for his Persian campaign that began in March of the following year (Ammianus Marcellinus 22.9.15; Sozomen, *H. E.* 5.19). The emperor soon alienated the ruling classes because of his ascetic life, interest in reviving paganism in a Christianized metropolis, reluctance to support the chariot races, and a serious conflict with the Antiochene curia concerning the proper solution to economic problems (Socrates, *H. E.* 3.17; Athanassiadi 1992: 216). The latter was the main cause of discontent among the citizens of the city (Libanius, *Or.* 15.8–19; Socrates, *H. E.* 3.1). When the emperor arrived in the city, food shortages had already occurred. Libanius tells us that an edict reducing the price of food coincided with a severe drought. Vendors left the city, famine ensued, accompanied by scarcity, and the Antiochenes blamed everything on Julian (Socrates, *H. E.* 3.1; Sozomen, *H. E.* 5.19; Libanius, *Or.* 15.8, 19, 21, 70; 18.195–6, 148). Having now become unpopular, he was constantly ridiculed by the people, yet it was during this period that many of his extant works were written (Smith 1995: 7–9). Within this situation of growing hostility Julian's anti-Christian posture was reinforced. During the winter of 362–3 he was doing research for his *Contra Galilaeos*. According to Theodoret an edict was issued at this time which expelled Christians from the army (*H. E.* 3.4). Whether this is true is rather unlikely, owing to the fact that since Diocletian the number of Christians in the military had increased, and Julian needed a large army for his Persian campaign. On 29 January 363, however, we hear that a number of Christians who served in the army were executed (Woods 1997; Jones 1963: 24–5). Other policies against the Christians were the edict forbidding daytime funerals (Julian, *Ep.* 56), in a context where pagan funerals occurred at night; and the support of pagan intellectuals in the East to revive the imperial cult by sacrificing to Julian (Libanius, *Or.* 15–36). Although scholars continue to debate the precise meaning of Julian's actions at this time, it is clear that the growing hostility towards the Christians from June 362 to March 363, and the concomitant favouritism shown to pagans, strongly indicates a movement of imperial policies towards an increasingly overt anti-Christian programme. And this appears to have been a driving force in Julian beginning at least with the death of Constantius II.[28]

Other significant events occurred while he resided at Antioch. Before launching the Persian campaign the emperor consulted the oracle of Daphne which was located about six kilometres south-east of Antioch (Lieu 1986: 51–7). Desiring to restore the shrine's Castalian springs which were believed to possess prophetic powers, Julian invoked the deity, who ordered that the bodies buried nearby be removed to another place.[29] Julian interpreted this to mean that the remains of St. Babylas, bishop of Antioch who was martyred during the Decian persecution, and who was buried close to the shrine, must be relocated. On 22 October 362 the temple of Apollo at Daphne, along with the cultic statue, was destroyed by fire.[30] Accusing the Christians of starting the fire, Julian retaliated by ordering the great church in Antioch to be closed (Theodoret, *H. E.* 3.6). Fresh persecutions against the Christians began under the leadership of the emperor's uncle Julian (Lieu 1986: 51–7).

Under Iamblichus Neoplatonism had evolved into a syncretistic system comprising metaphysics, ethics, and Chaldean theurgical rites (Simmons 1995: 216–303). This new religious philosophy was characterized by a strong belief in divine revelation (oracles) thought capable of giving to the recipient guidance for one's decisions, wisdom in the affairs of life, and even glimpses into the future. With respect to the history of religion in the ancient Mediterranean world, Julian the Apostate is very significant for our understanding of this mystical belief in 'personal prophecy'. Pagan and Christian sources inform us that early in his life Julian became obsessed with an interest in augury, sorcery, enchantments, dreams and visions, divination, extispicy, oracles, soothsaying, necromancy, horoscopes, prodigies, zodiac signs, seeking out seers, all kinds of omens, and many other prophetic 'signs' (Julian, *Ep.* 6; Libanius, *Or.* 12. 69; 13.14, 48–9; 15.53; Ephrem' s *Hymn against Julian, passim*). Indeed he offers to students of ancient religions, particularly those interested in 'prophetic revelation', a gold mine of information. For example, Julian tells us that the foundation of the Roman empire consists of the body of ancestral religious customs passed down from antiquity, the *mos maiorum*, which beginning in the Regal period (753–510 BC) came about by divine revelation. Under king Numa great blessings occurred because the Sibyl and others experienced 'divine possession' and 'inspiration' and gave oracles for the city from Zeus (Julian, *Contra Galilaeos* 194B; *Ep.* 20). By placing this concept of *Sacred History* in contradistinction with the Christian 'fulfilment from prophecy' argument, Julian aimed at dismantling a powerful weapon in traditional Christian apologetics to show that the Christian interpretation of Old Testament prophecies about Jesus was untenable (Julian, *Contra Galilaeos* 106C, 138C). But it was not just an academic argument. Owing to his strong belief that prophecy was a 'blessed gift' from the gods (*Contra Galilaeos* 106C), the extent to which it influenced both his personal affairs and, more importantly, his decisions as emperor should not be overlooked. Often prophecies, meaning here all means of acquiring important information from the gods, directly affected governmental appointments and military decisions (Ammianus Marcellinus 22.12.6–7; Libanius, *Or.* 18.180; Julian, *Ep.* 9). By prophecy Julian knew when people would die, including himself (Ammianus Marcellinus 22.1.2; Sozomen, *H. E.* 5.1; Eunapius, *Philos.* 475–6; Averil Cameron 1993: 91). Even though he alludes to the rare manifestation of the prophetic spirit in his own day, he stresses that it has altogether ceased amongst the Hebrews and Egyptians, and finds comfort in the 'sacred arts' of divination through which heaven can aid man now.[31] And if it was rare, oracular revelation did continue at a few temples of Apollo, and the incident at Daphne proves how zealously Julian sought out divine oracles.[32] Finally, Julian was significantly influenced by dreams and visions, and kept in his imperial entourage a group of experts who were adept at their interpretation (Ammianus Marcellinus 23.3.3; 25.2.3 – 4, 25.3.9; Julian, *Ep.* 4).

Julian's keen interest in prophetic revelation may shed some light on the edict which he issued at Antioch, probably late in 362, that ordered the rebuilding of the Temple at Jerusalem. A former vice-prefect of Britain, Alypius, was appointed to supervise the project, but shortly after it began an earthquake and a fire brought about its termination (Ammianus Marcellinus 23.1.2–3; Seaver 1978). Scholars have given several reasons for Julian's motives. First, he wanted to rebuild the temple as a part of his programmeme to revive animal sacrifices (Blanchetière 1980; Athanassiadi 1992: 164). Second, it was a part of his anti-Christian policies (Klein 1986: 287; Smith 1995: 193). Finally, Julian wanted to disprove Christ's prophecy of Matthew 24.2, Mark 13.2 and Luke 21.6 which predicted the destruction of the Jerusalem Temple (Browning 1976: 176; Bowerstock 1978: 89–90; Potter 1994: 171). One other motive that has never been investigated concerns an oracle, undoubtedly derived from Porphyry's *Philosophia ex oraculis*, and quoted by Augustine in the *De Civitate Dei*:

> For when they saw that it could not be destroyed by all those many great persecutions but rather increased amazingly because of them, they thought up some Greek verses or other, as if they were the outpouring of a divine oracle in reply to some one consulting it; in them they make Christ blameless, to be sure, of this charge of sacrilege (so to call it), but explain that Peter contrived by sorcery that the name of Christ should be worshipped for three hundred and sixty-five years, and then after the completion of that number of years it should immediately come to an end.
>
> (*Civ. Dei* 18.53)

The important elements of this prophecy are: (1) a pagan god gives 'prophetic revelation'; (2) it is a futuristic prophecy containing a specific date; and (3) it predicts the termination of Christianity exactly 365 years after Christ began to be worshipped. At least five data strongly suggest that the oracle derives from Porphyry's *Philosophia ex oraculis*: (1) The oracle was in a collection of Greek verses; (2) oracular revelation was given after someone inquired about Christianity; (3) the many 'Great Persecutions' are now in the past; (4) Christ is not criticized; and (5) Peter is a magician. During the winter of 362–3 Julian was doing research for the *Contra Galilaeos* (Lib., *Or.* 18.178) which he finished before March 363. While writing the work, it is highly possible that Porphyry's anti-Christian books were consulted, and the above oracle was discovered. Realizing that he could be instrumental in the fulfilment of the prophecy, Julian called a conference with Jewish officials which resulted in the Edict on Rebuilding the Temple in Jerusalem. Moreover, he will have perceived both the fulfilment of the prophecy and the rebuilding of the Temple as interrelated events that could bring about the realization of his dream to revive Hellenism. As a fervent anti-Christian, Julian will have viewed the rebuilding of the Temple as a historical confirmation of Porphyry's oracle and the crowning event of his imperial career. A comforting thought in his twilight years would have been that the gods used him to fulfil the prophecy given by a prominent Neoplatonic philosopher about the demise of a religion for which they possessed a mutual hatred. We may also give the following data to support this interpretation:

1 Even by pagan accounts Julian was very superstitious and possessed a fanatical interest in oracles.

2 Julian performed many kinds of rituals regularly in order to look into the future.

3 Julian personally believed in oracular (and other kinds of) revelation, and depended on it for guidance in his affairs.

4 Porphyry wrote *c.* 50–60 years before Julian, and was still considered the most famous anti-Christian writer of the period. His books were in circulation, and it would be unreasonable to think that he did not have a significant influence on Julian.[33]

5 The discovery of the '365–year oracle' may have resulted from the acquisition of George of Alexandria's library which Julian was keenly interested in procuring as early as July 362.[34] The oracle was most probably in the *Philosophia ex oraculis*, and its discovery was the main stimulus for the conference with the Jews. In *Ep.* 51, written in late 362, Julian refers to his plans to rebuild the Temple *after* his Persian campaign. The discovery of the Porphyrian oracle changed his mind to start the project *before* the campaign began in March 363.

6 Ammianus Marcellinus (23.1.2) informs us that Julian was eager to extend the memory of his reign by great works, and he planned *at great cost* to restore the Temple in Jerusalem. He also says that he entrusted the *speedy* performance of the work to Alypius. Why speedy? What made him change his mind not only about the timing of the project, but also what made him between July 362 and the following winter (December-February 363) feel compelled to do it hurriedly? The answer could very well be that he wanted to see the fulfilment of the prophecy *in his lifetime before the 365 years were terminated.*

7 From an early age Julian was familiar with the scriptures, including the Olivet eschatological discourse of Matthew 24, Mark 13 and Luke 21 which give Jesus' prophecy about the Temple. The Porphyrian oracle was perceived as divine

inspiration for the restoration of the Temple and retribution for Jesus' false prediction.

8   Julian constantly relied on Neoplatonic philosophers for prophetic wisdom, often in direct opposition to the traditional practices of his soothsayers.[35] Ephrem, in *Hymn against Julian* 4.22, describes Julian's attempt to rebuild the Temple as the *divination of a madman*. This may indeed imply that the Porphyrian oracle motivated him. 'Divination' was a word used in the preface of the *Philosophia ex oraculis* to explain the salvific benefits that Porphyry's readers would receive (see Eusebius, *Praeparatio Evangelica* 4.6–7).

9   Ephrem the Syrian is one of the earliest Christian writers to refer to Julian's Temple restoration, but he never mentions the Olivet discourse passages. He uses Daniel to argue from prophecy that the Temple would not be rebuilt. Cyril, bishop of Jerusalem, also uses Daniel's prophecy, which he says was confirmed by Christ, to show that the Temple would not be rebuilt. Porphyry's interpretation of Daniel in the *Contra Christianos*, combined with the 365–year oracle, motivated Julian to begin the project when he did. Both were integral to his desire to disprove Jesus' prophecy. Ephrem calls Julian the 'king of Greece' (Alexander) who 'rejected Daniel' and provoked God to anger. We have seen that Porphyry argued that Daniel was not a true prophecy, but simply a historical book.

10 Socrates (*H. E.* 3.23) says that both Porphyry and Julian were scoffers at those they disliked (the Christians), referring to Porphyry as Julian's 'father'. This strongly suggests that Porphyry had a direct influence on Julian's anti-Christian polemics.

11 Julian admits that the manifestation of the prophetic spirit in his day was rare. Yet he sought oracles for guidance and to know the future. He kept several collections of books on the proper interpretation of prophetic revelation in a chest which he took with him even while on campaign. One book was a 'Book of Oracles'. He also consulted the Sibylline Books in Rome. We hear of books on the interpretation of lightning, Tarquitian Books 'On Signs from Heaven', and Etruscan Books 'On War' for the precise interpretation of omens before battle. If these were consulted regularly, and he had a preference for Neoplatonic oracles how much more would he confide in the collection of oracles (*Phil. or.*) compiled by a renowned anti-Christian Neoplatonist (Porphyry)?[36]

12 Julian strongly believed that 'signs' in the form of concrete historical events must follow a prophecy in order to confirm its authenticity:

> It is not possible to behold the truth from speech alone, but some clear sign must follow on what has been said that will guarantee the prophecy that has been made concerning the future.
>
> (*C. Gal.* 358E)

Ammianus tells us that Julian was an expert in the discernment of such prophetic signs (21.1.6; also 22.1.2; 23.3.6–7, 23.5.8–9.), and the emperor wrote to Libanius on 10 March 363 that at the beginning of the Persian campaign Zeus showed many favourable signs from heaven (*Ep.* 58). Because he received oracles and accompanying signs, Libanius says that Julian carried out his plans 'with the end already in full view'(*Or.* 13.49). A project as vast as rebuilding the Temple presupposes two known facts about Julian's belief in prophetic revelation. First, an oracle motivated him to restore the Temple. Second, the rebuilt Temple could be a concrete sign to prove that Jesus' prophecy about the Temple was false, and Porphyry's oracle about Christianity's termination 365 years after Jesus began to be worshipped was true.

The date is arguably important. Augustine, who of course believed in the deity of Christ, dates the beginning of his worship at Pentecost (*Civ. Dei* 18.54) *c.* 29 CE in the consulship of the two Gemini. He calculates that the 365 years ended on the Ides of May in the consulship of Honorius and Eutychianus in 398. The next year (18 March 399) officials in Carthage demolished pagan temples and images.

Augustine then gives a concrete 'sign' that the prophecy was false. In the 30 years since that day, he says, Christianity has increased, and then he adds: 'Who does not see how much the worship of the name of Christ had grown during the period of nearly thirty years from then to the present, especially after many of those became Christians who had been held back from the faith by that supposedly true prophecy, which they now saw, after the completion of the specified number of years, to be foolish and ridiculous?' (*Civ. Dei* 18.54). This demonstrates clearly that many pagans during Augustine's day strongly believed in Porphyry's prophecy.

In 363 Julian had about two years left for the 'sign' confirming Porphyry's prophecy to occur, provided that he dated the beginning of Christianity at the birth of Christ. Porphyry's oracle declared that Christianity would expire *immediately* 365 years from the worship of Christ. Julian knew that according to Matthew, this began in Bethlehem when the Magi brought presents to the stable. Julian's insistence on calling Jesus the Galilean is not so much because he denied the Christians any claim to universality (Athanassiadi 1992: 161, n. 2) as it was to stress the mere humanity of Jesus. Yet if Julian dated the beginning of the worship of Jesus at Pentecost as Augustine did, he could still look forward to seeing the fulfilment of Porphyry's prophecy in his lifetime because in 394 CE (Augustine's calculations were inaccurate) he would have been 63. Even if he had not lived to see the Temple completed, he would have been given credit for it. Ammianus' remark that Julian was compelled to move forward hurriedly with the project is best understood as a decision that was motivated by his belief in the fulfilment of the Porphyrian oracle within two years from the time he finished the *Contra Galilaeos*. We may conclude that Julian wrote the *C. Gal.* during the winter of 362–3 in his palace, mainly at night, while dealing with growing discontent in Antioch, preparing for the Persian campaign, and meeting with Jewish officials concerning the rebuilding of the Temple. He had sent two letters months before to Alexandria demanding that books from George's library be sent to him immediately. This is one possible source of Porphyry's works on philosophy, which may have included polemical writings. It is logical to assume that Julian consulted the *Contra Christianos* and *Phil. or.* while writing the *C. Gal.*, and he may have discovered the prophecy that predicted the termination of Christianity 365 years after its beginning while reading the *Phil. or.* This motivated the emperor to convene a speedy meeting with Jewish officials to initiate work on the Temple project.

This helps us to understand why Julian moved the date for the beginning of the construction from *after* to *before* the Persian campaign, and why he moved forward with it hurriedly.

In March 363 Julian set out for his Persian campaign against the advice of his best soothsayers who admonished him both before and during the invasion that the gods did not favour the enterprise (Libanius, *Or.* 12.76; Socrates, *H. E.* 3.19–21; Ammianus Marcellinus 23.2.7, 23.5.11). As we have noted, the emperor increasingly relied on prophetic guidance, especially oracles, provided by Neoplatonic philosophers like Maximus of Ephesus (Rufinus, *Historia Ecclesiastica* 1.36; Ammianus Marcellinus 22.12.6–7; Ephrem, *Hymn against Julian* 2.8; Socrates, *H. E.* 3.21). Ammianus Marcellinus describes many 'signs' which occurred during the invasion to prove the divine disfavour expressed by the soothsayers (23.5.10, 23.3.6–7, 23.5.4–5, 23.5.12–14, 25.2.7–8). After an attempt to take Ctesiphon (May 363) failed, Julian ordered a retreat as Shapur II's army was approaching, and on 26 June 363 he was fatally wounded at the age of 32 while leading a counter-attack against the Persians. He died later in the evening in his tent (Ammianus Marcellinus 25.3.1–23; Libanius, *Or.* 17.23; Socrates, *H. E.* 3.21; Sozomen, *H. E.* 6.1), and his body was taken to Tarsus where it was given a customary imperial burial. The Christian Jovian became the next emperor (Ammianus Marcellinus 25.5.4–9).[37]

THEMES OF THE *CONTRA GALILAEOS*

As we have seen, during the winter of 362–3 Julian hurriedly wrote the *Contra Galilaeos* in the midst of economic problems in Antioch, planning the Persian campaign, and beginning construction of the Temple in Jerusalem (Libanius, *Or.* 18.178; Masaracchia 1986; Athanassiadi 1992: 362–3; Smith 1995: 190). The text of the *C. Gal.* is lost, though parts of Books 1 from an original three are preserved in Cyril of Alexandria's refutation which was written in the 430s (Masaracchia 1986). Lacking in original thought and not profoundly intellectual, the *C. Gal.* is described by Libanius as a work that was produced without any attention to elegance (*Or.* 18.178). Julian often irritates his readers by jumping from one subject to another, then back again to his original theme (*C. Gal.* 213B-C; 218 A-B). He sometimes promises that he will cover a subject later in his treatise, then proceed to do it (213A). It is indeed a disappointing work, often repetitive, and, according to one scholar, it demonstrates the emperor's inability to distinguish the fundamental from the trivial (Malley 1978). Julian possessed neither the analytical, theological, historical and linguistic expertise of Porphyry, nor the propriety and objectivity of Celsus. The whole work would have been well served by an efficient editorial revision.

Early in Book 1 Julian tells us the purpose of writing the *C. Gal.*:

> . . . to set forth to all mankind the reasons by which I was convinced that the fabrication of the Galileans is a fiction of men composed by wickedness.
>
> (*C. Gal.* 39A: Wright)

He says further that the Christian uses that part of the soul that loves childish fables to induce men to believe that a 'monstruous tale' is true (39B). Christians wail over the corpse of a Jew because they have abandoned the ever-living gods of the Romans. Their religion is absurd, and their doctrines are not divine (39B; 138C; 194D; 197C; 206A; 229D). The *C. Gal.* appears to have been written in association with Julian's attempt to revive Hellenism in the Eastern urban centres of the empire, and it was written with the twofold objective of demonstrating the superiority of Greek *paideia* to Christianity, and showing that the Christians lacked the support of ancient ancestral customs. To achieve his goal, Julian develops six major themes in the *Contra Galilaeos*. We now turn to these themes.[38]

Jesus

The purpose of Julian's criticism of Jesus is to show that he was not God, and he reinforces his argument first by proving the novelty of Christianity. The Galileans, he says, have abandoned both Hellenism and the ancestral teachings of the Jews. Just 'yesterday' Jesus' doctrine appeared, and it has done nothing to ameliorate the urban culture of the empire (*Ep.* 47; *C. Gal.* 106C; 194D; 197C; 201E; 238A). Christianity is an enormous pretension (*C. Gal.* 116A), primarily because the Christians have misinterpreted the Hebrew scriptures. Jesus was never recognized by God (in the Old Testament) as his 'Son' (159E). Of all the New Testament writers, it was only John who made up the 'evil doctrine' of the divinity of Christ (335B). Anyway, even the Jews themselves rejected Jesus, who brought an infectious disease to the world and actually opposed God's will for mankind to worship many gods (159E). The Logos Doctrine of Johannine theology, moreover, is contradictory: if Jesus is indeed God, why does John say: 'No man has ever seen God at any time' (333D)? Because the Christian teaching about Jesus is a myth, he cannot therefore in any way *save* mankind. Mankind has prospered much more from the worship of such deities as Helios (*Ep.* 47, 55; Ugenti 1992: 395–402; Smith 1995: 197–204).

Julian also criticizes the teachings and works of Jesus. For instance, to reinforce his claim that Hellenism is superior to Christianity because the latter has abandoned its ancestral customs, Julian mocks the assertion of Jesus that the Jews are God's 'Chosen people' (106B). Since Jesus neither lived a pure life, nor did he teach it to his disciples (205E), his teachings which are recorded in the evangelists would cause the disintegration of the Roman empire if everyone practised them (*C. Gal.* fr. no. 5). Hence the Galilean man-made myth is detested of the gods and will poison Hellenism, which is the true salvation of the world (*Ep.*147; Malley 1978: 12). Jesus' works are equally condemned. To prove that Jesus was not God, Julian develops further the argument of Celsus which attributed Jesus' miraculous power to the operation of magic by maintaining that Moses, the prophets, Jesus, and his disciples surpassed all the magicians and charlatans of every place and period in history (100A). (His penchant for hyperbole is evident here.) Julian thus greatly minimizes the soteriological value of Jesus' works:

> Yet Jesus, who won over the least worthy of you, . . . accomplished nothing worth hearing of, unless anyone thinks that to heal crooked and blind men and

to exorcise those who were possessed by evil demons in the villages of Bethsaida and Bethany can be classed as a mighty achievement (191E).

If Jesus did not offer any lasting benefits to his own people, who in the end rejected him, why should an erudite person not accept Hellenism which has been the fount of many divine blessings since ancient times?[39]

As we have already noted above, a classic theme in anti-Christian polemics was the rejection of the apologists' 'Proof from Prophecy' argument. Julian continued this tradition, and because of his sound knowledge of scripture, he was able to attack it from several perspectives. The major point he makes is that the Old Testament Messianic prophecies have been misconstrued by the Christians, who falsely applied them to Jesus. Nowhere in the Pentateuch, he argues, did Moses predict a Messiah who would be 'God born from God'. Moses taught the Hebrews to worship one God, not two (262B-C, E; 276E; 290C-D; 291A). Christian biblical theologians have eisegeted and now worship Jesus as a second (false) God. Besides, the Mosaic prophecies often apply to king David, and Isaiah 7.14 did not predict the virgin birth of a God (253B-E; 261E; 262B-D). Julian also asserts that the mythological tritheism expressed in the baptismal formula given by Jesus in Matt. 28.14 clearly contradicts the Mosaic monotheism of the Pentateuch (291A). Other examples of the New Testament doctrines that came about by the corruption of the original teaching of Moses and the prophets are the Incarnation; the deity, passion, and resurrection of Christ; the Pauline concept of Christ being the 'end of the Law'; the Mariological doctrine of Theotokos; and the cult of the martyrs which, to the emperor, was tantamount to witchcraft and violates Old and New Testament teaching (320; 320B-C; 327A-C; 335D; 339A-C; 262D; 276E-277A).

God

To Julian Christian teaching about God is absurd and trivial, and it lacks the superior rationalism of Greek philosophy (160E). Though some scholars have interpreted Julian's thought as based on a concept of natural theology which presupposes an innate knowledge of God, this does not, as we have already seen above, rule out any need for divine revelation (52B-C; Smith 1995: 192f.). Innate knowledge provided a general epistemology concerning the nature of the divine and helped to answer a number of teleological questions about the relationship between providence and the natural world. Revelation, whether it manifested itself by oracles, Chaldean-Neoplatonic theurgy, soothsaying, or extispicy, made the divine world and its otherwise inaccessible, mysterious, and secret knowledge relevant and accessible to the inquirer. The recipient of the revelation possessed the confidence that the personal decisions of his daily life were influenced and protected by supernatural guidance. 'Personal religion' of this kind was a symptom of the age; it affected pagans and Christians alike, permeated all classes in society, made contact with the gods possible, and it often degenerated into absurd practices. Neoplatonism supplied Julian with much of the conceptual basis for his understanding of God, and this would include the belief in the divinity of the cosmos (69C). Hence God does not increase or decrease, he is immutable, free from decay and generation. He is pure, immortal, eternal, and transcendent (69C). As an intellectual Julian rejected the Graeco-Roman myths which depicted (e.g.) Kronos eating his children and Zeus having sex with his mother (44A-B). Even more so will he call Hebrew myths absolutely incredible (75A; Meredith 1980: 1143), and the Judaeo-Christian God of scripture gave him plenty of ammunition for the *Contra Galilaeos*. He specifically criticizes the particularity of the Hebrew God which, he argues, prevents Christianity from being a truly universal religion (100C). In contradistinction to the Platonic doctrine of divine impassibility, Julian excoriates the irrational nature of the Christian God which is inferior even to the mildness of Lycurgus, the forbearance of Solon, and the benevolence of the Romans (168C; 171D). The God of scripture possesses weaknesses of character normally condemned in humans. He constantly expresses jealousy, anger, resentment, and other features inconsistent with divinity, which prove his indisputable irrationality (106E; 152B-D; 155C-D; 160D; 161A). The Hebrew God is best understood as one of the many national gods to whom the higher power has delegated responsibilities for their particular territories. The incorporation of the Hebrew God into his philosophical system can have benefited his attempt to revive Hellenism in the urban centres of the East in at least four ways. First, he was able to defend traditional polytheism and at the same time give a coherent explanation for the diversity of religious culture. Second, he could attempt to explain the tension between monotheism and polytheism based on a theology of the cosmos which was characterized by a Neoplatonic understanding of a hierarchy of Being. Third, on a broader scale, he could see it as an impetus for the revival of Hellenism in the urban centres of the East. Finally, he could show that Christianity should be abandoned because it lacks the support of ancient ancestral customs (115D-E; 116A-B; 143B-C; 148B-C; 155E). The Christian doctrine of God is therefore pure nonsense (155E).

Creation

Julian quotes Plato's *Timaeus* 30B to prove that Platonic cosmology is superior to the biblical account of creation in Genesis 1–2 (57B-C). The cosmos exists as a living creature with a soul and intelligence (57C-D). Exegeting *Timaeus* 41A-C, Julian maintains that the visible celestial planets and stars are likenesses of the invisible gods (65B-C). The immortal part of humans was given by the Demiurge as the rational soul, and the rest of the process of becoming consisted of weaving mortality and immortality (65D). In Genesis Moses fails to inform us of the immediate creator of the universe (66A). Julian follows Plato by saying that God is not the creator of material things, but only disposes of pre-existing matter (49C-D). The transcendent God who is the principle of ultimate reality is at the pinnacle of the hierarchy of being, and from him emanates all other ontological levels of reality.

As the creator of mortal beings and material reality, the God of Genesis was perceived by pagan philosophers as a being demoted in the metaphysical realm, and because of this Julian specifically castigates the creation stories in Genesis 1–2. For instance, on the creation of Eve, he asks whether God did not know that she would be a misfortune to Adam (75B). He further asks why God denied to humans the power to distinguish between good and evil (89A). To Julian this is a ludicrous myth for four reasons. First, it depicts God as being ignorant that the woman became a deceiver. Second, God refused something beneficial for Adam and Eve: the knowledge of good and evil. Third, God was jealous about the possibility of humans eating from the tree. Finally, God became envious when Adam and Eve knew good and evil, and expelled them from the garden (75B; 89A; 93E; 94A). Such concepts as sin, human free will, and choice were abhorrent to a Neoplatonist who believed that all levels of material reality are immutably ordered by providence for a world which is essentially eternal.

Criticism of scripture

Julian is similar to Porphyry in that both possessed a sound knowledge of scripture and used it against the Christians. To ascertain the nature of his knowledge, we may first observe that 98 scriptural passages are cited or alluded to in Julian's works, and most of these are found in the *Contra Galilaeos*. Fifty-seven are from the Old Testament and 41 from the New.[40] Forty-four of the Old Testament passages come from the Pentateuch: (16) Genesis, (11) Exodus, (9) Deuteronomy, (5) Leviticus, (3) Numbers; 13 derive from other books: (2) I Samuel, (3) I Kings, (1) 2 Kings, (5) Isaiah, (1) Psalms, (1) Hosea. Of the New Testament passages there are 28 from the evangelists: (13) Matthew, (5) Matthew or another evangelist (4) Luke (1), Mark (1), Mark or Luke (1), John (4); and 21 from the other books: (6) Acts, (7) Pauline, writings (3) I Corinthians, (1) Colossians, (1) Hebrews. Of the New Testament figures named we have Jesus (24 times), John (8), Matthew (7), Mark (4), Luke (4), and Paul (13).[41] The function of scripture in the polemics of Julian was probably influenced by Porphyry, and we may give four premises of his argument (Meredith 1980: 1147):

1 The Christians have abandoned Hebrew traditions and have misinterpreted scriptures (the Old Testament) (238B; *Ep.* 47).
2 Even if one trained a child in the scriptures from a young age, his character would not be any better than that of a slave (230A-235B). Scripture does not make one wiser, braver, or better than one was before he read it (230A). It is not therefore for the intelligent, nor for those seeking wisdom (229D).
3 Greek writings, which Christians often ascribe to the Devil, enable people to acquire courage, wisdom and justice. They actually produce virtue in those not endowed with the natural ability to apprehend them. To the person so endowed, he becomes a gift of the gods to civilization (229D; 230A-B).
4 Christians use Greek learning in their theology. If their scripture is sufficient, why do they nibble at Greek literature (229C)?

The church: doctrines and practices

The apostate emperor believed that the church is under a double curse because it has abandoned both the polytheism of the Greeks and the traditions of its Hebrew fathers (238A-B). Although Julian admits that he is not a Jew, he expresses respect for the God of Abraham and Isaac, and argues that the Christians rebelled against the Mosaic Law. For example, they do not keep the Passover, practise circumcision, sacrifice animals, or honour the food laws of the covenant (314C; 343C; 351A; 354A-B). Furthermore, the Galileans have not accepted a single admirable teaching from the Greeks or the Hebrews (43A), and the only thing that the latter have in common with the Christians is the rejection of polytheism (238C-D). This is very unfortunate, he claims, because the gods have sent many lawgivers to the Greeks who were superior to Moses (141D). At least the Christians would be following some sort of law if they had not abandoned Hebrew customs, although it is harsh and inferior to the humane laws of the Romans (202A), and in reality they have transgressed all the commandments that God gave to Moses (351B; also 42E-43A; 99E; 141C-D; 218B; 253A-B; 254B; *Epp.* 20).

In conjunction with this theme of the Christian abandonment of the truth Julian develops a protean attack upon the past and contemporary followers of Jesus. He says, probably following Celsus, that only the very base people of society like shopkeepers, slaves, maidservants and dancers become Christians (206A; 238D-E; 245A-C; 191D-E; *Ep.* 55). Christians are misguided and foolish, wicked and arrogant (194C; 229C; 230A; 238B). Julian focuses on the early leaders of the Apostolic Age, such as Peter (314D-E) and Paul (106B). For example, he maintains that Paul's teaching is full of contradictions, and his concept of Christian universalism is ridiculous. After quoting Rom. 3:29 and Gal. 3:28, he asks why did God neglect most of humanity for thousands of years, who in ignorance served idols, but only recently came to a small tribe in an isolated part of Palestine. If he is indeed the God of all alike, as Paul teaches, why did he neglect the Greeks (106D)?

Julian's criticism of Christianity often includes contemporary practices in the church. Calling Christians the most depraved of all people, for instance, he mocks those believers who make the sign of the cross and 'hiss at demons' (*Ep.* 19; Bolton 1968). Why should they adore the wood of the cross, he asks, but refuse to revere the shield that providentially fell from the sky during Numa's reign (194C)? The cult of the martyrs is based on witchcraft, it has caused the worship of many corpses, and it disobeys Jesus' teaching recorded in Matt. 23:27 (*Ep.* 41; *C. Gal.* 201E; 202A; 224E; 327B; 335B-C; 340A). Christian worship is maligned as impure, unholy, full of superstitions, an infectious disease, and basically atheistic (*Ep.* 20 and 47; *C. Gal.* 43B; 202A). He uses Nicene Logos theology against the Semi-Arians to prove that because of their disagreement over doctrines Christians certainly cannot possess the truth (206A). The rite of baptism is supposed to 'wash' sin away according to *I Cor.* 6:9–11, but in fact Julian says it is not conducive to the reformation of character (245D). *New Revelation* from God claimed by the Galileans is rejected because Moses made it clear that the Old Testament Law is for all time (319D-E; *Ep.* 47; *C. Gal.* fr. 1). Indeed, Christians have not even remained faithful to Apostolic doctrines, and evidence of this is the Johannine notion that Jesus is God (327A).

The superiority of Greek *paideia*

Julian's programme to revive Hellenism in the Eastern urban centres of the Roman empire[42] was predominantly motivated by the unswerving personal conviction that Greek *paideia* was a gift of the gods which had preserved civilization, caused the development of high culture, and blessed humanity with true salvation (Criscuolo

1986; Alan Cameron 1993: 25–9). This latter point – the soteriological implications of Julian's policy – has not been given the attention it deserves. For example, Julian was aware that some of the success of Christianity during its 300 years was attributable at least partly to the church's claim to a unique revelation from God (Ugenti 1992: 393), the application of the Hebrew concept of the 'Chosen People' to itself, and the belief that its religion was the only truly universal religion (Couloubaritsis 1995). To confront these notions, Julian stresses the sacred origin of Rome beginning with the Regal Period (753–510 BCE). Zeus brought about the birth of Rome and her great empire by setting over her Numa, the great philosopher-king who communed with the gods in pure thought and was inspired by divine oracles given by the Sibyl (194B-C; see Fouquet 1981: 196; Scott 1987: 345; Wallace-Hadrill 1981).

Julian builds on this conceptual foundation in a number of ways. We may first mention his conviction that Greek literature is far superior to Christian scripture, and educated Christian writers have borrowed much from it (171D; 229C). Julian also contrasts the Greek gods with the Hebrew God. Relying on Platonic soteriology, he says that men should not imitate the God of scripture, if indeed salvation is based on imitating God, the contemplation of the intelligibles, and freedom from passion, because this God often expresses anger, jealousy, wrath, resentment and grief (171E). Jews and gentiles are in agreement on many doctrines except monotheism, and actually Solomon, who was the wisest of the Hebrews, practised polytheism (141C-D; 171E; 176A-B; 224E; 306A-B). It must be emphasized here that for Julian, 'gods' does not refer to the deities of the Greek myths, but rather to Helios, Asclepius, and others which have been given a philosophical reinterpretation. Because they have a superior aptitude for the mysteries and theology, the wise men of the Greeks have given civilization a more noble concept of deity than that espoused by the Hebrews. Plato was more worthy than Moses of communion with God, the Greeks had an aptitude for theology, and therefore the Hebrews – and even much more the Christians – do not have a legitimate claim to a 'unique revelation' or to the status of the 'Chosen People of God' (49A-B; 171D; 176A-B; *Ep.* 3 and 36). The most profitable goal for all humanity is to pursue Greek philosophy (*Ep.* 3).

His concept of Greek *paideia* is not, however, restricted to religion, but rather encompasses every facet of Graeco-Roman civilization. In every area of the arts and sciences Greek learning greatly surpasses that of the Hebrews, and he gives examples of law, government, military science, medicine, philosophy, cosmology, astronomy, mathematics, music and, of course, theology (178A-B; 190C; 222A; 224C-D; 235C). Finally, Julian strikes at the central message of Christianity, the doctrine of Christ the saviour of the world, by referring to the 'greatest gift of the gods', the saving-deity Asclepius. Salvific theophanies of this god have been numerous in history. He has descended to earth as a man and visited Epidaurus, Pergamum, Rome, and many other cities. His salvation is even now universally available to all throughout the empire, and the benefits he gives to his worshippers far exceed the paltry number of miracles performed by the Galilean years ago in a dark corner of Palestine. Asclepius has healed many sick bodies, trained and educated many souls, and his oracles have been found everywhere on earth. Julian himself testifies that the god healed him of illnesses by prescribing remedies, and he will grant eternal salvation in the next life. He concludes that as a saving and healing deity, Asclepius is far superior to Jesus (200A-B; 235B-D).

NOTES

1 See Libanius, *Oration* 18.8 (Julian's funeral oration). The many writers who have covered the biography of Julian include Browning (1976), Bowersock (1978), Athanassiadi (1992) and Smith (1995). Vidal (1964) is an impressive novelistic account.

2 Libanius, *Oration* 13.8; 18.10–11; Socrates, *Historia Ecclesiastica* 3.1. Cf. Bowersock (1978: 23f.) and Smith (1995: 2, 23–48).

3 Libanius, *Orations* 12.3, 80; 13.13 (very religious); 12.94; 18.30 (studious); 12.95 (ascetic); Julian, *Epistle* 60, to Himerius (sensitive to human pain); *Ep.* 23, to Ecdicius (personal library); Ammianus Marcellinus 25.4.1–3 (sexually pure after his wife's death); 25.4.5–6 (moderation in eating and drinking); 25.4.7 (his wisdom); 25.4.8–14 (political and military skills); 25.4.16 (inconsistent); 25.4.17 (very talkative and superstitious); Socrates, *H. E.* 3.1 (self-controlled). Ammianus Marcellinus (24.4.27) says that after a Roman victory during the Persian campaign, Julian would not so much as look at the young virgins taken captive, even though Persian girls were known for their beauty. See also, in general, Browning (1976: 42), Bowersock (1978: 12–20), Smith (1995: 7). Bouffartigue (1989) tries – unconvincingly – to give a psychological sketch of Julian, especially concerning his 'paranoia'. On his love of applause, see Ammianus Marcellinus 25.4.18.

4 See Festugière (1957) and Smith (1995: 2). For this formative period, see Browning (1976: 40–41); Athanassiadi (1977); Bowersock (1978: 25); Paschoud (1980); Demarolle (1986); Klein (1986); Gauthier (1987); Buck (1990) and Bouffartigue (1992: 13–49).

5 Eunapius, *Lives of the Philosophers* 473. Sozomen says that Julian was brought up in the knowledge of the scriptures (*Historia Ecclesiastica* 5.2).

6 On being a reader see Socrates, *H. E.* 3.1; Theodoret, *Historia Ecclesiastica* 3.1. I find no reason to doubt that Julian was a sincere Christian early in his life, on which see Ammianus Marcellinus 21.2.3–4; Ephrem, *Hymn against Julian* 1.14; Libanius, *Or.* 13.12; Socrates, *H. E.* 3.1; Sozomen, *H. E.* 5.1; Theodoret, *H. E.* 3.1; Vogt (1963); Masaracchia (1990: 9) and Smith (1995: 182–89).

7 E. g., Ephrem, *Hymn against Julian* 1.1. For Ephrem, see Lieu (1986). Drinkwater (1983: 355) believes Julian was a Christian in outward appearance (see the preceding note). For Macellum, see (e. g.) Sozomen, *H. E.* 5.2; Browning (1976: 40); Smith (1995: 2). Bidez (1930) remains a good source.

8 Cf. Sozomen, *H. E.* 5.2. For Julian's Latin education see Lacombrade (1960).

9 *Ep.* 2, to Priscus. Ephrem, *Hymn against Julian* 1.16 calls Julian a 'Chaldaean'. For the influence of Iamblichus, see Alonso-Nunez (1973); Balty (1974: 267–69); Browning (1976: 51–62); Lewy (1978: 151 [n. 312] and 270); Saffrey (1981); Sheppard (1982); Penati (1982 and 1983); Marcone (1984); Shaw (1985); Dillon (1987), who gives a good survey of Iamblichean Neoplatonism, and Finamore (1988), Scott (1987) Athanassiadi (1992: 136) and Ugenti (1992).

10 Cf. Eunapius, *Lives of the Philosophers* 473 (Maximus was Julian's teacher); 475 (he used theurgy to make Hecate's statue smile); Socrates, *H. E.* 3.1 (Maximus influenced Julian philosophically); Sozomen, *H. E.* 5.1, says Julian renounced Christianity and purged

himself of baptism by pagan sacrifices); Libanius, *Or.* 18.18 (Julian's conversion to Neo-platonism); Sozomen, *H. E.* 5.2 and Theodoret, *H. E.* 3.1 (Julian's initiation). On Julian's initiation/apostasy see Athanassiadi (1977), Lewy (1978: 248), Fouquet (1981: 191–202), Gauthier (1987: 233) and Klein (1986: 278). Drinkwater (1983: 359) argues that from 351 CE Julian was not the centre of a pagan resistance movement, and Maximus 'stage-managed' Julian's formal apostasy, views with which I disagree on evidence given earlier in this essay. (cf. Averil Cameron 1993: 89; Smith 1995: 138). Athanassiadi (1977) argues for a conversion to Mithraism evidenced in Julian's *Hymn to King Helios*; for an opposite view, see Smith (1995: 139–62). On Mithraism, see Gordon (1972) and Ulansey (1989).

11 Cf. Libanius, *Or.* 18.24–7, 29: Socrates *H. E.* 2.34; Sozomen, *H. E.* 3.1, 5.2; Smith (1995: 3); Browning (1976: 64–6).

12 Cf. Julian, *Ep.* 26, early 362 from Constantinople for Julian's affection for St Basil.

13 Libanius, *Or.* 13.24–32; Eunapius, *Philos.* 476; Sozomen, *H. E.* 5.1–2; Socrates, *H. E.* 3.1; Browning (1976: 79–104), Bowersock (1978: 33–45).

14 Libanius, *Or.* 12.44–6, 13.24–32 for the Strasbourg and Gaul campaign in general; also 18.55, 18.75–91; Smith (1995: 3).

15 Libanius, *Or.* 12.65, 13.36; Ammianus Marcellinus 21.7–16.6, 20.10–11; Sozomen, *H. E.* 5.1; Socrates *H. E.* 3.1; Theodoret, *H. E.* 3.1. Browning (1976: 120) and Smith (1995: 3).

16 Ammianus Marcellinus 22.5.1–5; Libanius, *Or.* 18.126; Sozomen, *H. E.* 5.3, on restoring priests' tax exemptions; Theodoret, *H. E.* 3.3; Socrates, *H. E.* 3.1, 3.11; Eunapius, *Philos.* 478; Libanius, *Or.* 12.69, 17.9 and 17.18. Cf. Ephrem, *Hymn against Julian* 1.4, 2.1, 2.3, 2.27; Julian, *Ep.* 41, to the Citizens of Bostra 1 August 362, and *Ep.* 47, to the Alexandrians November or December 362. Also cf. Downey (1955, 1957), Arce (1975), Browning (1976: 178), Chuvin (1990: 43), Athanassiadi (1992: 181–89), Averil Cameron (1993: 93–4), Bradbury (1995).

17 *Oration* 4.64. Cf. Bidez (1930: 310), Downey (1957: 98), Hardy (1968) and Malley (1978: 205).

18 Socrates, *H. E.* 3.12; Libanius, *Or.* 18.122–4; Julian, *Ep.* 41, to the citizens of Bostra 1 August 362, from Antioch; also see Hardy (1968: 136), Chuvin (1990: 43) and Woods (1997).

19 Socrates, *H. E.* 3.1; Sozomen, *H. E.* 5.5; Theodoret, *H. E.* 3.2; Ammianus Marcellinus 22.5.2.

20 Libanius, *Or.* 18.126; Ammianus Marcellinus 22.4.3; Socrates, *H. E.* 3.1; Sozomen, *H. E.* 5.2, 5; Theodoret, 3.2; Lieu (1986: 45).

21 Socrates, *H. E.* 3.12: Julian told Maris, bishop of Chalcedon, who was suffering from cataracts, that he was a blind old fool, and the Galilean god would never heal him.

22 For instance, note his special hatred for bishops like Athanasius: Theodoret, *H. E.* 3.5 (exile ordered); Socrates, *H. E.* 3.14 (his flight); Julian, *Ep.* 24, An Edict to the Alexandrians (exile ordered); *Ep.* 46, to Ecdicius Prefect of Egypt, calling Athanasius 'the enemy of the gods' and ordering him to leave Egypt. For Julian's treatment of bishops see Fowden (1978).

23 Theodoret, *H. E.* 3.3, reporting that the bones belonged to John the Baptist. Cf. Sozomen, *H. E.* 5.10.

24 Cf. Athanassiadi (1992: 122) Graeco-Roman culture is a product of divine revelation. This is evidence that Julian was interested in prophecy.

25 See Julian, *Ep.* 20, to Theodorus the High Priest, spring 362, who is told to avoid innovations in religion and observe the customs inherited from their forefathers because the gods gave them to humanity.

26 See Julian, *Ep.* 22. Julian caused a number of Christians to apostasize (Theodoret, *H. E.*

3.8). Another reform was forbidding the religious curse: priests should be men of prayer and blessing (see Julian, *Ep.* 18). On his religious reforms see Alonso-Nunez (1973: 185) and the standard reference texts previously mentioned.

27 See Jones (1963: 30). I disagree with Hardy (1968: 138), who interprets the edicts as ancillary to Julian's political reforms and not as persecuting policy. Browning (1976: 174), Bowersock (1978: 83–4), Malley (1978: 27) and Meredith (1980: 1138) see it as at least partly anti-Christian. See also Klein (1986: 47); Masaracchia (1990: 11) and Smith (1995: 199).

28 Cf. Bidez (1930: 266–8): Julian desired to set up a pagan church centrally organized like that of the Christian which practised theurgy and Neoplatonism. For discussion see Browning (1976: 134–43), Bowersock (1978) who sensibly argues that Julian was decidedly anti-Christian from the start, Athanassiadi (1992: 181), Bradbury (1995) and Smith (1995).

29 Ammianus Marcellinus 22.12.7 and 22.13; Socrates *H. E.* 3.18; Theodoret *H. E.* 3.6f.; Julian, *Ep.* 29; Libanius, Or. 17.30. Also see Gregory (1983) and standard references.

30 Ammianus Marcellinus 22.13.1 says the fire was caused by a pagan philosopher who left burning candles by the cultic statue.

31 Cf. *C. Gal.* 198B-C; Eunapius, *Philos.* 475–6, says Julian prophesied the demise of Greek religion, including the oracles in his lifetime.

32 In *C. Gal.* 235C he refers to the oracles of Asclepius found everywhere in the world, an exaggeration no doubt, but it contained some truth none the less.

33 For various views on the extent to which Porphyry influenced Julian, see Demarolle (1986: 40–6), Masaracchia (1990: 15), Smith (1995: 40), Potter (1994: 104–5) and Chadwick (1985). A forthcoming article by me will analyse all textual and other technical data pertinent to this interpretation.

34 Julian, *Ep.* 23, *Ep.* 38 and *Ep.* 51. For George of Alexandria, see Sozomen, *H. E.* 3.2–3, 5.7. He was bishop of Alexandria and was murdered by a mob in 361 CE.

35 Ammianus Marcellinus 23.5.10–11 relates that Etruscan soothsayers repeatedly told Julian not to invade Persia, but he preferred the authority of his Platonic advisers. Cf. Smith (1995: 8).

36 Ammianus Marcellinus 22.12.6–7: Julian consulted many oracles; on the rarity of the prophetic spirit see Julian, *C. Gal.* 198B-C; on the 'Book of Oracles' (including the *Phil. or.?*) see Libanius, *Or.* 18.118; on the Sibylline books see Ammianus Marcellinus 23.1.7; the 'Books on Lightning', Ammianus Marcellinus 23.5.12–4; the 'Tarquitian Books', Ammianus Marcellinus 25.2.7–8; the 'Books on War', Ammianus Marcellinus 23.5.10.

37 For Julian's campaign and death see Browning (1976: 187–218), Bowersock (1978: 106–19), Lieu (1986: 92), Griffith (1987: 244–7) on Eastern Christians' interpretation of his death as God's ultimate triumph.

38 For some of the secondary literature on the *C. Gal.*, see Courcelle (1948: 64–5), Bartelink (1957: 37–48), Bolton (1968: 496–7), Malley (1978): *passim*; Meredith (1980: 1138–40), Demarolle (1986: 41–2), Gauthier (1987: 233) (the text); Masaracchia (1990: 20–1), Athanassiadi (1992: 161–9), Smith (1995: 190–207).

39 Cf. 213B; fr. no. 2: Moses fasted 40 days and received the Law; Elijah fasted 40 days and saw God; what did Jesus receive after his 40–day fast? Fr. no. 3: ridiculing Jesus' temptation; fr. no. 4: Why did Jesus need help from an angel if he was God?

40 On the whole, all figures come from Bouffartigue (1992: 156–70). For Julian's scripture references see his Appendix II: 683f.

41 See Bouffartigue (1992: 114–17). Demarolle (1986: 44) gives 180 references to scripture in the *C. Gal.*; cf. Meredith (1980: 1147), Klein (1986: 286) and Smith (1995: 205).

42 For the literature on this topic see the standard works cited above and Dostalova (1982).

BIBLIOGRAPHY

Alonso-Nunez, J. M. (1973) 'En torno al Neoplatonismo del Emperador Juliano', *Historia Antigua* 3: 179–85.

Ammianus Marcellinus. (See under Rolfe).

Arce, J. J. (1975) 'Recontrucciones de templos paganos en epoca del emperador Juliano (361–363 d.C.)', *Rivista Storica dell' Antichita* 5: 201–15.

Athanassiadi, Polymnia (1977) 'A Contribution to Mithraic Theology: The Emperor Julian's Hymn to King Helios', *Journal of Theological Studies* 28: 360–71.

—— (1992) *Julian: An Intellectual Biography*. London: Routledge.

Balty, Jean Ch. (1974) 'Julien et Apamée. Aspects de la Restauration de L'Hellenisme et de la Politique Antichrétienne de L'Empereur', *Dialogues d'Histoire Ancienne* 1: 267–304.

Banchich, Thomas M. (1993) 'Julian's School Laws: Cod. Theod. 13.3.5 and Ep. 42', *The Ancient World* 24: 5–14.

Bartelink, G. J. M. (1957) 'L'empereur Julien et le vocabulaire chrétien', *Vigiliae Christianae* 11: 37–48.

Bidez, J. (1913) *Vie de Porphyr.* Gand: E van Goethern; Leipzig: Teubner.

—— (1930) *La vie de l'Empereur Julien*. Paris: Belles Lettres.

Blanchetière, F. (1980) 'Julien Philhellène, Philosémite, Antichrétien: L'affaire du Temple de Jerusalem (363), *Journal of Jewish Studies* 33: 61–8.

Bolton, Charles A. (1968) 'The Emperor Julian Against "Hissing Christians"', *Harvard Theological Review* 61: 496–7.

Bouffartigue, J. (1989) 'L'État mental de l'Empereur Julien', *Revue des Études Greques* 102: 529–39.

—— (1992) *L'Empereur Julien et la culture de son Temps.* Collection d'Études Augustiniennes 133. Paris: Institute d'Études Augustiniennes.

Bouffartigue, J. and Patillon, M. (1977) *Porphyre De L'Abstinence Tome I Livre I.* Paris: Belles Lettres, *Bulletin de l'Association Guillaume Budé.*

Bowersock, G. W. (1978) *Julian the Apostate.* Cambridge, Mass.: Harvard University Press.

Bradbury, Scott (1995) 'Julian's Pagan Revival and the Decline of Blood Sacrifice', *Phoenix* 49, 4: 331–56.

Browning, Robert (1976) *The Emperor Julian.* Berkeley: University of California Press.

Buck, David F. (1990) 'Some Distortions in Eunapius' Account of Julian the Apostate', *The Ancient History Bulletin* 4: 113–15.

Cameron, Alan (1993) 'Julian and Hellenism', *The Ancient World* 24: 25–9.

Cameron, Averil (1993) *The Later Roman Empire.* Cambridge: Mass.: Harvard University Press.

Chadwick, Henry (1985) 'Oracles of the End in the Conflict of Paganism and Christianity in the Fourth Century', in E. Lucchesi and H. Saffrey (eds), *Memorial A. J. Festugière.* Geneva: P. Cramer, 125–9.

Chuvin, Pierre (1990) *A Chronicle of the Last Pagan*, trans. B. A. Archer. Cambridge, Mass.: Harvard University Press.

Couloubaritsis, Lambros (1995) 'La religion chrétienne a-t-elle influencé la philosophie grecque?', *Kernos* 8: 97–106.

Courcelle, Pierre (1948) *Les Lettres Greques en Occident.* Paris: Boccard.

Criscuolo, Ugo (1986) 'Guiliano e l'Ellenismo: Conservazione e Riforma' *Orpheus* 7: 272–92.

Demarolle, Jeanne-Marie (1972) 'Un aspect de la polémique païenne à la fin du IIIe siècle: Le vocabulaire chrétien de Porphyre', *Vigiliae Christianae* 26: 117–29.

—— (1986) 'Le Contre Galiléens: continuité et rupture dans la démarche polémique de l'empereur Julien', *Ktaema* 11: 39–47.

Dillon, John (1987) 'Iamblichus of Chalcis (c. 240–325 A.D.)', in Wolgang Haase (ed.) *Aufstieg und Niedergang der Römischen Welt*. Berlin: de Gruyter, II.36.2: 863–908.

Dostalova, R. (1982) Christentum und Hellenismus', *Byslav* 44: 1–12.

Downey, G. (1955) 'Philanthropia in Religion and Statecraft in the Fourth Century after Christ', *Historia. Zeitschrift für Alte Geschichte* 4: 199–208.

—— (1957) 'The Emperor Julian and the Schools', *The Classical Journal* 53: 97–103.

Drinkwater, J. F. (1983) 'The "Pagan Underground", Constantine II's "Secret Service", and the Survival, and the Usurpation of Julian the Apostate', in Carl Deroux (ed.) *Studies in Latin Literature and Roman History III, Collection Latomus*. Brussels: Latomus, 80: 348–87.

Festugière, A. J. (1957) 'Julien à Macellum', *Journal of Roman Studies* 47: 53–8.

Finamore, John F. (1988) 'THEOI THEÔN: An Iamblichean Doctrine in Julian's Against the Christians', *Transactions of the American Philological Association* 118: 393–401.

Fouquet, Claude (1981) 'L'hellenisme de l'empereur Julien', *Bulletin de l'Association Guillaume Budé*, 192–202.

Fowden, Garth (1978) 'Bishops and Temples in the Eastern Roman Empire A.D. 320–435', *Journal of Theological Studies* 29: 53–78.

Gauthier, Nancy (1987) 'L'éxperience religieuse de Julien dit "Apostat",' 27 August: 227–35.

Gordon, R. L. (1972) 'Mithraism and Roman Society: Social Factors in the Explanation of Religious Change in the Roman Empire', *Religion* 2:93–121.

Gregory, Timothy E. (1983) 'Julian and the Last Oracle at Delphi', *Greek, Roman, and Byzantine Studies* 24: 355–66.

Griffith, Sidney H. (1987) 'Ephraem the Syrian's Hymns "Against Julian": Meditations on History and Imperial Power', *Vigiliae Christianae* 41: 238–66.

Hardy, B. C. (1968) 'The Emperor Julian and his School Law', *Church History* 37: 131–43.

Jones, A. H. M. (1963) 'The Social Background of the Struggle between Paganism and Christianity' in A. Momigliano (ed.) *The Conflict Between Paganism and Christianity in the Fourth Century*. Oxford: Oxford University Press, 17–37.

Klein, R. (1986) 'Julian Apostata. Ein Lebensbild', *Gymnasium* 93: 273–92.

Kroll, W. (1894) *De Oraculis Chaldaici*. Breslau.

Lacombrade, C. (1967) 'L'empereur Julien emule de Marc-Aurele', *Pallas* 14: 9–22.

Lewy, Hans (1978) *Chaldaean Oracles and Theurgy* new edn. by Michael Tardieu. Paris: Études Augustiniennes.

Lieu, Samuel N. C. (ed.) (1986) *The Emperor Julian Panegyric and Polemic*. Translated Texts for Historians. Greek Series I. Liverpool: Liverpool University Press.

Malley, William J. (1978) *Hellenism and Christianity*. Rome: Università Gregoriana Editrice.

Marcone, A. (1984) 'L'imperatore Giuliano, Giamblico e il Neoplatonismo', *Rivista Storica Italiana* 96: 1046–52.

Masaracchia, Emanuela (1986) 'Sul testo del Contra Galilaeos', in Bruno Gentili (ed.) *Giuliano Imperatore*. Edizioni Quattro Venti di Anna Veronesi. Urbino: Società Italiana per 10 Studio Dell' Antichita Classica. 109–20.

—— (1990) *Giuliano Imperatore. Contra Galileos*. Rome: Edizioni dell'Ateneo.

Meredith, Anthony (1980) 'Porphyry and Julian Against the Christians', *Aufstieg und Niedergang der Römischen Welt*, Berlin: de Gruyter, II.23.2: 1119–49.

Paschoud, F. (1980) 'Trois Livres récents sur l'empereur Julien', *Revue des Études Latines* 58: 107–23.

Penati, Anna (1982) 'Le seduzioni della "potenza della tenebre" nella polemica antichristiana di Giuliano', *Vetera Christianorum* 20: 329–40.

—— (1983) 'L'influenza del sistema Caldaico sul pensiero teologico dell'imperatore Giuliano', *Rivista di Filosofia Neo-scolastica* 75: 543–62.

Potter, David (1994) *Prophets and Emperors*. Cambridge, Mass.: Harvard University Press.

Puiggali, J. (1982) 'La Démonologie de l'empereur Julien étudiée en elle-même et dans ses rapports avec celle de Saloustios', *Les Etudes Classiques* 50: 293–314.

—— (1987) 'La Démonologie de Celse Penseur Médio-Platonicien', *Les Etudes Classiques* 55: 17–40.

Quasten, Johannes (1953) *Patrology*. 4 vols. Vol. 2: *The Ante-Nicene Literature After Irenaeus*. Utrecht and Antwerp: Spectrum.

Rolfe, John C. (1937) *Ammianus Marcellinus I*. Loeb Classical Library. Cambridge, Mass.: Harvard University Press.

Saffrey, H. O. (1981) 'Les Neoplatoniciennes et les Oracles Chaldaïques', *Revue des Études Augustiniennes*, 209–25.

Scott, Stan (1987) 'L'Empereur Julien: Transcendence et subjectivité', *Revue d'Histoire et de Philosophie Religieuses* 67: 345–62.

Seaver, J. (1978) 'Julian the Apostate and the Attempted Rebuilding of the Temple of Jerusalem', *Res Publica Litterarum* 1: 273–84.

Shaw, G. (1985) 'Theurgy: Rituals of Unbification in the Newplatonism of Iamblichus', *Traditio* 41: 1–28.

Sheppard, A. (1982) 'Proclus' Attitude to Theurgy', *Classical Quarterly* 33: 212–24.

Simmons, Michael Bland (1995) *Arnobius of Sicca. Religious Conflict and Competition in the Age of Diocletian*. Oxford: Oxford University Press.

—— (1997) 'The Function of Oracles in the Pagan–Christian Conflict during the Age of Diocletian: The Case of Arnobius and Porphyry', *Studia Patristica* 31: 3 49–56.

Smith, Andrew (1993) *Porphyrii Philosophi Fragmenta*. Leipzig: Teubner.

Smith, Rowland (1995) *Julian's Gods. Religion and Philosophy in the Thought and Action of Julian the Apostate*. London: Routledge.

Ugenti, V. (1992) 'Altri spunti di polemica anticristiana nel discorso Alla madre degli Dei di Giuliano Imperatore', *Vetera Christianorum* 29: 391–404.

Ulansey, David (1989) *The Origins of the Mithraic Mysteries*. Oxford: Oxford University Press.

Vidal, Gore (1964) *Julian*. London: Heinemann Ltd.

Vogt, Joseph (1963) 'Pagans and Christians in the Family of Constantine the Great', in A. Momigliano (ed.) *The Conflict Between Paganism and Christianity in the Fourth Century*. Oxford: Oxford University Press, 38–55.

Wallace-Hadrill, A. (1981) 'The Emperor and His Virtues', *Historia* 30: 298–323.

Woods, D. (1997) 'The Emperor Julian and the Passion of Sergius and Bacchus', *Journal of Early Christian Studies* 5: 335–68.

Wright, W. C. (1922) *Philostratus and Eunapius*. Loeb Classical Library. London: Heinemann.

—— (1993) *The Works of the Emperor Julian*, 3 vols. (reprint) Loeb Classical Library. Cambridge, Mass.: Harvard University Press.

INDEX OF BIBLICAL REFERENCES

———— •✦• ————

OLD TESTAMENT

NEW TESTAMENT

INDEX OF CLASSICAL
REFERENCES

— •✦• —

INDEX OF JEWISH REFERENCES

———— •✦• ————

INDEX OF PATRISTIC
REFERENCES

———— •◆• ————

Epistle to Diognetus

Eunomius of Cyzicus

Expositio Fidei

First Apology

Second Apology (Apologia apologiae)

Fragments

Eusebius (Pamphili) of Caesarea

Contra Hieroclem

De ecclesiastica theologia

Demonstratio evangelica

Epistula ad ecclesiam Cæsariensem

SUBJECT INDEX

—— •◆• ——